A History of Gay

The Male Tradition

Gregory Woods

Yale University Press
New Haven and London

Set in Garamond by MATS, Southend-on-Sea, Essex
Printed in Hong Kong through World Print Ltd.

Library of Congress Cataloging-in-Publication Data

Woods, Gregory, 1953–
A history of gay literature: the male tradition/Gregory Woods.
Includes bibliographical references and index
ISBN 0–300–07201–5
1. Homosexuality and literature. 2. Homosexuality in literature. 3. Gays' writings—History and
criticism. 4. Literature—History and criticism. I. Title.
PN56.H57W66 1997
809'.89206642—dc21
97–28159 CIP

A catalogue record for this book is available from the British Library

1 3 5 7 9 10 8 6 4 2

Acknowledgements are due to the following for permission to quote copyright material:
Curtis Brown for Théophile Gautier, *Mademoiselle de Maupin*, trans. Joanna Richardson
(Copyright © 1981 Joanna Richardson)
David Storey, Jonathan Cape Ltd. and A. M. Heath & Co. Ltd. for David Storey, *Radcliffe*
(Copyright © 1963 David Storey)

Contents

Acknowledgements

....

In the writing of this book I have accumulated debts to helpful colleagues and friends, whom I must now thank. The Faculty of Humanities at the Nottingham Trent University, where I teach Cultural Studies and English, gave me sabbatical leave at a crucial stage in the preparation of the first draft.

Earlier versions of some chapters appeared, at length or in fragments, in various journals – *European Gay Review*, *Journal of Homosexuality*, per*versions* and *PN Review* – and in the following books: Gabriele Griffin's *Difference in View*, Mark Lilly's *Lesbian and Gay Writing*, Robert K. Martin's *The Continuing Presence of Walt Whitman*, Emmanuel S. Nelson's *Gay and Lesbian Writers of Color* and *AIDS: The Literary Response*, and Claude J. Summers's *Homosexuality in Renaissance and Enlightenment England* and *The Gay and Lesbian Literary Heritage*. I could not have functioned without the patience and encouragement of all these editors.

Susie Fischer and Michele Gregory gave me their hospitality in Jersey City, as did David Shenton in London. Sue Thomas fielded all my panic-stricken phone calls about a sinister new word-processor which knew more about my secret life than I did about its. And Tim Franks was consistently supportive throughout the period in which I was working on the book: much of its emotional strength is derived from him. He also drew my attention to a number of queer books which I would otherwise have overlooked. So did David Shenton and Geoff Whittaker.

At Yale University Press, Robert Baldock not only commissioned this book, but also provided the friendship and professional support I needed to bring it to fruition. I am more than grateful for his continuing confidence in my work.

In 1951 the Fleet Street editor Leonard Crocombe dedicated his book *Slow Ship to Hong Kong* to his elder daughter. *A History of Gay Literature* is dedicated to the same unique individual: my mother, Charmion Woods.

Chapter 1

The Making of the Gay Tradition

In September 1865 the pioneering sexologist and homosexual activist Karl Heinrich Ulrichs drafted a list of 'Bylaws for the Urning [i.e. homosexual] Union', a kind of premature gay liberationist manifesto. Among the principal goals of this as yet non-existent Union were:

   c. to found an Urning literature.
   d. to further the publication of appropriate Urning writings at Union expense.

Ulrichs was a poet himself, though not a very good one. He planned to publish *Nemus Sacrum* (*Sacred Grove*), an anthology of Greek and Latin classics of homosexual poetry, along with some of his own verses; but the plan never came to fruition.[1] Later Edward Carpenter, too, would combine the roles of poet and sexologist, though to rather more productive effect. The relationship between poetry and homosexual advocacy has a long history. After all, in Greek myth, the most prominent candidate for the honour of having been the first mortal man to love his own sex was the poet Orpheus. It was he who attempted to persuade the men of Thrace to start loving boys, an indiscretion for which he was dismembered by the Maenads. Another of the men reputed to have been the first homosexual mortal, Thamyris, was also a wonderful poet. He made the hubristic mistake of challenging the Muses to a contest; as a consequence of this impertinence, he was deprived of the powers of sight and song.

If we are to speak of a continuous, or even intermittent, 'gay tradition' in literature – and every gay theorist warns us to be careful if we wish to do so – it would be a tradition not of novels but mainly of verse. Brought together in one place, its constituent texts would look something like, but be even broader than, the contents list of Stephen Coote's *Penguin Book of Homosexual Verse*, beginning in the ancient world and progressing with great vitality – considering how widely stigmatised male–male love has been at various points in history – through the Middle Ages and Renaissance, beyond the modern world into the era of the postmodern; from pederasty to sodomy, from homosexuality to gayness, from pre-gay queerness to post-gay queerness, and beyond. More comprehensive than Coote, it might include the *Epic of Gilgamesh*, Hispano-Arabic love poetry, the meditations of Saint John of the Cross, the *Chanson de Roland*, Turkish *divan* poetry, and so forth.

We are not thinking of mere byways, obscure deviations from the mainstream. Male poets who loved boys or men do not always materialise as radical subverters of conservative traditions or as isolated eccentrics. Gay poetry does not always go against the grain; indeed, there have been many times when it *was* the grain. Again and again, if one examines the most deep-rooted traditions of love poetry, with the most strongly established conventions of both form and topic, not to mention etiquette, one comes across love poems addressed by men to boys (where 'men' and 'boys' tends to mean little more than a slight difference in ages). Such poems are often to be found nestling happily in the midst of heterosexual love poems. For instance, there is an anthology of 656 poems by Chinese court poets of the Southern Dynasties, entitled *New Songs from a Jade Terrace*. It was compiled by the poet Hsü Ling in about AD 545. As you work your way through the collection you occasionally encounter a poem which, although as conventional in its imagery and formality as any of the others, is about a desired boy rather than a woman. Yet these homo-erotic poems are not simply formal exercises, allowed into the very public space of the anthology because the 'friendship' they express is 'platonic' or 'chaste'. On the contrary, a poem like Wu Chün's 'A Boy' is explicitly dismissive of 'virtue'. A man invites a boy to bed – nothing could be less equivocal.[2]

One factor which helps to explain why some cultures produce a proliferation of love poems addressed to boys by men is, quite simply, male privilege. The sheer availability of boys makes their concrete presence amenable to transposition into erotic imagery. The poetry of the Ottoman Empire, for instance, is shaped by the fact of a society in which women's clothing and their segregation rendered them all but invisible to men; boys, on the other hand, might be seen in all their glory at the public baths. Moreover, with levels of male and female education and expectation maintained in a condition of pronounced and permanent inequality, such societies tended to offer men very little reason for wishing to befriend women. Intimacy was easier and more natural between pairs of males.

The problem for us today is to conceive of how the mind of a poet might work in a society with completely different sexual rules from our own. Consider the erotic range of a poet like Catullus (*c*.84–54 BC), the scabrous laureate of the late Roman republic. His verse includes tender and vibrant love poems addressed to Clodia Metelli ('Lesbia'), a married woman; enthusiastic epithalamia on matrimony; insulting epigrams accusing a man called Gellius of all manner of sexual transgressions, including incest and cock-sucking; what we might now (inaccurately) call 'homophobic' tirades against men who loved men instead of boys, or against men who took the 'wrong' part in oral or anal intercourse with boys; and so on. However, it is also clear that Catullus, true not only to the conventions of his society but also to the promptings of his own heart and genitals, loved sex with young men and loved one man, Iuventius, with greater ardour than the feeling was returned.

Perhaps this is not the work of a 'gay poet' in the contemporary sense; yet it offers the gay reader a broad range of interest, both in terms of identifiably shared emotions and as a documentary glimpse of 'our' sexual history. The two great virtues of Catullus' view of sexuality are his sense of humour – which leads him to laugh at himself as often as at others – and his seriousness, the depth of his commitment to his own desires. The tension between the two moods brings him close, at times, to a tone which we might recognise in certain types of modern gay irony. This may just be a coincidence; or it may demonstrate the influence of classical education in the late nineteenth century on men who were beginning to define themselves as belonging to a distinct human type, the homosexual; or it may just be an instance of retrospective wish-fulfilment (call it cultural appropriation) on the part of a gay reader like me.

The fact is that gay literature is not simply a matter of the emotional records of individual writers. Gay writers do not, on their own, 'make' gay literature. There are processes of selection, production and evaluation to be taken into account. Our canons of literature of quality are no more eternal than any other. Indeed, gay literary critics have been fairly explicit about the intentional social purposes behind their re-evaluations of past texts and canons. The contingencies behind the heralding of gay classics need to be acknowledged and made manifest. The canon of gay literature has been constructed by bookish homosexuals, most explicitly since the debates on sexuality and identity which flourished in the last third of the nineteenth century. Indeed, if one were seeking to erect a memorial at the birthplace of gay literature, it would make sense to site it, not on some Assyrian ruin from which the story of Gilgamesh and Enkidu first emerged, nor on the banks of the Nile where inscriptions speak of the relationship of Seth and Horus; but in one of Oxford's relatively unloved Victorian buildings. I am thinking of some space where impressionable youths sat at the feet of men like Walter Pater or Benjamin Jowett, or solitary garrets where the same youths read the classics in Greek and Latin and where they made lists of mythic and historical figures who felt the same as they did on catching sight of a muscular physique. Those lists would eventually turn into the contents pages of our gay anthologies and our histories of gay literature.

Actually, the writing of such lists pre-dates the Victorian age. Byrne Fone writes that 'it was in the latter [sic] eighteenth century that writers began compiling lists . . . to bring legitimacy to what the world called perversion'. A much earlier example is the moment in Christopher Marlowe's *Edward II* when Mortimer Senior compares the king's relationship with Piers Gaveston with Alexander's love of Hephaestion, Hercules' of Hylas, Patroclus' of Achilles, Tully's of Octavius and Socrates' of Alcibiades (I. iv, 390–96). In *The Faerie Queene* (1590, 1596) Edmund Spenser, too, lists male lovers in pairs: Hercules and Hylas, Jonathan and David, Theseus and Pirithous, Pylades and Orestes, Titus and Gesippus, and Damon and Pythias (Book IV, Canto X, 27). Fone argues that such lists show 'the first elements of a growing awareness, and even a slowly growing militancy about and pride in the homosexual past'.[3] There is a fine catalogue in the poem *Don Leon*, which dates from between 1823 and 1836 and is often attributed to Lord Byron. Here, the poet invokes the names of philosophers and poets who loved men or boys – Plato, Socrates, Bion, Plutarch, Virgil and Horace – in the hope of justifying his own sexual tastes. His argument boils down to its simplest elements in these two couplets:

> I love a youth; but Horace did the same;
> If he's absolv'd, say, why am I to blame?
> When young Alexis claimed a Virgil's sigh,
> He told the world his choice; and may not I?[4]

Oscar Wilde's short story 'The Portrait of Mr W.H.' similarly turns into a kind of bibliography of gay literature; and his famous courtroom defence of 'the love that dare not speak its name' on 30 April 1895 listed David and Jonathan, Plato, Michelangelo and Shakespeare.

At about the same time, lists began to appear in sexological textbooks. In *Homogenic Love* (1894), later incorporated into *The Intermediate Sex*, one of Edward Carpenter's first purposes is to name the 'homogenic' lovers from the ancient world, the classical and oriental authors in whose work 'homogenic' passages can be found, and then a number of key writers from the modern world: Michelangelo, Shakespeare, Winckelmann, Tennyson and Whitman. In *The Intermediate Sex* itself (1908), Carpenter wrote, long before it would become a cliché, that 'some of the world's greatest leaders and artists have been dowered either wholly or in part with the Uranian temperament – as in the cases of Michel Angelo, Shakespeare, Marlowe, Alexander the Great, Julius Caesar, or among women, Christine of Sweden, Sappho the poetess, and others'.[5] In *The Intersexes* (1910), Xavier Mayne (the pseudonym of the American Edward I. Stevenson) offered the following somewhat haphazard list as a demonstration of the fact that there are several varieties of 'uranism':

> Such types are Alexander the Great, Martial, Beethoven, Rafaello, Oscar Wilde, Robespierre, William Rufus, Nero, Lord Byron, Sir Isaac Newton, Gilles de Rais, David, Jonathan, Pope Alexander VI, General [Jan Tserklaes, Count of] Tilly, Prince Eugene of Savoy, Henri III, Shakespeare, [August von] Platen, Cellini, Heliogabalus, Jerome Duquesnoy, St Augustine, Molière, Frederick the Great, Michel-Angelo, Charles XII of Sweden, Peter the Great, Montaigne, Pausanias, [Theodore] Beza, Tschaikovsky, [Franz] Grillparzer, Gonsalvo de Cordova, Socrates, Hölderlin, Abu Nuwas, Hadrian, the Caesars, Alexànder I of Russia[.][6]

Mayne appears to be protesting the importance of his chosen topic. The eclecticism and unpredictability of the list, emphasised by its not being presented in any logical order, is part of the point: not only are we everywhere, but we always were. Moreover, the habit of making lists has been a hard one to break. A post-gay-liberationist project like *The Pink Plaque Guide to London* (1986) does not seem so very different in its essentials. Indeed, it formalises the idea of the list to the extent of turning the whole of London into a catalogue of the queer presence in metropolitan history.[7] The fact is that many supposedly radical, post-Stonewall, gay-liberationist texts were doing the same thing as the Victorian aesthetes felt needed doing. In *The Sexual Outlaw* (1977), John Rechy answers the accusation that homosexual man weakens the 'moral fabric' of society with the questions, 'Did Michelangelo? Da Vinci? Socrates? Did Proust? Did Shakespeare with the sonnets? Did Tchaikovsky?'[8] Holly Johnson's 1994 song 'Legendary Children' consists of little more than lists and the affirming claim that all the named individuals were queer.[9] Clearly, naming the major figures in the tradition had become a tradition in itself.

In essence, what we are talking about here is homosexual men's deliberate creation of a homosexual tradition. Eric Hobsbawm's lucid introduction to his and Terence Ranger's book *The Invention of Tradition* is helpful here. Hobsbawm writes that '"Traditions" which appear or claim to be old are often quite recent in origin and sometimes invented.' This process of inventing traditions 'is essentially a process of formalisation and ritualisation, characterised by reference to the past, if only by imposing repetition'. When Hobsbawm speaks of 'the use of ancient materials to construct invented traditions of a novel type for quite novel purposes', one inevitably thinks of the uses to which Victorian inverts put their classical learning.[10]

Thinking along these lines, then, we have to nominate as a most significant event in the history of homosexual cultures in England the moment in the 1840s when Benjamin Jowett introduced Plato into his lectures at Oxford. Linda Dowling puts the point succinctly when she writes that 'Greek studies operated as a "homosexual code" during the great age of English university reform'.[11] But although Jowett made the dialogues of Plato available not only through his lectures but also, much more widely, in his magisterial translations, he did not allow that they could have any valid significance within the moral life of Victorian England except when studiously appropriated and applied to the conditions of heterosexual matrimony. As he wrote in the introduction to the second edition of his translation of the *Phaedrus*, 'what Plato says of the loves of men must be

1. *Platonism vulgarised and Christianised for nineteenth-century tastes.* (Jean Delville, *Plato's Academy*)

transferred to the loves of [men for] women before we can attach any serious meaning to his words'.[12]

Notwithstanding such displays of dutiful squeamishness, the fact is that a strongly homo-erotic atmosphere grew up in certain parts of the university at this time, not uninfluenced by the fact that until 1884 college fellows in Oxford were not permitted to marry. The model of Socratic love – those educational affections which Plato's dialogues attribute to Socrates' relationships with beautiful boys – could be applied, without great distortion, to tutorial arrangements which already existed within the university. Linda Dowling points out that 'the gesture that was to become a central literary trope for imaginative initiation among late-Victorian Decadent writers' was when an older man gave a younger man a copy of a significant book.[13] Dowling uses the example of John Connington, the Corpus Professor of Latin, giving a copy of William Johnson's 1858 volume of homo-erotic poetry *Ionica* to John Addington Symonds. Earlier, in 1858 itself, the seventeen-year-old Symonds had discovered the *Phaedrus* and the *Symposium* and devoured them both in one feverish, transformative night. In E.M. Forster's novel *Maurice*, Clive Durham likewise faces up to his own inversion – before repressing it once and for all – on reading the *Phaedrus* for the first time. Comparing these two events, Richard Jenkyns remarks: 'There were no sensible little paperbacks then; the Platonic dialogues contained almost the only intelligent discussion of the subject [of homosexuality] to be found anywhere, and when inverts first lighted upon them, the sense of liberation was overwhelming'.[14]

Over a century has now passed since Wilde failed to impress the court, though he won the applause of some in the gallery, for invoking those famous lovers-of-the-same-sex. David Halperin has called the intervening period 'one hundred years of homosexuality'. Alan Sinfield calls it 'the Wilde century'.[15] The numbers are not exact, but the symbolism is no less precise for that. Homosexuality is in essence a construct of the (late) nineteenth and twentieth centuries; *as* an essence it is just as distinctively a characteristic of modernism as are atonalism in music, Cubism in painting, or interior monologue in the novel. (Alan Pryce-Jones said of Oxford in the 1920s that 'it was *chic* to be queer, rather as it was *chic* to know something about the twelve-tone scale and about Duchamp's "Nude

Descending a Staircase"'.[16]) The existence of homosexuality, not as a circumstantial matter of passing sexual whim, but as a shared condition and identity, raises the intriguing possibility of homosexual culture, or at least of a minority subculture with sexual identity as its base. At the very least, by sympathetic identification with cultural texts which appeared to be affirmative, homosexual people saw a way to shore up their self-respect in the face of constant moral attack, and they found materials with which to justify themselves not only to each other but also to those who found their very existence, let alone their behaviour, unjustifiable.

Moreover, once homosexual people developed a need for something identifiable as their own culture, they looked not only to the future – by producing 'a literature of their own' (to adopt John Stuart Mill's phrase about women writers) – but also to the past. In the late nineteenth century and throughout the twentieth, homosexual people have been involved in the retrospective creation of a culture of our own – which is to say, the appropriation of disparate cultural products and producers, and the elaboration of a fiction: that of a continuous 'male love' tradition descending to Victorian London (or Paris, Berlin, Vienna or New York) from Periclean Athens and beyond. While the ancient Greek language was still being widely taught in schools, male homosexuality was often known as 'Greek love'.

Lesbian literature never received such consistent endorsement and consolidation from readers in positions of intellectual power. While it may be true that the history of male gay literature is, in large measure, a history of acts of censorship, it is often, also, a record of self-affirming male élites with access to advanced education and the means of cultural production. There is at least as much power as powerlessness to be acknowledged in the history of male gay culture. Obviously, the situation of lesbianism is a completely different matter. Men's access to Greek and Latin literatures in the original language – and even to formal education itself – is probably the major determining factor here.

It is not insignificant that in the Anglo-Saxon cultures these developments coincided with the emergence of 'English', the discipline which would ultimately replace *literae humaniores* (classics) in the academy. The transition from classics to English – initially under the homophobic tutelage of Matthew Arnold – was instrumental in determining the future of the culture of homosexuality. (It was also during this period that prose fiction took over from verse as the defining centre of 'literature'.) Just as F.R. Leavis created the 'Great Tradition' (George Eliot, Henry James, Joseph Conrad) and F.O. Matthiessen created the 'American Renaissance' (Nathaniel Hawthorne, Herman Melville, Walt Whitman) – both critics working from clearly definable subject positions within debates on sexuality, Leavis the homophobic intellectual tough-guy opposed to nancy aestheticism, and Matthiessen himself secretly homosexual – so too had earlier figures like John Addington Symonds and Edward Carpenter started compiling lists in order to create the sense of 'a usable past'.

During this appropriative process, many different types of men, boys and cultural texts were, often without much attention to historical nuance, decisively relabelled: the Spartan pederast, the Japanese Samurai warrior, the pre-Columban native American *berdache*, the sodomite burnt at the stake, even the mere sentimental friend – for a long while, indeed until very recently, even if they could not all comfortably be called 'homosexuals', they could be co-opted even so into 'homosexual culture' as heroes in its evolving but monolithic tradition. This tendency to ignore historical and cultural boundaries was reinforced by anti-homosexual discourses which associate modern queers with ancient Sodomites or (via Gibbon) with the mythical constituency of degenerates who precipitated the decline and fall of the Greek and Roman empires.

· · ·

What was considered worth appropriating? Which authors began to appear on those lists of praiseworthy inverts? What written texts attracted the readers I have been referring to, and how did those texts ever become what we now recognise as a very strongly established canon of homosexual literature? The clearest canonisations have been effected, for many centuries, not only by critical appraisal but also by the assembling of anthologies. Anthologists have clearly hoped to create a sense of cultural continuity and an international community of shared sexual interest. Yet it is worth bearing in mind that, terminology apart, the notion of a sub-sector of literature devoted to homo-eroticism is not particularly new. History is littered with patrons who had specific erotic interests and tailored their commissions accordingly. At other times, artists took it on themselves to make entrepreneurial choices which affected the subsequent availability of specific types of art work.

In Greece, Phanocles wrote *Love Stories, or Beautiful Boys* (*Erastes e kaloi*), a series of elegies offering examples of boy-loving heroes and gods. Among editors working in Arabic, al-Tha'alibi (d. 1038) edited *The Book of Boys*, now lost. In the thirteenth century, Ahmad al-Tifashi produced *The Delight of Hearts*, and the enterprising al-'Adili edited both *A Thousand and One Boys* and *A Thousand and One Girls*. Ming-dynasty China gives us the anonymously edited *Records of the Cut Sleeve* (*Duan xiu pan*). But most famously and influentially in the West, Strato of Sardis, who lived in the second century AD and wrote lively epigrams expressing an interest in both women and boys, nevertheless edited a narrowly specific collection called *Pederastic Poems* (*Mousa Paidiké*). Almost one hundred of Strato's poems have come down to us because this anthology was absorbed into the so-called Palatine Anthology which, combined with the collection by Maximus Planudes, became that magnificent resource of 4,000 epigrams, *The Greek Anthology*. Whether one calls the *Mousa Paidiké* a gay anthology depends on the purity of the individual reader's sense of history.

Regardless of their definitional elisions and inaccuracies, anthologies have played a central role in the establishing of canons of homosexual literature. Furthermore, since the late nineteenth century they have actually provided homosexual readers with a broad kind of gay cultural education which would not have been on offer even in the English 'public' schools and Oxbridge colleges whose curricula were so heavily based on the Graeco-Roman classics. Such collections furnished extracts from a complete curriculum for the diligent, homosexual autodidact. Perhaps the most significant and original of them was Edward Carpenter's *Ioläus* (1902, enlarged in 1906), ostensibly an 'anthology of friendship' but actually an attempt to map out the cultural and historical roots of the people Symonds had called 'the third sex' and whom Carpenter called 'the intermediate sex'.[17] Wits in the book trade used to refer to it as 'The Bugger's Bible'.

Carpenter wastes little time on preliminaries. His Preface does not define Friendship (the capital F is his). The fact that he is dealing only with male friendship does not merit a mention – we are apparently supposed to take that for granted. The structure of the book is explained in one sentence: 'By arranging the extracts in a kind of rough chronological and evolutionary order from those dealing with primitive races onwards, the continuity of these customs comes out all the more clearly, as well as their slow modification in course of time.' The continuity of customs is the point. Carpenter is tracing his own heritage as a friend to other men. *Ioläus* consists of five chapters: 'Friendship-customs in the Pagan and Early World', 'The Place of Friendship in Greek Life and Thought', 'Poetry of Friendship among Greeks and Romans', 'Friendship in Early Christian and Medieval Times' and 'The Renaissance and Modern Times'.[18]

By the time Patrick Anderson and Alistair Sutherland had come to publish their book *Eros* (1961) – again named after a boy in Greek myth, and again an anthology of 'friendship', but this time explicitly male – the canon had greatly expanded.[19] Anderson's introduction is hardly more forthcoming than Carpenter's: 'The subject, as I grew to see it, was any friendship between men strong enough to deserve one of the more serious senses of the world [sic] "love"' (p. 8). Clearly a little self-conscious about this vagueness, he later remarks that 'I do not think it is the job of an anthologist to be too firm about his categories, at least when the collection is something of a pioneer' (p. 12). Homosexuality is not mentioned.

The chapters of this new collection are as follows: 'The Great Originals' (which lays the ground rules with the stories of David and Jonathan, Achilles and Patroclus, and Zeus and Ganymede), 'The Greeks', 'The Romans', 'The Dark and Middle Ages' (turning to the Christian and Islamic worlds), 'The Renaissance', 'Eighteenth Century and Romantics', 'The Nineteenth Century' and 'The Moderns'. The anthology ends with two thematic but rather haphazard chapters, 'Exotic Encounters' and 'The School Story'. Interestingly, the first chapter includes Oscar Wilde's courtroom plea on behalf of 'the love that dare not speak its name', a decision by which the editors clearly intend to link their ancient material not only with modern instances of 'friendship' but also with criminalised homosexuality. (Remember that *Eros* came out between the publication of the Wolfenden Report of 1957 and the Sexual Offences Act of 1967.) The fact that the medieval chapter begins by outlining the new proliferation of penalties for sodomy also, clearly, broadens the scope of the anthology beyond mere 'friendship'.

Several other survey anthologies appeared in the years subsequent to Stonewall and the birth of gay liberation.[20] The first major attempt at a cross-cultural and trans-historical survey of poetry was *The Penguin Book of Homosexual Verse*, edited by Stephen Coote and published in 1983. In his introduction, Coote sets out his parameters – or rather, their lack – with blithe unconcern for the problems he is raising with every sentence. He begins: 'This is a collection of poems by and about gay people. It ranges in time and place from classical Athens to contemporary New York.' He would like his book to be read primarily for pleasure, but also as 'a history of the different ways in which homosexual people have been seen and have seen themselves'.[21] The introduction's sub-sections follow a now fairly familiar historical path: 'Ancient Greece', 'Rome', 'Lesbians in Classical Poetry', 'The Making of Prejudice' (this covering the territory equivalent to Anderson and Sutherland's fourth chapter, 'The Dark and Middle Ages'), 'Renaissance and Enlightenment', 'The Making of the "Homosexual"', and 'Gay Today'. The body of the anthology itself is not subdivided.[22]

Coote's collection was widely reviewed because of its 'Penguin Book of . . .' status. More often than not, it was criticised for its inclusiveness, particularly for its inclusion of sexually celebratory verse of the post-Stonewall era. The problem is, of course, in the nature of canons: do we make our choices of gay culture according to aesthetic or socio-historical criteria? Clearly, any book which unapologetically places the likes of Olga Broumas and Chuck Ortleb next to Homer and Shakespeare is likely to cause aesthetes to shudder, particularly if it appears to include the latter pair for thematic reasons rather than for the fact that they were 'great' poets. But how else can a gay anthologist operate at all?

The main defence available to the compiler of such a broad survey must be located in the pleasure of the reader; and the reader in question should be assumed to be lesbian or gay. The gay anthology is addressed to the gay reader, both to induce enjoyment and to convey a sense of cultural solidarity. Given these functions of the 'pleasure principle' in the compilation of anthologies, academic-historical and academic-aesthetic complaints may prove irrelevant to the success or failure of the enterprise. In a nutshell, it may be completely beside the point whether William Shakespeare was 'gay' or 'queer' or a 'homosexual' or a 'sodomite'; or if he and the male addressee of his sonnets were 'just good friends'; or even if no such friend ever existed and the sonnets in question were – as so many heterosexually identified critics have claimed – mere poetic exercises, common to their time. All of this is irrelevant if any of the sonnets are amenable to being read by a gay reader *as if they were* 'gay poems'. If they work as if they were, they *are*. The reader's pleasure is paramount.

To this extent, anthologies like Coote's function well as capacious lucky-dips, in which any page one turns to will offer a potential gay text. And in the present context, at least, a potential gay text *is* a gay text. It is in their educational roles, on the other hand, that such collections really do raise problems. For instance, Coote's hope that his book will be treated as 'a record, a history' of representations of 'homosexual people' is obviously compromised by the editor's – and therefore the book's – willingness to assume a trans-historical and cross-cultural unifying definition of gay culture. This slippage has already occurred between the title's 'homosexual verse' and the first sentence of the introduction's 'poems by and about gay people'. Add to this the fact that Coote's own translations of the gay classics incorporate such culturally and historically specific epithets as 'faggot', 'queer', and 'queen', and one must reluctantly conclude that the academic uses of the book are limited; or, at least, that the book needs to be shelved next to a more sceptical volume of sexual history.

Of course, Coote's strategies are determined – or, to some extent, sanctioned – by the moment of their conception. *The Penguin Book of Homosexual Verse* was a response to a marketing need created by the growing currency of gay culture during the previous decade. In some sense, for all its faults, it represented the culmination of what some writers and readers had been working towards: the establishing of a canon; the continuation of a tradition. Although published in 1983, the book had its origins in possibilities raised by gay liberation. In some respects already a rather dated concept in 1983, this anthology of 'homosexual verse' nevertheless bore the stamp of 1969.

The latter date is the point in cultural history after which, at last, we can unproblematically speak about a certain kind of text as 'gay literature': that is to say, literature about being gay, by men who identify themselves as being gay. It was then – in the industrialised West at the end of the 1960s – that a systematic renaming occured, and 'queers' and 'homosexuals' became 'gay', in much the same way as, shortly beforehand, 'negroes' had become 'black'. Such redefinition at street level, of course, cannot fail to have its impact on the cultural forms which use language as their primary matter. 'Gay liberation' spawned 'gay literature'. Winston Leyland was not exaggerating when he spoke of a 'Gay Cultural Renaissance'.[23]

By the time one arrives at an event like the publication of Carl Morse and Joan Larkin's *Gay and Lesbian Poetry in Our Time* (1988), it is clear that the culture of homosexuality has been established for long enough to be able to sustain not only the replacement of one canon with another, but also the simultaneous implication that many younger writers are strongly placed to invade the new canon in due course. Thematically, it moves from quietly affirmative voices of the McCarthyite era to the more flamboyant celebrations of gay liberation – though this historical progression is obscured by the editors' decision to arrange the poets not chronologically but alphabetically – and it incorporates poetry of the AIDS epidemic seamlessly into its cross-section of cultural development. Its portentous title clearly expresses the seriousness of its canonising intent.

Even given the effects of homophobia on the production, distribution and evaluation of texts, we are increasingly in charge of our own culture. We have our own requirements, and set our own standards thereby. This is why gay-edited anthologies and gay-authored critical works are at the crux of the development of gay reading practices. Moreover, the specialist marketing of gay literature is greatly facilitated once specifically gay bookstores start opening in the major urban centres of the Western world: the Oscar Wilde Memorial Bookstore in New York, Gay's the Word in London, A Different Light in San Francisco, Los Angeles and New York, *Les mots à la bouche* in Paris, Lambda Rising in Washington DC. As important as the text itself are the ways in which we come to hear of it, find a copy of it, read it, and keep it to ourselves or pass it on to others. Gay newspapers provide gay book reviews; many run their own mail-order book clubs. Gay literature emerges from a network of readers as much as from poets, playwrights and novelists themselves. The book you are reading continues the process.

Then, of course, there is the development of specialist publishing houses. If gay publishers had not existed *as such* before the late 1960s, the fact remains that a number of publishers recognised in homosexuality a saleable theme. Some of them worked with idealistic motives. For instance, early in the century in Germany, the publisher Max Spohr issued a number of important homosexual texts, including Siegfried Moldau's *Wahreit* (1906), Hans Waldau's *Aus der Freundschaft sonnigsten Tagen* (1906), Theo von Tempesta's *Aus dem Liebesleben zweier Freunde* (1914) and Konradin's *Ein Jünger Platos* (1913). Spohr was a co-founder of the enlightened Scientific-Humanitarian Committee and an important figure in the homosexual rights movement. His publishing house held firmly to the line of Magnus Hirschfeld's theory of the 'Third Sex'.[24] By contrast, in England from the 1930s onwards the Fortune Press – run by Reginald Ashley Caton from 1924 to 1971 – put out novels about male homosexuality for opportunistic commercial reasons. Although pretty indiscriminate in his willingness to publish the extremes of quality and trash, Caton had the distinction of issuing the first books of Philip Larkin and Kingsley Amis. The Fortune list included editions of such classics as Plato's *Symposium* (1925), *Strato's Boyish Muse* (1932), Petronius' *Satyricon* (1933) and the anonymous *Don Leon*, unreliably reputed to be by Lord Byron (1934). Alongside these were such contemporary novels on homosexual themes as Terence Greenidge's *The Magnificent* (1933), Richard Rumbold's *Little Victims* (1933) and Reginald Underwood's *Bachelor's Hall* (1934), *Flame of Freedom* (1936) and *Hidden Lights* (1937), as well as all twelve undated volumes of the 'Boy' diaries of Aubrey Fowkes/Esmond Quinterley.[25] After the Second World War, publishers like Swan in Toronto, Ace in London and the Paperback Library in New York produced cheap paperback reissues of fiction on homosexual themes, keenly aware of the potential size of a homosexual market. Judging by their lists, and by the cover blurbs on these paperback editions, little distinction was made between degrees of quality: extremely distinguished and pioneering novels sit cheek-by-jowl with slender, sexy potboilers.

But gay publishing as we now know it dates from the moment of gay liberation. Consider the following sequence of events in the United States of America. Each may be, on its own, relatively trivial; but taken together they constitute a significant, even major, development. *E pluribus unum.* In 1969 the poet Paul Mariah founded *ManRoot* magazine and the ManRoot press in San Francisco. In 1970, also in San Francisco, Winston Leyland founded *Gay Sunshine* magazine. In 1971, the Boston Gay Liberation Front established *Fag Rag* magazine, and then, in 1972, the Good Gay Poets publishing house. In 1973, Ian Young's pioneering gay poetry anthology *The Male Muse* was published. In 1974, Andrew Bifrost founded *Mouth of the Dragon* ('A Poetry Journal of Male Love') in New York. In the same year *RFD* ('A Country Journal for Gay Men Everywhere') was established in Tennessee. New York's *Christopher Street* followed in 1976. In 1977, the novelist Felice Picano started the Sea Horse Press. Meanwhile, back in 1975, Winston Leyland had published the poetry anthology *Angels of the Lyre* under the new imprint of the Gay Sunshine Press; it was followed by a second anthology, *Orgasms of Light*, in 1977. In 1983, Ian Young followed up *The Male Muse* with *Son of the Male Muse*, a collection of much younger writers than had appeared in the earlier book.[26]

It was in the same period that gay literary studies began to flourish in the American academic world. Significant early publications included Louie Crew and Rictor Norton's special issue of *College English*, the official journal of the USA's National Council of Teachers of English, which they gave the one-off title *The Homosexual Imagination* (1974); Ian Young's ground-breaking bibliography *The Male Homosexual in Literature* (1975), complete with essays on gay fiction and poetry by Young himself, on drama by Graham Jackson, and on censorship by Rictor Norton; and Louie Crew's book *The Gay Academic* (1978), a collection of pedagogic and literary-critical essays by various authors.In 1979 Robert K. Martin's *The Homosexual Tradition in American Poetry* established a viable American gay canon and, despite a wave of homophobic reviews, set a high critical standard for gay academics in literary studies to follow.[27]

. . .

Alan Sinfield has said that 'gay men seem doomed to wrestle with the canon'.[28] The fact is that the situation of gay literature is far more secure than that of the literatures of other subcultural groupings (except those in obvious positions of dominance, such as straight white men, gay white men who write as if they were straight and, to an extent, straight white women who choose not write 'as' women). While it is true that post-gay-liberationist readers and critics have had to rediscover lost texts and reassess texts undervalued by straight critics, our task has greatly been helped by the fact that, unlike the work of women writers or non-white writers, texts which can loosely be categorised as 'gay literature' are extremely widely and securely represented in the mainstream Western canon. Many have remained in print. As David Bergman has said, with reference to the American canon, 'A literature which gives Whitman, Melville, Thoreau, and Henry James significant places cannot be said to underrepresent homosexual writers.'[29]

If you consult *The Western Canon* (1994), in which Harold Bloom not only provocatively reasserts the pre-eminence of the traditional canon but also presumes to provide a booklist stating exactly which texts that canon consists of, you soon notice that the canon would not look at all convincingly definitive without its gay content. Indeed, Bloom's list actually begins and ends with gay texts: *The Epic of Gilgamesh* and Tony Kushner's play *Angels in America*. The fourth section of the list, subtitled 'The Chaotic Age: A Canonical Prophecy', is extraordinarily weak in its representation of recent black and female writers, yet it includes the work of gay American poets like Robert Duncan, Frank O'Hara, James Schuyler, James Merrill and Richard Howard. There are two novels by Gore Vidal, and even two novellas by Edmund White, yet only one novel by Toni Morrison (*Song of Solomon*) and none at all by Alice Walker. Of course, one could easily argue with the gay writers and texts Bloom has chosen to include and exclude – as with many of his other choices – but the fact remains that gay writing is reasonably strongly represented here, in spite of Bloom's celebrated resistance to recent developments in subcultural literatures and subcultural literary criticism.[30]

On the other hand, one cannot help noticing that in the cases of many (but, admittedly, not all) of the relevant authors, Bloom is careful not to list the more explicitly gay-related of their books. Thus, he lists Giorgio Bassani's *The Heron* but not *The Gold-Rimmed Spectacles*, Michel Tournier's *The Ogre* and *Friday* but not *Gemini*, E.M. Forster's *Howards End* and *A Passage to India* but not *Maurice*, Christopher Isherwood's *The Berlin Stories* but not *A Single Man*, Reinaldo Arenas' *The Ill-Fated Peregrinations of Fray Servando* but not *Farewell to the Sea*, Patrick White's *Riders in the Chariot*, *A Fringe of Leaves* and *Voss* but not *The Twyborn Affair*, Truman Capote's *In Cold Blood* but not *Other Voices, Other Rooms*, Gore Vidal's *Myra Breckinridge* and *Lincoln* but not *The City and the Pillar*, and Edmund White's *Forgetting Elena* and *Nocturnes for the King of Naples* but not *A Boy's Own Story* or *The Beautiful Room is Empty*.

I am not for a moment suggesting that in all these cases Bloom has got it wrong – and deliberately, at that. I do not think that the whole dubious enterprise of his highbrow hit-parade would be brought nearer perfection by the inclusion of the gay texts I have just named. However, I do believe that, seen together in one place like this, so many such exclusions tell us something revealing and useful about how gay authors tend to be treated once they become good enough to force straight-identified critics to consider their works for inclusion in one canon or another. Let them make sure that they write at least one book which is *less* gay.

Much the same can be said about the selective policies of educators. To put it simply, homosexuality must not be allowed into the classroom; not even into the classroom which contains its average (or even above average) share of homosexual students. Until white readers discovered Toni Morrison and Alice Walker, how often did (gay) James Baldwin ever appear as the token black writer on a college syllabus of post-war American fiction, when (straight) Ralph Ellison would do? Or, if Baldwin had to be allowed in, how often were students asked to read *Another Country*, when the more circumspect *Go Tell It on the Mountain* was still in print? (Incidentally, James Baldwin's fiction does not make it into Harold Bloom's canon. Ralph Ellison will do.)

It is easy to tell where gay literature begins – in openly gay authors' writing explicitly about the experience of being gay – but where does it end? Unless it is to be confined to that one narrow class of texts, it cannot ultimately be confined at all. It must comprise any literary material which has anything to say about matters which we now think of as pertaining to gender roles and to the spectrum of sexual experience. The former, restrictive definition is virtually impossible to use in relation to pre-twentieth-century materials; but the latter is so general as to include virtually all literature of all cultures and all times, and is therefore also unworkable. Each has its own attractions, each its own uses; but neither is sufficient. However, it is the more open, generous definition that sanctions the raiding of the canon for whatever spoils it has to offer. Roland Barthes used to argue that it was not the job of a critic to detect and reveal the secret meaning of a work of art – a truth exhumed from the past – but to construct a way of understanding the work in the critic's own time ('l'intelligible de notre temps'). The 'common reader' does this all the time.

The implication of this approach is that the retrospective pleasures of reading past literatures are legitimate in their own right. For our present purposes, the main subjects of retrospection will be not dead authors but living texts. Once the 'personal' lives of authors are ruled out of the reckoning – as mere gossip, only irregularly supported by reliable evidence – we can concentrate on the lives of languages. It is often productive to follow the developing meanings of individual words or phrases. For instance, in western European cultures what happens to the concept of the 'third sex' between Lord Byron's *Don Juan* (1819–24) and Honoré de Balzac's *Le Père Goriot* (1834)? And what leap of the imagination does it take before Karl Heinrich Ulrichs adopts 'third sex' as a virtually scientific term? In the world-view offered by Byron, there are women, men and eunuchs. The phrase 'third sex' is used twice, once when referring to the singing of a castrato (IV, 86), and once to refer to the eunuch Baba (V, 26), who elsewhere is described as being 'neither man nor woman' (VII, 60). In Balzac's novel, the Maison Vauquer bears a sign advertising it as being a boarding house not only for the two sexes, but also for others ('Pension bourgeoise des deux sexes et autres'). It is here that Vautrin befriends Eugène de Rastignac.

In Book 1, chapter 3 of Thomas Hardy's *The Return of the Native* (1878), a man called Christian Cantle admits to being 'The man no woman will marry'. Thirty-one and still unwed, he says his condition 'makes me afeard'. All who are present agree that he is living confirmation of the old folk saying 'no moon, no man', for he was born at the time of a new moon. In a variant text, Hardy made one woman turn Christian down with the dismissive epithet 'maphrotight fool', meaning 'hermaphrodite fool'. Timothy Fairway shows a certain liberal sympathy for Christian's pitiable predicament by observing that 'Wethers must live their time as well as other sheep, poor soul.' Wethers are castrated rams.[31] In Book 3, chapter 7, to his embarrassment, Christian wins a woman's dress in a raffle. He says 'I – I haven't got neither maid wife nor widder belonging to me at all, and I'm afeard it will make me laughed at to hae it . . . What shall I do wi' a woman's clothes, and not lose my decency!'[32] With neither wife nor mother, the only alternative open to him, other than transvestism, would be to give the dress to a woman who is neither his wife nor his mother. Either way, the dress offers him nothing but a threat of sexual scandal. On both of these occasions, Timothy Fairway reacts with the same word, although in neither case does he directly apply it to Christian Cantle. On the first, when Christian makes his admission, under the mistaken impression that he is the womanless man he overhears the others referring to, Fairway calls the fact that there are as many as *two* such men 'the queerest start I ever know'd'. On the second, when Christian wins the dress, Fairway laughs and says, 'I'm damned if this isn't the quarest start that ever I knowed!' Moreover, it is worth noticing that on both occasions Christian, too, repeats a pertinent word: 'afeard'. He is frightened at the prospect of becoming irrevocably other – not just strange but, so much worse, sexually strange. The word 'queer' is the lexical bridge between late-nineteenth-century decadents' reverence for the *strange* and the mid-twentieth-century epithet for all that is homosexual, used as both insult and self-affirmation. We are staring at the moment in history when queerness comes close to denoting homosexuality.[33]

Of course, by noticing and isolating such incidents, we are talking about the history, not only of literatures, but of the languages in which they are written. Here is another. In Joseph Conrad's short novel *Typhoon* (1903), young Jukes, the chief mate of the steamer *Nan-Shan*, finds himself clinging to a solid object in the storm: 'he discovered that he had become somehow mixed up with a face, an oilskin coat, somebody's boots'. After a brief struggle for some secure purchase on this collection of objects, he 'was himself caught in the firm clasp of a pair of stout arms. He returned the embrace closely round a thick solid body. He had found his captain' – namely Captain MacWhirr. They are caught up together in a great rush of water and thrown over and over, meanwhile 'tightening their hug'. When the sea leaves them dashed against the wheelhouse wall, Jukes is 'rather horrified, as though he had escaped some unparalleled outrage directed at his feelings. It weakened his faith in himself.' All I want to point out about this brief passage is that Conrad deliberately leaves open the precise source of Jukes' horror. Is it the merely the obvious outrage of the wave that he has escaped, or is it the captain's embrace? And if there has indeed been the threat of some 'unparalleled outrage', why were his feelings its object rather than, or as much as, his body?

A little later, as the ship begins to founder, they renew their embraces: 'Jukes felt an arm thrown heavily over his shoulders; and to this overture he responded with great intelligence by catching hold of his captain round the waist'. While they are bracing themselves against the wind, 'cheek to cheek and lip to ear', they exchange a few words about missing crew members. The captain asks, 'D'ye know where the hands got to?' and Jukes, 'distressed' by the captain's wish to know, 'apprehensively' asks, 'Want the hands, sir?' Whereupon another huge burst of the typhoon forces them to intensify their grasp on each other. The ship begins to break up. 'Captain MacWhirr and Jukes kept hold of each other . . . and the great physical tumult beating about their bodies, brought, like an unbridled display of passion, a profound trouble to their souls.' Again, note that the attack is on the 'soul' as well as the body.

In a brief lull that ensues, Jukes does find some hands, if not the ones the captain was asking after: 'a hand gripped his thigh . . . It was the boatswain. Jukes recognised these hands, so thick and enormous that they seemed to belong to some new species of man.' In the enforced physicality of storm conditions, the boatswain 'began to explore Jukes' person upwards with prudent, apologetic touches, as became an inferior'. But Jukes does not embrace him; he does not like the man, and he resents his arrival on the scene. Back at the beginning of this tale, I now remember, Jukes complains twice to the captain about the Siamese flag they are about to sail under. Twice he calls it 'queer', and when the captain obtusely fails to see anything queer in it, Jukes petulantly storms off the bridge.[34] This is not a novel by a homosexual writer, as far as we know; nor is it explicitly about homosexual characters. Neither of these facts prevents its being amenable to gay readings. You might call this the process of queering the canon. It works in parallel with canonising queers.

And yet, nevertheless, there is always an element of tact involved in the job of the gay critic – not because the critic is gay, but because any critical reading depends on its plausibility to be persuasive. For instance, in chapter 20 of Edith Wharton's novel *The Age of Innocence* (1920) we encounter the following passage:

> Only once, just after Harvard, he had spent a few gay weeks at Florence with a band of queer Europeanised Americans, dancing all night with titled ladies in palaces, and gambling half the day with the rakes and dandies of the fashionable club; but it had all seemed to him, though the greatest fun in the world, as unreal as a carnival. These queer cosmopolitan women, deep in complicated love-affairs which they appeared to feel the need for retailing to everyone they met, and the magnificent young officers and elderly dyed wits who were the subjects or the recipients of their confidences, were too different from the people Archer had grown up among, too much like expensive and rather malodorous hot-house exotics, to detain his imagination long.[35]

You can already tell, no doubt, that I want to comment on Wharton's use of the words 'gay' and 'queer'. I almost *italicised* them, but in the present context they effectively italicise themselves. Now, it does not seem unreasonable for the active reader to speculate upon a deliberately ambiguous use of both key words – although, it has to be noted, Wharton uses both of them throughout the novel to mean only 'jolly' and 'strange' respectively. However, we know that 'gay' was commonly in use in post-First World War Harlem to denote a kind of fun-loving openness to sexual possibility that might well include same-sex love; and that 'queer', and even 'strange' itself, when applied to matters sexual, could already connote inversion. When they occur together, as here, and add up to a plausible sequence of sexual meanings, it is not a mere option for gay critics to attempt to construct such a sequence: it is incumbent on us to do so. That, after all, is our job.

What 'plausible sequence' is there, then, in Edith Wharton's two sentences? The ex-student Newland Archer goes to Europe with a bunch of Americans so un-American as to seem 'queer'. They move in circles characterised by everything that we are told the good

American democrat of the late nineteenth century had come to disapprove of in Europeans: aristocracy, inherited wealth, sophistication, decadence. The queerness of the women is barely distinguishable from what is cosmopolitan in their appearance and behaviour. Their love affairs, although presumably heterosexual, are nevertheless both 'deep' and 'complicated' – which is to say, both distant from and incomprehensible to the ordinary American. The worst thing that Archer gets involved in is listening to gossip and watching its protagonists. In this way, he saves himself from drifting into any situation serious enough to seem real. He participates in European life, but only as if attending a carnival which he knows will end, without consequences, as soon as he catches the boat home.

The 'queer cosmopolitan women', meanwhile, associate with men who are either 'magnificent young officers' or 'elderly dyed wits' (for I think it is correct to assume the maleness of the latter, whose dyedness and whose wit are separate parts of the same personality type). For the most part, the former are the 'subjects' of the women's confidences – that is, it is with them that the women have their affairs and it is, therefore, they who become worthy topics to be gossiped about – and the latter, the dyed wits, who receive their confidences. We may infer that the wits have as much interest in the young officers as the women have, even if they have less chance of having affairs with them – less chance of such public affairs, at any rate. Archer is too unimaginative to have space in his imagination for these painted, witty queens. They did not grow up where he did, and so the fact alone that they are Italians, even were they not also 'malodorous hot-house exotics', is enough to make them 'too different' for him to cope with. Thus, the American cultural narrowness which both Edith Wharton and Henry James found so irritating, and yet, in its innocent way, so endearing, has its sexual component – which the gay critic dare not leave unconsidered. The point I have arrived at, then, is the opposite to the point I made three paragraphs ago. It is not tact one needs as a gay reader, but a strategic lack of tact – a willingness to lay oneself open to accusations of 'reading things into' places where they do not belong.[36]

Anyone who objects to homosexual readers treating 'heterosexual writers' (if that is what they were) in such ways ought to take a look at the bizarre things 'heterosexual readers' (if that is what they are) do to books by homosexual authors. In John Sutherland's *Is Heathcliff a Murderer?* (1996), a book about various 'puzzles' in nineteenth-century fiction, we read the following remarks:

> one of the endeavours of homosexual love, with its cult of the marvellous boy, is to abolish sequence . . . *The Picture of Dorian Gray* fantasises a world where middle-aged hedonists can be forever boys, equated in a timeless plane composed half out of lust, half out of the wish-fulfilling visions of the fairy story. Dorian Gray is, to play with the word, two kinds of fairy – the Faustian hero who sells his soul for youth, and the middle-aged, mutton-dressed-as-lamb gay, who would sell his soul to look young again.[37]

Here, as so often when reading the unembarrassed ramblings of homophobic critics, one feels like genteelly responding: know thyself. Does Sutherland seriously believe that heterosexual men have not constructed their equivalent cult of the marvellous girl? Are we seriously expected to swallow the idea that heterosexual men (not to mention women) do not ever regret ageing? (Has he ever read William Butler Yeats?) I am not sure that Sutherland is completely wrong about the book, but the manner of his approach is prejudicial and near-sighted. The fact is that *Dorian Gray*, whatever its faults (and it is not a book I like), is not *Peter Pan*: it is not a fairy-tale (in the inoffensive sense), nor it is about a boy who never grows up. It is, of course, obsessively ageist, but that is another matter. Wilde was a mature man in his mid-thirties when *Dorian Gray* was published. He had written fairy-stories for his sons. I am interested in the way Sutherland uses these two facts against the Wilde who was a 'fairy' attracted to the beauty of male youth. This passage is no less insulting to the gay reader than it is to Wilde. That it was considered publishable by a respectable company in 1996 gives cause for concern. And yet, the reason why it was publishable was that it is not unusual. Literary critics are publishing this kind of complacent drivel all the time.

In the absence of stable definitions and the presence of unstable prejudices, the concept of 'gay literature' has to be seen as a movable feast. It often seems to exist in the spaces between texts, shaped by a debate between pro- and anti-homosexual historians and critics, continually reconstituted by new theoretical conceptions of both literature and sexuality. The 'gay canon' as passed down the generations contains a core of prestigious names (Virgil, Shakespeare, Proust) but is otherwise infinitely variable, like any canon, according to social fashion and individual taste. In a sense it was inevitable that this introductory chapter should have become a bibliographical essay, in its own way a list of lists. (Perhaps even this could be refigured, *post facto*, as a homage to Walt Whitman, the great list-man of American culture, for whom sheer quantity was always more thrilling than the distracting minutiae of quality, which he associated with snobbish class consciousness and the inhibiting effects of formal education.) What emerges from such accumulations of texts is the certainty of their cultural centrality. This is not a marginal tradition, even if it is sometimes marginalised. Merely to read the index pages of a book like this is to begin to retell one of the grandest of the grand narratives, the history of gay literature.

Chapter 2

The Greek Classics

In Greek myth there are several candidates for the honour of having been the first mortal male to love boys. Laius, the father and victim of Oedipus, is one; the poet Thamyris another. If not the first, Orpheus was another pioneer, after he lost Eurydice. Both Thamyris and Orpheus learned their craft as poets under Linus, the inventor of rhythm and melody. Thamyris made the mistake of rivalling Apollo for the love of Hyacinth. Worse still, he boasted within Apollo's hearing that he could outsing the Muses. Apollo told the Muses, who punished Thamyris by confiscating both his voice and his eyesight. He would never be able to see, or sing the praises of, Hyacinth again. Without the seeing and singing of beauty, love itself could no longer exist; Apollo had eliminated his rival as effectively as if he had had him killed. Love and poetry were thought to coexist. It was the poets who, as lovers of boys, expressed what the Victorians would later call, vaguely and rather ominously, Greek love.

There is an old argument which suggests that the acceptance of male–male sexual relations in Greek society post-dates Homer, who lived in the crystal purity of the eighth century BC. Even that Victorian pioneer of gay studies *avant la lettre* John Addington Symonds adhered to this view. In his essay on 'The Dantesque and Platonic Ideals of Love' (1893) he writes:

> Homer excludes this emotion from his picture of society in the heroic age. The tale of Patroclus and Achilles in the 'Iliad' does not suggest the interpretation put on it by later generations; and the legend of Ganymede is related without a hint of personal desire. It has therefore been assumed that what is called Greek love was unknown at the time when the Homeric poems were composed.[1]

However, Symonds adds that this argument is 'not conclusive'. What is undeniable is that the Homeric epics have far more to say about heterosexual than homosexual relationships. The men relate to each other principally as comrades in arms or as opponents. Most of the poems' sexual intensity is invested in men's responses to Helen of Troy or in Odysseus' responses to various women. William Ewart Gladstone, who was a devotee of Homer, was particularly comforted by the fact that Homer's world showed no signs of the shameful sexual behaviour between men which other Greek writers, notably Plato, dared to sanction.

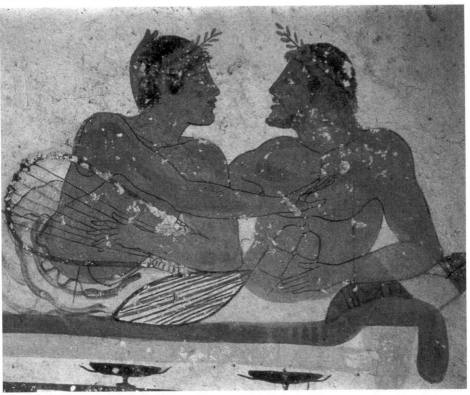

2. The Western ideal of platonic friendship suppresses its origins in homosexual desire.
(*Lovers*, fresco from the Tomb of the Divers, Paestum, *c*. 480 BC)

Be that as it may, the *Iliad* remains the source of one of the most famous examples of male love, at least between mortals, in Greek culture. The plain fact of the matter is that, contrary to Symonds and regardless of Homer's own understanding of the matter, the story of Achilles and Patroclus has indeed suggested 'the interpretation put on it by later generations'. Nor did it have to wait until the nineteenth century for this devious misinterpretation to take shape. In the *Amores*, a third- or fourth-century AD dialogue by pseudo-Lucian of Samosata, one speaker ridicules the idea that Achilles and Patroclus could possibly have been chaste. How but in physical pleasure did they express their love? What else did they spend their time doing – just 'sitting opposite each other'?[2] In the *Odyssey* (XXIV, 78) we are told that after the death of Patroclus, Achilles loved Antilochus, and that all three men were eventually interred together in the same grave. Hans Licht comments that 'Homer is unable to imagine the chief hero of his poem without a favourite'.[3]

Boys were already known to be a valuable commodity. In the *Iliad* (XIX, 193), the reconciliation of Agamemnon and Achilles is marked by the former's presenting the latter with a gift of several high-born youths. Twice (XIV, 297; XV, 449), the *Odyssey* refers to an extensive trade in boys across the seas frequented by Odysseus. Even the famous narrative of the rape of Ganymede, which Homer mentions in the *Iliad* (XX, 231), seems as much to do with material theft as it does with sexual desire.

Boy-lovers in (and after) ancient Greece were greatly advantaged and empowered by the fact that the father of their gods was said to have had a history of pederastic involvement.

(Of course, it may simply be that boy-lovers self-seekingly invented a boy-loving god.) Zeus' abduction of Ganymede becomes the most important model of mortal relationships, whether carnal or chaste, between men and boys. We can see what would become a typical use of the myth in the following lines by Theognis of Megara, who worked in the sixth century BC:

> The love of boys is sweet. Even the king
> Of gods, the son of Kronos, loved a boy
> Ganymede, and he took him to his home
> Olympus, and he gave divinity
> To him, because he had the lovely bloom
> Of youth. Don't be surprised, Simonides,
> To see me love and serve a handsome boy.[4]

This is one of the earliest examples of what was to become an extremely common argument, not only in Greece but later in Rome, then throughout the Middle Ages and the Renaissance all over Europe. The poet identifies with Zeus; the boy he loves is like Ganymede; their love is correspondingly divine. In its more debased uses, the myth could also be used to excuse abduction, rape and the use either of one's boyfriend as a mere waiter at table or of one's slave as a bedmate.

Commenting on these justificatory uses of the myth, Robert Graves credits it with having helped to institutionalise Greek misogyny. But Graves appears to be working in a distinctly twentieth-century spirit of objection to homosexuality. He writes:

> The Zeus–Ganymede myth gained immense popularity in Greece and Rome because it afforded religious justification for [a] grown man's passionate love of a boy. Hitherto, sodomy had been tolerated only as an extreme form of goddess worship [in the transvestite and transsexual rites associated with Cybele] . . . But this new passion . . . emphasised the victory of patriarchy over matriarchy. It turned Greek philosophy into an intellectual game that men could play without the assistance of women, now that they had found a new field of homosexual romance. Plato exploited this to the full[.][5]

There is very little evidence to suggest that prior to this point, mere 'game' or not, Greek philosophy welcomed the involvement of women. Nor is it clear how one pederastic myth could so easily win the day for boy-lovers, when so many, indeed most, of the sexual relationships enjoyed by the gods were heterosexual. However, this is not to deny that ancient Greek society was strongly misogynistic and that the idealisation of man–boy love had its part in maintaining this institutional sexual prejudice. Actually, the situation is much more complicated than a chicken-and-egg argument over which came first, pederasty or misogyny, would suggest.

It must be arguable that the most influential of all the Greek writers, if not of all their thinkers, was Plato (427–347 BC).[6] If it is true that, as Graves says, he exploited to the full 'the new field of homosexual romance', he did so in a manner which repaid his dues to homosexual romance itself. It is in Plato more consistently and more convincingly than anywhere else in Greek thought that pederasty is exalted from the status of a sexual outlet to a philosophical system claiming access to divinity. Furthermore, this system's arguments are presented, as if by way of pre-emptive proof, in dialogues which are themselves evidence of the rational love-making which may occur between man and boy.

3. The educational dialogue
between inspirer and hearer. (Detail
of youth and man in vineyard on
black-figured cup, *c.* 520 BC)

A good example of what is meant by the phrase 'Socratic dialogue' in the context of the
cultural history of homosexuality is *Charmides*, in which Socrates enters into dialogue with
the eponymous boy in order to find out if his inner, spiritual and intellectual beauty could
possibly be as great as that of his lovely face and body. As the philosopher says to Critias,
his host, 'before we see his body, should we not ask him to show us his soul, naked and
undisguised?' (p. 11). When the boy enters the room and sits down, his clothing swings
open for a delightful moment. Catching sight of the boy's body, Socrates is almost
overcome by desire and has to struggle to control himself. In the conversation which
follows, Socrates typically educates the boy, not by teaching him a string of facts which he
must remember and repeat, but by asking him questions and thereby subtly eliciting from
him a range of philosophical deductions, all born out of the boy's own capacity for logical
reasoning.

Similarly, in the *Lysis*, Socrates discusses with a beautiful boy a topic closely related to
the beauty of boys – friendship, in this case. In this type of dialogue the line here between
education (Latin root: *e-ducere*, to lead out) and seduction (*se-ducere*, to lead aside) is both
narrow and faint. As much for late Victorian inverts as for Plato's contemporaries, this is
the very model of the educational pederastic relationship. The adult Greek lover acts as
inspirer (*eispenelas*) and his adolescent beloved responds as hearer (*aïtas*). (Xenophon
spoke of *breathing* love into beautiful boys in order to strengthen their modesty and self-

control.) Their verbal love-making develops the boy's mind as effectively as their physical exertions, if any, might help to tone up his physique. Relationships with girls or women would be irrelevant to this process. Eva Cantarella has outlined the complex educational purpose of pederasty, and its superiority over marital relations, as follows:

> Love between men dates back to a time in Greek history when . . . the man–woman relationship, for all its importance and its indispensable reproductive function, did not lie at the centre of social organisation. What occupied the central position was the relationship between men. In other words, heterosexual relations provided physical life, but the function of giving life within the adult male group, the function of creating a man as a social individual, belonged to the homosexual relationship, set up for this purpose, almost as an institution, between a grown man and a boy. But this relationship was supposed to last only for a well-defined period of time.[7]

The principal act of homosexual expression was intercrural intercourse (that is, the insertion of the man's penis between the boy's thighs). The man was expected to be invariably active, the boy correspondingly passive. Indeed, the boy was not strictly meant to show any particular interest in having sex with his lover, and when they did make love, always at the lover's instigation, the boy was not meant to make any demonstrative expression of pleasure. In pictorial representations of homosexual intercourse, the penis of the boy is only rarely shown erect.[8] Fellatio and anal intercourse were not generally considered to be appropriate to the moderation and dignity required of a properly educational relationship.

The most influential of the dialogues upon the development of homosexual culture and subcultures is the *Symposium*, Plato's account of a banquet at which the diners agree to entertain each other by giving speeches on the topic of love. In subsequent centuries this dialogue has been used to support two completely opposed views of the moral viability of homosexual relationships. On the one hand, Plato is said only to approve of friendships between males – 'platonic love' as it apocryphally came to be called – and to deplore physical expressions of same-sex desire. On the other hand, the *Symposium* has been extensively exploited by apologists for male homosexuality, who cite the many signs of its approval of male–male love, regardless of physicality, and its implication that this sort of love is inevitably superior to that which may develop between a man and a woman. The same two parties have chosen either to use other dialogues such as the *Gorgias* – in which the figure of the passive and effeminate homosexual male (*kinaidos*) is taken as proof that the pleasures associated with love are not automatically to be equated with goodness – or conveniently to ignore them.

The *Symposium* begins with the speech of Phaedrus, according to whom Love is the oldest of the gods. He confers on us the greatest benefits. Nothing inspires a sense of honour and nobility, as opposed to dishonour and shame, so readily as love: for any man is particularly sensitive to such things in front of his lover. It is for this reason that an army of pairs of male lovers would be invincible. Only a lover will sacrifice his life for someone else – hence the great distinction with which the gods treated Achilles when he died for Patroclus. The lover is possessed. In this respect, he comes closer than the one who is loved to being divine; but when he acts heroically the latter, because he is not possessed, is a greater hero than the former. In leading men towards the acquisition of merit, both here and in the hereafter, Love is the most powerful of the gods.

Pausanias, who speaks next, argues that since there are two Aphrodites (one the daughter of Uranus, the other the daughter of Zeus and Dione), there are also two distinct types of love, the common or vulgar sort and the heavenly sort. Love is not inherently good; it is good only if it impels people to love in a correct manner. Common love is physical, is directed by men to women as well as to men, and prefers its object to be unintelligent. Its effect, whether good or bad, is purely a matter of chance. But heavenly love – ruled by the Aphrodite who was born not by woman but monosexually from the sea, out of the dismembered fragments of the body of her father, Uranus – develops between two males – and develops maturely, between an older and a younger man, rather than between a man and a boy. This is because boys are still unpredictable and inconstant. We condone in lovers the kind of behaviour which we would not be able to accept in others, but we encourage the loved one to flee the attentions of his lover. We use this as a test of both the lover's nobility of purpose and the beloved's interest in the pursuit of wisdom and virtue. The attainment of excellence is the proper end of Love.

At this point in the narrative Aristophanes has an attack of hiccups, so his turn is taken by Eryximachus, according to whom good health is caused by mutual love existing between the various elements of the human body. Musical harmony, too, exists under Love's influence. Indeed, Love holds sway over all things, whether human or not, and is the author of all our happiness.

When Aristophanes has recovered from his hiccups he gives what may be the most famous speech in the whole of the *Symposium*, in which he speaks of the origins and purposes of Love. The degree of seriousness with which Plato expects this speech to be taken is open to question; at any rate, we should certainly not assume that Plato actually believed in the myth which he has the comic dramatist propound. However, it has its importance in as far as it demonstrates an early conception of distinct sexual orientations.

According to Aristophanes, of all the gods Love is the most friendly to humankind. Originally, there were three sexes: the male, from the sun, the female, from the earth, and the two combined, from the moon, which shares the characteristics of both sun and earth. At the same time, all human bodies, of whichever sex, were spherical. Finding that these creatures were rebellious in spirit, Zeus decided to weaken them by cutting them all in two. This was done, and its incidental effect was to reduce the number of physical sexes to two. Subsequently, each human individual yearned constantly to be reunited with his or her other half. It follows that the halves of what had originally been the hermaphroditic sex, whether now female or male, became heterosexual (to use the twentieth-century term); but those who had originally been of a single sex were now homosexual, seeking to find an other half belonging to the same sex as their own.[9]

When any half did happen to find its other half, it could do nothing but lovingly cling to it in an unsatisfiable manner: for these creatures still had their sexual organs on what had been the outside of their spherical bodies and they now had no way of uniting themselves with their other halves. Therefore, Zeus compassionately saw to it that their sexual organs were transferred to the front of their new bodies, thereby enabling united halves to conjoin sexually. The heterosexual halves were empowered to reproduce – 'or if man came to man they might be satisfied, and rest, and go their ways to the business of life'. Aristophanes argues here that man-loving young men are 'the best of boys and youths, because they have the most manly natures'.

Countering an apparently quite common argument, he adds: 'Some indeed assert that they are shameless, but this is not true; for they do not act thus from any want of shame, but because they are valiant and manly, and have a manly countenance, and they embrace that which is like them' (p. 561). In their maturity, they are not generally inclined to get married and beget children – although many do so, in obedience to the law – but prefer to live with each other in an unmarried state. People of whichever sex or sexual orientation who do manage to find their other halves are thenceforth inseparable. Their most fervently held wish is to be melted into one being again. Thus, to conclude, Love is 'the desire and pursuit of the whole' (p. 562). As Eryximachus said, on it depends the happiness of the human race.

Agathon speaks next. Love, he says, is the happiest of the gods. He is young, and hates old age. He is self-controlled and courageous. The principal evidence of his wisdom lies in the constant reproduction of living things. Furthermore, all worthwhile human endeavour stems from Love.

Here, Socrates finally says his piece; yet what he says consists not of his own original views, but of those of a woman called Diotima, by whom he has obviously been impressed and with whom we can take it that he agrees.[10] According to Diotima, then, Love is half god and half human – a mediator between the two conditions. The state of love is a desire for the perpetual possession of the good. Using the metaphor of pregnancy, Diotima argues that all men are in a state of both physical and spiritual pregnancy. When they come to maturity it is in their nature to feel the need to give birth, but they can do so only in beauty and never in ugliness. Indeed, it is Love's object to achieve 'birth in beauty, whether of body or soul' (p. 577).

Both Love and generation have the common goal of immortality. Now, some men, Diotima says, have a creative instinct which is physical; and it is they who have recourse to reproductive sexual intercourse with women. They believe that by producing children they can secure immortality for themselves in the memory, and in the very existence, of subsequent generations. On the other hand, there are those whose creative instinct is more spiritual. They conceive not in the body but in the soul; and their progeny is not a child but wisdom and virtue. The poet is an example of such a man. Throughout this part of the discussion, the implication is that physical creativity is clearly inferior to the spiritual; and, therefore, that male–male love is superior to male–female love. This latter point applies, in the first place, because male–male friendships are being contrasted with male–female reproductive sexual relationships; however, the same point appears to apply even if like is being compared with like, and the two males do have a physical relationship: for, given the institutionalised misogyny of Greek society (even when the speaker is, as here, a woman herself), the understanding is that men have a greater capacity for spirituality – even in their physicalities – than any woman has. As Aristophanes' speech reminds us, men were associated with the sun, women with the earth.

When a man associates himself with the beauty embodied in the man he loves he will produce spiritual children (such as poetry or philosophy or statesmanship) which the two lovers will then nurture as if they were bringing up children. Such children as these are likely to be superior to human children in being both more beautiful and immortal. This must be the goal in a lifetime of loving, even for men who do enter into reproductive relationships with women. Any man's life should involve an eventual movement away from the love of merely physical beauty towards that of moral beauty. The former is little more than a pale simulacrum of the latter.

Just as Socrates concludes this account of his dialogue with Diotima, Alcibiades arrives, the worse for drink. Hearing the topic of the evening, he gives a tipsy speech in praise of Socrates, the only man who ever shared a couch with him for the night but made no attempt to make love with him. (Both beautiful and correspondingly experienced at fending off or egging on would-be seducers, Alcibiades was clearly amazed by such modest restraint.) Thus, the philosopher himself is unwillingly held up to the assembled company as the final exemplar of the kinds of spirituality which they have been discussing. When a crowd of revellers arrives, the dinner party breaks up.

There are certain moments of subdued bawdiness in Plato's dialogues which draw our attention to the fact that not all Greeks were as philosophically cool as Socrates when confronted either with extremes of physical beauty or with evidence of other people's sexual interest in such beauty. Contrary to certain idealising representations, most of which are loosely based on the atmospheric effects of the Platonic dialogues – deeply serious discussions in the gymnasium or in the moderating shade of the plane trees – the Greeks were not a race of philosophers. It would make more sense to think of them as a barrack-bound people, the men at least as likely to spend their spare time exchanging dirty jokes and gossip as seeking to refine their abstract ideas. For a taste of this aspect of their civilisation one has to turn to what made them laugh. Aristophanes' comic dramas give us the best impression of this side of their lives and shared attitudes.

In the words of K.J. Dover, 'The reader who turns from Plato to comedy is struck not only by the consistent comic reduction of homosexual eros to the coarsest physical terms but also by its displacement from the centre to the periphery of Athenian sexual life; for comedy is fundamentally heterosexual.'[11] The popular playwright Aristophanes (c. 448–c. 388 BC) is unrelenting in his satirisations of high-born men who are effeminate, who take a passive role in homosexual intercourse, and who prostitute themselves for material gain. But what he is criticising in such representations is not pederasty itself – which he appears to have taken for granted as being capable of both giving healthy, manly pleasure and rising to the levels of nobility claimed for it by the likes of Socrates and Plato – but what he regarded as its increasingly debased manifestations in the society of his time. Aristophanes reserved many insulting expressions, most often anally based, for those responsible for this perceived decline in moral standards: white-arse (*leukopygos*), black-arse (*melanpygos*), rough-arse (*dasuproktos*), wide-arse (meaning overused: *europroktos*) and so forth. But the leading male characters in the plays almost invariably have an eye for a beautiful boy – the eye of the active male philanderer – in much the same way as they are often diverted by the beauty of young women and girls. So it would be an error to suppose that the drag-wearing politicians and voracious pathics Aristophanes ridicules are in any way intended as clauses in a general argument against same-sex relationships. This must have been perfectly clear to his audiences: for there is no reason why they would have been expecting any such perversity of thought.

· · ·

Just as it is virtually impossible to imagine the direction English literature would have taken had it never been able to draw on the insights of Plato, so it is equally difficult to conceive of an English poetic tradition uninfluenced by the bucolic Idylls of the Sicilian poet Theocritus (c. 308–240 BC).[12] Along with somewhat fewer, but similar, works by Bion and Moschus, these are the poems which definitively establish Western culture's preferred version of pastoral life; and they thereby exert a far greater influence on subsequent literary production than is strictly merited by their own (admittedly not inconsiderable) aesthetic merit. They deal with a world based partly in the everyday realities of the herdsman's life – excretion, reproduction, death and all – and partly in an idealised Arcadian space closely watched and sagaciously cared for by benevolent gods. They are peopled by simple folk, as completely untainted by book-learning (although sensitively receptive to the muses of sung poetry) as they are highly educated in the ways of Nature. Their time is spent tending their herds and crops, appreciating the beauty of their natural surroundings, and falling in love. Their main recreational activity is song, often indulged in competitively, with something like a set of pan pipes as a prize. And the songs they improvise concern their own lives: hymning the beauty of someone they love, lamenting a friend's death, lulling their flocks to sleep.

Theocritus makes a distinction between lust and love – the former is quick and crude, the latter lingers and causes as much pain as eventual pleasure – but he never claims that love is entirely lacking in a certain element of lust. The boys in his poems have all seen sheep and goats mounting each other, and the implication is that they are turned on by the sight because of its inherent suggestion that bodies are meant for sexual apposition. There is even a suggestion that animals might be turned on by human intercourse in a brief passage of Idyll V which English translators used to render only into Latin. The goatherd Comatas and the shepherd Lacon are in competitive mood. The former says to the latter:

> When I bugger you, you'll feel it. Your she-goats
> will bleat, and your rams will screw them.

– to which Lacon replies with what must be one of the most effective of all improvised insults:

> May you be buried no more deeply than you bugger,
> you old hump-back.

However, these men's familiarity with the natural world may also give them a strong sense of appropriate and inappropriate behaviour. And they do not generally see the mounting of a desired body as a sufficient end in itself. Their randiness is not decadent in the manner of spoilt city-dwellers. Everything in Arcadia is conducted in accordance with natural law. And everything includes love between men and boys. In the singing competition which follows on from the combative dialogue I have just quoted, Comatas sings about the girl he is courting, while Lacon sings of the boy Cratidas, who is playing hard to get. But then Comatas asks Lacon, still singing:

> Don't tell me you've forgotten
> when I got you on the ground
> and you raped me blissfully against the oak?

The evident mutuality of this rough encounter – which Lacon claims to have forgotten – has now given way to a plaintive longing on both their parts for the individuals they are in love with. Longing is, of course, the perfect mood for song.

To my mind, the most delightful aspect of Theocritus' Idylls is their association of the oral pleasures of improvised love poetry with those of making love itself. We come back to the theme with which I began this chapter: the aptness of poetry to the shaping of love. In Theocritus' work the sight of a lovable person inspires a flow of celebratory language. The dialogues, even the competitive ones, are courtships. A beautiful poem earns the kisses of a beautiful girl or boy. A sexy poem may arouse even more delicious physical responses and rewards. The young people in these poems are all usefully but modestly employed, generally herding sheep or goats, and are correspondingly poor. But they never yearn for greater riches than a fresh honeycomb, a new set of pipes, or the honey and harmony of a beautiful lover. Most poems represent them as being in a combined state of watchfulness over their flocks and careless leisure. There is a lot of what Walt Whitman might call 'loafing' going on. Much of their time is spent in time-consuming courtships, conducted at length and at leisure. Sexual arousal comes and goes.

Some of the Arcadian festivals and customs reported or invented by Theocritus give the impression of a culture almost intoxicated by its own burgeoning sexuality. Take as an example the following passage from Idyll XII:

> Nisaeans, men of Megara, first among oarsmen,
> may you prosper and be blessed for the honour
> you have shown to Diocles, the Attic stranger,
> lover of young men. Always in the early spring
> the boys still gather round his tomb and hold
> their contest in the art of love. And he whose kissing,
> lip on lip, is judged most sweet, will return home
> to his mother, dressed in victory garlands.
> It is a lucky man they choose as judge!

Diocles was an Athenian who died while attempting to save the life of a boy he loved. The boys who honour his grave with their teasingly erotic competition do so by way of preparation for the honour of being loved by such a man – if another such man exists. They are making themselves ready to provide a sweetness of kisses in keeping with such an honour. The point is that, by associating their erotic games with Diocles' memorial, they are committing themselves to their society's standards of heroism, manliness and manly fidelity. The last line I have quoted, of course, barely needs saying at all. The lucky man who judges these boys can honourably toy with promiscuity, even if only for the duration of the competition, and even if only imagining the even sweeter pleasure that making love with them could generate. The reader, of course, is placed in a similar position – but without even the kisses.

The tomb of Diocles reminds us of one of the key themes, not only in Greek literature, but in love poetry ever since: that of the passage of time and the inevitability of death. As one of Theocritus' men says to the recalcitrant boy he is courting (XXIX):

> By your gentle lips, I beg you recall
> that you were younger twelve months ago:
> before a man can spit, we're old and wrinkled.

This darkness of mood always alternates with a cheerfully resigned *carpe diem*. Given that death is inevitable and is likely to occur sooner than expected, love is all the more important and all the more urgent. Far from offering a trivial, idealised vision of love, set in an impossibly perfect world, Theocritus' poetry can, without warning, suddenly wound the unwary reader with a moment of depressive reflection. In fact, perhaps the best way of summarising his fundamental attitude to love, after the prettiness of the pastoral context has been admired and set aside, is to quote two lines from Idyll XXX:

> But the man in love can feed only on memory
> as desire consumes him to the very bone.

This image of love as a wasting disease, or even as post-mortem decay, far from seeming inappropriate to the erotically celebratory tone of so many of Theocritus' poems, actually serves to confirm and underscore that mood. Life is all the more beautiful for the contrast with what it must become. This is a world where, although the grapes are abundant on the vine and wine is forever plentiful, and although the bodies of the boys and girls who tend their flocks on fertile slopes are invariably slender and beautiful, nevertheless 'Grapes become raisins. Roses wither and die' (XXVII). Death can turn up at any moment – and no moment is opportune for such a visitation – to repeat its perennial threat: *Et in Arcadia ego*.

So Theocritus, this most lambent and lucid of erotic poets, is also the first of the great elegists. His account of the death of Hylas and the consequent grief of Heracles (XIII) is far more touchingly erotic than Apollonius' matter-of-fact report of the same events in *The Voyage of the Argo*. Along with Bion I (the lament for Adonis) and Moschus III (the lament for Bion), his first Idyll (Thyrsis' lament for Daphnis) sets the pattern for centuries of European mourning.

When the circumstances and personalities of Theocritan pastoral are reworked by Theocritus' contemporary Longus, we can see that the balance has begun to tilt against a simple acceptance of the bucolic naturalness of homosexual activities. Longus' *Daphnis and Chloe* is essentially the story of a boy and a girl's development through puberty, and their love's maturation from sibling-like affection, through innocent and ignorant caresses, to a wedding night of heterosexual intercourse proper – all occurring in the most manifestly natural of circumstances and at a natural slowness of pace in tune with the cycle of the seasons.[13] The story is like a precursor to Bernardin de Saint-Pierre's *Paul et Virginie* (1788) or even H. de Vere Stacpoole's *The Blue Lagoon* (1908). You might say it propagandises heterosexuality; it certainly idealises it.

Centred on the budding beauty of its two protagonists' physiques, *Daphnis and Chloe* is often in danger of drifting over into prurient voyeurism, but never quite lingers long enough to do so. Longus makes much of the scenes in which Chloe first takes notice of the sight, and feel, of Daphnis' naked body. The boy is bathing, and we watch him from the girl's point of view: 'It seemed to Chloe, as she watched him, that Daphnis was beautiful; and as he had never seemed beautiful to her before, she thought that this beauty must be the result of washing. Moreover, when she washed his back, she found that the flesh was soft and yielding; so she secretly touched her own body several times to see if it was any softer.' The next day, she persuades him to have another wash: 'and while he was washing she looked at him, and after looking at him she touched him. And again she went away full of admiration, and this admiration was the beginning of love' (p. 20). It is crucial to note that these, and subsequent, bathing scenes take place in the open air, at a natural spring.

These sequences of watching and touching constitute a natural education in heterosexual consciousness, leading from early puberty to a wedding night of sexual bliss (just after the book's final sentence). In addition, Daphnis receives lessons from two other teachers. The first, Lycaenion, gives him the benefit of her experience of heterosexual intercourse by allowing him to experience it for himself with her – a lesson the details of which he re-uses on his wedding night with Chloe. But the second teacher is Gnathon, an importunate boy with a taste for wine and other boys; he is 'nothing but a mouth and a stomach and what lies under the stomach'. Gnathon takes a fancy to Daphnis and tries to seduce him:

he asked him to present his backside, as a she-goat would to a he-goat. When Daphnis finally realised what he meant, he replied that it was quite all right for a he-goat to do that sort of thing to a she-goat, but no one had ever heard of a he-goat doing it to another he-goat, or a ram to another ram, or a cock to another cock. So Gnathon actually tried to rape him; but Daphnis pushed him away – he was almost too drunk to stand – and knocked him down. (p. 124)

Daphnis already knows about the (supposedly) heterosexual orderliness of the natural world; but what he learns from Gnathon is that some people's desires controvert nature, and that one vice is often accompanied by others (drunkenness, violence and so forth).

His defence of his own virtue is conducted in terms of aptness to nature rather than of individual wish: he appears to be secure in the assumption that nature's sexual requirements coincide exactly with his own. His knowledge of Chloe's harmony with the bucolic world they both inhabit can only have confirmed this in his mind. It is what sets her so clearly apart from Gnathon's literal lack of balance.

. . .

Hardly any Greek writers do not refer to pederasty. This does not mean that they all liked boys. On the contrary, many mentioned boy-love only to point out that they preferred women. But pederasty was such a significant institution in Greek society that it cropped up in the written texts not only when the subjects of sex or love arose, but also in the much wider political context of power relations between the sexes and the social classes. The pederastic system was a defining aspect of the structure of Greek social life, no less important than the military institutions, and its influence extended far beyond the privacy of the individual man's sleeping quarters.

Greek mythology was correspondingly well stocked with homosexual myths, often about boy-loving deities, and we know that the Greeks were themselves already compiling lists of famous boy-lovers and famous lovable boys, just as Victorian Englishmen would later seek to compile similar lists if not always for quite the same reasons. One of the fullest of these catalogues was put together by, of all people, Saint Clement of Alexandria: 'Zeus loved Ganymede; Apollo Cinyras, Zacynthus, Hyacinthus, Phorbas, Hylas, Admetus, Cyparissus, Amyklas, Troilus, Branchus, Tymnius, Parus, Potuieus, and Orpheus; Dionysus loved Laonis, Ampelus, Hymenaeus, Hermaphroditos, and Achilles; Asclepius loved Hippolytus; Hephaestus Peleus; Pan Daphnis; Hermes Perseus, Chryses, Therses, and Odryses; Heracles Abderus, Dryops, Iokastus, Philoktetes, Hylas, Polyphemus, Haemon, Chonus, and Eurystheus'.[14] The list is not complete, but it gives a good impression of both the proliferation of such mythic narratives of male love and Clement's interest in that proliferation. He seems to be impressed, even if he does not approve.

Greek literature is full of gay texts, from Pindar's pious celebrations of the athletic prowess of Greek youths to the erotic lyrics of Theognis of Megara, who was wont to ride (or at least to describe riding) boys' arses as if they were frisky colts. It is not possible to analyse, or even to mention, them all here. The many epigrams on boy-love preserved in Book XII of the *Greek Anthology* – a massive storehouse of gravestone inscriptions, love letters, graffiti, scurrilous personal remarks and ejaculations of desire – give a rich impression of the different moods boy-love was able to evoke throughout the Greek diaspora. Among these pages are the contents of Strato's *Mousa Paidiké* (c. AD 140), the earliest of the gay anthologies to have survived.

But there is a paradox which forces itself upon the reader's attention throughout the *Anthology*. It is not confined to the poems themselves: for it lies at the heart of Greek attitudes to the love between men and boys, which they so insistently exalted. It manifests itself in the tonal modulations of the *Symposium*. It is most eloquently summarised by Michel Foucault, who really makes it the cornerstone of his study of Greek sexual history:

> On the one hand, young men were recognised as objects of pleasure – and even as the only honourable and legitimate objects among the possible male partners of men: no one would ever reproach a man for loving a boy, for desiring and enjoying him, provided that the laws and proprieties were respected. But on the other hand, the boy,

4. Adult pleasure takes
its licensed course.
(Scene of a man
titillating a young boy
from a red-figure cup by
the Brygus Painter,
500–475 BC)

whose youth must be a training for manhood, could not and must not identify with that role. He could not of his own accord, in his own eyes, and for his own sake, be that object of pleasure, even though the man was quite naturally fond of appointing him as an object of pleasure. In short, to delight in and be a subject of pleasure with a boy did not cause a problem for the Greeks; but to be an object of pleasure and to acknowledge oneself as such constitutes a major difficulty for the boy.[15]

The problem with boys is that they are unresponsive – which is precisely as it should be. Men should love boys, but boys should resist men. We shall recognise this pattern repeating itself, later, in the Latin and Arabic literatures. It accounts for the great degree of frustration expressed in the most highly developed literary traditions of boy-love, and for the intensity of desire expressed by the disappointed poet/lover. It partially accounts for the fact that so many modern cultures think of loving as a matter of yearning for an absent beloved, rather than of enjoying the comforts of his or her presence.

A number of the poets represented in the *Anthology* are in the happy position of recalling the unresponsive behaviour of particular boys they once courted, at a time when those boys have since become lovers in their turn and are finding themselves duly courting unresponsive boys. There is a great deal of vengeful satisfaction expressed on the topic of a cruel boy's come-uppance. If the tone is often slightly bitter, the pleasure is no less sweet. Nowhere is this more succinctly expressed than in an epigram by Statilius Flaccus (XII, 12):

> Just as he gets a beard,
> Lado, the lovely, a bitch to lovers,
> loves a boy. Justice is quick.

Thus, although the moment of the boy's first stubble is so often conceived in poetry as a time of great loss, when a beloved boy is suddenly too old to be respectably the object of a man's passion, and must be allowed to find a boyfriend of his own, it can also be a moment of more or less vindictive relief. He is now little more than his ex-lover's competitor in the search for younger flesh.

As anyone knows who knows boys, reluctance can be undermined by a timely gift. This is where the austere conventions of Greek boy-love can be seen to degenerate into a materialistic system of the bartering of adult wealth for adolescent sexual favours. Boys could accept gifts in homage to their loveliness – indeed, a suitor would rarely appear empty-handed if he expected his assertions of sincerity to be taken seriously – but a boy who accepted money for sex was a whore. The line between a boy's being admired for the lavishness of the gifts he attracted and reproached or ridiculed for prostituting himself was narrow. The *Anthology* is full of references to the gift economy and its less desirable consequences, such as the destruction of the reputations of high-born boys, the reduction of courtship to mercenary negotiations about sexual favours and material rewards, competitiveness between boys for the attentions of generous suitors, and so forth.

In spite of all we know about the unwritten conventions and written laws governing the sexual behaviour of both men and boys, it is clear that, like any city, Athens developed its own networks of meeting places and cruising grounds, both indoor and out, and that plenty of homosexual action occurred outside the conventions of the single suitor courting the single boy. Boys gathered in certain places – barbers' shops, physicians' quarters, the gymnasia, the baths – and men were attracted to the same places at least as much by the prospect of casual sex as by that of a more formally negotiated and recognised relationship. At night, hustlers could be found on the Pnyx, a dark hill west of the Areopagus.

What I am saying is that, then as now, the rules were made to be broken. It may be that historians like Foucault do not pay enough attention to this fact. That reservation notwithstanding, it is as well to give Michel Foucault the last word, since in the passage which follows he appears actually to be addressing himself to gay men with an interest in the culture of Greek pederasty. He seems to be trying to discourage the kind of Graecophilia that flourishes, perhaps especially in France, among men who are more strongly attracted to boys than to other men. He is delivering what they may take to be, after the familiar good news, the bad. The aim is to shatter the illusion of a Greece in which boy-love flourished without restriction. Foucault writes:

> To this male love, and more precisely to this love of young boys and adolescents – a love that was later to be so severely condemned for such a long time – the Greeks

granted a legitimacy, which we are fond of seeing as proof of the freedom they granted themselves in this domain. And yet it was in connection with this love, much more than with health (which also preoccupied them) and much more than with women and marriage (the orderliness of which they nevertheless sought to maintain), that they spoke of the need to practise the strictest austerities.[16]

Chapter 3

The Roman Classics

It is not possible to name an exclusively homosexual – or rather, boy-loving – male writer in ancient Rome. While Roman culture shows abundant signs of the presence of man–boy love – to such an extent that, ever since Edward Gibbon's *Decline and Fall of the Roman Empire* (1776–88), it has been taken by many people as self-evident that homosexuality destroyed 'the glory that was Rome' – the fact is that the Roman writers who show a sexual interest in boys tend to show an even greater interest in women. This was a society which took for granted what we now know as 'bisexuality'. Beauty tended to be determined by age, not gender.

Consider the odes of Horace (65–8 BC). Virtually all of Horace's poems about boys also mention women or girls. (The converse is not the case, though, when he is writing about women.) Less rude than Catullus or Martial, he nevertheless maintains a quiet involvement in and enthusiasm for the erotic life, even when he claims to be beyond it. For instance, in IV, 1, he claims no longer to hope for a mutual love affair with either woman or boy – and yet he is in thrall to Ligurinus, a boy who shows no interest in him. He dreams about the boy and when in his presence is unable to speak. The equal balance of his reference to women and boys ('nec femina nec puer') is typical, and is clearly not the mere rhetoric of anti-sexism that such constructions later appear to be in (say) the poems of Walt Whitman. In Horace, such balanced references to both sexes convince one that they are related to lived experience. Moreover, the poems themselves are presented as taking part in the erotic life to which they refer. In III, 1, Horace speaks of his audience as consisting of both (female) virgins and boys ('virginibus puerisque canto'). To all of them he speaks of love; and to certain individuals he actually addresses love poems. (The disdainful Ligurinus is one of these.)

Catullus (*c.* 84–*c.* 54 BC) is a similar case. He was one of the first poets, certainly one of the first whose works have survived, to write a connected sequence of love poems which go into detail about the emotional complexities of a love affair with a single, named individual. The individual is a woman, Clodia Metelli, whom Catullus refers to as Lesbia (though apparently without the intention of raising lesbian connotations). But he also wrote love poems to a named man, Iuventius, and many scandalous, gossipy epigrams in which he refers to the homosexual habits of other men. In a sense, it is Catullus who brings the tradition of the homo-erotic epigram down to earth. Where the Greek poets had tended to heighten and beautify, Catullus uses what one might call the language of the streets and often adopts a searingly mocking tone. He is insulting and argumentative, yet also capable of the sweetest outbursts of lyricism.

Above all, he is a realist, in the sense that he is dealing with real people and real events. Unlike his great admirer Martial, who had fewer connections and lived under the Emperor Domitian's tyrannous regime, Catullus was from a wealthy background and lived in a political era, under the First Triumvirate, when it was possible not only to speak one's mind in public, but to do so, as Catullus did, bluntly. So in one poem (XXIX) he addresses Pompey as a high-born queer ('cinaede Romule'), while in another (LVII) he attacks both Caesar and his chief engineer Mamurra, again as queers ('improbis cinaedis,/ Mamurrae pathicoque Caesarique').[1] Catullus had enough influence in Roman society to be able to get away with this sort of thing.

Catullus is always at his most sexually outspoken when lampooning other people's behaviour. And when he is in this mood any sexual taste becomes fair game, apparently including his own. He demands various possessions back from Thallus, whom he denounces not only as a flabby queen, but as a rapacious one to boot (XXV). He accuses Gellius of cock-sucking (LXXX) and Vibennius and his son of various sexual misdemeanours in the public baths (XXXIII). When Aurelius and Furius have the effrontery to infer Catullus' sexual tastes from his epigrams, he calls them queers and threatens to bugger them both by way of punishment (XVI).

The two main terms of insult to appear in these bawdy satires are *pathicus* and *cinaedus*, the former denoting a passive man beyond the youthful age up to which sexual receptivity could be seen as charmingly accommodating; and the latter a kind of hustler catering to the requirements of the pathic. There is no doubt that, in Roman culture as in so many others, phallic power was cherished more highly – at least by the social collective – than individual pleasures and affections. A man who was known to have abdicated his position of sexual superiority (as insertor) to a man either younger or from a socially inferior position could be treated as having relinquished his right to be taken seriously as a Roman citizen. Hence (as in XVI) Catullus' tendency to wield the phallus as a punitive weapon. The most light-hearted and erotic instance of this is the epigram (LVI) in which he claims to have happened on a boy and girl making love. The poet makes his presence felt, without interrupting them, by buggering the boy. The verb Catullus uses for the latter act (*cecidi*) constitutes a pun on beating and fucking, which in the original underlines the punitive aspect of the poet's intervention while nevertheless acknowledging the potential pleasure involved, for both man and boy. Buggery is treated as a joke – but a sexy one. Importantly, the joke is, as it were, bisexual rather than merely homo-erotic. Both males, particularly the boy at the centre of the sandwich, will get the best of both worlds in this impromptu threesome.

Catullus was a compulsive kisser. His most affecting love poems are those in which, losing all sense of proportion and restraint, he quantifies the kisses required to demonstrate the extent of his love for a particular individual. The most famous of these lyrics (V) is addressed to Lesbia and demands hundreds and thousands of kisses. But there are comparable poems addressed to men, too. When his beloved Veranius returns to Rome from Spain, Catullus proposes to kiss him all over his face and eyes, and asks who, of all happy people, could possibly now be happier than himself (IX).[2] In a poem to Iuventius, the poet says that three hundred thousand kisses would not exhaust his love (XLVIII). One is well prepared for the moment when the faltering of a relationship is signalled by the fact that kisses can turn sour: when Catullus snatches not three hundred thousand but just a single kiss, Iuventius ostentatiously washes out his mouth. For the rejected lover, honey turns to bile (XCIX).

Another boyfriend, unnamed this time, crops up in XV and XXI. Catullus entrusts the boy to Aurelius' care while at the same time worrying that the boy's virtue most needs guarding against the guard: for, Catullus claims, Aurelius' penis represents a threat to both good boys and bad ('infesto pueris bonis malisque'). Should Aurelius succumb to temptation and lay hands on the boy, Catullus will personally truss him up and shove radishes and mullet up his arse. In XXI, Catullus threatens, for the same reason, punitively to bugger Aurelius.

Catullus' best long poems are epithalamia – celebrations of marriage – and it is clear from one of these (LXI) that the poet held, or at least laid claim to, perfectly orthodox views on the relationship between homo- and heterosexual relationships. Not only did he subscribe, as we have seen, to his society's beliefs about masculine power and the imperative that a respectable adult male should never willingly relinquish it by subjecting himself to penetration by another man, but he also believed that boy-love was for bachelors. Ideally, once married, a man should cleave to his wife alone; and she should ensure, by maintaining his sexual pleasure, that he never err. In LXI, the bridegroom is urged to give up boys, however hard that may be: for husbands no longer share the legitimate sexual rights of single men. What is otherwise a consistently jolly poem is clouded only by this passing moment, in which the husband's loss and the wife's responsibility are emphasised.

Like Catullus, Tibullus (c. 54–c. 19 BC) wrote love poems to both a female and a male addressee.[3] There are more to the female, Delia; but the few to his boyfriend, Marathus, are no less intense. They are also, to my mind, subtler than the equivalent poems by Catullus. But as is so often the case with homo-erotic poetry, modern critics have repeatedly attempted to play down Tibullus' sincerity in the Marathus poems: he was just following a literary fashion, they claim, or performing an exercise. (This critical strategy is most succinctly performed by W.R. Paton when commenting on the boy-loving epigrams of Meleager: 'These attachments were in his case rather a matter of fashion than of passion.'[4]) In fact, Tibullus' poems to Marathus are neither as artificial nor as formulaic as such claims might suggest. We have no reason to doubt their depth of sincerity – if biographical authenticity really must be our main aesthetic criterion – other than the overpowering reason of our own culture's distaste for same-sex relationships.

In the poem beginning 'Sic umbrosa tibi contingant tecta, Priape' (I, iv), Tibullus presents an argument on boy-love distinguished by its ironic reversals and frailties. He puts the case, at first, in the voice of no less an authority on matters sexual than Priapus himself, the god of fecundity. In summary, what Priapus says to the poet is this: don't trust boys; each of them will provide you with a distinct and convincing reason for loving him; don't be put off if he resists your advances, he's bound to come round in the end; promise him anything, even if you don't mean to deliver; beauty and youth last only a brief time, so refuse your boy nothing he asks of you; eventually it will be he who is pleading and you who give; nowadays, however, boys are so brazen they haggle for gifts from their prospective lovers; Venus protects all lovers. Thus, Priapus' train of thought performs a broad, circular swoop from untrustworthy boys, via the untrustworthiness of the men who try to woo them, back again to the untrustworthy boys. Tibullus closes the poem with his own additional argument: the god has urged me to give this advice to lovers; I'll be famous even in old age for my advice to the young men I desire; oh Marathus, spare me the worst of your tortures; I don't want to be ridiculed as the authority on love who was himself inept at loving.

This wonderful poem offers a really sophisticated impression of the devious operations of desire. What is so impressive is an effect – which Tibullus may have learned from

Catullus, whom he admired – whereby lyricism and irony work in opposite directions to generate a unified tone which accurately represents desire's ambivalence. The poem also expresses what appears to have been a very common view, so often discernible in the poetry of male love from both Greece and Rome, of boys as both victims and victimisers, both bribable and extortionate, alternately coy and shameless, pure and insatiable – above all, unpredictable. This is exactly their charm; it is also the source of their power.

Boys will eventually get their come-uppance, firstly from time itself, which must inevitably turn them into men (unless they die first, which many of the subjects of erotic verse do), and secondly, as they themselves fall in love, from the boys and girls whom they desire. In the poem beginning 'Non ego celare possum, quid nutus amantis' (I, viii), we find that this has happened to Marathus himself: for he loves a girl who does not love him in return. No great diplomat in these matters, Tibullus takes a certain pleasure in reminding the boy of how he once teased the lovelorn poet. When he was loved, he mocked love; but now that he loves, he is mocked in his turn. It is far too late to regret his mistreatment of Tibullus. In the subsequent poem (I, ix: 'Quid mihi, si fueras miseros laesuros amores') it turns out that it was the poet who introduced the unresponsive girl to Marathus. He seems both pleased with having done so, as a satisfying act of loving vengeance, and to regret it for the pain it is causing the young man. In any case, the whole experience is represented as being the virtually inevitable consequence of ageing: boys become lovers (of girls and/or younger boys); their erstwhile lovers lose them as boyfriends but continue to love and educate them; the boy learns the pains he once caused in the man. The cycle continues.

Rome's other major, innovative poet of boy-love was Martial, the Spanish outsider who scrutinised and satirised the sexual habits of the Romans with a fearlessness which seems to have been its own defence against criticism. Martial's reputation for producing obscene poems is, perhaps, somewhat exaggerated: for, while it is true that the twelve books of his epigrams, published between AD 85 and 103, are an extremely useful source of information on sexual behaviour in first-century Rome, he has other interests than sexuality, and when he does speak of sex he is by no means uncritical of other people's habits. Thus, although his general attitude is one of benevolent permissiveness, he is careful to protect his own reputation: my works may be lascivious, but my life is pure ('lasciva est nobis pagina, vita proba' – I, 4). Catullus had made similar disclaimers, and others have made them since.

Furthermore, Martial's celebrations of urban lust are shaped within an extremely conventional framework of social rules. A bachelor himself, he promoted the married state as being both orderly and proper, and he urged husbands to concentrate on their wives rather than on ephemeral relationships with younger men. Adultery figures in his verse as a transgression, even if a mild one. And although Martial is indulgent to man–boy relationships, he does not stray from his society's rigid conventions about the roles and acts such relationships may involve: men who are passive partners to younger men or to slaves are ruthlessly lampooned, and fellators are invariably said to be afflicted with a kind of semeniferous halitosis.

On the other hand, as in Catullus, the existence of male–male desire is taken for granted as a rewarding and necessary aspect of life, to be enjoyed both first- and second-hand, by lovers and gossips. Daily life is full of opportunities – to observe beautiful boys, to seduce them, to befriend them, to betray or be betrayed by them, and to move on to the next. Sometimes in place of beauty one may encounter the far more straightforward prospect of the spectacularly well-hung. (In IX, 33, when applause is heard coming from the direction of the public baths, Martial surmises that the other bathers must have caught sight of

Maron's enormous penis.) It is clear that the baths, which men visited daily, offered opportunities far beyond those of personal hygiene. In I, 96, Martial mentions a man whose lips tremble at the sight of the bodies he spies on in the baths.

In accordance with the morality – and, indeed, the aesthetics – of the time, Martial allows his roving eye to appreciate only certain physical types of young men; and these types are dictated, in general, by age; but more precisely, by degree of physical maturation. In II, 36, the poet is precise about the desirability of different types of hair, whether on a young man's head, his face or his body. As did the Greeks, the Romans scrutinised boys' bodies with a meticulous, almost fussy, attention to body hair. Depending on how a particular relationship was going, the arrival of hair could cause either regret or relief. In IV, 7, a boy called Hyllus draws attention to his beard, his age, and body hair ('barbamque, annosque, pilosque') as reasons for withdrawing from a relationship; whereupon Martial laments the fact that a boy can become a man, and therefore, strictly, unavailable, literally overnight.

It is clear that Martial – or perhaps just the fictional 'speaker' of his epigrams – could treat his boyfriends with great tenderness, even if (as in IX, 60) he had to pretend that the roses he had bought for a boy were grown on his own farm. This small deception offers a clear instance of how, in his poems, moments of sincere sentiment are generally treated with good-natured irony: when a private moment of love becomes a public moment of poetry Martial is already located at a distance from the original emotional impulse. Perhaps the best example of this tendency occurs in I, 46, which is a four-line poem about the technicalities of the approach to orgasm when two males are making love. In terms of sexual rhythm and pace, Martial and Hedylus have been proving incompatible. When the latter is about to come, the former loses his erection. The greater the urgency of the one, the less the other is equipped to deal with it. An insoluble paradox. But Martial suggests an ideal solution: Hedylus must mislead him. When about to come, instead of urging Martial to hurry, Hedylus should ask him to slow down – and Martial will duly speed up. Thus, whilst Hedylus falsifies his own needs, Martial's body will act against the false instructions. By a process of mutual betrayal, the lovers will thus achieve simultaneous orgasm.

That, at least, is the theory. Of course, the poem is a joke. But it is not dismissive of the problem it confronts. Nor does its diagnosis of what today we are inclined to call a failure of communication cast the relationship itself in a poor light. There is respect for the boy in every line, even if his ardour is seen ironically as being counterproductive. In one sense, this is an apologetic poem, the admission of an older partner that the younger is too fit for him. What the poem gently demands is compatible sexual action, to be achieved by compromising between the ages of the two lovers. It is an appeal for, and offer of, negotiation.

Other poems are apparently less emollient. In IV, 46, for example, Martial claims to prefer kisses snatched by force to those freely given. He is turned on more by the anger of the boy he is addressing than by his face – so he beats him. This, of course, turns out to be counterproductive since it results in the boy's neither fearing nor loving him. Despite what I have already said about the poet's conventionality and his reinforcing of established Roman sexual taboos, a number of epigrams give us an insight into his ability to comprehend, if not always necessarily to share, other people's sexual perversity. Why should the boy he spanks fear him – or, indeed, love him – when there is the spanking itself to compensate? All profundities of emotion appear to have been put on hold for the duration of a simple erotic game.

Martial is aware that Roman sex lives are many, varied – and funny. In one poem (VII, 87), having listed a number of people whose relationships with their pets are suspiciously

5. The divine predator
sanctions the love of boys.
(Ganymede and the Eagle,
4th century AD)

close, he goes on to ask a boy called Labycas why, in the face of such overwhelming evidence of the variety and abundance of love, he should not submit to being loved. The argument is not convincing, but its desperate tenuousness may be: perhaps Labycas can be seduced by laughter. The fact is that, for all the claims on spirituality in much of the erotic poetry of Rome, poets were rarely solemn about the prospect of sexual transcendence. Moreover, they usually laughed at sex which remained firmly rooted in the unsatisfactory, but no less beguiling, physical world. For both Catullus and Martial, people's sexual obsessions were hilarious, and rarely reprehensible to any serious extent. What makes the tone of the poetry so pleasant is that, even when they mock other people's behavioural extremes, both poets recognise that nobody is immune to the spell of sexual attraction. Anyone may succumb to its dementia – themselves included.

Connected with these beliefs is the idea, which would much later be given scientific backing by psychoanalysis (or by the more popular versions of it), that trying to opt out of one's sexual existence was futile. Despite all the sexual problems, or the problems in personal relationships, that Martial diagnosed, he nevertheless believed that celibacy makes you unhappy. In XI, 56, he criticises a Stoic whose austere claims to virtue make him grumpy and, therefore, inclined to praise death and despise life. Martial ridicules the philosopher's acts of self-deprivation (no fire in the hearth, no straw on the bed) as mere vanity, delusions of high-mindedness. With a pitiless thrust of tempting logic, Martial proposes that if the Stoic were to go to bed (and not just to a strawless pallet) with a rosy-lipped serving boy, he would not only begin to take new pleasure in life but would even pray for greater longevity than Nestor's. Martial's clinching contribution to Stoical debate is that it is all too easy to be dismissive about life when things are working out badly for you ('Rebus in angustis facile est contemnere vitam').

To Martial, grumpiness is the deadliest sin. In XII, 75, he briskly lists several types of boy: the girl-chaser, the self-hating queer, the boy who could have been a girl, the boy who rejoices in taking it up the arse. For all their troublesome querulousness, they are at least engaging with life. Martial says he would rather endure a lover such as these than have to endure the company of a rich but miserable woman. The money could never compensate for the misery; whereas, it is implied, in the boys' cases, good sex could help one to overlook all kinds of shortcomings. In a similar mood elsewhere (XI, 104), Martial encourages an uptight woman to discard her inhibitions. She is motionless in bed, and insists on extinguishing the lamp. Martial invokes famous precedents – Hector and Andromache, Ulysses and Penelope – for the idea that sex should be enjoyed: so noisily passionate were the former pair, it is said, that the slaves outside the door used to masturbate while listening to them. He also argues that his mistress, who refuses to be buggered ('pedicare negas'), should look to the example of Juno, who played Ganymede to Jove before Ganymede himself appeared on the scene. It is clear that already, in the ancient world, one of the most practical uses of myth was to justify the mortal desires of human beings, even if the justifying argument was, as here, presented in a light-hearted way.

Sexual humour helped poets to reach a wider audience than was available for serious lyrics. So, since the wrong type of homosexual activity, whether in bed or in the way a man presented himself within society, was one of many topics seen as deserving the deployment of scathing humour, poets were literally able to capitalise upon jokes about homosexuality. The sixteen verse satires of Juvenal (AD c. 55–c. 140) are a case in point. For all that he moralistically berated the vices and other social failings of Rome, railing against a range of enemies including women, Jews and men who were sexually passive with male lovers, Juvenal was essentially most interested in self-publicity. His poems have served as influential models, ever since, for satirical attacks on political complacency, materialistic extravagance and urban squalor. Their caricatures of homosexual degeneracy are presented in a tone of apoplectic ridicule; and yet Juvenal's withering scorn often reflects badly on himself, to the extent that the clearer subject of a given satire may suddenly appear to be, not the matter ostensibly being satirised, but the poet's own soaring blood pressure.

One gets a similarly vivid impression of the kinds of moral excess to which Juvenal was referring, but from a much more indulgent – indeed celebratory – point of view, in the *Satyricon* by Petronius (who died in AD 66). This is an extraordinary text which manages to be something like a satire, something like a picaresque novel – although fragmentary and unfinished, full of wild variations in mood – and nothing like any other book you might choose to read. Only about a tenth of the original has survived. At its heart is the competitive friendship between the narrator Encolpius and the hugely-endowed Ascyltus ('you'd think the man was just an attachment to his penis'), who runs off with Encolpius' boyfriend, sixteen-year-old Giton. When Encolpius tries to take the boy back, Ascyltus threatens to saw him in two so that each of them can keep half of him. The story of the boy of Pergamon, which forms a discrete narrative within the book, is worth reading for its ironic attention to the treacherous sexuality of young boys. The breathtaking speed at which puerile resistance turns into both sexual voracity and mercenary acquisitiveness is at once this story's central joke and its most disquietingly accurate insight.

The *Satyricon* has a pretty exaggerated reputation as a dirty book. Certainly, in terms of the language used, it is more restrained than either Catullus or Martial.[5] But in the condition in which it has survived it is still an important account of homosexual themes and variations. As Cecil Wooten rather eccentrically puts it, 'in spite of the fact that much of Roman literature deals with homosexuality in one way or another, the *Satyricon*, or at least what we have of it, is the only extensive piece of Latin literature in which the characters are predominantly homosexual (probably 4 or 5 on the Kinsey scale)'.[6] One can readily appreciate how a text which gives this impression, once read alongside other supposedly shocking historical evidences, might have led the likes of Edward Gibbon to within an inch of concluding that homosexuality was responsible for the fall of Rome. Indeed, from the viewpoint of eighteenth-century England, hardly any other possible cause can have been visible at all. The book's levity alone must have seemed conclusive.

One writer who never made jokes about homosexuality was Virgil (70–19 BC). Although male love is not as prominent a guarantor of courage in the *Aeneid* as in Virgil's great model, the *Iliad* – where Achilles' pre-eminence in battle and his demonstrative love for Patroclus combine to form a central theme – Virgil's poem does include a pair of lovers, Nisus and Euryalus, whose closeness in battle follows the familiar pattern. Euryalus, the younger, is famous for his beauty; Nisus for his love of the boy. None of Aeneas' men is lovelier than Euryalus, whose face has just begun to show the down of adolescence. The two of them are inseparable. In battle they work as a team, each aiding and protective of the other. But their final venture, in Book IX, is ill-judged.

Nisus plans a daring night raid on the enemy camp, intending to go alone; but Euryalus insists on accompanying him. Together, therefore, they hack their way through large numbers of enemy men without rousing them from their deep, wine-induced slumbers. The boy Euryalus is the more bloodthirsty of the two, and when the killing is finished he puts on Messapus' helmet as a trophy. As the two lovers are returning to their own camp, this ornamental headdress glints in the moonlight and gives away Euryalus' position to a troop of Latin cavalrymen. Nisus does not notice until too late that the boy has been surrounded. He witnesses the moment when Volcens, the leader of the Latin troop, plunges his sword into Euryalus' breast. Raging for instant vengeance, Nisus charges forward and thrusts his own sword into Volcens' mouth. The others overcome Nisus, who, dying, throws himself across the body of his boyfriend. Calling them a 'fortunate pair', Virgil promises them that they will be remembered for as long as Aeneas' descendants inhabit Rome.

Virgil's real contribution to gay literature is not an epic but a lyric: the second of his *Eclogues*. This pastoral love song, in which Corydon yearns in vain for the unresponsive (or under-responsive) Alexis (possibly expressing Virgil's own love for his slave Alexander), eventually became one of the most influential male–male love poems of all time. Both Richard Barnfield and Christopher Marlowe were enchanted imitators of it, and their imitations were imitated in turn. Traces of Virgil's poem can be found throughout the English elegiac tradition (see Chapter 9). In the ultimate homage, André Gide gave his Socratic dialogue on male homosexuality the Virgilian title *Corydon* (1924).

The other great Roman narrative poet whose work needs to be considered here is, of course, Ovid (43 BC–AD 17). He may appear unpromising if one starts with the didactic poems about love and sex, *Amores* and *Ars Amatoria*. The former has nothing relevant to say; the latter hardly refers to homosexuality except in passages about men who are over-concerned with their appearance. For instance, he advises men to look after their hair and nails, to trim nasal hair and make sure that their breath always smells sweet. Any more elaborate preening should be reserved 'for wanton women – / Or any half-man who wants to attract men' (I, 523–4). Later, he warns women away from men who 'are always fixing their hair', and he asks, 'What's a woman to do when her lover's smoother than she is,/ And probably has more men on the side as well?' (III, 434, 437–8). Speaking less superficially, on the topic of sexual mutuality, Ovid says he believes that lovers should reach orgasm simultaneously – and he offers this as the reason why he personally is not interested in making love with boys (II, 683–4). One editor explains this remark by inferring, without evidence, 'an assumption on Ovid's part that boys submitted to sodomisation, or indeed any sexual approaches, not out of desire, but for profit'.[7] It is significant that the point is made by Ovid as a matter of personal preference: he allows that others may find their pleasure with boys, even lacking mutuality. But the type of homosexual preference he will not countenance (as in I, 524) is an adult preference for adult men.

Knowing of this routinely grudging approach, one might be surprised to discover that another of Ovid's books, the *Metamorphoses*, contains some of the most influential homo-erotic narratives ever written. It is not just that Ovid tells the stories of famous mythological couples – Jove and Ganymede, Apollo and Hyacinthus, Apollo and Cyparissus – but that the manner of the telling, with such lyric grace, in the midst of so many hetero-erotic myths, offers them to future readers and writers, particularly during the Renaissance, as a limitless source book of erotic and poetic images and archetypes. Spinning a continuous narrative to link the creation of the world, the loves of the gods, the siege of Troy, the founding of Rome, and the rule of Caesar, *Metamorphoses* integrates pre- and post-Homeric mythology with the new Roman mythology and the history of Rome. In so doing, this book constitutes a massive and authoritative cultural project, endorsing Roman imperialism with the resources not only of Olympus itself but also – in the materials of Homeric and Virgilian epic – of Parnassus.

It is Ovid's version of the myth of Orpheus (censoriously omitted from Book X of George Sandys' 1626 translation into English) that suggests Orpheus was torn to pieces by the vengeful Maenads for having taught the men of Thrace how to love boys. Orpheus is represented as a master of the two related arts, love and love poetry. As such, he is an appropriate patron to the poets of the ancient world, endorsing their passionate interest in both the love they express and the means of its expression.

> Meanwhile he taught the men of Thrace the art
> Of making love to boys and showed them that
> Such love affairs renewed their early vigour,
> The innocence of youth, the flowers of spring.[8]

The men of Thrace and the Maenads represent two opposed constituencies of poetry readers. Both groups are intensely attentive to whatever he sings. He changes the lives of both, acting on the female and the male to an equal extent but in opposed ways. His legacies are the poetry itself and the loved or hated love of boys.

Chapter 4

....

The Christian Middle Ages

....

The common view of the Middle Ages is of an illiberal space between the orgiastic decadence of Rome and the airy, experimental humanism of the Renaissance. These are (or include) the so-called Dark Ages between two periods of light, governed by super-stition, policed by a corrupt army of quasi-Christian clerics, and continuously burdened with the threat of pestilence. Sexuality was no more acceptable than witchcraft. Sodomy was not to be mentioned, still less to be practised. All that awaited the sodomite who did speak was the stake.

While there is an element of truth in all this, it is hardly truer as an overall picture of the age than any grotesque caricature. (It also depends on caricatures of the eras on either side.) In fact, as the magisterial researches of John Boswell have conclusively shown, the period between Rome's decline in influence and its Renaissance is little less fruitful than many other periods in its production of gay writing as an expression of gay desire. Indeed, Boswell speaks of an 'astounding amount of gay literature' emerging from this period, expressive of an 'extraordinary flowering of gay love'.[1]

Boswell makes a convenient distinction between three medieval periods. First: 'During the early Middle Ages gay people were . . . rarely visible. Manifestations of a distinctive subculture are almost wholly absent from this period, although many individual expressions of homosexual love, especially among clerics, survive. . . . Legal enactments were very rare and of dubious efficacy.' Second: 'The revival of urban economies and city life notable by the eleventh century was accompanied by the reappearance of gay literature and other evidence of a substantial gay minority.' Third: 'Beginning roughly in the latter half of the twelfth century . . . a more virulent hostility appeared in popular literature and eventually spread to theological and legal writings as well.'[2] So the common version of anti-sodomitic medievalism is, essentially, a representation of the third period only. The fact is that medieval literature deals with male love in many different ways, at least one of which may be surprisingly positive.

Furthermore, as is true of any period and most cultures, the literature of the Middle Ages can provide radically different treatments of the same subject. Take just one example, that of references to the myth of the destruction of Sodom in two English poems of the late fourteenth century. There is a reference to the people of Sodom in *The Vision of Piers Plowman* which suggests that to William Langland this myth bore no connotation of sexual transgression. In Passus XIV, the figure of Patience states that 'the misery and misfortune among the men of Sodom / Grew through abundance of bread and plain slothfulness'. It was the fact that they were 'immoderate in meat and drinking' that attracted vengeance on 'their vile living' (ll. 83–90). This is so far from later versions of the story as, now, to seem odd – perhaps, even, an obtuse denial of the story's sexual meanings. And yet, apparently, Langland's sexless reading of the Sodom story is not untypical of his time – though it was quickly going out of fashion.[3]

In contrast, the version of Sodom we are offered in the Gawain poet's *Cleanness* (sometimes known as *Purity*) specifies the sexual sin which caused God's wrath. Indeed, it is specified as in God's own words. He says to Abraham:

> They han lerned a lyst that lykes me ille,
> That thay han founden in her flesch of fautes the werst;
> Uch male mas his mach a man as hymselven,
> And fylter folyly in fere on femmales wyse.
>
> (lines 693–6)

(Roughly: they have learned a practice that pleases me ill, having found in their flesh the worst of all faults. Each male takes as his mate a man like himself, and they wantonly unite in female fashion.) Two points are of interest here: firstly, that sodomy is considered by God to be the worst of all possible human faults; and secondly, that God considers that both men who unite in this manner are lowering themselves to the level of female wantonness. There is a certain ambiguity as to whether 'mas his mach a man' refers to taking a mate as a single sexual act or as the forming of a sexual relationship. (Are we talking about mating or mateship?) The reason for my having raised this question is that it seems to open up a further issue concerning the poet's view of homosexual roles. I would suggest that he appears to conceive of sodomites as consorting in pairs of 'female' men – that is, in pairs who may exchange active and passive sexual roles according to the taste of the occasion. They are not simply passive, effeminised men who seek to be penetrated by otherwise 'heterosexual' and manly men. Be that as it may, the Father concludes his account as follows:

> Now haf thay skyfted my skyl and scorned natwre,
> And henttes hem in hethyng an usage unclene;
> Hem to smyte for that smod smartly I thenk,
> That wyyes schal be by hem war worlde withouten ende.
>
> (lines 709–12)

(Now they have altered my purpose and scorned nature, and taken up in contempt an unclean usage; I intend to punish them for that filth, so that all shall be warned by them, world without end.) The story of Lot and the two angels is then told in some detail, and the destruction of the city ensues. This is a familiar account, though the poet has added his own unique embellishments. It is this version of Sodom and sodomy, not Langland's, that will eventually prevail.

In the introduction to his indispensable anthology of *Medieval Latin Poems of Male Love and Friendship*, which prints many of the texts referred to in John Boswell's classic study, Thomas Stehling argues that the subject of male love was uncontroversial enough to have become commonplace: 'The topic of love between men in the Middle Ages was simply more traditional and less fraught with personal anxiety' than it is today. By way of Christian use of the Greek and Latin languages, many pre-Christian attitudes and themes

6. The Christian archetype of the platonic lover holds His beloved disciple. (Jesus and St John, fourteenth-century)

had been inherited throughout Europe, the negative with the positive. Thus, again according to Stehling, 'Throughout the Middle Ages, poems insulting homosexuals, particularly as men who make women of themselves, coexist with love poems written between them.'[4] Moreover, what we might call gay poetry was included within the general currency of written texts in circulation: 'Perusing a manuscript, a medieval reader might have found a complaint against Fortune, a hymn to the Trinity, a love poem [from a man] to a young boy, a riddle, and maybe an epitaph for a famous medieval bishop' (p. xxvi). However, it is less easy to accept the facility with which Stehling comes to his conclusion that 'The survival of all these poems suggests a literary world unembarrassed by homosexuality' (p. xxv).

The institutions of monasticism contributed to an atmosphere in which men saw other men (or boys) as the most suitable objects for their higher affections – not to mention, in many cases, their lower passions. Close relationships between 'brothers' were tolerated, even encouraged, as contributing to the spiritual education of novices and younger monks. As Boswell says, 'The loving relation of teacher and student in religious communities was very much a medieval ideal, despite its obvious parallel to Greek homosexuality, and many of the greatest teachers of the period were known especially for the intensity of their love for their students.'[5] Even risking reference to New Testament precedent, a single teacher might gather around him several intimate 'disciples'.

Although we have no reason to suppose that homosexuality was confined to the social spheres of the educated, and plenty of evidence to suggest otherwise, it is true that the homosexuality of literate men, for obvious reasons, left stronger traces. Apart from any other consideration, those who could read could identify their own pleasures with precedents to which only they and their peers, endowed with a classical education, were privy. As John Boswell puts it, 'Where Ovid was enjoyed, Vergil quoted, Plato read, there gay passions and sentiments were known and studied and often respected.'[6] Such authors provided crucial alternatives to Leviticus and the myth of Sodom.

Not surprisingly, poets who wrote in Latin in the medieval period were just as likely to invoke pre-Christian learning in their works as they were to quote or cite particular scriptural narratives. The lovers of boys among them seem to have been far more likely to refer to Jove and Ganymede than to David and Jonathan. (Indeed, John Boswell convincingly argues that the name of Ganymede actually came to *mean* what we now call 'gay'.[7]) Hildebert of Lavardin (*c.* 1055–1133), the Archbishop of Tours and the most famous poet of his time, wrote a poem briefly telling the story of how Jove turned from his wife to the Trojan boy, and how the heavenly pleasures he experienced with Ganymede – pleasures consisting of wine by day and embraces by night – finally persuaded him of what he must have doubted until then, that he really was a god ('et se tunc tandem credidit esse deum'). In another poem, Hildebert warns that boys are never safe in great houses, for such places are always full of Joves (Stehling, pp. 58–9).

A French primer on composition dating from around the turn of the twelfth and thirteenth centuries contains two exemplary letters, one from a man who is trying to persuade a boy to have sex with him, the other replying that the boy will do no such thing. While the man, unsurprisingly, invokes Jove and Ganymede – not to mention Hyacinth, Cyparissus and their lovely bodies – the well-educated boy indignantly reminds him not only of the terrible fate of Orpheus, but also of Sodom and Gomorrah (Stehling, pp. 90–93).

But the most sustained of the Ganymede invocations comes in an early thirteenth-century manuscript which reprints a poem probably written in France, late in the twelfth century: the so-called 'Debate between Ganymede and Helen' (Boswell, pp. 381–9; Stehling, pp. 104–21). When the boy and the girl lie down in the grass together in order to make love, the heterosexually inexperienced boy arranges his body as if to take the passive role ('applicat se femine, tanquam vellet pati'). Helen instantaneously understands what he has hitherto been up to, and it is she who instigates the discussion which follows, she denouncing his past vices, and he, with mixed fortunes, attempting to defend them. Appointing Nature and Reason as their judges, they symmetrically set about their incompatible arguments with equal verve: 'The more she praises women, the more he praises young boys.'

Few if any of their arguments are new; most are borrowed from similar discussions in classical Latin literature (and many will reappear in much later texts, especially during the Renaissance period). When Helen scolds him for failing to take procreation into account, Ganymede playfully replies:

> Let old men eager for children beget sons;
> Let tender youth play freely in their lust.
> The sport we play was invented by gods,
> And is still played by the worthiest men.

This, then, is a temporary position he is adopting: the generation of children will follow in due course. For the time being, he is content to allow desire to lead him where it will – namely, into the arms of other males. The reference to the gods has the effect of adding authority to the boyishness of his pleasures. Helen counters that unless he marries, Ganymede's great personal beauty will die when he dies. (Readers will anticipate that this is to be one of the first themes in Shakespeare's sonnets.) His looks are, in any case, already threatened by the very process which has led him to want to have sex with Helen in the first place: she taunts him with the approach of whiskers, wrinkles and a hairy chest – all supposedly grotesque developments in a male-loving male – and says she wishes he could be turned into a female by way of revenge for his having declared war on womankind.

Ganymede reminds Helen that Jupiter prefers him to Juno: when in bed between the two of them, he would always rather turn to Ganymede than to his wife. Several times the boy misogynistically details the characteristics he deplores about the female sexual organs, to the extent that Helen finally loses her temper and allows herself to speak immodestly. Her clinching insult – which brings both a blush to Ganymede's cheeks and tears to his eyes – is that whenever he ejaculates between a man's thighs he is throwing away a human life ('inter crura . . . ibi fit hominis iactura'). I suppose we should note, incidentally, that she is now imagining Ganymede as the active partner in a most un-Greek manner. Be that as it may, not only is the boy finally won over by this argument, but so are Apollo and Jupiter himself, who vows to go back to Juno. The poem ends with another, climactic, un-Greek touch: the poet calls on the Cities of the Plain to reflect with shame upon their vices and, by implication, to recant ('erubescant Sodome, fleant Gomorei'). The implication is that the medieval sodomite no longer even has the dubious precedent of Jove to rely on in his pursuit of eternal happiness: for from now on, even ungodly Olympus is barred to his sort.

Again and again in poems from the early medieval period, boyish beauty is explicitly associated with that of the opposite sex. And, as in both Greece and Rome, the implication must be that, if a boy can be so easily mistaken for a girl, his body will just as satisfactorily provide the sexual pleasures which a man could never have had with an unmarried high-born girl of the same age: in the insistent moment of his desire for such beauty, he could easily 'mistake' a boy's body for a girl's.

Ausonius (c. 310–c. 394) laments the recently dead Glaucias as only just having passed that moment of young puberty when he could be taken for a boy or a girl; his beard was just starting to grow. In another epigram, Ausonius writes about a boy during whose construction Nature was undecided until the last moment as to whether to make a girl or a boy; so the beauty in question, although decidedly male, seemed almost female ('paene puella, puer') (Stehling, pp. 2–3). Baudri, the abbot of Bourgueil (1046–1130) speaks of a boy whose voice could be a boy's or a girl's ('Incertum an pueri sit vox tua, sive puellae'), but whose girlishness will soon be erased when his beard starts to grow (and, presumably, the voice starts to break). Indeed it is age itself – the age of puberty – that finally activates the distinction between male and female ('aetas a pueris quae dat differre puellas'). Until that happens and the boy becomes unequivocally masculine, certain delightful possibilities offer themselves: 'The touch of your snow-white body sports with my hands' (Stehling, pp. 38–9). Hilary the Englishman, a pupil of Peter Abelard, also speculates on the initial indecisiveness of Nature ('se proferret te puellam, an proferret masculum') during the creation of a particularly lovely boy. Indeed, the subject of this poem is so very lovely, even if now decisively male, that he is strongly admired by both girls and young men (Stehling, pp. 70–71).

In a boy such girlishness may be a sign of great value, whether aesthetic or erotic; but in a man it may become scandalous and enfeebling effeminacy. As in Martial or Juvenal, such figures attract the derision of more masculine satirists. One such man is denounced, by Ennodius (*c.* 473–521) as follows: his face is masculine but his gestures are feminine – and his thighs are both ('Vir facie, mulier gestu, sed crure quod ambo'). This is the essence of the effeminate man: no one could really mistake his face for that of a woman, but his gestures are revealingly womanish, signalling a potential sexual ambivalence: between his legs are sexual organs both male and 'female'. The implication is that he prefers to use the latter. In another of Ennodius' epigrams a man is described as being of common gender, or rather of all genders at once ('communis generis, satius sed dicitur omnis'). And in a third epigram, Ennodius again denounces the reversibility of the queer physique: a woman when passive, but when active, no less shamefully, a man ('femina cum patitur, peragit cum turpia, mas est'). The sixth-century Luxorius, a Carthaginian imitator of Martial, writes about an effeminate lawyer ('advocatus effeminatus') whom he characterises as a Paris to be used as if he were a woman ('uso femineo Paris') (Stehling, pp. 6–7).

A number of poems from the period – as, I guess, from any period – bemoan the fact that sodomy is becoming increasingly widespread and threatening to undermine the moral health of the body politic. In a poem on 'The Wickedness of the Age' (*De malitia saeculi*) the aforementioned Hildebert of Lavardin claims that sodomy is the most prevalent of the sexual vices, a veritable plague ('Omnibus incestis super est sodomitica pestis'), what with men turning away from their wives and Ganymedes taking over women's position at the domestic hearth. Not surprisingly, Hildebert reminds such sinners of the lesson of Sodom (Stehling, pp. 54–7). In the mid-twelfth century, Bernard of Cluny wrote a 3,000-line poem called 'Contempt for the World' (*De contemptu mundi*), in the third book of which he fulminates against the openness of sodomites in his day. None of these sinners either hides his sin or expresses a sense of shame about it; 'he becomes she' ('ille fit illa'); numberless Ganymedes keep materialising, taking over every bedroom; Juno has been deserted, and even female goats have been usurped by billies; hermaphrodites are all the rage ('est moda plurimus hermaphroditus'). The law of nature ('Lex genii') has been overruled, and legions of half-men ('semiviros') are busy giving each other the attention they owe to their wives (Stehling, pp. 76–9).

Once biblical injunctions against physical expressions of sexuality come into play, all literature about sodomy becomes extravagant in its warnings of eternal torture. As the body is thrust from time into eternity, all its pleasures will turn into protracted agonies; for one thing is said to be beyond doubt: the body of the sodomite – as opposed to that of the sentimental friend – will burn in Hell. Marbod, the bishop of Rennes wrote a poem entitled 'An Argument Against Copulation between People of Only One Sex' (*Dissuasio concubitus in uno tantum sexu*) in which he gives a graphic account of the end to which the sodomite must come:

> There that wretch rages, roasted by eternal flames:
> Brow, eyes, nostrils, neck, ears,
> Mouth, throat, and breasts become fodder for flames.
> Back, sides, and belly blaze without relief;
> Guilty hips and cock never cool.
> [*nec frigent coxae nec mentula conscia noxae*]
>
> (Stehling, pp. 34–7)

The physicality of this list is the crux of the matter: bodily sin merits bodily punishment – in perpetuity. Every item listed has taken its due part in the sin: first the face with its initial attractiveness and its access to the five pleasurable senses; then the body itself, front, back and sides; and finally the groin, the point at which the white heat of sin is generated. But the heat of illicit passion is nothing compared to the heat of its consequences, as any number of medieval paintings so graphically demonstrate. Any of the body's sites of pleasure is a potential site of pain.

This Christian fascination with the punishment of the body is not just some kind of reasonless collective aberration, mass sadism before Sade. It has to be seen in the context of a history of gruesome martyrdoms and subsequent canonisations. Inventive violence is present throughout the Old Testament, of course; but it was written into Christian history from the moment of the arrest of Jesus. Medieval Christian culture is understandably obsessive about the fates of the early Christians: all those curious methods of execution, each making its uniquely cruel mark on that particular body. There is a logical symmetry to the way in which such torturous responses to virtue were answered with a new Christian mythology which promised much worse, and infinitely lengthier, tortures as the punishment for vice.

The Christian literature of bodily punishment reaches its highest point of achievement, and its most systematic inventiveness, in Florence on the eve of the Renaissance. Dante Alighieri started writing the *Divina Commedia* at some time between 1307 and 1314, beginning with the *Inferno*. The whole poem, including the *Purgatorio* and the *Paradiso*, was not completed until a short time before his death in 1321. As well as being a detailed account of the topography of its three spiritual locations, narrated as a kind of fascinated travelogue, the *Commedia* is a richly gossipy summation of Dante's culture, faith and personal affections and animosities. And every item of gossip (apart from the *Paradiso*'s virtue-based gossip, which hardly merits the name) is accompanied by promises of the most hideous spiritual and bodily humiliations to come.

In *Inferno* XV and XVI the 'violent against nature' – writers and clerics in XV, politicians and military men in XVI – are seen eternally running through a rain of fire on a barren, plantless desert appropriate to their sexual habits. Among them Dante recognises his old teacher Brunetto Latini. (Joseph Pequigney has playfully suggested that this may be 'the first – and the classic – instance of "outing"'.[8]) Brunetto tells him that all the men in his group have been fouled by the same sin ('d'un peccato medesmo al mondo lerci' – XV, 108). In *Purgatorio* XXVI another category of sodomites is observed moving through fire on the upper level of the lustful (that is, the level of the least culpable), circling in the opposite direction to their heterosexual, but equally guilty, counterparts. Here, their perpetual motion constitutes a willing, repentant working-off of their purgative sentence rather than Hell's unchanging and unstoppable punishment. They are being refined by the fires that engulf them. They call out the name of their sin ('*Soddoma*') as they pass. It is worth pointing out that in both Hell and Purgatory, Dante places the sodomites in close-knit groups – subcultures, you might call them – rather than in the isolation that they are so often condemned to in the condemnatory literatures of later centuries.

Joseph Pequigney has observed that 'Dante's thinking about homosexuality obviously and demonstrably evolved, drawing farther and farther away from the thought of [Thomas] Aquinas and the other scholastics as composition of the Commedia proceeded, and finally reaching a position that was extraordinary for his own age and so advanced even in ours that *dantisti* [Dante scholars] have yet to catch up with it.'[9] (Dante scholars have been outraged for centuries by what they perceive to be Dante's leniency to certain categories of sinners, the sodomites principal among them.) Pequigney's point is that nowhere in the *Purgatorio* does Dante treat sodomy as being unnatural. Instead, he categorises it as a sin of excess.

7. The sodomite body is given an earthly foretaste of the refining fires of Hell. (Nicholas Hogenberg, *Punishment of the Sodomites*)

It is possible, therefore, to infer that, if not carried to excess, sodomy might conceivably be regarded as virtuous, or at least not sinful. It is, after all, a category of love, and Dante always treats love as a potential good. And his sodomites include a number of figures who are worthy of considerable honour. As Pequigney says, 'In fact, all of the sodomites identified [in *Inferno*], with the single exception of the bishop Andrea de' Mozzi, are impressive and accomplished personages. The view would seem to be taken that most homosexuals are exceptional men rather than deranged or depraved, and on this matter [Dante] Alighieri may well be making a point of dissenting from Aquinas and the other Christian writers of like bias'.[10] Of course, we ought to remember that the *Commedia* consists of three parts, and that no matter how well respected the sodomites are in the first two, nothing can detract from the fact that they are altogether absent from the *Paradiso*; or, at least, it may be that Paradise contains only those who have got away with it. Remember that Dante's guide throughout the *Divina Commedia* is, of all people, that renowned lover of boys, Virgil.

In a very different text, the *Mabinogion*, the Welsh collection of stories committed to paper in the fourteenth century after an unknown period of oral development, one story develops the theme of retributive tortures in a way that demands our attention. It contains a fascinating instance of metamorphosis, whereby homosexual intercourse is inflicted as a means of punishment for a heterosexual transgression. In the tale called 'Math Son of Mathonwy' two brothers, Gwydion and Gilvaethwy, are severely punished for the rape of a female virgin in their Uncle Math's protection. In the first place, Math magically transforms Gilvaethwy into a hind and Gwydion into a stag, and says to them, 'Since you are in league with each other I will make you go off together; you shall mate, and you shall have the nature of wild deer, and when those animals bear their young you shall bear yours. Return here a year from today.' When they do return they are accompanied by a fawn, which Math transforms into their human son; he calls the boy Hyddwn and has him baptised and fostered.

Meanwhile, Math changes Gilvaethwy into a boar and Gwydyon into a sow. As before, he sends them away for a year. They mate and return with a piglet which Math transforms into their second son, Hychdwn ('a handsome lad with thick auburn hair'). Next, Math changes Gilvaethwy into a female wolf and Gwydyon into a male. When they come back after a year, Math changes their cub into a third son, Bleiddwn. Finally, he returns the two brothers to their original form, and says to them, 'Men, if you wronged me you have been punished enough – it is a great disgrace that each of you has had children by the other.'[11]

Of course, I am bound to say that this tale conjures up, even if it does not explicitly detail, the image of two males copulating, of their taking it in turns to be active or passive, and of their being subjected to shame as a consequence of their sexual metamorphoses. In other words, this may appear to be, as it were, a homosexual fable. (Incest, too, is pertinent.) However, it seems more plausible that the 'great disgrace' which Math calls down on the heads of his nephews is less to do with sodomy than with their having become female and given birth. They were, after all, turned into 'heterosexual' pairs of animals and never copulated *as* males. It is their masculinity, rather than what we would call their heterosexuality, that has been compromised by their uncle's harsh and inventive punishment.

The fact remains, though, that at the heart of their shame lies their having been fucked, each by the other. Like vanquished soldiers in certain cultures, they have been unmanned by being raped. Where they were virgins, they have been deflowered – hence the aptness of their punishment to the original crime. We are glimpsing a system of gender values in which the thought of homosexuality is virtually unthinkable, even though, as we have seen, at some level in this story it *is* being thought. It is not sufficient simply to assume that nobody would have made a connection between a fiction about two copulating males and the existence of such creatures in 'real' life: for the fact is that, as well as existing as a threatening presence within biblical mythology – roared into the popular consciousness from the pulpit – the sodomite could actually be encountered in person. And because he could be met in the street, he started to appear, if only fleetingly, in the literature of daily life. Was he recognised for what he was? John Boswell has stated the case as follows: 'At many points in the Middle Ages gay people seem to have been rare to the point of exciting wonder – although people seem to have known what they were when they encountered them – and at other times heterosexual writers expressed concern that gay people were taking over the world.'[12]

In some texts he is apparently still invisible, even when forbidden sexual acts might have identified him to any reader. In others he is visible as a distinct type, even though there is no evidence that he is actually involved in any sexual activities at all. We can find examples of these two types in two closely related and quite similar texts, Boccaccio's *Decameron* and Chaucer's *Canterbury Tales*. Giovanni Boccaccio (1313–75) wrote the stories in *The Decameron* (*Il decamerone*) over an indeterminate period, but the collection was not completed until 1358. His tone is consistently daring, yet always held within the bounds of what might conceivably be told to an audience of relatively sophisticated, high-born ladies. He is not held back by the expected proprieties. Nothing in the Bible prepares us for the relaxed bawdy of the tale (day 5, story 10) in which a cuckolded husband comes to terms with his wife's infidelity by going to bed with both her and her male lover at once. The story ends as follows:

8. Entry into solid flesh, the ultimate proof of spirituality. (Detail from the Syon Cope, *The Incredulity of St Thomas*)

9. (facing page) Beardlessness as social and sexual stigma. (*Chaucer's Pardoner*, woodcut from Thomas Caxton's 2nd edition of Chaucer's *Canterbury Tales*, 1484)

After supper, what Pietro devised for the satisfaction of all three hath escaped my mind; but this much I know that on the following morning the youth was escorted back to the public place, not altogether certain which he had the more been that night, wife or husband. Wherefore, dear my ladies, this will I say to you, 'Whoso doth it to you, do you it to him'; and if you cannot presently, keep it in mind till such time as you can, so he may get as good as he giveth.'[13]

The disingenuousness of the storyteller Dioneo's claim that 'what Pietro devised' has slipped his mind is blatant, and we are led to assume that the ladies he is addressing are at liberty (and perfectly able) to imagine the boy-sandwich he has invoked. Dioneo began by warning his audience that what he was about to narrate was 'in part not altogether seemly', but added that nevertheless it might 'afford diversion'. The ladies do laugh, but apparently less than at earlier stories they have been told, by reason of their embarrassment: for the teller has called to mind unthinkable pleasures and no lady wishes to appear to be able to think of them. The fact remains that the joke depends on such thought. It relies on the image of a young man both transgressing and transgressed, penetrating and penetrated. He is getting his come-uppance.

Sodomy is presented here as a laughably appropriate method of domestic revenge. But all it appears to have done to the boy is leave him in a condition of intrigued perplexity. He moves back into the public space disturbed in his sense of self-definition – husband or wife? – but this is not at all a question of his basic essence. He is no different now from what he was the day before. What he is trying to remember and define is a matter of actions, not essences. While it may offer him future possibilities for sexual pleasure, whether or not with the same couple, it is not likely to alter his selfhood in any fundamental way.

Geoffrey Chaucer planned *The Canterbury Tales* in about 1387, but had not completed the massive sequence by the time of his death in 1400. Many of the tales are based on those of Boccaccio, but as a rule Chaucer does not share Boccaccio's moments of sexual explicitness. His bawdiness is altogether more hyperborean and chilly than the Italian's. Needless to say, Chaucer was familiar with the official version of sodomy. In his tale the Parson mentions 'thilke abhomynable synne, of which that no man unnethe oghte speke ne write' – though he adds, 'nathelees it is openly reherced in holy writ' (X, 909).

But the issue of homosexuality gathers most detail in the figure of the Pardoner. I suppose we could call him the first gay character in English literature, certainly the first major one. That is to say, unlike the men in the Boccaccio story, who commit an act, or night-long sequence of acts, which in the younger of the two involves a confusion of roles but in neither involves any question of fundamental being, the Pardoner is apparently characterised and stigmatised by personal essence, regardless of whether he ever acts on that identity with the bodies of other men. In the General Prologue, he is famously described as 'a geldyng or a mare' (I, 691), which most commentators take to mean, after

all the niceties of definition have been worried over for a sufficient period, that he is homosexual. His unmanly beardlessness is given as a further defining sign.

Monica McAlpine regards Chaucer's treatment of the Pardoner as exemplifying 'the medieval confusion of [male] homosexuality with effeminacy'. She speaks of his 'tortured and theatrical self-image' and characterises him as being 'isolated from his heterosexual and homophobic peers by a condition of homosexuality'. As for his relationship with his travelling companion, the Summoner, McAlpine writes:

> The Pardoner may be seen as a frustrated heterosexual who associates himself with the lecherous Summoner in order to deny his own impotence and to acquire symbolically the Summoner's virility; or he may be seen as a homosexual, ambivalent about disclosing his status, who nonetheless becomes suspect through the public display of this ambiguous friendship.[14]

McAlpine adds that these two possibilities correspond with Chaucer's own offering of the 'geldyng'/'mare' alternatives. The person of the Pardoner is never free of his written context, not simply and obviously as one of Chaucer's fictional characters, but as a living emblem of certain sorts of potential or actual sinfulness. Glenn Burger calls him 'a theological sodomite or hermeneutical eunuch'.[15] The first phrase seems tautological, since 'sodomite' is already itself a theological term. The individual cannot escape the scriptures which have been inscribed on his body; nor does he try to. Think of the blame that seems to be attached to the mere fact of the Pardoner's beardlessness. Already, we see the unmanly man who is deemed guilty by the mere fact of his appearance. But although he speaks, in his due turn, as one of Chaucer's narrators, he never really speaks for himself. By contrast, the cries of '*Soddoma*' on the lips of Dante's sinners in Purgatory sound like an expressive self-identification, an assertion of difference. Even through the tones of shame and repentance, one can hear the voice of a culture which will not be silenced.

Chapter 5

The Orient

The third chapter of Edward Carpenter's anthology *Ioläus* (1902, 1906) is entitled 'Friendship in Early Christian and Mediaeval Times'. It concludes with an eleven-page sequence subtitled 'Eastern Countries'. Carpenter opens these pages with the following remarks: 'It may not be out of place here, and before passing on to the times of the Renaissance and Modern Europe, to give one or two extracts relating to Eastern countries. The honour paid to [male–male] friendship in Persia, Arabia, Syria and other Oriental lands has always been great, and the tradition of this attachment there should be especially interesting to us, as having arisen independently of classic or Christian ideals'.[1] There follow a few poems by Rumi, Hafiz, Sa'di and Nesim Bey; plus short extracts from two travel books. Similarly, Patrick Anderson and Alistair Sutherland's 1961 anthology *Eros* has a chapter on 'The Dark and Middle Ages' which contains subsections on 'The Persians' and 'The Moors'.

I am adopting a similar policy here, even if, for two obvious reasons, this must be regarded as little more than a strategy of convenience. Firstly, the so-called Orient is not a single culture. To treat it as one entity is to distort the reality of its diversity, but is also to comply with Western constructions of the East as uniformly mysterious, dangerous and exotic. (In this sense, the Orient is, indeed, a single cultural construct.) Secondly, the Orient does not conform to conventional European periodisations of history: while Europe was in its 'Dark' and 'Middle' Ages, the cultures of Arabia and China were, arguably, at far more advanced stages of development. For them, a Renaissance beginning in the quattrocento would have been more or less superfluous.

We do not yet, in the West, fully understand the 'gay' literatures of the East except as distorted in the glass of our own image. It often seems that the best we can do, as gay readers of Eastern texts, is to recognise signs of our own kinds of gayness and assume, or hope, they are what they seem. This is the essence of orientalism: finding what we want to find. It might not, therefore, seem unreasonable to impose our own gloss upon the following remarks from Edward Said's definitive book, *Orientalism*:

> The Orient is *watched*, since its almost (but never quite) offensive behavior issues out of a reservoir of infinite peculiarity; the European, whose sensibility tours the Orient, is a watcher, never involved, always detached, always ready for new examples of what the *Description de l'Égypte* called 'bizarre jouissance.' The Orient becomes a living tableau of queerness.[2]

The influence of the Islamic cultures' homo-erotic literatures on the northern European cultures in the eighteenth and nineteenth centuries demands to be read in the light of Said's influential work. Among the great documents of this tendency, many of them imbued to a greater or lesser extent with a homo-erotic ethos, are the homosexual Edward Fitzgerald's ungendered translation of *The Rubaiyat of Omar Khayyam* (1859) and the bisexual Sir Richard Burton's translations of the *Arabian Nights* (1885 and 1886–88) and of *The Perfumed Garden* of Shaykh Nafzawi (1886).

These men were starting to find in the East rich veins of what they and other Victorians had already mined from the Greek and Roman cultures. After all, the same pattern repeats itself among the ruling classes wherever an advanced civilisation segregates the sexes, setting male above female in terms of status, and conjoins them only in the reproductive institution of marriage and the masculinist recreational institution of prostitution. Virtually all men who can afford to do so get married and produce children – and therefore seem, in terms of twentieth-century sexual institutions, to be heterosexual. But virtually all also form their closest bonds, as friends or lovers, within the high-status all-male institutions of the military, of religious worship, of sporting activities and of the arts – and therefore might seem to be homosexual. Thus, as in ancient Greece, so also in pre-twentieth-century China and Japan; and as in the Greek diaspora, so too in the Arabic: segregation of the sexes; women relegated to an emphatically subordinate role in all things; male friendship as virtually the highest good; in cases of homosexual activity, respectability invested only in taking the 'active' part, and preferably with boys on the cusp of puberty; growth of facial hair as a meaningful sign of a boy's suitability for love-making; the necessary evanescence of the moment of love with such a creature.

At first, the advent of Islam left Arabic poetry relatively unchanged. But when the Abbasids took over from the Umaiyads in 749 and the capital moved from Damascus to Baghdad, a period of urban sophistication followed, supplanting many of the values of the old Bedouin courts (and holding sway until the sack of Baghdad by the Mongols in 1258). United not nationally but by a common language, Arabic, and by a common scripture, the Qur'an, the fast-developing culture of Islam in the so-called Middle East was yet, in the great cities that dotted its trade routes, extremely cosmopolitan. The literature of this fresh ethos is perhaps best represented by the work of one of its great mavericks, Abu Nuwas (*c.* 760–*c.* 815), the legendary poet at the court of the Abbasid caliph of Baghdad, Harun al-Rashid.

Abu Nuwas has always been most famous for his incomparable verses in celebration of wine (*khamriyyat*) and boys (*mudhakkarat*) – neither in great favour with stricter adherents to Islamic law – and in general his willingness to go against the grain, standing out against many aspects of Islam as well as against the earlier Bedouin traditions. In this sense, he was a great innovator. It is he who appears in some of the most well-known stories in the so-called *Arabian Nights*. These stories, parables and fables date mainly from the tenth century, though some are from as early as the eighth; the collection as a whole took something like its present shape in the thirteenth.

In a typical story about the poet, when Harun al-Rashid summons him at night, Abu Nuwas is eventually found in a tavern, unable to leave because he owes a boy there money. The boy is wearing three tunics (white, red and black), for each of which Abu Nuwas improvises a poem. After the white poem the boy takes off the white tunic; after the red he takes off the red; but, disappointingly, he never takes off the black tunic. Harun has the boy paid off so that the poet can return to the palace, where he is urgently needed to extol the beauty of a slave girl to whom the caliph has taken a fancy.[3]

However, Abu Nuwas himself is absent from what is possibly the most famous of the stories in which his celebrated love of boys takes a central role.[4] When the wise woman

Dahia ('the Mistress of the Masters') challenges an old man called al-Salihani to justify his claim that boys are preferable to girls ('my tastes have always led me to prefer the perfect to the imperfect'), he quotes various poets to back up his view, and of these the only poet named is Abu Nuwas. At first the old man's arguments seem, within the context of the *Nights*, persuasive enough:

> Surely you will admit that a woman has nothing which can be compared with the beauty of a youth, his supple waist, his fine drawn limbs, the tender mingling of colour in his cheeks, his gentle smile, the charm of his voice? The Prophet himself, in putting us on our guard against so evident a danger, said: 'Do not look long upon beardless boys, for their eyes hold more of temptation than the eyes of huris.' Remember, too, that the greatest praise that a man can find for the beauty of a girl is to compare it with the beauty of a boy (p. 411).

He recites one of Abu Nuwas' poems, in which a girl is praised for having thighs like a boy's, before continuing:

> Also a youth is not content only with his beauty; he can ravish our hearts with his language and the perfection of his manners. And how delicious a thing it is to see young down beginning to shade his lips and cheeks, those marriage beds of roses! Is anything in the world comparable with that charming period of transition (p. 411)?

He quotes several poems in praise of this ephemeral moment of sublime beauty, including one in which Abu Nuwas riskily defies strict convention (coming close to praising young men rather than mere boys) by arguing that the hairiness of puberty signifies growing strength – all the more attractive in the limbs of a sexual partner:

> And as the hair grows longer
> It's a sign his thighs are stronger.
> (p. 411)

Dahia is persuaded by none of this. She gives a long and elaborately erotic speech in praise of girls, and reminds her interlocutor that his quotation from the Qur'an was actually more in praise of the female 'huris' than of the 'beardless boys' it compared them with. Also, she reminds him that there are other verses in the scripture which take a very different line on man–boy sexual relations. She quotes a relatively mild one: 'Why do you seek out male love? Has not Allah created women for the satisfaction of your desires, that you may enjoy them as you will?' Although she congratulates the old man on his wide knowledge of pederastic poets – acknowledging Abu Nuwas as the 'greatest of them all' and the 'king of pederasts' – she delivers a peroration dismissing boy-love as having no place in either Heaven or the life of the Prophet. To conclude her speech, Dahia lowers the tone of the debate from the heights of scripture by indecorously quoting a scatological poem in which the nether regions of girls and boys are contrasted, the one being a source of 'suave incense', the other of 'a deep brown offence'.

This story's way of using poetry as evidence to support logical argument is repeated throughout the *Nights*. Poetry is like wine insofar as it enchants the senses and can seduce the soberest intelligence to fall for any stated opinion. In another story the Princess Budur, having disguised herself as her own husband, marries and makes love to a young girl.

Then, still in drag, she courts him, the husband, with a torrent of pederastic verses. These prove so effectively seductive that he shifts from his initial reluctance to an eager curiosity about buggery; whereupon, Budur leads him to bed – and reveals her true identity.[5] In much the same spirit as *The Ring of the Dove*, the great treatise on love by Ibn Hazm (994–1064), the *Nights* appear to be based on the general assumption that no man can resist beauty in either woman or boy.[6]

The lavish eroticism of the *Arabian Nights* became highly popular in nineteenth-century Europe; and its popularity was much deplored by moral arbiters, mostly self-appointed. Even though, as Richard Burton rather disingenuously says in his Terminal Essay, 'the proportion of offensive matter bears a very small ratio to the mass of the work', the bawdy spirit of the *Nights* was almost more than late Victorian society could bear. On the other hand, since the whole book concerned not one wayward Englishman, its perversities could be put down to the fact that all of its characters were foreigners. The eroticism could be viewed as relating only to something far from home – as if Victorian London did not have far more brothels and dives than Abbasid Baghdad could ever have dreamed of – and its tastes could be stigmatised (if also envied) as being merely 'exotic' and not, therefore, entirely serious.

Abu Nuwas is the most significant presence in another collection of stories and poems, *The Delight of Hearts, Or What You Will Not Find in Any Book*, collected by Ahmad al-Tifashi (1184–1253) in the first half of the thirteenth century. Of the twelve chapters of this work, five are about 'homosexual' topics (V, VI, VIII, IX and XII).[7] Here again, Abu Nuwas is celebrated both for his exuberant and open love of boys and for his ability to express his enthusiasms in consummate verse. According to one of the stories here, when asked by a slave merchant how he could possibly prefer boys to women, the poet improvised the following reply:

> There are men who like women
> and who make women glad;
> but, as for me, all pleasure comes
> in the body of a lad!
>
> When, barely past his fifteenth year
> tendrils of hair begin
> to form on his cheeks: a tender down
> reluctant to hide the skin.
>
> A boy at that age no longer fears
> the things we dream of doing
> with him, and he's lost his childish soul
> that never thought of screwing![8]

The tone is typically uncompromising. It is the mark of one of the most fearless 'gay' writers of all time. Abu Nuwas never ceased to praise the attractions of boys; he never recanted; and he never allowed those who so often questioned the validity of his tastes to interfere with his basic belief, that more pleasure was to be had from a bottle of wine, a boy and the improvisation of a love (or sex) poem than in any other sphere of human enjoyment. The sheer sense of unquenchable appetite and unlimited joy is his gift to the tradition within which he was working. Victorian inverts would find him both hard to believe and hard to put down.

As time passes, however, innovations become conventions. The erotic themes come to be expressed in entirely predictable metaphors. Indeed, the skill of a really accomplished poet comes to lie not in inventing completely new modes of expression, but in finding a fresh way of stating the old, incontrovertible truths of sexual desire: that women are like the sea, boys like the solid earth; that beautiful boys and girls are like gazelles; that their promisingly flexible bodies bend like the trunks of young willows; that roses of natural modesty and good health glow in their cheeks; that pearls adorn their toothy smiles; that their faces (or arses) merit comparison with the full moon; and so forth. These conventions developed, or continued to be followed although left undeveloped, throughout the Arabic-speaking world.[9]

· · ·

The greatest of the Persian mystic poets is Jalaloddin Rumi (1207–73). The intensity of his love poetry derives from well-documented, and extremely well known, circumstances in his life. In October 1244 in Konya, he met Shamsuddin Tabrizi, the wandering dervish who inspired him to the heights of spiritual love. Indeed, for six months after their meeting, Rumi was so engrossed in his new love – they cut themselves off from the outside world in a narrow cell and are said to have discoursed continuously with each other without eating or drinking – that his family and disciples finally lost patience and forced Shams to leave town. The separation proved insupportable to Rumi, who eventually had Shams recalled from Syria. When the two men met again, they embraced each other with such ardour that they fell in a heap on the floor, 'so that one did not know who was lover and who was beloved'. Rumi's great outpouring of mystical love poems was principally inspired by his involvement in this relationship. When Shams was assassinated on 5 December 1248 – perhaps with the culpable involvement of Rumi's own son – the truth was kept from Rumi, who twice travelled to Syria in search of his vanished beloved. His poems represent this period of separation in terms of the most intense yearning for the absent one.

Eventually, however, peace of mind came to Rumi as he recognised that Shams existed within himself: he had achieved complete identification with the one he loved. As Annemarie Schimmel comments, 'Rumi's poems which resulted from this experience show all the stages of mystical passion – longing, yearning, searching, and again and again hope for union, love without limits'.[10] Hence Rumi's greatness: for in the tradition to which he belongs, longing is considered superior to union. If the soul is in a state of longing, creativity results, whereas union brings about the complacency of silence. Rumi's love for Shamsuddin represented, for the poet, no less than a glimpse of divine beauty and splendour. His love poetry, therefore, constituted not an individualistic expression of physical and emotional desire so much as a prayer – tens of thousands of verses in length – to the divinity whom Rumi regarded as both the cause and the object of true love.[11]

The fact that the second of the great Persian poets, Sa'di of Shiraz (born c. 1213–19, died 1292), wrote two distinct types of love-based poetry – in the mystical *Bustan* and the more unabashedly physical *Gulistan* and *Hazliyyat* – raises a familiar problem:

The modern reader is puzzled by the disparity between the orthodox sentiments of the religious writings or the refined passion of the mystical poems on the one hand, and the lustful pornographic pieces on sodomy and seduction of boys on the other. The modern editor resolves the conflict by omitting the latter from the *Kulliyyat*. Faced with the same dilemma, English translators even in the tamer episodes of the 'Gulistan' turn boys into girls and change anecdotes about pederasty into tales of heterosexual love.[12]

In both the *Bustan* (1257) and the *Gulistan* (1258), Sa'di's heterosexual anecdotes deal much less with love and courtship than with marital discord. Boys are held in higher regard than women; and, with women, anal intercourse is said to be superior to vaginal. But boys offer Sa'di a broader and richer range of opportunities for different types of love. In some works he simply lusts after their bodies; in others he is lyrically romantic about their personalities; and in yet a third type, the boy represents a transcendent ideal, a momentary glimpse of the divine.

In any case, the pederastic poet had to choose his vocabulary with care. As Schimmel points out, 'The boy one loved passionately was the *shahid* [witness], but the boy one sodomised was the *mukhannas* or *amrad*'.[13] The latter term, *amrad*, meant beardless, but it could also be used to mean cowardly, crafty, disgraced, ignoble, infamous, spiritless or stupid. As in Rome, the passive partner (*maf'ul*, or 'the done') was subject to far greater disapproval than the active partner (*fa'il*, or 'the doer'), largely because the former was regarded misogynistically as having taken on the function of a mere woman. But the *shahid*, catamite though he might actually be, was invariably celebrated as a great beauty and a worthy object of any man's love. It was therefore possible for Sa'di to write a *ghazal* celebrating his own reputation as a boy-lover: 'Sa'di's fame has spread everywhere for his love of boys [*shahidbazi*];/ In this there is no blame among us but rather praise.'

Hafiz of Shiraz (1319/20–1391) is thought to have been familiar with both Rumi and Sa'di's poetry. Hafiz became the undisputed master of the *ghazal*, the short love lyric – some five hundred of them are attributed to him. Through a fashion for his work among eighteenth- and nineteenth-century writers and readers of German, he ultimately became the most influential of all the Islamic poets. His works were most extensively translated by the Austrian orientalist Joseph von Hammer (1774–1856). As Annemarie Schimmel has wryly observed, Hammer was 'honest enough to translate the object of love as male, for he was "afraid of getting entangled in contradictions by praising girls for their green sprouting beards." Here, he is certainly superior to most of the translators and imitators of Hafiz in the 19th and early 20th centuries.'[14]

Needless to say, once Hafiz's verse started to be read in Europe the usual reservations were expressed by those who could not cope with the idea of an earthly love between two males. Because the poems could not respectably be sensual, they must be mystical. Of course, the truth of great poetry is much more complicated. What Schimmel has to say on Hafiz is relevant, also, to other poets. In most of his verse there is 'a constant oscillation between the worldly and the spiritual level'. She continues: 'The object can be the beautiful beloved, preferably a fourteen-year old boy who is as cruel as he is charming and hence called with the traditional term, a Turk; or the object can be the Divine Beloved Who Acts as He Wills, and who is loved by the poet because He combines jamal and jalal, Beauty and Majesty . . . ; the object can also be the prince, whose whims are endured by the subject and who has to be flattered in terms of utter subjection (as has the beloved) and expects high praise' (p. 30). The point to be emphasised and remembered, here, is that the fact that a poet wrote mystical love poems does not excuse the reader who insists on reading his more earthly (and fleshly) love poems as being purely spiritual – which is generally to say, *not* homosexual – any more than the enthusiasm of gay readers should be allowed to pornographise those poems which are, indeed, mystical. Most of these poets wrote both. Indeed, the situation is further complicated by the fact that they often wrote *both at once*: for, as is the case with most good erotic art, the physical and the spiritual exist in concert (if not always in harmony), and it is more or less impossible to write well about either without invoking the other.

The later the commentator, the more likely he or she is to perform insistently mystical readings of physical signs. A good example of this tendency is the work of the seventeenth-century Persian author Mushin Fayd Kashani, who reads previous writers' references to the face (*rukh*) as pertaining to 'the revelation of Divine Beauty in Attributes of grace'. References to the tresses (*zulf*) pertain to 'the revelation of Divine Majesty in Attributes of Omnipotence', whereby the reality of the divine is deliberately veiled as if a beautiful face were to be obscured by hair; and references to the tavern (*kharabat*) mean, not places where one may get drunk on wine and flirt with the waiters, but 'Pure Unity, undifferentiated and unqualified'.[15] One is reminded of the strategies of much later literary critics when faced with homo-erotic texts.

In the introduction to *The Penguin Book of Turkish Poetry*, Nermin Menemencioglu briefly (parenthetically) acknowledges the fact that in *divan* poetry the loved one may be of either sex:

> The beloved is a moon-faced, almond-eyed beauty with a cypress-like figure. Her (or his) eyes may also be likened to a narcissus, and her figure to a lance. Her cheeks are rose or tulip, her locks hyacinth, her eyebrows two bows, her eyelashes arrows, her teeth pearls, etc. Her waist is thinner than a hair and her ruby lips are the Fountain of Youth.

But Menemencioglu feels the need to add, given that the mystical reading is always available to explain away disturbingly hedonistic poetry, '*divan* poets are not necessarily homosexual when they give human beauty the masculine attributes considered more decorous in a society in which women veil all but their eyes'.[16] Considering the fact that moon, cypress, rose, tulip, hyacinth and pearls have already been mentioned in relation to parts presumably not decorously visible when a woman is so heavily veiled, this argument seems not to function. Its only purpose appears to be to disabuse the English-speaking reader of the suspicion that homosexual desire may be expressed, alongside heterosexual desire, in some of the most famous of all Turkish poetry. Apparently, it would be as indecorous today for an editor to speak about bisexuality – or about the bifurcation of sexualities which may occur when a society segregates men from women and values women so much less highly than men – as it might have been in the fifteenth century for a poet to mention a woman's pudenda.

Having said that, one must acknowledge that it is indeed possible to appropriate a sufficiently long-standing erotic tradition for entirely non-erotic purposes. The twentieth-century Soviet poet Lahuti, for instance, took as his textual beloved a certain notorious homophobe, one Joseph Stalin.

· · ·

As in the ancient Mediterranean cultures, the Chinese and Japanese segregated the sexes and tolerated or even encouraged intense emotional relationships between members of the same sex. The Chinese regarded celibacy as perverse and unnatural (as the Jesuits discovered, to their dismay, when they arrived in China and were regarded as recruiting sexual partners when they sought to convert young men) and they condoned male promiscuity even in tandem with matrimony: any married man who could afford it could respectably attach a courtesan to his household; any wife who objected could be divorced on the grounds of jealousy. Men who preferred boys could take a male slave. Richer men could take multiple courtesans or boys.

Classical Chinese did not have a concept of 'homosexuality' as either condition or identity. Poetic metaphor and the reference back to famous precedents (individuals or events) took the place of such terminology. For example, male homosexuality came to be known as 'the cut sleeve' (*duanxiu*), so named after the famous incident when the Emperor Ai cut off his own sleeve rather than disturb his boyfriend, Dong Xian, who was asleep on it. Male lovers also picked up the epithet *long yang*, after the Prince of Wei's lover, Longyang Jun.[17] In a famous anecdote the latter, having bitten into a particularly delicious peach, handed the rest of it to the prince to eat. In later years the phrase 'the love of shared peach' (*fen tao zhi ai*) was used to denote male homosexuality.

One of the consequences of this common type of reliance on the written past is a certain stylisation, one might say artificiality, which leaves the reader all the more eager to watch out for moments of departure from the given script: for it is in these moments of innovation that one most clearly sees through the literature to its origins in personality and event. Moreover, the Chinese literary tradition is almost entirely concerned with the lives of, and concerned to cater for the reading needs of, an extremely narrow élite of literate members of court and their immediate retinue. In general, therefore, this is a literature of limited social aims and achievements, but with an intense concentration on and immense subtlety of approach to those relatively narrow areas of life to which it does address itself.

Many of the emperors cultivated 'favourites' – that is, male lovers – in addition, and often in preference, to their harems of wives and concubines. Given the institutional nature of favouritism, and its prevalence, it follows that the most constant written sources of anecdotes on such relationships are the court chronicles – to all intents and purposes the history books of the Chinese, or at least of their imperial dynasties. Among the common themes of these texts are the fickleness of rulers' affections and the regrettable tendency of favourites to distract rulers from the affairs of state. Where the records are critical of such relationships, they tend to be criticising not homosexuality as such, but influence.

Many of the early texts, even love poems, deal with prostitution, either literal (sex for money) or virtual (sex for favour, influence or just a place to live). A poem by Zhang Hanbian, writing in the Jin dynasty (AD 265–420), hymns the delicacy and fragrance, the bodily purity and the light-hearted sociability of a fifteen-year-old actor-cum-prostitute called Zhou Xiaoshi. It ends as follows:

> Inclined toward extravagance and festiveness,
> gazing around at the leisurely and beautiful.
> A pleasant expression delights in laughter,
> a handsome mouth delights in talking.

Bret Hinsch has argued that this passage hints at 'a network of patronage and even outright prostitution'.[18] If so, it is a network with which Zhou appears to be both familiar and at ease. However, the later poem 'Multitudinous Blossoms', by Liu Zun (d. AD 535), begins with a very different line about the same boy: 'How pitiful the young boy Zhou is!' For all the earlier text's closing point about Zhou's love of speech, it is clear that such a boy might not be entirely free to speak his own mind. As Liu Zun puts it,

> From an early age he knew the pain of scorn,
> Withholding words; ashamed to speak.

This poem's lyrical homage to Zhou's beauty and its conventional references to precedent (including shared peaches and the cut sleeve) only render more poignant the hard-hitting first line and the even harder last: 'New faces stream steadily through the palace'. In other words, the boy's beauty is breathtaking but mundane. He can be replaced. Indeed he must be, if the beauty of the palace is to be maintained. Mere boys lose their looks; bought boys lose their positions.[19]

The Tang period (AD 618–907) saw fewer references to favourites and correspondingly more to egalitarian friendships between men of more or less equal ages and social positions. In spite of the facts that, as in so many other cultures, the use of ungendered – or ambiguously gendered – language serves to obscure the gendered substantiality of the love in question, and that a tradition existed whereby male writers would adopt a female persona in writing heterosexual love poetry, nevertheless there remain identifiable love poems in which a male poet appears to be speaking *in propria persona* to a loved one of equal status who is also male. For instance, the prolific poet Bo Juyi (772–846) wrote texts celebrating moments of closeness to his friends – as when sharing a bed with Qian Hui:

> Drawing up the green silk coverlets,
> placing our pillows side by side;
> like spending more than a hundred nights,
> to sleep together with you here.

Or lamenting their absence – as when writing to thank Yu Shunzhi, who was away on business, for a present the latter had sent: 'I think of you as if I'm with you, / day or night'. There are also some particularly affecting poems, written at a distance, to his otherwise closest friend Yuan Zhen.[20] Certain fragments of a more sexually explicit poem by Bo Juyi's younger brother Bo Xingjian have survived – they use the conventional imagery, though, of shared peaches and cut sleeves – but it is to later, increasingly popular works that one must turn, both for greater sexual openness and for the painfully slow emergence of details about the lives of ordinary Chinese people, let alone details of ordinary Chinese homosexuality.

Bret Hinsch quotes a passage from an early piece of prose fiction: 'When Wu Sansi saw his beloved's pure whiteness, he was immediately aroused. That night Wu summoned him so they could sleep together. Wu played in the "rear courtyard" until his desire was satisfied.'[21] This kind of text comes as close to explicitness as a language lacking in sexual vocabulary could manage. It remains ambiguous, if not exactly opaque. The word translated here as 'summoned' (*jiao*) could also mean 'hired', in the sense of prostitution. The phrase 'rear courtyard' (*hou ting*) refers, of course, to the rectum of the beloved; but one can imagine, I suppose, a reader to whom this would not be clear. One should never underestimate the obtuseness of certain kinds of reader when it comes to overlooking homo-erotic texts or to castigating gay readers for reading homo-eroticism into 'innocent' texts.

Be that as it may, during the Tang period a more specifically sexual vocabulary does develop alongside traditional metaphors. Hinsch quotes another story, about a boy who becomes a prostitute, which uses 'the first recorded derogatory term for a homosexual act' in classical Chinese: *jijian*. The word literally means something like 'chicken lewdness', but it is translatable as sodomy. The short story uses this term in the sentence 'Because of his exceptional good looks he was repeatedly sodomised', but also uses *hou ting* a few sentences later: 'Day and night men excitedly played in his rear courtyard.' It was *jijian*, rather than any of its more picturesque metaphorical predecessors, that was used in legal texts when certain homosexual acts were outlawed under the Qing dynasty (1644–1914).[22] The neo-Confucian stress on asceticism and the virtue of family life tended to hasten this shift into legal sanctions and derogatory terminology.

It was under the Ming dynasty (1368–1644) that an anonymous anthologist put together a collection of texts about male homosexuality from two thousand years of

Chinese cultural history, the *Records of the Cut Sleeve* (*Duan xiu pan*). This fact alone gives us a strong idea, not only of the availability of suitable material, but also of the presence of a suitable audience. The very existence of this one anthology – it has been called 'the first history of Chinese homosexuality, perhaps the first comprehensive homosexual history in any culture'[23] – argues the presence of what we would now call a gay subculture with its own interests and needs.

Among authors catering to these at the end of the Ming period – and writing in the vernacular rather than classical Chinese – is the major figure of Li Yu (1611–80), whose stories and plays deal with homosexual relationships in some depth. His first play, *Pitying the Fragrant Companion* (*Lian xiangban*), deals with a wife who falls in love with a younger woman and persuades her husband to welcome her into the family as a concubine. A later play, whose title off-puttingly translates as *A Male Mencius's Mother Educates His Son and Moves House Three Times* (*Nan Mengmu jiaohe sanqian*), contains an only half playful account of the origin of sexual intercourse between men, justifying the fact that it does not produce children:

> This practice was created when there was suffering and poverty among the people. How was this practice useful? Once in ancient times, as a result of unfortunate circumstances two men happily began to live together. Why were they happy? Because one suddenly thought up this practice! The other joyfully consented to doing it.[24]

This is unlikely to have weakened the confidence of neo-Confucian logic, but it is a good try. Certainly, for all that it is presented humorously, this is touching evidence that the moral argument in favour of same-sex relationships had been engaged in seventeenth-century China. It would be wiped out three centuries later.

Li Yu's short stories also deal with male homosexuality, albeit in somewhat hectic plots, often enlivened by moments of violence. In 'The House of Gathered Refinements' two friends, Jin and Liu, both married with families, share a young male lover called Quan, with whom each in turn enjoys 'the flowers of the rear courtyard'. However, when the faithful Quan rejects the advances of a corrupt official, Yan Shifan, the latter has him castrated. Quan eventually denounces Yan to the emperor, who has Yan beheaded. Subsequently, Quan uses Yan's skull to piss in. In 'Chronicle of Extraordinary Love', when the young widower Jifang falls in love with the beautiful boy Ruiji he asks (and pays) the boy's father for permission to marry him. (There is evidence that such formalisations of male relationships could occur in Fujian province.) They do so, and the boy, in order to avoid the day when he will have to marry a woman, castrates himself and lives as a woman. The couple arouse strong resentment locally, and when it is discovered that Ruiji has mutilated himself he is sentenced to a beating. Jifang volunteers to take his place and is beaten to death. The widow Ruiji brings up Jifang's young son Chengxin, and when in due course he, too, is courted for his beauty, Ruiji takes the boy to a region where homosexuality will be less of a threat to him. Both of these examples demonstrate an ambivalence, if not in relation to the moral value of male love itself, at least to its place in the broader social pattern. Although the rear courtyard is shown to be a potentially dangerous place, the danger derives from those who do not frequent it.[25]

The most famous and easily the most extensive treatment of male homosexual themes in nineteenth-century Chinese literature is Chen Sen's novel, *Precious Mirror of Ranking Flowers* (*Pinhua baojian*, 1849). This narrative of loves between actors and their scholarly patrons distinguishes clearly between moral and immoral behaviour, yet does not do so around a simplistic opposition of heterosexual virtue and homosexual vice. Instead it proposes a range of types of passion – extreme, shrewd, tasteful, pure, virtuous, impetuous, straightforward, drunken, voluptuous, seductive – to be judged by the degree and nature of the passion itself, rather than by the mechanics of genital apposition. However, it is clear that Chen Sen is arguing against the grain of social morality, and that his is an argument which was gradually being lost. By the time Western versions of sexual orientation had been absorbed into the Chinese language – in particular, with the coining of a medical equivalent to 'homosexuality' (*tongxinglian*/*tongxingai*) – the very idea of the 'cut sleeve' had been replaced by a far more judgemental distinction between reproductive heterosexuality and corruptive sodomy.

. . .

The monk Kobo Daishi is said to have introduced man–boy love to Japan on his return home from China in AD 806.[26] Whatever the truth of this tradition, it does show how Japanese conventions both of pederasty itself and of pederastic writing follow on from those which developed in China. All the way through Japanese literary history, we can find stories and poems of gay relevance, often unobtrusively published in general anthologies. Hsü Ling's poetry anthology *New Songs from a Jade Terrace* (c. AD 545) contains a scattering of man–boy love songs. The eleventh-century *Tale of Genji* (*Genji monogatari*), written by a woman, the Lady Murasaki, contains an episode in which, having been rejected by the woman he loves, the Lord Genji consoles himself by sleeping with her younger brother. A famous tale in the *Heike Monogatari* tells of the death of the beautiful youth Atsumori at the battle of Ichinotani, beheaded by an enemy who had instantaneously fallen in love with him at the moment of first seeing him.[27] The thirteenth-century anthology *Kokonchomon-shu* includes many stories of man–boy love. The fourteenth century saw the publication of an increasing number of *chigo monogatari*, stories about beautiful, well-educated, upper-class novices in Buddhist monasteries; a monk's love affair with such an acolyte would enlighten him as to the ephemeral, illusionistic nature of all merely emotional ties. The seventeenth-century *Tale of a Country Bumpkin* (*Dembu monogatari*, c. 1624–43) debates the relative advantages of women and boys as sexual partners. And so forth.

Differing fashions in boy-love have prevailed at various periods in Japanese history. In the twelfth century, for instance, the love of the *chigo* became fashionable at court. (A *chigo* was a boy between the ages of ten and seventeen.) But in the Samurai tradition the beloved is conventionally a slightly older youth between the ages of thirteen and twenty, known as *wakashu*. The latter kind of boy-love was known as *shudo*. (This word first appears in a document dating from 1485.) In the way of *shudo*, as in Greece, the lover was considered to be under an obligation to ensure the education of the boy he loved, especially his moral education. All samurai were expected to marry, but matrimony existed in parallel with *shudo*: it did not replace any aspect of the love of boys. In contrast to Greek conventions, sexual intercourse with a boy, whether *chigo* or *wakashu*, was likely to have been anal: the literature does not contain references to fellatio, mutual masturbation or intercrural intercourse.

The greatest of the Japanese classics of boy-love is *The Great Mirror of Male Love* (*Nanshoku okagami*, 1687), which is subtitled 'The Custom of Boy Love in Our Land'.[28] The author was Ihara Saikaku, the first Japanese writer to live exclusively on his income as a writer. Although his book speaks of two relevant types of men, connoisseurs of boys (*shojin-zuki*) and woman-haters (*onna-girai*), the former bisexual and the latter exclusively homosexual, Saikaku concentrates his attention on the exclusives. He claims that the love of boys pre-dates that of women, and he mentions Chinese precedents for Japanese homosexual behaviour.

As among the Greeks, Japanese pederasty was closely circumscribed by conventions. We have seen that the facial and bodily hair of growing boys had great significance in Greece and, if to a lesser extent, in Rome; but in Japan the sexual significance of a boy's hair was further formalised by the development of rigidly observed conventions of hair-cutting and scalp-shaving. At eleven or twelve, as a boy took his first step towards adulthood, his crown was shaved, thereby drawing attention to his forelocks. At fourteen or fifteen his temples were partially shaved, but the forelocks were again left to grow. At eighteen or nineteen, the forelocks and pate were shaved clean. At this crucial stage, the boy was strictly no longer available to be loved by older males, but he was now at liberty to take a younger boyfriend.

The suitability of the sexual arrangements of youngsters was closely policed. For instance, in 'Within the Fence' (*The Great Mirror*, 1: 3) a boy who is engaged in an inappropriate affair with a man is ordered to undergo the coming-of-age ritual, and its related haircut, after which he will no longer legitimately be able to be the beloved of any adult male. If couples of boys or men of equal ages ever were accepted – and they were – it would be on the important condition that one was clearly and exclusively the 'man' of the relationship and the other the 'boy'.

A strong distinction was maintained between romantic love and the love associated with a boy's social duties. This is demonstrated with awful clarity in the story entitled, with such deceptive charm, 'Though Bearing an Umbrella, He Was Rained Upon' (2: 2). A lord takes a beautiful boy, Korin, into his bed and has sex with him. The boy, who is subject to his authority and ought to make a formal show of gratitude for the great honour that has been shown him, instead complains to the lord: 'Forcing me to yield to your authority is not true love. My heart remains my own, and if one day someone should tell me he truly loves me, I will give my life for him. As a memento of this floating world, I want a lover upon whom I can lavish real affection' (p. 98). The lord does not forget this impertinent indiscretion, and when, in due course, Korin does indeed take such a lover as he spoke of, and does refuse to betray him, the lord unambiguously cuts off one of Korin's arms, then the other, and finally cuts off his head.

Again as in the Greek tradition – for obvious reasons, closely connected with the age-related conventions I have mentioned – eligible boyhood in Japan was regarded as being tragically evanescent. According to the story called 'Love Letter Sent in a Sea Bass' (1: 4), 'All told, loving a boy can be likened to a dream that we are not even given time to have' (p. 69). On the other hand – and despite all the conventions favouring the love of boys over that of men – the story called 'Two Old Cherry Trees Still in Bloom' shows that relationships which began in boyhood can last a lifetime, and the storyteller honours their endurance: 'Mondo was now 63 and Han'emon 66. Their love for each other had not changed since the days of their youth [when one was 16, the other 19]; neither of them had ever gazed at a woman's face in his life. Having lived together all these years, they truly deserved to be emulated as models of the way of love for all who love boys' (p. 181). Note, again, that these two men are exclusively homosexual, rather than bisexual.

As one reads through this rich, and often richly moving, material, one begins to see the lineaments of what one might describe as a distinct gay subculture, with its own styles, tastes and codes. According to the story called 'His Head Shaved on the Path of Dreams' (2: 3), boy-lovers were identifiable by a certain style of appearance. Consider the following description of one man:

The man looked to be under 30. The pate of his head was shaved well back with a short topknot. Both inner and outer robes were made of a black dragon-patterned weave bearing the chrysanthemum-leaf crest on the back, sleeves, and chest. He bore a plain sash of braided silk and sported two swords, long and short, in the foppish Yoshiya style. In short, he appeared to epitomise the connoisseur of boy love. (p. 105)

We also learn, from 'Who Wears the Incense Graph Dyed in her Heart?' (8: 5), that periodically there were major changes in the styles of male love. As this narrative puts it, 'In the old days, boy love was something rough and brawny. Men swaggered when they spoke. They preferred big, husky boys, and bore cuts on their bodies as a sign of male love. . . . Boys these days are expected to be delicate, nothing more' (p. 307).

One of the distinguishing signs of subcultural solidarity was the demonstrative misogyny with which the 'woman-haters' marked themselves off from the mere 'connoisseurs of boys'. This same story ends, and with it the whole collection, as follows: 'Because there is female love, the foolish human race continues to thrive. Would that the love of boys became the common form of love in the world, and that women would die out and Japan become an Isle of Men. Quarrels between husband and wife would cease, jealousy disappear, and the world enter at last into an era of peace.' A likely story.

The first act of Chikamatsu Monzaemon's play *Double Suicide in the Middle of the Night* (1721) tells a discrete story about Yamawaki Koshichiro, a beautiful boy who attracts many love letters from four suitors. Three of these men arrive one day, each hoping to persuade the boy to come away with him. All three are samurai. But when Koshichiro's elder half-brother, Hanbei, inspects the letters, he sees that there is a fourth suitor, Koichibei, a servant in the house. He summons him. Testing the depth of the suitors' love, Hanbei asks which of them will commit himself to an eternity alongside the boy by dying with him by the sword. None of the samurai is man enough to contemplate such a fate. Koichibei, on the other hand, declares the intensity of his love by snatching up a sword and preparing to kill himself with the boy. Impressed, Hanbei has to intervene to disarm the two lovers. He gives his brother to the servant. In tears, they embrace each other.

Theatrical traditions are central to the history of male homosexuality in Japan. The travelling Noh companies acquired a reputation for the erotic flavour of their entertainments: 'To attract their clients, they relied on the sexual attractions of their young men, rather than on their art. They often went so far even as to prostitute their younger members in order to survive.'[29] Indeed, by one of those happy accidents which often place sexual attraction at the centre of cultural change, official patronage was first granted to Noh after the shogun Yoshimitsu, aged sixteen, was turned on by the performance of a twelve-year-old boy, Zeami (1363–1443). Under Yoshimitsu's patronage, Zeami flourished as both actor and dramatist, the key figure in the founding of the classical Noh tradition.

The more secular tradition of *kabuki* at first included girls dressed as boys, but *onna kabuki* (women's *kabuki*) was banned in 1629 on the grounds of its tendency to corrupt public morals. Its plays were considered excessively erotic; its actresses had a reputation for involvement in prostitution. It was replaced by *wakashu kabuki*, with boys playing the female roles. But they too had to be banned, for the same reasons, in 1652. The theatre companies were allowed to go back into business in the following year, but only on the condition that their boy actors cut off the forelocks (the *mae-gami*, or frontal hair) which had made them seem so sexily girlish. The actors compensated for their enforced head-shaving, and made themselves all the more sexy, by adopting a cap called a *yaro*. The success of this ploy, of *yaro kabuki*, can be measured by the fact that the very word *yaro* came to signify a male prostitute. Subsequently, wigs were worn and certain actors became specialists in playing female roles. In contrast to the player in the English theatrical tradition, the specialist actor of female roles, the *oyama*, continued playing women throughout his career. Indeed, he would live as a woman in daily life off stage. The aim of the great artists in this tradition was to perfect a completely artificial femininity, 'the femininity that only men can bring into being'.

Between the eighteenth and twentieth centuries, under the related influences of Western imperialism, the rise of the bourgeoisie, the growth of capitalism and the Japanese industrial revolution, *shudo* went into decline. The drive for Westernisation and modernisation during the Meiji period (1868–1912) included strenuous efforts to bring Japanese sexual morality into line with the supposedly enlightened standards of the Victorians. This meant doing away with such archaic practices as *shudo*. In their place, Western legal and medical discourses began to prevail. Of course there have been important homosexual writers since then: Tahuro Inagaki (b. 1900), who wrote an *Aesthetics of Adolescent Love*, would be one such; more famously in the West, Yukio Mishima (1925–70) is another. Both belong to this intermediate period of repression, and both write accordingly.

Yukio Mishima's *Forbidden Colours* (*Kinchiki*, 1951–53) shows clear evidence of how Japanese gay culture might be influenced by Western patterns and archetypes. Mishima was an extreme case, of course. Notwithstanding his fascistic calls for a return to samurai ideals, he had a broad knowledge and deep love of certain aspects of Western culture, many of them clearly manifested in his novels. One of the more curious things about *Forbidden Colours* is the way in which Mishima, as if he were an Englishman of the late nineteenth or early twentieth century, keeps comparing modern male beauty to that of the famous boys in Greek mythology.[30] Only very rarely does Mishima represent homosexual men in such a way as to make one feel he could be anything but extremely uncomfortable to have to identify his own sexuality with theirs. There is a certain grudging respect in the following passage, for instance:

> Only the Jews were a match for them when it came to fortitude. In the abnormal degree to which they held fast to a single, humiliating point of view they were like the Jews. The emotion proper to this tribe gave birth to fanatical heroism during the war. After the war it embraced a pride at being in the van of decadence. It thrived on confusion. In that riven ground it grew clumps of tiny, dark violets. (p. 103)

The comparison with the Jews is not original – it comes from Proust. Nor is it, I think, a point of which Mishima much approves. Far more likely, it is the reference to 'fanatical heroism during the war' that really resonated with the author: it ties in so closely, not only with the kinds of reference to ancient Greece that evoke the comradeship of warriors and the fortitude of the Spartans, but also with the samurai traditions Mishima revered to the point of his own ritual suicide. We have to understand all of his references to ancient Greece – and to traditions of martial pederasty in particular – in a spirit of cross-cultural identification between the samurai and the Greeks. And yet, it seems to have been becoming increasingly clear to him that his classical references were largely redundant. In the Westernised culture of the gay bar and the 'Gei Pa-ti' (for Mishima's characters have already learned the emergent American use of the word 'gay'), as in the wider stretches of Japanese society, decadence had set in; and reference could be made to the likes of Narcissus and Apollo in a spirit of womanish camp. Once one calls a young man Apollo merely in order to convey an impression of his prettiness, one has lost touch with the power of the cultural tradition from which such a reference derives. All that is left is the sexy male body, but it is a body in decline: into decadence, into unfitness, and into middle age. These are the major threats from which the theatricality of Mishima's suicide so effectively released him.

It is difficult to think of Mishima as a gay writer in the Western sense. Much closer to that recognisable type would be a poet like Mutsuo Takahashi (b. 1937), whose extraordinary poetry often out-flaunts even the likes of Allen Ginsberg, by whom he appears to have been influenced, as well as by Walt Whitman. The jauntily defiant title of one of Takahashi's collections was *You Dirty Ones, Do Dirtier Things* (*Yogoretaru Mono wa Sara no Yogoretaru Koto o Nase*, 1966) and his characteristic topic is the unseemly but transcendent physical beauty of urban sexual rituals. His development of this theme reaches its qualitative peak in his lengthy 'Ode' (1971), a rhapsodic celebration of fellatio in which he subsumes the orality of sucking a cock into that of composing and reading a poem.[31] Takahashi is very widely travelled, and makes explicit use of the cultural materials he has picked up on his way. The footnotes to the Afterword to 'Ode' typically contain references to Egyptian hieroglyphics, W.H. Auden, Sigmund Freud and Norman O. Brown, the Old and New Testaments, Lao Tzu and the *Tao-te Ching*, James Frazer's *The Golden Bough*, Guillaume Apollinaire, Gertrud von Le Fort's *Die ewige Frau*, Albert Moll's *Die homosexuelle Liebe*, Rilke and Plato. ('Ode' celebrates an exceedingly bookish blow-job.) This conscious turning away from Japanese cultural traditions may be a necessary concomitant to becoming a gay writer in the Western sense. It also spells out, for better or worse, the obliteration of *shudo*.

Chapter 6

....

The European Renaissance

....

Although he claimed to be attracted to beauty in any human age or sex ('d'ogni età, d'ogni sesso'), Michelangelo Buonarotti made no bones about his belief that male love was superior to the love of women. As one of his poems states the case,

> L'amor di quel ch'i' parlo in alto aspira;
> donna è dissimil troppo; e mal conviensi
> arder di quella al cor saggio e verile.
> L'un tira al cielo, e l'altro in terra tira;
> nell'alma l'un, l'altr'abita ne' sensi,
> e l'arco tira a cose basse e vile.

(The love of which I speak has high aspirations; / woman is too different; and it ill becomes / the wise and manly heart to burn for her. / One love pulls you heavenwards, the other earthwards; / one is located in the soul, the other in the senses, / and draws its bow towards things which are low and vile.) This is not an unusual distinction for a man to be making during the Renaissance period in Europe. Ultimately, it derives from Plato. Specifically, in this case, it derives from readings of Marsilio Ficino's commentaries (1469) on Plato's *Symposium*. The argument is the inevitable consequence of a virtually inbred misogyny. While woman is *all* physique, the prime site for sin and for lust in particular, man is naturally more spiritual, better equipped to transcend the baseness of physical matter and its attendant vices. It follows that this is not an argument about the superiority of homosexual intercourse over heterosexual intercourse – though many men who were predominantly homosexual adopted it, including Michelangelo himself.[1] Rather, it suggests that men are essentially too good for sex, and that they are only dragged into it by the unworthy pursuit of the love of women. If they would only love each other, and each other alone, men would not have to be dragged down to the level of such a filthy business. The more refined the man, the less likely he is to become embroiled in the earthly pleasures of heterosexual intercourse.

Giovanni Dall'Orto has examined the widespread concept of 'Socratic love' (*amor socraticus*) in Italian Renaissance texts and concluded that the history of this idea 'became a struggle against the identification of same-sex love with same-sex behaviour'.[2] But for some men the struggle was also against the identification *of* same-sex behaviour – that is,

10. Self-portrait of the artist defeated by his lover, Tommaso Cavalieri. (Michelangelo's *Victory*)

a struggle to disguise sex as friendship for fear of the consequences of being denounced as a sodomite. There were very good, pragmatic reasons – the avoidance of gibbets and jails – for spiritualising the literature of male love. In readings not only of Marsilio Ficino himself, but also of the likes of Giovanni Pico della Mirandola, Baldassare Castiglione, Giordano Bruno and Michelangelo himself, Dall'Orto identifies the *amor socraticus* as a field of contestation in which an early version of the fixed sexual orientations had been established. For instance, Dall'Orto quotes a passage in which Giordano Bruno speaks of Socrates' 'natural leaning towards the filthy love of boys' ('la sua natural[e] inclinatione al sporco amor di gargioni'), (p. 49). One thing is certain: it is not only today's axe-grinding and filthy-minded gay critics who discern carnal meanings in supposedly 'chaste' texts. One Girolamo Muzio wrote of the poetry of Benedetto Varchi: 'Concerning the sonnets by Varchi ... they are more wanton and filthy than chaste and honest; moreover, his dealing always with eyes, forefront, cheeks, lips and neck in my opinion has nothing holy, nor has his "big kiss" anything chaste no matter what the Platonists say.'[3]

What of the Renaissance in England? In a moment of genuinely informative bafflement, the literary critic Bruce Smith asks: 'What are we to make of a culture that could consume popular prints of Apollo embracing Hyacinth and yet could order hanging for men who acted on the very feelings that inspire that embrace?'[4] He means the culture of Renaissance England, though he could just as well be speaking of Italy. The disparity he points out is not just an interesting curiosity. On the contrary, it signals a structural characteristic of English society at the time – a fault line cutting right across many aspects of the development of the English institutions: incipient English nationalism, fashionable Greek revivalism, the restraints of Christian scripture, tensions around the status of Catholicism, the imperialist adventures of the great explorers and their reactions to what they witnessed among the savages, the impertinent emergence of English as the dominant language in literature even while Greek and Latin remained the languages to be read by the most highly educated, courtly dandyism and the manly requirements of military expansionism, and so forth.

If one reads much of the poetry of the time, one gets the impression that the English countryside was a pastoral haven from all ills. Nothing could be further from the truth for

11. Desirable boyhood receives
his just desserts at the hands of a
vengeful morality. (Bartolomeo
Manfredi, *Cupid Chastised*, *c.* 1605)

ordinary people. Even court poets would have to avert their eyes from a lot – not least, the
climate – in order to persuade themselves that the great parks of their experience were
easily comparable with what they (and not the illiterate rustics) had read of a place called
Arcadia. The traditions of Graeco-Roman pastoral lyric were imported wholesale to
English culture, with variable regard to geographical likelihood, at the very time when
English poets were attempting to establish a distinctive national (and nationalist) literature
in the English language. And, to some extent, the sexual mores of classical pastoral were
imported into a society whose rules were, to say the least, different from those of Athens
or Rome.

Elizabethan homo-erotic pastoral is possibly at its most unrefined, some critics say
naïve, in Richard Barnfield's poems from the years 1594 to 1598. This is presumably why
his work is so often dismissed as consisting of imitative exercises – obviously far easier to
argue in his case than in that of Shakespeare's much more inventive and subtle sonnets.
On the other hand, Barnfield's unguarded enthusiasm for the bucolic love poem provides
its own charm and its own outspokenness. Dating from when the poet was in his early

12. Renaissance man meets his nemesis, Renaissance boy. (Donatello's *David*)

13. The physical peak of tragic passivity, painted by a self-declared sodomite. (Sodoma, *Jesus at the Column*)

twenties, the poems have a slightly raw quality that itself seems endearingly boyish. Bruce Smith is reacting to something similar when he writes:

> In their rhetorical teasing and relentless sexual punning there is something pornographic about Barnfield's poems. They are completely self-absorbed. They never get beyond sexual desire. They are, in effect, poems of masturbation.[5]

Smith also calls them 'campy', which seems both anachronistic and reductive. Barnfield is not generally regarded as an important poet, except in one respect: he can be contrasted with Shakespeare – or rather, Shakespeare can with him. Not only do Barnfield's sonnets show up how subtle Shakespeare's are, but their puerile homosexual effusiveness can be used to point out the supposedly universal sophistication of Shakespeare's more mature, platonic friendliness. (Barnfield's pederastic eros is inauthentic when contrasted with Shakespeare's mature marital status.) On the other hand, Barnfield's sonnets can be cited as demonstrating that boy-love was one of the fashionable subjects of the age, and that Shakespeare was merely outdoing fellow-poets in treatment of a conventional theme, rather than expressing any real depth of personal emotion, when he wrote his equivalent sequence. (When it comes to poems of boy-love, Shakespeare is less authentic than Barnfield – and is all the better for it.)

In other words, Barnfield is a useful poet to have around when you are trying to bolster up Shakespeare's position as heavyweight champion of the literary world. On the one hand, Barnfield is the rather feeble, homosexual poet. On the other, Shakespeare is the coolly Apollonian bard, somehow above passion except when attributing it to his dramatic characters or to himself in poems which so artfully express the feelings not of one man but of 'us all'. Shakespeare is regarded as heterosexual, of course – since how else could he represent first England and then Great Britain so respectably? – but his heterosexuality is domesticated, represented in the details of Anne Hathaway's cottage and the bed in Will's will, rather than a matter of unstable passion.

It is true that Barnfield's sonnets do not survive comparison with Shakespeare's: both stylistically and emotionally they seem far less complex, less adventurous and less expertly controlled. Paradoxically, this can give them the look of being mere exercises, forcing emotion into unaccustomed patterns of rhythm and rhyme. If so, however, they come across as exercises driven by genuine emotion which renders the poet less able to control his stylistics. That is to say, as exercises they fail; as expressions of emotion, in spite of themselves, they begin to succeed. In Sonnet 12 Barnfield explicitly denies that his love is merely a literary exercise, derived from classical examples, and asserts that he is writing from personal experience:

> Some talk of *Ganymede* th' *Idalian* Boy,
>   And some of fair *Adonis* make their boast,
>   Some talk of him whom louely *Læda* lost,
> And some of *Ecchoes* loue that was so coy.
> They speak by heere-say, I of perfect truth[.]

Of course, this is itself a lie: for Barnfield cannot stop himself from writing as if he were living in Arcadia rather than England, and all of his references are to Greece rather than to his own cultural surroundings. Indeed, this stanza really deserves to be inverted, since Barnfield is addicted to writing classical pastoral – and nothing else.

Throughout the sequence, the poet (speaking as Daphnis) is noisily aching for a kiss. Sonnet 5 ends: 'Then if thou hast a mind still to annoy me,/ Kill me with kisses, if thou wilt destroy me'. In Sonnet 6 he calls on the boy's 'Sweet Corrall lips' to 'Come quench my thirst or els poor *Daphnis* dies'. Sonnet 8 begins: 'Sometimes I wish that I his pillow were,/ So might I steal a kiss, and yet not seene'. In Sonnet 16 he complains that 'Weening to kisse his lips, as my loues fee's,/ I feele but Aire: nothing but Aire to bee him'. Two poems list the loved boy's physical parts and attributes, mainly concentrating on the kissability of the face: Sonnet 2 speaks of his cheek, chin, brow, lips, eyes, locks and 'gate' (gait) and Sonnet 17 his limbs, cheeks, lips, mouth, tongue and teeth. Indeed, in the latter poem, having inventoried these parts, he says that 'such a body' is 'sinne-procuring'. (This phrase is one of a number of moments when Barnfield's anachronisms allow his Englishness to show through its Arcadian costume.)

If the face is the synecdochic representation of the whole boy, then it follows that a mere kiss represents more general forms of physical intercourse. The poet craves a sexual possession which is justified by the sheer physical beauty of the desired object. It is a body built, in the Greek manner, for physical consummation – and built for the Greek manner of consummation. But the boy will not give way, not even with kisses. As the poet complains in Sonnet 10: 'But as for his pure, spotles, vertuous mind' (as opposed, I suppose, to Sonnet 17's 'sinne-procuring' body), 'Hit wholy is to chastity inclined./ And thus it is: as far as I can proue,/ He loues to be beloued, but not to loue'. He is a prick-teaser, as determined to fend off his suitors as he was to attract them in the first place. Whether this can legitimately be called 'chastity' is a matter for theology.

Bruce Smith writes that 'Arcadia is a place apart, but it is also a time apart, during which personal identities are not fixed and desire is free to wander'.[6] As we have seen, this is not entirely true: Longus' Daphnis and Chloe showed that when desire begins to wander in the wrong direction it needs to be resisted. What is true, though, is that Arcadia holds out the *promise* of such fluencies of identity and desire, even if it does not actually deliver them. In Barnfield's work, the Ganymede poems appear to be superseded by 'An Ode', in which a young swain says:

> Loue I did the fairest boy,
> That these fields did ere enioy.
> Loue I did, fair *Ganymed*;
> (*Venus* darling, beauties bed:)
> Him I thought the fairest creature;
> Him the quintessence of Nature:
> But yet (alas) I was deceiu'd,
> (Loue of reason is bereau'd)
> For since then I saw a Lasse
> (Lasse) that did in beauty passe,
> (Passe) fair *Ganymede* as farre
> As *Phoebus* doth the smallest starre.

There is a suggestion, here, of the mythology of the 'passing phase': the swain has grown out of the deception of his homosexual stage. Suddenly, the scales are lifted from his eyes and he is able to recognise the true extent of female beauty. Of course, to read the poem in this negative way, we have to take this poem as legitimately coming after the homo-erotic ones; and also to read it as referring not just to one lass who happens to be more beautiful than Ganymede, but to the generality of female beauty outstripping male beauty. To read it in this way is to argue, contrary to Bruce Smith, that this particular administrative district of Arcadia, like so many others, follows conventions of restraint imported from elsewhere. It is true that certain freedoms are allowed, but they are strictly limited; and heterosexuality must, eventually, prevail.

Whether or not Barnfield was homosexual does not concern me. All I know is that he was married and had at least one child, which proves and disproves nothing. In any case, knowing, or believing we know, that a particular writer was what we would now call homosexual does not necessarily provide easy access to his work as 'homosexual literature'. Sir Francis Bacon (1561–1626) is an interesting case in point. We have it on the questionable authority of both John Aubrey's *Brief Lives* and Sir Simon D'Ewes' *Autobiography* that Bacon loved men. D'Ewes speaks of his sexual relationships with his manservants and suggests that Bacon was almost brought to trial for sodomy. If we allow ourselves to suppose that the evidence is sufficient to confirm that Bacon was, in the words of H. Montgomery Hyde, 'a thorough invert' (as opposed to a slipshod one?), it may seem a logical next step to turn to Bacon's writings for whatever literary evidence they afford. But how is this to be done?

Two similar instances come to mind. In *The Other Love*, his 1970 history of homosexuality in Great Britain, H. Montgomery Hyde mentions no positive evidence but asserts that Bacon's work does not 'show any interest in or attraction towards the other sex'. Hyde adds, though, that it is not without significance that 'his essay "On Beauty" [*sic*] in the celebrated *Essays* deals exclusively with masculine beauty'.[7] Likewise, the entry on Bacon in the *Encyclopedia of Homosexuality* sketches in the details of the life and then adds: 'In accord with Greco-Roman and Renaissance predecessors, his essay "Of Friendship" confines itself to relations between men. "Of Beauty" discusses the matter exclusively in terms of male exemplars.'[8] Joseph Cady, too, backs up his assertion that Bacon 'hints at his attraction to other males' in the essays by remarking on the fact that 'Of Beauty' 'discusses examples of male beauty only'.[9]

I think we can dismiss the point about the essay on friendship (1607) quite firmly. In Bacon's day the word 'friendship' referred, virtually by definition, to relations between males; so the essay's lack of reference to male–female relationships reveals hardly anything useful about the writer. It certainly does not prove that he is discreetly referring to sexual affection – though it may be that he is.[10] The claims about Bacon's essay on beauty provide a more complex problem. While it is perfectly true that this short piece contains only references to men, the men in question are a peculiar selection: 'Augustus Caesar, Titus Vespasianus, Philip le Bel of France, Edward the Fourth of England, Alcibiades of Athens, Ismael the Sophy of Persia' (all 'the most beautiful men of their times') and no one else. One looks in vain for the staple currency of the Renaissance version of male beauty, all those familiar figures from Greek myth (Adonis, Apollo, Ganymede, Hyacinth, Hylas, Narcissus) or pastoral lyric (Alexis, Corydon, Daphnis). Perhaps the main reason for this is that Bacon specifies the superiority of maturity over youth – 'persons in years seem many times more amiable . . . no youth can be comely but by pardon' – and most of the Greek archetypes are boys rather than men. But he is also steering his topic away from a purely sensual consideration of beauty, which, he appears to acknowledge, would confine his examples to the young. He is also, of course, dealing with historical rather than mythical figures. In other words, this essay is not really about what Hyde and the encyclopaedist want it to be about. Perhaps 'handsomeness' would more clearly express to today's readers the physical side of the mature distinctiveness that Bacon is hoping to convey.

Needless to say – as we have seen and shall see in abundance elsewhere – it does not take an author whose homosexuality or bisexuality can be proved with, or may creatively be inferred from, documentary evidence to provide us with an authentic gay literature. For one more or less random example, there is a spectacularly intense moment of homo-eroticism in

Andrew Marvell's poem 'The Last Instructions to a Painter' (1667). Indeed, Marvell was sufficiently proud of this passage to repeat it wholesale in 'The Loyal Scot', which dates from about two years later. The lines in question are 649–96, about the death of one Captain Archibald Douglas in June 1667, when the Dutch fleet daringly sailed right into the Medway. Marvell's tribute to Douglas begins with a pseudo-classical bathing scene and ends with a strange account of his burning to death as though he were merely languishing in the embrace of a particularly ardent and powerful lover. Perhaps contemporary readers would have understood this as suggesting the purifying fire of God's (or Christ's) love.

Douglas is presented as being a beautiful youth 'on whose lovely chin / The early down but newly did begin,/ And modest beauty yet his sex did veil,/ While envious [female] virgins hope he is a male'. Well, he is; but that does not prevent his being ravished and taken away from them before long. As long as his manhood remains veiled, any pretty man in this period is seen as being potential competition for women. Until his 'down' becomes bristly he will continue to be desirable to men. There is a certain introversion about Douglas' beauty – 'His yellow locks curl back themselves to seek,/ Nor other courtship knew but to his cheek' – which, as well as suggesting narcissism, implies that he, too, is a virgin still, too young to have tasted love, though not, judging by his 'down', meant to seem actually pre-pubertal.

In the lines which follow, the poet imagines Douglas bathing – and being watched bathing, night-time notwithstanding, as we who read the poem also watch: 'Oft, as he in chill Esk or Seine by night / Hardened and cooled his limbs, so soft, so white,/ Among the reeds, to be espied by him,/ The nymphs would rustle.' The voyeurism of the nymphs, then, is unlike ours, since their purpose is to be noticed by him; even, with luck, admired by him. They hope their interventive admiration will become interactive, provoking him to attain his first heterosexual moment. In a sense, although they are attracted to the equivocal nature of his present beauty, their aim is to accelerate his growth. One might say, it is the down they desire but the bristles they must encourage. In that respect, their ploy has the potential to spoil the reader's view of him – if the reader is a man: for, at the moment of the bathing scene, the boy Douglas is on the verge of becoming a man, available only to the female gaze.

The nymphs address him – 'Fond boy, why so untame / That fliest love's fires, reserved for other flame?' – accusing him of a kind of amorous cowardice. However, the fact is that he really does have more mature matters to deal with than flirtation, and fiercer flames to cope with than those of the love the nymphs can bring to bear on him. Presumably having 'Hardened and cooled' his deceptively soft, white limbs in a bathing scene less languor-ously pastoral than purposefully virile, he goes back to his ship to face his patriotic fate. His body is caught in the subsequent conflagration:

> Like a glad lover, the fierce flames he meets,
> And tries his first embraces in their sheets.
> His shape exact, which the bright flames enfold,
> Like the sun's statue stands of burnished gold.
> Round the transparent fire about him glows,
> As the clear amber on the bee does close,
> And, as on angels' heads their glories shine,
> His burning locks adorn his face divine.

This is an extraordinary prettification of horrendous suffering, which is not even acknowledged. The intensity of the eroticism derives from its incongruity with the circumstances of the death. Douglas' heroism – his turning from the safety of the land to a glorious death in battle at sea (or offshore, at least) – is figured by Marvell as a rejection of the bucolic sufficiency of the nymphs in favour of a more rigorous and glorious love. This is also, of course, a boy's decision to make love for the first time, not in a woman's arms, but in a man's – not cooled by moonlight but seared by the sun – and the boy will be the willingly dominated, passive partner. It is the moment to which the beautiful development of his body has brought and suited him.

The moment of initiation is eternal: it remains to define Douglas, as amber defines the bee, for ever. Although only momentarily cast in gold as 'the sun's statue', his shape is commemorated in the poem, also for ever. The flames around his face are both a brighter version of the 'yellow locks' that seek to kiss his cheeks and the halo of an angel – in either case, the appropriately 'divine' adornment to such beauty, the ephemeral, earthly version of the heavenly glory to which his being burnt alive has sent him. One is meant to imagine him as if in a painting, static and preserved, for ever brave, for ever beautiful – and never wed.

· · ·

When we turn from Renaissance poetry to drama, we are confronted with an immense potential for homo-erotic representations, but they do not necessarily exist in the manifest directness of the printed word. While in poetry, too, it is always incumbent on the reader to do what is popularly known as 'reading between the lines', in drama there is the added dimension of theatrical practice to be taken into account. And theatrical practice does not exist simply as a record of how plays were performed in Shakespeare's day – even if such a record existed and could be trusted as being accurate to all performances – but has accumulated its own history, in parallel with texts, but not always strictly in accordance with their stage directions. Renaissance drama exists on the page and on the stage, and its existence on the stage has evolved through several centuries, each of which has seen the development of new conventions of production and performance.

The first and most significant difference between performances then and now is, of course, in the conventions surrounding the representation of women. Then they had boy actors, now we (usually) have girls and women. Although the precise extent of the difference is difficult to gauge, no one should attempt to play down its importance. Renaissance audiences saw dressed-up boys where we see women. Two simplifying hypotheses can be offered at this point: firstly, that audiences at the time were so used to the convention of boys dressed as women that they simply did not consider the boy visible; they refined him out of existence in order to see nothing more than the woman he was playing. Secondly, on the contrary, audiences were so used to the convention of boys dressed as women that they were completely at ease with the sexual connotations (to do with androgyny and bisexuality) which were so visible in every scene; audiences saw boys in drag and enjoyed their performances, but never lost sight of the fact that they were boys; in effect the theatre at that time was 'gay theatre', and the reputation the buildings themselves acquired as male brothels was often deserved.

Some of the Puritans' attacks on theatre and theatricality suggest that, at least to some spectators, the latter hypothesis may have rung true. Consider the following passage from Phillip Stubbes' *The Anatomie of Abuses* (1583):

Marke the flocking and running to Theaters & curtens, daylie and hourely, night and daye, tyme and tyde to see Playes and Enterludes, where such wanton gestures, such bawdie speaches: such laughing and fleering: such kissing and bussing: such clipping and culling: Suche winckinge and glancing of wanton eyes, and the like is used, as

14. Androgyny makes friends with spirituality. (Follower of Verrocchio, *Tobias and the Angel*, *c*. 1470–80)

is wonderfull to behold. Than these goodly pageants being done, every mate sorts to his mate, every one bringes another homeward of their way verye freendly, and in their secret conclaves (covertly) they play the *Sodomits*, or worse.[11]

This vision of the theatre as the site of purposeful titillation leading to actual sexual encounters is possibly paranoid. It reminds one of today's periodic panics about the dissemination of pornography on satellite television or the Internet. But we know that other theatrical traditions which used boy actors – in the Far East, for instance – gained similar reputations, not only for the immorality of the plays they put on, but also for their willingness to service the audiences they had so deliberately inflamed. Women did not play women on the English stage until after the Restoration of Charles II to the English throne in 1660 – a change introduced, possibly, in order to reform the morals of the theatre, which so often seemed to be threatening to teeter over into sodomitical practices.

It should never be forgotten that playwrights write *for* the conventions of their day, and are therefore heavily influenced by them. Shakespeare did not write for the Memorial Theatre at Stratford which bears his name, nor even for the facsimile of the Globe which was built in London in the mid-1990s. Every one of his women characters is written on the assumption of the boy within the costume. On this topic, Juliet Dusinberre has written that 'The boy actor encouraged the dramatist to observe the similarities between the sexes, the way in which boyishness itself formed an element in femininity' (and femininity, one might add, in boyishness).[12] This is interesting enough, though most Elizabethan playwrights were in no need of such encouragement: as we saw in our glance at the poetry of the Christian Middle Ages in Europe, the girlishness of beautiful boys had long been a cliché of poetic utterance. That female and male beauty were more or less interchangeable until the height of puberty was certainly taken for granted. Dusinberre reiterates her useful point, that the convention of male playing of female characters allowed and encouraged playwrights like Shakespeare to imagine some particularly spunky women. 'The boy actor was a spur to the creation of heroines of allegedly masculine spirit,' she says, and: 'Shakespeare's women are both women and boys' (p. 251). And again: 'The boy actor prompted the creation of boyish heroines' (p. 271) And yet there is always going to be a down-side to this effect, given that no female character on the stage was ever more mature than the young boy who played her. In Dusinberre's words, 'Some of the finest Shakespearian women are still schoolboys' (p. 253).

Shakespeare's gender comedies depend on the hypothesis of totally convincing – or rather, deceptive – gender performativity. A girl dresses as a boy and easily passes as such. The modulation of a voice is lowered or raised and becomes instantly unrecognisable. In some near-to-literal sense, it is taken as being true that the apparel *proclaims* the woman or man. Clothing is an announcement, not only of social status, but of gender: change your clothes and, to all appearances, your body will change with them. Sexual attraction is determined, not by the essentialist and binarised 'orientations' of twentieth-century understanding, but by a manipulable beauty. By implication, if one is not of the 'appropriate' gender to effect a particular courtship, one can dress as if one were and start paying court. Whether one succeeds will depend, not on the homosexuality of the loved one, but on the success of the performance.

Most of the sustained sequences of plausible cross-dressing in Renaissance drama involve female characters passing as boys. Only rarely does the opposite situation take a major part in the narrative structure of a play. An example would be the way in which, in John Day's *The Isle of Gulls* (1606), Lisander remains dressed as an Amazon through most of the play, from Act I, Scene iv to the last scene, Act V, Scene i.[13] That he does so has no significant homosexual connotation in relation to his character: he dresses as a woman in order to gain access to the woman he desires, the Princess Violetta, whose father is keeping her on an island away from men. However, it has been argued that in the figure of Lisander dressed as a woman, much wider issues are being marshalled into view: 'the new nobility, the king, the queen, their favourites, and the homosexuality of the English court were satirised through the use of a man disguised as a woman'.[14]

References to sodomy are not exactly abundant in early seventeenth-century drama, but nor are they particularly rare or hard to find. In Cyril Tourneur's *The Revenger's Tragedy* (published in 1607) Vindice says rather forwardly to Lussurioso, 'How dost, sweet musk-cat – when shall we lie together?' – to which Lussorio reacts in an astonished aside: 'Sfoot, the slave's / Already as familiar as an ague / And shakes me at his pleasure' (I. iii, 35–8). In Tourneur's *The Atheist's Tragedy* (1611) the Puritan chaplain Languebeau Snuffe leaps on the corpse of Borachio, thinking it the living body of the gentlewoman Soquette, and says: 'Verily thou liest in a fine premeditate readiness for the purpose. Come, kiss me, sweet Soquette. – Now purity defend me from the sin of Sodom! This is a creature of the masculine gender' (IV. iii, 206–9). Then he notices that the body is dead and cries murder.

Sodomy tends to be seen as a practice associated more with power than with mutual pleasure, and submission to it as either a sign of irredeemable weakness or a knowing step on the road to influence. In John Webster's *The White Devil* (1612) Flamineo says 'Give me a fair room yet hung with arras, and some great cardinal to lug me by th' ears as his endeared minion' (V. i, 122–4). This charming fantasy of being fucked from behind by a corpulent prince of the Church has at least as much pragmatic humour in it as distaste. If influence is to be bought in such ways, so be it; the price may well be worth paying. It is a serious joke, about both the debauchery of the powerful and the relatively modest sacrifice a man might make so that some of that power would rub off on him.

A sodomite with real power appears in Ben Jonson's play *Sejanus His Fall* (first performed in 1603). Sejanus has grown powerful through having been the 'minion' and bedfellow of the emperor Tiberius. In Act Four, Scene Four, Arruntius describes some of the libertine excesses enjoyed by Tiberius on Capri. In a speech which Jonson based on Tacitus' accounts of the carnal amusements of Tiberius at his spectacular island bolthole, the Villa Iovis, Arruntius speaks mainly of murder, but the choice of victims is important:

> Thither, too,
> He hath his boys, and beauteous girls ta'en up,
> Out of our noblest houses, the best formed,
> Best nurtured, and most modest: what's their good
> Serves to provoke his bad. Some are allured,
> Some threatened; others (by their friends detained)
> Are ravished hence, like captives, and, in sight
> Of their most grievèd parents, dealt away
> Unto his spintries, sellaries, and slaves,
> Masters of strange, and new-commented lusts,
> For which wise nature hath not left a name.
>   (IV. iv, 391–401)

Like a Sadean libertine, Tiberius uses his wealth and power to violate the social hierarchy he has placed himself above. In doing so – in Elizabethan if not precisely in Roman terms – he violates the Great Chain of Being, that mythic construct which naturalised the existing social order. His destruction of the children of the nobility is not just more shocking than the destruction of slaves: it is more unnatural. So the emperor is unnatural twice over – yet in ways which are not thought to be unrelated – as sodomite and subverter of the social order. Interestingly, though, in these lines there is no precise indication that he himself actually enjoys at first hand the bodies he has ordered kidnapped; instead, he is said to pass them over to his 'spintries, sellaries, and slaves'. As my edition of the play footnotes them, 'spintries' and 'sellaries' are 'Male prostitutes and practitioners of unnatural vice'.[15] (Both words appeared in R. Greneway's 1598 translation of Tacitus' *Annals*.)

Arruntius reaches the crux of his critical speech with the accusation that the emperor has become 'the ward / To his own vassal, a stale catamite' (403–4). This remark hardly differs from so many tropes in Renaissance drama (Shakespeare is full of them) whereby the apparently stable order of the world is said to have been suddenly overturned. It certainly fits in with what has just been described: a place where the children of the nobility are handed over to the murderous enjoyment of slaves. In a single, more or less chaste utterance, Arruntius manages to conjure up the perfect image of social inversion: a greater man presenting his arse to the penis of a lesser. Even if the accusation is not meant to be taken literally (as it is in Marlowe's *Edward II*), that the head of state is being buggered by his power-hungry favourite, the image is used to conjure up the horror of a manipulated emperor. Nothing could better express the vulnerability of the very empire to unnatural acts of social inversion. The later account of Sejanus' dismemberment at the hands of the mob (V. vi, 808–35) is detailed and gruesome, evoking the visceral pleasures of a justifiable revenge. It may remind us of the fate of Orpheus, or the tortures some medieval Christian texts promised would befall the unrepentant sodomite. Terentius' speech revels in the extremity of the ultimate degradation of the sodomitic body.

Jonson's comic play *Epicoene, or The Silent Woman* (1609–10) is altogether more relaxed about its sexual conundra. For instance, in the opening scene Truewit appears to regard the keeping of a boyfriend as little more than a kind of rich man's idleness. He says: 'Why, here's the man that can melt away his time, and never feels it! What between his mistress abroad and his ingle at home, high fare, soft lodging, fine clothes, and his fiddle, he thinks the hours ha' no wings or the day no post horse' (I. i, 22–6). This may be disapproving, but it regards having a boyfriend (ingle) as no greater a vice than wearing fine clothes or wasting one's time playing the fiddle. This is a gently satirical way of starting a play about a man, Morose, who is tricked into wooing a boy (who is dressed as a woman) by the fact that boys chatter and nag less than women and therefore make for a quieter home life: the supposed 'Epicoene' is both pretty and silent, a jewel among women. As it turns out, however, once the wedding is over Epicoene starts nagging with a vengeance. This only serves to compound the deception: for, in Morose's eyes (or ears) her scolding makes her all the more a woman. 'A manifest woman!' he exclaims, as though while she remained silent she had been, to all intents and purposes, an honorary man.

One of the Restoration texts most frequently cited as representing a loving and possibly sexual relationship between two men is Thomas Otway's play *Venice Preserved, or, A Plot Discovered* (1682). The two characters in question are Pierre and Jaffeir. It is certainly true that they are extremely demonstrative in their affection for each other. For instance, when Jaffeir is lamenting the way he and his wife Belvidera are being cruelly treated by her father Priuli, he says to his friend,

> Bear my weakness,
> If throwing thus my arms about thy neck,
> I play the boy, and blubber in thy bosom.

The main point of Pierre's reply is, 'Command my heart: thou art every way its master' (I, 274–6, 283). Each friend considers himself the other's protector, as if each is father to the other, or else his adult lover, and the other is a vulnerable boy. They believe they understand each other's needs and desires implicitly. As Jaffeir says to Pierre, 'thou art so near my heart that thou mayst see / Its bottom' (II. ii, 78–9). They are committed to remaining loyal to each other whatever circumstances arise. Jaffeir again: 'By love and friendship, dearer than my life! / No pow'r or death shall make me false to thee' (II. ii, 115–16). And yet there appears to be a limit beyond which they cannot step. Having handed over Belvidera to his co-conspirators as a hostage and guarantee of his loyalty, Jaffeir says to Pierre:

> Oh Pierre, wert thou but she,
> How could I pull thee down into my heart,
> Gaze on thee till my eye-strings cracked with love,
> Till all my sinews with its fire extended,
> Fixed me upon the rack of ardent longing;
> Then swelling, sighing, raging to be blest,
> Come like a panting turtle to thy breast,
> On thy soft bosom, hovering, bill and play[.]
>
> (II. iii, 228–35)

He imagines making love with Pierre; he even puts the fantasy into words. Yet his opening words are an efficient disclaimer. Having prefaced his speech with 'wert thou but she', he is free to say virtually anything he wants. On the face of it, Jaffeir is declaring a sexual love for Belvidera of a kind which he does not feel for Pierre; but he is also addressing the same statement of love, albeit in conditional tenses, to his friend. He expresses the thought in language whose ardour, if he were really only reporting to a third party an intense emotion felt for the absent wife, would seem redundant. To some extent, the longing, swelling, sighing, raging and coming must apply to the man whom he is imagining in the woman's place. We cannot help but conclude that the speech, ambiguously, both expresses a sexual convention and, in the very same words, transgresses it.

On finding, after all, that Jaffeir has betrayed him to the Duke of Venice, Pierre is understandably distraught. He says to his erstwhile friend *about* his erstwhile friend:

> the man, so called, my friend,
> Was generous, honest, faithful, just, and valiant,
> Noble in mind, and in his person lovely,
> Dear to my eyes and tender to my heart;

– but the Jaffeir to whom he is speaking is a loathsome coward (IV. ii, 188–91). This is an important utterance because it acknowledges the physical as well as the spiritual aspect of his admiration for Jaffeir: Jaffeir looks 'lovely' to the eye as well as to the heart. The loveliness of his person was as significant to the friendship as the nobility of his mind. Physical appreciation is not proof of sexual intercourse, however. For the play's only more manifest reference one has to go back to an exchange between Bedamore and Pierre in the second act. When Bedamore says, 'I'd forgo the hopes of a world's empire,/ Rather than wound the bowels of my friend', Pierre replies:

> I must confess you there have touched my weakness.
> I have a friend; hear it, such a friend!
> My heart was ne'er shut to him.

He adds, 'W' have changed a vow to live and die together, / And he's at hand to ratify it here' (II. iii, 103–7, 110–11). The curious point about the wounding of the bowels is not unambiguous. It has all the signs of being a bawdy joke, though it does not occur at a particularly suitable moment for one. Of course, one can be wounded in the bowels from a number of different directions, but the most obvious of these is the one from which Christopher Marlowe's Lightborn delivers death to Edward II: through the anus. If this is not an unjustifiable conclusion to come to – and I think it is not – one begins to see an open reference to sodomy in Bedamore and Pierre's exchange. But, given the vitriol with which the topic of sodomy had to be spoken of – if, and only if, it had to be spoken of at all – how can this possibly be the case? Bedamore does not respond to any such sodomitic confession. So it appears that his reference to the bowels and Pierre's response (unless Bedamore is simply not hearing its sexual meaning) are not related to sodomy at all, but to a metaphorical depth of hurt, an emotional hurt so deep that it penetrates downwards to the very bowels of the mistreated friend. This is not to say, however, that in certain productions Thomas Otway's audience would necessarily have been deaf to the sodomitical double meaning I have suggested.

The characters who have most mistakenly been seen by twentieth-century readers and audiences as homosexual – because of their flamboyance, which is so easily called 'camp' –

are the fops and dandies of Restoration comedy. But they are not sodomites. On the contrary, they tend to be voracious womanisers. This was already true of such characters in Shakespeare, but as the seventeenth century passed the fops became foppier, and their womanising became more extreme. Their effeminacy derives from excessive contact with femininity. They are emphatically *not* what we might think of as flamboyant queens. (Some twentieth-century productions muddle this distinction by giving their fops the mannerisms, and occasionally even the modern dress, of screaming queens.) Perhaps nowhere is this clearer than in John Vanbrugh's play *The Relapse* (first performed in 1696). There is what you might call a gay character in *The Relapse*, but it is not Lord Foppington. He is, 100 per cent, the womaniser – unlike Coupler, the pander and arranger of marriages. The latter has no personal attachment to the institution of matrimony other than as a way of making money and settling scores. (Foppington, it is true, wants to marry for money – but he is also looking for a compatible sexual partner in a presentable wife.) Women do not interest Coupler, but young men do. When Coupler meets Young Fashion after the latter's prolonged absence he exclaims, 'Ha! you young lascivious rogue, you. Let me put my hand in your bosom, sirrah.' But Fashion rebuffs him with 'Stand off, old Sodom!' and 'Keep your hands to yourself, you old dog you, or I'll wring your nose off' (I, iii, 181–6). When Fashion begs his help in a scheme against Foppington, Coupler calls Fashion 'my Hephestion' (the name is that of the boyfriend of Alexander the Great). When they have agreed on a suitable course of action – when Coupler has proposed that Fashion steal the young heiress Foppington wants to marry – Fashion is so delighted that he allows himself a moment's flirtation with his fellow conspirator: 'Egad, old dad, I'll put my hand in thy bosom now.' Taking him at his word, Coupler kisses him: 'Ah, you young hot lusty thief, let me muzzle you – (*Kissing*) Sirrah, let me muzzle you.' But Fashion tears himself away and mutters in a disgusted aside, 'P'sha, the old lecher!' A few moments later, Coupler kisses him again, and Fashion again makes his feelings known to the audience: 'Um! P'sha!' (I, iii, 264–76).

This is the only scene in which the text as written shows us that Coupler is a lover of men, but it can be taken as sanctioning a gay reading (by producer and actor) of the character's motivation and behaviour in all the other scenes in which he appears. (What this generally means, in practice, is that he is played for laughs as a distinctly twentieth-century camp stereotype.) Act I, scene iii also seems to demonstrate a certain continuity of expected behaviour between the seventeenth century and the present day. Fashion's threat of violence when Coupler seeks to touch him – albeit, perhaps, not seriously meant – and his spitting-out of Coupler's kisses, enact a type of anti-homosexual defensiveness in men with which we are now so familiar.[16]

Finally, I must remind the reader that there are times, many times, when the very absence of the homosexual theme in literature is worth commenting on. Take, for instance, northern European reworkings, for the theatre, of Greek and Roman mythological or historical narratives. Most of them heterosexualise the bisexual social structures of the ancient world. Shakespeare's *Julius Caesar* provides plenty of scope for the reader or producer to perform homosocial readings, but shows no sign either of the title character's sexual notoriety or of Roman society's institutional tolerance of a range of male homosexual behaviours.[17] Or take a later example, Jean Racine's *Britannicus*, first produced in 1669. Although Racine's source for this great narrative of political intrigues was Tacitus' *Annals*, in which a sexual relationship between Nero and Britannicus is made explicit, the text of Racine's play needs to be put into strongly suggestive production before the erotic nature of the power relations between these two men can be clear to any but the most subtle audience member. Roland Barthes writes that 'Britannicus, hated by

15. Virile power centres itself in the phallus. (Hercules and Diomoedes)

Nero, is nonetheless in a certain erotic relation with him, for it is enough that hate coincide with Power for sex to be ambiguous; Nero delights in Britannicus' suffering as in that of a woman loved and tortured.' But Barthes clearly believes that Racine was adopting censorious strategies to please the French audiences for whom the play was intended. (Racine's Britannicus does not get repeatedly fucked by Nero as he does in Tacitus.) And Barthes adds a footnote: 'As for Hippolytus, Racine has made him Aricia's lover to keep the public from taking him for an invert.'[18] To represent accurately Roman sexual mores and their political consequences as related in his historical sources, Racine would have had to turn his audiences' attention away from the Roman power struggles he was interested in to the *scandal* of sodomy in seventeenth-century France. It is arguable that nothing else would have been visible to them. The logic of Racine's decision to expunge sodomy from history is in this sense understandable.

Chapter 7

Christopher Marlowe

Our familiarity with Christopher Marlowe starts, in the anthologies, with a simple lyric of amorous invitation: 'Come live with me, and be my love'. Like so much English pastoral and elegy, 'The Passionate Shepherd to His Love' is shaped by Virgil's second Eclogue, one of the most influential of all homo-erotic poems. In Virgil's poem, Corydon tries to persuade the boy he loves, Alexis, to come and live with him, by promising him gifts: equal share in his livestock and the milk they produce, a set of pan-pipes, two young deer, flowers gathered by the nymphs, ripe fruit gathered by Corydon himself, fragrant cuttings to wear. But Alexis is not impressed and does not respond. It may be that these riches are altogether too bucolic for his tastes.

Marlowe, in his turn, was fascinated by the figure of the gilded boy, the boy lacking in shame, who demands to be spoilt by a rich and indulgent patron; in short, the boy who – even if his price is high – can be bought. Before a man can strip such a boy he must first adorn him with signs of admiration, deck him out with jewels. In the famous lyric, the passionate shepherd promises his love (ungendered, but generally and logically assumed to be female, at any rate since Walter Ralegh wrote 'The Nymph's Reply') a cap, a 'kirtle' (smock/coat), a woollen gown, a pair of lined slippers with gold buckles, a belt decorated with coral and amber. Clinching the offer, he concludes:

> And if these pleasures may thee move,
> Come live with me, and be my love

– thereby returning to the proposition with which he started. Ralegh's nymph is not taken in by the promise of such gifts: she dismisses them as ephemera.[1]

Marlowe's boys, on the other hand, tend to be as dazzled by promises of such wealth as he by the boys themselves. An adorned boy is one who likes to attract the eye. He is a narcissistic flirt. He dresses, not to hide his nakedness, but to draw attention to it. A richly costumed boy proclaims the success of his own beauty, proving it with the wealth that some besotted patron has spent on him. The more florid, the more feminine his apparel, the more Marlowe seems to feel a boy is amenable to being undressed. Such boys fancy themselves in jewels and want more of them.

In the opening lines of *Dido, Queen of Carthage*, Jupiter tries to secure the continuing love of Ganymede by offering to feather his nest. The god promises the boy feathers from Juno's peacock and Venus' swans, and actually plucks him a feather from the wings of the sleeping Hermes. Perhaps this is a cunning way of getting the boy to think of feather beds and what goes on in them; it is certainly, also, a threatening reminder of the ornithological manner of his rape. Jupiter then gives him jewels which Juno wore at her wedding, urging him to 'trick thy arms and shoulders with my theft'. For his part, Ganymede, without a word of thanks, takes the jewels and asks for more:

> I would have a jewel for mine ear,
> And a fine brooch to put in my hat,
> And then I'll hug with you an hundred times.
>   (I. i, 46–8)

The sale is blatant: affection costs gifts. Jupiter does not haggle, but agrees to Ganymede's price at once, in words which echo those of the passionate shepherd: 'And shall have, Ganymede, if thou wilt be my love'.[2]

When Venus enters and finds Jupiter cuddling the boy in his lap, she refers scornfully to Ganymede as 'that female wanton boy'. There are several reasons for this. Firstly, of course, she calls him female because of his implied sexual role as passive partner to Jupiter's activities. But she is also alluding to the effeminacy of his appearance, bejewelled as he already must be in recognition of services rendered. Partial to feathers and gems, the boy is, to all intents and purposes, in drag. His feminine ornaments are the outward signs – the bridal jewels – of the gender role he adopts in relation to Jupiter. Venus is also, implicitly, contrasting this 'female' boy with Aeneas, the beautiful and unequivocally manly hero whose champion she is. It is a contrast that Marlowe reinforces later on, when Dido adorns Aeneas with her crown and sceptre. Neither toyboy nor queen, heroic Aeneas is not tempted by such finery. He says firmly:

> A burgonet of steel, and not a crown,
> A sword, and not a sceptre, fits Aeneas.
>   (IV. iv, 42–3)

(A 'burgonet' is a helmet.) That Dido ignores this protest and likens his kingly appearance to Jupiter's serves to underline the contrast with Ganymede. Indeed, she calls for a mere Ganymede to be this new king's cup-bearer. She sees in Aeneas' very manliness a divinity that could do for her what Jupiter did for Ganymede:

> For in his looks I see eternity,
> And he'll make me immortal with a kiss.
>   (IV. iv, 122–3)

In the purity of his virile physique lies all the spirit she considers she requires for an eternity of bliss. She seems to believe that Ganymede's effeminacy is wanton, trivial and ephemeral by contrast. The beauty of her Aeneas requires no decoration, since it shows itself to best effect in the exertion of heroic deeds.

Love, also, has the effect of augmenting physical beauty. Marlowe sees love itself as an adornment, a kind of cross-dressing in the aptness of the loved one's garb. In *Hero and Leander*, after the lovers' first night together, Leander heads for home, quite incapable of hiding his love: for he is wearing it.

> With Cupid's myrtle was his bonnet crowned,
> About his arms the purple riband wound
> Wherewith she wreathed her largely spreading hair;
> Nor could the youth abstain, but he must wear
> The sacred ring wherewith she was endowed
> When first religious chastity she vowed[.]
>
> (II. 105–10)

As well as being a literal adornment, this ring is Marlowe's representation of the rupture of Hero's maidenhead. Leander wears her hymen on his penis; they are wed.[3] All the more disruptive, then, is the virtual adultery of the famous sequence (which follows some forty lines later) when Neptune mistakes the naked Leander for Ganymede and almost drowns him while caressing him. The god tries to woo the youth, in a typically Marlovian scene, by putting Helle's bracelet on his arm and giving him 'gaudy toys to please his eye'. But Leander is not seduced, and says to Neptune, rather primly, 'You are deceived, I am no woman, I' (II. 192). Evidently used to dealing with this error ('Some swore he was a maid in man's attire,/ For in his looks were all that men desire' – I. 83–4), Leander is polite but firm. Not for him the glittering finery of Ganymede, effeminised by acquisitiveness.

Even naked, though, Leander is clad. His body is a prime locus for mythology. For sheer richness, his uncut hair rivals the Golden Fleece. Cynthia, or the moon goddess Diana, yearns to be held in his arms, as she yearned, also, for Endymion. His body itself is 'as straight as Circe's wand', a bewitching instrument of seduction. Jove could, dog-like, lap nectar from Leander's hand, as though from Ganymede's most lavish and shapely receptacle. Leander's shoulder is as white as the ivory in which Hermes fashioned a new shoulder for Pelops, yet as tasty as Pelops' original flesh, which Demeter ate. The 'immortal fingers' of an unnamed god have left their imprint on his spine, the 'heavenly path' that leads directly to the paradise of his behind. His eyes, cheeks and lips are lovelier than those of Narcissus. Even the celibate Hippolytus could not have resisted falling in love with him (I. 55–78). None of him is his own. All has been prefigured in Greek myth and its Roman revisions. All Leander can do is outdo immortal beauty, but for all too mortal a span.

This proliferation of myth is unsurprising, coming from the pen of so devoted a fan of Ovid as Marlowe was. The body of his Leander is no blank sheet: it is fully inscribed with the text of *Metamorphoses*.[4] The boy himself has none of the privilege or understanding of authorship; nor has he even chosen, as though ordering tattoos, the myths to which his body will refer. Only those who desire him can read him, and he is no Narcissus. He is innocent of his own beauty.

Others in Marlowe are, as we have seen, far more aware, even in literal economic terms, of their erotic worth. Gaveston, in *Edward II*, is typical of Marlowe's gilded boys, as spoilt by Edward as Ganymede by Jove. (In fact, Gaveston was a year older than Edward, but Marlowe clearly prefers to cast his male–male love affairs in a classical, pederastic mould, with the richer, more powerful man as the elder.) Edward proves his love by dishing out, not jewels, but political honours (though there are, indeed, bejewelled insignia that go with some of these).[5] The younger Spenser receives similar, if less lavish, treatment later on.

Twentieth-century critical responses to the Edward–Gaveston relationship have been unsurprisingly negative. Typically faint in its praise is John E. Cunningham's remark: 'If we can overcome the repugnance most of us feel for the whole subject [of homosexuality], the parting between Edward and Gaveston is a truly moving one'.[6] That dates from 1965. It is depressing that this kind of view continues to be expressed, as in the following – albeit more sinuous – version, from Judith Cook, published in 1986: '*Edward II* is not often performed today . . . and it is not too difficult to see why. . . . We have to accept in Marlowe's world that the Edward who has been shown as so unsympathetic in the first half of the play becomes sympathetic to us in the second in spite of his proclivities and his weaknesses, but there is no logical link to show us how this comes about.'[7] We know what is meant by 'proclivities' and can see how, like Cunningham, Cook tries to recruit all contemporary audiences into her homophobic 'us'. Just as wrong-headed is the apparent assumption that a tragic hero's 'weaknesses' militate against an audience's sympathy. Perhaps Cook has never seen *Hamlet* or *Othello* or *King Lear*.

Occasionally, however, we find a more measured response, such as Harry Levin's remark that 'Gaveston is more and less than a friend to Edward, who devotes to him an overt warmth which Marlowe never displays toward the female sex'.[8] There is in the relationship a degree of emotional balance which could not have been established if Gaveston were merely a gold digger. He has an eye for the main chance, to be sure, and is seeking both advancement and wealth; but he also, crucially, loves the king. For all its fragility, their balance has its effect on audience response. As A.L. Rowse has written, 'Marlowe's sympathy is distributed between Gaveston and the king, his interest is in the relationship between the two; and so the most memorable scenes of the play are those that depict the king's infatuation, and those of his downfall and end'.[9] But it is the 'end' that is most likely to stay with the audience when they go home.

If Gaveston is the love of Edward's life, in comparison with whom young Spenser is a pale but much needed imitation, the king's nemesis appears in the gorgeous and frightful shape of one last lover, Lightborn, the love of Edward's death. In even the most restrained production, Lightborn is – has to be – the last man Edward sees, speaks to and touches. He is the last lover to penetrate the king. In Gerard Murphy's 1990 production for the Royal Shakespeare Company at Stratford-upon-Avon, the assassination scene was fully played as a seduction, with a leather-clad Lightborn (George Anton) lying with the king (Simon Russell Beale) and embracing him before stripping him naked for the rapacious murder. Murphy insisted on the full physicality of the action, arguing that 'The physical can only happen when Edward is bereft of all political and regal power. In my eyes, the play primarily questions the price you have to pay for kingship, fame, power, success.' Simon Russell Beale said of his interpretation of the scene: 'It's a love scene. It's the first time someone treats Edward with apparent affection and the first time we see any sexual thrill on stage'.[10]

Like all the other sexy men and boys in Marlowe, Lightborn is an inscribed text. His face gives away his purpose, even while he is acting out such false kindness as 'Lie on this bed, and rest yourself awhile' (V. v, 74). As he leads Edward to bed, Edward says 'I see my tragedy written in thy brows' (76), as if the whole play were tattooed thereon. But Edward's need for a last moment of love is even stronger than his terror, and for a fleeting moment his incorrigible sugar-daddy instincts reassert themselves: he offers the seducer the last of his jewels. This gesture is an attempt at a bribe –

> O, if thou harbour'st murder in thy heart,
> Let this gift change thy mind, and save thy soul!
> (89–90)

– but also, inevitably, calls to mind all those earlier gifts the king showered on his lovers. Lightborn's response, 'lie down and rest', is apt to either reading of the giving of the jewel. This is the reply of the paid hustler, about to do what he was paid for, but also, since the bed is to be the scene of the crime, a cynical enticement into a deadly trap. As it happens, however, Lightborn is less in control of the sequence of events than he imagines, and his seduction of the king results in death that is mutual.

It is illuminating to compare Lightborn with another seductive figure who appears at a play's tragic climax in intimate connection with the downfall of its hero. I am thinking of Helen of Troy in *Doctor Faustus*. The two scenes are similarly bare of detail. They do not work well on paper – they are, after all, written for the stage. In both scenes, language defers to action, or at least to visual representation. The main consequence of this shift from the spoken is a concentration on physicality: the violation of Edward, the beauty of Helen. By this point in each play, temporal life asserts itself in a last brief spurt of carnality (in which mortality is implicit), before the question of the survival of the soul is re-established as pre-eminent.

Critics often discuss Helen as a theatrical problem, hardly less extreme than that of enacting Edward's assassination on stage. John E. Cunningham describes Marlowe's stratagem as follows: 'Marlowe was faced with the problem of presenting an adolescent boy on the stage in full daylight, and persuading the audience that they were seeing the most beautiful woman who ever lived. He therefore reduced the actor's movements to a minimum, gave him no speech at all, and put all the beauty into Faustus' lines.'[11]

In this scene Marlowe's use of boy actors as women does, indeed, become risky and reflexive. The boy actor must be seen as the devil in the flesh. Paradoxically, the evil spirit who plays the role of Helen, like the actor who plays him playing her, is more substantial than the womanly flesh he adopts as his disguise. This is not a virtuous beauty, but suggestive and subversive: vice cross-dressed, all the more vicious for being in drag, at once visibly sinful and deceptively innocent. It is the *boy* in 'Helen' that Dr Faustus desires. Boyishness signifies the sins of the flesh, since to Marlowe that is what boys meant. It is as natural to Faustus to lust after this 'Helen' as it might have been to Marlowe himself.

Twentieth-century attempts to solve the scene's potential problem have veered between extremes, of which two are worth mentioning here. In Clifford Williams' production for the Royal Shakespeare Company at Stratford-upon-Avon in 1968, Maggie Wright played Helen completely naked, and therefore unquestionably female in her beauty. On the other hand, in Christopher Fettes' 1980 London production (at the Lyric Theatre, Hammersmith, and then the Fortune Theatre), Helen was played by a boy. Critical accounts of the latter version are varied. William Tydeman says this male Helen was 'controversial but effective': she 'achieved an extraordinary erotic rapport with Faustus'.[12] But Michael Scott is less positive: 'Wearing a white linen trouser costume with gold fastenings around the ankles and the back slit to the waist, this Helen was exquisitely decadent . . . . Faustus was a slave to her but the audience was far from convinced of her beauty and was rightly uneasy at her appearance.'[13]

Looking at the text – from which Helen, as Cunningham suggested, is virtually absent, since she has nothing to say – one notices that Faustus never comments on her body. What little he says about her is located above the neck: 'Was this the face . . .' and 'heaven is in those lips'. As far as the hero's concentration is concerned, then, hers is an ungendered beauty. Boys, too, have faces and lips; there is no reason why a boy should not convey this much of her attractiveness. It does not take a naked actress to do the trick.

Echoing *Dido, Queen of Carthage* – indeed, 'quoting' Dido's words precisely, as though expressly making a classical reference to shape his lips to the times from which Helen has been summoned – Faustus begs Helen to 'make me immortal with a kiss'.[14] What follows, although expressed in metaphysical terms, is strangely puerile:

Her lips suck forth my soul: see where it flies.
Come, Helen, come, give me my soul again.
Here will I dwell, for heaven is in those lips,
And all is dross that is not Helena.

(V. i, 100–103)

This reminds me, anachronistically, of a distinctly adolescent erotic mode: the passing of chewing gum from mouth to mouth. There is as much spittle as soul in these kisses. Faustus is deceived, by the taste of a devil's tongue, into believing that his soul is being sucked to Heaven, when it is actually on its way to Hell. Kissing the 'dross' that he does not see within 'Helen', Faustus ejaculates his spirit into damnation. Unable to tell woman from boy, angel from devil, Heaven from Hell, and spirit from physique, he sets the seal on his own fate.

Marlowe's texts, and the characters within them, are continually establishing cross-references to each other. Faustus 'quotes' Dido; Gaveston likens himself to Leander (I. i, 8); Neptune mistakes Leander for Ganymede (II. 157–8); Isabella likens Edward and Gaveston to Jove and Ganymede (I. iv, 181); Lancaster says Gaveston is 'like the Greekish strumpet', Helen of Troy (II. v, 15). One begins to see in such references the threads of Marlowe's interests and the purposeful, if somewhat enclosed, nature of his learning. His texts seem to conjoin, self-consciously, as an *oeuvre.* One gets into the habit of following the connections between them. So when Faustus, having kissed Helen, embarks on his fantasy of re-enacting the Trojan wars in Wittenberg, and mentions Achilles, I immediately start turning pages until I come to the reference to him in *Edward II* (II. i, 396).[15]

After the initial burst of eroticism there follows a macho tirade in which Faustus' motives are shown to be, rather than heterosexual, homosocial. His attempt to impress Helen with the strength of his desire relies on homosocial proofs: he will relate to the woman via the men in her life. He will take the part and place of Paris. He will fight 'weak Menelaus' – not a very impressive promise, this, if his opponent's weakness is a foregone conclusion. And he will 'wound Achilles in the heel' – again, not much of a promise, since he *knows* that Achilles' weak point is his heel – for which heroic act he will expect Helen to reward him with a kiss. It may be useful to recall the reference in *Edward II.* Marlowe knew of Achilles as a homosexual lover: he is one of the men brought up to justify the Edward–Gaveston relationship. Perhaps one of Faustus' thrills, here, is to be that of queer-bashing. As a last affirmation of the doctor's heterosexuality – that is to say, of his desire for women and not for men – the Helen scene does not truly involve an exchange of spirit. Faustus uses his desire for Helen to place himself above other men, a distinctly worldly manoeuvre. That Helen is a mere illusion – spirit, indeed – is beyond Faustus' under-standing. He is interested only in the apparently physical surface: the look of her, the feel of her. He is completely unaware of, even if attracted to, the youthful devil within.

Joseph A. Porter has spoken of how, in the world of Marlowe's imagination, 'the human body of either gender is the most insistently corporeal of objects: it realises with peculiar provocativeness the renascent and newly problematic (because newly secular) appreciation of the body that had come up from the Italy of Botticelli and Michelangelo to an England comparatively starved for pictures and statues of nudes'.[16] Marlowe's classical references, coming as they do against a lush background of Mediterranean pastoral set in temperate weather, solidify this impression of the visibility and erotic abundance of flesh. And, by constantly voicing such classical allusions, many of his characters become involved in the same welcoming of Greek and Italian sunshine into northern European life. For instance, as Claude J. Summers has said, in *Edward II* 'Gaveston conceives elaborate, Italianate spectacles designed to translate the dour English court into a homoerotic theatre in which pages become nymphs and men satyrs'.[17] There is a real cultural *frisson* of horror in his being exiled to Ireland (I. iv) so soon after he has returned to England from France.

But there is a far deeper horror to be borne as the play reaches its climax. Physicality taken to extremes can, no doubt, become intolerable. This, at any rate, is what happens to Edward. With all the signs and comforts of his status confiscated, his lover killed, and his body defeated by humiliation and unaccustomed hardship, he is visited in the castle cistern by an apparent angel of mercy. More wary than Faustus with Helen – and for good reason – Edward suspects that Lightborn is truly a devil; but he clearly *wants* him to be an angel, lover and liberator. Lightborn plays on this desire, like an importunate lover, in order to gain access to the king's anus. He is meticulous in his choice of an 'apt' death for the sodomite, a deadly rape to be carried out in the place of excrement: cistern and rectum. The king is expected to consent to his own death as if to the loving intercourse he craves.

Remember what W.B. Yeats' Crazy Jane said to the Bishop: 'Love has pitched his mansion in the place of excrement'. In the finest of recent revivals of *Edward II* – Nicholas Hytner's 1986 production at the Royal Exchange Theatre, Manchester – the excremental version of sodomy was made all the more explicit by a set designed by Tom Cairns. The early court scenes were performed in an arena of dry dust on which bootprints were immediately obliterated by the sweep of the king's long, scarlet robes. But as the play progressed and the joy of Edward's love turned inevitably to its tragedy of sodomitic degradation, the dust turned to sludge – the more so after Edward, being dethroned, was humiliated under a running faucet and left to crawl about through the mud in wet underwear. Thus the lavish court turns into the stinking castle cistern of the closing scenes. The king is assassinated in a pit of excrement that is used by his captors to represent his physique.

There have been some curiously muted responses to the assassination scene's representation of violent homophobia. Referring to reactions in Marlowe's day to the red-hot poker, Harry Levin writes: 'The sight of the instrument would have been enough to raise an excruciating shudder in the audience; and subtler minds may have perceived, as does William Empson, an ironic parody of Edward's vice.'[18] In a more recent essay, Alan Bray is similarly tentative; he speaks of 'the hideous murder of Edward at the play's end, whose form seems to ape his sexual sin'.[19] Surely the issue is more clear-cut than this would suggest. Lightborn is delivering Edward's come-uppance for everything he has done with Gaveston. While it may be true that the noblemen show little overt homophobia during the play, it is not they who choose the manner of the king's death; it is Lightborn. He dispatches Edward with a queer-basher's mockery. His violent erotic imagination is no more inventive than the kind that, these days, produces violently anti-gay graffiti. He pretends to seduce the faggot king, and then gives him what every faggot needs: a red-hot poker up the arse. It no more takes 'subtler minds' to read such signs than it does to scrawl them in the first place.

Marlowe does not allow this awful scene to be diluted. Take away the essential action, and there is virtually nothing left. He has, and is, determined to portray the crude violence to which the alliance between virility and political skulduggery is liable to lead. In a convincing reading of the linked themes of manliness and sodomy in Marlowe's work, Simon Shepherd has characterised these texts as 'problematising the male and masculinity'. This goes against a more general, and reductive, critical trend, which Shepherd outlines succinctly as follows: 'The association between masculinity and violence is regarded by most commentators not as a critique but as a personal kink of Marlowe's deriving from his homosexuality.'[20]

In *Edward II*, there is no choice so straightforward as that between jewels (Ganymede) and armour (Aeneas), which we saw in *Dido, Queen of Carthage*. Edward's court is no safe haven for sybarites. It is located in fortresses; its luxuries are heavily defended. If there are pretty boys here, most will be soldiers, too. For all its beauty, the male body is a fighting machine. Even a lad as young as the king's son is practised at arms, and knows already how to gird himself in masculinity.[21] Nor is it only bodies that can be bought with jewels; it is also swords (or, for that matter, a red-hot poker). Power and passion are inextricably confused. There is no clear opposition between dressing and undressing: one can just as well dress for love and undress for combat as put on armour and strip for bed.

Although in one of his translations of Ovid's elegies Marlowe writes that 'Love is a naked boy' (X. 15), in most of his work this is not strictly true. His boys are generally seen in either fancy dress or drag, and it is this adornment that shows they are either beloved already, or available to be loved. Cupid may go naked, but mortal boys are heavily clad. Their trinkets are the coinage of desire's transactions.

There is, however, a peculiar exception to this in *Edward II*; we receive it from the lips of Gaveston. The 'Italian masques' he is planning for the king's delight include the following:

> Sometime a lovely boy in Dian's shape,
> With hair that gilds the water as it glides,
> Crownets of pearl about his naked arms,
> And in his sportful hands an olive-tree,
> To hide those parts which men delight to see,
> Shall bathe him in a spring[.]
>
> (I. i, 61–6)

This is a fascinating paradox – a naked boy in drag. Blond, he is either long-haired or wearing a wig. His arms are bejewelled in a feminine, or effeminate, manner. But there can be no doubt that this is a boy. His genitals can hardly be properly concealed by a mere olive branch – the leaves of the olive, unlike those of the fig, are unsuited to the purposes of modesty – still less by such a branch in teasing, 'sportful hands'. This 'lovely boy' is 'in Dian's shape' only by the most sophisticated, symbolic criterion. At least the boy playing Isabella is fully clothed and, perhaps, strategically padded. But this Diana is in drag only insofar as he is being signalled as an object of male desire. The reference to 'those parts which men delight to see' is a succinct celebration of universal bisexuality: it refers to both Diana's and the boy's 'parts' with equal gusto. Whether the boy's genitals are visible, and so self-evidently male, or momentarily concealed by olive leaves, and so presumably female, the fact remains that they are being offered as a focus for powerful men's desire. More sportful hands than his/her own are assumed to be reaching out towards them. This Diana is a huntress eminently huntable.

This boy marks a crucial spot in Marlowe's erotic geography, equidistant between devilry and innocence, pastoral and decadence. He is caught, in the moment of Gaveston's dreaming him up, in that quintessentially Ovidian moment of metamorphosis, between one state and another. On the cusp of adolescence, he is neither child nor man; unmistakably male when his loins are exposed, but otherwise as girlish as any but the most choosy Humbert Humbert could wish. He is on the verge of becoming something plainer, less equivocal. He will probably be a soldier. By the time he comes to desire as well as to be desired, he will have embarked on manhood proper. But for now he is held in a state of imaginary suspension between real boyhood and apparent girlhood, boyhood past and manhood to come. He is there to be desired. That is what his adolescence means.

Age, therefore, is a crucial signifier, not only in these texts – as in the classical literature to which they incessantly refer – but also in their performance. The majority of the desired used to be played by adolescent boys or very young men; most desirers were men in the prime of manhood. Before and after these come, respectively, pre-pubertal boys and old men, virtual spectators around the arena of the erotic. They have had, or are still waiting, their turn. The teens of boys have significance for Marlowe both for their classical resonances (the ages at which Greek and Roman boys were thought capable of being loved and then of loving), and also in accordance with the theatrical conventions of his day (the ages at which English boys could play beloved women and then loving men).

There is no plain love-making in this dramatic vision. Every embrace is a cultural sign and involves an assertion or adjustment of power relations. Just as Edward II's last bedchamber, which he shares with the glamorous Lightborn, is 'the sink / Wherein the filth of all the castle falls', so, too, do all bedchambers – and, indeed, the nether regions of all human bodies – become the conduits of mortality. No aspect of the lives of lovers does not pass through these narrow, fetid spaces in which bliss finds its cradle. Money, power, status, violence; even, at times, love itself.

Chapter 8

William Shakespeare

What we read in Shakespeare is never pure text, any more than the staging of one of his plays can ever be innocent of the hermeneutics of production. As so many recent critics have pointed out, William Shakespeare is far from being just an author with a body of texts to his name. He is a major cultural institution. In ways which are not true of Christopher Marlowe, he is expected to serve the purposes of countless vested interests. His plays come with introductions and footnotes, and are pestered by whole libraries of commentary. In Britain especially, people's enjoyment of the plays is often restricted by the prospect or memory of exams. Rather than add much to this peripheral noise by performing my own readings here, therefore, I have chosen to concentrate on following some strands of other commentators' thoughts about how the issue of homosexuality relates – or, as some critics will apoplectically insist, how it *does not* relate – to that monolith of high cultural self-confidence, *The Complete Works of William Shakespeare*. The point is to signal the sense of controversy that pervades most straight-identified critical material when addressing these topics, especially in relation to the sonnets, and the ways in which gay critics have therefore had to address such topics as though they were controversial indeed.

The sonnets are the centre of controversy, but we begin with the plays. It is not difficult to see which characters or which incidents in a play might be most likely to recommend themselves to a producer or actor as being available for plausible interpretation as relating to bi- or homosexuality. Every case I mention here will be more plausible in production than any of the anachronistic settings – *Macbeth* in the wild West, *Romeo and Juliet* in the American Civil War, *The Merchant of Venice* in Berlin, *Henry V* on the sands of Iwo Jima – one can see on some stage somewhere during virtually any month of a given year. And yet they are not treated as such by academic critics. (Audiences are always another matter.)

In *Romeo and Juliet* (which dates from the mid–1590s) the relationship between Romeo and Mercutio could be played as an erotic relation between post-adolescents who know that the future direction of their adulthood will involve marriage and the concurrent, perhaps consequent, weakening of such male–male bonds. As Paul Hammond has said of the two youths' easy badinage, 'Homosocial play includes homo-erotic play.'[1] To some readers, *Henry IV* Parts One (printed in 1598) and Two (printed in 1600) conjure up the spectre of a Hal, corrupted by low-life companions, ascending the throne as Henry V. It would not be merely fanciful to stage a production in which one source of this corruption would be an excessive sexual familiarity between the prince and his unsuitable friends: for, as Jonathan Goldberg has argued, 'the plays forever transgress even as they seem to be producing the boundaries between illegitimate and legitimate male/male relations'. When it comes to *Henry V* (probably written in 1599, printed in 1600), Goldberg points out that Hal has a bedfellow (see II. ii, 8), but that we do not know who he is. (Falstaff himself, perhaps?) What matters here is not so much the sex of the bedfellow as his class: 'For if, on the one hand it would be unremarkable for men to be sleeping with each other, it would be unspeakable if the wrong men were, if the sex between men was not conducive to maintaining social hierarchies and distinctions.'[2]

If there are characters in Shakespeare who could, without undue distortion, convince us as being predominantly 'homosexual', one of the first to come to mind would be Antonio in *The Merchant of Venice* (printed in 1600).[3] Indeed, there might be good reason for raising the issue of Antonio's sexuality in a coherent production of a play that does, after all, take social prejudice as one of its central themes. A twentieth-century audience is likely to want to connect the various sources of oppression in the play, and to contextualise them within what we know of our own recent history. As Alan Sinfield very reasonably puts it, 'Of course *The Merchant of Venice* doesn't anticipate the Holocaust, or, indeed, Nazi persecution of homosexuals, but we may find it hard to approach the text without such an issue coming to mind.'[4] Who is to say that this is an illegitimate way of experiencing the relevance of drama in performance?

In Seymour Kleinberg's 1983 reading, *The Merchant of Venice* is not only about anti-Semitism, but also 'about homosexual eroticism in conflict with heterosexual marriage, about the rivalry of romantic male friendship with the claims of conventional marriage'. Pairing Shylock and Antonio as 'psychological counterparts', Kleinberg writes of the latter:

> Antonio is a virulently anti-Semitic homosexual and is melancholic to the point of despair because his lover, Bassanio, wishes to marry an immensely rich aristocratic beauty, to leave the diversions of the Rialto to return to his own class and to sexual conventionality. Antonio is also in despair because he despises himself for his homosexuality, which is romantic, obsessive, and exclusive, and fills him with sexual shame.[5]

Textually, there may be problems with certain details of this view, but one can see how it might easily be incorporated into the understanding of a staging of the play without violence having to be done to the script. Kleinberg continues:

> What Antonio hates in Shylock is not Jewishness, which, like all Venetians[,] he merely holds in contempt. He hates himself in Shylock: the homosexual self that Antonio has come to identify symbolically as the Jew. It is the earliest portrait of the homophobic homosexual.[6]

This is, without doubt, a strongly post-Nazi (and post-Proustian) reading – as all of today's readings must be, unless they are merely complacent, or even ignorant. Kleinberg says that 'The happy ending of the play is the triumph of heterosexual marriage and the promise of generation over the romantic but sterile infatuation of homoeroticism.'[7]

As such, this ending might be no less uncomfortable to a gay spectator than (say) the ending of *The Taming of the Shrew* to a conventional feminist. So many of Shakespeare's so-called 'resolutions' seem to flatten out the emotional complexities of what has preceded them with this kind of imposition of apparently incongruous, but undoubtedly tidy, institutional endings. (The institutions in question, to the values of which each play is shown to return, are usually those of matrimony and the divine right of kings.) John Clum has commented on the place of the homosexual character in such resolutions, as follows:

> In Shakespeare, bisexuality, hinted at, seems to be happily, if cautiously, absorbed by society, but the characters who feel exclusively homosexual desire (the Antonios of *Twelfth Night* and, perhaps, *The Merchant of Venice*) suffer the typical stage homosexual's fate of isolation when the traditional finale of coupling is enacted. Yet Shakespeare's comedies can hover at the brink of polymorphous perversity.

This depends on the production. Clum goes on to mention John Caird's 1989 production of *A Midsummer Night's Dream* for the Royal Shakespeare Company, in which the administering of the love potion almost resulted in Demetrius' falling in love with Lysander. Only Puck's officious intervention could literally turn Demetrius to face Helena at the appropriate moment. Clum comments:

> Homosexual desire is barely averted. The moment got one of the production's biggest laughs, but it also reminded one of the possibility of homosexual desire lurking very near the surface in many of Shakespeare's comedies.[8]

It is difficult not to think of the *Dream*, in particular, as having as one of its central themes the sheer contingency of sexual object-choice.

The most prominent male 'couple' in Shakespeare, enjoying a lasting sexual relationship and resisting all pressure to part them, are, I suppose, Achilles and Patroclus in *Troilus and Cressida* (probably written in 1602 but not printed until 1609). Gregory Bredbeck reports the craven evasiveness of Kenneth Palmer's annotations to the 1982 Arden edition of the play. Famously, Thersites calls Patroclus 'Achilles' brach', 'Achilles' male varlet' and his 'Masculine whore'. Commenting on the fact that the word 'brach' had a specific sexual meaning, Palmer writes that 'it seems unlikely that Thersites meant (or was taken to mean) that Patroclus was a catamite'. And on 'male varlet', the meaning of which he can neither deny nor hide, Palmer says that, even if Thersites is accusing Patroclus of having sex with Achilles, 'there is no certainty' that his 'imputation' is 'correct'. As Bredbeck correctly comments, these annotations are made to erase precisely what is the crux of Thersites' scurrilous remarks, 'the political discourse of Renaissance sodomy'.[9]

Not only do Achilles and Patroclus absent themselves from war; but what particularly hurts the Greek old guard is the manner of their abstention. Withdrawn into the privacy of Achilles' tent, they are nevertheless regarded as *ostentatious* in their attention to the sufficiency of their own relationship. The nature of their offence, or its ostensible nature at least, is outlined at some length by Ulysses:

> The great Achilles, whom opinion crowns
> The sinew and the forehand of our host,
> Having his ear full of his airy fame,
> Grows dainty of his worth, and in his tent
> Lies mocking our designs. With him, Patroclus,
> Upon a lazy bed, the livelong day
> Breaks scurril jests,
> And with ridiculous and awkward action,

> Which, slanderer, he imitation calls,
> He pageants us

– 'us' being, on this occasion, Agamemnon, Nestor, Menelaus and Ulysses himself, though Ulysses only specifies imitations of Agamemnon and Nestor (I. iii, 142–51). It appears that, in the opinion of Ulysses at least, Achilles has been disarmed by flattery: his fame as a hero has given him an inflated sense of his own worth, and this has had the effect not of spurring him on to further and greater deeds of heroism, but of allowing him to rest on his laurels. It is as though he had been effeminised overnight, his valour reduced by excessive praise to daintiness. He spends all day reclining on a bed with Patroclus, making not love but mischief. In its imitative theatricals, their idleness is creative but unproductive, a perversion of the way in which young warriors should respect and be influenced by their elders. By mimicking the older men 'with ridiculous and awkward action', Achilles becomes in their eyes as 'ridiculous and awkward' as he thinks them. After all, they may be old, but they are not sacrificing national pride to a childish pageant.

Ulysses gives examples of the two lovers' performances, in which Achilles plays spectator to Patroclus' performer; but in narrating these offences in such detail, offering plausible direct quotations from Achilles and a precise record of the tone of Patroclus' voice, Ulysses himself turns into a performer. The sheer extent of his indignation – this is a long speech – takes his mind as much off the war as he is claiming Achilles' has lately been. Indeed, there is not a little evidence that he actually relishes his account of the mocking of Agamemnon and Nestor. He sums up as follows:

> And in this fashion,
> All our abilities, gifts, natures, shapes,
> Severals and generals of grace exact,
> Achievements, plots, orders, preventions,
> Excitements to the field or speech for truce,
> Success or loss, what is or is not, serves
> As stuff for these two to make paradoxes.
> (lines 178–84)

This is not elegant – Shakespeare's Ulysses is very much the military man – but his list builds up to a splenetic ending in the dismissive, coupled anonymity of 'these two' and the horror of the paradox. We may be reminded of how scandalised by Oscar Wilde's use of 'brilliant paradoxes and corrosive epigrams' the leader-writer of London's *Daily Telegraph* claimed to be (6 April and 27 May 1895); but what resonances does the concept of paradox have when spoken by an exasperated Greek hero in front of an audience in early seventeenth-century England?

The 1957 Cambridge edition of the play glosses 'to make paradoxes', merely, as signifying to 'turn into absurdities', which is, indeed, part of the story. By making fun of their ageing seniors, Achilles and Patroclus are turning epic into farce, at the same time as their confining themselves to a comfortable tent is turning epic warfare into chamber theatre. Seeing absurdity in heroes past their best, they are making absurdities of them. Worse still, the habit is catching: for, as Nestor now reports:

> in the imitation of these twain,
> Who, as Ulysses says, opinion crowns
> With an imperial voice, many are infect.
> (185–7)

By imitating the lovers' imitations, others in the Greek army (Ajax and Thersites are named) are infected with their insubordination. The older heroes' authority is being threatened by an epidemic of satirical theatricality. There are connotations, here, of both contemporary Puritan objections to theatre itself and, of course, distrust of male love. Achilles and Patroclus are, at the very least, seeing too much of each other, homo-erotically forsaking their homosocial obligations. So serious is this transgression that it could lose the Greeks the war. There is far more to paradox than mere absurdity of speech: it threatens to overturn the 'natural' order of the body politic (see chapter 32).[10]

Other plays have recently kept returning to the stage in partially 'homosexual' interpretations. One of these is *Othello* (performed at court in 1604 but not printed until 1622). Ever since Tyrone Guthrie's 1937 production at the Old Vic, with Ralph Richardson as Othello and Laurence Olivier as Iago, it has been blandly acceptable to suggest that Iago's hatred and envy of Othello arises from an unacknowledged and unreturned erotic attraction. The other main reading, also now common, is possibly best represented by one of its earliest adherents, Leslie Fiedler, who argues that, in what he regards as Iago's ambivalent feelings for Cassio, 'there are equivocal hints of a repressed passion between males turned destructive, rather like the relationship more frankly treated by Herman Melville in *Billy Budd*'. Fiedler speaks of the 'glimmerings of homosexuality' in Iago's account of Cassio's dream.[11] This is the key moment, because the most explicitly if misdirectedly erotic, in any homosexual reading of the play, whether critical or in production. In Iago's words to Othello:

> I lay with Cassio lately,
> And being troubled with a raging tooth
> I could not sleep.
> There are a kind of men so loose of soul
> That in their sleeps will mutter their affairs:
> One of this kind is Cassio.
> In sleep I heard him say: 'Sweet Desdemona,
> Let us be wary, let us hide our loves';
> And then, sir, would he gripe and wring my hand,
> Cry 'O sweet creature!' and then kiss me hard,
> As if he plucked up kisses by the roots,
> That grew upon my lips; then laid his leg
> Over my thigh, and sighed and kissed, and then
> Cried 'Cursèd fate that gave thee to the Moor!'
> (III. iii, 410–23)

Sleeping together means little: beds were routinely shared, even by strangers, in Shakespeare's time. What is revealing, if the story is true, and even more revealing, whether or not it is true, insofar as Iago does not appear to notice that it reveals anything about himself, is Iago's submission to being made love to as Desdemona's surrogate. He does not push Cassio away, or shake him as one might a disturbing snorer; but silently submits, firstly to caresses, then to insistent kisses on the mouth (indeed, the image of uprooting them suggests these kisses are invasive: these men are kissing with tongues), and finally to the scandalous indignity of lying *underneath* another man.

There are productions which act out this incident at some point during the sleepy drunkenness of Act II, scene iii, thereby removing any doubt about the veracity of Iago's report. This seems regrettable, particularly since Iago's paradoxical and duplicitous nature ('I am not what I am,' he says at one point) is made manifest by his skills at ambiguous double-dealing, and doubt would seem to be one of the most useful intellectual and emotional conditions for a production to instil in its audience if they are productively to respond to Iago as his machinations take their toll. The problem is, though, that to make him a repressed, perhaps self-hating, homosexual is to attempt to explain away his bad behaviour pseudo-psychoanalytically, basing the explanation on the rather feeble notion that homosexuality itself is reason enough for a man to seek to destroy a heterosexual relationship. I am not objecting as much to the facile version of homosexuality that this represents – though it clearly is objectionable – as to the trivialisation of Shakespeare's complex portrayal of Iago. There is no doubt that a crass, simplistic production can destroy the play; and presenting Iago in this manner, with homosexuality itself as a bogus villain, would probably amount to such a production. No wonder Jonathan Dollimore has been so vehement in pressing his argument that, as one of the chapter subheadings in his book *Sexual Dissidence* puts it, we should 'Forget Iago's "Homosexuality"'.[12] Elsewhere, Dollimore has distinguished between the cliché of twentieth-century productions and a more plausibly sixteenth-century perspective, seen from which 'Iago embodies not "sublimated" homosexuality but militant maleness and a virulent contempt for women'.[13] Even this, though, may not set him apart from the masculinist institutions he serves to an extent that could begin to provide motivation for his extraordinary malice.

The more militaristic the context of the individual play, the more Shakespeare demonstrates his interest in passionate relations between men. As we have already seen, however, it was not possible serenely to wander into such dangerous territory without, at the very least, showing an awareness of potential risk. Jody Greene has argued that the 'fragmentary qualities' of *Timon of Athens* do not derive from an aesthetic failure on the author's part – a failure, that is, adequately to 'polish' or 'finish' the play – 'but rather from the impossibility of writing a play about the limits of male friendship in the Renaissance without recourse to the vocabulary of sodomy'.[14] Greene claims that this play is eminently suited to the kind of critical scrutiny characteristic of such readers within gay studies as Bruce Smith, Gregory Bredbeck and Jonathan Goldberg, and is evidently perplexed by their never having addressed *Timon*: 'it takes place in a world virtually absent of women, and treats such themes as male friendship, prodigality, usury, unnatural reproduction, and "diseased" sexuality'. It is 'an all-male drama in which the boundaries of friendship and sodomy collapse'.[15]

Any of these remarks might be applied, also, to *Coriolanus*. Consider the sheer extravagance of Aufidius' words on meeting up with Coriolanus, hitherto his arch-enemy:

> here I clip
> The anvil of my sword, and do contest
> As hotly, and as nobly with thy love,
> As ever in ambitious strength, I did
> Contend against thy valour. Know thou first,
> I lov'd the maid I married: never man
> Sigh'd truer breath. But that I see thee here
> Thou noble thing, more dances my rapt heart,
> Than when I first my wedded Mistress saw
> Bestride my threshold.
>
> (IV. v, 110–19)

First and foremost, this is an expression of male privilege, in the face of which a mere wife is hardly visible at all. But it is also, undoubtedly, an avowal of love. Furthermore, Aufidius has been dreaming – or are these nightmares? – of Coriolanus.

> Thou hast beat me out
> Twelve several times, and I have nightly since
> Dreamt of encounters 'twixt thyself and me:
> We have been down together in my sleep,
> Unbuckling helms, fisting each other's throat,
> And wak'd half dead with nothing.
> (IV. v, 122–7)

When he immediately uses a sodomitic metaphor in reference to the business of waging war – he speaks of 'pouring war / Into the bowels of ungrateful Rome' – one is inevitably inclined to refer it back to what has just been said. The two warriors' having been, as Aufidius puts it, 'down together in my sleep' makes deliberate play with the idea of two men in a bed, even though he is only speaking of himself, alone, dreaming of the other. Contrary to twentieth-century critics who do not wish to talk about such topics, intense homosocial relationships do, in Shakespeare, veer towards the topic of sodomy. It may be that the men involved resist sodomy with all the fear and loathing of the critics themselves. But the fact that the topic arises at all tells us a great deal about certain social attitudes. We are not dealing with what homophobic critics like to think of as a prelapsarian age, 'innocent' of 'deviance'. And gay critics are not 'reading things into' texts which are so palpably interested in that heavily policed boundary between friendship and sexual love.

. . .

While Shakespeare's plays are interesting enough, to varying degrees, as gay literature, nothing in them can compare, quantitively or qualitatively, with the sonnets, either as pure text or as the site of an enduring controversy about sexual meaning. These poems date from the mid–1590s but were printed in 1609. There are 154 of them. They are love poems. According to the order in which they are almost invariably published, the first 126 are addressed to a young man, the rest to a woman, the so-called 'Dark Lady'. They are either deeply emotional expressions of love or subtle imitations of such expressions. That is to say, they are either private love poems (albeit later put into publication) or flamboyant public exercises in literary expression. They either constitute the greatest of the gay texts in English literature – or they do not. If they were addressed to actual individuals, it should be possible for the curious literary historian to come up with the names of the individuals concerned. And if the young man is named (for the Dark Lady hardly matters), and if it can be proved that he was of a much higher rank than the poet, or that like the playwright he was happily married and had children, then his naming can be used to disprove the scandalous impression that the first 126 poems express same-sex(ual) desire. Hence much of the dreary research which has been done into the identity of the collection's supposed dedicatee, the famous but unnameable 'Mr. W.H.', who is possibly, in any case, a misprint for Shakespeare's own initials.

Simon Shepherd has pointed out that people have responded in significantly different ways to the suggestions that, on the one hand, any given character in one of the plays is homosexual and, on the other, that the sonnets to the young man represent homosexual desires. Shepherd writes:

Homosexuality in the plays has only been found in the last few years, and doesn't cause much worry. The Sonnets are different because, instead of showing a *fictional* world, they apparently depict [their author's] real feelings. It might be expected that a great artist can deal with all manner of unsavoury topics, but can a great artist *be* homosexual? Especially if that artist is the national poet, who represents all that's best in English writing.[16]

The debate on the sonnets has been vigorous and committed. Much is at stake. A national poet is at far greater risk of censorious distortion than any merely good writer who happens to work in a national language. In Shakespeare's case, the manhood of Englishness is at stake.

In the 'literary and psychological essay' with which he introduces his glossary of *Shakespeare's Bawdy* (1968), Eric Partridge takes a firm line against homosexual readings of Shakespeare.[17] In his very first sentence on the topic he dismisses them all by invoking his own heterosexuality as a guarantee of authority: 'Like most other heterosexual persons, I believe the charge against Shakespeare; that he was a homosexual; to be, in the legal sense, "trivial": at worst, "the case is not proven"; at best – and in strict accordance with the so-called evidence, as I see it – it is ludicrous.' Quite apart from the eccentric punctuation, there is a lot going on here. In the first place, there is a veiled threat to straight and closeted readers, that if they fail to reject gay readings, they will themselves be assumed to be homosexual. Secondly, of course, no reasonable person (which seems to mean, no heterosexual person) could be happy with such a 'charge' being laid 'against' them. Thirdly, Partridge is eliding gay readings of Shakespeare's sonnets with biographical claims that Shakespeare himself was 'a homosexual' – though in what follows, he is unable to quote a critic who actually makes this claim. Fourthly, there is a discrepancy between the suggestion that only homosexual readers perform homosexual readings and the idea that such a reader is laying a 'charge against Shakespeare' rather than sympathetically identifying with him. Finally, for all his claims to (hetero) objectivity and, in a footnote, to 'possessing an open mind', Partridge is speaking in a tone which is itself distinctly unscholarly. Indeed, so intemperate is his approach to the subject of homosexuality that he has relinquished control over the logic of his language: 'at worst' and 'at best' appear to have been misplaced.

In his second sentence on the subject, Partridge outlines a brief history of homosexual readings: 'The charge was first brought in 1889 by a homosexual (Oscar Wilde); it was renewed, exactly a decade later, by another [Samuel Butler]; it was again renewed, at a second interval of ten years, by yet a third; and, roughly three decades later still, the subject – if we ignore several unimportant intermediate attempts – was, not very convincingly, re-opened.' Partridge does not go on to name the author of the last case, presumably, because he was alive when *Shakespeare's Bawdy* was being compiled. However, most painful to Partridge is the fact he has to acknowledge next: that since the First World War 'the theme has . . . been touched on by several notable writers whose heterosexuality is not in doubt'. These notables he neither quotes nor even names, for he feels he has a far more persuasive case in denouncing other critics' homosexual partiality. Not that he ever engages with the arguments of Wilde, Butler and so forth. On the contrary, he dismisses them out of hand. In an extraordinary sentence, he argues that 'To re-examine the "evidence" adduced by the homosexuals . . . would be a waste of time' (p. 12). If by any chance anyone should disagree with this approach and want to engage more fully with the debate, Partridge refers people whom he calls 'my heterosexual readers' to two firmly hetero biographies of Shakespeare, by Hugh Kingsmill and Hesketh Pearson respectively. He offers no help to his homosexual readers, either because to do so would be another waste of time, or because he knows they will already have scurried off to the library to waste their time consulting the likes of Oscar Wilde and Samuel Butler.

Partridge wastes the next page of his essay asserting that Shakespeare would have 'subscribed in full to the sentiments expressed' in Kenneth Walker's *The Physiology of Sex* (1940). He quotes one such sentiment – 'There, in the unfortunate intersexual whose method of expressing his urge disgusts us, walk ourselves, but for the grace of a more satisfactory complement of hormones' (p. 13) – in the evident belief that attending to the minutiae of the history of medicine would be yet another waste of time. That Partridge is content to rely on Walker in 1968 says little, either, for his willingness to keep up to date with the debate on sexuality in the twentieth century, let alone that in the seventeenth.

In the case of Shakespeare's sonnets, about which, although they form the centre of his case, he has no ideas of his own, Partridge can only quote Hesketh Pearson: 'Most of the sonnets can be read as literary exercises' – by which Pearson means that the emotions expressed in the poems are merely conventional, not sincere, and should not be taken at face value as apparently intense and obsessive expressions of passion. Partridge calls this a 'no nonsense' approach (p. 14). He then quotes Pearson's opinion that 'Homosexualists have done their utmost to annex Shakespeare and use him as an advertisement of their own peculiarity. They have quoted sonnet 20 to prove that he was one of themselves. But sonnet 20 proves conclusively that he was sexually normal.' Rather than actually quote Pearson's explanation of how the sonnet does any such thing, and rather than offer his own gloss on it, Partridge simply quotes Sonnet 20 in full, as if fully confident that 'my heterosexual readers' will only have to read it to agree. He says nothing further about it, but rushes on to sonnet 144 in a sentence beginning 'As if that were not enough . . .' (p. 15).

I am working with a copy of *Shakespeare's Bawdy* borrowed from my university library. A student has annotated this section of Partridge's introduction – in pencil, I am glad to say. In the margin next to the claim that Shakespeare would have 'subscribed to' the views of Kenneth Walker, the student has written: 'One reader would be *very* dissatisfied if anyone touched his hormones.' At the end of Partridge's essay, the student has added: 'And if Shakespeare had been a homosexual, you my poor perverted & ignorant man, would never have had the opportunity of writing this silly little article because you would have written him off as an "unfortunate intersexual".' I mention these annotations because they strike me as being no less interesting than the essay itself. The student's anger is just as worthy of serious consideration as Partridge's. Neither is speaking from an objective position, but only Partridge is pretending to do so. For me, they symbolise opposite sides of a more general debate about gay culture and gay studies.

Of course, what Eric Partridge says about gay critics is correct: we represent, as it were, a vested interest, and the readings we perform are shaped accordingly. It was, indeed, homosexual readers who resisted the anti-homosexual tendency to read the sonnets as a mere fashionable exercise, and who read them instead as passionate love poems.[18] It has to be said that, as literature, the sonnets were all the better for it. Neither the various identifications of 'Mr W.H.' (William Herbert, Earl of Pembroke? Henry Wriothesley, Earl of Southampton? Willy Hewes? A misprint?) nor speculation on the poet's own sexual identity or habits has any substantive effect on the sonnets' availability to gay readers and openness to gay readings; and only the most obdurate, even desperate, anti-homosexual reading strategies will allow the sonnets to be read as a formal exercise by a red-bloodedly heterosexual writer. It is the latter reading which is the more perverse.

Another version of the dismissal of gay readings of the sonnets occurs in a book by Alfred Harbage. It is briefer than Partridge's, but no less firmly opposed. Harbage mentions that the issue of 'strange love' (he uses a phrase which is Elizabethan, but which is not the only Elizabethan phrase available) 'was at last brought into the open by Oscar Wilde and others who had a personal interest in establishing its presence'. Personal interest is, presumably, to be contrasted with the *im*personal objectivity of the heterosexual. Harbage adds:

> The consequence is that it is now impossible to say anything right about the emotional content of the sonnets. Homosexuals are inclined to share Wilde's view, and it would be inhumane to deny them its comfort, but since our humane impulses should be inclusive, we must recognise that endorsing the view will not contribute to the greatest comfort of the greatest number. Attacking the view is an equally dubious tactic. Needless defenses of Shakespeare's heterosexuality can only advertise that it has been questioned, while a notably vigorous defense might seem intended to advertise the speaker's own sexual normality.[19]

Far be it from me to suggest that such a standard example of homophobic liberalism, with its consistent references to homosexual readers as 'them' and everyone else as 'us', must have the effect of advertising Alfred Harbage's own 'sexual normality'. That is not a matter of much interest here. Nor do I have time to debate whether it is really the task of literary criticism to 'contribute to the greatest comfort of the greatest number'. (We have television and Prozac for that.) Harbage's regret that he can no longer 'say anything right' about the sonnets represents, in miniature, the growing unease among certain types of critic when confronted by any subcultural viewpoint that enables the universalising coercion of the mainstream to be challenged. Harbage appears to believe that our whole system of meaning has been demolished by the raising of the question of homosexuality in the same breath as the answer of Shakespeare.

The bottom line is always the sexual orientation of the so-called Bard. As Simon Shepherd suggested, it is not the sonnets themselves which are being so resolutely defended against scandalous imputations of sodomitic yearning so much as the reputation of the sonneteer. Indeed, by contrast, the sonnets are mere literature, a relatively trivial matter when national pride is at stake. As a chapter subtitle by Katharine Wilson succinctly and insistently puts it, 'SHAKESPEARE NOT HOMOSEXUAL'.[20] Of course not; but, as Alan Sinfield has said, 'the early-modern organisation of sex and gender boundaries, simply, was different from ours. And therefore Shakespeare couldn't have been gay. However, that need not stem the panic, because, by the same token, he couldn't have been straight either.'[21] *Ergo*, SHAKESPEARE NOT HETEROSEXUAL. Commit it to memory.

The sonnets remain. And they are still 'love poems', still spoken by a male persona, and their two addressees are still respectively male and female. I was going to add that nothing can change these basic facts, but some efforts have been made in the past to do precisely that: as in Michelangelo the Younger's 1623 edition of his great-uncle's *Rime*, certain radical editorial changes could be made to render love poetry safe. John Benson famously published a heterosexualised version of Shakespeare's sonnets in 1640, leaving out altogether Sonnets 19, 56, 75, 76, 96 and 126. In 101 and 108 he changed 'he' and 'him' to 'she' and 'her'; and in 108 'sweet boy' became 'sweet love'. In 14 'fair friend' became 'fair love' – clearly indicating that to Benson (and contrary to many anti-homosexual critics in the twentieth century) the word 'friend' was male but was not necessarily chaste.

However, tellingly, Sonnet 20 survived intact, apart from an insignificant misprint. Benson was clearly one of those who read Sonnet 20 as an unambiguous disavowal of sexual intent.

Reading the sonnets addressed to the boy and those to the lady as having interconnected meanings, some readers take the logical step of relating the poet's affection for the boy to the misogyny which puts into doubt his affection for the lady. To Leslie Fiedler, 'The point is that the poet confesses to sleeping with women and considering it filthy, while chastely (but passionately) embracing an idealised male.'[22] Joseph Pequigney makes roughly the same point at a later date: 'Fundamental and pervasive in Shakespeare's two-part sequence is the contrast between "two loves" in two senses of the word: two "loved ones" . . . the male and the female; and "two types of love," the homoerotic true love and the heterosexual lust.'[23] The latter distinction should not be confused with homosexuality and heterosexuality as we think of them nowadays. Eve Kosofsky Sedgwick draws back to take a wider social view, in order to define the distinction between the two loves with greater precision. She writes:

> there is not an equal opposition or a choice posited between two such institutions as homosexuality (under whatever name) and heterosexuality. The Sonnets present a male–male love that, like the love of the Greeks, is set firmly within a structure of institutionalised social relations that are carried out via women: marriage, name, family, loyalty to progenitors and to posterity, all depend on the youth's making a particular use of women that is not, in the abstract, seen as opposing, denying, or detracting from his bond with the speaker'.[24]

The necessary recourse to woman – but not for woman's sake – is virtually the first theme of the whole sequence. In Sonnets 1 to 17 the speaker urges his beloved friend to get married and have children, in order thus to preserve his beauty beyond its mortal span. The mood here is demoralised, partly because the lover is reflecting on the speed at which his loved one's beauty inevitably must fade, but also because the poet has not yet hit upon the glorious fact that the intensity of his own love can do physical reproduction's job far more efficiently: for the poet is a poet, which conventionally means that he can offer the young man a ticket to immortality. It is not until later in the sequence, though, that he will suggest this. For now, heterosexual intercourse looms.

In yet another attempt to establish that the sonnets cannot possibly have any queer connotations, Paul Ramsey has argued that 'Sonnets 1–17 are not very apt to have been written by an active homosexual to his lover'.[25] This appears to be an anachronistic view of the matter. In a world where beloved adolescent boys were simply *assumed* to be due to graduate to courting women at the moment of entry into manhood proper, the repeated sentiment of these opening poems would be read as routinely recommending, not a change in exclusionary 'sexual orientation' but the necessary next step into adulthood. It is an initiatory sentiment, proud of the boy's growth at the same time as it is, perhaps, quietly regretful of it.

Valerie Traub is referring to the move beyond these opening seventeen sonnets – whereby the speaker gives up the idea of children and, instead, privileges the poetic creativity of men above the reproductive creativity of women – when she writes: 'The logic of the sonnet sequence is, I believe, thoroughly misogynistic, and its homoerotics seem utterly entwined with that misogyny: a debased female reproduction is excised, and its creative powers appropriated, by the male lover-poet who thereby celebrates and immortalises his male beloved.'[26]

If the sequence as a whole has always been controversial, all of its controversies have centred on a single poem, Sonnet 20. Twentieth-century readers in particular have tended to fight out the sexual issues raised by the whole sequence, mainly, on the scuffed and bloodied arena of number 20. Here the poet refers to the young man he loves as 'the master mistress of my passion', endowed with the face and heart of a woman, but without a woman's fickleness. The concluding six lines go as follows:

> And for a woman wert thou first created,
> Till Nature as she wrought thee fell a-doting,
> And by addition thee of me defeated,
> By adding one thing to my purpose nothing.
> > But since she prick'd thee out for women's pleasure,
> > Mine be thy love, and thy love's use their treasure.

The 'one thing' for which the poet has no use is, of course, the young man's prick – pricked out by Nature to provide women with the pleasures of penetration. Whether this last point is to be taken ironically or dead-pan is open to question. This is the only sonnet in the whole sequence with only 'feminine' line-endings (that is, lines which end on an unstressed, 'weak' syllable).[27] Thus, in rather a literal sense, the body of the poem enacts a certain sexual flexibility: masculine language in a feminine structure, virility in drag. The boy is girlish – which is to say, he is desired by men – in a manner which reminds us of a literary convention going back at least as far as Homer. The poem certainly does not mean that he is effeminate.

Sonnet 20 has not always caused embarrassment: we have seen that John Benson kept it in the 1640 edition. But it soon began to do so; and the embarrassment has rarely faded since. In 1780 George Steevens said, 'It is impossible to read this fulsome panegyrick, addressed to a male object, without an equal mixture of disgust and indignation.' In 1840 D.L. Richardson said, 'I could heartily wish that Shakespeare had never written it'.[28] Samuel Taylor Coleridge felt the need, even in his private marginalia, to defend the whole sequence of the sonnets as Philip of Macedon had defended the Theban Band against 'those, whose base, fleshly, & most calumnious Fancies had suspected their Love of Desires against Nature'. Coleridge went on:

> This pure Love Shakespere appears to have felt – to have been no way ashamed of it – or even to have suspected that others could have suspected it / yet at the same time he knew that so strong a Love would have been made more compleatly a Thing of Permanence & Reality, & have been blessed more by Nature & taken under her more especial protection, if this Object of his Love had been at the same Time a possible Object of Desire / for Nature is not bad only – in this Feeling, he must have written the 20th Sonnet, but its possibility seems never to have entered even his Imagination. It is noticeable, that not even an Allusion to that very worst of all possible *Vices* (for it is wise to think of the Disposition, as a *Vice*, not of the absurd & despicable Act, as a *crime*) not even any allusion to it in all his numerous Plays – whereas Johnson, Beaumont & Fletcher, & Massinger are full of them. O my Son! I pray fervently that thou may'st know inwardly how impossible it was for a Shakespere not to have been in his heart's heart chaste.[29]

Coleridge's parenthetical distinction between the 'Disposition' and the 'Act' is interesting in itself. (Like so many other pieces of evidence, it puts paid to crude post-Foucauldian claims that before the invention of homosexuality as a state of being there were only individual homosexual acts.)

More recent critics have made every (often contortionate) effort to read this key sonnet as proving that the speaker has no physical interest in the young man. In his 1963 'psychosexual analysis' of the sonnets, H.M. Young argues that Sonnet 20 'simply could not have been written by a homosexual'. He continues, ignoring strong precedents in classical literature: '"A woman's face" would add no charm in the eyes of a homosexual, and the one thing which nature so carelessly added would not have been to his purpose nothing. It would, so far from defeating him, have been the one thing absolutely essential.' Young does concede, however, that Sonnet 20 is fiendishly ambiguous and proves nothing about the poet's sexual orientation: for the whole poem could be an elaborately contrived 'smoke-screen, a haze expressly contrived to obscure that homosexual feeling which the poet's keen interest in his friend's physical beauty repeatedly suggests'.[30] One cannot help adding that, if so, it is an extraordinarily inept piece of smoke-screenmanship. Surely Young believes Shakespeare is a better poet than that.

Hallet Smith is willing to acknowledge the presence of love, but not of sexual desire: 'The attitude of the poet toward the friend is one of love and admiration, deference and possessiveness, but it is not at all a sexual passion. Sonnet 20 makes quite clear the difference between the platonic love of a man for a man, more often expressed in the sixteenth century than the twentieth, and any kind of homosexual attachment.'[31] Paul Ramsey, on the other hand, acknowledges the presence of sexual desire, but not of sexual activity: 'Shakespeare says that there is a sexual element in his feeling for the young man' but that 'the relation was not physically overt'; to argue that it was 'is to call Shakespeare a liar'. He adds, with an implicit sideswipe at those who perform more explicitly gay readings of the sonnet, 'It would be pleasant to accept the testimony of Sonnet 20 and consider the matter closed.'[32] But unlike Ramsey, the sonnet is obdurately resistant to closure.

Peter Levi says that 'In the sonnet (20) about [the Earl of] Southampton as a boy-girl or a girl-boy, Shakespeare makes it clear what kind of love he is talking about, but clearer still that this is sublimated, unconsummated love.' In fact, the sonnet does not refer to the essentialist binaries boy–girl and girl–boy, but rather to a matter of sexual roles. The 'master mistress' might be understood as being, in terms of passion, both subject and object – by which I mean both lover and beloved – and, in sexual terms, both active and passive. At no point is sublimation 'clearer still' than desire itself. Levi also says, still apropos of the sonnets, that 'homosexual love was to Elizabethans inevitably chaste'.[33] This is actually no truer of Elizabethans than of Reaganites.

Robert Giroux, having referred to number 20 as the sonnet which is 'most explicitly homosexual', nevertheless concludes that such sentiments as are expressed in it 'do not represent the feelings of an active homosexual' and that, on the contrary, lines 13 and 14 are the poet's way of saying 'that physical love between him and the young man is out of the question'.[34] This compromise, at once acknowledging and dismissing the possibility of a gay reading, creates as many new problems as those it glosses over. In particular, one would want to ask Giroux whether he wishes to engage seriously with the possibility that either a latent or a chaste homosexual desire is operating in the poem. Either way, Giorgio Melchiori calls Sonnet 20 blatantly homosexual ('schiettamente omosessuale').[35]

A number of commentators attempt to distinguish between different types of homosexual desire in order to make some sense of this poem's ambiguity without rendering it down to banal unambiguity. For instance, Martin Seymour-Smith writes: 'In the unique Sonnet 20 Shakespeare tries to come to terms with what is an extremely complex situation. The poem can be understood only as a declaration, by a person who has previously imagined himself to be heterosexual (and whose experience has been totally heterosexual), that he is experiencing homosexual feelings.'[36] Elsewhere, Seymour-Smith extends this point to cover the sequence as a whole, which provides, he says, 'a poetic insight into what may be described, paradoxically, as a heterosexual's homosexual experience'.[37] But this is the critic's own paradox; it would not be comprehensible to anyone whom its key terms post-dated.

I myself once implied that the youth is 'chiefly admired for the delightful promise of his backside', and that in Sonnet 20, therefore, 'Shakespeare is not interested in his boyfriend's penis'.[38] Much remains to be made love to. There is, after all, a lot more to a boy than his penis. What about his arse? In this respect, I was suggesting a pederastic sexual relationship on the Greek model, where the man's pleasure was paramount, the boy's virtually unmentionable. Eve Kosofsky Sedgwick reminds us that 'here again as elsewhere in the Sonnets, "nothing" denotes, among other things, female genitals'.[39] For the speaker's purposes, then, the boy's arsehole might prove to be 'nothing' indeed – a sexual organ lacking in intrinsic status, dedicated solely to the pleasures of its penetrator. By contrast, the boy's penis would be undesirably demanding.

Bruce Smith says that Sonnet 20 represents the moment at which 'Homosocial desire changes by degrees into homosexual desire.'[40] Claude Summers quotes this point and adds: 'For all the speaker's temporising in the concluding couplet, what is most interesting in the sonnet as a whole is his genuine sense of bewilderment as he attempts to understand his newly awakened passion.'[41] In these readings, the poem constitutes a reflexive statement of the poet's coming-out to himself: he is beginning to realise the enormity of the presence of a supernumerary penis in his consciousness. No mere 'friendship' poem would need to have raised this topic at all.

Rictor Norton uses his reading of Sonnet 20 to take issue with those critics who claim the sequence is merely conventional:

> The sonnet reveals a man who is nearly obsessed by the fact that his lover has a penis. By expressing this awareness on paper, he has violated all the decorum proper to the missives between a faithful friend and his alter ipse. I can find no other example in Renaissance literature, either in England or on the Continent, in which a gentleman even hints at, much less so blatantly, his friend's genital endowment and its relation to his own pleasure. The tacky dismissal of its usefulness to him raises an issue that should otherwise have gone unnoticed.[42]

That last point is certainly persuasive. Having brought the beloved's penis into the account – and having thereby inadvertently kept it under phallocentric discussion for several centuries – the poet has effectively sexualised the young man, whether lover or friend, and has therefore sexualised the account of the relationship, whether actively physical or not. It has never been wrong for critics to bear the boy's penis in mind.

Once a decision has been made about Sonnet 20, or once the reader has opted for indecision, readings of the other sonnets follow in due order. Effectively, the struggle for ownership of the sonnets is won or lost in the fourteen lines of number 20. The love-or-friendship question resurfaces only occasionally in relation to the chastity or physicality of later poems. There are few surprises to come. So it is the expected critics who point out later moments of sexual ardour. For example, Martin Seymour-Smith writes that 'It is not easy to explain [Sonnet] 36 ['Let me confess that we two must be twain . . .'] by any other hypothesis than the physical one.' Reading it in accordance with this hypothesis, he infers that 'Shakespeare acknowledges that the sensual side of himself has won. Therefore they can never meet again.'[43] And it is with familiar exasperation that Joseph Pequigney says of Sonnets 52 ('So am I as the rich, whose blessèd key . . .'), 87 ('Farewell, thou art too dear for my possessing . . .') and 75 ('So are you to my thoughts as food to life . . .') that they 'can be perceived as chaste only at the cost of their considerable attenuation'.[44]

Reading the sonnets will always flush out the reader's attitudes to homosexuality. To that extent if no further, this sequence of poems is *the* key gay text in English literature. (And Sonnet 20 is *the* key individual poem.) For centuries the sequence has been testing the extent to which canonical English literature will ever be allowed to be 'gay literature' at all. The sonnets cannot easily be consigned to oblivion – as has effectively happened to Richard Barnfield's poems – so the queerness has to be sent there instead. Hence the importance of Mr W.H.'s identity. Once he can be proved to be a mere patron, whom Shakespeare is seeking to flatter and thank, then the heat of the passion in the words is proved satisfactorily temperate. Be that as it may, it seems that many critics would agree with D.L. Richardson in wishing these love poems from a man to a boy had never been written at all. Remember what the not-so-foolish Fool says in *King Lear* (III. vi, 19): 'He's mad that trusts in the tameness of a wolf, a horse's health, a boy's love or a whore's oath.' The love of boys will lead to endless trouble. Perhaps only writing about it leads to worse.

Chapter 9

The Pastoral Elegists

After its consistently profound contributions to general theories of love, it is arguable that gay literature has taken as its most insistent, solemn theme the relationship between love and death. How, our writers have asked, can love survive a lover's dying, other than by the literalistic means of the leaving of children? Bone-headed commentators tend to deduce from homosexual writers' expertise in this field that homosexual love is *itself* deathly, even causes death. In this chapter we shall focus our attention on the tradition of the 'friendship' elegy, which English poets of various sexual orientations derived from their readings of the Greek classics, and which American writers eventually derived from their English forebears. We shall see that, although so closely concerned with death, far from tending deathwards, the love expressed within this tradition is intensely life-enhancing. Moreover, it has exerted a much stronger influence on people's responses to the quotidian experience of death and mourning than one might ordinarily expect of 'mere' poetry. To put it plainly, the pastoral elegy has shaped what we expect from graveyards.

Relatively speaking, the classic elegies are young men's poems. Edmund Spenser was thirty-four when Sir Philip Sidney, two years his senior, died in 1586; but *Astrophel* was probably written at the beginning of the following decade. John Milton was twenty-nine when Edward King died, aged twenty-five, in 1637; *Lycidas* was published in the following year. Thomas Gray and Richard West were both twenty-six when the latter died in 1742; but the *Elegy Written in a Country Church-Yard* was not published until 1751.[1] Percy Shelley was twenty-nine when John Keats died, aged twenty-six, in 1821; *Adonais* was written and published in the same year. Alfred Tennyson was twenty-four when Arthur Hallam died, aged twenty-two, in 1833; but *In Memoriam* took many painful years to write, not reaching completion and anonymous publication until 1850. Matthew Arnold was a rather more mature thirty-nine when Arthur Clough died, aged forty-two, in 1861; *Thyrsis* was published in 1866. T.S. Eliot was twenty-seven when Jean Verdenal, one year younger, died in the Dardanelles in 1915; *The Waste Land* came out in 1922.

As well as the elegists themselves, most of the young men who died were also poets. One of the matters lamented is the silencing of their voices. (The demise of Orpheus may be invoked as precedent, the point being that, even after death, he sang on.) A number of their deaths are associated with water. Edward King was literally drowned in the Irish Sea; Arthur Hallam was lengthily shipped back to England after dying in Vienna; 'Death by Water' is one of the major themes, and subtitles, of Eliot's poem. (Orpheus again: his severed head continued singing as it floated down the river Hebrus and out to sea, ultimately to be washed up on the shore of Lesbos.) All of the poems are intended either to record the apotheosis or themselves to ensure the immortality of the beloved friend. Several of them end with him entering the firmament as a brilliant star.[2]

Most elegies in the English tradition make some reference, explicit or not, to the classical myth of the vegetation god Adonis. Having been killed by Ares in disguise as a wild boar, Adonis spent half of each year with one of the rivals for his love: with Persephone in the darkness of the underworld and with Aphrodite/Venus in the light of summer. He came to preside over, and symbolise, the cycle of the seasons. The midsummer rites associated with his name involved a period of mourning (by women), followed by rejoicing at his rebirth (see Theocritus, *Idyll* 15). Associated rituals included the planting of short-lived plants in pots, so-called 'Gardens of Adonis', the seasonal deaths and rebirths of plants being the central point of the allegiance to this particular deity. Of course, elegists make much of the fact that he was a beautiful boy, his beauty eternally preserved in the cycles of Nature by an early death.

The gender of the loved one in this tradition is neither immaterial – as one modern, liberal argument would have it – nor always proof of mere 'friendship'. We know that a number of ancient laments take the fact that the dead person was male as being central to the nature of the intimacy that once existed between mourner and mourned. In the Bible, David sings: 'I am distressed for you, my brother Jonathan; very pleasant have you been to me; your love to me was wonderful, passing the love of women' (2 Samuel I:26). In the epic known by his name, Gilgamesh sings: 'Hear me, great ones of Uruk,/ I weep for Enkidu, my friend,/ Bitterly moaning like a woman mourning / I weep for my brother.'[3] We should not forget that much of the most emotionally expressive homo-erotic literature from the pre-'homosexual' world took the form of personal laments like Achilles' for Patroclus, David's for Jonathan, and Roland's for Olivier in the *Chanson de Roland*. For all the male–male love affairs recorded in the ancient world, there was no sure convention of definitions. David has to compare his love with heterosexual relations, or with those of mother and son. Gilgamesh runs swiftly through the friendship–widowhood–brotherhood gamut to give some impression of how he feels. But these comparisons are also, crucially, contrasts. It is *because* the dead loved one was male that the lover's grief is so intense. Their shared gender is understood to have intensified the degree of their identification with each other. This is not to say that all the commemorated relationships were what we would now understand as 'homosexual'. Some were. Others were 'merely' homosocial. But most were, to varying extents, homo-erotic.

In its consolatory role, elegy is required to perform a change of mood, from grief, through fond remembrance, to hope. This process is generally achieved by simple means: a sequence of changes of tense. Typically, an elegy will pass through four stages: (a) *present* (he is dead), (b) *past* (I loved him), (c) *present* (but he is dead), and (d) *future* (but he will live hereafter). Even when, in Bion's 'Lament for Adonis', the mourner cries out, 'Let all nature die,/ now Adonis is dead', his curse is of limited duration. The flowers he calls for, to be strewn on the boy's grave, represent the year's descent from summer into autumn. An unspoken future springtime is understood. The mourner curses the natural world, not to an eternal death, but to six months' mourning in an uncomfortable winter.

So the most stupendous miracle of the traditional English elegy – the breathtaking revelation on which the change of mood from grief, through resignation, to hope is hinged – occurs when the poet understands that the loved one *will live again*: if not here and now, 'hereafter'. (This can come as a slow realisation or as a dramatic flash.) Such a transition from loss to confidence in eternal life happens, in Milton's *Lycidas,* between the forlorn declaration 'Lycidas is dead, dead ere his prime' (line 8) and 'Weep no more, woeful shepherds weep no more,/ for Lycidas your sorrow is not dead' (lines 165–6). A far longer and more difficult transition happens, in *In Memoriam,* between the moment when Tennyson imagines himself as a distraught girlfriend in her lover's absence, crying 'all is dark where thou art not' (VIII, 12), and the consoling confidence of:

> Dear heavenly friend that canst not die
> Mine, mine, for ever, ever mine[.]
> (CXXVIII, 7–8)

It is then not long before the poet realises that even his own future death will not end their friendship:

> Far off thou art, but ever nigh;
> I have thee still, and I rejoice;
> I prosper, circled with thy voice;
> I shall not lose thee tho' I die.
> (CXXIX, 13–16)

Tennyson's poem is probably the most insistently possessive elegy of them all – whatever knell he hears seems to ring out that repetitive 'mine, mine, for ever, ever mine' – but its forthright closing statements of continued ownership do constitute a valid counter-argument to the initial emotion of irretrievable loss. This is the point towards which any elegist who tries to represent the emotional changes which occur over a prolonged period of grieving appears to be striving. As soon as it is clear that the beloved has not, after all, vanished for ever, it is possible to become reconciled with death. Indeed, it may be that death can then be regarded as having preserved the very love it once appeared so cruelly and purposelessly to have destroyed.

· · ·

Edmund Spenser's 'Astrophel' makes an important point, which is taken up by subsequent elegists. No matter what he really looked like when alive, the elegised subject is invariably presented as having been beautiful, not only in character but in face as well. His physical loveliness was but the outward sign of his moral perfection. In the case of Philip Sidney, as espoused by Spenser:

> He grew up fast in goodness and in grace,
> And doubly fair wox both in mind and face.

> Which daily more and more he did augment,
> With gentle usage and demeanour mild:
> That all men's hearts with secret ravishment
> He stole away, and weetingly beguiled.

It is the physical beauty that, in the first place, seduces the viewer into friendship with the subject. The superficial impetus of physical desire leads towards moral desire, which is supposedly more profound and longer lasting. Having won men over with his 'mind and face' at an age when he was still growing up – that is, at the ideal age by the standards of the Greeks – Astrophel then died, at the worst time and the best, prematurely. Men's 'secret ravishment' suddenly became public mourning.

Notwithstanding all the men and women who appear in the rest of the poem, all mourning for Astrophel with apparently equal vigour, there is a moment of convincing selfishness when the speaker claims the greatest pain: for Astrophel was 'dearest unto me!' Whether the pastoral elegy is merely a means by which a male poet may respectably say such things is open to question. (That would seem to be a rather reductive way of regarding the genre as a whole, but it may be an accurate account of just one of the motives for writing one's commemorative verse in this vein.) What is certain is that, once Arcadia has been evoked, the subject of male love will, as it were, naturally arise; and a poet will either confront and use it, or he will rather vaguely just refer to it in passing, unacknowledged, as if it were little more than a decorative device or atmospheric effect.

It is likely that in Spenser's *The Shepheardes Calender* (1579) we hear the least distorted echoes of Theocritus in English literature. These twelve eclogues, one for each month of the year, are evidently shaped by a genuine urge to represent some of the varied pleasures and exertions of rural life. They do not read as mere exercises in pastoral. They are, however, far less frank on sexual themes than Theocritus was, and the poems are accompanied by an explanatory gloss (by one E.K., probably the poet's friend Gabriel Harvey) in which the reader is warned against drawing the wrong inferences from the main text. When, in 'January', Colin Clout mentions Hobbinol, the youth who is in love with him but whose love he cannot return, E.K.'s gloss is severely defensive of Spenser's meaning – one might almost say excessively so. The verse in question is mild enough:

> It is not Hobbinol wherefore I plain,
> Albe my love he seek with daily suit;
> His clownish gifts and court'sies I disdain,
> His kids, his cracknels, and his early fruit.
> Ah, foolish Hobbinol! thy gifts bene vain:
> Colin gives them to Rosalind again.

Lest we should misconstrue this as referring to the wrong kind of male–male affection, the gloss is insistent:

> In this place seemeth to be some savour of disorderly love, which the learned call *paederastice*; but it is gathered beside his meaning. For who that hath read Plato his dialogue called *Alcibiades*, Xenophon, and Maximus Tyrius, of Socrates' opinions, may easily perceive, that such love is much to be allowed and liked of, specially so meant, as Socrates used it: who saith, that indeed he loved Alcibiades extremely, yet not Alcibiades' person, but his soul, which is Alcibiades' own self. And so is *paederastice* much to be preferred before *gynerastice*, that is, the love which inflameth men with lust toward womankind. But yet let no man think, that herein I stand with Lucian, or his devilish disciple Unico Aretino, in defence of execrable and horrible sins of forbidden and unlawful fleshliness. Whose abominable error is fully confuted of Perionius, and others.

Placing the gloss immediately next to the stanza it comments on, one is struck by some incongruity between the evidence in the poem and the strictness of the note. After all, this is the first mention of Hobbinol; it shows little evidence of his importunity (more, but not much more, comes later); and Colin Clout is firm in his rejection of both 'foolish Hobbinol' and his 'clownish gifts'. So what seems most interesting here is the fact that – regardless of the 'real' meaning of the stanza and the poet's original intention – E.K.'s note raises the hypothesis, or is possibly reacting to first-hand experience, of the kind of reader who takes Hobbinol to be a sodomite. Now, such readers come in two main sorts: E.K. is defending the poem either against the accusations of those who might take it to be obscene because it refers to an obscenity, or against the enthusiasm of male readers who share what they take to be Hobbinol's sexual taste in young men. Today, we might call these readers anti-gay and gay. In his insistence on the spirituality of the love in question, E.K. is dismissing both – or making a show of doing so, at least – while claiming himself to belong to the anti-gay camp.

With Plato and Socrates on the one side, and Lucian and Pietro Aretino on the other, E.K. offers his readers a divided bibliography (albeit a brief one) on two incompatible but coexistent versions of pederasty. He does so, in the first place, to emphasise his own and Spenser's erudition: the poem and its notes, together, constitute an education in classical pastoral, with brief accounts of certain pertinent myths, recommended reading (Angelo Poliziano's Latin translation of Moschus, for instance, and Virgil's second Eclogue) and exercises in rendering pagan themes appropriate to both Christian belief and English nationalism. The note on pederasty, of course, may be taken as a contribution to this latter aim. The point is that Spenser's and E.K.'s erudition, their knowledge of the Greek and Latin classics, is not indiscriminate: it will not do moral damage to the English *polis*. They know what not to read. And, like all warnings about dangerous books, E.K.'s gloss is likely to have drawn as much attention to Lucian and Aretino as to Plato and Socrates.

The reference to Plato is narrowly selective. Why the *Alcibiades* and not *Timaeus* or *Symposium*? (Marsilio Ficino's Latin rendering of the latter dated from 1482.) The answer seems obvious: neither *Timaeus* nor *Symposium* could be cited as being sufficiently firmly opposed to the love of one man for another's 'person', which is to say his body. In any case, this is a point which E.K. gives away somewhat in the confusion of his note's references to 'paederastice': in his first sentence he uses this word to mean, according to 'the learned' among whom he seems to include himself, 'disorderly love'. But by his third sentence he is suddenly and rashly affirming the superiority of 'paederastice' to 'gynerastice', the sexual love for women. It then takes the quick back-pedalling of the fourth sentence to redefine 'paederastice', contrary to the first sentence, as being not only those 'execrable and horrible sins of forbidden and unlawful fleshliness' but also the nobler passion for the soul with which the love of a woman can never compete.

What the gloss tells us is that the relocation of Greek and Latin pastoral in Renaissance England stirred up certain clear anxieties about the spectre of sodomy. The classics were to be recommended for their humanistic philosophies, not to mention their often pleasure-loving tone; but many Greek and Latin texts had a reputation for immorality which could rub off on educated English readers – most of whom had honed their reading skills in all-male academies at an impressionable age. Spenser wrote *The Shepheardes Calender* after Cambridge, in his mid-twenties, in the year of his marriage. In a sense, these eclogues marked the beginning of the poet's respectable maturity. E.K.'s rather edgy gloss helps them to make that mark.

In 'April', Hobbinol is still lamenting his unrequited love for Colin Clout, but also Colin's unrequited love for Rosalind:

> Nor this, nor that, so much doth make me mourn,
>   But for the lad, whom long I loved so dear,
> Now loves a lass that all his love doth scorn:
>   He plunged in pain, his tressèd locks doth tear.

To an extent, the tables have turned. Hobbinol's mood has mellowed. It is Colin who is tearing out his hair. It is he who now might be accused of being 'clownish' and 'foolish' – not that Hobbinol, who still loves him, is ever so cruel as to say so. But some readers might think, on the contrary, that by enforcing this mature discretion on Hobbinol, the poet makes sure that the two types of love – no matter that they are unrequited, with comparably painful consequences for the one who loves – are left seeming quite different. The man who loves a man remains accused of being undignified; the man who loves a woman – whose behaviour is, in the long run, much the same – is never so accused.

However, the supposed foolishness of Hobbinol does not give us the full measure of Spenser's approach to male love. There is a passage in *The Faerie Queene* (1590, 1596) that takes a very different tone, glorifying and idealising a familiar list of gay couples from classical mythology. Arriving at the temple of Venus in search of his (female) beloved Amoret, Scudamor catches sight of 'another sort / Of louers lincked in true harts consent', men who have 'grounded their desire' not in lust for women but 'on chaste virtue' of such a type as fires their spirits to aspire to 'Braue thoughts and noble deeds' rather than mere physical dalliance and reproduction. As we have already noted, Scudamor names some eminent exemplars of this loving capability: Heracles and Hylas, David and Jonathan, Theseus and Pirithous, Orestes and Pylades, Titus and Gesippus, and Damon and Pythias ('whom death could not seuer'). Spenser's main point follows – an unequivocal recommendation of eternal 'friendship':

> All these and all that euer had bene tyde
> In bands of friendship, there did liue for euer,
> Whose liues although decay'd, yet loues decayed neuer.

Looking on, Scudamor begins to envy these pairs of men their 'endlesse happinesse'. Living in a space from which 'feare and gealosye' are absent, they 'Might frankely there their loues desire possesse' (Book IV, Canto X, 26–8). However, the supposition is that 'their loues desire' is absolutely chaste. That is what makes it so much to be desired; that is why it involves neither fear nor jealousy. Because physical, sex would be as subject to death as is the physical life itself. This is decidedly not a scene of unfettered homosexual relations. It *is* a scene of incomparably passionate male love.

Consider this question of heavenly love, as John Milton later raises it in *Paradise Lost* (completed 1665, published 1667). Responding to Adam's curiosity about how the heavenly spirits express their love, the angel Raphael, 'with a smile that glow'd / Celestial rosy red, love's proper hue', says:

> Let it suffice thee that thou know'st
> Us happy; and without love no happiness.
> Whatever pure thou in the body enjoy'st,
> (And pure thou wert created) we enjoy
> In eminence; and obstacle find none
> Of membrane, joint, or limb, exclusive bars:
> Easier than air with air, if spirits embrace
> Total they mix, union of pure with pure
> Desiring; nor restrain'd conveyance need,
> As flesh to mix with flesh, or soul with soul.
> (VIII, 620–29)

It is interesting that Milton has to locate the happiness of love, as soon as it is mentioned, in the body, albeit in bodies more pure than those of human beings. He presents us with a conundrum: angels have the desirable beauty of the human, an appearance of membrane, joint and limb, all glowing with 'love's proper hue'; but that appearance is not solid; nevertheless, they are able to love each other in what amounts to a physical manner – entering each other to the extent of actually mixing – even if they are without physique. Far from being disappointed that they cannot actually touch the surface of each other's beautiful apparent flesh, they are able, unlike humans, to achieve the perfect consummation of the admixture of beings. In other words, their intercourse takes them to a part far beyond that which they desired when they were first attracted by each other's angelic appearances. Commenting on this oblique and complex passage in 1961, C.S. Lewis complained that it had aroused a 'certain amount of critical prudery'. He added:

> The trouble is, I think, that since these exalted creatures are all spoken of [elsewhere in the poem] by masculine pronouns, we tend, half consciously, to think that Milton is attributing to them a life of homosexual promiscuity. That he was poetically imprudent in raising a matter which invites such misconception I do not deny; but the real meaning is certainly not filthy, and certainly not foolish. As angels do not die, they need not breed. They are not therefore sexed in the human sense at all.[4]

Whether they are sexed in any other sense is not made clear.

In an excellent essay called 'Milton's Sodomite', Gregory Bredbeck writes that 'Milton's sexual epistemology . . . is informed by what might best be called an intense skepticism of the flesh'.[5] This is true of many Christian writers, of course. And yet, to have formed such an opinion of human flesh, one must first have considered the attributes and tendencies of that very flesh itself. One does not develop a horror of flesh without first having encountered, or at least having considered, not only how horrible it can be, but *how* it can be horrible. Milton is not simply dismissive of carnality: he is far too committed to the implications of his topics for that. Male beauty raised sexual connotations which he was incapable of ignoring. Bredbeck points out, for instance, that one of his commonplace books contains an entry on 'Lust for boys or men'.[6] Bredbeck quotes C.S. Lewis' remarks about Milton's angels in order to establish that his insistence on the absence of sexuality from Milton's formulation of angelic pleasure (in Bredbeck's terms, his erasure of Milton's sodomite) is itself distortingly anachronistic. The point is that, whenever he has to think of either heavenly beauty or heavenly pleasure, Milton cannot but call sexual desire and consummation to mind. If nothing else, sex will provide the reader with a point of comparison, a measure of bliss which Heaven will immeasurably exceed.

It is in this intellectual context, in which the spectre of sodomy is always a dangerously distracting presence, that we must read Milton's massively influential elegy. (*Lycidas* is Milton's most literal elegy, but he was an elegiac poet in a much broader sense. After all, does all pastoral elegy not partake of the mood implicit in the very title, let alone the central theme, of *Paradise Lost*?) The very name of *Lycidas*, the young man and the poem both, is enough to access a whole library of connotations; but it chiefly sends the reader scurrying back to Theocritus. Countless other references lead to Virgil. Milton had a very literary imagination, forever referring back to the books he had read and taking inspiration from them. There is no escaping his reverence for his sources. He recommends them as often and as strongly as he recommends the scriptures. The miracle is that he manages to produce a poem which is both lively and affecting from such a wealth of book-bound materials. By comparison, John Cleveland's poem 'On the

Memory of Mr. Edward King, Drowned in the Irish Seas' is a far more stilted and conventional affair.

Milton's poem begins with his addressing the evergreens of the English landscape, thereby establishing both the pastoral thematics of what is to follow and the major point of the survival of Nature beyond the deaths of individual creatures. (This theme is far less convincing in a post-nuclear world given over to the well-being of the motor car.) It is to the enduring greenery that Milton addresses his grievous announcement, the occasion of the poem:

> for Lycidas is dead, dead ere his prime,
> young Lycidas, and hath not left his peer.
> Who would not sing for Lycidas? He knew
> himself to sing, and build the lofty rhyme.
> He must not float upon his watery bier
> unwept, and welter to the parching wind
> without the meed of some melodious tear.
>
> (lines 8–14)

Taking the key words of this sequence (Lycidas, dead, young, peer, sing, tear) one can plot the course of Milton's self-justificatory argument, the premise of which is Lycidas himself. A poet must speak of the deaths of poets, just as a lover must weep when he loses his beloved. The deaths of the young are all the more to be deplored and ritualised than those of people who have lived out a full span of experience and succumbed to old age. Far from feeling self-conscious about the depth of his grief (as Tennyson will, later), Milton presents his act of mourning as a matter of duty, almost of piety. The claim that Lycidas has 'not left his peer' is a particularly interesting one because, of course, he has: a host of peers are mourning him, the principal among them being the speaker of this poem; and yet none of them is his peer in the other sense, his equal. In the sense of this duality, he is already taking on certain Christ-like characteristics: as a man he had peers, but he is peerless in his immortality.

Having invoked the help of the classical muses, Milton sets about his first task, that of reminiscence: he and Lycidas rose early and tended their flocks together, often singing together to pass the time (lines 25–36). The scene is obviously Theocritan, but unlike so many poets who were merely accomplished imitators of classical models, Milton does not dwell on it. The reason for this may be, simply, that he did not wish to construct false reminiscences. He was, after all, experiencing real grief for Edward King, and while the poem was expected to perform a necessary task of commemoration after a pastoral model, we can assume it was not Milton's intention to erase King's life by fictionalising it.

He attempts to blame the nymphs for King's death – 'Where were ye nymphs when the remorseless deep / closed o'er the head of your loved Lycidas?' (lines 50–51) – but instantly withdraws that train of thought as being futile. In the demoralised moment which follows, he questions the worth of his own trade, poetry – 'what boots it with uncessant care / to tend the homely, slighted shepherd's trade / and strictly meditate the thankless muse?' (lines 64–6). Would there not be more point in making love? The love he thinks of making is, of course, heterosexual – 'to sport with Amaryllis in the shade, / or with the tangles of Nëæra's hair' (lines 68–9) – and he expresses it as a frivolity, a mere matter of sporting with surfaces, thereby answering his own question. Poetry is now of greater use to him than any amount of hetero-erotic play. While the latter might temporarily serve to take his mind off the death of Lycidas, only the writing of poetry can take him through his grief for his male friend into some form of consolation.

In 1639, the year after *Lycidas*, Milton wrote the *Epitaphium Damonis* (Damon's epitaph), a pastoral reflection on the death of another close friend, Charles Diodati. Written in Latin, this lament, too, is spoken as though by a shepherd – its refrain, repeated seventeen times, is 'Lambs, go home unfed; your shepherd does not have time for you now', a modification of the last line of Virgil's second eclogue, 'Ite domum saturae, venit Hesperus, ite capellae'; and a number of other phrases are borrowed from others of Virgil's texts. The dead friend's Greek name is presumably chosen to remind the reader of the famous lovers Damon and Pythias. He and the man who mourns him were friends since boyhood ('a pueritia amici erant'); and what is now to be established is whether such friendship can survive the death of one of them.

As in *Lycidas*, the mourning voice works its way eventually around to that point at which lamentation can cease: 'Ite procul lacrymae'. He reconciles himself to the fact that Damon/Diodati , having led a blameless life, has now surely taken his place in Heaven, where he will remain throughout eternity. As the poem reaches its close, the speaker focuses on Damon's virginity: 'Because the blush of modesty and a youth without stain were your choice, and because you never tasted the delight of the marriage bed, see – virginal honours are reserved for you!'[7] Again, we see male friendship being presented as proof of purity and, therefore, morally superior to heterosexual relations. The manly virgin is as close as Milton could imagine a human individual's being able to approach, here on earth, the condition of those happy, blushing angels in *Paradise Lost*.

In *Paradise Regained*, Satan tries to tempt Jesus with a banquet attended by, in addition to nymphs, 'Tall stripling youths rich clad, of fairer hue / Than Ganymed or Hylas' (II, 352–3). Needless to say, the temptee is not tempted. But it is interesting that the tempter tried – or, at least, that Milton thought this a worthy test for Christ to have passed. The mixture of Christian and pagan mythologies is one we recognise from *Lycidas*, in the closing section of which Milton makes use of the pastoral connotations of Christ's role as shepherd. According to Bredbeck, *Paradise Regained* 'reveals gendered meaning in general to be a product of the fall, a system distinctive of a separation from God' and also shows that C.S. Lewis' erased sodomite, although 'frequently devalued during the Renaissance', was also 'constantly in play' (p. 230). He may, indeed, have been in play in ways which related directly to current affairs. For instance, it has been argued that *Comus* (1634) was written, if not exactly in response to the Castlehaven scandal of 1631 – when the second Earl of Castlehaven and two of his servants were executed for buggery and rape – at least with the scandal at the back of his mind.[8]

· · ·

Percy Bysshe Shelley wrote *Adonais*, his elegy on John Keats, in Pisa at the beginning of June 1821. It opens by stating the facts of the matter – you might say, by stating the obvious: 'I weep for Adonais – he is dead!' And the speaker enjoins his hearers straight away to do the same as he does: 'O, weep for Adonais!' What follows is an account of collective mourning, usually personified in the figures of Greek goddesses and nymphs. Only one clear homosexual reference creeps in: 'To Phoebus was not Hyacinth so dear / Nor to himself Narcissus, as to both / Thou, Adonais' (XVI). By stitching Keats into the fabric of Greek pastoral mythology, Shelley invokes an idea of immortality which is more physical, more picturesque, less vague, than Christian versions of Heaven. For all that it is a mythical space, Arcadia can be located in a specific geography: in this case, either the Italy Keats died in or the England he came from. But it is a space that must be peopled with pre-Christian deities – even if, as in *Lycidas*, Christ then appears among them as another of the denizens of the Arcadian pastures.

Having concluded that Adonais is now 'made one with Nature' (XLII) the mourner is able to proclaim the survival of his seductive beauty:

> He is a portion of the loveliness
> Which once he made more lovely[.]
>   (XLIII)

This assertion of the continuity of beauty is the strongest consolatory note Shelley strikes. The loveliness of the natural world, though now diminished by the absence of Keats from it (for he used to intensify its beauty not only by writing beautifully about it, but also by being beautiful in his own person), remains, and he remains in it. This is a compromised consolation, for Shelley never renounces that claim that Keats' death has lessened the beauty of the world, even though it may contain him still. It seems that this slight dimming of the light is to be permanent.

We know that Shelley thought about male homosexuality in considerable depth. Indeed, he wrote about it – and not only at second hand, as when he was translating Plato's *Symposium*. While reading the *Phaedrus* during the summer of 1818, he wrote 'A Discourse on the Manners of the Antient Greeks Relative to the Subject of Love'.[9] Arguing that, because Greek civilisation was predicated upon both 'personal slavery and the [institutionalised] inferiority of women', Greek men found that their feelings of 'sentimental love' had been 'deprived of their natural object', Shelley represents homosexual love as being a necessary, if unnatural, expedient. Degraded and uneducated, women were unable fully to reciprocate such feelings, so Greek men 'sought a compensation and a substitute' in each other, or rather in younger members of their own sex. The consequence was that 'beautiful persons of the male sex became the object of that sort of feelings, which are only cultivated at present as towards females'. Subdued to such an extent, Greek women were fit only either to produce children or to serve men's baser desires. The more high-minded forms of love were inappropriate to the low status which women were accorded.

In the next stage of his argument, Shelley treads carefully around the question of sexual acts. In the first place, he pleads lack of historical evidence for whatever it was that Greek men did with the bodies of their boyfriends: 'We are not exactly aware . . . what that action was by which the Greeks expressed this passion'. That said, however, he allows himself to rule out certain possibilities: 'I am persuaded that it was totally different from the ridiculous and disgusting conceptions which the vulgar have formed on the subject, at least except among the more debased and abandoned of mankind. It is impossible that a lover could usually have subjected the object of his attachment to so detestable a violation or have consented to associate his own remembrance in the beloved mind with images of pain and horror'. This appears to be a reference to anal intercourse, which so often evokes 'images of pain and horror' in those who have not had the pleasure of trying it out. Although Shelley does not say so – and probably never *would* (or could) have said so – this passage suggests an implicit approval of other forms of sexual expression, presumably including those which, as we now know, were the usual sexual modes between males in Greece, mutual masturbation and intercrural intercourse. One thing is unambiguous: Shelley is taking it for granted that 'the Greeks expressed this passion' between man and boy with more than mere kisses. They had sex – but not anal sex.

Shelley is presumably referring to anal intercourse again, a little later; but by this point in the essay he appears to have shifted his ground. He seems to be assuming that the Greeks *must* have made love anally; and he sets out a meagre defence, comparing their immorality with that of early nineteenth-century Englishmen. He writes: 'The action by which this passion was expressed, taken in its grossest sense, is indeed sufficiently detestable. But a person must be blinded by superstition to conceive of it as more horrible than the usual intercourse endured by almost every youth of England with a diseased and insensible prostitute. It cannot be more unnatural, for nothing defeats and violates nature, or the purposes for which the sexual instincts are supposed to have existed, [more] than prostitution.' This is the most daring moment in the essay – or would have been, had he published it. His assertion that anal intercourse is unnatural only to the extent that heterosexual intercourse outside marriage is unnatural introduces a useful – and, at that time, rare – element of relativity into the argument about sexual morality. Not that Shelley is being at all positive about men who make love in this particular way; but he is, at least, spreading his disapproval rather more thinly than was the habit of his era.

In the next paragraph, Shelley demonstrates that he is familiar with the Latin literature of male–male sexuality (he mentions Catullus, Martial, Juvenal, Suetonius, Lucretius, Virgil and Horace) but evidently not with the Greek: he claims that Greek literature contains none of the sexual details he has seen in the Latin: for 'the Greeks seemed hardly capable of obscenity in a strict sense'. Even Aristophanes, he claims, is 'innocent' compared with Catullus. We can infer from this passage that he would not have felt safe writing a Virgilian elegy on Keats. It appears to have been important to him to refer only to Greek culture, since Latin – even the relatively austere Latin of Virgil – was liable to bring with it too many undesirable associations.

In the penultimate paragraph of what remains of the essay, Shelley mentions that even England has produced a literature of male love – and what a literature! – but he does not allow that the best of it was ever expressive of sexual desire (still less reactive to sexual pleasure): 'in the golden age of our own literature a certain sentimental attachment towards persons of the same sex was not uncommon. Shakespeare has devoted the impassioned and profound poetry of his sonnets to commemorate an attachment of this kind, which we cannot question was wholly divested of any unworthy alloy.' In this way, Shelley reaches a point at which the subject of sexual activity has been dropped as being irrelevant to the higher-minded sentiments he wishes to commend in Greek culture – and perhaps to recommend in English. He has consistently been talking about chaste, 'platonic' affairs between men. But, I repeat: he has not felt able to do so without acknowledging that 'Greek love' was open to sexual expression in a manner no more appalling than were the sexual habits of most young Englishmen of his day.

It is vital to take into account that, for writers such as Milton, Keats and Shelley, references to ancient Greek culture did more than locate a source of usable materials pertaining to male love; they were also intended to connote *republicanism*. So such poems as these are often imbued with a radical spirit which makes nonsense of claims that English uses of pastoral are uniformly conservative in their nostalgia. In America Walt Whitman's elegiac work, too, is imbued with a spirit of radicalism which explicitly espouses ideals of democratic egalitarianism and individual liberty. Even if pastoral is always to some extent elegiac, often regretful of a loss of simplicity in the face of urban encroachment on rural spaces, it does not automatically follow that it cannot also be forward-looking and capable of envisaging positive change.

· · ·

One of the premises of Alfred Tennyson's *In Memoriam*, as of most elegies, is the early line, 'Let Love clasp Grief lest both be drown'd' (I, 9). Survival is at stake. The mourner wonders how he will ever survive in the absence of the young man he loves. More anguished still, he wonders how, even if he does survive, his love will survive the loved one's absence. Might it be the case that he will, one day, actually *forget* the dead man? The writing of the poem – all 132 sections of it – will be a significant factor in ensuring that this does not happen.

Alan Sinfield has written that 'The emotions represented in *In Memoriam* should be understood as in uneasy relation to the dominant notions of proper manly behaviour.'[10] In particular, Tennyson's assumption of widowhood in relation to the dead Hallam, with its imagery of cross-dressing and its 'inappropriate' effusions, looked distinctly suspect to certain readers. The very length of the poem, its continental talkativeness on the theme of bereavement, was enough to make it seem both un-English (or rather, un-Victorian) and unmanly. Throughout the poem Tennyson refers to his own condition as that, sometimes of a widow, sometimes of a widower. He thereby demands the right to mourn with demonstrative expressions of grief rather than just a manly grimace.

Tennyson invokes the imagery of classical pastoral when describing the English churchyard to which Hallam's body is brought home. But when he actually names Arcadia and its presiding deity, Pan, as he does in section XXIII, he is immediately stricken by doubt. The following section begins with the lines:

> And was the day of my delight
> As pure and perfect as I say?

This is not just an anticipation of the objections of sceptical readers. Far more interestingly, it is an open expression of personal doubt. Having fallen into the convention of Arcadian references, Tennyson feels self-conscious about the extremes of happiness he is laying claim to having enjoyed in Hallam's company. Even having experienced it for himself, he finds himself asking how such bliss could possibly have been generated in the real world – that is to say, in Victorian England. Nineteenth-century pastoralists were under some pressure, if only imposed by their own scruples, to justify ignoring or erasing the industrial revolution. After all, purity and perfection are a lot to ask of the world of Blake's 'dark, satanic mills'.

In this search for an acceptably unforeign precedent for extreme feelings of bliss generated by male love, where else does an Englishman go but back to Shakespeare? In section LX he makes the proud, and perhaps quite risky, assertion:

> I loved thee, Spirit, and love, nor can
> The soul of Shakespeare love thee more.

Of course, Tennyson has defused the potential risk by disembodying both Hallam and Shakespeare. (The fact that they are dead is convenient at this point.) Much would be altered in the balance of the whole poem if he were to address Hallam, in lines like these, as 'Arthur'; and much would change if it had been the body, not the soul, of Shakespeare that was invoked. What the poem does offer us, though, is a glimpse of a competition between two men's souls for the spirit of a younger third (plus, of course, a hubristic tilt at the Bard's pre-eminent reputation as a love poet). This moment of identification relies on the critical mass which had been established to rescue Shakespeare's sonnets from the potential 'taint' of accusations of physical passion. Tennyson hopes to capitalise on patriotic defences of Shakespeare, thereby ensuring that his own poem will be read as befitting the emotional requirements of English manliness.

There is a defensiveness in Tennyson which did not seem to be present in Milton or Shelley. Victorian standards of masculine respectability provide grounds for really strong anxieties, and yet Tennyson does resist the pressure to stay silent. Indeed, he resists it more resolutely than any of the other poets in this chapter. The outcome, whether intentional or not, is a very productive inner tension. In the words of Richard Dellamora, 'Despite explicit attempts in *In Memoriam* to conserve the pure love of comrades and the preeminence of marriage, countertendencies destabilise the ideological givens of the poem. Invisible but disturbing, connotations of sexual danger energise the poem while remaining unspoken.'[11] This is true, but the important thing to note is that the poet survives the risks he takes, in spite of the fact that the poem did attract some distinctly suspicious reviews. Above all, Tennyson's triumph is to have found his way to a position from which it is possible plausibly to claim that it is 'better to have loved and lost / Than never to have loved at all'. This is a position of strength from which he has managed to banish any hint of sodomitic transgression. After all, from the point of view of Victorian orthodoxy, in the case of the sodomite it would be better to be dead himself than *ever* to have loved at all.

Arthur Clough died in 1861, but Matthew Arnold did not start writing his elegy, 'Thyrsis', until 1864, and did not complete it until January 1866. He had written commemorative verses before – I am thinking in particular of his 1850 poem 'Memorial Verses', on the death of Wordsworth – and he had written pastoral poetry before, most notably 'The Scholar-Gypsy' (1852–3), on which 'Thyrsis' is actually based. It gives the impression of being much less grief-stricken than the Tennyson, and is certainly much shorter and therefore less open to risk. The bucolic name Thyrsis appears in Theocritus' first Idyll, and Virgil used it again in his seventh Eclogue. The subheading of the poem consciously echoes Milton's subheading to *Lycidas*. So, in these and other respects, Arnold's poem is very much the self-consciously intertextual effort of a donnish intellect; and yet, like all the other elegists we are considering here, Arnold strives to create the impression of an untutored, naturally cultured simplicity of intelligence: the mind of a bereaved shepherd. Like Cambridge in *Lycidas*, Oxford becomes Arcadia. It is possible to scoff at this. After all, what do these poets really know of the kind of outdoor life a shepherd has to endure, or of the wages that come with it? But we have to remind ourselves that no post-medieval Arcadian literature – not even that which coincides with the realist movements in nineteenth-century fiction – is meant to be realistic. The very premise of these poems is idealistic; so it makes no sense to criticise them for their lapses into implausibility.

There is a moment in the poem when the speaker says, as if to the dead Thyrsis, 'Time, not Corydon, hath conquered thee!' By referring back in this way to the simple pastimes of bucolic life – in the Theocritan world, singing competitions, or competitions to win the favours of unattached boys or girls – Arnold casts Clough not as a lover but as a close friend with whom he shared his most intimate sexual desires, both by exchanging poetry with him (the improvised songs) and by discussing sex with him. The competitions which are thus imagined between Thyrsis and Corydon, Clough and Arnold, are ways in which male friends can get close to each other without their friendship's veering off into illegitimate forms of intimacy. Competition is the viable way of protecting the individual's masculinity against the creeping effeminacy of overt affection for his male friend. (You can wrestle with your friend, but not make love.) It is while imagining this kind of circumscribed male friendship that Arnold conceives of his own role, now, as the dead friend's elegist: 'Alack, for Corydon no rival now! – / But when Sicilian shepherds lost a mate / Some good survivor with his flute would go, / Piping a ditty sad for Bion's fate; / . . . / And flute his friend, like Orpheus, from the dead' (lines 81–90). This is the role the elegist always takes on himself – if not literally to raise the dead, at least to keep his memory alive. Arnold models himself not only on Moschus, elegising Bion, but also on Orpheus, daring to venture into the underworld, if only in vain. But, as I have suggested already, there is little sense of real daring here.

In the days that followed the assassination of Abraham Lincoln on 15 April 1865, Walt Whitman realised that he was going to have to add to *Drum-Taps*, his volume of Civil War poems, a substantial reaction to this conclusive event before they could be published. Where the earlier poems had been brief but intensely packed with personal emotion and sexual attraction, the Lincoln elegy 'When lilacs last in the dooryard bloom'd' is a lengthy meditation, not only on the death of a single individual, but on the death of a representative individual within a democracy in which (at least theoretically) any one death is as significant as any other. Since Lincoln himself represented this political ideal, his death makes the perfect example of the passing of ordinary lives as being, not trivial, but of overarching significance. Few poets could have managed this representation of a great public event, the assassination of a President, as if it were a purely personal tragedy. Whitman's characterisation of Lincoln as 'him I love' ran the risk of sounding hubristic and ridiculous. But his concentration on the smaller scale of things – the dooryard itself, for instance – while yet recounting the slow procession of the coffin across the nation, helps to effect the poem's impression of unforced intimacy.

Whitman's *Drum-Taps,* the Civil War section of *Leaves of Grass,* was reissued in Great Britain in 1915 with an introduction which related the themes of the poems to the land war on the continent. But Whitman was not the most widely read poet in the trenches of the First World War. The tones of simultaneous yearning and regret that characterise virtually all the poems of A.E. Housman, and which make his collected poetry read like a dignified cross between *In Memoriam* and the gravestone inscriptions of the *Mousa Paidiké,* help explain why it was his verse that was so often included in the personal belongings of the young British men who went to war. And when those men died, new poets set to work. Collectively assessed, the English poetry of the First World War constitutes an extraordinary document in the developing history of what some commentators have liked to call a 'homosexual sensibility'. Teachers do not say so in British schools – where the poetry of the Great War is just about the only literature in verse that students will put up with – but the three most famous war poets were either bisexual (Rupert Brooke) or homosexual (Wilfred Owen and Siegfried Sassoon). And it shows. This is, perhaps, the most popular gay literature in English culture, although many readers would be furious if they heard you saying so.[12]

The war was also, as it were, the primary cause of T.S. Eliot's *The Waste Land* (1922). Its effects are stamped all over the poem, visible both in the general theme of the (self-) destruction of the great civilisations and in the narrower, personal theme of grief over the loss of a single individual. In 1952, when John Peter published an essay arguing that *The Waste Land* was an elegy on the death of a young man – hardly a scandalous claim, given the canonical strength of the elegiac tradition in English literature – Eliot's reaction was, you might think, somewhat extreme: he threatened to sue unless all remaining copies of Peter's essay were pulped. Given Eliot's influence at the time, his demands were met in full, and Peter even sent him an apology. Peter kept the essay, of course, and sensibly republished it, with an even more interesting afterword, in 1969.[13]

The essay's premise is, as I have just said, apparently uncontroversial: 'At some previous time the speaker has fallen completely . . . in love [with] a young man who soon afterwards met his death, it would seem by drowning. . . . Enough time has now elapsed since his death for the speaker to have realised that the focus for affection that he once provided is irreplaceable.'[14] But even this, and even at a time of national grief for lost young men, touched a raw nerve in Eliot. It seems reasonable to assume that the nerve in question was linked with Eliot's mourning for one man in particular. The biographical facts are few. All we know is that, while studying at the Sorbonne in Paris in 1910–11, Eliot made friends with the young Frenchman Jean Verdenal. Verdenal died in the war in 1915 at the age of twenty-six. Eliot's poetry collection *Prufrock and Other Observations* (1917) was dedicated to his memory. The dedication carries a quotation from Dante's *Purgatorio* (XXI): '*Or puoi la quantitate / comprender dell'amor ch' a te mi scalda, / quando dismento nostra vanitate / trattando l'ombre come cosa salda*' (roughly: you can see the extent of the love which warms me towards you when I forget our lack of substance, treating the shades as if they were solid).[15]

Eliot's key autobiographical utterance on the beloved friend is a sentence he published in the *Criterion*: 'I am willing to admit that my own retrospect is touched by a sentimental sunset, the memory of a friend coming across the Luxembourg Gardens in the late afternoon, waving a branch of lilac, a friend who was later (so far as I could find out) to be mixed with the mud of Gallipoli'.[16] What appears to be Eliot's point of sensitivity is Peter's daring to suggest that 'a sentimental . . . memory of a friend' (please note how my ellipsis purposefully distorts the original text) constitutes a matter of 'love', far too dangerous a word to be applied to male friendship. In his later afterword, Peter convincingly relates the lilac boy to the poem's hyacinth girl. It is she who represents an ideal, if sentimentalised, form of love throughout the poem; and yet she, no less than Tiresias, appears to change sex at several points. Traditionally, of course, hyacinths call to mind a dead male, their beautiful namesake. And, indeed, the manuscript confirms 'her' maleness, linking her with the line (125) quoted from *The Tempest*, 'Those are pearls that were his eyes.'

The Waste Land is never positive about sex, hetero- or homosexual. The sequence (lines 202–14) in which the speaker encounters Mr Eugenides merely underlines how things have worsened since the moment in the hyacinth garden. A quotation from Paul Verlaine extolling the voices of choirboys (*Et O ces voix d'enfants, chantant dans la coupole!*) leads straight into the frenzied, lusty jug-jugging of birds, then a reminder of Tereus' rape of Philomel; whereupon Eugenides is introduced: 'Under the brown fog of a winter noon / Mr Eugenides, the Smyrna merchant / Unshaven, with a pocket full of currants / . . . / Asked me in demotic French / To luncheon at the Cannon Street Hotel / Followed by a weekend at the Metropole.' Nothing could be further from the homo-erotic pastoral of the hyacinth garden than Eugenides' proposition, spoken 'in demotic French'. The air is polluted, the suitor unshaven, and, worst of all, Jean Verdenal's language is reduced, from expressions of love in the hieratic or poetic, to a lewd proposition in common speech, the dreadful demotic.

Eliot chooses his sources with meticulous care. A number of them have homo-erotic resonances. For example, the fragmentary line 'To Carthage then I came' (line 307, at the end of 'The Fire Sermon') is, as the notes tell us, a quotation from Saint Augustine; and the notes tell us that Augustine adds, 'where a cauldron of unholy loves sang all about mine ears'. This is, in fact, the opening sentence from Book III of the *Confessions*. Augustine arrived in Carthage in AD 371, to study there, as a teenager on the lookout for love: 'I had not yet fallen in love, but I was in love with the idea of it'. And it was in Carthage, therefore, that 'I muddied the stream of friendship with the filth of lewdness'. His second visit to the city in AD 376, to teach there for the next seven years, followed closely on the death of a male friend. This had been, as he subsequently wrote, 'a friendship that was sweeter to me than all the joys of life'.[17] Eliot is able to compare his own bereavement with Augustine's.

The climax of the poem's personal theme (lines 402–6) is at once the most open and the most reticent part of it:

> My friend, blood shaking my heart
> The awful daring of a moment's surrender
> Which an age of prudence can never retract

> By this, and this only, we have existed
> Which is not to be found in our obituaries

– nor, for that matter, in Peter Ackroyd's biography of Eliot. It can be found in 'our' poems and their manuscripts, however. The manuscript's earlier version of line 402 is somewhat more passionate ('My friend, my friend, beating in my heart'). Similarly, the original manuscript's 'friend, my friend I have heard the key' became just 'I have heard the key' (line 411); and the manuscript's 'your heart responded' became the vaguer and less revealing 'your heart would have responded' (420). These expurgations of feeling, mostly advised by Ezra Pound, only begin to purge the poem of its homo-erotic emotions.[18] Much remains. It was, after all, the version as published, and not the manuscript, that persuaded Hart Crane, when he first read *The Waste Land*, that T.S. Eliot must be homosexual.[19]

Until a time when the premature deaths of comrades, friends and lovers become commonplace – as in a large-scale war or in an epidemic – the 'friendship' elegy is going to be among the most intense and anguished literature of male love. This has been the case in English culture ever since the Renaissance. During, and for a while after, the First World War, elegiac writing became the principal mode of poetic expression in English literature. Similarly, during the AIDS pandemic, elegy has been moved to the centre of gay poetry's palette. But such elegies have tended to discard pastoralism as being inappropriate to the predominantly urban nature of gay liberationist lifestyles in the 1970s. Moreover, by the mid-1980s gay elegies would largely have lost the element of surprise. What used to be so rare (other than in wartime) and barely credible – the premature deaths of young men – is now one of our literature's most insistent themes.[20] I shall return to this in my penultimate chapter.

Chapter 10

....

From Libertinism to the Gothic

One of the principal identifying marks of the libertine is indiscriminacy. He (for the assumption usually is that the psychological and physical conditions which result in libertinism are best accommodated by maleness) does not idealise and venerate a single individual or confine his desires to a single type. Rather, he obtains his satisfaction by cumulative means. Like Don Giovanni boasting of his *mille e tre* successes, he is the sexual equivalent of the adding machine. Little discrimination is made between the beautiful and the ugly; any flesh will do. The only discrimination between character types is not between (say) the clever and the dull, or pleasant and unpleasant, but between moral types, the virtuous and the vicious: for, although any object is a mere number in the libertine's cumulative scheme, he always finds that the deflowering of a virgin affords him a far keener enjoyment than does the mere pleasuring of an already experienced physique. The literature of libertinism is full of violated nuns.

At one of its extremes the mythology of sexual indiscriminacy is eager to invoke the figure of the bisexual, the individual to whose desires gender does not pose a barrier, any more than do the laws of church or state. So often represented as being dedicated to hedonism, bisexuality supposedly doubles the libertine's opportunities for pleasure, not only by adding males to females as available flesh, but also by opening up – to the male libertine – the possibility of being fucked as well as fucking. Don Giovanni's body is a penetrating machine, but the bodies of many of the Marquis de Sade's libertines are also, as it were, reversible.

The literary history of libertinism takes us back at least as far as Suetonius' *Lives of the Twelve Caesars*, and particularly to his accounts of the lives of Nero (the lover of his mother Agrippina; lover of such women as Acte and Sabina Poppaea; husband of Sporus, the youth he ordered castrated for his spousal role; and wife of Doryphorus) and Tiberius (whose orgies on Capri are detailed, also, in Tacitus' *Annals*). The modern period tends to produce more modest forays into pleasure-seeking – although, as we shall see, it amused the Marquis de Sade to imagine the extravagant consequences of the combination of vice and enormous wealth: Gilles de Rais (1404–40) was one of his greatest heroes.

The better-known literature of libertinism appears always to be produced by men who themselves have reputations as libertines. In some cases, of course, the reputation may be a consequence of the writings rather than of actual hedonistic behaviour. But it is significant (let us say, in the period from Pietro Aretino in the sixteenth century to Lord

Byron in the early nineteenth) that the spirit of libertinism is best evoked in writing by men who themselves had inclinations in that direction. Writing about their conquests, as Don Giovanni sings about his, may be an important part of the pleasure of conquest. Imagining further pleasures may either spur the author on to fresh conquests in actuality, or obviate the need for them.

Pietro Aretino (1492–1556) was lustily interested both in women themselves and in writing about them (as in his *Ragionamenti*, a series of dialogues between two women about the sexual lives of nuns, wives and whores), but he was also the subject of accusations of sodomy which obliged him to flee Venice in 1538, and he wrote a jauntily positive comedy about what we would now call homosexuality, *Il marescalco* (1533). In this play the Duke of Mantua's master of the horse is told he must marry – this despite, or else because of, the fact that he is said to be 'reluctant with women'. A practical joke of a wedding is arranged for him, at which his reluctance turns to relief when it is revealed that his bride-to-be is his young page Carlo, dressed as a woman. It appears that both his misogyny and his homosexuality are amply satisfied by this timely revelation.

Théophile de Viau (1590–1626) also developed a reputation for libertine morals in both his life and his poetry. In 1623 he was imprisoned, untried, for the portmanteau crime of *lèse-majesté divine* (an accusation aimed at the combined abominations, in this case, of sodomy and atheism). He remained captive for two years before being released but banished from Paris. Meanwhile, however, he was to become the most often published poet in seventeenth-century France: between 1621 and 1696 no fewer than eighty-eight editions of his work appeared. Théophile regarded pleasure as the highest good, and sexual pleasure as potentially the most joyous of all. Among his many erotic epigrams about heterosexual intercourse are a number on male homosexual topics, including one ('Par ce doux appetit des vices . . .') which begins with an explicit avowal of sexuality ('Par tant de foutre repandu / Qui t'a cent fois lavé les cuisses') before offering one of those lists from which man-loving men have so often sought both justification and solidarity: among others, he names Apollo and Hyacinth, Corydon, Julius Caesar, James I of England and the Duke of Buckingham.[1]

John Wilmot, Earl of Rochester (1647–80) was, as they say, a notorious rake. Even though a degree of libertinism was very much the fashion of the Restoration period in England, Rochester often overstepped the mark of impropriety; but whether his own behaviour or his scabrous and scatological poetry was more scandalous is open to question. Rochester's verse expresses precisely the kind of indiscriminate voraciousness which I have mentioned as being the mark of the libertine. In 'The Imperfect Enjoyment', a poem about impotence, he speaks about the behaviour of his own penis when he and it were both younger:

> Stiffly resolv'd, 'twould carelessly invade
> Woman or man, nor ought its fury stayed:
> Where'er it pierced, a cunt it found or made[.][2]

This designation of any penetrable orifice as 'a cunt' is revealing of several libertine tendencies. In the first place, all receptive orifices are regarded as being qualitatively identical and interchangeable: a boy can have 'a cunt' in this sense, and it makes him no less or more satisfactorily fuckable than any woman. In the second place, no sexual partner consists of anything but 'a cunt', and none has any purpose other than to receive the invasive prick. Thirdly, the libertine's prick is insatiable and has a will of its own: he speaks of it as if it makes his decisions for him, and he admires its unambiguous, pitiless 'fury'.

The penis is so important that it defines all the elements in the world around it. Everything is either 'a cunt', can be turned into 'a cunt', or is of no interest whatsoever. In an earlier passage from the same poem, speaking of intercourse with a woman, Rochester writes:

> In liquid raptures I dissolve all o'er,
> Melt into sperm, and spend at every pore.
> A touch from any part of her had done't:
> Her hand, her foot, her very look's a cunt.
>
> (p. 38)

This even more forthright display of the reduction of the partner's personality and body to 'a cunt' – meaning a stimulus, *any* stimulus, to ejaculation – is not so much misogynistic, perhaps, as misanthropic. Neither female nor male is of interest to the speaker except insofar as she or he can generate pleasure; and yet, however, this makes the partner of paramount importance, if only for the duration of her or his frictive presence.

In the famous 'Song' which begins with the dismissive line 'Love a woman? You're an ass!', Rochester produces one of the most famous and outspoken English statements of male-to-male sexual attraction. The song ends with the following lines:

> Then give me health, wealth, mirth, and wine,
>   And, if busy love entrenches,
> There's a sweet, soft page of mine
>   Does the trick worth forty wenches.
>
> (p. 51)

There is something both charming and repulsive about this verse. It is not, of course, meant too seriously and should not be overburdened with critical anxieties; but, on the other hand, its very frivolity is part of what is disturbing about it. For a start, Rochester's inimitable pleasure-loving mood is sustained not only by health, mirth and wine, but, far more importantly, by wealth. This brings us to a crucially defining characteristic of libertinism in general: it always consists of *bought* pleasures, in part if not entirely. The one thing that might well stay the 'fury' of the Earl of Rochester's penis would be pennilessness. When he speaks of his 'page' or of 'forty wenches', Rochester is enumerating cunts which are either already on his payroll or available for temporary purchase. The point about the accommodating and indefatigable pageboy is not only that he could generate the required multiplicity of orgasms, but also that he would do so more cheaply.

Strictly speaking, libertinism is an aristocratic phenomenon. It cannot survive democracy. This is why Rochester, at least as he presents himself in his own writing, is such a perfect exemplar of the libertine personality. Note how, in the lines I have just quoted, the anonymous wenches are dismissed in favour of the particular employee whose 'sweet, soft' disposition and physique have selected him out of however many other individuals the earl employs; but how this delightful boy is only turned to if 'love' – an above-stairs word – fails to provide what is required of her. In other words, when his own social equals decline to assuage the libertine's lust, he has servants to turn to; and in the last resort he can collect, or send for, other bodies from beyond the walls of his own home. Even in Rochester's pleasantest rhymes, we are beginning to see the elements of Sadean fantasy.

The play called *Sodom, or The Quintessence of Debauchery* (Antwerp, 1684) is usually attributed to Rochester. It was written either by him or by a reasonably skilled parodist. As drama, *Sodom* is no less unperformable than Sade's *Philosophie dans le boudoir* (1795). But as a sustained sequence of erotic jokes, it adds flesh to our overall conception of the libertine world-view. Such as it is, the play's plot needs briefly to be summarised. King Bolloxinion rules his realm by decree of desire: 'My Pintle only shall my scepter be;/ My laws shall act more pleasure than command / And with my Prick, I'll govern all the land'. Thus taking to their extremes the phallocentric tendencies of patriarchal power, the king commands an end to heterosexual intercourse. Instead, he allows the women to adopt the use of dildoes, both on themselves and on each other, and the men to turn to buggery. Now, true to the misogynistic bias of libertine bisexuality, it turns out that the women are left frustrated and unsatisfied by each other, even when armed with bigger and bigger dildoes, whereas the men enjoy their sodomitic interregnum with enthusiasm and vigour. In the end, however, it transpires that buggery is spreading the pox throughout the land. So the king has to reverse his decree. The men and women return to each other's arms and beds.[3]

Clearly, regardless of its pleasure-loving veneer, *Sodom* is structured on misogynistic and anti-sodomitic principles. Its tributes to the joys of buggery are thoroughly compromised in a manner which cannot be attributed to the pressures of convention – the whole text is too far beyond the pale for that to apply. The King's proclamation of a return to heterosexual relations restates a very familiar argument, but in the frankest vernacular:

> To love and nature all their rights restore –
> Fuck women and let buggery be no more:
> It doth the procreative End destroy,
> Which nature gave with pleasure to enjoy.
> Please her, and she'll be kind: if you displease,
> She turns into corruption and disease.
>
> (V, ii)

All that is left here of the libertine spirit is 'Fuck women', but even this is somewhat negated by the subsequent line on procreation. No libertine ever wanted babies – unless by his wife at a safe distance from the locus of his unabated pleasures. It may be that these lines are meant to be parodic; but even so, they come at such a decisive moment in the play that dramatic structure seems to need them to be spoken in earnest. The time for a new line in joking is past. For all its superficial celebration of omnisexual chaos, the play is no less in need of a fifth-act restoration of order than any Shakespearean comedy where clothing is returned to the appropriate gender before the final curtain. As *Sodom* comes to its compromised and conservative ending, the queen is dead, the princess has gone mad, and everyone without exception is consumed by the fires of Hell. This is, of course, the end that will come to Mozart's Don Giovanni a century later.

Although the likes of Aretino, Théophile and Rochester produced texts which broke certain taboos and scandalised the readers they were intended to scandalise, all of them compromised in one way or another with the values of their respective times. This is only to be expected. Few but the most extreme moments in their texts can prepare us for the systematic outrages of the one author who monopolised libertinism in the late eighteenth and early nineteenth centuries: the Marquis de Sade (1740–1814). Although the majority of his work was not published until certain manuscripts were released by his family in the twentieth century – a remarkable event, when you consider the lengths to which so many families have gone to suppress the unacceptable voices of their black sheep – Sade represents an extraordinarily dynamic moment in European cultural history, when darkness is discovered at the heart of the Enlightenment, and the so-called Age of Reason lurches into unreason.

Imprisoned at Vincennes and then in the Bastille for sodomy and poisoning, Sade was in the middle of revising the manuscript of his pornographic masterpiece, *The 120 Days of Sodom* (*Les 120 journées de Sodome*, 1785), when he was removed from the Bastille to the Charenton asylum. Soon afterwards, on 14 July 1789, the Bastille was stormed. Sade assumed that his manuscript, which he had left behind in the prison, was lost for ever. Indeed, he himself never saw it again, and he spent the rest of his life making various attempts to distil the libertine essence of *The 120 Days* in novels like *Justine* and *Juliette*. But the hidden manuscript was later found in what had been Sade's room (it was no mere cell) in the Bastille and was preserved until it was first published in the 1930s. There is evidence that Sade spent several months of 1794 in the same prison as Choderlos de Laclos, whose great novel *Les liaisons dangereuses* (1782) serves up a much diluted version of libertinism, with no sodomy and precious little sadism. By contrast with Sade's book, it is a primer for marital harmony.

Dedicated to the task of outraging the laws of both Nature and Religion, *The 120 Days* was intended as a kind of *Summa Pornographica* of perversity.[4] Its systematic structure gives an impression of inclusiveness, even though the effect of reading it may be to suggest that the very few pornographic plots in existence can be varied *ad infinitum*. Four rich libertines, each married to an appropriately debauched wife, recruit four highly experienced older women to narrate all possible human sexual excesses; plus eight young girls, eight young boys, eight massively well-hung young men, and four female servants. All of them are closed away in a massive château, to hear and enact the full range of sexual permutations. (I almost wrote 'permutilations'.)

The body of the book is in four parts, divided according to the extremity of the sexual events they contain: Part 1 contains Madame Duclos' narration of the 150 'simple passions', told at a rate of five a day for the period of a complete month; Part 2 contains Madame Champville's narration of the 'complex pleasures'; Part 3 contains Madame Martaine's narration of the 'criminal passions'; and Part 4 contains Madame Desgranges' narration of the 'murderous passions'. (I hardly need add that Sade's idea of what constitutes a 'simple' pleasure is likely to be a good deal more complex than that of most readers; and the following three categories are correspondingly advanced.) The proceedings are governed by strict statutes, which regulate every detail of the daily routine. Not one act of ingestion or excretion goes unsupervised; not one is allowed to pass without contributing to the pleasure of the four masters. These statutes are, of course, written out in full. Anyone who believes that writing pornography is a spontaneous, libido-led process must surely be dissuaded by this book.

The four libertines who instigate and orchestrate these goings-on include the Duc de Blangis, who is succinctly sketched as follows: 'a liar, a gourmand, a drunk, a dastard, a sodomite, fond of incest, given to murdering, to arson, to theft, no, not a single virtue compensated that host of vices'. As far as his energetic addiction to sodomy is concerned, the duc's body is reversible: 'For roughly twenty-five years he had accustomed himself to passive sodomy, and he withstood its assaults with the identical vigor that characterised his manner of delivering them actively when, the very next moment, it pleased him to exchange roles'. With him is his brother, the Bishop of X***, likewise an 'idolater of active and passive sodomy, but eminently of the latter'. Indeed, we are told, 'he spent his life having himself buggered'. The third of the libertines is another pillar of society, the Président de Curval, who 'would glide into every hole to be found, indiscriminately, although that of a young lad's behind was infinitely the most precious to him'. Sade later says of him, ' Men, women, children: anything was fuel to his rage'. As well as having many sexual tastes in common, and being of noble rank, the four libertines are also – it hardly

16. The indiscriminate acrobatics of libertinism.
(Illustrations from the Marquis de Sade's *La Nouvelle Justine*, 1797)

needs saying – immensely rich. As the narrative rather blandly puts it, 'Their excessive wealth put the most unusual things within their reach' (pp. 194–209).

Even while they are making the initial preparations for their retreat into pleasure in the sealed château, the four libertines hold regular sexual feasts, five a week to be exact. One of these is an all-male affair:

> At the first of these gatherings, the one exclusively given over to the pleasures of sodomy, only men were present; there would always be at hand sixteen young men, ranging in age from twenty to thirty, whose immense faculties permitted our four heroes [the rich libertines], in feminine guise, to taste the most agreeable delights. The youths were selected solely upon the basis of the size of their member, and it almost became necessary that this superb limb be of such magnificence that it could never have penetrated any woman; this was an essential clause, and as naught was spared by way of expense, only very rarely would it fail to be fulfilled. But simultaneously to sample every pleasure, to these sixteen husbands was joined the same quantity of boys, much younger, whose purpose was to assume the office of women. These lads were from twelve to eighteen years old, and to be chosen for service each had to possess a freshness, a face, graces, charms, an air, an innocence, a candor which are far beyond what our brush could possibly paint. No woman was admitted to these masculine orgies, in the course of which everything of the lewdest invented in Sodom and Gomorrah was executed. (pp. 194–5)

Importantly, while the well-endowed men chosen to stay in the château may be of any class – and Sade derives some amusement from their cloddish gormlessness – none of the young boys is from a peasant background: both Zélamir and Cupidon are the sons of otherwise undefined gentlemen, Narcisse's father 'filled an honorable post compatible with his nobility', Zéphire's father is 'a ranking officer', Céladon's is a magistrate, Adonis' a judge, Hyacinth's a retired officer, and Giton's 'a man of consequence'. So every violation of these boys' backsides – and there will be many – is one in the eye for the social hierarchy.

Among the group's written statutes is the following: 'The salon shall be heated to an unusual temperature, and illuminated by chandeliers. All present shall be naked: storytellers, wives, little girls, little boys, elders, fuckers, friends, everything shall be pell-mell, everyone shall be sprawled on the floor and, after the example of the animals, shall change, shall commingle, entwine, couple incestuously, adulterously, sodomistically' (p. 246). However, this delightful representation of domesticated polymorphous perversity is not typical of the whole of *The 120 Days*. As the book progresses it becomes more and more extreme, passing through elementary acts of sadism, coprophilia and sacrilege, or combinations thereof ('In order to combine incest, adultery, sodomy and sacrilege, he embuggers his married daughter with a Host'), to the most elaborately inventive tortures and lingering executions. The shapely exterior of the body – all those bodies so carefully chosen at the start of the narrative – ceases to be as attractive as its exposed innards.

It makes no sense to write Sade off as a 'mere' pornographer. In her classic essay 'Must We Burn Sade?' (*'Faut-il brûler Sade?'*, 1951), Simone de Beauvoir makes out a case for his sophistication, both as a philosopher and as a writer. For me, one of her most telling observations is the following: 'he was too deeply rationalistic to lose himself in fantasy. When he abandons himself to the extravagances of his imagination, one does not know which to admire the most, his epic vehemence or his irony'.[5] It is also worth noting that

Sade was keenly aware of the social context governing the development and regulation of sexual manners. Despite his fiction's concentration on implausible Grand Guignol, many details demonstrate that he knew what was happening in the real world outside his imagination and his jail. For example, he leaves us with one of very few references from this period to the apparently common practice of queer-bashing. In *Philosophy in the Bedroom* (*La philosophie dans le boudoir*, 1795), one of his well-endowed male characters denies being homosexual, adding, 'I favor women. But, at the same time, I'm not one of those impetuous lads who feels [*sic*] that a male's advances are to be answered with a beating.'[6]

Many of Sade's generalisations about the attractions of vice (or sin or crime) apply well to popular developments in European fiction at the time. He knows perfectly well that virtue is less interesting as a sustainable topic than vice. As he says at one point in *The 120 Days*, 'if crime lacks the kind of delicacy one finds in virtue, is not the former always more sublime, does it not unfailingly have a character of grandeur and sublimity which surpasses, and will always make it preferable to, the monotonous and lackluster charms of virtue?' (p. 197) Particularly in its invocation of the sublime, this reads like a statement of the generally hidden subtext of all Gothic fiction. As with Milton and Satan, so too with the Gothic novelists and their dark-haired, foreign villains. It is to early Gothic fiction that we now turn.

· · ·

William Beckford's orientalist fantasy *Vathek*, written in 1782, is a text which readily attracts the catch-all epithet 'camp'. Its combination of fairytale shallowness with lavish descriptions of ornamentation and behavioural excess, intensified by a certain amount of sexual suggestiveness, leave it open to appropriation by devotees of camp with little attention to historical process. Philip Core describes it as 'a precious mosaic of Middle Eastern daydreams and mysticism', but his entry on Beckford in *Camp: The Lie that Tells the Truth* is more concerned with the author's extravagant and scandalous way of life than with his writings.[7] Much the same is true of the references to Beckford in Mark Booth's *Camp*, but Booth does offer one useful insight into how so early a text might legitimately take its place in the history of what came to be known as camp:

> The unresolved opposites in the camp mind sometimes result in uncomfortable ambiguities; in *Vathek*, William Beckford clearly did not resolve conflicting desires to write beautifully and humorously, with the result that an idyllic oriental scene will be punctured by an ill-defined joke, creating something that is neither beautiful nor funny. The equivocation of the camp personality does not always transfer well into literature.[8]

The problem here, as in the case of so much camp literature, is one of intentionality. By what aesthetic criterion is the critic making his judgement, and is it the same criterion by which the writer judged that his book was finished? Is what Booth finds 'uncomfortable' a flaw in the text, caused by the author's yoking of conflicting aims, or a deliberately provocative indeterminacy of tone – both beautiful *and* funny – designed by the author to cause discomfort in readers trained in the consumption of more conventional prose? Must camp fail in order to succeed? Or does it succeed by provoking failures of reception in its audiences? Certainly, in the last sentence I quote, Booth is being unhelpfully critical: for what kind of personality, as a general type, always does 'transfer well' into literature?

Booth is right, though, to identify humour as one of the most significant points at issue. There is a section of Beckford's narrative in which the caliph Vathek is instructed by the Giaour to whom he has sold his soul to pick out the fifty most beautiful sons of his courtiers and sacrifice their lives. In the welter of sentimental homo-eroticism that follows the boys to their deaths, there are one or two off-colour jokes. Booth might account for their incompatibility with the sadder general tone of the passage by blaming Beckford's 'conflicting' aesthetic 'desires'. This does not appear to be an adequate response. Let us examine two moments in particular. To entice the boys towards the edge of the chasm into which he is going to hurl them, Vathek proposes to give each of them in turn an item of his jewellery or opulent clothing. The narrative continues: 'This declaration was received with reiterated acclamations; and all extolled the liberality of a prince who would thus strip himself for the amusement of his subjects and the encouragement of the rising generation.'[9] If we disregard the straightforward irony of the discrepancy between Vathek's murderous intentions and the apparent generosity of his promises – to which the reader reacts in the ironic security of superior knowledge, knowing more than the soon-to-be-bereaved – there remains a second level of irony, less tragic, more bawdy, which seems to be presenting itself to a readership familiar with, and appreciative of, socially unacceptable sexual practices: the 'corruption' of boys by men. Read at this level, the idea of a man stripping naked for 'the encouragement of the rising generation' (who are actually about to *fall*) is a joke about puberty, youthful erections, mutual masturbation and cross-generational sexual dalliance. What is camp about the joke is, firstly, that it is tonally 'inappropriate' to its genocidal moment; and, secondly, that one can conceive of its being either entirely overlooked by earnest (dare one say, heterosexual?) readers, or deplored by them as being tasteless. Whether the conception of such obtuseness in uninitiated readers is fair or even plausible does not affect the brief shiver of superiority which camp humour must grant its appreciators.

When the parents realise that their sons have been flung over the clifftop by Vathek to appease his Giaour, they threaten instant revenge. Bababalouk, the chief of the eunuchs, is instructed by the vizier to protect Vathek's life; whereupon, as the narrative puts it, 'Bababalouk and his fraternity, felicitating each other in a low voice on their having been spared the cares as well as the honour of paternity, obeyed the mandate of the vizier' (p. 214). The joke about the advantages of castration over parenthood also appears to be (if one may briefly use the anachronistic terminology) about the advantages of homosexuality over heterosexuality. Remember the common association, in the eighteenth and nineteenth centuries, of eunuchs and sodomites, united in their unmanliness. The humorous effect is derived from an evident disproportion between the mass slaughter of the boys and a phrase as bland as 'the cares . . . of paternity'. For once, the tables have been turned, and eunuchs, themselves so often subject to the contempt of bawdy humour, think themselves lucky they have been unable to father sons. That they say so 'in a low voice' rather than a high one is a further disruption of the expected.

Beckford combines such moments of sexual humour with a farrago of violence and sentimentality which only gestures in the direction of profundity, rather than ever putting in much effort actually to be profound. Later in the book the story of the boy Gulchenrouz, 'the most delicate and lovely creature in the world' (p. 239), combines decorative sentimentality with moments of what you might call sadistic camp – as when Carathis, speaking on behalf of the Giaour, says that 'There is nothing so delicious . . . as the heart of a delicate boy palpitating with the first tumults of love' (p. 260). This is no symbolic heart – unless, perhaps, symbolic of a teenager's penis – but a living organ torn from the breast of puberty, ready for eating. It is in moments like this that one recognises not only the black humour of the divine Marquis but also the more hysterical fits of the Gothic novel.

As Mario Praz so definitively established in *The Romantic Agony* (1933), Gothic fiction is essentially an erotic genre, all the more so, retrospectively, in the glare of the post-Freudian spotlight. So many of the Gothic plots could have slipped over, had their authors been inclined (or allowed), into pornography: all those vulnerable single women confined to massive private houses or castles by darkly handsome men; irresponsible rich men at a loose end; feudal social structures in which people are no harder to purchase than livestock; emotional extremes of fear and desire; and so forth – all these elements are present in Sade's novels, where 'sadism' is never held back for propriety's sake but becomes what we know it as today.

Some critics are inclined to make biographical connections here. For instance, in an essay on Horace Walpole, William Beckford and Matthew Lewis, George E. Haggerty remarks: 'It is impossible to chronicle the suffering that went into the creation of the Gothic novel, but the very emergence of anti-homosexual feeling, so evident, for instance, in the case of Beckford, hints at the source of such misery.' The novels of these three writers 'can be seen as an attempt to come to terms with the kinds of inner conflict that the emerging crisis of homosexuality made inevitable'. The madness which their novels explore 'is the mode of discourse which answers the intense private anxieties that these novelists could barely disguise in their fictions'.[10]

Gothic fiction by men, who were so much less restricted by propriety than women, even those women who dared to write Gothic fiction, is full of erotic tension, not only centred on the single girl at risk of rape or worse, but also, if more fitfully, in flashes of attention to the bodies of young men. Take the example of the following short scene in Charles Maturin's *Melmoth the Wanderer* (1820):

> A naked human being, covered in blood, and uttering screams of rage and torture, flashed by me; four monks pursued him – they had lights. I had shut the door at the end of the gallery – I felt they must return and pass me – I was still on my knees, and trembling from head to foot. The victim reached the door, found it shut, and rallied. I turned, and saw a groupe worthy of Murillo. A more perfect human form never existed than that of this unfortunate youth. He stood in an attitude of despair – he was streaming with blood. The monks, with their lights, their scourges, and their dark habits, seemed like a groupe of demons who had made prey of a wandering angel, – the groupe resembled the infernal furies pursuing a mad Orestes. And, indeed, no ancient sculptor ever designed a figure more exquisite and perfect than that they had so barbarously mangled.[11]

It is difficult to imagine Maturin setting such a scene in his present day, the early nineteenth century. Propriety requires its pseudo-medievalism, as if by claiming that such a scene is a realistic representation of the arcane and archaic practices of the Spanish Inquisition, the author can evade responsibility both for having imagined it in the first place and for delivering it to his readers as a source of excitement. Propriety is also served by Maturin's recourse to Greek mythology and the history of art: the figure of Orestes and that of Murillo grant the scene a spuriously 'cultured' seriousness whose main purpose is to diffuse any suspicion of titillation. Such references to Greek myth and Renaissance art crop up throughout the history of modern pornography. But their actual effect – particularly in scenes of violence, like this one – is to pornographise the body. This is not a scene in which obscene violence against the person of a defenceless boy is being deplored, either by author or narrator. The victim's torment is abstracted to the extent of seeming beside the point. The tableau has been aestheticised in such a way as to relieve the reader of the burden of having to care about the boy: his limbs are beautiful, his blood mere spots of paint. We know, and need to know, nothing about the boy himself. Like so many female rape victims throughout Western cultural history, he is not an individual, but mere *frisson* fodder.

Leslie Fiedler once wrote that the early Gothic novelists were working 'at a time when the sole name for the unconscious was "hell"'.[12] This is, I guess, the post-Freudian reading of Gothic in a nutshell. It presupposes what may be considered somewhat implausible similarities between the eighteenth- and the twentieth-century unconscious; but that does not mean we can easily dismiss the persuasive power of Gothic fiction's constant yoking of sexual desire with the threat of violence. Mario Praz convincingly identified the influence of Sade in all of Gothic sensationalism.

An even better exemplar of Sade-ism in Gothic fiction is the earlier novel *The Monk*, written by Matthew Lewis when he was only nineteen and published in 1796. This lavishly intemperate book has as its central character a monk, Ambrosio, 'so strict an observer of Chastity, that he knows not in what consists the difference of Man and Woman'.[13] Since the book begins with an epigraph from *Measure for Measure*, the reader is put on guard by such reports of extremist chastity: for Ambrosio is doubtless to be compared with Shakespeare's Angelo, initially icy but easily melted. As the verses recited by Lewis' Gypsy put it, 'Fair Exteriors oft will hide / Hearts, that swell with lust and pride!' (p. 38). Sure enough, in a plot which relies on the possibilities of disguise – as when a girl called Matilda enters the monastery as a boy called Rosario – and extreme moral reversals, Ambrosio is ultimately tortured by the Inquisition and condemned to be burnt for having committed murder.

The novel's constant recourse to sex and violence to titillate an audience ostensibly more amenable to the persuasive force of Christian piety leaves a vivid impression of moral contingency. The whole narrative equivocates between the high-mindedness of scriptural law and the low-bodiedness of a teenager's sub-pornographic fantasies. There is a characteristic passage, worth quoting in full, when Matilda conjures up the apparition of a 'Daemon' in front of the monk:

> It was a youth seemingly scarce eighteen, the perfection of whose form and face was unrivalled. He was perfectly naked: A bright Star sparkled upon his fore-head; Two crimson wings extended themselves from his shoulders; and his silken locks were confined by a band of many-coloured fires, which played round his head, formed themselves into a variety of figures, and shone with a brilliance far surpassing that of precious Stones. Circlets of diamonds were fastened round his arms and ankles, and in his right hand He bore a silver branch, imitating Myrtle. His form shone with dazzling glory: He was surrounded by clouds of rose-coloured light, and at the moment that He appeared, a refreshing air breathed perfumes through the Cavern. Enchanted at a vision so contrary to his expectations, Ambrosio gazed upon the Spirit with delight and wonder: Yet however beautiful the Figure, He could not but remark a wildness in the Daemon's eyes, and a mysterious melancholy impressed upon his features, betraying the Fallen Angel, and inspiring the Spectators with secret awe. (pp. 276–7)

It is the kind of passage which, in the days when novels were routinely illustrated, must have cried out for illustration. Like the passage I have just quoted from *Melmoth the*

Wanderer, this is clearly intended to appeal to the reader's sense of the visual, although here the picture is not stated to be in any particular artist's style. Having said that this teenage boy is 'perfectly naked' – where 'perfectly' means both completely and in a flawless condition of beauty – the narrative immediately decks him out with ostentatious trinkets. A rather gaudy angel, ornamented with various symbols of eternal health and wealth, he cannot quite carry off the pose without showing signs of internal corruption: the wildness of his eyes and melancholic set of his face betray the fact that he has fallen from grace. One sees this kind of youth in so many later representations of homosexual men: he has kept himself well – but only in body. The sadness of his spiritual condition will always overrule mere physical beauty. The fallen angel may be desirable, but his condition is not to be desired. He may be beautiful, but his beauty is self-consciously constructed to conceal a far uglier reality. The eye is beguiled by this apparition, but the soul is left in a state of indeterminate anxiety by it. He is a vision of moral decay.

Be that as it may, the narrative dwells more on the physical beauty than on the moral ugliness. The reader is seduced by a biased record. And seduction is the point, of course. This demon is the very creature, not only to undermine the resistance of the chaste, but to do so whatever their gender. His very purpose is to weaken the moral fibre of both monks and nuns. In other words, looking at him not only in this instance but also in his many other manifestations elsewhere, this figure is the embodiment of bisexuality. A threat to both sexes – like the mythic 'bridge' conveying HIV from gay men to straight women – he is potentially even more dangerous than the merely homophile sodomite.

Eve Kosofsky Sedgwick's famous work on literature and male homosocial/homosexual desire developed out of her early work on Gothic fiction.[14] According to Sedgwick, 'the Gothic was the first novelistic form in England to have close, relatively visible links to male homosexuality, at a time when styles of homosexuality, and even its visibility and distinctness, were markers of division and tension between classes as much as between genders'. Later in her argument, she adds: 'The Gothic novel crystalised for English audiences the terms of a dialectic between male homosexuality and homophobia, in which homophobia appeared thematically in paranoid plots.'[15]

No less than the violent plots of pornographic libertinism, Gothic fiction has, from the start, dared to speculate, not only on socially unacceptable permutations of flesh, but also on the points of convergence of pleasure and pain, fear and desire, strength and ill health and, of course, love and death. It has put the reader's own sense of security or threat to the test in relation to all of these topics. We know that one of Gothic fiction's principal pleasures derives from the intense feelings of panic it generates. A paranoid panic akin to that of the man who will not turn his back on a gay man is ever reliably generated by the appearance of the Gothic villain. It may come from the breath of the vampire, hotly erecting the hairs on the back of our necks. Do we have time to run away, or would we rather turn and wait? This ultimately self-defining question may govern our reactions to both sadistic pornography and the Gothic plot. It is raised by the infernal attractiveness of the Count in Bram Stoker's *Dracula* (1897), and it is still being raised by the knowing, post-Freudian fantasy/horror novels of Clive Barker or by the homo-erotic antics of the vampire Lestat in Anne Rice's vampire chronicles.

Chapter 11

New Bearings in the Novel

Gay readers seem used to thinking of the novel as the principal site of gay literature. As we have seen, this was not always the case. Gay poetry has the far longer track record. But it is true that towards the end of the nineteenth century, at very roughly the same time that the existence of 'the homosexual' as a distinct type of individual was being definitively established, the novel started to take over from poetry as the best place in which accessibly to express the quotidian realities of homosexual lives. None of this happened suddenly. Looking back on the history of the novel – and much more such looking back needs to be done before gay critics have established a full inventory of the material in question – we find that homosexuality has made its presence felt in various (usually enforced) disguises, even in the most apparently unlikely of texts.

As the pre-eminent 'social' literary medium of the bourgeois-capitalist era, the novel has kept a record not only of changing social attitudes, but even of the minutiae of individual lives. Above all, during the course of the nineteenth century, realist fiction became increasingly adept at representing a broad range of human types, including many – such as members of the working classes – who had made little impression upon previous literatures. As part of the same development, the homosexual person eventually became the homosexual character, a visible presence in the cultures of the industrial revolution.

Since its earliest days the novel has raised issues of relevance to our quest for representations of the lives of same-sex lovers. Tobias Smollett, for instance, included in his novel *Roderick Random* (1748) what Rictor Norton has called 'the earliest extended defence of homosexuality in [English?] literature'. In fact, it is a seduction scene played largely for laughs, in which Earl Strutwell attempts to seduce Roderick Random by urging him to read Petronius and by arguing that male homosexuality is the best defence against the corruption of womankind. In the later novel *Peregrine Pickle* (1751), Smollett gives us early evidence of the practice of blackmailing same-sex lovers in English society: a number of extortioners carry out their business 'by prostituting themselves to the embrace of their own sex, and then threatening their admirers with prosecution'.[1]

Care must be taken, as ever, not to distort such references, or the very tone of whole books, by coming to them with anachronistic assumptions. Retrospective impositions of twentieth-century concepts on early novels are not helpful to anyone. For instance, I remain unconvinced by Pamela Bacarisse's argument that 'Cervantes' treatment of chivalric literature in *Don Quixote* is actually an example of a "Camp" approach'. Since

Bacarisse never treats sexuality as having any crucial bearing on the nature of camp, she never has to consider Hispanic sexual mores in Cervantes' day in justification of her apparently anachronistic use of 'camp' as a critical term in relation to Cervantes' work (published in 1605 and 1615). Instead, she performs a sketchy comparison of Cervantes with the Argentine novelist Manuel Puig on the grounds that 'both of them are parodying themselves, and that this is the essence of "Camp"'. In fact, it looks as though the word she is seeking throughout her essay is the somewhat unfashionable term 'irony'. For irony to become camp a further dimension is required, to do with gender roles and sexuality; and Bacarisse shows no sign of believing that such a dimension exists in Cervantes. This may, indeed, be the major *difference* between the parodic modes of Cervantes and Puig.[2]

There are times when one feels an overwhelming urge to expand the boundaries of what is meant when one speaks of 'gay literature', or the 'gay novel', at least as far as to include not only representations of queer people by writers of whichever sexual orientation, but also characters who are merely regarded by others as being, even slightly, 'strange' in ways related if not to sexuality itself, then to gender identity or marital status. Let me try to clarify this point in relation to one example, that of Henry Tilney, in Jane Austen's *Northanger Abbey* (finished in 1803 but not published until 1818).[3]

It seems to have been clear to Austen that there are two branches of discourse, the male – which regarded itself as the serious mainstream – and the female – which men regarded as trivial and marginal. There is a men's way of talking and a women's. What makes Henry Tilney perfect in the role of suitor to Catherine Morland is that he does not fit the pattern; and what makes John Thorpe odious is that he does. When Thorpe takes Catherine out for a drive, his conversation ('or rather talk') is completely taken up with dreary anecdotes about horse races and boasts about his own prowess at betting, shooting and hunting (p. 85). Catherine is bored. On the other hand, what makes Henry Tilney such pleasant company is that he is not so single-mindedly wrapped up in what Jane Austen sees as entirely male concerns. He is both able and willing to meet women on their own ground. Thus, when Mrs Allen asks him, apropos of the gown she is wearing, 'Do you understand muslins, sir?', he is able to give an informed reply about both quality and cost. Mrs Allen is impressed by the extent to which he differs in this respect from her husband ('I can never get Mr Allen to know one of my gowns from another'). Wanting to hear more of this prodigy of approachable masculinity, she asks him what he thinks of Catherine's dress. His reply – 'It is very pretty, madam . . . but I do not think it will wash well; I am afraid it will fray' – is so unusual that, for all the equanimity of her light-heartedness, Catherine appears to be a bit shocked by it: '"How can you," said Catherine, laughing, "be so – " she had almost said, strange'.

While not wishing to make too much of this scene (pp. 49–50), I do feel that it betrays a slight shudder of anxiety, in Catherine, of course, but also, perhaps, in Jane Austen herself. To be sure, Catherine respects the aspect of Henry which this conversation reveals, partly because she too has experience of not fitting snugly into her gender role. (We know that, as a child, she was a tomboy – p. 37.) But by virtue of the fact that she is almost rude enough to call him 'strange' – and that the rudeness of the epithet is proven by her suppression of it – we can see that Henry has come close to a point of true strangeness, where eccentricity threatens to become transgressive. Why, he is so strange that he is almost . . . not the marrying kind.

Remember that in Austen's world a single man above a certain age – a bachelor, though, not a widower – is a very strange figure indeed, particularly if he has chosen to live in that condition. It may be that the opening sentence of *Pride and Prejudice* (1813), so famous for its irony, is not ironic at all. Or rather, it is ironic only at a superficial level. 'It is a truth universally acknowledged, that a single man in possession of a good fortune, must be in want of a wife.' The hyperbole of the first six words does not undo the fact that the rest of the sentence is meant in earnest. While I admit that the scene in *Northanger Abbey* may not quite conjure up the extreme of homosexuality, it certainly does raise the issue of effeminacy in men. Probably, Austen is thinking of that eighteenth-century brand of effeminacy which involved liking women's company too much, rather than not enough; but what matters – both in the scene in question and at this stage in my argument – is that, allowed to become extreme, such effeminacy might make a man unmarriageable. Briefly, subliminally, Jane Austen has conjured up the spectacle of Henry Tilney *dressed in drag*.

Jane Austen does refer to buggery at least once, however. There is a moment in *Mansfield Park* (1814) when Mary Crawford, a relatively worldly woman brought up among naval folk, lets slip an obscene joke while genteelly disclaiming responsibility for doing so. She says: 'Certainly, my home at my uncle's brought me acquainted with a circle of admirals. Of *Rears* and *Vices*, I saw enough. Now do not be suspecting me of a pun, I entreat.' All Edmund can gravely say in reply is 'It is a noble profession.'[4] This joke – Mary Crawford's and Jane Austen's – should be appreciated in the context of the fact that, after the 1797 mutinies at the Nore and the Spithead, executions for buggery were greatly increased by the Navy.[5] Mary's crude remark has a degree of topicality.

Perhaps the narrative moment at which anxieties about insecure manifestations of masculinity are most commonly aired (and more and more so later, as the homosexual *Bildungsroman* begins to flourish in the twentieth century) is when a boy begins to arouse the suspicions of his elders, that he is failing to attain the virile goals demanded of him by the mere fact of his sex. The spectre of the over-protected boy is conjured up in the third chapter of Anne Brontë's *The Tenant of Wildfell Hall* (1848) in the person of Arthur Graham, a child in danger of being permanently weakened by his excessively solicitous mother.[6] That, at least, is the opinion of Mrs Markham, the mother of the narrator. When little Arthur's mother says she does not like to leave him alone at home when she goes out, Mrs Markham replies: 'You should try to suppress such foolish fondness, as well to save your son from ruin as yourself from ridicule.' Clearly, ruin is a somewhat extreme extrapolation from close parenting, and Mrs Markham does not specify what kind of ruin it is that she is predicting as the outcome of 'spoiling the child'; but the main point here appears to be the one which would be made more explicit and become a matter of even greater popular anxiety in the twentieth century: boys with over-loving mothers are liable to end up leading unmanly manhoods.

The two mothers' opposed views develop into a discussion or, as the chapter's title has it, 'A Controversy'. When it transpires that Mrs Graham has been nurturing in her son a distaste for wine – so as to save him from at least one 'degrading vice' in adulthood – Mrs Markham is reduced to tears of laughter. Wiping her eyes, she says: 'I really gave you credit for having more sense – The poor child will be the veriest milksop that ever was sopped! Only think what a man you will make of him, if you persist in – '. Mrs Graham interrupts at this point, but it is the first half of Mrs Markham's last sentence that is of interest. The over-protected boy's upbringing appears to be raising the possibility that his mother will 'make of him' a man who is flawed.

As their argument continues, Mrs Markham makes her point for a third time, now more explicitly: 'Well, but you will treat him like a girl – you'll spoil his spirit, and make a mere Miss Nancy of him – you will indeed, Mrs Graham, whatever you may think.' This is the crux of the issue. The suitable upbringing for a boy is different from that for a girl: less interventive at the parenting stage, but more so at the schooling. If a boy is treated 'like a girl' – narrowly, in the context of this chapter, if his mother refuses to leave him at home on his own, discourages in him a taste for alcohol, and attempts to educate him herself – then he will never develop the appropriate 'spirit' for manhood. Worst of all, he may turn into 'a mere Miss Nancy'.

The *Oxford English Dictionary* refers to the use of this phrase in William Carr's *The Dialect of Craven, in the West-Riding of the County of York* (1824): 'A Miss-nancy is an effeminate man.' That much is obvious. Our problem is, as ever, to determine what 'effeminate' meant at the time. It is not possible to be exact about when, in Britain, 'Nancy' came to denote a specifically homosexual type of effeminacy. At any rate, the discussion in Anne Brontë's novel goes no further in its explicitness than I have already reported. It may be that sexuality is not relevant at all to Mrs Markham's vision of the wrong kind of man – though in most such cases in nineteenth-century fiction the question is raised, albeit left implicit, whether such a man, flawed in his very manhood, might not make a particularly good husband and father.

Rounding off the chapter, Gilbert Markham reflects on his own relationship with his mother: 'Perhaps, too, I was a little bit spoilt by my mother and sister, and some other ladies of my acquaintance; – and yet, I was by no mean a fop – of that I am fully convinced, whether *you* are or not.' Regardless of the aggressive defensiveness of the closing phrase, there is a concession here which cuts across Mrs Markham's argument: she too pampers her son, even if only 'a little bit', and yet he – although he is speaking as his own defensive witness – shows no sign of becoming a 'fop'. This term is not usually related to homosexuality – as we have seen, the fops and dandies of English culture are generally aggressive womanisers – and it may be that Gilbert's reference to foppishness at this stage in the argument is conclusive. Excessive interest in fine clothing, while eventually a suspect trait in any man, is not the same thing as a propensity for sodomy.

Girlish boys have certain uses, however. The capability that beautiful boys have of seducing heterosexual men who believe them to be beautiful women is often taken for granted in nineteenth-century French novels, requiring neither explanation nor excuse. An episode of this kind takes place in chapters 37 and 38 of Alexandre Dumas' *The Count of Monte Cristo* (*Le Comte de Monte-Cristo*, 1844–5) when Albert de Morcerf is kidnapped during the Roman carnival by the brigand Luigi Vampa.[7] Albert flirts with an unknown woman – she is masked at first, but she does grant him a glimpse of her face, which he finds 'charming' – and, by exchange of notes in bouquets of flowers, arranges to meet her on his own. He thereby falls into a trap. As is subsequently explained when Monte Cristo intervenes to have him released, the 'woman' is not 'Teresa' at all, but Beppo, a fifteen-year-old boy. But as one of the bandits explains to Franz d'Epinay, 'it was no disgrace to your friend to have been deceived. Beppo has taken in plenty of others.' Apparently, then, it does not require the Bakhtinian conditions of a carnival for this trick to work: Beppo is performing it constantly.

However, the main point I wish to make about this sequence is related to what Dumas does not bother to say. Although Albert is soon 'in love with' the masked woman he pursues through the streets of Rome, Dumas wastes no effort in actually describing the beauty which proves to be so dangerously seductive. When Beppo is, in either sense, eventually unmasked, no attempt is made to suggest that his looks are exceptional. Indeed, through the course of two whole chapters, we are really only given two fleeting signs to convince us that such a man as Albert could so easily mistake a boy like Beppo for such a woman as he imagines 'Teresa' to be. In the first place, we have that maskless moment when the apparently female face is described as being 'charming' – hardly an effusive or excessive epithet. And secondly, when the seductress turns out to be a mere boy – not even a boy explicitly described as being beautiful – we learn that Beppo is fifteen. Presumably, these two facts alone are thought to be enough to account for the incident. Indeed, so little anxiety about gender is provoked in Albert by these events – none at all, in fact – that it seems one is meant to assume that *any* man would willingly have danced his way into the same trap. A fifteen-year-old boy will be charming enough.

A slightly earlier French novel, Théophile Gautier's hauntingly erotic *Mademoiselle de Maupin* (1835), allows the theme of disguised gender much more room for development.[8] The narrator, a young man called d'Albert, has never yet had a love affair; but, being in love with the idea of love, he fully intends to have one. He seems primed for an unusual experience, to say the least – or he is rather voguishly posing as being so primed. Like a late-nineteenth-century decadent, he establishes his individuality with certain outspoken assertions of distance from bourgeois domesticity: 'I adore everything which is singular, dangerous and excessive' (p. 56); 'Whatever I am waiting for, it is certainly nothing ordinary or commonplace' (p. 59). But the question arises as to whether he really has the strength of character and purpose to confront excess when it presents itself to him, or whether he will anxiously fall back on the ordinary and the commonplace.

Still a virgin at the age of twenty-two, d'Albert is yearning to take his first mistress. This is stated, at one point, in what seems to be a curiously defensive way: 'after all, what I want is legitimate, and nature owes it to every man' (p. 62). This invocation of both legitimacy and naturalness in the same breath suggests that the existence of love affairs which are neither legitimate nor natural has occurred to him. (As we shall see, in fact, he is quite well read in the classical literature of male love.) His heterosexuality seems by no means a foregone conclusion. He is conscious that it may lapse – even if his statement of this consciousness tends to look like an overstated pose: 'To tell the truth, I have so many daydreams and aberrations, that I'm terribly afraid of degenerating into the monstrous and the unnatural' (p. 90).

Furthermore, even while searching the streets of Paris for a mistress, d'Albert openly admits to finding the generality of women ugly: 'I must confess that what we have agreed to call the fair sex is devilishly ugly; out of a hundred women, hardly one was passable'. One is not surprised to find that he is applying a classic double standard to the question: 'how much uglier a woman is if she is not beautiful than a man if he is not handsome!' (p. 71).

As his sexual career develops, he is not satisfied by the emotional sufficiency of his status as a mere man. He has transsexual fantasies: 'I have never wanted anything so much as to meet on the mountain, like Tiresias the prophet, those serpents that make you change your sex'. He amplifies this thought as follows: 'I began by wanting to be another man. Then I reflected that I could, by analogy, pretty much foresee what I should feel, and I shouldn't know the changes and surprises which I expected. I should therefore have preferred to be a woman; this idea has always occurred to me, when I had a mistress who wasn't ugly; for an ugly woman is a man to me' (p. 102). There is a good deal of narcissism involved in this fantasy: for he only wants to be the kind of woman whom he himself would desire – indeed, the very mistress he is yearning for, a woman whom he himself could fuck. What he does not mention, perhaps because he does not yet know it, is that, conversely, a beautiful man is a woman to him. He names the sexes according to the location of his desire.

A crucial turning-point occurs in chapter 5. Much of the chapter consists of d'Albert's thoughts on the topic of beauty. Like a dutifully narcissistic aesthete, he begins by applying the concept to himself: 'The only thing in the world which I have wanted with some consistency is to be beautiful. When I say beautiful, I mean as beautiful as Paris or Apollo' (p. 139). As an ambition, this is both grandiose and shallow. He elaborates on it a little while later, still using classical references to establish his high standard of male beauty; but by this point it is no longer clear that he is only speaking of the beauty which he himself would aspire to. He appears, also, to be speaking of the kinds of men he would wish to see and to admire: 'And if a man had supreme beauty and supreme strength as well: if, under the skin of Antinous [beloved of Hadrian], he had the muscles of Hercules [lover of Hylas, Eurystheus and Ioläus], what more could he desire?' (p. 141). Not only would such a creature be homosexually approachable; but he would also be sexually flexible, both lover and beloved, fucker and fucked – ideally beautiful not just visibly, but also in bed.

Soon after reaffirming his transsexual fantasy – 'I have wanted to be a woman so that I might know new sensual pleasures' (p. 143) – d'Albert finds a new opportunity for reflexive speculation opening up before him. A young man of singular, androgynous beauty arrives in the household he is staying in.

> No one could be more graceful; he isn't very tall, but he's slim and shapely; there is something gentle and undulating about his gait and movements which I find extremely agreeable; many women would envy him his hands and feet. His only fault is to be too beautiful, and to have features which are too delicate for a man. He is endowed with the darkest and most beautiful eyes in the world; they have an indefinable expression, and their gaze is difficult to bear. But, as he is very young and has no sign of a beard, the softness and perfection of the lower part of his face somewhat temper the sharpness of his eagle's eyes; his glossy brown hair floats in big curls over his shoulders, and gives his head particular character. There is one of those types of beauty that I dreamed of, realised at last, before my eyes. What a pity that it is a man, or what a pity that I'm not a woman! (p. 146)

This effeminate youth, then, raises the core question of sexual roles. Since sexual intercourse would require one male body and one female, what kind of intercourse could possibly come of d'Albert's desire for this boy? One of them would have to play the man and one the woman – the manliness no less of a role than the womanliness – but which would be which? Although this man's youth excuses his beardlessness (unlike the stigmatic situation of Chaucer's Pardoner), there is something potentially culpable about the sheer extent of his facial beauty. Male prettiness involves connotations of sexual transgression: precisely, of the potential for submission to being sodomised.

Now, the beautiful newcomer, who is called Théodore, appears already to be involved in some kind of homo-erotic relationship: for he has brought with him his page, a boy of fourteen or fifteen, as beautiful as his master – and equally feminine: 'The master was as beautiful as a woman, the page was as beautiful as a young girl' (p. 148). (D'Albert has changed his tune since he spoke of the ugliness of woman; now she is the standard even of male beauty.) When d'Albert first gets a chance to observe the two of them together, the master has adopted a distinctly unmasterly position at the feet of the servant:

> The young man, who was still on his knees, contemplated these two little feet with loving and admiring attention; he bent down, took the left one and kissed it, then the right one and kissed that, too; and then, kiss by kiss, he went up the leg to the place where the material began. The page slightly opened his long eyelids, and cast a drowsy and benevolent glance at his master, a glance which revealed no sense of surprise. (p. 148)

The page dozes off; and while his young master watches him sleeping – for two whole hours – d'Albert in turn watches this touching tableau of man and boy, apparent lovers masquerading as master and servant. As he rather superfluously says to himself and the reader, 'What were the links that bound the master to the page, the page to the master? Certainly there was more between them than the affection which can exist between master and servant' (p. 149). He speculates on their being friends or brothers, but seems to feel that the fact of their disguising their true roles must suggest a relationship in much greater need of secrecy.

The tone of d'Albert's observation – and Gautier's creation – of this scene becomes increasingly voyeuristic, particularly with regard to the pageboy's chest. It seems to be that of a pubescent girl: 'two or three buttons on the jerkin had been undone to make breathing easier, and they allowed one to glimpse . . . a lozenge of plump and buxom flesh of admirable whiteness, and the beginning of a curve which was difficult to explain on the breast of a young boy; if you looked closely, you might also have found that the hips were a little too developed'. Presumably, d'Albert did 'look closely' with that stern, measuring glance, and he clearly expects the reader to do so too. Moments later, he actually takes the liberty of challenging the (male) reader to imagine this curve of white flesh in greater detail than he himself is going to divulge: 'If the reader is less short-sighted than we are, let him cast his eyes under the lace of that shirt and decide honestly whether that curve is too rounded or not' (p. 149). By this stage, the novel has become avid in its generation of a pornographic atmosphere whose purpose is to make the reader imagine in detail the shapes, beginning with that ambiguous curve, of an androgynous physique.

Without realising that he is being watched by d'Albert and all the rest of us, Théodore continues to gaze at his sleeping page and says out loud to himself:

How beautiful he is like that! If I weren't afraid of waking him, I should devour him with kisses. What an adorable dimple in his chin! What a white and delicate skin! Sleep well, my darling. I am really jealous of your mother, I wish that I had given birth to you. (p. 150)

These extremely unmanly sentiments, switching as they do from ardent homo-eroticism to emasculatory uterus-envy, perplex d'Albert's residual sense of the masculine proprieties; but they may also offer him some hope: for he is beginning to fall in love with the newcomer. The latter's susceptibility to male charms, albeit those of a very young boy, may encourage d'Albert even as it plagues him with worries about the direction his love-life appears to be about to take.

The moment of truth comes in the final paragraph of chapter 8, when d'Albert's growing emotional panic is addressed in a letter to his friend Silvio:

You pitied me for not loving. Pity me now for loving whom I love. What misfortune, what an axe-blow on my life, which was already cut in so many pieces! What senseless, guilty, hateful passion has taken hold of me! It is a disgrace, and I shall never cease to blush for it. It is the most deplorable of all my aberrations, I can't begin to understand it, I don't comprehend it in the least, everything in me is upside-down and in confusion; I no longer know who I am or what others are, I wonder if I'm a man or a woman, I have a horror of myself, I feel singular and inexplicable urges, and there are moments when I feel that my mind is going, and the sense of my existence has quite gone. For a long time I could not believe what had happened. I watched and listened to myself attentively. I tried to unravel this tangled skein which had become caught up in my soul. At last, through the veils which shrouded it, I discovered the appalling truth . . . Silvio, I love ... Oh, no, I could never tell you . . . I love a man! (p. 181; ellipses in the original)

So this is how a Frenchman came out to himself (and to his closest friend) in 1835. Note that he believes his life has fundamentally changed. He is not simply disturbed at the thought that he has, just this once and temporarily, been physically aroused by a man's body, nor even by that thought's implication, that he could act on that arousal and make love with the male body in question. No, the issue goes much deeper than that, and is a question of the essence of his personality, rather than just a fleeting physical aberration. His very identity seems to have changed ('I no longer know who I am'), as may his biological sex ('I wonder if I'm a man or a woman'). The situation has also raised a fundamental question about his mental health ('I feel that my mind is going').

Thus, suddenly, in the all too real presence of what would later come to be called homosexuality, all of his modish pretensions to aestheticism and decadence are dashed to pieces on the anvil of homosexual panic. As the next chapter opens d'Albert elaborates on both his feelings for Théodore and how he feels about those feelings. His observations on the appearance of the man he is in love with turn into an essay on homosexuality. What has developed between them is not what would be expected between two men: 'I love that young man, not in friendship, but with love – yes, with love'. The oddity of the situation is underlined by the fact that d'Albert is heterosexually inexperienced, and cannot even compare what he feels now with what he has felt, heterosexually, in the past: 'never have I found any woman so singularly disturbing' (p. 182).

He tries, perhaps rather forlornly, to persuade himself that his original impressions were correct, and that the womanish man is, after all, a woman dressed as a man. He looks at Théodore in his dressing gown ('which looked rather like a woman's dress') and is convinced of the opposite of his conclusions the previous night: 'he seemed not the handsomest of men, but the most beautiful of women' (p. 183). An excess of beauty has ambushed the unsuspecting aesthete, who writes to his friend Silvio: 'Théodore must be a woman in disguise; otherwise the thing is impossible. That beauty is excessive, even for a woman. It is not the beauty of a man, were he Antinous, the friend of Adrian, or were he Alexis, the friend of Virgil. It is a woman, I am sure' (p. 184). If nothing else, in these anguished passages he establishes that his reading on these matters is quite extensive:

> Those strange loves which fill the elegies of the ancient poets, those loves which so surprised us, those loves which we could not conceive, are, then, probable and possible. In the translations we made of them, we put women's names in place of the names that were there. Juventus ended as Juventia, Alexis was changed into Ianthe. Beautiful boys became beautiful girls, and so we recomposed the monstrous seraglios of Catullus, Tibullus, Martial and gentle Virgil. It was a very gallant occupation which only proved how little we had understood the classical genius. (p. 186)

This understanding of the systematic eighteenth- and nineteenth-century hetero-sexualisation, and indeed bourgeoisification, of the literature of classical pederasty shows that d'Albert is quick to think of himself within a much wider context than the limits of his own sexual desire.

D'Albert continues to agonise about the potential shame of his situation, even after having claimed: 'What is remarkable is that I hardly think about his sex any more, and that I love him with perfect confidence' (p. 197). He has clearly been determined to overcome his initial scruples, but always in the hope that his suspicions will prove well founded, and that his beloved will turn out to be a woman after all. Every now and then, however, that confidence falters and he returns to the nagging issue of homosexuality: 'suppose my presentiment deceived me, and Théodore were really a man, as all the world believes!'

Testing this uncomfortable hypothesis yet again, he looks set to come down on the side of love rather than that of conventional, bourgeois morality: 'If I came to know for certain that Théodore was not a woman, alas! I am not at all sure that I shouldn't love him still' (pp. 199–200) – and he means, in accordance with his earlier distinction between love and friendship, that his love would continue to derive from a root in physical desire.

Meanwhile, Mademoiselle de Maupin – for it is she – gives an epistolary account of her secret life as the dashing young chevalier Théodore. Writing to her friend Graciosa, she tells how she came to be living as a man, and how she came to be employing a young girl as her pageboy. Like d'Albert, along the way she has stumbled across the strangeness of her own desires. Unlike him, she acts on them, all the time pretending to be a man. Not that she is entirely reconciled to the exact kind of love she has been experiencing: 'I have been loved, O Graciosa! And it is sweet, although I have only been loved by a woman, and, in a love so deviant, there was something painful not to be found in ordinary love' (p. 272). However, there is a suggestion, as so often in subsequent gay literature, that the pain is worth having.

She compares herself, as d'Albert has previously been comparing himself, with those around her, and finds that 'Many men are more feminine than I am' (presumably, d'Albert himself is one of the men she means). Throughout her account she shows herself to be a keen observer of sexual behaviour. It is she, not d'Albert, who turns out to be the novel's truly pioneering theorist of sexuality: for it is she who is the novel's true queer. Generalising on what she has observed on her travels, she says: 'It often happens that the sex of the soul is not the same as that of the body, and this contradiction cannot fail to produce a great deal of confusion' (p. 273). And she later gives voice to certain ideas which would be commonplace much later in the century:

> I belong to a third sex, a sex apart, which has as yet no name: higher or lower, inferior or superior; I have the body and soul of a woman, the spirit and the strength of a man, and I have too much or too little of either to be able to couple with the other. (p. 330)

Different in essence from all the people she encounters, she can really only conceive of satisfactorily coupling with another creature like herself, a creature sufficiently different from the bourgeois models of masculine and feminine to contain the supposedly incompatible qualities of both.

When d'Albert finally writes a love letter to 'Théodore', announcing that he knows she is a woman, he oddly does not stop addressing her as a man, and he appears to be maintaining, unaltered, his original distaste for the generality of women. He seems still to want the manliness that so attractively fused itself with her body, but he is relieved not to have to cope with his own deviancy any longer. It may be that he wants the pleasure of a boyfriend without the inevitable guilt and shame that having a boyfriend would involve. Again he has recourse to classical homo-erotic references when he asks his beloved, 'What loving nymph has fused her body with your own, in the midst of a kiss, O beautiful young man, more charming than Cyparissus and Adonis, more adorable than all women?' Such beauty might have been acceptable in a male in classical times, but d'Albert proves himself far more conventional than he ever admits in disallowing the aptness of male beauty – despite his susceptibility to it – to the times he is living in.

He relieves his own anxiety by declaring his beloved to be of the proper sex, which is to say female: 'But you are a woman, we are no longer in the age of metamorphoses. Adonis and Hermaphroditus are dead – and this degree of beauty may no longer be attained by a man' (pp. 296–7). His guilt and confusion have evaporated, at least for as long as what he here maintains remains true. As he says, 'You are a woman, and my love is no longer reprehensible, I can give myself to it without remorse, and abandon myself to the tide which bears me towards you; however great, however wild the passion that I feel, it is permissible and I can confess it' (p. 300).

The outcome of this comedy of inadmissible desires is that 'Théodore' comes to d'Albert wearing female clothes – they have been staging a performance of *As You Like It*, and 'he' comes dressed as Rosalind – and they make uncontroversially heterosexual love, even if, somehow, there remains something of a man called 'Théodore' in the spaces between them. However, Gautier does not provide a happy ending of loving bliss for this multi-faceted couple. On the morning after Mademoiselle de Maupin has made love with d'Albert, Théodore and his pretty little page take their leave, and d'Albert is left to balance out the satisfactions of the night against the disappointments of that morning and of mornings to come.

. . .

Midway between the evil libertine of Sadean pornography and the morally blameless homosexual man of mid-twentieth-century apologist fiction is one of the great characters of the realist novel, Honoré de Balzac's Vautrin (real name Jacques Collin, also known as 'Trompe-la-Mort', Carlos Herrera, etc.). The main predecessor to Marcel Proust's Baron de Charlus, he is without doubt the most complex and compelling queer character in nineteenth-century fiction. His main appearances are in *Père Goriot* (*Le Père Goriot*, 1834) as Vautrin, in *Lost Illusions* (*Illusions perdues*, 1837–43) as Herrera, and in *A Harlot High and Low* (*Splendeurs et misères des courtisanes*, 1839–47) as Herrera and Collin. In simplistic gay liberationist terms he definitely constitutes a 'negative image' of homosexuality, being a murderer and a thief. But he is also disturbingly attractive. Balzac may have based Vautrin on an ex-convict called François-Eugène Vidocq, who ended up running an early manifestation of the French Sûreté.[9]

The key encounter in *Lost Illusions* occurs in a very famous scene towards the end of the book, when the supposed Abbé Herrera (Jacques Collin, aged forty-six, has stolen the identity of a man he has murdered) meets the suicidal young poet Lucien Chardon at the roadside and picks him up: 'the stranger turned round and seemed to be struck by the poet's profoundly melancholy beauty'; indeed, in this revealing moment of recognition, Herrera looks like 'a hunter coming upon a prey long and vainly tracked' (p. 635). On hearing that Lucien is an atheist, the older man grabs hold of his arm 'with maternal eagerness' (pp. 635–6). Within minutes, Lucien reveals that he is about to kill himself, and Herrera offers him, instead of death, both wealth and power.

This moment of motherliness is characteristic of the way Herrera always treats his young protégés. The filial role is one of several he demands of them. As he says to Lucien, 'You want to be a soldier? I will be your commanding officer. Obey me as a wife obeys her husband, as a child obeys her mother, and I guarantee that in less than three years' time you'll be the Marquis de Rubempré' (p. 649). Each will be of each sex, swapping roles in a continuity of emotional flexibility, now one the master of the other's heart, the master now the victim of the other's systematic humiliations, and yet each the equal of the other insofar as they exist and flourish in mutual dependency.

As they walk along the country lane, still arm in arm, Herrera speaks of vice: 'How does a vice get such a stranglehold? From its inherent strength or from human weakness? Are there certain cravings which border on insanity?' (p. 639). These are precisely the questions which his experiment on Lucien will be seen to raise. A few moments later, he manhandles the boy into his carriage and they drive off together. Lucien is not at all concerned at this rapacious turn of events – he had, after all, been at an extremely low point before Herrera happened along, and he is being offered an alternative of the implausible type that he could never seriously have anticipated. Indeed, he allows himself to be persuaded by the stranger's pleasantness and infected by his insistent optimism: 'The Spanish priest seemed so genuinely affectionate that the poet did not hesitate to open his heart to him' (p. 640). He is already in Herrera's power.

Vulnerable or not, Lucien is in no mood to resist the glamorous stranger's blandishments: 'the diplomat's effort at corruption made a deep impression on a man only too disposed to welcome it' (p. 645). Herrera expects, and has good reason to expect, everyone he encounters to be amenable to corruption, just so long as the moral weak point of that person can be located. According to Herrera's cynical philosophy, 'we are all at the beck and call of something, perhaps a vice, perhaps a need' (p. 648). He himself is mainly driven by his desire to control the lives of certain attractive younger men like Eugène de Rastignac in *Père Goriot* and Lucien, here. And his main way of gaining influence over such youths is to identify their own vices or needs. Essentially, he seduces by blackmail. Adding to the above remark, he urges Lucien to 'observe the law of laws: secretiveness!' The greater the developing need for discretion, the more effective the possible future threat of a strategic indiscretion.

Apparently establishing the basis of their future relationship, Herrera gives Lucien a brief lesson in gay literature and, thereby, in gay love: 'Have you pondered over Otway's *Venice preserved*? Have you understood the deep friendship between man and man which binds Pierre to Jaffeir, makes them indifferent about women and alters all social relationships for them?' (p. 654). But in fact Herrera also wants his relationship with Lucien to work in a very different way: 'I want to love a creation of my own, shape it, mould it to my purposes so that I may love it as a father loves his progeny' (p. 655). This is much more to the point: for Herrera wants, not power over Lucien himself (though that too will be necessary), but to exert power *through* Lucien. By the end of the novel the younger man knows that he is no longer in control of his own destiny. In a letter to his sister, he writes: 'Instead of committing suicide, I have bartered my life. I belong to myself no longer. I'm nothing more than the secretary of a Spanish diplomat [Herrera]. I'm his creature' (p. 673).

In *A Harlot High and Low*, Herrera gives the 'harlot' Esther a lecture on a certain kind of love 'unconfessed before men'. His vehemence looks like a kind of sincerity that may be based in personal experience. When Esther asks what kind of love he means, he replies:

> The love which is without hope, when it is the inspiration of a life, when that life is governed by its devotion, when every action is ennobled by the thought of reaching an ideal perfection. Yes, the angels approve such a love; it leads to the knowledge of God. To perfect oneself unceasingly in order to be worthy of the loved one, to make a thousand hidden sacrifices for him, adore him from a distance, give one's blood drop by drop, for him to destroy all self-love, all pride and anger, to spare him even the knowledge of whatever pangs of jealousy he may cause, give him whatever he wishes, even to our own detriment, love what he loves, to keep one's face turned towards him and to follow him without him knowing; religion would have forgiven you such a love, it offended against neither human nor divine law, and led to other courses than that of your filthy pleasures. (p. 43)

His meaning is that Esther's kind of love is unworthy of Lucien. To her ears, the male pronouns throughout the speech make sense, since they refer to the man who might thus be loved by a woman – if not by a woman like her – but from his own point of view, it appears, he is speaking of a kind of love which he, unlike her, is capable of giving a man. This reads like one of those old arguments promoting 'spiritual' relationships between men above the irredeemably physical relation of man and woman. Herrera certainly shows evidence, despite his need to exert control, that he is capable of a devotional kind of love, in which any action may be justified as having been performed for the sake of the loved one. His power over his protégés is protective to a maternal degree. Slightly later, the older man says to the younger: 'Child, you have in old Herrera a mother absolutely devoted', to which Lucien obligingly replies: 'I know, my dear' (p. 65).

Like Mademoiselle de Maupin, Herrera is beginning to formulate a theory of deviant sexualities. He too has come up with the metaphor of the soul of one sex existing within the body of an individual of the opposite sex. He says that Lucien has 'the soul of a woman' (p. 372). I think it would be uncontroversial to say that their relationship is infused with an eroticism which does not really seem to be present in other such emotional transactions between powerful, older benefactors and their young male beneficiaries in nineteenth-century fiction. (For instance, consider the relationship which develops between Pip and Magwitch in Dickens' *Great Expectations*, 1860–61.)

During the fascinating prison episode at the climax of this book – which anticipates so many of the themes of Jean Genet's novels – we learn that 'Trompe-le-Mort' (Dodgedeath, his prison nickname) has another boyfriend: 'Théodore Calvi, a young Corsican, sentenced to life imprisonment for eleven murders, at the age of eighteen, thanks to influence which had been dearly bought, had been Jacques Collin's chain mate from 1819 to 1820' (p. 427). The boy's prison name is Madeleine. They escaped from jail together but then got separated, and Collin was searching for Théodore at the time when he first encountered Lucien. Now, as Collin is in prison again – but still in disguise as the priest Herrera – he hears from certain convicts, once his own cellmates, that Théodore, now twenty-seven, is on death row. The news almost causes this pillar of strength to collapse.

This section of the book gives the reader a brief but invaluable education in prisoners' slang, starting with the most useful noun, 'queen' (*tante*):

> For the benefit of those readers who don't know what a *queen* is, we may recall the words of the governor of one of the central prisons to the late Lord Durham, who visited all the prisons during his stay in Paris [. . .] The governor, having shown him round the whole prison, the yards, the workshops, the dungeons, etc., pointed to one building with an expression of disgust.
> 'I shan't take Your Lordship there,' he said, 'for that's the *queens*' quarters . . .'
> 'Really!' said Lord Durham, 'and what are they?'
> 'That's the third sex, my lord.' (pp. 453–4)

This institutional recognition and segregation of a major new sexual category makes the prison the perfectly appropriate place for the climax of a criminal relationship between two men. The very language of the place is suitably deviant. (In this section of the novel Rayner Heppenstall's 1970 translation makes a valiant effort to substitute British queer slang of the 1960s for the arcane mysteries of the original. Indeed, he makes a better job of this than most of Jean Genet's translators.) The prison authorities themselves are aware of, and seem to tolerate, the intense love that may develop between two men. When Lucien eventually does commit suicide, Herrera grieves as a parent. Given the terrible news, he says to the prison governor and the doctor, 'If you're fathers, you're only that and no more; . . . I'm a mother too!' (p. 430, ellipsis in the original). Taken to see the boy's body, he embraces it passionately, convincing the doctor that this is his son, but leaving the governor, who knows more about these things, doubting it: he can recognise homosexual love when he sees it.

The authorities leave Herrera alone with Lucien's body for five hours, and Balzac invites his readers, even the most homophobically hostile among them, to imagine the intensity of his grief, rather than passively to have it described to them. This is an interesting strategy of involvement, in keeping with the very fact of Balzac's having raised the topic of male love in the first place. He positions Herrera, as it were, between two corpses:

> Even those who are least susceptible to any feeling of sympathy with this strange world may yet imagine Jacques Collin's state of mind, between the corpse of the idol he had worshipped five hours that night and the impending death of his old chain-mate, the future corpse of the young Corsican Théodore. (p. 459)

It is not made clear which 'strange world' is being referred to here. Presumably, it means both the prison in general and the 'third sex' wing in particular. The reader is asked to identify, if only for a fleeting moment, with both. Later in the same day, Herrera begins to articulate his grief, and he does so by invoking familiar roles – 'Ah! never did a good mother tenderly love her only son as I loved that angel' – though he is, in virtually the same breath, critical as a mother may be critical: 'He was weak, that was his only fault . . . Lucien should have been a woman' (p. 514). (One of his pet names for the boy had been Lulu.) Referring to his agonising encounter with Lucien's corpse, he waxes sacrilegious in a pre-Genetan way: 'the body I was kissing like a madman, like a mother, as the Virgin must have kissed Jesus at the entombment' (p. 515). This is as sacred as his rhetoric ever gets; it revels in intentional profanity.

Even in the depths of his grief, Collin sets about plotting to save his beloved Théodore from execution. Still dressed as Herrera, he gets to visit the young man. The narrative sets out the twenty-seven-year-old Calvi's appearance as follows:

> Théodore Calvi, a young man of sallow complexion, fair-haired, with deep-set, ambiguously blue eyes, well-proportioned, of prodigious muscular strength beneath that lymphatic air which is often found in those from the South, would have displayed the most attractive physiognomy but for arched eyebrows and a somewhat low forehead, sinister in their effect, but for red lips of a savage cruelty, and but for a muscular habit in which is revealed that irritability peculiar to Corsicans, the explanation of their readiness to kill in a sudden quarrel. (p. 474)

This routine mix of tribal prejudice and pseudo-scientific objectivity cannot hide the possibility which has already been raised, that this is a man who could be passionately loved, that he could love in return, and that his lover could be another man, albeit a master criminal. Indeed, one recognises in the sight of him – precisely in the apparent cruelty of his lips and the suppressed violence in his overactive limbs – a desirable and lovable type: for if the cultivated, lady-like Lucien ('this man half woman', he is called at one point – p. 94) was the presentable side of Herrera's passion for young men – a presentable 'son' he could take to the theatre – Calvi is his unadulterated bit of rough. Yet he is no less lovable, no less in need of saving, for all that. His is the first skin Collin saves in the hours of wheeling and dealing that follow; but Collin does not neglect to save his own: he blackmails his way into a post as head of the Sûreté, changes his name again, and gives his newly pardoned boyfriend a job in his office. The first of the queer happy-endings.

· · ·

An interesting example of a text whose silences are fleetingly voluble about urban homosexuality is Charles Dickens' *Oliver Twist* (1837–8). Think of how this novel represents the risks to which the vulnerable little boy, Oliver, is subjected when he is set adrift in the great Victorian metropolis of London. Of course, children at risk constitute one of Dickens' favourite topics – indeed, his interest in the deaths of children is extreme to the point of perversity – but although he is able to suggest the sexual risks to which young girls are vulnerable, particularly in his portrayal of the harassment of Little Nell by the rampantly phallic Quilp in *The Old Curiosity Shop*, he can never go quite that far with his boys. The fact is, however, that poverty and homelessness had made of London a vast brothel, where the flesh of adults and children, both female and male, was available for sale at low cost. Dickens appears to convey some awareness of this fact when, in chapter 19, Bill Sikes says to Fagin, apropos of Oliver, 'wot makes you take so much pains about one chalk-faced kid, when you know there are fifty boys snoozing about Covent Garden every night as you might pick and choose from?'[10] Boys come cheap and plentiful, in other words, and the criminal underworld is just as willing to exploit them as are the apparently law-abiding bourgeoisie. While they remain on the streets, they are open to extremes of abuse.

That innocent boys are subject to some sexual risk has already been suggested, in chapter 10. When Oliver is forced to live among working-class boys who have already been mightily corrupted, one of his new companions is a boy called Charley Bates, a skilled pickpocket like so many of the rest. Just once in the novel, Dickens refers to this lad not with his first name but by a slightly more formal appellation: 'Master Bates sauntering along with his hands in his pockets' (p. 80). In this single phrase, Dickens conjures up not only that quintessentially Victorian bugbear 'self-abuse', but also the even more unthinkable prospect of mutual masturbation. Charley Bates' jaunty gait, with that suspiciously casual apposition of hands and loins, hints subtly at potential moral decline of a sort which Victorian sexual mythology associated so closely with both physical weakness and the descent into imbecility. However, unwholesome though the habits of such boys were perceived as being, the fact is that the young pickpockets have been saved from worse fates – starvation or prostitution – by being taken off the streets. To that extent, one should credit Fagin (but not the far more brutal Sikes) with having given the boys some kind of home, albeit primitive, some kind of family, albeit exploitative, and some kind of economic hope. Fagin's endearments have criminal ulterior motives, but at least he seems not to be a paedophile or a pimp.[11]

Other fiction from late in the century refers quite explicitly to homosexuality, mainly in its manifestation – often treated as being both comical and diabolical – as a crime. In his novel berating the moral decline of tsarist Russia, *Resurrection* (1899), Leo Tolstoy intensifies the impression he is conveying of widespread corruption with a few moments of gossip about homosexual scandals. When a group of senators idly dismisses Maslova's appeal against her wrongful conviction for murder, they ring for some tea and turn their attention to St Petersburg's most pressing current topic of gossip. The head of an unnamed government department has been accused of 'the crime provided for in Article 995'. (Articles 995 and 996 of the penal code dating from the 1830s were anti-homosexual laws.) Senator Bay reacts with an expression of disgust, but his colleague Skovorodnikov says: 'Why, where is the harm of it? I can show you a Russian book containing the project of a German writer, openly proposing that it should not be considered a crime, and that men should be allowed to marry men.' Having said this he laughs 'boisterously', but he is able to give full details of the book's title and place and date of publication. When Bay mentions that the accused man has been appointed governor of a town in Siberia, Skovorodnikov replies: 'That's splendid! The bishop will meet him with a crucifix. They ought to appoint a bishop of the same sort.' And he adds: 'I could recommend them one'.

Three chapters later, as Nekhlyudov is leaving the Senate, the advocate tells him about the same case: 'how the thing was found out, and how the man, who according to law should have been sent to the mines, had been appointed governor of a town in Siberia'. Later, when Nekhlyudov visits the Countess Catherine Ivanovna, on entering the room he overhears the countess and Mariette talking about the new Siberian governor. Something that Mariette says about the case is 'so funny that the Countess could not control herself for a long time'. Her hilarity brings on a coughing fit.[12]

However, even such sketchy references are quite rare. It is not until early in the twentieth century, first of all in Germany, that homosexuality becomes a common theme in many novels, and the central theme in some. In having to deal with the preceding period, we come back, as ever, to the matter of silences. Two of the most potentially fascinating homosexual novels of the nineteenth century were never written. Two incomparable naturalist novelists, Émile Zola in France and Stephen Crane in the United States, both planned to write novels centred on homosexuality. But Zola passed on his materials to a friend, who used them in a non-fictional account of sexual perversions; and Crane was dissuaded by horrified friends. Imagine a novel even remotely like a cross between *Maggie: A Girl of the Streets* (1893) and *The Red Badge of Courage* (1895) and you will begin to sense the enormity of this loss.

Chapter 12

....

The American Renaissance

....

In 1849, six years before the first edition of *Leaves of Grass* came out, a rather lurid novel called *City Crimes*, by 'Greenhorn' (George Thompson), was published in Boston. Its rambling subtitles give an impression of its author's and its publisher's populist intentions: *Or, Life in New York and Boston. A Volume for Everybody: Being a Mirror of Fashion; A Picture of Poverty, and A Startling Revelation of the Secret Crimes of Great Cities.* This was just one of a series of sensationalist novels by 'Greenhorn' ('Author of "The Housebreaker," "Dissipation," "Venus in Boston," "The Gay Deceiver," & c., & c., & c.'). Purporting to offer a realistic account of the excitements and dangers newly available in the two great eastern cities, the novel used many rhetorical tropes which were being used in popular newspapers at the time. That it should be so explicitly aimed at 'Everybody', apart from being a pretty forlorn plea for more readers than ever did grant it their time, is a sign of a moral intention – if, perhaps, a cynical one, fashioned both to conceal and to justify plainly commercial motives. The author claims a message that all should hear and learn from – including, presumably, the inhabitants of the very cities under scrutiny. It is a message about moral degeneration.

Among the 'Secret Crimes' so startlingly revealed in *City Crimes* is that of sodomy. Two separate passages bring this distasteful topic to the reader's attention. In the first, a young woman called Josephine attends a costume party dressed as a boy. She is approached by a man in the costume of a Spanish cavalier, who addresses her 'in a slightly foreign accent' as a young lady. Deciding to play a game with the man, and thereby unwittingly drifting into a situation the like of which she has never imagined before now, Josephine declares that she is not a lady but a boy. The cavalier, who later turns out to be the Spanish ambassador, immediately surprises her with the vehemence of his admiration: 'By heaven, I took you for a female; and though you are a boy I will say that you are an extremely pretty one.' He asks for an assurance that he is not being deceived; she gives it. He even tests her out by 'passing his hand over the swelling outlines of her bosom, which no disguise could entirely conceal', and he says, 'there seems to me to be something feminine in these pretty proportions'.

Still unaware of the situation she is getting herself into, Josephine presents herself as being a boy with a 'naturally very effeminate' appearance, who occasionally enjoys giving the false impression that he is female. Clinching the point, she claims that this is one of those occasions and that her bosom is padded. All doubts removed, the Spaniard declares

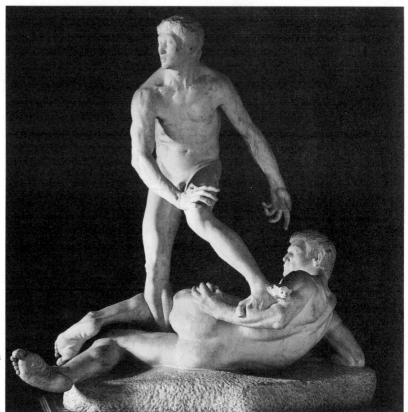

17. Torn between pioneering and settling, white American manhood wavers between homo-eroticism and domesticity. (George Gray Barnard, *Struggle of the Two Natures of Man*)

himself: 'Were you a lady, you would be beautiful, but as a boy you are doubly charming. Be not surprised when I assure you that you please me ten times – aye, ten thousand times more, as a boy, than as a woman. By heaven, I must kiss those ripe lips!' So, one metamorphosis has led to another: the beautiful female turns into a beautiful male, thereby provoking the apparent gentleman to turn into a predatory sodomite. When Josephine protests, asking if she is (as she had hoped he would be) the victim of a joke, he replies: 'you may pronounce my passion strange, unaccountable, and absurd, if you will – but 'tis none the less violent or sincere. I am a native of Spain; a country whose ardent sons confine not their affections to the fairest portion of the human race alone, but – '. The rest of his declaration being, strictly, unspeakable, he whispers it in her ear; whereupon she draws back 'in horror and disgust'.

It is now that he declares his high rank in the hope of impressing the 'boy' into granting the asked-for kiss. It may be that this revelation of aristocratic status is meant to seem as naturally untrustworthy to the young woman in democratic America as is his nationality. Why, the fellow is both a Spaniard and a nobleman – a combination of misfortunes which is itself tantamount to sodomy. Outraged, Josephine admits to having deceived him about her sex; but she adds that her playful deception 'has developed an enormity in the human character, the existence of which I have heard before, but never fully believed till now. Your unnatural iniquity inspires me with abhorrence.' She threatens to broadcast his indiscretion if he does not leave her alone. So he does – but with bad grace, muttering threats of vengeance.[1]

The author refers back to the Spanish ambassador's 'diabolical proposal' to Josephine when, later in the book, a similar man makes a similar attempt to seduce a boy – but this time a real boy, 'very handsome' and 'twelve or fourteen years of age'. The incident takes place on a steamboat. Again, the man is 'a gentleman', and again his complexion is 'very dark'. He keeps feeding the boy with cake and fruit; eventually he gives him a gold ring from his own finger. Lest any reader should have misunderstood what is going on here, the narrator makes the situation clear: 'The man was a foreigner – one of those beasts in human shape whose perverted appetite prompts them to to [sic] the commission of a crime against nature.' The syntactical structure which enforces an association of foreignness with this particular variety of beastliness, the mythic 'crime against nature', is the perfect instrument to serve a very American – or very Anglo-Saxon, rather – type of xeno/homophobia. The man's foreignness accounts for his 'perverted appetite'. I am reminded of those passages in Nathaniel Hawthorne's *The Scarlet Letter* (1850) when the very market days which keep the Puritan community of Boston commercially alive also threaten its moral death by drawing both Native Americans and European sailors into the vulnerable heart of the town. That novel is set in the mid-seventeenth century; but, as *City Crimes* shows, the anxieties it portrays are still strongly felt, in the cities of the Eastern seaboard, two centuries later.

At this point in the narrative, while the foreigner is paying court to the handsome American lad, George Thompson interposes a report on the dreaded presence of sodomy in New York. He begins with an avowal of squeamishness which serves as a moralistic apology to those readers who reckon the subject should not have been broached at all: 'It is an extremely delicate task for a writer to touch on a subject so revolting; yet the crime actually exists, beyond the shadow of a doubt, and therefore we are reluctantly compelled to give it place in our list of crimes'. The sensational novelist does not invent; he merely investigates areas of human degradation that already exist. He must always lay claim to what are conventionally journalistic motives. Having thus prepared his ground, Thompson continues with the following account:

> We are now about to record a startling fact: – in New York, there are boys who *prostitute* themselves thus, from motives of gain; and they are liberally patronised by the tribe of genteel foreign vagabonds who infest the city. It was well known that the principal promenade for such cattle was in the Park, where they might be seen nightly; and the circumstance has been more than once commented upon by the newspapers. – Any person who has resided in New York for two or three years, knows that we are speaking the truth. Nor is this all. [T]here was formerly a house of prostitution for that very purpose, kept by a foreigner, and splendidly furnished; here lads were taken as apprentices, and regularly trained for the business; – they were mostly boys who had been taken from the lowest classes of society, and were invariably of comely appearance. They were expensively dressed in a peculiar kind of costume, half masculine and half femenine [sic]; and were taught a certain style of speech and behaviour calculated to attract the beastly wretches who patronise them. For a long time the existence of this infernal den was a secret; but it eventually leaked out, and the proprietor and his gang were obliged to beat a hasty retreat from the city, to save themselves from the summary justice of Lynch law.

I quote this passage at length because it gives such a clear glimpse – albeit with tantalising lack of detail – of a thriving sodomite subculture in Manhattan, though one supposedly made up entirely of 'genteel foreign vagabonds' preying on good-looking but needy

American boys from the working class. While the suggestion that the cruising grounds in Central Park were well known to many inhabitants of the city – if not necessarily to 'Any person' who lived there – is quite plausible and implies both that more men than 'foreign vagabonds' used these areas and that their cruising was more or less openly conducted; on the other hand, one wonders how the novelist-as-reporter came across his more specialised information about the male brothel – not just about its existence, but also about the splendour of its furnishings, the costumes of its working boys, and even certain tones of speech they used. Hearsay, no doubt. The important thing about the passage, though, is the way in which the author associates the boy-loving man in the narrative around it with these two manifestations of organised homosexuality in New York. By 'organised homosexuality' I mean the recognised cruising grounds and the brothel, two efficient ways of bringing together males who wish to have sex with other males. So the man on the steamboat and the Spanish ambassador who appeared earlier are not presented as being uniquely depraved individuals. Depraved, yes; but not necessarily isolated. Such men have set up their own networks and institutions alongside those of the heterosexual mainstream. This tendency to associate with each other is, of course, a large part of what makes them seem dangerous.

Back on the steamboat, the foreign gentleman invites the American boy to share his comfortable stateroom – an offer which the boy gratefully and naïvely accepts. But: 'Half an hour afterwards he rushed from the state-room with every appearance of indignation and affright.' He reports the foreigner to one of the boat's officers – 'and the result was that the foreign gentleman and his baggage were set ashore at a place destitute of every thing but rocks, and over ten miles from any house; very inconvenient for a traveller, especially at night, with a storm in prospect'. Furthermore, although this inconvenience is presented as being thoroughly deserved – and the tone of the narrative seems grateful for the fortuitously punitive bad weather – the author cannot resist making a harsher final comment: 'The miserable sodomite should have been more rashly dealt with.' Perhaps he was referring to 'the summary justice of Lynch law' which he mentioned in connection with the New York brothel.[2]

The foregoing account of two brief episodes in an obscure and not very well written text are offered, here, by way of an introduction to the literary context in which Walt Whitman, himself a working journalist with certain investigative skills, came to start writing (and publishing) as openly homo-erotic a book as *Leaves of Grass* eventually turned out to be. In particular, Thompson's themes of foreignness and (less emphatically) effeminacy were ones which Whitman would deliberately steer away from in his attempt to celebrate a quintessentially manly and American vision of the homo-erotic relations he would refer to as 'adhesiveness' and 'the love of comrades'. We may also observe at this juncture – in the hope that it will not seem completely irrelevant – that the New York of *City Crimes* and *Leaves of Grass* is also the city to which Horatio Alger fled from Brewster, Massachusetts, in 1866, after being accused of 'the abominable and revolting crime of unnatural familiarity with *boys*'. It was in New York that he struck up many more such friendships, and it was here that he became one of the most successful commercial novelists in the United States. New York inspired the formula of the classic Alger story: 'luck and pluck' combine with many other attractive features of boyhood to raise the central character, a boy, from the gutter to one of many versions of success. In this particular series of manifestations, the American Dream arises, with seamless aptness, from the wish-fulfilling dreams of an active pederast.

· · ·

The successive editions of Walt Whitman's *Leaves of Grass* (1855, 1856, 1860, 1867, 1871, 1881 and the so-called 'Death-bed Edition' of 1891) have turned out to be the most

18. Democratic comradeship in the privacy of the American landscape. (A Margaret C. Cook illustration for Whitman's *Leaves of Grass*, 1913)

influential of the American homo-erotic texts, and indeed influential *as* homo-erotic texts. David Reynolds has pointed out that the erotic agenda of Whitman's work was to a large extent reactive to a context in popular culture. Reynolds writes: 'a primary reason heterosexual love does not have more prominence in *Leaves of Grass* is that Whitman above all wanted to avoid the deceit, the artificiality, the amorality that he associated with the heterosexual love plot of popular novels'.[3] This is reasonably convincing, but it cannot override what I take to be *the* 'primary reason', namely Whitman's own homosexuality. And yet, writing in an environment where any 'miserable sodomite' might run the risk of being 'rashly dealt with', Whitman was both astonishingly outspoken and expediently circumspect. His natural morality of male comradeship *had to* avoid deceit, but bodily safety probably depended on it to some extent. Lynch law is no respecter of fine distinctions.

Whitman's dream of democratic comradeship was, perforce, as much influenced by his actual experience of the city of New York as by his fantasies about the open prairie, or the Rocky Mountains, or the Great Lakes. Even if the geography is often based on secondary sources, he is essentially a geographical writer whose versions of personal relations are strongly determined by his (and his culture's) perceptions of space, both private and public. It is Michael Moon who most usefully addresses this topic. He writes: 'In engaging directly in the furor of the times over the increasing availability to young men in cities of novel spaces, both private and public, in which to enjoy the opportunities for pleasure ("dissipation") afforded by the brothel, the tavern, and the extrafamilial privacy of boarding-house rooms, Whitman was exceptional among American Renaissance writers.'[4] This question of spaces, as Moon so rightly perceives, is crucial to Whitman's perception of other men. Representing American democracy as they so often have to, these men are always carefully placed in significant American spaces, whether urban or rural, generally out of doors. (It is, of course, woman who presides over the domestic spaces in the *Leaves*.) Each man's attractiveness is assessed in relation to his physical setting. Indeed, there is a strong association between physicality and space in everything that Whitman wrote, perhaps even stronger in him than in other nineteenth-century male American writers. The American individual and the American continent are one; together they constitute the nation.

Like other writers of the same period, Whitman makes some effort to demonstrate that the urban industrial revolution cannot obliterate the virility of the pioneering spirit. Much depends on his portrayals of urban manhood. The city has to be as amenable a location, when it comes to love, as the prairie or the open road. The relation between the urban crowd and the pair of individuals is central to both versions of 'Once I Pass'd through a Populous City', the straight and the gay. This is the poem which commemorates Whitman's 1848 trip to New Orleans, where he appears to have had a brief affair with, in the version most often published, a 'woman who passionately clung to me', or in the original version, another man:

> Once I passed through a populous city, imprinting my
>   brain, for future use, with its shows, architecture,
>   customs and traditions,
> But now of all that city I remember only the man who
>   wandered with me, there for love of me,
> Day by day and night by night, we were together – all else
>   has been long forgotten by me,
> I remember, I say, only one rude and ignorant man who,
>   when I departed, long and long held me by the hand,
>   with silent lips, sad and tremulous.

This evocation of an uneducated man so fascinating as to have distracted the poet from his self-educative tourism through New Orleans is meant to impress us with a sense of the poet's overriding dedication to matters of the heart rather than to those of the intellect; but, more importantly, it emphasises Whitman's constant argument that the culture of the United States exists in the hearts of the people rather than in institutions. That is how the poet feels he came to know the 'populous city' so well – through one of its citizens, not as a tourist but as a peripatetic lover.

I find it hard to disagree with Camille Paglia's view that 'There is no true intimacy in Whitman. His poetry is a substitute for intimacy and a record of the swerve *from* it.'[5] Many of his more 'private' poems (like this one) actually appear to have public, political points to make. The better-known voice of Whitman is, of course, far from being an intimate one. The 'barbaric yawp' is self-consciously brazen and public, addressing itself to a much wider audience than the poet could ever plausibly have expected his work to reach. It is aimed at the generic category of *strangers*, as if Whitman needs above all to believe that he can use his poetry as a medium through which actually to *meet* every other American. In these public poems there is indeed, as Paglia suggests, an affectation of intimacy which is wholly bogus. For example, there is the famous moment in the poem 'So Long!' when Whitman addresses the reader as follows:

> Camerado, this is no book,
> Who touches this touches a man,
> (Is it night? are we here together alone?)
> It is I you hold and who holds you,
> I spring from the pages into your arms[.]

The association of poem and flesh was not new, of course; and Whitman's insistence that he himself was manifest between the pages of his book is entirely in harmony with his overall strategy. But it is when he actually starts to imagine the space in which the reader and he hold each other (dark or light? public or private?) that his strategy becomes intrusive – particularly, I guess, to women readers – and even imperialistic. He is intent on colonising the reader, body and soul, without prior consultation. If there is any intimacy in this kind of gesture, it is the limited intimacy of anonymous sex. Contact is established – and that is enough.

In 'Whoever You Are Holding Me Now in Hand', with impressive presumption, Whitman engages the unknown reader as his comrade or wife:

> Here to put your lips upon mine I permit you,
> With the comrade's long-dwelling kiss or the new husband's kiss.
> For I am the new husband and I am the comrade.

He imagines engaging in this kiss on a high hill, or out at sea, or on a beach or a quiet island, 'lest any person for miles around approach unawares'. The openness of nature is invoked as a closed, private space – even a guilt-ridden one. The reader is thus inveigled into an uncomfortable conspiracy of kisses which ill accords with the avowal of openness which occurs in virtually all of the poems. That open spaces are used as closets is a deeply disruptive trope throughout *Leaves of Grass*.

It is true that Whitman does not write love poems of the sort in which the first person singular addresses the second person singular in tones of private avowal. (One reason for this may be that the men he loved were, above all, men he loved *talking* to, and men who were not normally comfortable with books.) But a poem like 'When I Heard at the Close of the Day', if not really a direct expression of true intimacy (as how many poems ever are?), does at least record such intimacy. Its dismissal of public honours ('how my name had been receiv'd with plaudits in the capitol') is rather a grand gesture, to be sure; but as the poem enacts the wait for the approaching loved one, it also performs the move away from the public arena (and the city) into an emphatically natural intimacy beneath shared bed covers, within hearing distance of the sea. It is here that, contrary to Camille Paglia, by shifting the locus of the poem from capitol to bed, Whitman most convincingly swerves *towards* intimacy. This is one of the most beautiful of gay love poems. It dismisses the formalities of democratic civics as an irrelevance – albeit, perhaps, temporarily – to the free play of sexual closeness. In doing so, it fires a shot across the bows of interventive politicians.

When Whitman writes, in 'In Paths Untrodden', 'in this secluded spot I can respond as I would not dare elsewhere', he is referring not only to an imagined landscape of overgrown paths and the reedy banks of ponds, a place where one might 'celebrate the need of comrades' in the most obvious way without fear of interruption, but also to the site of the poem itself. The poem, that is to say, is a safe space, for all that it is so manifestly public. This is possibly because he feels he can control the reception of his desires better when publishing them in a poem than, say, when cruising the streets (not that he ever expressed any difficulty in this latter respect). The somewhat mischievous irony with which he thus declares his blaring poetry to be a 'secluded spot', set apart from the democratic multitudes he is so famous for celebrating, is a further example of his attempt to draw the reader into a private space with a promise of public friendship. It is important to remember, also, that Whitman's version of pastoral is often associated with the male body. In section 24 of the 'Song of Myself', not only does he celebrate his own body as a landscape, but he then imagines himself inhabited by the kinds of men he is inclined to love. If, he writes, he will ever worship one thing more than another, 'You sweaty brooks and dews it shall be you! / Winds whose soft-tickling genitals rub against me it shall be you! / Broad muscular fields, branches of live oak, loving lounger in my winding paths, it shall be you!'

The Civil War poems present adhesiveness in practice. It so often takes a war to persuade men to love each other at all demonstratively. Like so many homosexual writers before and since, Whitman found his war as erotic as it was tragic. This is not to accuse him of insensitivity; on the contrary. There is little inhibition about *Drum-Taps*. From the start, the poet invests his faith in the men in Yankee blue. In 'First O Songs for a Prelude' he enthuses: 'How good they look as they tramp down to the river, sweaty, with their guns on their shoulders! / How I love them! how I could hug them, with their brown faces and their clothes and knapsacks cover'd with dust!' Many of the poems that follow celebrate purposeful groups of men; indeed, in 'Eighteen Sixty-One', the year itself is praised as having a 'masculine voice'. But as soon as Whitman comes to the effects of war, the injuries and deaths, he starts to focus on individuals: in 'Vigil Strange I Kept on the Field One Night' a killed boy ('dearest comrade', 'boy of responding kisses'); in 'A Sight in Camp in the Daybreak Gray and Dim' a 'sweet boy with cheeks yet blooming' although dead; in 'As Toilsome I Wander'd Virginia's Woods' a soldier's grave bearing the scrawled inscription 'Bold, cautious, true, and my loving comrade'. They are (or were) individuals, but they are many. When Whitman ends 'The Wound-Dresser' with the lines

> Many a soldier's loving arms about this neck have cross'd and rested,
> Many a soldier's kiss dwells on these bearded lips

he sounds like a prolific lover, boasting of his promiscuity. His point is more than the usual one in war poetry – that the bodies of potential lovers have been wasted as corpses. The loveliness and the lovingness of the Union soldiers is a significant factor in their subsequent victory; it is also a substantial part of what they are fighting for. Given that Whitman proposes in 'For You O Democracy' (in the 'Calamus' section of the *Leaves*) to 'make the continent indissoluble' by instituting the 'manly love of comrades' wherever he turns, it is clear that he associates a Union victory, and hence the very existence of the States as one nation, with his own prolific experience of male love, both at war and in time of peace.

In December 1994 the *National Geographic* magazine published a 'photo essay' feature on Whitman.[6] The opening double-page spread, on which the title 'America's Poet: Walt Whitman' is overlaid, consists of a photograph captioned as follows: 'Bucking stormy seas, a [young, male] lifeguard rides the surf off Montauk, New York – Walt Whitman's youthful swimming grounds'. Twenty pages later, another seashore photograph is captioned: 'Towed by a plane, an underwear ad hails a [naked, male] sunbather on Long Island. Whitman's odes to sex and homoeroticism shocked many 19th-century ears – but not all'. The ad in question is the famous photograph of Marky Mark Wahlberg dressed in nothing but his pristine Calvin Klein underpants. The accompanying essay by Joel Swerdlow eventually comes round to the topic of gayness by a circuitous route. Having described Whitman's nursing and visiting work during the Civil War, Swerdlow adds: 'If Walt were alive today, we would probably find him with those dying "amid strangers" at facilities such as those that care for people with AIDS' (p. 137). The poet's own sexuality is not broached until the penultimate page of the essay (p. 139), as follows:

> During his lifetime, censors and critics focused on 'I turn the bridegroom out of bed and stay with the bride myself' and other heterosexual lines. 'I never read his book –

but was told that he was disgraceful,' Emily Dickinson wrote to a friend. Whitman's letters and poems, however, indicate a physical attraction to men. This has received considerable scholarly attention, reflecting, in large part, the intimacy of Whitman's writing. Readers feel they know him.

This interest in Whitman's sexuality is unusually intense. Who did Michelangelo or Mark Twain love? Few people know or care, yet Whitman's private life can stimulate bigotry. I wander into a bar on Camden's water-front, much like those that Whitman frequented. It is dark at noon, and full of men with no pressing engagements. As I leave, the bartender stops wiping glasses. 'You're not going to say Whitman's a faggot, are you?' he says. 'I like his poetry, and I don't like people saying he's a faggot.'

This odd sequence of *non sequiturs* and half-truths makes for a rather mealy-mouthed tribute. Its messages are mixed. It blames any discomfort connected with Whitman's gay status on anonymous 'bigotry', but never attempts an argument against that position. The national bard is thus protected in an international forum – the *National Geographic* – by recourse to the passing opinion of a New Jersey bartender, who is allowed to stand in for all those Americans who remain uneasy when the Good Gray Poet is said to have been gay. Not a word of the homo-erotic poetry is ever quoted. I offer this text as exemplifying the extent to which Whitman's homosexuality both must and yet cannot be acknowledged in the United States. Manifestly, his destiny is to be treated as the embarrassment which, for much of his career, he sought to become. In that sense, the unease he still causes is a measure of his continuing success.

· · ·

The canon established by F.O. Matthiessen in his 1941 book *The American Renaissance* is drawn from a narrow fund of white, male New Englanders. The titles of the book's four main subsections tell it all: 'Emerson to Thoreau', 'Hawthorne', 'Melville' and 'Whitman'.[7] Several recent essays have discussed the relevance of Matthiessen's own homosexuality to what may now seem a very subjective sequence of choices.[8] (I do not mean to suggest, however, that the choices of a homosexual critic are any more subjective than those of the unexceptional heterosexual misogynist he might otherwise have appeared to be.) What is certain is that, notwithstanding its many qualities, his version of the 'renaissance' he defined has had to have a lot of authors and texts added to it in order to remain a convincing account of mid-nineteenth-century cultural development in the United States. Yet Matthiessen's canon has remained resilient, particularly once a handful of important additions – Emily Dickinson being the most obvious – are taken into account. It still provides the basis of how nineteenth-century American literature generally gets taught.

Given how it generated a critical cliché about the puerility of American literature – or rather, how it allowed a cliché which already existed to be developed in a new direction – Leslie Fiedler's influential book *Love and Death in the American Novel* (1960) is worth examining in greater detail than Matthiessen's. It is when he is discussing James Fenimore Cooper's Leatherstocking novels that Fiedler first raises the issue for which his book first became so famous: 'This is the pure marriage of males – sexless and holy, a kind of counter-matrimony, in which the white refugee from society and the dark-skinned primitive are joined till death do them part.'[9] At this point, Fiedler is referring specifically to the relationship between Natty Bumppo and Chingachgook in Cooper's *The Last of the Mohicans* (1826), but it soon becomes clear that he is taking this relationship as an example of a major American literary trope. Furthermore, although he describes such homo-erotic miscegenation between white and non-white males as 'sexless and holy', Fiedler does not hesitate to perform psychoanalytic readings which winkle out the carnality implicit in such representations of male friendship. A mere page after having used the word 'sexless', he appears to have changed his mind: 'the passion that joins male to male in Cooper is not in its implications as innocent as he wants to think' (p. 210).

Whether sexual or not in themselves, these fictional relationships between men are read by Fiedler as being resolutely anti-heterosexual – or, more accurately, anti-female. Indeed, 'the very end of the pure love of male for male is to *outwit* woman', largely because of what she represents: a trinity of evils comprising matrimony, civilisation and Christianity, each of which is, in its own way, apparently designed to delimit the liberty of the male individual (p. 210). Fiedler finds this tendency even more clearly on display in the novels of Mark Twain:

> In our national imagination, two freckle-faced boys, arm in arm, fishing poles over their shoulders, walk toward the river; or one alone floats peacefully on its waters, a runaway Negro by his side. They are on the lam, we know, from Aunt Polly and Aunt Sally and the widow Douglas and Miss Watson, from golden-haired Becky Thatcher, too – from all the reduplicated symbols of 'sivilization'. (p. 268)

Fiedler is referring, of course, to both *Tom Sawyer* (1876) and *Huckleberry Finn* (1884). What is remarkable about this passage is the way in which he opens it by referring, rather pompously, to the whole of the 'national imagination', as if no other narrative had ever been put together since the American Revolution. When a boy like Huck Finn decides to 'light out for the territories' he is enacting the great American myth of the West (even if he heads south). The implication is that the myth itself is puerile, and is ideally represented by Twain's two boys. As Fiedler adds at a later stage in the exposition of his argument, 'It is maturity above all things that the American writer fears, and marriage seems to him its essential sign' (p. 330). And woman is the essential sign of marriage. It is she who lays the trap of settlement and domesticity.

Wherever he turns among male authors, Fiedler finds much the same pattern. There it is again – it hardly needs saying – in the novels of Herman Melville: 'Marriage to a woman would have seemed to Melville's hero [Ishmael, in *Moby-Dick*] intolerable; only through a pure wedding of male for male could he project an engagement with life which did not betray the self' (p. 344). And again: 'it is clear that the absence of women in *Moby Dick* indicates not the absence of love from the novel, but its presence in the peculiar American form of innocent homosexuality'. He calls the story of Ishmael and Queequeg 'perhaps the greatest love story in our fiction' (p. 531). Even when he reads Nathaniel Hawthorne's *The Scarlet Letter* (1850), that novel which so remarkably makes up for what one might complain of as American fiction's relative 'absence of women' (when contrasted with European novels of the same period) by focusing on Hester Prynne with such impressive sympathy, Fiedler is convincingly sceptical about the importance of the novel's heterosexual themes:

> Surely no loving tie is closer than the one established between [the male protagonists] Chillingworth and Dimmesdale in *The Scarlet Letter*, as the cuckold penetrates in icy intimacy his cuckolder's psyche. Hester, Chillingworth, and Dimmesdale stand to each other in that odd relationship which European critics call the unnatural triangle, in which two men are bound to each other through the woman they jointly possess, as they cannot . . . possess each other. (p. 360)

Nowadays, following Eve Kosofsky Sedgwick's *Between Men*, we would recognise this as a 'homosocial' triangle; but the point to be made about the two men's relation to each other through the woman remains persuasive. If, even in this most woman-centred of American Renaissance novels, heterosexual relations are somewhat shunted aside by a homosocial intimacy, how fragile an institution American heterosexuality appears to be, at least as represented in classic nineteenth-century fiction. Fiedler seems disappointed by this.

One thing puzzles him. Why did nineteenth-century readers put up with literature which so often comes so close to endorsing male homosexuality? 'How could Antinoüs come to preside over the literature of the nineteenth-century United States, which is to say, at a time and in a place where homosexuality was regarded with a horror perhaps unmatched elsewhere and ever?' The answer Fiedler hypothesises is that 'so violent a disavowal of male inversion' as existed at the time 'fostered an ignorance of its true nature': because the 'sin' or 'crime' of sodomy was understood to be so horrendously degenerate in its physical expression, no merely affectionate 'friendship' between two males seemed anything like the unthinkable vice which had taken vague shape in people's fearful imaginations. Indeed, Fiedler claims that 'In our native mythology, the tie between male and male is not only considered innocent, it is taken for the very symbol of innocence itself' (p. 346). Where the male–female relation was obviously subject to lust, the male–male relation could appear to be beyond reproach.

Fiedler's maverick analysis of his nation's literary heritage is still important to the gay reader today, mainly by virtue of its rudimentary 'gay readings' of classic texts. *Love and Death in the American Novel* gave an indication of what gay literary criticism might become, but, importantly, it was not itself gay literary criticism. Fiedler regarded American literature's failure to deal with heterosexual relations in sufficient depth as a sign of arrested development. The insistent theme of male–male affection, despite its obvious fascination not only for Fiedler himself but for generations of American readers, was dismissed as 'juvenile and regressive, that is, narcissistic; for where woman is felt to be a feared and forbidden other, the only legitimate beloved is the self' (p. 344). This puerile narcissism is the version of male homosexuality which prevails throughout Fiedler's thesis.

In his later book, *The Return of the Vanishing American*, Leslie Fiedler adds an important further detail to his outline of the narrative in which white man bonds with red man in the wilderness: 'There are, finally, two archetypal versions of the Fall in the Garden: one inherited from the Old World, one created in the New. In the first, Man and Woman are portrayed living at peace in an Earthly Paradise until the Serpent enters; in the second, Man and the Serpent are presented as cohabiting amicably until Woman comes on the scene. For the Indian *is* the serpent.'[10] He adds that Chingachgook, the name of Fenimore Cooper's Indian, means 'great serpent'.

The American Renaissance sees one line of its natural succession in recent gay reworkings of the mythology of the West. I am thinking of several types of fiction, some gay-authored and some not, all containing gay male characters. There was an aptness to the ways in which, in the 1960s, Richard Amory harnessed the West to the purposes of soft pornographic romance and produced his 'Loon' novels, starting with *Song of the Loon* in 1966. As if he were deliberately constructing retrospective fictional proof of Leslie Fiedler's thesis, Amory was eroticising the meeting between white man and Native American at a time when television and the movies were still reluctant to represent the 'red man' as having anything about him worth loving.

William Burroughs said in a 1965 interview that he was going to write a Western, but did not do so until *The Place of Dead Roads*, which was published in 1983. And yet this novel meshes in so closely with the themes and techniques of Burroughs' other fiction that it reveals him to have been a Western writer all along. Certainly, none of his early 'science

fiction' (so called by categorisers) could have taken shape without the influence of an already firmly established tradition, according to which American masculinity depends on the existence of one frontier or another. More recent, substantial Western novels in which gay male characters play a major role include Leslie Marmon Silko's *Almanac of the Dead* (1991), Tom Spanbauer's *The Man Who Fell in Love with the Moon* (also 1991) and William Haywood Henderson's *Native* (1993). Further down market is the explicitly gay and unashamedly populist cowboy fiction of Cap Iversen.

The cowboy occupies a crucial position in American gay culture, in terms of both styles and ideals. One thinks of the 'clone' look which became so popular – and not just in the United States – during the 1970s: blue jeans, plaid shirt, leather boots, masculine facial hair. Like the Marlboro Man himself, any disco queen could look as if he had drifted into town from some distant spot beyond the frontier, where men were men and women were, too. If the West plays a major part in the States' conception of themselves as 'the land of the free', one of the institutions Westerners were initially free of was the family. Prior to permanent settlement, the West always signified a space beyond the family and its 'feminine' constraints. To some writers the mythic West is still the only place where male friendship, whether homosocial, -erotic or -sexual, can flourish without the domesticating interference of bourgeois femininity.

However, the West's most interesting futures must be imagined in the resurgent potentialities of Native American culture. Reading books like Walter Williams' *The Spirit and the Flesh* and Will Roscoe's anthology *Living the Spirit* (both 1988), one can see the outline of how a gay American Indian culture might emerge from late twentieth-century reappraisals of pre-twentieth-century native traditions.[11]

· · ·

19. (facing page) The pioneering male body settles the American landscape . (Thomas Eakins, *The Swimming Hole*, 1883)

20. Insipid classicism unequal to the pioneering spirit. (Thomas Eakins, *Arcadia*, 1887)

If Whitman is the Good Gay Poet of the American Renaissance, his nearest equivalent among novelists is Herman Melville. Best summarised in a passage by Robert K. Martin, Melville's interest in gender roles and male sexuality is at once emotional and scholarly:

> Melville clearly disliked effeminate men; like Whitman his literary sexual ideal involves a love between two men, and not a man and a boy, or a man and a pseudo-woman. The effeminate man was the over-civilised man, who had adopted the values of civilisation (i.e., woman) over those of the primitive (i.e., man). The ideal therefore becomes an androgyny that represents the integration of the values of civilisation and the primitive, or of female and male. This androgyny should not be confused with effeminacy; for Melville, androgyny indicates self-sufficiency and wholeness, whereas effeminacy indicates weakness, indulgence, and partialness.[12]

Like Whitman, Melville is interested in dynamic masculinity, expressed and fulfilled in physical action. (His representation of decisive paralysis, the great short story 'Bartleby the Scrivener', actually serves to underline this interest.) His narratives of seaboard life are designed, in part, to dramatise the contrast between different male types. In this sense, Melville is an informed connoisseur of working men. As well as the contrast between types, his narratives dramatise the relationships between individuals. One of the more striking examples of this tendency is chapter 94 of *Moby-Dick*, entitled 'A Squeeze of the Hand', where Ishmael gives an account of the manual processing of whale sperm. This rhapsodic passage is justly famous:

Squeeze! squeeze! squeeze! all the morning long; I squeezed that sperm till I myself almost melted into it; I squeezed that sperm till a strange sort of insanity came over me; and I found myself unwittingly squeezing my co-laborers' hands in it, mistaking their hands for the gentle globules. Such an abounding, affectionate, friendly, loving feeling did this avocation beget; that at last I was continually squeezing their hands, and looking up into their eyes sentimentally; as much as to say, – Oh! my dear fellow beings, why should we longer cherish any social acerbities, or know the slightest ill-humor or envy! Come; let us squeeze hands all round; nay, let us all squeeze ourselves into each other; let us squeeze ourselves universally into the very milk and sperm of kindness.[13]

The sense of affectionate male togetherness built up in this short chapter stands in a crucial relation to the rest of the novel. Work and leisure merge to the extent that the men's efficient working relations and their affections are functionally indistinguishable from each other. Ishmael's liking for his shipmates in general – in addition to his particular love for Queequeg – is foregrounded here in a manner that locates male love at the very heart of whaling itself. The sperm-squeezing scene has to be one of the most openly and unashamedly homo-erotic pieces of nineteenth-century writing. And yet, how can it possibly be? To me, now, it reads like a virtually pornographic description of a circle-jerk. I find it difficult to conceive of a reader to whom it would not suggest a rhapsodic episode of mutual masturbation. How can there not have been such readers? How can they not have been – if numbers matter – in the majority?

I am inclined to agree with Robert Martin that 'every positive depiction of sexuality in Melville is a depiction of male masturbation, frequently mutual. There is never any portrayal of sexuality involving . . . penetration'. Martin illustrates his point with detailed reference not only to the sperm-squeezing episode, but also to the passages on Carlo in *Redburn* ('probably the most extravagant paean to masturbation to have appeared in respectable literature') and to the chapter entitled 'Killing Time' in *White-Jacket* ('in which it appears that masturbation is one of the principal ways of killing time on board ship') (pp. 63, 55, 62). But time is not all that is killed when men relate emotionally to each other in the intimacy of shipboard life. As Robert Martin so succinctly puts it, 'Melville was not able to imagine what it might have been like for two men to love each other *and survive*' (p. 7). Ishmael's life is saved not by his beloved Queequeg but by Queequeg's buoyant coffin. And in *Billy Budd*, completed just before the author's death in 1891, desire comes to fruition not in love-making but in fatal violence.[14]

The eponymous Billy is portrayed as being vibrantly, alluringly ambiguous. Although his body is 'heroic' (p. 354), he is 'not presented as a conventional hero' (p. 332). Although his body is miraculously virile and strong, capable of killing with a single blow, his face is beardless and 'feminine in purity of natural complexion', his smile is 'ambiguous', and narrative credibility is not strained when he is compared with either a (female) 'rustic beauty transplanted from the provinces and brought into competition with the highborn dames of the court' – which would well describe one of Genet's young delinquents in the company of older convicts – or with one of Hawthorne's beautiful but flawed women characters (p. 329), or with 'a condemned Vestal priestess in the moment of being buried alive' (p. 376). Although his voice is 'singularly musical', when he is emotionally provoked it shatters, being 'apt to develop an organic hesitancy, in fact more or less of a stutter or even worse' (p. 331). This invisible defect, like Macbeth's ambition or Othello's jealousy (if that is what they are), serves as Fate's means of bringing about a tragic conclusion. Insofar as Billy's ambiguity consists of both transgressing strength and transgressed weakness, respectively destructive and self-destructive, it is terminal: literally, fatal.

The comparisons with women are pertinent to Billy's suspect passivity, which is explicitly manifested in his general behaviour and implicitly extended to whatever sex life he might have had. He is a man, however, and amply furnished with proof of virility: 'our Handsome Sailor had as much of masculine beauty as one can expect anywhere to see' (p. 331). When Claggart suggests to Captain Vere that there may be 'a man trap' hidden under the 'ruddy-tipped daisies' of Billy's facial beauty (p. 372), he adapts a commonplace description of pretty but sexually voracious women to a matter in which real danger is involved: for Billy's graceful physique is endowed with enormous *active* strength. While his beauty is a homosexual trap, his strength is a potential murder weapon. Since the whole ship is effectively 'worked by muscle alone', its sailors are employed as items of power (p. 337). Like all the men engaged to work aloft, Billy has been chosen for his 'youth and activity' (p. 346). Indeed, neither his physique nor his temperament can easily accept the opposition of sophistication to his naïvety: 'being of warm blood he had not the phlegm tacitly to negative any proposition by unresponsive inaction' (p. 359). There are times, in fact, when he seems capable of conventional heroism after all.

Billy is repeatedly compared with mythical figures, as if his lack of significant personality required frequent denial for the story to work. He begins as an Apollo (p. 326) and a statue of Hercules (p. 329). But it is to the role of Adam that his innocence and vulnerability suit him best. His primitive behaviour, while in some sense morally perfect, is prelapsarian to the extent of containing within itself the promise of lapse. Adam and Eve can be considered innocent only in the light of subsequent events, since innocence is not an issue in Paradise. To say they are innocent, therefore, is to begin the account of their Fall. (Innocence is a creature of hindsight. The idea of future innocence – common to most versions of a heavenly life to come – is a contradiction in terms.) Likewise, Melville's comparison of Billy Budd with Adam 'ere the urbane Serpent wriggled himself into his company' is both avowal of innocence and promise of guilt (p. 331). There is always a suggestion of destructive carnality in his grace, as there is when Captain Vere thinks of him as 'such a fine specimen of the *genus homo*, who in the nude might have posed for a statue of young Adam before the Fall' (p. 372). The fact that the captain tries to imagine him naked is a reminder of why, according to the biblical myth, he is clothed at all. In part, Billy's perfection is flawed because it inspires the imperfections of others.

The outcome of this novel's plot is explicitly and repeatedly referred to as a tragedy – and remember that it was written long before the words 'tragedy' and 'tragic' came to be used indiscriminately, for any unfortunate event in daily life. This is crucial to our understanding of Billy's behaviour. The book's portrayals of character are governed by questions of choice or its lack. Melville uses them definitively when describing nautical life (p. 364):

> Yes, as a class, sailors are in character a juvenile race. Even their deviations are marked by juvenility . . . Every sailor, too, is accustomed to obey orders without debating them; his life afloat is externally ruled for him; he is not brought into that promiscuous commerce with mankind where unobstructed free agency on equal terms – equal superficially, at least – soon teaches one that unless upon occasion he exercise a distrust keen in proportion to the fairness of the appearance, some foul turn may be served him.

Even the officers, according to Captain Vere, 'ceased to be natural free agents' the moment they received their commissions (p. 387). It is the man who steps out of his place in the structure, by making or seeking to make moral decisions of his own, who destroys himself or is destroyed. The only choice open to him is to take that transgressive step. But once he has done so, he is no less 'externally ruled' – by gods or masters or whoever – than when he obeyed orders with the more circumspect pack. He has no further say in his future.

This is why Billy is a 'fatalist' (p. 327) and 'Fated boy' (p. 377: the first words spoken to him after he has struck Claggart down). The motive for his crime is irrelevant. As Captain Vere says at the impromptu trial, 'Budd's intent or nonintent is nothing to the purpose' (p. 389). The point is reiterated even when he is hanged. The fact that the suspended body makes none of the expected, graceless movements of a hanged man, but remains motionless 'to the wonder of all', leads the purser to comment on Billy's extraordinary self-control. But the ship's hard-headed surgeon attributes the motionless-ness to 'mechanical spasm in the muscular system', which is 'no more attributable to will power . . . than to horsepower' (p. 401).

Billy Budd's tormentor, the victimising victim Claggart, has small, shapely hands, unaccustomed to labouring, a beardless chin, and a colourless complexion which, when contrasted with 'the red or deeply bronzed visages of the sailors', seems 'to hint of something defective or abnormal in the constitution and blood' (p. 342). He is an unsavoury representation of repressed desire. As Robert Martin has put it, 'Writing now as a contemporary of the early Freud, Melville sees his villain Claggart as a repressed homosexual whose desires for Billy can only be translated into a false accusation against him'.[15] If Claggart is the serpent in Eden, and if his presence anticipates a fall, the moral catastrophe implicit in the tale symbolically coincides with the official closure of the frontier. Similar homosexually repressed bullies will appear in later American novels of military life: for instance, Captain Penderton in Carson McCullers' *Reflections in a Golden Eye* (1941) and Sergeant Callan in Dennis Murphy's *The Sergeant* (1958). In their envious desire for the virility of younger servicemen, these men represent a perceived failure in American masculinity which, despite two world wars and countless imperialist skirmishes, began anticipating Vietnam the moment the frontier was closed.

Chapter 13
....

Muscular Aestheticism

....

In 'The Portrait of Mr W.H.', his story about Shakespeare's sonnets, Oscar Wilde drew a line of descent from Plato to himself, via Marsilio Ficino's translation of the *Symposium*, Michelangelo's sonnets to Tommaso Cavalieri, Montaigne's essays, Christopher Marlowe, Shakespeare himself, Richard Barnfield, Johann Winckelmann and Walter Pater.[1] I have already raised this list as an example of how Victorian inverts had started laying claim to a literature of their own. Wilde shows he has been reading these authors in order to prove that his own writing is derived from an established tradition. At this point in my argument, I am especially interested in the last two names on the list: for it was through Walter Pater that Wilde felt able to lay claim to both the Renaissance and ancient Greece – the Rome of paganism, as opposed to Catholicism, did not interest him very much – and it was through Winckelmann that Pater had been able to develop his distinctive views on Platonism and Greece.

Pater's essay on Winckelmann dates from 1867; it was subsequently collected in his *Studies in the History of the Renaissance* (1873). A key figure in European neo-classicism, Johann Winckelmann (1717–68) produced his history of classical Greek art, *Geschichte der Kunst des Alterthums*, in 1763. Pater particularly respected him for the personal enthusiasm he brought to his work:

> That his affinity with Hellenism was not merely intellectual, that the subtler threads of temperament were inwoven in it, is proved by his romantic, fervid friendships with young men. He has known, he says, many young men more beautiful than Guido's archangel. These friendships, bringing him in contact with the pride of human form, and staining his thoughts with its bloom, perfected his reconciliation with the spirit of Greek sculpture.[2]

Wolfgang von Goethe had admired Winckelmann for similar reasons – his espousal of the aesthetics of friendship and young, male beauty – and published a biographical essay on the art historian in 1805.

Walter Pater himself coloured the fabric of his critical work with 'subtler threads of temperament'; he too encountered 'the pride of human form' in young men. To the second edition of *The Renaissance* (1877) he added his famous exercise in what you might call gay literary criticism, the essay 'Two Early French Stories', which deals in part with the medieval French story of love between men, *Li Amitiez de Amis et Amile*.[3] It is here, too, that he asks whether Chaucer's Knight's Tale is not more concerned with Palamon and Arcite's love for each other than with their pursuit of Emelya.

The lectures Pater eventually collected together in *Plato and Platonism* (1893) were among his most influential work. As with Winckelmann, so too with Plato: those 'subtler threads of temperament' which Pater discerns in the German art historian were also present in the Greek philosopher. In Pater's view, Plato's work, like Dante's, was fundamentally shaped by the fact that he was a lover. Love affected his powers of perception; it was love that made him sensitive to visual detail. Pater argues that Plato's aesthetics anticipate the late nineteenth-century notion of art for art's sake, but without the modern unlinking of ethics from aesthetics. The resulting view of art is masculinist and misogynistic. (This hardly needs saying – we are talking of both ancient Greece and Victorian men's taste for ancient Greece.) He defines it as follows:

> Manliness in art, what can it be, as distinct from that which in opposition to it must be called the feminine quality there, – what but a full consciousness of what one does, of art itself in the work of art, tenacity of intuition and of consequent purpose, the spirit of construction as opposed to what is literally incoherent or ready to fall to pieces, and, in opposition to what is hysteric or works at random, the maintenance of a standard.[4]

It is no easy task, in reading this packed sentence, to disentangle what is Greek in it from what is staunchly Victorian. That, I suppose, is the most useful point one can make about it: it is sometimes hard to distinguish the rhetoric of the *palestra* from that of the public school.

In the passage quoted, Pater's contempt for what is feminine or effeminate begins to seem defensive. To lack manliness is to be, or to be at risk of becoming, unconscious, artless, obtuse, purposeless, incoherent, fragmented, hysterical, random and lacking in worthwhile standards. This implied critique of womanliness is devastating – but routine, nonetheless. (Pater was not uncommon in this respect.) By thus associating artistic and intellectual control with 'manliness', and thereby with male physicality, Pater proposes an aesthetic which is as much for homo-eroticism's sake as for art's alone.

The extraordinary eighth lecture in *Plato and Platonism*, simply entitled 'Lacedaemon', turns out to be an intense rhapsody on virility and homo-eroticism. Pater imagines an Athenian paying a visit to neighbouring Lacedaemon. (He thereby defensively disavows the intensity of his own fervour in what follows. He is just pretending to be Greek.) In Lacedaemon the Athenian finds the best conditions of slavery, under which a slave develops a close relationship with his masters, 'including a sort of bodily worship, and a willingness to share the keen discipline which had developed the so attractive gallantry of his youthful lords'. Lacedaemonian beauty is preserved by law – they 'forbade all that was likely to disfigure the body' (p. 219) – and was subjected to a rigorous physical regime. The Athenian heartily approves of the fact that Lacedaemonian boys are not allowed to take warm baths, but instead have daily to plunge into the cold (and public) waters of a river. He comments:

> Yes! The beauty of these most beautiful of all people was a male beauty, far remote from feminine tenderness; had the expression of a certain *ascêsis* in it; was like un-sweetened wine. In comparison with it, beauty of another type might seem to be wanting in edge or accent. (p. 222)

Given that this is 'a male beauty', it does not seem unreasonable to infer that this last remark really addresses not just 'another type' but *the* other type – that is to say, female beauty. The 'edge' and 'accent' that are to be derived from asceticism are to be compared, in art, with the spare and efficient beauty of the wet bodies of young men.

On the topic of relationships between such youths, Pater again waxes eloquent – although still ventriloquising through his fictitious Athenian. He speaks of the Lacedaemonians' respect for the heavenly twins Castor and Pollux, the Dioscuri:

> Brothers, comrades, who could not live without each other, they were the most fitting patrons of a place in which friendship, comradeship, like theirs, came to so much. Lovers of youth they remained, those enstarred types of it, arrested thus at that moment of miraculous good fortune as a consecration of the clean, youthful friendship, 'passing even the love of woman,' which, by system, and under the sanction of their founder's name, elaborated into a kind of art, became an elementary part of education. A part of their duty and discipline, it was also their great solace and encouragement. The beloved and the lover, side by side through their long days of eager labour, and above all on the battlefield, became respectively, [*aitas*], the hearer, and [*eispenelas*], the inspirer; the elder inspiring the younger with his own strength and noble taste in things. (pp. 231–2)

This is one part history, two parts humbug. It is also an important statement of Walter Pater's cultural drift. The awkwardness of the biblical phrase in the middle of it all – 'passing even the love of woman', referring to the story of David and Jonathan – is a reminder that these are the sentiments of a Christian Englishman, not a pagan Athenian. We should remember, also, that two years after the publication of *Plato and Platonism*, in the Central Criminal Court of the Old Bailey, Oscar Wilde would invoke David and Jonathan in a vain attempt to pass off his sexual escapades with rent boys as mere 'clean' friendships between spiritual equals.[5] No one believed him.

Once pederasty is 'elaborated into a kind of art' and becomes not only 'an elementary part of education' but also a part of young men's 'duty and discipline', we can see the route by which male homosexuality came so strongly to feature in the intellectual life of Britain in the later decades of the nineteenth century. Education in the classics, such as boys and young men received from older men in the nation's public schools and universities, might also be an education in the possibility of pederasty. Boys who learned Greek also learned about Greek love. If they had the privilege of going to Oxford and attending the lectures of men like Walter Pater and Benjamin Jowett, that learning might be especially intensive and detailed.

· · ·

This is not the place to relate in detail the history of the Oxford Movement (or the Tractarians), from John Keble's 1833 sermon on 'National Apostasy' in the Church of England, to John Henry Newman's entry into the Roman Catholic Church in 1845. (Newman became a cardinal in 1879.) This is not the place, either, for an account of the Roman Catholic revival in England. The oddity of the Oxford Movement's early espousal of celibacy is inevitably perceived to have combined with its adherents' propensity for forming intense friendships to give the movement its distinctive psychological and cultural profile. David Hilliard draws a fairly obvious inference: 'It seems inherently possible that young men who were secretly troubled by homosexual feelings that they could not publicly acknowledge may have been attracted by the prospect of devoting themselves to

21. The paradoxical wedding of manliness and effeminacy. (Oscar Wilde photographed by Napoleon Sarony, 1882)

a life of celibacy, in the company of like-minded male friends, as a religiously sanctioned alternative to marriage'.[6] Both Newman and Frederick Faber established religious brotherhoods, at Littlemore and Elton respectively, and were followed into Catholicism by the brothers they had gathered. Nor should we overlook the fact that a similarly intense, if rather less overtly demonstrative, homo-erotic trend developed within the ethos of the so-called 'muscular' Christianity of men like Thomas Arnold of Rugby school. Traces of it are present in such mid-century school-based novels as Thomas Hughes' *Tom Brown's Schooldays* (1857) and Frederic Farrar's *Eric, or Little by Little* (1858).

For all its strictures against sodomy, nineteenth-century Christianity – muscular or otherwise – developed some distinctly pagan streaks. As Hilliard has pointed out, Roman Catholicism eventually attracted a significant number of homosexual writers from the *fin de siècle* in England, among them Alfred Douglas, John Gray, Lionel Johnson, André Raffalovich, Frederick Rolfe ('Baron Corvo') and Oscar Wilde himself; and an equally significant number of the Uranian poets were Church of England clergymen, among them Edwin Emmanuel Bradford, Samuel Elsworth Cottam, George Gabriel Scott Gillett, Edward Cracroft Lefroy and Edmund St Gascoigne Mackie.[7]

Frederick Faber (1814–63) was educated at Shrewsbury school and Harrow, before going up to Balliol College, Oxford, in 1833. It was when he was an undergraduate, if not before, that he developed what was to become a lifelong taste for sentimental friendships with other men. Fellow student Roundell Palmer later wrote of Faber, 'The attraction of his looks and manners . . . soon made us friends, and our affection for each other became not only strong but passionate. There is a place for passion, even in friendship; it was so among the Greeks; and the love of Jonathan for David was "wonderful, passing the love of women".'[8] These remarks are worth quoting because they are so characteristic of the era in which they were made. Both the vague, general reference to Greece and the specific quotation from the Book of Samuel (2 Sam. 1: 26) are commonplaces of defensive self-justification. The reader should note that Palmer raises both of these precedents not, as we might today, to effect a kind of cross-cultural gay identification, but, on the contrary, secure in the knowledge that they will help deflect suspicion of sexual wrongdoing between himself and his soulmate.

Throughout his life, Faber was a prolific poet. At Oxford in 1836 he won the Newdigate, the poetry prize which Oscar Wilde would be awarded for 'Ravenna' in 1878. From the start, one of his favourite themes was friendship; but he never seems to have felt that his writing was inappropriate to his position as a deacon and then a priest in the Anglican Church (he took orders in 1837 and 1839). Poetry was the respectable medium in which men could quite openly express affection for each other. That it was also the principal medium of prayers and hymns was helpful, and no mere coincidence. Faber would become one of the best writers of Roman Catholic hymns in English, using techniques he had honed in what were essentially love letters to student friends.

Gerard Manley Hopkins went up to Balliol College, Oxford, in 1863. There he heard Benjamin Jowett lecture on Thucydides. There, too, in 1866, he was tutored by Walter Pater. In 1865, Robert Bridges introduced Hopkins to a seventeen-year-old poet called Digby Mackworth Dolben, a great admirer of Faber's verse. Hopkins fell in love with him; they exchanged poems. It was probably from Dolben that Hopkins caught the habit of thinking of the manhood of Jesus Christ in distinctly physical terms. Dolben drowned in 1867, and his influence on Hopkins became all the more lastingly intense in the refining fire of grief. I offer these biographical notes only to demonstrate that Hopkins, too, belonged to that culture of sentimental and erotic male friendships shaped by both Greece and (Catholic) Rome to which Newman and Faber had belonged before him. His poems emerged from the same confluence of trends.

In 'The Lantern Out of Doors', Hopkins watches men passing by in the night. His attention is drawn to them by 'either beauty bright / In mould or mind or what not else'. At any rate, there is something about each of them that makes him 'rare'. However, there is also something about Hopkins' response that draws itself to our attention, where it has to be found wanting. I am referring to the phrase 'beauty bright / In mould or mind'. The afterthought of the phrase 'or mind' is unconvincing except as a cover-up of an entirely visual appreciation of men's forms. The fact is that when men are passing, whether lit by lanterns or in the full light of day, it is not possible without at least stopping their procession to tell whether their minds are beautiful. Hopkins is thinking of beautiful men and then rather carelessly rationalising the thought as also pertaining to spiritual beauty. The plain fact is that he had a visual imagination – indeed, this is what makes his great spiritual poetry and saves it from abstraction. It was through sight that he perceived the consummate beauty, and proof, of God's handiwork; but likewise, it was through the sight of beauty that he encountered his most shaming temptations.[9]

As the poem continues, he makes the point that all these men are cared for by Christ as any man would care for his closest friend. The Saviour's interest and affection are asserted in the following words:

> Christ minds; Christ's interest, what to avow or amend
> There, éyes them, heart wánts, care haúnts, foot fóllows kínd,
> Their ránsom, théir rescue, ánd first, fást, last friénd.

The striking thing about this and many other passages in Hopkins' poetry, letters and sermons is that he envisages Christ's love in such intense and intimate terms. This is his attraction to orthodox Catholics, though they hardly dare say so: he puts the love of God into terms the immediacy of which our own physical lives have led us to comprehend. In 'The Soldier', Christ is portrayed as one who routinely comforts and spiritually protects soldiers with kisses. ('For love he leans forth, needs his neck must fall on, kiss . . .') This physical interventionism was both deeply attractive to Hopkins, who was always yearning for such love in his own life, and ultimately no less deeply disturbing. This poem raises a point which pertains to the whole of Hopkins' career. Beautiful men remind him of Christ. It hardly needs saying, though, that we could put a far more negative spin on such a statement. When he sees beautiful men, he desires them; his desire makes him feel guilt; and his guilt draws his attention to the moral system, to which he himself so strongly subscribes, which denounces male–male desire in the name of Christ, the name which now therefore springs to mind.

The other reason for this association of ideas is, simply, an association of physiques: Hopkins often found himself becoming excited at the sight of a well-carved body of Christ on a crucifix, and he was often dismayed to find that he was becoming sexually excited when trying to meditate in a more spiritual vein on the events of Christ's Passion. Beautiful men remind him of Christ because Christ was a beautiful man. In an 1879 sermon he freely avowed: 'I make no secret I look forward with eager desire to seeing the matchless beauty of Christ's body in the heavenly light'.[10] His religion asked him to worship such a man, and its iconic conventions invariably put such a man on central display in its churches. This was a perversity of unconscious thought from which, it seems, Hopkins was never entirely free.

The more one reads Hopkins, the more one becomes convinced that his particular torture was to have realised the intensely carnal nature of his own spirituality. He tried to discipline it by scourging himself, both literally and figuratively; but as is so often the case, this may have had the contrary effect, of drawing his attention more urgently to his own sensitised flesh. The other striking point about Hopkins was his uncomfortable sense of personal oddity. He never thought of himself as belonging to the confident Victorian majority. Indeed, one of his justly most famous shorter poems, 'Pied Beauty', is dedicated to the notion that there is something to be prized in contrariety and strangeness – 'All things counter, original, spare, strange; / Whatever is fickle, freckled' – for they are fathered on us by Christ himself, the patriarch of strangeness.

Hopkins is keenly aware of the sheer filthiness of mortality. He often thinks about dirty bodies. As he asserts in 'The Sea and the Skylark', humanity has long outgrown its purity. We are terminally 'breaking, down / To man's last dust, drain fast towards man's first slime'. From slime to dust, our physical lives can never escape their basis in dirt. In 'God's Grandeur', he laments humanity's materialism as a matter of soiling:

> And all is seared with trade; bleared, smeared with toil;
> And wears man's smudge and shares man's smell[.]

Yet he knows that the smudge and smell of male mortality are intensely attractive. His most moving poetic appraisals of physical beauty are famously about adult working men:

the farrier Felix Randall and Harry the ploughman. Their sweat, though disturbingly material, is also evidence of their virtue. It is both filthy and clean. It signals simplicity, which Hopkins finds trustworthy.

Even though, in 'Felix Randall', the dead farrier is referred to as being 'big-boned and hardy-handsome', and even though he is remembered at work in the forge, 'powerful amidst [his] peers', Hopkins addresses him as 'child'. 'Harry Ploughman' is even more forthright in its admiration of the power and sinews of manliness, and yet it too speaks of Harry awkwardly as the 'child of Amansstrength'. If he had to conceive of a virtuous man, he tended to do so by imagining within the virile physique a boyish spirit. Boyishness and membership of the working class were closely associated in his mind. The combination of puerile simplicity and massive strength is held to be virtually angelic in its capacity to prove God's miraculous creativity. Joseph Bristow has spoken of how so many of the poems 'raise the question of how male strength might be invested with a glory that unites man and God, dissolves class differences, and, what is more, enables same-sex desire'.[11]

Hopkins eventually had the priesthood which Frederick Rolfe could only fantasise about; and Rolfe had the sex life that, it seems, poor Hopkins could only dream of – and only in a torment of guilt and bodily self-loathing. Hopkins, of course, was a much better poet. Perhaps that is some kind of compensation. This is a glib way of putting a far more profound point about the extent of Hopkins' achievement. The fact is that, by contrast, other homo-devotional poets like Frederick Faber, Digby Mackworth Dolben and Frederick Rolfe produced work that, whatever its superficial pleasures, was banal in the extreme. Where Hopkins excelled was in his ability to combine a complex poetic persona with an innovative voice. (Emily Dickinson was the only contemporary who outper-formed him in this respect.) His technical innovations are the key to the actual expression of an eroticism which, for all his struggles against the temptations of voyeurism and masturbation, he could not conceive of suppressing altogether. The triumph of his poems is in their exuberant orality.

Sprung rhythm was not just some newfangled way of prettifying poetry. It introduced a degree of physicality to texts which Hopkins never wanted to seem merely intellectual. It usually represents physical movements in space, not to mention the bodily exigencies of breath and rhythm itself. The breathiness (or is it breathlessness?) of the opening line of 'The Wreck of the Deutschland' – 'Thóu mastering mé, God' – reduces deity to a mere unstressed syllable after the dramatic personal relationship between 'Thou' and 'me'. That it is a relationship of mastery and subordination makes the inequality of the two personae seem all the more dynamic. The poet's own inactive passivity is ardent in its demand for the potent intervention of the more creative spirit than his own.

· · ·

As a young poet, Oscar Wilde was more Faber than Hopkins, even if he was a far more ambitious writer, in worldly terms, than either of them. Most of his poetry dates from his youth. To my mind it scotches two oddly widespread myths: firstly, that he somehow only became interested in boys after meeting Robbie Ross at Oxford in 1886; and secondly, that he was a great poet. Because it largely pre-dates the development of his interest in paradox, it deserves much closer attention than gay critics have yet bothered to give it. Looked at as a body of work, the verse consists of a mixture of sentimental paganism and devotional Christianity – not a particularly uneasy or unusual juxtaposition in the late nineteenth century. It is, of course, in the 'Greek' poems that Wilde so clearly divulges his yearning for youthful masculinity. As representations of ancient Greece, these are derivative and entirely conventional; but coming from an undergraduate in Victorian

England, and being published without significant scandal, makes them rather interesting as a manifestation of peculiar cultural circumstances. We need to try to determine what it is about the poems that makes them less suitable to be raised in evidence against Wilde at the trials than *Salomé* and *The Picture of Dorian Gray*. What is it about their sexiness that was not so clearly apparent?

Scattered throughout the poems are references to familiar myths: Heracles mourns Hylas in 'The Garden of Eros'; Hylas dies again in 'Canzonet', as does Hyacinth; Hylas reappears in 'Ravenna', and Hyacinth in 'The Burden of Itys' along with Adonis, who himself reappears in 'The Sphinx' in close proximity to the Emperor Hadrian and his boyfriend Antinous. One of the claims Wilde makes in 'The Burden of Itys', and which he seems to be trying to support in so many of the poems, is that 'they are not dead at all,/ The ancient Gods of Grecian poesy; / They are asleep'.[12] If woken, they would take little persuasion to make themselves at home on the Thames and in the landscape around Oxford. (Matthew Arnold had already made this point, not much more subtly.) By this stage in the poem, indeed, the English pastoral landscape has already called a number of them to mind, including Narcissus and a figure who seems particularly to have interested Wilde, but who does not often appear in other poets' work, Salmacis –

> Who is not boy nor girl and yet is both,
>   Fed by two fires and unsatisfied
> Through their excess, each passion being loth
>   For love's own sake to leave the other's side
> Yet killing love by staying[.]
>
>   (p. 789)

The image of this hermaphrodite's self-defeating bisexuality might influence speculation on how Wilde felt about his own sexual orientation at the time of writing – did he feel he was making himself unlovable? – but I am more interested in the cumulative effect of all these references in the texts. What were they meant to convey, and how might they have been received? Salmacis crops up again later in the same poem ('lonely Salmacis / Had bared his barren beauty to the moon' [p. 793]) alongside an equally sad but also 'voluptuous' Antinous; and yet again in 'Panthea', still congenitally sad, jealously watching Venus disport with a shepherd and sighing 'for pain of lonely bliss'. In this latter case, Salmacis' jealousy seems all the more intense coming after an invocation of the rape of Ganymede. Apparently it takes a clearly defined gender to be so demonstratively desired, other than by oneself.

Despite its awfulness, the poetry is fascinating: for it shows the young Wilde trying to become a serious writer according to the models he knew best. All the evidence from his life suggests that he wanted to be a great writer and that he felt he had the ability to become one. His later problem, as a playwright, was a lack of models: the only suitable major figure in his lifetime was Ibsen (Shaw was two years younger than Wilde), and he did not quite fit the Wildean requirements. Much of the awkwardness of Wilde's camp over-confidence at the height of his success seems to spring from this problem: he was trying to be the greatest English (*sic*) dramatist since Shakespeare (Marlowe never interested him very much) but also wanted to get on in society and to dazzle the crowds. These are incompatible aims. Yet their very incompatibility contributed to the characteristic brittleness of Wilde's tone.

Wilde's plays established a camp style which now, more than a century later, any third-rate British script-writer can passably imitate when called on to represent middle-to-upper-class speech. Moreover, as Brigid Brophy established in her book on Ronald Firbank, an even more important strand of influence passed, through the transformative offices of Firbank himself, from Wilde to such major English novelists as Evelyn Waugh, Graham Greene and Anthony Powell.[13] The plays may not be about clearly homosexual characters – the nearest Wilde comes to representing homosexual desire on the stage is in *Salomé*, in Herodias' pageboy's love for the Syrian captain of the guard – but they deal with markedly relevant social themes: the living of double lives in *The Importance of Being Earnest*, for instance, and blackmail in *An Ideal Husband*. (The Labouchère Amendment of 1885, which introduced the concept of 'gross indecency' between men to the statute books in England and Wales, had quickly become known as 'the blackmailer's charter'. Blackmail was topical.) It is difficult to disagree with Neil Bartlett, who comes much closer to understanding Wilde than Richard Ellmann, for all his virtues, ever managed: 'When I started all this, I thought Wilde was a comic writer, but now I know better. All of his characters are in terror of being discovered. Their elegance of diction is only a front; anything rather than speak the truth.'[14] In all of the plays in modern settings, beneath the glossy surface of the wit, the fear of scandal looms large; and yet Wilde's characters are continually tempting fate by testing the limits of what they can get away with.

Moreover, as Alan Sinfield has pointed out, in so many of his male central characters, whether in the plays or in *The Picture of Dorian Gray*, 'Wilde is exploiting the indeterminacy of the dandy image; it represents less a distinct entity than a device for unsettling conventional ideas'.[15] In this sense, one could say that Wilde's version of homosexual literature depends entirely on the presence of the heterosexual reader or spectator. (The same must be said of the plays of Joe Orton, some seventy years later.) Had he ever written for homosexual readers, his books would have been classed as pornography, and would have had to be published (if at all) as such – privately and anonymously. So it might as well have *been* pornography – or liberationist advocacy, which would have amounted to much the same thing. The novel *Teleny* (1896), which is sometimes attributed, at least in part, to Wilde, gives us some idea of what a homosexually direct *Dorian Gray* might have looked like. But it would have lacked the edge which the need for indirection and the desire for provocation give the plays. The fact is that Wilde wrote a transgressive literature which thrived on the conditions of oppression and yet courted the approval of the oppressor. This latter position is neither abject nor cowardly; on the contrary, it represents a courage that could not indefinitely go unpunished. In a man who was leading a dangerous double life it may have been foolish; but then so is climbing Everest, if you happen to fall.

In the context of European homosexual writing, Wilde and Lord Alfred Douglas demand to be contrasted with Paul Verlaine and Arthur Rimbaud. The latter were, in terms of quality, by far the more productive couple. Both Wilde and Verlaine ended up being sentenced to two years' hard labour: in 1873 Verlaine was convicted of an assault on Rimbaud, whom he had shot in the wrist when they were both drunk, and was given the maximum sentence after a medical report, read out in open court, affirmed that his body showed signs of recent homosexual intercourse; and in 1895 Wilde was convicted of 'gross indecency'. Wilde was destroyed, but Verlaine soldiered on. Wilde wrote *De Profundis*, it is true; but Verlaine wrote some of *Sagesse* in jail – it was published in 1880 – and went on to publish *Jadis et Naguère* (1885), *Amour* (1888), *Parallèlement* (1889), *Dédicaces* (1890), *Bonheur* (1891), *Chansons pour elle* (1891), *Odes en son honneur* (1893) and *Le Livre posthume* (1893–4). It was not Verlaine but Rimbaud who gave up writing, not long after the shooting incident in 1873, at the age of nineteen. Of course, Verlaine was in the much happier position than Wilde, for a while, of having found a boy who had a beautiful and very smelly body which was available to be put to unspeakable uses, but who was also a breathtakingly beautiful poet. Wilde, on the other hand, fell for a boy who was beautiful but vain, with more aristocratic airs and graces (which flattered Wilde's own vanity) than real poetic talent, and who was never as good a lay as the nearest telegraph boy.

As he is now, Wilde survives as a cultural monument rather than a writer. It is important that he wrote, of course: for that is what gave him his confidence and his vulnerability. But, as he was always at pains to insist, he put more of his genius – muddled and mad as it was – into his life than into his art. I suspect that his reputation as a gay cultural figure is not fully merited by his writings, which are often second-rate. Let me try to put it another way. It is hard to rid oneself of the impression, on rereading him, that Oscar Wilde was a great writer with no great writings to his credit. He was the very queen of performativity, *posing* as a 'somdomite', while also going through the relevant motions, and likewise *posing* as a poet.

Neil Bartlett makes the point that 'Wilde did not create out of an intimate, heroic sense of himself as an individual or as a homosexual. He was prolific, public, commercial, promiscuous, shallow and repetitive. He was a plagiarist.'[16] *The Picture of Dorian Gray* could have been a great novel – if only it had been written by Henry James. But he was too busy writing *The Tragic Muse* (1890) and the stories in *The Lesson of the Master* (1892). Muddled by its heterosexual pretexts, there are times when it seems a timid, mealy-mouthed novel in comparison with, say, Joris-Karl Huysmans' *À Rebours* (1884). And yet it did not fail to make its point. Neil Bartlett reminds us that 'The Cleveland Street scandal was only eight months old, and that too featured boys in the Guards and a disgraced Lord who had to leave England. The charges against Dorian are dangerously topical and almost specific'.[17] In the plea of justification filed by Queensberry and signed by Charles Gill on 30 March 1895, *Dorian Gray* is not only described as 'a certain immoral and obscene work in the form of a narrative' but is said to have been 'understood by the readers thereof to describe the relations[,] intimacies and passions of certain persons of sodomitical and unnatural habits[,] tastes and practices'.[18] This understanding was no mere 'subtext' but was derived from the very fabric of the text itself. It was obvious to those who had need of solid evidence that this was a book which, by their standards, had an unashamedly immoral purpose which went beyond its aesthetic integrity. According to Alan Sinfield, 'The book should be viewed not as the cunning masking of an already-known queerness, but as reaching out towards formulations of same-sex experience that were . . . as yet nameless'.[19] Far from working as art for its own sake, it was an experiment in unspeakable articulations.

We must not underestimate how difficult it was to speak out at this time. Some of Wilde's most forceful utterances were, paradoxically, also tentative. His peroration on 'the love that dare not speak its name', given under cross-examination by C.F. Gill, has been celebrated, quite rightly, ever since, as a significant public expression of homosexual pride, albeit expressed in terms of sexless spirituality. One aspect of the speech, though, has generally gone unacknowledged. It was not delivered with the usual confidence of the man renowned as a great public speaker. The reporter for the *Star* called it 'an explanation which unfortunately was not at times perfectly audible'.[20]

· · ·

The most influential modern homosexual writer in late nineteenth-century Britain was no Greek scholar, and no Anglo- or Roman Catholic; but the Good Gray Poet himself, Walt Whitman. In the last years of his life, the most enthusiastic readers of Whitman's poetry were not Americans at all, but Englishmen.[21] And it was not primarily for the innovation of his poetic line that they read him, but for his exuberant homo-eroticism. These English gentlemen were his fans because they were the first generation of homosexuals – who still tended to call themselves Uranians – and because, all soundly educated in the classics, they saw in his poems a vigorous re-flowering of Greek love in representations of modern life. They shuddered, and not with horror, at the thought of how manhood might blossom, unrestrained. Only theoretically committed – if at all – to egalitarian principles, many of them envisaged thrilling forays across the boundaries between the classes.

Whitman thus sent shock-waves through the furtive gentility of Britain's Uranian community. He transformed their nostalgia for pastoral Greece into yearning for a utopian New World of open frontiers and open-necked shirts. Oscar Wilde said that there was 'something so Greek and sane' about Whitman's poems. He did not mean the form of the verse, of which he did not approve. (Not that Wilde was English; in many ways, no one was more Irish. He was, however, a central member of an English literary élite.) Wilde had been familiar with Whitman's work ever since his enlightened mother had read *Leaves of Grass* to him when he was thirteen. We do not know to what extent she expurgated the text. When he took the 'Final Schools' exam at Oxford in June 1878, one of the questions Wilde had to answer was on what he believed Aristotle would have made of Whitman. But the 'Greek' poetry that Wilde himself eventually came to write – the sentimental 'Charmides', for instance – is insipid stuff; nothing could show *less* of the American poet's influence.

When he met Whitman in Camden in 1882, Wilde told the older poet that he and his friends at Oxford used to carry the *Leaves* with them when they went for walks. After their meeting Whitman referred to Wilde as being 'so frank and outspoken and manly'. It may come as a surprise to witness Whitman's use of the epithet 'manly' to describe Wilde, whom we have come to think of as being effete and effeminate. But the fact is that Wilde was a big, strong man. His effeminacy was part pose, part media myth. It was not the aspect of himself he presented to the maestro. He evidently satisfied those high standards of manliness which the great democratic connoisseur had been establishing over the previous three decades.[22]

An even greater devotee of Whitman was John Addington Symonds; but his enthusiasm did not make his verse any more receptive to the American's revolutionary poetic ideas. In 'The Song of Love and Death' (1875), Symonds addresses Whitman as follows:

> Thou dost establish – and our hearts receive –
> New laws of Love to link and intertwine
> Majestic peoples; Love to weld and weave
> Comrade to comrade, man to bearded man,
> Whereby indissoluble hosts shall cleave
> Unto the primal truths republican.[23]

This impresses me now, if at all, purely on the strength of its sincerity. While it is clear that Symonds was taking no lessons from the master in poetic technique, that is not what had struck him most about Whitman's project. The crux of the matter was those 'New laws of Love'. Symonds was (and is) all too easy a target for mockery. Algernon Swinburne called him and his followers 'Calamites', a wonderful sneer, neatly combining 'calamities' with 'catamites' in its reference to Whitman's holy writ *Calamus*. But, no matter what the waspish Swinburne may have thought, Symonds did have a serious project in mind, and a determination to carry it out, even if he did not have the policy for doing so. What interested him were Greek love and the possibility of its survival in modern society. He considered Whitman's social thinking the key to the matter, but he wanted reassurance that he was not reading *Leaves of Grass* at crossed purposes.

In a letter of August 1890, Symonds took the bull by the horns and asked the question he had been dying to ask for years: 'In your conception of Comradeship, do you contemplate the possible intrusion of those semi-sexual emotions and actions which no doubt do occur between men?' This is hesitantly put, but does – just – get to the point. Whitman was, or affected to be, shocked. In his reply he referred to 'such gratuitous and quite at the time entirely undream'd & unreck'd possibility of morbid inferences – wh' are disavow'd by me & seem damnable'. A couple of paragraphs later, presumably apropos of the same topic, he made the famous claim: 'Tho' always unmarried I have had six children – two are dead – One living southern grandchild, fine boy, who writes to me occasionally'.

Edward Carpenter told Symonds he should never have addressed the issue to Whitman point-blank. He said Whitman's denial was a lie, clearly intended to shake the obstinate Symonds off, once and for all. Oscar Wilde came home from America and told the poet George Ives that Whitman made no secret of his homosexuality. 'The kiss of Walt Whitman,' he said, 'is still on my lips.' I dare say one must choose between the evidence of the two men who met Whitman face to face, and that which he put in writing for a correspondent on the other side of the Atlantic.

In his book of the following year, *A Problem in Modern Ethics* (1891), Symonds did his duty by Whitman, saying of him: 'At the outset it must be definitely stated that he has nothing to do with anomalous, abnormal, vicious, or diseased forms of the emotion which males entertain for males.' But Symonds could still not resist putting as positive a gloss on this as he could: 'Whitman never suggests that comradeship may occasion the development of physical desires. But then he does not in set terms condemn these desires, or warn his disciples against them.' This is a compromise of sorts. It allowed Symonds to go on to quote the famous footnote from *Democratic Vistas* (1871), which so many homosexual apologists would eventually turn to. The note in question speaks of 'threads of manly friendship' running through the warp of American life, 'unprecedentedly emotional, muscular, heroic, and refined', and ends as follows: 'I say democracy infers such loving comradeship, as its most inevitable twin or counterpart, without which it will be incomplete, in vain, and incapable of perpetuating itself'. Thereafter, Symonds could quote Whitman's 'I dream'd in a dream', 'To the East and to the West', and 'For you O Democracy', in order to establish that Whitman's poetry calls to mind the story of the Theban Band at the battle of Chaeronea – which is Symonds' supreme example of the intensity, purity and masculinity of male homosexual love.[24]

Gerard Manley Hopkins, too, was strongly attracted to the content of Whitman's verse, but he dared not submit to the implications of that attraction. Writing to Robert Bridges on 18 October 1882, he said: 'I may as well say what I should not otherwise have said, that I always knew in my heart Walt Whitman's mind to be more like my own than any other man's living. As he is a very great scoundrel this is not a pleasant confession. And this also makes me the more desirous to read him and the more determined that I will not'.[25] To identify thus with so complete a scoundrel cannot have occurred lightly. But to repudiate the idea completely would have been a far greater denial: for Hopkins' poetry reveals how intimately his love of men and boys was connected with his love of Christ.

The main responsibility for the introduction of Whitman to Britain lies with Edward Carpenter. Carpenter himself first encountered Whitman in 1868 or 1869, in William Rossetti's selection from *Leaves of Grass*. He went on to try, in his lifestyle and his writing

22. The patriarch of American manliness meets his match. (Walt Whitman and Harry Stafford, *c.* 1876)

alike, to show that Whitman's democratic ideals could operate to beneficial effect even in the Britain of empire and Victoria. In his opinion, there already existed in the hearts of the British the conditions under which a saner, more egalitarian society could thrive. Men loved men, in Britain as elsewhere, but this love had not yet been properly recognised as a creative force. Like Symonds, Carpenter mentions Whitman and the Theban Band in the same breath, in a poem called 'Into the Regions of the Sun'. Like Wilde, he saw in Whitman a trace of the Greek – but enlightened by American constitutional democracy.

In *Homogenic Love* (1894, the year before Oscar Wilde's trial) Carpenter quotes the famous *Democratic Vistas* footnote on the relationship between democracy and comradeship. Of Whitman himself, Carpenter writes: 'Like all great artists he could but give form and light to that which already existed dim and inchoate in the heart of the people.' What Carpenter means by this is 'homogenic love'; and this passage moves straight from the mention of the poet to the following detailed remarks on the presence of the 'intermediate sex' in everyday life in Britain:

To those who have dived at all below the surface in this direction it will be familiar enough that the homogenic passion ramifies widely through all modern society, and that among the masses of the people as among the classes, below the stolid surface and reserve of British manners, letters pass and enduring attachments are formed, differing in no very obvious respect from those correspondences which persons of opposite sexes knit with each other under similar circumstances; but hitherto while this passion has occasionally come into public notice through the police reports, etc., in its grosser and cruder forms, its more sane and spiritual manifestations – though really a moving force in the body politic – have remained unrecognised.[26]

Like Symonds before him, Carpenter was at pains to point out that Whitman was a *healthy* lover of men. Whitman was living proof, if anybody was, that the state of being homosexual was not necessarily neurotic, not necessarily a 'condition'. Carpenter's anthology *Ioläus* (1902) includes Whitman's poems 'Recorders Ages Hence', 'When I Heard at the Close of the Day' and 'I Hear it Was Charged against Me'. It also re-quotes the *Democratic Vistas* footnote. *Days with Walt Whitman* (1906) records visits to the master in 1877 and 1884.

However, it is in his own poetry that Carpenter's admiration for Whitman really catches fire. His huge book *Towards Democracy* was closely modelled on *Leaves of Grass*, not only in style (which eventually becomes laboured and forced in Carpenter's thoroughly English cadences) but also in content and in the manner of its appearance in successively enlarged editions (1883, 1885, 1892, 1902, 1905). He ended up writing a book that was, if not aesthetically, *politically* magnificent. Insofar as he believed that, without new attitudes to sex – to contraception and homosexuality in particular – the redistribution of capital could have only superficial effects on the structure of society, Carpenter's thinking was decades in advance of that of most other British socialists.

Carpenter also realised that there was more than aesthetics to Whitman's poetic line. The escape from metrics was a crucial sign that the poetry was no mere academic exercise, and that the poet was not going to be hidebound by the obsolete rules of a narrow, literate class. Even if, in the execution, Carpenter's imitations of Whitman occasionally looked more like parodies, it is important that he, unlike Symonds, felt able to take this radical step in his writing. (Why, after all, should a socialist be writing with the good mannered measure of Lord Tennyson?) It was a signal of the more important breaks with convention that he was eager to make in his personal life. Reading someone like Whitman could involve a major commitment. The literature of homosexuality was moving far beyond mere aesthetics.

Chapter 14

Spirit Versus Physique

The homosexual novel or play – that is, the novel or play *about* homosexuality as a central topic, rather than that which merely contains a homosexual character or two – was most seriously developed by writers in Germany throughout the era of psychoanalysis. A didactic fictional tradition emerges, with individual novels often drawing heavily on the arguments of contemporary sexual theorists. For example, Adolf von Wilbrandt's *Fridolins heimliche Ehe* (1875; published in New York as *Fridolin's Mystical Marriage* in 1884), which James W. Jones describes as 'the first novel in German to present homosexuality as a phenomenon deserving of acceptance because it is natural for the person involved', clearly follows Karl Heinrich Ulrichs' theory of the 'third sex' with a female soul in a male body.[1] This novel tells of Fridolins, a professor of art history who, at the age of forty, finds his life's fulfilment in the person of Ferdinand, a younger man who becomes his student and moves in with him. Their relationship is never presented as being erotic – it is intellectual – but the book's happy ending is no less remarkable for that.

In the pseudonymous Konradin's *Ein Jünger Platos: Aus dem Leben eines Entgleisten* (1913), when two schoolboy lovers are forced to part, one of them commits suicide. The other, Theodor Reinhold, goes through various short-term relationships as a student. It is not until he is thirty that he falls in love with a boy he is tutoring, sixteen-year-old Lorenzo. Together they read not only Plato's *Symposium* but also, even more tellingly, Wilbrandt's *Fridolins heimliche Ehe*. Eventually, at the moment when they are about to make love, they notice that the boy's younger brother is watching them. Theodor has second thoughts about the relationship and moves to Italy. He has sex with a boy in the Blue Grotto on Capri, but has to pay for it. When he subsequently hears that Lorenzo has drowned – whether by accident or by his own hand not being clear – Theodor tries in vain to kill himself. In the end he decides to have only non-sexual relationships, and he moves to America to have them.

These are the beginnings of the novel of homosexual apology. In a sense, unlike (say) *The Picture of Dorian Gray*, they have no other point to make. The pathos of the homosexual predicament *is* the point. And yet, in Wilbrandt's book, the protagonists do not have sex; nor do they even explicitly desire to do so. Even in Konradin's book the viability of an actively homosexual life is not exactly endorsed. The second point of all these early novels is that the protagonist's homosexuality is natural to him and does not deserve to be constantly denounced as somehow having come into existence in contravention to natural law. Needless to say, this argument is much easier to pursue in the face of prejudice with reference to fictional characters for whom the desire for sexual action – and especially for anal intercourse – has been refined out of the account.

It was always possible, though, to make use of the fact that homosexuality was seen as being against nature. The most common strategy towards the end of the nineteenth century was to associate the unnatural, via the artificial, with the arts; and to value 'man'-made things more highly than the banality of nature. The nearest thing a purposeful aesthete came to nature might be in a *pose* of natural behaviour. A line of influence running down from Wilde's generation, through Ronald Firbank's, to the likes of E.F. Benson in fiction and Noël Coward in drama, developed one distinct strain of camp writing in English fiction. Much of this work is sexually suggestive, but sex between men does not actually take place in it. The worship of artifice is often presented as part of a pose of celibacy, particularly since sex involves so much stickiness and filth. Thus, the aesthete often constructed the image of himself as a paradoxical combination of *mens insana in corpore sano*: the embodiment of unquenched (but not necessarily frustrated) desire.

Furthermore, since women were regarded as being particularly in thrall to nature – most particularly insofar as they were menstrually led by lunar cycles – it became possible to regard boys as being somehow less physical than women, and, *ipso facto*, more spiritual. Even sexual intercourse between two males might be imagined as more spiritual than heterosexual intercourse, precisely because it served no mechanical, propagative purpose. Just as art for art's sake was of a higher aesthetic value than (say) mere journalism or propaganda, so too might sex for sex's sake transcend the mundane purposefulness of reproduction. Within this context of aestheticised sexuality and intellectually justified love, boys became confused with angels; seduction with prayer; and the bedroom with the hinterlands of Paradise.

Spirituality could also be claimed as a triumph in the face of legally enforced sublimation. Indeed, in most Western nations from the late nineteenth century onwards, the law implicitly demanded that relationships between men be no more than 'platonic' or, to use the Churches' word, celibate. Rather than be defeated and have to avoid close same-sex relationships altogether, men could, as it were, spell 'platonic' with a capital 'P' and convince themselves – and others, should the need arise to defend themselves against the accusation of indulging in more fleshly pursuits – that their loving relationships, far from excluding the physical element for reasons of defensive expediency, were actually celibate by choice, and motivated not by physical desire ('lust') but by the philosophies of classical revivalism. Like Plato's Socrates, their minds were on higher things. Love was a transcendence of physique, a meeting of minds. We have already seen how this tendency dominated the Renaissance mind after Marsilio Ficino's versions of Plato came out. An excellent example of the same tendency in early twentieth-century thought occurs on the final page of *The Intermediate Sex* (1908) by Edward Carpenter:

> Unwilling as the world at large is to credit what I am about to say, and great as are the current misunderstandings on the subject, I believe it is true that the Uranian men are superior to the normal men in this respect – in respect for their love-feeling – which is gentler, more sympathetic, more considerate, more a matter of the heart and less one of mere physical satisfaction than that of ordinary men.[2]

Oddly enough, Carpenter attributes this reduced physicality to 'the presence of the feminine element' in Uranian men.

23. Always the more beautiful of the two, the body makes sure that the soul is aware of it. (John Gibson, *Love Tormenting the Soul*, c. 1839)

One would be rather more willing to accept these voluble claims of spirituality, from Plato himself no less than from legally constrained homosexual men of the modern world, if their philosophical underpinnings, and the texts in which their philosophies were propounded, were not so clearly and explicitly dependent on physical beauty. What chance did an *ugly* boy ever stand of developing a Platonic relationship with one of the latter-day Platos? (For that matter, indeed, once physical, homosexual desire is out of the picture, what chance of such a relationship did any *girl* ever stand?) Needless to say, in many cases biographical evidence, such as letters and diaries, has subsequently shown that the pose of spirituality did indeed serve as cover for sexual relationships.

It is at the beginning of the twentieth century that the *closet* comes into play in literary production (although it is not named as such for many decades). For each writer there are personal choices to be made, related to the risk of scandal. It was not only in England that the figure of Oscar Wilde now represented a terrible warning to inverts who sought to express themselves. Now was not the time to be daring. One strategic choice which could enable the homosexual writer to continue to write about the nature and the objects of his desire without putting himself at great risk of scandal was to sublimate the sexual theme and concentrate, instead, on the possibilities of spiritual comradeship. I do not mean to write of all work of this spiritualising tendency as mere closetry, invariably expressing only a fraction of what the author would have expressed had he not been censoring himself – but nor do I want to lose sight of that possibility. Certainly, as far as the homosexual reader is concerned, a novel about 'spiritual' love between two persons of the same sex may be a pertinent and effective representation of one part of what it means to be homosexual. For the homosexual author, to write this kind of text may be an expedient compromise with censorship – a way of saying something rather than nothing at all.

Bear in mind that critics with an anti-homosexual agenda have made a point of separating love between men from sex between men. They call the former 'friendship' (or, at most, 'platonic love') and only the latter 'homosexuality'. Their aim is to appropriate all texts about male love for the institution of heterosexuality, and, at the same time, to diminish the literature of homosexuality by allowing it only to be about sex. This leaves them in a position to extol the finer virtues of 'platonic' relationships between 'normal' men, while deploring the fact that queers only ever think about physical satisfaction. Having stolen our expressions of love, they depict us as incapable of expressing love. But the fact is that 'platonic' texts belong no less to gay literature than do our more explicitly homosexual texts.

In this context it could be productive to set up contrasting pairs of contemporaneous writers, the one making mileage out of the spirit, the other attempting to create a new kind of respectable (as opposed to pornographic) literature which confronts homosexuality head-on. We could, for instance, contrast the works of Thomas Mann (1875–1955) and André Gide (1869–1951), the former neither willing nor, one suspects, able to think of male–male love in any other way than in the Platonic model, but the latter ever struggling to arrive at the point where he could write what he regarded as his greatest book, *Corydon*, a platonic dialogue in shape but in content a strictly twentieth-century discussion of the scientific phenomenon of homosexuality.

Gide's *L'Immoraliste* (1902) is more explicitly pederastic in its protagonist's desire for boys than Mann's *Death in Venice* (*Der Tod in Venedig*, 1913), which is ostensibly concerned more with platonic aesthetics than with the earthly pleasures a boy's touch might provide. Similarly, *The Counterfeiters* (*Les Faux-Monnayeurs*, 1926) might be contrasted with *The Magic Mountain* (*Der Zauberberg*, 1924), that sublimely boring book about terminal illness. The latter's central character, Hans Castorp, only ever desires one woman, Madame Chauchat, who happens to remind him of a boy, Pribislav Hippe, from whom he once borrowed a pencil at school. The constant references to Pribislav throughout the novel, whenever Hans admires Madame Chauchat, suggest a great intensity of suppressed regret, but never cause the topic of homosexuality *per se* to be raised by the narrative. By contrast, Gide's novel is dripping with adolescent testosterone, most of it responding not to girls but to boys. Mann is a great writer – one cannot simply dismiss him for timidity – but his interest is clearly different from Gide's. This difference may be cultural as much as personal.

But the two divergent possibilities, spirituality and physicality, are even more conveniently represented by the work of two major European poets, one German and one Greek, whose lives coincided but whose gay poetry could hardly be much more different. I am thinking of Stefan George (1868–1933) and Constantine Cavafy (1863–1933). While the former developed an elaborate system of mystical idealism – some have said, a smokescreen – to express his yearnings for young male perfection, the latter wrote about sex. This is a loaded way of putting it (for I much prefer Cavafy) but, most importantly, we should bear in mind that whereas George was able to publish his work during his lifetime, Cavafy was not.

Stefan George was working in a German poetic tradition of neo-classicism, involving the exaltation of platonic friendship, descended from Winckelmann and Goethe. It was entirely in harmony with the cultural development of German nationalism, posited on combined glorifications of youth and masculinity. George believed in the creative, intellectual and spiritual power of boys throughout history. ('We know that the great expeditions that changed the face of our world were planned by the schoolboy Alexander, that the twelve-year-old son of Galilee instructed the scribes in the capital, that the Lord of the longest world rule we know of, did not die in his thirties, but as a youth . . .'[3]) He was widely read in high cultural boy-lore. His poems relate this learning to his own observations of living boys. When his writing is at its weakest its balance leans somewhat too far towards the bookish sources; but at its best it integrates book and boy.

In 'Day-Song' he speaks of being enraptured by the sight of a boy whom he then and therefore courts with extreme reverence. Similarly, in the poem beginning 'Ich forschte bleichen eifers nach dem horte . . .' he speaks of being inspired by a naked angel bearing and wearing flowers. When the flowers spill on the ground, both angel and speaker kneel to gather them up again, the former smiling, the latter blushing as pink as the roses. As if the ages of man and boy, lover and loved one, had been reversed, it is the ephebic angel who has all the confidence in this scene, and the poet all the adolescent nervousness. As throughout his career, George treats the young boys he exalts as though they were his masters, and abases himself to them. Indeed, they are the masters of nature – as in the poem beginning 'Gemahnt dich noch das schöne bildnis dessen . . .', where a swan vulnerably but voluntarily lays its neck in a boy's caressive hand. George appears to have located the dynamo of his spiritual eroticism in the erasure of his own ego at the feet of an imperious boy's. That he called each successive manifestation of this youth the Saviour does not detract from this fact.

In 'Encomium' ('Lobgesang') the poet addresses a loving prayer to his lord ('mein herr') in the shape of a naked boy with a wreath in his hair. It seems that this mythological figure, when previously seen, was clothed, winged and armed. The fact that he no longer has wings suggests he is a humanised angel – that is to say, a mortal boy. The fact that he is now naked and has laid down his weapons suggests he is a boy who is ripe for seduction: he is virtually offering himself to that end. Touched by him – emotionally and physically – the poet recoils in pain. Touched not only by the boy's finger but also, humiliatingly and honorifically, by his heel, the poet is defeated and blessed at once. It is a cleansing and healing hurt he feels. While the boy's breath stinks of a rank and beast-infested jungle, it is also sweetly and strangely reassuring. Paying homage at his lordly feet, the poet is enchanted by a vision of the desire he most fears. The boy in this poem is no mere cherub, but a masterful vision of animal lust.

George's boys would seem somewhat akin to the dressed-up (but usually still naked) Sicilian boys in the photographs of Wilhelm von Gloeden and his imitators – garlanded in a pseudo-classical manner and set against some appropriately unmodern backdrop of vineyards and broken columns – were it not for the fact that they are less likely to be the dark-haired, tanned sons of fishermen, with crusted feet and work-worn hands, than the pale, blond scions of the Prussian bourgeoisie, cultured schoolboys with manicured nails and a habit of composing insipidly romantic verses. One such, the Munich schoolboy Maximilian Kronberger, is commemorated in George's 'Maximin' poems, as his principal muse. George was capable of extraordinary presumption when writing about this boy's early death as if it had been a spiritual choice ('To the colorful and diverse destiny of a splendid mortal, he preferred the calm and quiet reign of the celestials'). This suggests either that he never gave much thought to the actual lives of the adolescents he idolised, or that he did, indeed, encounter some very rare types of boy. In the poem 'On the Life and Death of Maximin', in the volume *Der siebente Ring* (1907), Kronberger is spirited away beyond death by a god as desirable as himself, their union sealed with a kiss. The poem closes with this laudatory couplet:

Preist eure stadt die einen gott geboren!
Preist eure zeit in der ein gott gelebt!

(Praised be your city where a god was born, praised be your era in which a god breathed.)
This god is Maximin himself, the spirit of youth and beauty, altogether too perfect for the
place and times he lived and died in, though they were blessed by his passing presence.

Even if not by death, a beloved boy will in any case be taken from his adult lover by the
routine workings of time. George would have been all too aware of this from having read
widely in the Greek classics, even if he had not experienced it for himself in his actual
relationships. The song beginning 'My child came home' ('Mein kind kam heim') raises
the theme of puberty as a moment of loss to the one who loves, whether parent or lover:
for this is the time when a beloved boy grows up and leaves home. It is a moment of
culmination and success, towards which upbringing and education have been leading from
the start; and yet it is also, of course, a moment of parting and – for the adult rather than
the insouciant youth himself – of poignant grieving.

Only very few of the poems seem at all explicitly to address any aspect of the specific
social circumstances – as opposed to the isolated personal circumstances of the individual
in love with another – of male homosexuality in the late nineteenth and early twentieth
centuries. I would suggest that one such poem is 'Ripening', in which two lovers, the first
and second person singular, dare not embrace each other for fear of some unstated
intrusion of external forces; nor do they dare express themselves in words (not that they
seem to need to). Although the poem is set in a vineyard, ripe with the grapes of desire, at
sunset – this is no Munich park – nevertheless the lovers seem nervous of something more
like the legal situation in Germany than the social expectations of ancient Greece.

George's concept of a new nobility ('Neuen adel') can seem not dissimilar to the 'new
chivalry' of John Addington Symonds and the democratic comradeship of Whitman and
Edward Carpenter. It is exclusive, insofar as it appears to be an entirely male affair, but
inclusive, insofar as it is based on a community of classes, if with particular interest in the
elemental nature of the working man. It could be argued that the poem beginning 'New
nobility you wanted' is 'actually' a celebration of cruising as a kind of classless free-for-all:

Neuen adel den ihr suchet
Führt nicht her von schild und krone!
Aller stufen halter tragen
Gleich den feilen blick der sinne
Gleich den rohen blick der spähe[.]

(New nobility you wanted / Does not hail from crown or scutcheon! / Men of whatsoever
level / Show their love in venal glances / show their greeds in ribald glances.) Did I say
celebration? Well, this is as near as George gets. These libidinous exchanges of glances are
not supported, as in Whitman, by the constant endorsement of democratic freedoms.
Indeed, by the evidence of other George poems, they seem to occur even within a hierarchy
of rigid classes and degrees of beauty (or lack thereof). For this reason, the celebration is
unconvincing. It might even benefit – dare I say – from a programme of law reform with
regard to the public expression of erotic affection between men. But George's concept of a
new nobility is hardly ever stated in mass terms. It is much more likely to be imagined
taking shape between single pairs of men or in tight clusters of privileged initiates.

More characteristic of George's sight-based poems is 'The Dancer' (Der Taenzer). One
man focuses on one boy. Among a group of dancing children there is one who dances most

beautifully. Indeed, he is entire: he is the whole of youth ('die ganze jugend'). Certain physical details are mentioned: 'soft and lithe' his hip, his nimble feet, the way his hair shimmers in the darkness. That is all, but it is detail enough for the poet to generalise the whole of youth from it. This move from the fragmented physical to the integrated abstract is typical of George. It shows how his mind moves from the enchanting effects of a few observed details of boyish beauty – fragments then reassembled as if in the purposive concentration of a masturbator – to the rationalised harmony of an abstraction, in this case 'youth' – which represents far more than just 'young people'. What I am saying is, in short, that bodily detail vanishes from the typical George poem, and one sees it go. It was not absent in the first place. On the contrary, it is central to George's trains of thought: it inspires him. The boy acts as his muse, from whose form he deduces his own meditations on art and spirituality. But in the end it is the spirit that matters more.

These Platonist poems are not merely hiding lust behind intellectual comradeship, or dirty minds in clean bodies. George genuinely thinks of his homosexuality in spiritual terms, as a form of love with the capability of transcending mere physicality, even if its highest ideals are expressed in physical terms, with reference to the bodies of adolescent boys. As I have already suggested, to dismiss Stefan George and his like as mere closet cases will get us nowhere. In fact, the work of this kind of writer, at this moment in European history, makes a significant political plea for male–male relationships to be taken seriously. The ability to transcend is offered as an assimilationist counter-argument in the face of constant accusations of filthy, corrupting perversity. It may be a limited argument, and it may, at times, be transparent – give us your sons and we will do nothing worse than educate them – but it deserves to be respected as one logical strategy at an early stage in the continuing struggle for homosexual equality.

By contrast, Constantine Cavafy chose to write *as* a homosexual, with homosexual desires, within a homosexual tradition. This meant he had to circulate his poems privately. It was a limitation he accepted, if unwillingly, rather than compromise the poetry itself. Sex was so much a part of his self-identity that it could not be left out. After quoting Cavafy's poem 'Their Beginning', Rex Warner once briefly but usefully contrasted Cavafy's eagerness to find value in ephemeral sexual encounters with T.S. Eliot's unproductive rejection and denigration of 'one-night cheap hotels'.[4] The quotation is from Eliot's 'The Love Song of J. Alfred Prufrock', but Warner could just as well have quoted from *The Waste Land* the lines (208–14) in which Mr Eugenides invites the speaker for a presumably dirty weekend at the Metropole Hotel in Brighton. Eliot's fastidious distaste for the sheer physicality of sex seems to have prevented his acknowledging its potential value even between silk sheets, let alone in the sordid settings which he was apparently unable to imagine being transcended by any kind of intercourse. For him the body was the object of fear and revulsion, perhaps especially when most intensely desired.

Nothing could be further, as Rex Warner suggests, from Cavafy's representations of homosexual encounters in the modern world. While Eliot tends to regard sex as an ineffable source of ugliness and degradation, Cavafy is more likely to treat it as both a source of immediate impressions of beauty and the inspiration for the eternal beauty of works of art. 'Their Beginning' is a case in point. After an illicit encounter, two protagonists get dressed in haste and, saying nothing, separately leave the building. The unease with which they walk away betrays, not the secrets of the mattress they have just shared, but the fact that they suspect their unease *might* be betraying them. However, one of them is an artist, and he takes away with him more than a mere memory of sensual pleasures.

Tomorrow, the next day or years after will be written
The lines of strength that here had their beginning.

However slow the germination – or should I call it parturition? – even if the memory weakens, the impressions that replace it will retain, or augment, the 'strength' of the encounter itself. Furthermore, the work of art will itself be strong – far more so than might have been suggested by the nervousness with which the two men (since that is what they are) scurried away from the moment which redefined them. 'Their Beginning' dates from 1921, the year before *The Waste Land*. It may not have the technical bravura that makes Eliot's poem look so superficially modern, but its attitude to sexuality, as well as coming from a different culture, might as well have had its origin in a different world, at once more ancient and more modern – certainly less Edwardian.

In a manner of speaking, of course, it did. Cavafy's work has far stronger links with ancient culture than Eliot's, which is, by contrast, distinctly dilettantish in its approach to the cultural heritage it so demonstratively lays claim to. Cavafy has the advantage of writing in Greek, even if not from Greece itself but from the Alexandria of Theocritus and Bion. It is clear that he sees no distinction between his Greekness and his homosexuality in the manner in which each, though much modernised, seamlessly matches up with the condition of the ancient Greeks, not only in Athens itself but in its imperial adventures and post-imperial diaspora.

Cavafy is insistent that desire should lead to action; and then, in the case of the artist, that action should be turned into the enduring work of art. In 'Desires' he says that 'desires that have grown cold / And not been satisfied' are like the dead bodies of beautiful young virgins – 'never vouchsafed one sweet / Night time of pleasure or one gleam of morning' (*P*, p. 13). By implication, this loss affects not only the dead virgin himself (for Cavafy is thinking of boys, not girls) but also those who see him and therefore desire him. To this extent, Cavafy often speaks of beautiful young men as if they were public property, and certainly as if they were a significant contribution, in themselves, to the Alexandrian cultural heritage. To miss out on making love with any one of them leaves the poet with a very real sense of deprived sadness. Worse still, if one should suppress all desires and live on to an unfulfilled old age, one ends up like the protagonist of 'An Old Man', tricked by Prudence, left with the insistent memory of 'Ardours restrained, the sacrifice / Of joy' (*P*, p. 17). What follows from all the above is that one should seize the day. The *carpe diem* theme is prominent in all of Cavafy's work. In 'An Old Man', lying Prudence tricked a man with the words 'Plenty of time. Another day'. It is only now that he is old, and lonely, that he understands he should have acted on his sexual impulses. The motto should have been *Little time, only today*.

In his book on *Gay Men's Literature in the Twentieth Century* Mark Lilly has complained – I think, rather oddly – that 'The overriding importance of physical beauty in Cavafy's celebrations of the erotic is a problematic one for modern readers.' Lilly criticises Cavafy for his tendency 'to exalt beauty to such an extent, that it is represented as an indispensable attribute for a successful human life'.[5] He never mentions that this is true of virtually every gay writer his book deals with. (Why criticise Cavafy for this, and not Tennessee Williams?) Besides, should he not also be complaining about ageism? The ages of Cavafy's desired men are usually specified in the poems: they range from twenty to twenty-nine.[6] The point is not at all that the ugly, or the thirty-year-olds, are lacking in the attributes necessary for 'a successful human life' – nowhere, of course, does Cavafy say any such thing – but that desire, which does indeed, for better or worse, impose its own standards on him who desires, creates its own standards of beauty. You might say it is the

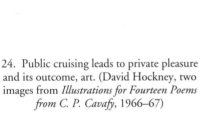

24. Public cruising leads to private pleasure and its outcome, art. (David Hockney, two images from *Illustrations for Fourteen Poems from C. P. Cavafy*, 1966–67)

desire for the beautiful young man that creates him – there, where he is most needed, among the contingencies of modern, urban life.

I would argue that, as I have already suggested, this insistence on physical beauty is far more problematic in the work of poets like Stefan George – and perhaps even in that of Plato himself – who lay such claims on spirituality. Why should a spiritual relationship be so heavily dependent on physicality, when a good brain and pleasant personality ought to do the trick? Cavafy, on the other hand, is so explicitly writing about sexual desire that his insistence on visual beauty is entirely consistent with every level of his thought. This is not to say that he ever actually defines the types of male beauty he desires (other than by age) or that he has a *Vogue* picture-editor's narrow view of bodily perfection. It may be that Lilly's retrospective imposition of narrowness on Cavafy's use of the word beauty – which, after all, notoriously takes unconventional shapes in the desires of the individual – is itself far more problematical.

Cavafy's depiction of urban life includes a rich variety of detail about the ways in which gay men conduct their sexual lives within and around the familiar institutions of the city. His narratives of urban encounters are solidly rooted in the reality of social conditions. His poetry is full of details about cruising and the contingent circumstances which can lead to unexpectedly momentous sexual events in what might have seemed inauspicious locations. Strangers meet in cafés; they become lovers in cheap rooms above bars; as their affair develops, they continue to meet in cafés and to retire to private rooms. In 'To Remain', two men make love at the back of a wine-shop, only half undressing, while the waiter dozes (*P*, p. 107). One corrupt-looking youth, seen 'At the Theatre', is all the more interesting for the scandalous reputation which has preceded him (*PAD*, p. 40). In 'The Tobacco-Shop Window', two men cruise each other's reflections in a shop window, walk a short way along the pavement, hesitate, smile, nod, and then take a cab together, already beginning to explore each other's physiques (*P*, p. 90). Two others meet over the merchandise in a store where one of them is employed. They discuss the quality of cheap handkerchiefs, investing their conversation with impenetrable double meanings and running their hands through the handkerchiefs so as to touch each other's fingers out of sight of the shopkeeper ('He Was Asking About the Quality' – *P*, pp. 188–9). Everywhere, economics affect the erotic life. Poor boys sell their bodies: one worker supplements his income in this way whenever he wants to buy some expensive new item of clothing (*P*, p. 175). A mainly heterosexual brothel provides 'secret rooms / considered shameful even to name' for those clients whose tastes and needs do not conform to those of the 'commonplace' majority (*PAD*, p. 51).

This is a world of palpable physicality, no less in those poems set in the past than in those about modern Alexandria. The relationships Cavafy deals with are always either sexual or missed opportunities for sex. Whether they last a lifetime or a frenzied half-hour, their physicality is highly valued. If spirit is involved at all, it is spirit that resides in the flesh and cannot be accessed by any but fleshly means. As in 'December, 1903' – where it is 'your hair, your lips, your eyes' that keep the memory of a lover alive in the poet's mind (*PAD*, p. 38) – the importance of physique outlasts the embraces themselves. If spirituality is remembered at all, it is preserved in the shape of a man. Hence the importance of homo-erotic art.

Cavafy's own artistic practice forms the central motif in his poetry. The homosexual artist takes centre stage, perfecting the perfectible. In 'Sculptor of Tyana' the artist shows us round his studio, pausing by a figure of Patroclus '(I must give him another touch)' and leading us towards his favourite piece, a figure of the youthful Hermes, all the more effective for its having been based on true affection: 'affection sanctified / My workmanship and greater care refined' (*P*, p. 44). For the artist in 'Representation', who has done a sketch of a particularly pretty boy, 'My work is in my heart and in my mind'. That is, it derives from a balance between affection and intellect. His joy in his work comes from restful moments after the completion of the drawing, when he can simply contemplate his achievement in the beautiful representation of the object of its inspiration (*P*, p. 70). In 'When They Awaken', Cavafy urges a poet to preserve the 'visions of your loving' by inserting them into his sentences, 'half hidden' (*P*, p. 77).

Good art does not emerge, in Cavafy, from a theoretical or 'spiritual' appreciation of human beauty. It is always based on experience, even if only the experience of having caught sight of a particular human beauty. In a number of the poems the artist, now ageing, looks back to the erotic experiences of his youth as the major source for his art. In 'Perception', for instance, a poet thinks back to the moral dilemmas which beset him when his active sexual life led to frequent, futile renunciations of pleasure. He now sees that those weak-willed resolutions to give up his vices have served a profound purpose after all:

> Under the dissolute living of my youth
> Were being formed the intentions of my poetry,
> The province of my art was being planned.

Had he actually ever managed to renounce his pleasures, the art would never have come to fruition (*P*, p. 99). In 'Silversmith' too, the artist, carving a naked boy into the side of a bowl, uses as his model the memory of 'The boy I used to love'. The extent of his effort and achievement can be measured against the fact that the youth in question died in battle as long as fifteen years ago (*P*, p. 127). Moreover, Cavafy knows perfectly well that homoerotic art is created, principally, for a homosexual consumer. A picture found 'In an Old Book' supposedly, according to its caption, represents Love; but what kind of love? To the speaker it is clear that the drawing of this boy was not intended for those who 'love more or less wholesomely, / Within the bounds of what is at all permissible'. The boy's face is not just routinely beautiful: for it both contains and recommends 'The beauty of unnatural attractions'. Some of these phrases are distinctly negative, but Cavafy always uses them with great irony. It is his purpose to exalt the soaring beauty of what so many others dismiss as degenerate and unnatural. Indeed, the figure of the boy in this poem is beautiful precisely because he dedicates his body to transgressive pleasures. It is as if he embodies homosexuality in some way that is physically different from – both aesthetically and erotically superior to – the bodies of heterosexual boys. This refined form of homoerotic beauty is perceptible only to those whom it will attract – namely, fellow homosexual boys and men. The picture exists to beguile and seduce such males,

> With those ideal lips which bring
> Delight to a body that they love;
> With those ideal limbs modelled for beds
> Called shameless by current morality.

There is an ideal masculinity, in other words, which is specifically homosexual (*P*, p. 133). Transgression intensifies both beauty and the pleasure one takes in it. In the words of the writer of erotic poetry in 'Theatre of Sidon', there is an 'Exquisite joy that comes when / The love of it is sterile / And rejected of men' (*P*, p. 136). This is Cavafy's triumph. It justifies his attention to sex and represents a strong line of defence against rejection itself. The rejection is taken for granted. If it is shaming, shame is accepted with pride. Hostility from outside renders the pleasure of being inside, in the arms of a beautiful lover, all the more affirmative.

Chapter 15

....

Marcel Proust

....

It would be difficult – though many critics have managed it, perhaps inadvertently – to take an overview of the flourishing of Modernist fiction without acknowledging the emergence of male homosexuality as a significant issue in the make-up of incidental characters and even, in many cases, of central characters. The Modernist canon is scattered with minor homosexual characters, such as the Greek sailor in the 'Eumaeus' episode of James Joyce's *Ulysses* (1922); or the unnamed victim whom Miss Lonelyhearts and Ned Gates taunt and torture for being queer in Nathanael West's *Miss Lonelyhearts* (1933); or Luis Campion in F. Scott Fitzgerald's *Tender is the Night* (1934); or Commendatore Angeloni in Carlo Emilio Gadda's late Modernist novel *That Awful Mess on Via Merulana* (*Quer pasticciaccio brutto de via Merulana*, 1957). In some novels, the presence of these minor characters, even so minor as to remain unnamed, throws significant light on the attitudes of central characters. For instance, in Ernest Hemingway's *The Sun Also Rises* (1926), the narrator Jake Barnes' hostile response to a bunch of young queens in a Paris bar says a great deal about his own sense of diminished virility as a consequence of the genital wound he has suffered in the Great War.[1]

A few of the Modernist authors, other than those who were themselves homosexual men, give significant and sizeable roles to homosexual characters: I am thinking of Tony Hunter in John Dos Passos' *Manhattan Transfer* (1925), Neville in Virginia Woolf's *The Waves* (1931) and Daniel in Jean-Paul Sartre's trilogy *The Roads to Freedom* (*Les Chemins de la liberté*, 1945–49). Other major authors from the Modernist period reward subtle gay readings of their fiction, even if their characters are not explicitly stated to be in homosexual relationships. Relationships worth reading in this light include that between Kim and the Tibetan lama in Rudyard Kipling's *Kim* (1901), the student friendship between Quentin Compson and Shreve McCannon in William Faulkner's *Absalom, Absalom!* (1936),[2] the erotic interest that develops between the poet and the boy in Hermann Broch's *The Death of Virgil* (*Tod des Vergil*, 1945), and any number of homosocial relationships which veer towards homo-eroticism in such novels by Joseph Conrad as *Heart of Darkness* (1902) and *Victory* (1919).[3] Another obvious source of important fiction about varyingly sentimental, spiritual and erotic friendships between males is Hermann Hesse, whose monumental novel *The Glass Bead Game* (*Das Glasperlenspiel*, 1945) follows in a long line of German examinations of 'men without women' (to use Hemingway's phrase).

Of course, in terms of gay literature, Modernism's real jewels are the works of authors who were themselves homosexual or bisexual: Jean Cocteau, André Gide, Marcel Proust, Ronald Firbank, E.M. Forster, Henry James, Federico García Lorca, Thomas Mann and so forth. These constitute the first major cohort of homosexual writers, the first conceptually post-Freudian generation. Their subjectivist, psychological fictions did far more than merely offer case studies in homosexuality – though that is more or less what Forster tried to do in *Maurice*, which he then considered unpublishable. More than this, they gave us a literature in which sexuality becomes both complex and varied, never fixed by a single pattern of heterosexual courtship and marriage.

The first of the great novels in which homosexuality takes centre stage, as both concept for discussion and behaviour for observation, is Proust's *A la recherche du temps perdu*. Proust began it in about 1909 – although the first volume, *Du Côté de chez Swann*, was not published until 1913, the year of Mann's *Der Tod in Venedig* – and went on working on it until his death in 1922, the year of *Ulysses*. As gay literature, the *Recherche* is remarkable for its insistence that inversion exists in great abundance everywhere, throughout society, even though it will often remain invisible to the untrained eye; and for Proust's apparent recognition that his readers may share the sexual interests of his characters.

The main characters around whom Proust teases out the topic of homosexuality are Robert de Saint-Loup, the Baron Palamède ('Mémé') de Charlus, Albertine Simonet, and the narrator himself. Saint-Loup first appears to Marcel, and therefore to the reader, as a lover of women: his affair with Rachel is protracted and intense. But later in life, despite the fact that he marries Gilberte Swann, Saint-Loup develops his interest in men, and his last great love is Charles Morel. Little information reaches us about his affairs with men, because Marcel hears only rumours of them, often at third hand. More visible is the Baron de Charlus, the great comic character Proust based on the poet Robert de Montesquiou, among others. He, too, appears first as if heterosexual – he is reputed, early on, to be the lover of Odette de Crécy – but he becomes Proust's most detailed representation of a man-loving man. His loves are many and varied, but the affair to which the narrator has clearest access is the one with Charles Morel (prior to Saint-Loup's liaison with the same).

Charlus is vain and snobbish, by turns demonstratively masculine and abjectly effeminate, both silly and profound. His life spans the whole period of the novel, and his intimacies bridge the social spectrum from palace to gutter. His erotic interests are especially varied as he grows older towards the end of the novel, when he develops a taste for small boys (XII, p. 95)[4] and pays working-class men in Jupien's brothel to whip and humiliate him. In his relations with Marcel, he is both generous and haughty, and always unpredictable.

André Gide had turned the novel down for publication by the *Nouvelle Revue Française* on the spurious grounds that Proust was a vapid socialite whose book was probably little more than fictionalised gossip about the *beau monde*. Although it is that indeed, it is a lot more besides, and Gide lived to regret his careless decision when he discovered what the *Recherche* was really like. However, he never approved of its representations of what he regarded as the negative aspects of homosexuality. Footnoting his 1922 Preface to *Corydon* in 1924, Gide acknowledged that Proust's work had 'accustomed the public to consider more calmly a subject which they previously pretended or preferred to ignore', but he dismissed Magnus Hirschfeld's theory of the 'third sex' ('with which Marcel Proust seems to agree') as being relevant only to a narrow range of cases of 'inversion, effeminacy and sodomy', whereas he was more interested in 'what we customarily call Greek love – "pederasty" which contains no element of effeminacy on either side'.[5] The Baron de Charlus represented most of the things

25. The nineteenth-century dandy/aesthete becomes the twentieth-century queen. (Jean Boldini, *Count Montesquiou*)

from which, in both his writings and his own life, Gide was at pains to distance both Corydon and himself. As he said in a letter to Proust (14 June 1914), he was worried that readers would take the complex individual Charlus as the uncomplex representative of a degenerate type. He did not want to be tarred with that brush.[6]

Because Marcel, the narrator of the *Recherche*, is fascinated by those who do not fit into strictly heterosexual patterns of social and sexual intercourse, *A la recherche du temps perdu* returns to the topic of homosexuality again and again. Lesbianism is raised, chiefly as a phantom, when for hundreds of pages Marcel fusses about whether his beloved Albertine has had affairs with other young women. As suspicion turns to paranoia, lesbianism is thus defined in a context of heterosexual jealousy. (Similarly, Charles Swann lengthily interrogates Odette, when she is still his mistress, about whether she has had affairs with other women. She has [II, pp. 200–15].) As it turns out after her accidental death, Albertine was indeed predominantly lesbian (XI, pp. 179–83); but by this time, for Marcel, the heat has gone out of the matter. The book's most haunting lesbian scene occurs in the first volume but echoes throughout the rest of the book: this is the occasion which Marcel witnesses at Montjouvain – characteristically prying through the window of a private house – when Mlle Vinteuil makes love with her girlfriend while desecrating a photograph of her own father (I, pp. 218–27). The scene is supposed to give Marcel a lasting insight into the cruel side of the human heart.

In truth, the account of the relationship between Albertine and Marcel is far less about a woman's sexuality than about a man's obsession with it. His suspicions turn him into something of an expert – at least, to his own satisfaction – on the culture and customs of Gomorrah. Likewise, his abiding interest in the Baron de Charlus gives him an education in the customs and culture of the Sodomites. As a consequence, the novel contains several long essays on homosexuality, which display a fascinating combination of speculation, invention, ignorance and solid information. Whether one should blame the ignorance on Marcel or Proust is a moot point. The generous view is to regard many of Marcel's utterances as being written by Proust at a considerable ironic distance.

Among the views expressed at various points in the novel are the following. Homosexual people – or rather, 'inverts', the term with which Proust was most comfortable – constitute not only a race apart, like the Jews, but a cursed race (*la race maudite*) who often support each other by the secretive means of a kind of international freemasonry. Inversion should not be categorised as a vice, even if there are plenty of inverts who are vicious. Some remain solitary; others socialise and organise with their own kind. Inversion has extensive parallels, both literal and symbolic, within the world of botany. It is possible to detect such people by observing details of behaviour and physique; they are adept at recognising each other. A distinction should be made between people who are homosexual by convention, as in ancient Greece, and those of the modern world whose homosexuality is involuntary. Male inverts make good husbands. Above all, however, the narrative keeps coming back to the figure of the homosexual man who is attracted only to heterosexual men and can therefore never find a partner who is able or willing to return his love. Charlus is the embodiment of this conundrum.

As André Gide noticed, the major problem with Proust's representations of homosexuality is that he used his own most abiding and precious memories of love to flesh out the novel's picture of heterosexual relations and was inadvertently left, when it came to writing about homosexuality, with predominantly negative themes and events. This is where the *Recherche* may be said to reveal the gaping flaw in its construction. It is a flaw imposed on the artist by the homophobia of his times. By the time Proust became aware of the consequences of his initial decision to heterosexualise his narrator (and himself), it was too late to adjust the disproportionately negative view the book conveys of its homosexual characters and the relationships they form.

In order to restore one's complete respect for the book, it may be useful both to approach Proust *du côté de chez* Roland Barthes, and to look out for signs of the ironic distance between Proust and his self-portrait, Marcel. Barthes makes some particularly revealing comments on the scene in *La Prisonnière* when Albertine accidentally lets slip the first half of an obscene expression. She covers her mouth, as if to cram the obscenity back into the silence of her body, but she cannot hope to hide her always very expressive blushes or to censor the eloquence of her sudden speechlessness. Marcel, her lover and captor and – inasmuch as he keeps confiding in us his doubts about her fidelity and virtue – her betrayer, is at first puzzled by her half-utterance; and when she refuses to complete her sentence, he mentally tries out several possible endings, none of them making any sense. When he finally understands what she said, he deduces from it proof that she is lesbian (X, pp. 185–8). Roland Barthes comments that Marcel is horrified, 'for it is the dreaded ghetto of female homosexuality, of crude cruising, which is suddenly revealed thereby: a whole scene through the keyhole of language'.[7]

One has to assume that Barthes is taking a characteristically ironic step beyond the common view of the *Recherche* as a *roman à clef*. If there is a key to this novel, we are invited not to turn it, but to remove it and peek through the hole. This phrase 'the keyhole of language' ('le trou de serrure du langage') is what impresses one as going straight to the heart of Proust's method. Of course, Barthes is preparing the ground for a conventional post-structuralist reading of the book as an unstable text open to an infinity of subjective readings, based on a free discourse between writer and reader. His point about the 'keyhole of language' has a general application, insofar as when we read fiction and 'see images' of fictional characters, we are not looking though the author's eyes or the narrator's eyes at an existing and complete reality; we are not holding a mirror up to an already detailed scene, nor are we looking into a mirror held by author or narrator. What flashes and fragments we 'see', or imagine we see, we see through and in the medium of the language in which they are presented to us.

This may be mildly interesting as a general proposition; but, applied to Proust, it has more particular and literal reference to narrative technique and our readings of it. To understand and enjoy the *Recherche* one must have an ear for gossip – not merely in order to follow up the real life equivalences of Proust's characters and events – that is, not to treat the book as autobiography and biography, a grand soap opera based on a true story. The book is that, to be sure; and, as such, it is *actually* an act of gossip. But that may be its least compelling aspect. More interesting are the technical aspects of the matter, the way in which the book is narrated: for it is here that Proust really innovates as a gay writer.

The usual narrative mode in Proust involves the relaying – with rhetorical flourishes and personal opinions of varying relevance – of information gained either by hearsay and eavesdropping, or by the visual observation of a partially obstructed scene (between figures across the distances of a drawing room; through peepholes; between the curtain and the window frame; and so forth). Most of Marcel's information comes to him *incomplete*. In the best tradition of gossip, his inferences and inventions fill the gaps.

Marcel is an obsessive detective of secrets, a follower of the most minute clues. (In a sense, since he learns everything piecemeal, all of the information he absorbs functions as a clue to the final picture.) He is most consistently involved in the great Gay Soap Opera quandary of wondering *Is-he-or-isn't-he?* and *Is-she-or-isn't-she?* That is to say, which of the other characters are homosexual? Although he wishes to be known as heterosexual, innocent of such affairs, Marcel claims to know all the little secret signs that *mean* 'perversion'. He finds visible, physical signs of homosexuality, generally based around the loins. One thinks, in particular, of the muscular wave which ripples over Legrandin's hips outside Combray church, a 'wholly carnal fluency' which draws Marcel's attention to 'the possibility of a Legrandin altogether different to the one whom we knew' (I, p. 169). And we must not forget the 'almost symbolical behind' of Charlus (VIII, p. 10).

Tones of speech, also, lead Marcel into sexual conjecture. On the very day when he first finds out about Charlus, he hears behind him the voice of Vaugoubert and decides at once, 'He is a Charlus.' Indeed, he already has the confidence, or the arrogance, to speak of his own 'trained ear' in this connection (VII, p. 89). There seem to be other points at which his ear responds in this way, not to voice alone, but to language. Could this be why he consistently misunderstands the lift-boy in the hotel at Balbec (IV, pp. 137–8); or why he says Jupien uses 'the most ingenious turns of speech' (V, p. 18)? There can be no doubt as to why, during the Great War, Saint-Loup learns the slang of as many servicemen as possible, regardless of nationality and rank (XII, p. 122).

There are two types of clue in operation throughout the book: those to which Marcel responds (or fails to respond) when analysing other characters; and those which he leaves as clues for us readers, rather than state the facts outright. One of the reasons he gives for merely hinting at character in this way is that 'the truth has no need to be uttered to be made apparent, and that one may perhaps gather it with more certainty, without waiting for words, from a thousand outward signs, even from certain *in*visible phenomena, analogous in the sphere of human character to what in nature are atmospheric changes' (V, p. 82).

So, as we have seen, Marcel can draw profound deductions from a movement in a man's hips. And we are expected to read such clues as he does, unprompted, when, for instance, one man greets another 'with a smile which it was hard to intercept, harder still to interpret' (XI, p. 344); or when Saint-Loup darts at a waiter a glance which 'in its limpid penetration seemed to indicate a kind of curiosity and investigation entirely different' from that of an 'ordinary' diner (XI, p. 360). In such cases, Marcel simultaneously infers and implies a sexual situation, without any certainty whatsoever, in his mind or in ours.

Marcel's hints to the reader often take shape as unspecific promises, accompanied by an 'as we shall see', which sometimes, perhaps deliberately, gets lost in his other plans and never comes to pass. We are promised certain 'quarrels' between Charlus and 'people wholly unlike Mme de Villeparisis' (V, pp. 369–70); a vision of 'Highnesses and Majesties' not of the Blood Royal but 'of another sort altogether', again in connection with Charlus (VI, p. 162); proof that homosexuality is curable (VII, p. 35); Charlus 'doing things which would have stupefied the members of his family and his friends' (X, p. 13) and appeasing 'his vicious cravings' (X, p. 49); and troubles brewing for the Saint-Loup marriage, not in a social but 'in another connection' (XI, p. 350). Even if such promises do come to fruition (as some of them do), given the book's length, the reader has often forgotten the promise by the time it is fulfilled. Perhaps its original suggestiveness is sufficient on its own; no further evidence is required. Whether or not the book duly and dutifully delivers, the reader's suspicious imagination will already have done the trick.

The whole book is packed with errors of conjecture, particularly in connection with the matters of sexual status and event. Consider a few examples, all with reference to Charlus. The Marquis de Saint-Loup, himself bisexual, keeps referring to Charlus, his uncle, as a great womaniser, a petticoat-chaser (V, p. 228; VII, pp. 127, 135); and so, on one occasion, does Swann (VII, p. 150). Part of Charlus' reputation for evil is based on a general public confusion, whereby he is associated with another Charlus, who was arrested in a disreputable house (VIII, p. 68). Charlus himself fondly imagines that only a handful of privileged initiates is aware that he is homosexual, whereas, in fact, this is very widely known or suspected (VIII, p. 259). In *Sodome et Gomorrhe*, there is a running joke at Charlus' expense, whereby, whenever anyone says, in a perfectly innocent context, that he is 'one of them' or 'one of us', Charlus immediately bristles with defensive indignation, under the mistaken impression that it is his sexuality that is being referred to (VIII, pp. 120, 159, 263). In the same volume, Charlus wrongly imagines that Cottard is making eyes at him (VIII, p. 90). Finally, Marcel tells us that Charlus' whole lifestyle is in error, since the baron confuses his 'mania' (that is, his homosexuality) with sentimental friendship (X, p. 1). The issue seems much more complicated than Marcel realises, and this may well be a mistake on his part rather than the baron's. If so, the logical outcome would be that Marcel has consistently misjudged Charlus throughout the book in his efforts to portray him as the personification of Vice.

In any case, the important thing about the book's great network of mistakes is that conjecture – which leads as often into error as to truth, and does so purely by chance – is shown to be, in its way, far more creatively functional than the self-consciously 'scientific' or 'objective' approaches Marcel often dutifully adopts in deference to the twentieth-century *Zeitgeist*.

In speaking of the 'creative' aspect of gossip, one should not include the kind to be found in the *Divina Commedia*, a dead gossip about dead people, which Dante presents as a *fait accompli*, a last judgement against which there can be no arguing. In Proust – and this is where the whole technique takes its place among the preoccupations of Modernism – the process of putting a character together with more or less unrelated fragments of suggestion and suspicion evolves in front of our eyes, as the fortuitous result of opinion and luck, resulting in a literature of subjectivity and contingency.

No characters ever achieve that monolithic certainty of definition that any self-respecting omniscient narrator could have granted them. Take the relatively solid heterosexuality of Swann, for example. While it remains the dominant impression, it is not the whole story. One of the most consistently homo-erotic set pieces in the whole novel is narrated (by Marcel, as ever) from Swann's point of view. This is when he enters the Sainte-Euverte household and, heading upstairs with leisurely reluctance, appraises the lavish and ornamental display of servants on the staircase. There are 'enormous footmen' with 'greyhound profiles', drowsing on benches; a statuesque, 'strapping great lad in livery', who seems useless, 'purely decorative', with hair like that of a Greek statue painted by Andrea Mantegna; colossal men whose 'decorative presence and marmorean immobility' suggest to Swann that this should be named the 'Staircase of the Giants'; and a young footman who resembles an 'angel or sentinel' by the bisexual Benvenuto Cellini. Finally, he recovers 'his sense of the general ugliness of the human male' when this spectacle of monumental attendants gives way to that of his fellow guests on the upper floor (II, pp. 147–51). Swann's dreams, too, are revealing. In one, a young man weeps to be losing him as he departs on a train (II, p. 189); and in another he has to console a tearful youth, who turns out to be himself (II, pp. 223–5). Swann tells Marcel that the friendships of Charlus are 'purely platonic' (VII, p. 150); but, some time after Swann's death, while discussing with Brichot whether or not Swann was homosexual, Charlus says, 'I don't deny that long ago in our schooldays, once by accident' – at which point discretion interrupts, and Charlus merely reveals that Swann had 'a peach-like complexion' as a boy, 'as beautiful as Cupid himself' (X, p. 126). That is all. What remains is a cluster of suggestions, as substantial as rumour, which Marcel is always glad to repeat but often reluctant to substantiate.

Even Marcel's 'scientific pronouncements', far from being objective and detached, actually tend to be opinionated and explicitly reactionary. For instance, the dull and intermittently ignorant lecture he gives us on homosexuality at the start of *Sodome et Gomorrhe* was evidently designed as Proust's invert-conservative reply to André Gide's much more radical (and more convincingly scientific) book *Corydon*, which had been published in the previous year, 1920. Marcel's warning 'against the lamentable error of proposing . . . to create a Sodomist movement and to rebuild Sodom' appears to presuppose a Sodom modelled on the aristocratic Faubourg Saint-Germain (VII, p. 45). The whole passage really only makes sense, in terms of the novel's structural integrity, if we read it as being historically and personally specific to Marcel in his time. In that case, it throws some very useful light on Marcel's own closeted yearning after teenage boys.

Although he is forever trying to provide one, Marcel seems temperamentally unsuited to giving a complete overview of the people and events he describes. It seems quite wrong, therefore, to speak of this as a 'panoramic' novel. On the contrary, it is a narrowly specific *peephole* novel (or, as Barthes might put it, a *keyhole* novel), whose narrator is a spy. Marcel's habit of *looking-through* becomes a narrative mannerism. Observations made from his windows in the hotel at Balbec or in the Hôtel de Guermantes may seem natural enough, and unforced. But when, as the psychological climax to *Le Temps retrouvé*, he peeks through a hole in a brothel door to watch Charlus being whipped by a male whore, Marcel's powerful imagination provides us with a wealth of details he could only have seen if the peephole had been movable and equipped with a zoom lens. For once, his account is impossibly complete (XII, pp. 155–6).

Throughout the book, amorous and sexual processes (such as flirtation and cruising) are associated with espionage. The cruising eyes of Charlus are occasionally 'shot through by a look of intense activity such as the sight of a person whom they do not know excites only in men to whom . . . it suggests thoughts that would not occur to anyone else – madmen, for instance, or spies' (IV, p. 69). When Marcel sees Saint-Loup leaving Jupien's brothel in a suspiciously quick and covert manner, he asks himself, 'Was this hotel being used as a meeting-place of spies?' (XII, p. 150). The idea is mistaken but not inappropriate. As Roland Barthes says, the novel is 'a tremendous *intrigue*, a *farce* network', in which all characters (particularly, of course, Marcel himself) are informants, stool pigeons, definitively indiscreet.[8]

What this does to our position as readers, in our 'discoursing with the text', is the novel's real *tour de force*, since we are involved in the intrigue as its principal beneficiaries. We are the point to which all the gossip flows, and it is our presence that attracts it. However, we do not get away with this lightly: we press our eye to the keyhole and, assuming we are healthily self-conscious, we see a keyhole-shaped reflection of our own eye staring back. The point is that, in order to appreciate the full quality and resonance of Marcel's gossip, we ourselves have to become fully involved *as gossips* in the process of drawing conclusions from his clues. We are ourselves implicated in the intrigue.

Proust's trick of turning all his readers into inveterate gossips is closely linked to one of his main themes: the relation between aesthetic creativity and male homosexual intercourse. One of the book's longest-running jokes persistently nudges the arts into a realm suggestive of sexual irregularity. The liaison between Charlus and the violinist Morel gives rise to a barely straight-faced equation of music and sodomy. 'I should like to listen to a little music this evening,' says Charlus when he first picks Morel up; 'I pay five hundred francs for the evening' (VIII, p. 11). Later, when Charlus and Morel play together for the Verdurins and their guests, Marcel comments that the baron's keyboard style has its 'equivalent' in his 'nervous defects', by which is meant his inversion (VIII, p. 137). When Mme Verdurin puts the two lovers in communicating bedrooms, she cannot resist this innuendo: 'If you want to have a little music, don't worry about us, the walls are as thick as a fortress' (VIII, p. 261). (See also X, p. 15.) At times the equation broadens to include artistic activities in general. Something of the kind seems to occur when a woman says she loves 'artistic' men because 'there is no one like them for understanding women' (I, p. 104). The whole issue of Bergotte's apparent 'vices' is concerned with 'a literary solution' to the moral problems raised by 'really vicious lives' (III, pp. 185–6).

By obsessing us with the *Is-he-isn't-he?* question, in the end, Marcel forces us to ask it of him. (The usual line on this matter of their sexualities has been that Proust was homosexual, his narrator heterosexual; but one is not obliged to follow it.) We may feel the need to ask such questions as the following. Why does Marcel find Albertine most sexy when she is sleeping? Why does he keep accusing her of being lesbian? Why does he become the most accomplished invert-spotter in the book? Why does he keep spying on the flirtations of male inverts? Why, in his only general pronouncement on the appearance of the male body, when he says it is 'marred as though by an iron clamp left sticking in a statue that has been taken down from its niche' (IX, p. 98), is he so clearly thinking of men as being in a perpetual state of erection?

Marcel is certainly not beyond reacting positively to male beauty. He shows us a young servant with 'a bold manner and a charming face' (V, p. 271); a pageboy 'as beautiful as Endymion, with incredibly perfect features' (VII, p. 268); and a 'handsome angel' of a butcher, up to his elbows in gore (IX, p. 180). Young men on the beach at Balbec are 'demi-gods' (III, p. 366), while the Comte d'Argencourt and the Duc de Châtellerault – both tall, blond, young and homosexual – look 'like a condensation of the light of the spring evening' in which they appear (V, p. 289). The two sons of Mme de Surgis, to whom Charlus will later take a fancy, are described by Marcel as possessing 'great and dissimilar beauty', inherited from their mother (VII, p. 119). Marcel, rather lamely, excuses his own tendency to admire good-looking men and boys as 'the mania which leads [male] people who are innocent of inversion to speak of masculine beauty' (VIII, p. 283).

Furthermore, there are equivocal moments in all of Marcel's infatuations with beautiful women. There is the occasion, for instance, when he dreams of Gilberte as a treacherous young man (III, pp. 289–90). He sees something of Mme Swann 'in the masculine gender and the calling of a bathing superintendent' at Balbec (III, p. 369); and, conversely, he sees in a portrait of the same woman, at first, 'a somewhat boyish girl', then 'an effeminate youth, vicious and pensive' (IV, p. 206). Saint-Loup reminds him of his beloved Mme de Guermantes (V, p. 101). And the relationship with Albertine fails (if it tries) to resist the intrusion of the author's autobiography: whatever one's theoretical principles, it is as difficult to separate Albertine from Alfred Agostinelli as Marcel from Proust.

Certain non-explicit remarks seem comprehensible to Proust, rather than to the Marcel who makes them, unless the latter has the former's inside knowledge of a relatively hidden homosexual subculture. One should include among these a description of Legrandin as 'a Saint Sebastian of snobbery' (I, p. 175); and of the Emperor William II as a green carnation (VI, p. 298).

It may be that, as André Maurois once said, Marcel's love for Albertine is 'nothing but a morbid curiosity'. He loves her in order to get close enough to observe her, to find out about her; and he does so in order to spy on himself. He is testing his own heterosexual resolve. Furthermore, it is hard not to conclude that he is testing it in a manner which prejudges the issue. The imprisoned Albertine (the *prisonnière* Marcel hides in his most private sanctum in order to contemplate her dormancy at his leisure) calls to mind the metaphor with which that era made a kind of sense of the homosexual male: the female soul *imprisoned* in a male physique. The monstrous act of appropriation whereby he incorporates her into his own domain – ostensibly an expression of desire – seems more clearly a sign of Marcel's homosexuality: he steals and keeps her precisely because he does not desire her. (Whether or not he knows this is another matter.)

As soon as we have established the *Is-he-or-isn't-he?* doubt about Marcel – with whom, remember, we are in conspiracy to inform/misinform ourselves about all the other characters – we have to understand that exactly the same doubt arises about *us*, and directly affects our competence to participate in the text. It appears that Proust is consistently aware of, and plays with, the fact that the book is openly, ostensibly chattering with heterosexuals from a heterosexual (Marcel's) point of view, but that it has a closeted *homo*sexual subtext of exchanges between a sexually equivocal Marcel and his *homo*sexual readers. This gives the *Recherche* a pre-eminent position in the as yet unwritten history of literary camp and in the history of homosexual culture. Its place in straight male Modernism may be a red herring.

Chapter 16

Homosexual Men by Women

Many of the classic early fictional representations of homosexual men were written by women, and it is on these that I mean to concentrate in this chapter. As with male writers, so with female. The 'private' lives of those who practise sodomy on and in each other's persons are not fit material for public speech. The British Empire preferred to think of itself, no less than the Soviet Union or the People's Republic of China, as an astringent desert of manly virtue surrounded by an otherwise effeminate oasis. It was easier for writers to set novels about homosexuality either far from Britain or in some equally distant period in the past. Like many male writers of the inter-war period, and of times since, Naomi Mitchison found the cultures of classical Greece and Rome an apt arena – safely neutral territory – in which to display aspects of male love. Her Greek stories 'Krypteia' and 'O Lucky Thessaly!' and the Roman story 'A Matter of No Importance' read like preparatory studies for the later and more ambitious gay fictions of women like Mary Renault and Marguerite Yourcenar.[1]

In 'Krypteia' the Spartan Geranor kills a subversive goatherd and takes his son captive, hauling him back to the Spartan camp. Geranor's beloved Charilas begs in vain for the boy's life to be spared: Geranor ignores him and has the boy interrogated and killed. Charilas, weeping into the Spartan soil, declares that he can no longer love a man who could do such a thing. In 'O Lucky Thessaly!' the young poet Pindar arrives in Thessaly, commissioned by the Grand Duke Thorax to write a celebratory ode on the boy Hippokleas, who has won the race at Delphi. The poet and the boy fall in love. Hippokleas becomes broody and stops playing with his friends. When the poem is finished and the chorus has been rehearsed, Pindar declares himself to the boy, but his intellectual detachment interferes with the pleasure of their love-making. Once the poem has triumphantly been performed at a great feast, Pindar decides to leave Thessaly. He feels that he must move on in order to hear the Muses speaking through another love. When he leaves, the heartbroken Hippokleas reluctantly goes back to the company of his friends.

In the Roman tale, 'A Matter of No Importance', the tribune Marcus Trebius returns to Rome from Britain, accompanied by Rudd, a young male slave whom he has grown to love. However, Decima, the rich heiress to whom Marcus Trebius has become engaged in order to further his political ambitions, demands the boy as a gift. The tearful Rudd is reluctantly handed over. Later, during Marcus Trebius' absence in Gaul, Decima swaps the boy for a brooch. By the time Marcus Trebius returns to Rome, Rudd has been sold to a foreigner and taken abroad. The political marriage goes ahead, but in spite of it Marcus Trebius is not elected as consul.

These are stories about broad moral dilemmas, rather than specifically about homosexual relations. In a way, that is what makes them so positive: for, having set the stories in the ancient world, Mitchison is able to take the male–male relationships entirely for granted. She is able, without risk of scandal, to represent a routine intensity of emotion between the male lovers which is both unexceptional and powerfully affecting. If there is an argument in favour of the acceptance of male homosexual love here, it is left unspoken, implicit in the way the story's relationships are accepted by the narrative voice and are presented as such. Readers who wish to call them into question will have to do so for themselves. Although all three of Mitchison's stories end unhappily, with the parting of the lovers, it is clear that the author does not believe that the temporary griefs she portrays are at all a *necessary* part of homosexual love, as homophobic myth – then as now – would dictate. At no point does she kill off her characters to punish their sin, as many other writers in this century have chosen, or felt they were forced, to do. To that extent and further, these early stories are positive in an exemplary manner.[2]

Similarly distant from the British social context of its day, Sylvia Townsend Warner's short novel *Mr Fortune's Maggot* (1927) is set on a South Sea island, far from the restraints of Anglo-Saxon morality. In tone and atmosphere, the story partakes of some of the camp exoticism and eroticism of Ronald Firbank's *Prancing Nigger* (1924). But Warner's book is, at heart, far more seriously charged: it has much to say about religious imperialism and, in general, the disruption of the equilibrium of 'primitive' societies by the civilising zeal of the developed world. It is also acutely conscious of how 'love' itself is, so often, a colonising process, ultimately as destructive to lover as to beloved. The beloved body may itself be treated as an inviting tropical island, a site of pleasure to be colonised, settled and subsequently exploited.[3] At the same time, it provides about the nearest we get to a rhapsodic version of man–boy love from the pen of anyone other than a man who loves boys.

However, although Warner was willing privately to refer to the book's central character, a missionary, as being 'fatally sodomitic',[4] in the novel itself Mr Fortune describes his love for the boy Lueli not as 'what is accounted a criminal love' but as a 'spiritual desire'. It is to the book's credit, though, that its subjects are harmony and hope, not the depredations of repression. The genteel missionary eventually leaves the island and his beloved boy behind, but he leaves enchanted and enriched. Having lost his faith through contact with the humane paganism of the islanders, he feels liberated into a truer spirituality, unencumbered by the Church. He leaves his God, or what is left of him, on the island as a souvenir for the boy. He also carves the boy an idol to adore. On the boat back to civilisation, he receives the news of the Great War, the ultimate sign of what horrors virility can contrive to support its own vanity.[5]

Of novels set in Britain at the time of their writing, one might have expected those most fully involved in the Modernist experiment with representations of consciousness to provide fruitful explorations of deviant states of mind. But this is not necessarily so. Virginia Woolf, for instance, seems to take her preoccupation with psychological reality as an excuse for representing love between men as a private affair, so emphatically divorced from the social realm as not to require the definition 'homosexual'. In *The Waves* (1931), she represents Neville's love of Percival as a lifelong obsession – perhaps a less traumatised form of the kind of obsession which ties Septimus Warren Smith to his dead wartime comrade, Evans, in *Mrs Dalloway* (1925) – from which Neville never emerges for long enough even to label himself homosexual.[6] It is true that, on leaving school, he is aware that he will 'pass, incredible as it seems, into other lives', and that his love of Percival is 'a prelude only' (p. 43). But, even though Neville does later have a lover, he still thinks constantly of Percival as his lost ideal; the lover, in any case, is faithless (pp. 126–7). Louis, who himself goes through a boy-loving phase at school, predicts Neville's future life as a stable but intense sequence of comfortable scenes 'with many books and one friend' (p. 48). What he fails to predict is the degree of the intensity: the friend will always be the same boy, even long after his accidental death.

There is certainly no awareness at any point in the book, none in any of the book's characters, that male homosexual acts were illegal. There is no sense of oppression; but, rather, of a *sup*pression of overt feeling voluntarily inflicted by Neville on himself, and the consequent image of him, within the minds of the other characters, as one whose destiny is irredeemably sad. When the news arrives that Percival has died in India, Neville says to himself: 'From this moment I am solitary. No one will know me now' (p. 108).

What Woolf depicts here – though she shows no clear sign of being aware of the fact – is male homosexuality at its most palatable to the British status quo (by which I mean, to the values of the upper-middle and upper classes). The Neville/Percival relationship is an entirely conventional 'public' (private) school romance: unrequited, sublimated, with the desired boy conveniently killed off and remembered thereafter, by the boy who desired him, in sentimentally nostalgic soft focus. There is no homosexual subculture to support Neville in his extended moment of bereavement. He has no queer friends.

As a consequence of this solitary condition, Neville's sexual identity really only takes shape in fantasy. He sits at home and roams the empire, daydreaming of Mediterranean boys sprawling naked in the dust beneath fig trees. He imagines Percival thrashing little boys with a birch (p. 25). He thinks of Percival 'naked, tumbled, hot' on his bed in the moonlight (p. 35). Later in life, he has a recurring fantasy about naked cabin boys squirting each other with lubricious hoses (pp. 128, 140). But unlike other bourgeois, homosexual characters of the period (Forster's Maurice, for instance), who meet their sexual needs among the working class, Neville is too much of a snob to soil his bookish, pseudo-classical dreams with the vulgarity of real life. In a characteristic moment he says, 'I cannot read in the presence of horse-dealers and plumbers . . . They will make it impossible for me always to read Catullus in a third-class railway carriage' (p. 51). Forster, like D.H. Lawrence, would have had him trying to strike up a conversation, at least. After all, a horse-dealer or a plumber might, more vividly even than Catullus himself, bring fantasy to life.

That other great Modernist, Gertrude Stein, was far less interested than Woolf in fictional character, so it is not surprising that one does not find in her work the kinds of detailed representation with which this chapter is concerned. In any case, Stein's attitude to homosexual men – or rather, in the customary manner of the homophobic, to what homosexual men *do* with each other – seems to have been negative. Ernest Hemingway says she told him, presumably referring to anal intercourse and ignoring other possibilities:

The main thing is that the act male homosexuals commit is ugly and repugnant and afterwards they are disgusted with themselves. They drink and take drugs, to palliate this, but they are disgusted with the act and they are always changing partners and cannot be really happy . . . In women it is the opposite. They do nothing that they are disgusted by and nothing that is repulsive and afterwards they are happy and can lead happy lives together'.[7]

Stein's only written representation of homosexual men is in a short piece called 'Men', in which a trio of men enact an emotional drama involving kisses, tears and physical violence.[8] In her characteristic fashion, Stein teases out the meanings of phrases by repetition and revision, until meaning itself seems a superfluous indulgence. But she does, here, grant some significance to what singles these men out from others:

> He was meaning again and again in being such a one and he was remembering that he had meaning again and again that he was such a one. He was remembering again and again that he was such a one and he was remembering again and again that he was having meaning. He was such a one. (pp. 314–15)

One thing that the piece makes clear, intentionally or not, is that the three creatures Stein portrays are quite alien to Stein's own equilibrium. Her verbal patterns have the effect of distancing her voice from the men's emotions, with which, as a lesbian, she does not even begin to identify. It could be that the tortuous repetitions of this piece were associated in her mind with the sexual promiscuity which (in Hemingway's account) she regarded as such a clear sign of homosexual male self-loathing.

By and large, the homosexual characters in men's novels were tragic loners, outcast in their own land, bewildered at being denied their birthright of patriarchal power. One has to turn to the non-Modernist women writers for a substantial development of the idea of solidarity between oppressed groups.[9] Even lesbians have appeared only relatively rarely in the male literature. But a number of women's novels, during and between the wars, made a point of discussing the commonality of interests between such groups as female and male homosexuals, the Irish in Britain, black people, Jews, pacifists and the working class. The bravest of these is *Despised and Rejected* by Rose Laure Allatini, writing as the pseudonymous 'A.T. Fitzroy' (1918), the publisher of which was convicted for promoting, not an obscenity, but a book likely to prejudice the recruiting of persons to serve in His Majesty's Forces, and their training and discipline. Indeed, questions of homosexuality and pacifism have to wait to be so seriously yoked together again until Mary Renault's *The Charioteer* (1953). Fitzroy's sophisticated association of the rituals of heterosexual courtship with social pressures on men to go to war proves to be the perfect context for her liberal arguments on sexuality. Hers is a more broadly conceived, *social* vision of virility, love and warfare than is found in more personal writings such as Wilfred Owen's or even Siegfried Sassoon's poems. It comes as no surprise to find that both the author and one of her central characters, Alan, have read and absorbed Edward Carpenter's *Towards Democracy* (first edition 1883, complete edition 1905).

Whereas, in men's fiction, it was so often seen as being important to represent homosexual men, at least for part of the narrative, from the viewpoint of the heterosexual homophobe, women writers were generally more concerned to offer the viewpoint of a sympathetic woman character, perhaps representative of the author herself. The clearest example of this type is June Westbrook, in *Strange Brother* by the pseudonymous 'Blair Niles' (1932). Healthily curious – or perhaps, at times, inquisitive to the point of intrusiveness – she observes, and then seeks out, homosexual men in Harlem bars. She questions and studies them. When she has won their trust, she is supportive. Her friendship with one, Mark Thornton, becomes the main relationship in the book:

> They were friends without any complication of sex. It was a different relationship from any that June had ever known before, closer than any which had ever existed between her and a woman friend, and more serene, June felt, than would ever be possible in any equally close friendship with a normal man.[10]

Mark reads a lot of the literature of homosexuality (Plato and Walt Whitman are named) and at one point he decides to compile 'an anthology of manly love'. What inspires him to embark on this task is his copy of Alain Locke's *The New Negro* (1925), the key anthology of the Harlem Renaissance. He reads in it the following lines from Countee Cullen's poem 'Heritage' and is moved to tears:

> Thus I lie, and find no peace
> Night or day, no slight release
> From the intermitten[t] beat
> Made by cruel padded feet
> Walking through my body's street.

June observes that 'he always identified himself with the outcasts of the earth. The negro had suffered and that bound Mark to him' (p. 234). She finds this identification curious, at first, but the novel presents it as being both logical and desirable. June's warming to the idea of such identification is the instrument with which the author seeks to persuade the uncommitted reader to accept it. It is through June's well-balanced female normality, rather than Mark's potentially self-pitying male deviance, that the book's pleas for tolerance are voiced.

Far more notorious – and therefore, perhaps, more effective – is Radclyffe Hall's novel *The Well of Loneliness* (1928), which has no mediating hetero voice to comfort the reader who seeks touchstones of normality.[11] Instead, it presents the homosexual mediation of its central character, who is sufficiently self-hating to be almost palatable to certain types of anti-homosexual readers. Hall's main portrait of a homosexual man, Jonathan Brockett, is no less of a stereotype than the manly lesbian Stephen Gordon herself; if perhaps no more so, either. Although brilliant, he is 'curiously foolish and puerile' at times, and his hands are 'as white and soft as a woman's' (p. 227). When he is in his foolish mood, his hands make 'odd little gestures', and his laugh becomes revealingly too high, his movements too small, for his unquestionably male physique. He is liable to compromise his body even further by playing such indiscreet tricks as putting on the parlourmaid's apron and cap (p. 230). Not unexpectedly, he is an aesthete: art is said to be the one thing in life he respects, the one thing which gives him much-needed consolation (p. 233). Be that as it may, his favourite activity is gossip – a fact which Hall even finds symbolically reflected in his appearance: he is described as having 'sharp eyes that were glued to other people's keyholes' (p. 235). When he gossips, his voice takes on an 'effeminate timbre' which Stephen hates (p. 245). Unstoppable, he gushes 'on and on like a brook in spring flood' (p. 247).

This is not to say that Hall is insensitive to the situation of such a man in such an era. Her account of Brockett's changing moods is unlike Virginia Woolf's depiction of Neville insofar as it carefully registers his reactions to oppression. There are times when he gets sick of 'subterfuge and pretences' (p. 241); and if he is cynical it is because he spends much of his time 'secretly hating the world which he knew hated him in secret' (p. 242). When he speaks of heterosexual people ('the so-called normal'), his voice, not unreasonably, becomes 'aggressive and bitter' (p. 350).

As a lesbian, Stephen Gordon observes Brockett from a certain distance, but also with sympathetic identification. When they first meet she feels at ease with him, 'perhaps because her instinct divined that this man would never require of her more than she could give – that the most he would ask for at any time would be friendship' (p. 228). But when the Great War breaks out, she discovers that, for all his marginalisation and difference as a homosexual man, he is still privileged *as a man*: he is allowed by his country to enlist in its service. (Hall does not mention, however, that he would have been rejected had he been open about his sexuality when enlisting.) Whatever he may think of this dubious honour, the reaction of a patriotic but redundant woman is clear: 'Stephen had never thought to feel envious of a man like Jonathan Brockett' (p. 271). There is, of course, a good deal of disdain in this sentiment: for Stephen usually only envies 'real' men. But in time of war, despite his effeminacy, Brockett is officially considered man enough to die for king and country – which Stephen is not.

After the war, when Stephen has, after all, distinguished herself in a women's ambulance unit and won the Croix de Guerre, and Brockett too has returned, changed in all aspects except 'those white and soft-skinned hands of a woman' (p. 333), Stephen seems increasingly to resent, but is forced to accept, a sense of fellowship with other queer people. Near the end of the book there is a complex, depressive scene in a gay bar – a kind of Purgatorio for melancholy inverts – where a grey-faced youth whispers to Stephen, 'Ma soeur' (my sister). Her immediate, macho impulse is to hit him in the face with her fist; but, although she thinks of him as 'it', a mere creature, barely human at all, she restrains herself, apparently realising that she has no choice but to identify with him. Digging her nails into her own palms, she reluctantly identifies him as an unwanted brother and replies, 'Mon frère' (p. 394). It takes the cultivated Jew Adolphe Blanc to calm her down and persuade her that the men in the bar are fully human. She never loses this antagonistic relation to effeminate men. Indeed, the book virtually closes with a dream in which a cluster of reproachful pansies accuses her of having stolen their masculine birthright of strength (p. 446).

The ostentatiously feminine man is, of course, always a potential problem to women if his performances ever threaten to slip over from self-expression into parody. And yet, on the other hand, women writers have often shown admiration for men who, even if they do despise the femininity they adopt, hate masculinity even more. So the shameless sodomite is always a useful character for highlighting both antagonisms and potential alliances between women and men. Djuna Barnes provides one such, Dr Matthew O'Connor, in *Nightwood* (1936).[12] He is an unlicensed gynaecologist who goes to bed in full drag: nightgown, wig and make-up. His bedroom is untidily packed with old scent bottles and rusty gynaecological instruments. At the head of the bed is a bucket 'brimming with abominations'. The whole room has taken on the air of its occupant's ambisexuality: it is described as 'a cross between a *chambre à coucher* and a boxer's training camp'. It no more resembles a real woman's boudoir than it does a real man's (p. 116).

However, what seems to interest Barnes most about the doctor is his way of speaking. He is, of course, pathologically indiscreet. He is sometimes heard to shout after a man's departing shadow in the street, 'Aren't you the beauty!' (p. 49) Asked what he remembers of Vienna, he describes Austrian boys on their way to school, 'rosy-cheeked, bright-eyed, with damp rosy mouths, smelling of the herd childhood' (p. 33). He claims to be able to tell men apart in pitch darkness, and even what quarter they frequent, by the 'size and excellence' of, one supposes, their genitals. Some 'come as handsome [and edible] as *mortadellas* slung on a table' (p. 136). Above all, he talks to women about men, on whose sex lives he is an authority. His knowledge is arcane and expansive, but is just as likely to be sharpened down to the point of a paradox: 'It's the boys that look as innocent as the bottom of a plate that get you into trouble' (p. 231).

In this case, then, the homosexual man constitutes a bridge across the gap between men and women, conveying information about the former to the latter, at once enthusing about men as sexual partners and proving their peculiarities alien and exotic. But he is, above all, an untrustworthy informant, far too much of a man: deceitful in bed, when dragged-up to be penetrated by men, and deceitful at work, when penetrating women under false pretences. Shari Benstock speaks of how the 'Gossipy and garrulous' doctor 'parodies woman's language, steals her stories and her images in order to teach her about herself'.[13] The problem is that, however sincere and convincing his drag, it still conceals the phallus; however brightly lipsticked his mouth, it still contains a patriarchal tongue. Even as an unlicensed doctor in a frock, he has learned to speak with the authority in which doctors are wont to dress up their speculations. Although demonstrably 'other' than heterosexual, heterosexist man, from the perceptive point of view of female otherness he is nonetheless *the same*. He is homosexual, but a man.

Many readers will have noticed that among the women writers I have mentioned in this chapter are many, a majority indeed, who have since been celebrated as contributors to the lesbian heritage of the Modernist period: Virginia Woolf, Gertrude Stein, Radclyffe Hall and so forth. Marguerite Yourcenar and Mary Renault follow in the same line. From an early moment in the twentieth century, lesbian writers have consistently shown a greater interest in the lives of homosexual men than has generally been shown in lesbian lives by homosexual male writers. (There are obvious exceptions like Proust.) But the main point of interest, here, is that we are seeing an incipient sense of interests shared by members of different minority groups. Some of these texts represent the first steps taken to develop a sense of resistant solidarity between the victims of patriarchy.

Women writers have not, of course, been immune to homophobia, as its carriers any less than its victims. For instance, there is a somewhat gratuitous passage in Winifred Holtby's *South Riding* (1936) which explains the unpleasantness of Alderman Snaith by identifying him as a survivor of predatory homosexual child abuse. Snaith watches, mesmerised, as his cat gives birth on his hearth rug, and is impressed by the 'neatness and economy' of the natural process. ('This, then, was nature – this amusing, tidy and rather charming process.') As the cat finishes licking her kittens clean, Snaith feels released from a burden of suppressed memory:

> Within that brief period of time a thousand half-formed images had been destroyed, a hundred nightmares broken. A serenity of liberation began to dissolve the horror surrounding all thoughts of mating and procreation haunting him since that one hideous initiation, when, a little pink and white boy, brought up by a maiden aunt, too soft and pretty and innocent for safety in Kingsport streets, he had fallen into the hands of evil men and fled from them too late, a psychological cripple for life.[14]

While a passage like this clearly reflects a general female concern about the consequences of child abuse, it performs two negative tasks as well. Firstly, given its brevity but the decisive confidence of its last five words, it somewhat ambiguously both absolves Snaith of responsibility, and yet blames him, for his subsequent personality and deeds, flashing on to the reader's consciousness with a virtually subliminal insistence, which takes no real account of the complexities of such a case. Secondly, as the novel's only reference to male–male sexual relations, its formulations of the conquest of nature by unnature, child by adult and innocence by evil take on a stereotypical resonance, echoing the most negative representations of homosexuality within the society to which the book claims reference; the result being, in an otherwise consistently reformist and liberal text, to suggest that anti-homophile vigilance can itself have significant reforming powers, eventually, to rid local communities and councils of the likes of Alderman Snaith.

In this text, then, if woman herself is 'other', the homosexual man is more 'other' still. His distance from woman is used, if only in passing, to punctuate the argument that heterosexual women and men have a close commonality of interests and should, therefore, share equally in the privileges of democracy. Only then can women, as mothers, adequately protect boys, as sons and potential fathers, from being raped by sonless men. If I overstate the case by isolating this passage from its humane contexts, I do so, not to accuse Holtby of an uncommon malice, but to offer a mundane example of how women writers too, even the most aware, may fail their gay readers by using homosexuality as a representative evil. This is a careless moment, from which I do not seek to excuse Holtby, but in contrast with which I would prefer to affirm the superiority of the rest of her book.

The most interesting of the systematically anti-homosexual texts by women in the inter-war period is Katharine Burdekin's *Swastika Night* (1937), originally published under the male pseudonym 'Murray Constantine'.[15] Burdekin's book is remarkable for its definitive association of Fascism with patriarchy; and one can recognise the logic of the next step, whereby she proposes that extreme male privilege must result in a culture like that of the ancient Greeks, in which women are enslaved and boys are exalted. The masculinist cult of boy-love is depicted as the logical consequence of a post-Hitlerian downgrading of women to the status of higher animals. Men have no memory of a time when women could be physically admired, even as mere sex-objects: here, woman is a shorn, cowed figure dressed in brown rags and fit only for the bearing of sons. The Knight who is the only character with access to any historical information curls his lips in disgust when he realises 'that women had once been as beautiful and desirable as boys, and that they had once been *loved*' (p. 11).

For relationships of any intimacy, men turn (spiritually) to each other and (physically) to boys. Even the dissident central character, the English mechanic Alfred, has only male friendships (though there is a woman he visits for strictly reproductive purposes) and he does not disapprove of the exclusive homosexuality of Thomas, his second son. Indeed, he even appears to envy the boy his special freedom: '*He* wouldn't be in the sickening atmosphere of the Women's Quarters. . . . He'd be off with the [male] friend of the moment, free to go where they would, with the whole clean night-country before them' (p. 166). This contrast between the enforced squalor of the women's quarters and the cleanliness of the masculine 'night-country' in which youths make love with each other helps to reinforce, in Alfred's mind, a sense of male love's harmony with nature.

In this novel, then, we see the other extreme of women's responses to male homosexuality. For some novelists, male inverts had seemed to be less implicated in the machinations of patriarchy than heterosexual men were; and it followed that such men, partially denied the rewards of orthodox masculinity, might be taken as potential allies in the struggle for sexual equality. For others, though, male homosexuality seemed like an extremist commitment to masculinity, an aversion to femininity virtually synonymous with misogyny. A man who loved men might be demonstrating his hatred of women. While recognising the logic of this point of view, it is important not to overlook its destructive potential. When we come to examine the literature of the Holocaust, we shall have cause to deplore the complacency of many commentators who accused the Nazis of mass homosexual perversion.

Chapter 17

The Harlem Renaissance

Eric Garber has spoken of 'a homosexual subculture, uniquely Afro-American in substance', which took shape in Harlem after the First World War.[1] To speak of the Harlem Renaissance and its participants in a gay cultural context is to speak, uniquely, of a cohesive gay community whose texts have been inherited not only by its most legitimate heirs – lesbian and gay African-Americans today – but, indirectly, by gay communities throughout the Western world. I mean 'texts' in the broadest sense, including languages and styles, songs and fashions, as well as novels and poems.

However, until early in the 1990s this unique subcultural heritage went largely unrecognised, even by African-American commentators, whose critical practice tends to be no less heterocentric than that of their white equivalents. As Emmanuel Nelson has written,

> Almost all the major figures of the Harlem Renaissance were gay: Alain Locke, Countee Cullen, Langston Hughes, Claude McKay. Yet among black scholars of the Harlem Renaissance there is a remarkable reticence about the sexualities of these pioneering artists and a determined unwillingness to explore the impact of their gayness on their literary constructions and on the forms and directions of the Renaissance'.[2]

To Nelson's list of names one would want to add the novelist Wallace Thurman and the white novelist-entrepreneur Carl Van Vechten who did so much to help get black gay writers into print.

One is persuaded of the urgent need for the Harlem Renaissance poets to be reappraised by and for gay readers when a gay black writer like Daniel Garrett says, of the Harlem writers, that 'many . . . were homosexual, though none but for Bruce Nugent expressed this in his work'.[3] In this chapter I intend to explore various gay reading strategies in relation to these writers, to suggest to contemporary readers likely meanings which had to be kept concealed at the time of their writing – concealed, that is, from hostile readers, but always accessible to perceptive, sympathetic readings. Such readings must be carried out, even today, in the face of obstruction on the part of some of the writers' estates, which would seem to prefer questions of non-standard sexuality to remain buried in obscurity. The case of the Langston Hughes Estate's interference in Isaac Julien's film *Looking for Langston* is only the most visible example of this tendency.[4]

The simplest way to begin a search for 'gay poems' by the Harlem writers is to consult them on the topic of attractive men and boys. There are many such figures in Langston Hughes' poems, but it should be remembered that they appear among at least as many, if not more, beautiful women.[5] In a sense, to turn some of these poems into 'gay poems' one must take the simple, and entirely excusable, step of isolating them from the rest. Disapproving heterosexual readers may complain that this is cheating, and that it has the effect of falsifying Hughes' output. My considered reply is that gay readers have had to make themselves, with practice, adept at such strategies, in order to step around the barriers which gay poets have often been forced to erect around themselves. If anyone is involved in the falsification of gay poets' work, it is the censorious and homophobic critical voices within the dominant, heterosexual community.

Hughes is particularly good on sailors. Like Billie Holiday, he covers the waterfront – that site of promiscuous social interaction and continental drift, where heavy labour and frantic leisure are equally at home, and where violence is no more than an expression of passionate release, no less than a way of life. As glimpsed in 'Water-Front Streets' (p. 51), this is potentially an ugly place, yet its ugliness is tempered by its conduciveness to dreaming. The waterfront is, by definition, on the margin of the city. It is also, by temperament, on the margin of urban social structures. Although the city's wealth must pass through this place, it does not itself accumulate wealth. Most who work here are poor. But they are rich in experience. Some have travelled on ships; others, who have had to stay behind, have travelled in the mind. It is its association with travel, its links with the rest of the world (in the present context, with Africa in particular), that make this a place in which the imagination holds sway, and even in which reality itself can meet the standards of the imagination. The dreams Hughes has in mind seem to be distinctly un-American. They are dreams of another place, where 'life is gay'.

One can read this poem as a slight lyric of rather sentimental Garveyism. But the language in which it is expressed is clearly intended to take us further. The poem's adjectives are 'beautiful', 'dream', 'rare', 'gay', and 'beautiful' again. The adverb 'wondrous' qualifies and intensifies 'rare'. This is no picture of squalor or poverty. As the imagery solidifies in the second stanza – with two of the adjectives becoming nouns, 'beauties' and 'dreams' – one receives an impression of nothing less than glamour; not so much the glamour of the waterfront streets themselves, which are 'not so beautiful', as that of the 'lads' who embark from here and who, in due course, will disembark again, laden with fresh experience.

The ships on which these sailors sail are 'dream ships' to those who stay behind, not only because of the exotic places they sail to, but also because of their exotic cargo, the sailor 'lads'. Like ships themselves, these boys' hearts are freighted with 'beauties' and 'dreams'. In such dreams, they reimagine the amorous encounters they enjoyed in port and conjure up hypothetical future encounters. In the last two words, 'like me', the speaker both compares his experience with theirs – he, too, is laden with dreams since encountering beauty – and identifies himself as the possible subject of an absent sailor's dream.

The international trade in dreams is also, of course, a trade in flesh.[6] Whether the sailors are buying or being bought, they participate physically in a commodification of dreams, of which Hughes seems heartily to have approved (but which was deplored by his critics in the black bourgeoisie, which was so earnestly trying to underpin its limited economic successes with racial 'respectability'). In other poems, then, sailors are associated with cash: when they hit the waterfront they have both energy and money to burn. So 'Port Town' (p. 71) is spoken, jauntily, by a whore of unspecified sex, to a sailor, enticing him with promises of a night of alcohol and 'love'. It begins as follows:

26. Gay subculture flourishes in the jazz age. (Invitations for drag balls at Harlem's Manhattan Casino and Rockland Palace)

Hello, sailor boy,
In from the sea!
Hello, sailor,
Come with me!

This jovial little poem, luxuriating in its own unapologetic shallowness, is a typical product of pre-Stonewall homosexuality: safe in the complacent assumption that it is spoken by a woman, but daring in the possibility that it is not. The distance between its two possible versions produces an ironic, stereoscopic effect which is authentic camp.

'Young Sailor', too, concerns the moment when a man on shore leave tries to decide what to spend his accumulated wages on (p. 73). Alcohol and women are the two alternatives mentioned. But remember that gay mythology of available sailors, while acknowledging that such men generally consider themselves heterosexual, depends on frustration and drunkenness to deliver the prize. Hughes' sailor goes to sea for 'strength' and returns to port for 'laughter'. At the point where sea and land so productively meet, on the waterfront, he 'carries' both strength and laughter, in a balanced combination which makes him irresistible. While the strength of his physique may be menacingly attractive, his relaxed laughter is positively inviting. It may be that he will continue to laugh while one engages with his strength. So be it. Both sailor and poem ignore the future, focused as they are on momentary delight, having 'nothing hereafter'.

Interestingly, these poems do not specify the skin colour of the sailors. On the other hand, for obvious reasons, the politicised Harlem street-poems often depend for their persuasiveness on Langston Hughes's clear attraction to young black men and his concern at their plight. I do not necessarily mean that these are all 'gay poems' in the narrow sense of statements of homosexual attraction; but there is, surely, a gay element to the poet's attitude to his male subjects. In the long sequence of poems 'Montage of a Dream Deferred', for instance, the recurrent evocation of 'Little cullud boys' is deeply affectionate. Hughes likes them. The tone of his voice wears a smile, even as he acknowledges their anxiety at reaching their 'draftee years'. As much as they may be a part of his own dreams, his poem concerns their dreams of genuine access to opportunity in the United States, and the deferral thereof (pp. 221–72).

The readings one performs on such texts depend on the degree of investigative creativity one is willing to expend upon them. In the case of Hughes's 'Trumpet Player', it could be judged both impertinent and counterproductive, not to mention heavy-handed, to read the whole poem as a conscious or unconscious paean to orality, and to oral sex in particular. The man in the poem is, after all, blowing a trumpet, not a penis. The fact remains, however, no matter how tactful the reader wishes to be, that the poem expresses its celebration of jazz in terms of ecstasy, desire, and pursed lips. (We should also remember that the word 'jazz' itself has sexual origins.) In other words, the trumpeter may not be having sex – or not at the moment of the poem – but he is sexy: both desirous and desirable (pp. 114–15).

Another textual homage to black manhood, Claude McKay's poem 'Alfonso, Dressing to Wait at Table', might be read as having an exclusively 'racial' agenda, to the extent that it protests against the confining of an active, black life to the service of rich white people. But the degree of its admiration for Alfonso, long prior to its mildly politicised, racial ending, leaves an impression more of an erotic *frisson* than of protest. The two aspects are, in the end, inseparable: for it is the sheer beauty of Alfonso's life and liveliness that makes his confinement especially shocking. Although his eyes are 'made' to attract women, it is clear that they have a similar effect on such men as the poet. While preparing to wait at table, Alfonso sings in a revealingly versatile voice which rises from mellow and seductive low notes to a trilled falsetto. And while singing, he blows 'Gay kisses' in the direction of 'imaginary lasses' – either he imagines women he might be kissing; or his audience wrongly imagines he intends his kisses for women; or the members of his audience, men like the poet, imagine themselves in the place of the women he likes to kiss. Whichever way one reads the scene, it constitutes a moment of shared joy which is interrupted by the greed of white people and the consuming culture they dominate.[7]

Countee Cullen's long poem 'The Black Christ' also routes its anti-racist message through a paean to the beauty of the black man, in this case Joe.[8] Although its speaker is Joe's brother, the whole text is essentially a love poem. When Joe is lynched, Cullen gives the subsequent lament a homo-erotic cultural focus by referring to the dead man as Lycidas (Milton's Edward King), Jonathan (lover of David), and Patrocles (Patroclus, lover of Achilles), all prematurely dead and volubly mourned by the men who loved them. The death itself is also eroticised: Joe is 'raped' by sleep; even when hanged, his corpse is 'lusty'. Joe's brother adorns him with such adjectives as 'young', 'beautiful', 'comely' and 'lovely' (pp. 132–133). His moral force is conveyed, almost entirely, in terms of wasted physical beauty.

A characteristic which all these writers share with white gay writers, but which is given a doubled intensity by the context of racism, is their interest in the related themes of oppressed beauty and of love under threat. White lesbian and gay readers are likely to be able to follow, and quite readily comprehend, the logic of the thought that leads, by however circuitous a route, from beauty to tragedy. I have already mentioned the episode in Blair Niles' 1932 novel *Strange Brother* when Mark Thornton is moved to tears on reading Countee Cullen's poem 'Heritage', thereby demonstrating to his woman friend that he identifies himself, as a homosexual man, with 'the outcasts of the earth'.[9] This sympathetic identification with oppressed African-Americans intensifies Mark's anti-racism, but also suggests that he will find in Harlem – as he has already found, in the book's scenes in the Harlem clubs – a return of sympathy from black people for his own anomalous relation to the dominant order.

Clearly, this episode posits a reading stratagem based on solidarity. It suggests, furthermore, that a black gay reader should be encouraged to make cross-references between his own racial and sexual status, identifying not only directly with the poet's disadvantaged race, but also making Mark's transverse association of America's racism with its homophobia. Had Blair Niles known (as she may have done), or been able to state, that Cullen was homosexual, she might have pointed out that he, doubly oppressed, was able to express himself openly only in reference to race, but that he may be assumed to have invested in this expression the frustration and anger generated at the other source, his sexuality. If he could construct a text in this manner, it follows that, working in reverse, the black gay reader should be able to extrapolate from the 'racial' text the sexuality-based anger which he and the author share.

If such associative readings work, for both white and black gay readers, I see no reason why one should not apply them, also, to other famous statements of racial oppression by gay black authors. It should be possible, for instance, to read Claude McKay's defiantly angry 'If We Must Die' as referable to homosexual oppression. Given the author's own sexuality, such a reading would do far less damage to the text, which is usually and sensibly read in reference to racial prejudice (or, more specifically, to the race riots of 1919), than Winston Churchill did it when he used it to represent the situation of Britain forced into a corner by Nazi Germany.[10]

In a similar way, there is no reason why one should not apply Countee Cullen's 'From the Dark Tower' (p. 47) to both racism and homophobia. While the imagery of light and dark is clearly intended to refer to white and black, it also works well as a representation of openness and enforced closetry. Taking the latter view of the poem, one can effortlessly read it as celebrating the hidden 'twilight world' of homosexuality. Moreover, not only does Cullen deplore oppression and celebrate the concealed lives which resist and survive it, but he also, in the closing couplet, offers some hope for the future, however distant. We 'hide', he says, and 'wait'. But our waiting is not without purpose: we bide our time and pass the time by tending our 'agonising seeds'. Of course, this last image, for all its assertion of pain, promises future growth and an emergence into light and life.[11]

When writers' enumerations of the absurdities of race prejudice focused – as they often did – on the miscegenation taboo, their texts inevitably arrived at a theme which was of particular interest to those of them who were homo- or bisexual: forbidden love. McKay's poem 'The Barrier' (p. 80), for instance, could seem to be addressing any barrier to love in the first ten of its twelve lines. By repetition of the phrase 'I must not', the poet reminds someone he loves that neither sight nor speech – still less touch, which is not mentioned – may be exchanged by them on any but the most formal basis. Only in the final two lines does he make it explicit that this embargo on love is caused by racial difference: the poet is 'dark', the loved one 'fair'. Until this point, the reader has been free to perform a gay reading. Indeed, even after the poem has imposed its closure, conclusively focusing on the one social issue rather than the other, one is left with an impression of the ambiguity which has thus been disengaged. As a gay reader, one may at least derive from the poem an associative reading which results in a comparison of the effects, on love, of racism and homophobia.

McKay's poem 'Courage' (p. 110) has a similar theme, and both gains and loses by treating it with consistent ambiguity. Neither the racial nor the sexual reading is closed off, but the sexual prevails. Much of the imagery corresponds with that of other poetry by homosexual men in this period: a 'lonely heart', warm but sad glances, a 'guarded life', the forlorn search for a shared refuge, and so forth. Yet, for all its conventional distress, the poem does reach quite a positive and assertive conclusion in the image of a joined pair of 'understanding hands'. This determined clasp is what is referred to in the poem's title. Despite all forces to the contrary, the speaker and his beloved courageously link hands, thereby affirming their 'ardent love and life'. Whether this courage is enforced by racist or homophobic objections to the affair is not stated, and is therefore, although not immaterial, generously left to the focus of the individual reader.

Nathan Huggins has said, of Countee Cullen's 'Harsh World That Lashest Me', 'There is, here, no real evidence that the poet is black, yet one has to know that fact to have the romantic sentiment make any sense.' In relation to the generalised complaints about oppression, one could say the same about his homosexuality.[12] One should add the caution, however, that this kind of transference between race and sexuality depends on ambiguity in the text – or on vagueness, to put it more negatively. White gay readers, in particular, should not be tempted to believe that their homosexuality necessarily gives them much of an insight into the oppression experienced by black people. Race and sexuality are transferable terms only in the most general sense. As soon as one approaches the specifics of either, one begins to see the dangers in the tendency to confuse the two. We need to be continuously aware of and awake to the dangers of appropriation. To read the work of writers like Hughes as 'gay poetry' alone would be offensively reductive, yet little more so than to read it as 'black poetry' alone. A new wave of readers is now prepared to perform creative re-readings on a literature which must be seen *fully*, as poetry *by gay men of colour*, if it is to receive the value and respect it deserves. After all, a readerly practice which involves denial as one of its principal strategies can hardly be called 'reading' at all.

Among the most accomplished of the ambiguous poems is Countee Cullen's elegant and unfussy 'Tableau' (p. 7), which celebrates the sight of a black boy and a white boy crossing the street, arm in arm, followed by disapproving glances. The poem offers a perfectly harmonised counterpoint of the two themes, sexuality and race, in a manner which, while saying nothing explicitly gay to the inattentive reader, nevertheless broaches the scandalous topic of homosexual miscegenation without subterfuge or disguise. To be so discreetly indiscreet is an excellent feat of anti-homophobic irony only rarely achieved in the pre-Stonewall conditions which provoked it. No amount of paraphrase can do it justice. The poem manages to negotiate its passage between safety and risk in a manner which seems almost as light as it is actually solid and secure.

Another text which manages this balancing trick is Hughes' 'Joy' (p. 57), a poem which presents itself as a rudimentary narrative, in the first person and past tense. The speaker goes looking for a certain vibrant, young woman, and finds her in scandalous circumstances and bad company – in the arms of the butcher's apprentice. Thus far – and here the story has already ended – the poem is a lilting, merrily hetero tale. But read it again; read its *title* again. The poem is called 'Joy' because the young woman's name is Joy. It is also called 'Joy' because it is not merely about a young woman, but about *joy*. On this second reading one sees the point: a male speaker celebrates the fact that he has found *joy* ('Slim, dancing Joy, / Gay, laughing Joy, / Bright-eyed Joy') in the arms of the butcher's boy.

Such company, such company,
As keeps this young nymph, Joy!

The heterosexual poem becomes a no less explicit homosexual poem by means of a sophisticated but uncomplicated reversal. The heterosexual poem depends upon its personification of joy as a young woman; the homosexual poem depends on the young woman's *un*personification as the abstract noun, joy. The woman is, as it were, the poem's cover. While she acts as decoy to inattentive homophobes, who are led up the garden path of their own complacency, the speaker is free to assert the joy of homosexual desire to those readers whose trained ears are receptive to the modulations of his camp tone.[13]

More clearly autobiographical lyrics, no matter how discreet, should supply fruitful material to the active gay reader, particularly when they concern the growth from childhood, through adolescence, into maturity. In the wistful poem 'Home Thoughts' (p. 21), McKay remembers the joys of his native Jamaica in terms of named schoolfriends: Davie, Cyril and Georgie, one agilely shinning up mango trees, the second hauling bananas on his back, and the third stripping off his clothes for a swim. This celebration of the physical activities of boys is, of course, a straightforward instance of nostalgia: that of the adult for boyhood, and that of the exile for his boyhood home. However, in the poem's final couplet, McKay briefly switches from reminiscence to a moment of associative eroticism, in which, between a gasped 'Oh' and the terminal exclamation mark, he indulges in the realist daydream of a new generation of boys, all climbing trees, hauling weights and taking off their clothes, now, at the very moment of the poem. This closing line conveys a great intensity of desire and despair. Home is a place the poet has left (Jamaica and boyhood), which he might possibly revisit (Jamaica), but to which he can never return (boyhood).

McKay creates a similar mood in 'Adolescence' (p. 27), a recollection of a remarkably untroubled period, through which he claims to have drifted as if in a state of suspension, an idyllic interim between childhood and adulthood, rather than the difficult metamorphosis which so many other writers describe adolescence as being. The poem situates the youth, prone and semi-naked, under a sky which deepens continually into warm, moonlit and starry nights. These are not nights of writhing, frustrated sleeplessness, endured on sheets reeking of semen and sweat; on the contrary, they bring peace and peace brings sleep, undisturbed by dreams.

The sense of balance and order which McKay thus imparts to the experience of puberty is strongly contrasted, in the third and last stanza, with his mood at the time of writing. Here, where he speaks of having to endure nights of feverish restlessness which neither drink nor drugs can calm, he appears to have exchanged an adolescence of sagacious equilibrium for a distinctly lonely and embittered adulthood. The principal effect of the difference is located on his palate: whereas his youth was 'sweet', his present condition fills his mouth with 'acrid brine'. Whereas sleep used to be as delicious as 'early love', the lack of it is now – and 'forever' – a source of agitation and enforced nostalgia. The solipsistic joy of youth has turned into a kind of lonely resentment – even, once McKay has emigrated to the great northern city, in the midst of crowds.

The theme of loneliness recurs in the poem 'On Broadway' (p. 67), where McKay describes feeling excluded from the vibrantly 'gay' (in both senses?) street life of Broadway by the youth and carelessness of the crowd. Indeed, the adjective 'careless' seems to be the crux of the matter: for McKay is in inhibited mood. What he sees on the sidewalk is a couple, represented by the whole of the youthful crowd: personifications of Desire and Passion, the former 'naked', both 'brazen'. There is at least a hint, here, of the discomfort of closetry. The poet is lonely because he cannot make an open declaration of himself. Carefulness has been imposed on his emotions to an extent that serves to stifle them. All that he can do, the only response available to him, is to 'gaze' at the sheer glamour of

Broadway, as if it were the creation of his own deprived but fertile imagination, a 'dream'. No doubt, the social geography of Manhattan should also be taken into account when one reads this poem. The theme of race is inevitably suggested by the fact that Broadway is not Harlem. It may be that the young people in this crowd are not only 'brazen' in their heterosexuality, but also brazenly, carelessly white. The poem conveys a sense of multiple exclusions, of exile.

The twentieth century's literature by homosexual men often raises the theme of exile, even if only of the internal sort. At its most intense, this association of outlawed sexuality with exile leads to a self-pitying view of homosexuality as *meaning* the enforced exclusion from love itself. Love, at best, is seen as being beset by difficulty. Langston Hughes' post-coital poem 'Desire' (p. 90) speaks of the 'double death' of consummation, involving a dying away of breath and the evaporation of the partner's disconcertingly unfamiliar scent. It is not clear whether this refers to the estrangement of an established couple or a one-night stand between literal strangers. In 'Café: 3 A.M.' (p. 243) he mentions the 'sadistic eyes' of vice squad members whose job it is to entrap and harass 'fairies'. The former of these poems utilises a poetic cliché, common since before the time of Shakespeare. The latter is much more to the point: for all its brevity, it exposes with a sudden crystal clarity the reality of how lesbians and gay men have to love in the face of adversity. Countee Cullen, in one poem's title and substance, calls on the reader to 'Pity the Deep in Love' (p. 54). Possible reasons for this may be found in other poems which depict lovers who must bury their love in order to allow it to grow – see 'The Love Tree' (p. 59) – or deny it altogether – see 'Magnets' (p. 143). Similarly, in the 'Song in Spite of Myself' (note the inverted reference to Walt Whitman), Cullen personifies love as a male, but claims that it inevitably falters, to end in 'aching' (p. 98). You can love Love, but, as like as not, he will repay you with shame and heartbreak.

David Levering Lewis has said 'Cullen's homosexuality was to be a source of shame he never fully succeeded in turning into a creative strength'.[14] It may be that, in the last analysis, we shall have to say much the same of McKay. Both poets chose the line of least resistance: discretion; and while their sexuality did find expression in their work, it does not seem to have functioned therein as a major shaping or modulating force. Both wrote poetry whose formal constraint does, to be sure, give an impression of voices stifled and held back – even at the same time as it expresses itself with perceptible passion and daring on racial matters. Only Langston Hughes managed a sassy and incisive voice, with many tonal levels, which he appears to have developed, not by reading Shakespeare and Keats, but by allowing himself to relax into the very different (and thoroughly American) influences of Walt Whitman and the Blues. The result is often recognisable to the trained ear as intentionally camp.[15]

However, it feels appropriate to conclude this chapter with a brief reference to the prose poems of the gay maverick Richard Bruce Nugent. Nugent provided an exotic and evocative story, 'Sahdji', for Alain Locke's anthology *The New Negro*, in which one man who loves another, unbidden, kills for him, but thereby effectively kills him.[16] Yet it was the story 'Smoke, Lillies, and Jade' which won notoriety for Nugent in 1926, when it was published by Wallace Thurman in the first and only issue of the journal *Fire!!* Langston Hughes later called it, rather coyly, 'a green and purple story . . . in the Oscar Wilde tradition'.[17] What such texts and the reactions to them demonstrated then, and remind us now, is that the voices of out gay men can often be heard over even the most strident demands that they be silenced.[18]

Chapter 18

The Tragic Sense of Life

In his biography of Michelangelo, John Addington Symonds surmised that 'the tragic accent discernible throughout Michelangelo's poetry may be due to his sense of discrepancy between his own deepest emotions and the customs of Christian society'.[1] It is possible that this tells us more about Symonds' time, the late nineteenth century, than about Michelangelo's. Symonds seems to be projecting his own rationalisation on to the Renaissance artist in a manner which could have the severely reductive effect of using Michelangelo's homosexuality *to account for* not only his depressive moods but even his greatness. Be that as it may, it is certainly true that at the end of the nineteenth century male homosexuality (and lesbianism less often and less emphatically) starts to be written about as an essentially tragic condition. Sadness, loneliness and a tendency to end in either suicide or worse have been regarded by many – and not only hostile heterosexuals – as being inherent in the condition. Hence the number of people who, even today, continue stupidly to begrudge our use of the word 'gay' as being wholly inappropriate to an unvaryingly joyless condition.

When I speak of tragedy in the present context, I am referring to far more than just unhappy endings – though these are by no means insignificant signs of a major cultural tendency. More importantly, I am referring to some of the main characteristics of tragic drama: the fatal imperfection or error of the hero (Oedipus' club foot, Macbeth's impotence, Edward II's homosexuality); the hero's key discovery or revelation (Oedipus discovers he has killed his father and married his mother as the prophecy foretold); the hero's fall, consequent on both of the above; emotional catharsis; and the conflict between fate and free will – in particular, the question of how far the hero's suffering is preordained or self-inflicted. An essential model to which many narratives of homosexuality refer is the story of Christ's Passion, especially the physical facts of His bodily wounds, His public humiliation, His naked exposure on the cross, and the inventive tortures of the flagellation, the crowning with thorns, and the Crucifixion itself. I am also referring to Oscar Wilde's least amusing and most convincing paradox – echoing through 'The Ballad of Reading Gaol' – that 'Each man kills the thing he loves'.

Joseph Bristow has argued that virtually all of Oscar Wilde's writings 'engage with doom or fate, often of the most unlikely kinds in the least plausible conditions'. As his first example, Bristow offers *The Picture of Dorian Gray*, 'which most obviously displays his perennial anxiety that the Hellenic ideal enshrined in a boy with consumingly beautiful looks must, in the end, face inescapable tragedy'. The latter is the key word here: Wilde's novel keeps returning to the noun 'tragedy' and the adjective 'tragic' as measures of a certain kind of intensity observable in the presence of beauty. At times the novel's gloomy preoccupation looks pretty trivial, little more than the paranoid ageism of an author who has reached his mid-thirties and become increasingly conscious of his admiration for the bodies of teenagers. But there is more to it than this. Wilde clearly had, to use Miguel de Unamuno's phrase, a 'tragic sense of life' which permeated every level of his thought, even when he seemed at his most frivolous. Bristow adds: 'It could be said, then, that the trials that led to Wilde's imprisonment uncannily enacted the fatalistic narrative structure that even cast its shadow across his comedies'.[2] This is a fair analysis, though I think we can discard the idea that the process was at all uncanny. It was not. It combined a purposeful risk of self-exposure on Wilde's part with the coldly deliberate vindictiveness of state law.

Wilde was, in a very broad sense, a tragedian, even though he has since been best loved as a writer of comedy. In the same way as his downfall influenced subsequent notions of effeminate queerness for a whole century, his sense of tragedy was also passed down – to homophiles and homophobes alike – as though it were a natural and inevitable side-effect of homosexuality itself. Wilde is the model of the twentieth century's tragic queer. When I use the word 'tragic' here, I do not simply mean unfortunate, sad or condemned to die. I am referring to a specifically literary quality of fatedness which casts the queer as an inglorious version of the tragic hero. (Marlowe's King Edward II could neatly fit this bill; but he, literally the hero of a tragedy, long pre-dates the developments with which the present chapter is concerned.) This characteristic and these characters have appeared most consistently in novels published between the Wilde trials in 1895 and the growth of the liberalising social movements of the late 1960s and early 1970s.

We know that one of the strongest imperatives behind the composition of E.M. Forster's *Maurice* was the search for a happy ending. Harder still, it was the search for an ending that seemed happy but not mawkish or forced. That this was going to be, literally, the main *end* of the novel – which is to say, both its ending and its objective – was clear to Forster from the very first moment in which he conceived of the book – the moment in the autumn of 1913 when George Merrill, Edward Carpenter's lover, so intrusively and effectively touched Forster on the backside. The first 'completed' version of the manuscript had a closing scene with Maurice and Alec living together in a woodcutter's cottage; but Forster's friends persuaded him to cut what they regarded as a ridiculous vision of bucolic harmony. We know that Forster was still revising the ending in 1958, and perhaps even later. It had to be possible, he thought, to offer a plausible denouement in which two adult male lovers settled down together and lived – as in so much hetero-marital fiction – happily ever after. (The problem was all the more intractable because he had chosen central characters from separate, incompatible classes.)

Maurice is about an ordinary man with a 'suburban soul', who happens also to be an 'outlaw' because he is homosexual. This is the whole point of the book – and yet it is also one of its major problems: for Maurice is intolerably boring. Moreover, his dreariness is directly related to what Forster knew was the book's major flaw: the laughable implausibility of its 'happy' ending. It is hard to be convinced that a man like Maurice could ever head for the greenwood in such an irresponsible way (he is not an American lighting out for the territories), homosexuality or no homosexuality. It is even harder to accept that a man like Alec Scudder would put up with Maurice for long. I do not mean that this could never happen; but that Forster has not established his case. Forster knew this, of course.

The more interesting homosexual man in this novel is Risley, the aristocratic aesthete, richly endowed with both money and intellect. But his main role is to be what Maurice is not: camp, distinguished, conspicuous. When he speaks he does so 'continually', making liberal use of 'strong yet unmanly superlatives'. His utterances seem all the more dramatic for the fact that 'in each of his sentences he accented one word violently'. His interest in talking ('It is my forte. It is the only thing I care about, conversation') is excessive, even for a university student.[3] It is the superficial mark of his more fundamental difference. Maurice feels dull next to him – as well he might – although their class difference accounts for much of this sense of inferiority. It is the aristocrat who is better able to express, whether in words or behaviour, his sense of difference from the mainstream.

Contrary to those critics who loftily dismiss the whole novel, as opposed to its central character, as a bore and, therefore, not worth thinking about, it is the very flaws in *Maurice* that make it so interesting. One of its major failings is common to a good deal of later gay fiction: boring men make boring central characters. And yet Maurice *has to be* dull. The very 'ordinariness' of the invisible, masculine, homosexual man can kill a novel whose central theme is the potential respectability of homosexual love. Who would not read about Proust's Charlus in preference to Forster's Maurice? True, the former is a more 'negative' representation than the latter, if bourgeois respectability is to be the principal standard by which one negotiates one's sexual politics. But Charlus *does* more. He has more opinions. His self-absorption is more extravagant. And his sex life is far more varied and inventive. Both date from the same period – Forster was working on *Maurice* just before the First World War, in 1913–14, when *Du Côté de chez Swann* was published but Proust was already writing, or at least beginning to sketch out, *Le Temps retrouvé*, the final volume of the *Recherche* – but whereas Maurice is the model of the undistinguished, middle-class man of the twentieth-century suburbs, in one sense the very essence of modernity, Charlus is both ancient and modern, Sadean libertine and Freudian queer. As such, he commands a greater range of emotional textures than Maurice's one.

I shall return to the question of the elusive happy ending in a later chapter. For the moment, I simply want to point out the difficulty Forster had in writing such an ending during the period in question; and the equal difficulty the different versions of such an ending presented to the manuscript's readers – who were virtually all, let it be noted, sympathetic homosexual men with a vested interest in happy endings. Apparently, none of the solutions to this intractable problem in *Maurice* ever seemed much less than implausible. The fact is that, given a 'tragic' ending, notwithstanding the novel's earlier positive representations and its author's shyness, *Maurice* might well have been published without much fuss at the time of the First World War. Without one, Forster felt, it could not. Very early in the century, then, Forster recognised what was happening in the literature of the newly-named 'homosexual' individual, but he could not find the resources with which to counter the trend. It had become a truth almost universally acknowledged that a young man neither possessed of nor in want of a wife must, instead, be setting himself up to become the tragic victim of his own fate.[4]

I have chosen as this chapter's two main examples of tragic fictions a novella and a novel, both about destructive relationships between military men, the first written just before the First World War, the second during the Second. It is important to note that both are about apparently virile men. That is the problem. Overt affection for another male, particularly another virile (and therefore apparently sexually active) man threatens to bring the whole edifice of his impressive masculinity crashing down around him. The first of these stories was written by a bisexual man, the second by a lesbian woman. D.H. Lawrence's novella *The Prussian Officer* was written in Bavaria in the spring of 1913 – before, but not long before, Forster started *Maurice* – and originally called 'Honour and Arms', but retitled by Edward Garnett, Lawrence's publisher. The Prussian officer himself, aged about forty, is unmarried – 'his position did not allow of it, and no woman had ever moved him to it' – but Lawrence is at pains to ensure the reader does not think him homosexual: 'Now and then he took himself a mistress.'[5] This characterises him as, to all intents and purposes, self-sufficient. Although he has to associate sexually with women, he does so only occasionally and, apparently, when he chooses. Even in the few phrases I have quoted here, he is shown to be single-mindedly dedicated to his military role – will subordinating nature – not only capable of mastering his physical desires but emotionally so superior to mere woman as to be unmovable by love. His brand of stoical masculinity is perfectly suited to soldiering.

The orderly's relationship to his superior is entirely passive. As military discipline requires of him, he submits completely to the older man, and obeys his orders without question. Indeed, he is expected, as far as possible in matters of daily routine, to anticipate what those orders might be and to have carried them out before they are given. A relationship develops in which each man is unwaveringly aware of the presence of the other. As the officer rides ahead of his marching men, 'The orderly felt he was connected with that figure moving so suddenly on horseback: he followed it like a shadow, mute and inevitable and damned by it. And the officer was always aware of the tramp of the company behind, the march of his orderly among the men' (p. 8). The intensity of the relationship is there from the start, as if necessarily ordained by its position within military structures of rank and favour. The younger man's fate seems ordained as he follows his master, 'mute and inevitable and damned'.

The captain is broodily aware of his orderly's physicality. (There is nothing else to him: no personality, no preferences, no choice.) As described by the narrative and observed by the officer, 'The orderly was a youth of about twenty-two, of medium height, and well built. He had strong, heavy limbs, was swarthy, with a soft black, young moustache. There was something altogether warm and young about him. He had firmly marked eyebrows over dark, expressionless eyes, that seemed never to have thought, only to have received life direct through his senses, and acted straight from instinct' (p. 9). One of Lawrence's purposes here and in subsequent descriptions is to absolve the boy's passivity of any hint of effeminacy (though there is something equivocal about those 'firmly marked' eyebrows). It helps that he is not an intellectual, and therefore not an aesthete. What is unmanly in him – his warmth, the softness of his moustache – is simply the attribute of his youth: he will grow out of it. So, despite the fact that he is so passive – even 'receiving' life 'through' his senses as if in a sexually receptive role, rather than actively living it – the orderly is like the officer insofar as neither of them is queer.

However, the younger man's body is enough to arouse the senses of the older – and he is irritated by this fact. Presumably he is discovering that his self-sufficiency is not unassailable after all. He is affronted by the 'warm flame' of the youth, acting on his own 'tense, rigid body that had become almost unliving, fixed'. So although his body is warmed by the orderly's presence – although and because – his mind reacts against it. 'He did not choose to be touched into life by his servant' (p. 9). And yet he cannot help observing the boy in close detail. There is a scar on the boy's hand. It arouses what will eventually turn fate, the officer's sadism; but Lawrence describes his response to it in a paradoxical way: 'The officer had long suffered from it, and wanted to do something to it. Still it was there, ugly and brutal on the young, brown hand.' One man suffers from the other man's wound; he wants, not to do something about it, but to do something to it; the wound is brutal as if what caused it (an axe) had not been. The officer 'had to use all his will-power to avoid seeing the scarred thumb. He wanted to get hold of it and – A hot flame ran in his blood' (p. 11).

Contrary to the earliest impression of the youth, there is a fluidity about him that the officer finds offensive: 'he was infuriated by the free movement of the handsome limbs, which no military discipline could make stiff' (p. 11). How we read this depends on how far we wish to take the connotations of the word 'stiff', which encompass both the incapacity of old age and the potency of sexual arousal, as well as the more obvious meaning of regimental self-discipline, the rigidity which is square-bashed into the bodies of marching men. There is, after all, a hint of effeminacy in the orderly's fluent movements, which the officer finds both threatening, in terms of his own virile security in a potentially queer boy's presence, and not threatening enough, in terms of the boy's physical aptness to the rigours of soldiering. Yet the boy is still detached. When bullied, he only becomes even more 'mute and expressionless' than ever, refusing to respond. As I meant when speaking of the use of the word 'stiff' to connote erection, no amount of the officer's 'military discipline' – which is to say, mental and soon physical cruelty – will arouse him. The officer is incensed by the lack of mutuality in their relationship, the lack of visible emotional response to himself. As a consequence of this frustration, he hits the boy in the face with a belt – which has the desired effect. The orderly weeps, even if only by reflex, and the officer is thrilled: 'When he saw the youth start back, the pain-tears in his eyes and the blood on his mouth, he had felt at once a thrill of deep pleasure and of shame' (p. 12).

Pleasure and shame go together more or less automatically in post-Wilde-trial references to male–male relationships: if the prospect of inevitable shame does not put a man off seeking pleasure altogether, his pleasures will be paid for with shame. Rather than do anything to assuage his guilt at having hit the orderly, the officer compounds it by spending the whole evening kicking him around. In the morning his thighs are covered in bruises; but there is no question of complaining to anyone, or even of allowing anyone to see he is in pain. 'No one should ever know. It was between him and the Captain. There were only the two people in the world now – himself and the Captain' (p. 17). We consistently find, in the 'tragic' accounts of destructive, or mutually destructive, relationships between men, that the moment in which the pair cut themselves off from the rest of society may be the most dangerous, the moment after which there is no turning back. When they turn their backs on society the protagonists of these narratives are moving beyond the compass of the rule of law into a new realm where only their own inexorable and solipsistic versions of morality hold sway. By accepting, or avowing, that only he and his master exist, the slave or the victim of torture allows that the master is no longer to be ruled by common standards of morality.

It is true that, in the morning, Lawrence's two men temporarily re-enter the routine life of their company, experiencing again its familiar atmosphere ('a hot smell of men, of sweat, of leather') and resuming their rightful positions in the corps: the captain 'a dominant figure' on his horse, looking down on 'his men', and the orderly 'a nonentity among the crowd' (p. 20). But this is no reintegration into the unit. The two men are irrevocably, and only, bound up in each other's fate. Violence is soon the inevitable outcome: the orderly breaks the officer's neck over a tree stump,

> pressing, with all his heart behind in a passion of relief, the tension of his wrists exquisite with relief. And with the base of his palms he shoved at the chin, with all his might. And it was pleasant, too, to have that chin, that hard jaw already slightly rough with beard, in his hands. . . . Heavy convulsions shook the body of the officer, frightening and horrifying the young soldier. Yet it pleased him, too, to repress them. It pleased him to keep his hands pressing back the chin, to feel the chest of the other

man yield in expiration to the weight of his strong, young knees, to feel the hard twitchings of the prostrate body jerking his own whole frame, which was pressed down on it. (p. 23)

Here is real pleasure without apparent shame. This is the first time the boy has touched the man, and he finds the experience 'pleasant' – an oddly non-committal adjective in a context where the (abstract) 'heart' and 'passion' are invoked, along with fright and horror. He touches the chin, the stubbly jaw, the chest, and indeed the 'body' itself, which becomes a corpse in his embrace. And it pleases him to have effected this reversal, to be on top, symbolically and literally. The relationship is consummated in a moment of fatal retaliation. Vengeance is a kind of mutual pact – a risk the tormentor may have known he ran – and it is sufficiently 'pleasant' to round off the avenger's life. Looking at the corpse of the captain, the orderly feels 'It was a pity *it* was broken. It represented more than the thing which had kicked and bullied him.' In fact, by now, it bears a particularly heavy burden: for it represents his own mortality, his life. 'Here his own life also ended' (p. 24).

Indeed, he duly dies, and doctors lay the two bodies out side by side: 'the one white and slender, but laid rigidly at rest, the other looking as if every moment it must rouse into life again, so young and unused, from a slumber' (p. 29). So the officer's body 'white and slender', is the less manly of the two, even though it has the rigidity – in being laid out at 'attention', and in being in a state of rigor mortis – which he required of a soldier but found obscenely lacking in his orderly; but the orderly's body, presumably neither white nor slender but tanned and muscular, is in the purer condition because younger and 'unused', although visibly bruised. Quite what the word 'unused' means here, apart from virginal, is not clear: for he certainly has been used, and visibly so. (The doctors choose to suppress the fact of his bruising.) However, what is apparent is that this joint lying-in-state, both bodies evidently naked, ends the story and seems intended by Lawrence to bear the full burden of whatever poignancy one can find in this particular tragedy. Only in death do the two men lie together, their bodies naked together only as corpses. As unhappy endings go, however, this is relatively happy. Lawrence seems to regard this unclothed togetherness on the mortuary slab as an appropriate culmination of their union – a consummation saved from sodomitic impurity and unmanliness by the profoundly pure virility of a violent death.

My second model narrative of tragic homosexuality was written by an American lesbian during the Second World War. Often simply included as one among many on lists of gay-related novels with 'unhappy' endings – but, reworked as a film by John Huston, peculiarly omitted from Vito Russo's necrology at the end of *The Celluloid Closet* – Carson McCullers' highly-strung novel *Reflections in a Golden Eye* (1941) is, in fact, a rather superior work, self-consciously presented from the start as 'this tragedy'[6] and summed up from Leonora Penderton's shocked point of view, at the very end, as 'some tragedy that was gruesome but not necessary to believe' (p. 125). Believable or not, the tragedy McCullers contrives is powered by suppressed homo-eroticism and reaches its denouement in a burst of loving violence. Certain elements in the narrative prove to be variations on familiar themes.

Captain Penderton is a small man with a 'nervous, finicky manner' (p. 10). The first chapter of the novel provides a lot of very explicit information about his character, beginning with the apparently rather vague premise that 'this personality differed in some respects from the ordinary', but then elaborating with sufficient detail to show that 'in some respects' is an ironic understatement. 'Sexually,' we are told, 'the Captain obtained within himself a delicate balance between the male and female elements, with the susceptibilities of both the sexes and the active powers of neither' (pp. 14–15). This inappropriate constitution contributes to the eventual breakdown of his two principal roles, those of army officer and husband. One should not underestimate the significance of both roles, martial and marital, in United States society at the time of the book's composition, and the perceived threat which failures of masculinity might pose to the virtue of American democracy. The publication of *Reflections in a Golden Eye* narrowly pre-dated the bombing of Pearl Harbor in December 1941, but not Roosevelt's call for the United States to become the 'arsenal for democracy', nor the conscription Act of September 1940. America was in a non-interventionist state of readiness for whatever display of unassailable masculinity the nation might be called upon to provide.

As the first chapter progresses, more and more evidence emerges of Penderton's constitutional weaknesses. Not only can he not enforce his wife's fidelity, but he does not even seem to want it; indeed, he is said to have 'a sad penchant for becoming enamoured of his wife's lovers'. Before he married, 'his fellow officers tended to avoid his room in the bachelors' quarters or else to visit him in pairs or groups' (p. 15). His wife is able to deploy the most withering humiliations to defeat him. For instance, on an occasion when he threatens to kill her for walking past their open front door in the nude, she replies: 'Son, have you ever been collared and dragged out in the street and thrashed by a naked woman?' The very fact of her making this threat in this contemptuous manner is almost as destructive to his self-esteem as if she had actually carried it out.

Needless to say, their marital estrangement is sexual in origin. It dates back to their honeymoon: 'When she married the Captain she had been a virgin. Four nights after her wedding she was still a virgin, and on the fifth night her status was changed only enough to leave her somewhat puzzled' (p. 20). To my eye, this appears to be a joke about anal intercourse. If so, it reinforces the way in which the narrative justifies Leonora Penderton's reliance on lovers in the face of her husband's inappropriate desires. Furthermore, to compound what we already know about his unacknowledged homosexuality, McCullers makes him a coward, a condition caused by a fundamental moral imbalance which will precipitate the novel's violent conclusion: 'In his balance between the two great instincts, towards life and towards death, the scale was heavily weighted to one side – to death' (p. 15).

Leonora Penderton is much closer to two other men than to her own husband: her current lover, Major Morris Langdon, and her servant, the camp Filipino aesthete Anacleto. In a limbo between the virility of the former and the effeminacy of the latter she contemptuously locates the equivocal captain. To see his wife in the company of either, as so often he must, is a humiliating accusation to Penderton: for he is demonstrably neither one thing nor the other. In ways which remind us that Carson McCullers was a friend of W.H. Auden, who was always so insistent that psychological ailments are likely to have physical outcomes, Penderton is given certain outer signs of his inner malaise. Like Proust's M. Legrandin, he has unmanly buttocks which when he rides, 'spread and jounced flabbily in the saddle' (p. 27). He wears a truss (p. 51). He develops toothache and a tic (p. 107). Like the airman in Auden's *The Orators*, Penderton's sexual obsessions are linked with another form of compulsive behaviour, kleptomania. In the box the truss came in he keeps a stolen silver spoon.

It happens that when Leonora appears naked at the front door she is seen by Private Ellgee Williams, an agile youth with a face which shows the 'watchful innocence' (p. 8) of an animal. In his innocence, he has never seen a naked woman before, while in his watchfulness he determines to see more of her. He starts to hang around the Penderton house, and even to enter Leonora's bedroom at night to watch her sleeping. An ominous pattern of voyeurism develops as Williams watches Leonora, and Penderton watches

Williams. Nakedness intervenes on a second fateful occasion, when Penderton unwisely decides to ride his wife's horse Firebird, which he is unable to control. The horse bolts through the woods and when Penderton eventually manages to bring it to a halt, he dismounts and starts whipping it, before bursting into tears and throwing himself to the ground. What happens next is both an erotic dream and a humiliating nightmare. Penderton has dismounted at the very spot where Williams goes to sunbathe in the nude. 'At first the Captain did not believe what he saw. Two yards from him, leaning against an oak tree, the young soldier whose face the Captain hated looked down at him. He was completely naked. His slim body glistened in the late sun' (p. 73). With no attention to the prostrate officer's dignity, the youth steps over him and wordlessly leads the horse away. Penderton's reaction is revealing, and begins to account for what follows:

> It had happened so quickly that the Captain had not found a chance to sit up or to utter a word. At first he could feel only astonishment. He dwelt on the pure-cut lines of the young man's body. He called out something inarticulate and received no reply. A rage came in him. He felt a rush of hatred for the soldier that was as exorbitant as the joy he had experienced on runaway Firebird. All the humiliations, the envies, and the fears of his life found vent in this great anger. (p. 74)

So being out of control initiates contradictory responses in him – joy in the case of the horse, fury in the case of the young man – but the contradiction is in keeping with the paradoxical nature of his manhood as McCullers has outlined it. As an unmanly man in a position of virile responsibility, he is vulnerable to humiliations but cannot fight them. One possible response would be to give himself up to them, as a passive, homosexual masochist, in a spirit of joyful resignation. But since he is forbidden, and he forbids himself, this alternative, only one further option is open to him: that of impotent rage. His response to the sudden vision of the naked youth culminates as follows: 'In his heart the Captain knew that this hatred, passionate as love, would be with him all the remaining days of his life' (p. 74).

From now on, Penderton is obsessed with Williams, and it again seems to be under the influence of Auden that McCullers imagines the obsession operating within him as if it were a physical illness. 'His preoccupation with the soldier grew in him like a disease. As in cancer, when the cells unaccountably rebel and begin the insidious self-multiplications that will ultimately destroy his body, so in his mind did the thoughts of the soldier grow out of all proportion to their normal sphere' (p. 108). As in so many gay texts when an older man dreams of socialising as an equal with a younger man, or an upper-class man wishes he did not have to condescend to the working-class man he desires, so too Captain Penderton has fantasies of being reduced to the rank of the enlisted man. Instead of being isolated in an officer's house, and more importantly in the feminine atmosphere of the company of his wife and Anacleto, he longs for the masculine ease of barrack life: 'the hubbub of young male voices, the genial loafing in the sun, the irresponsible shenanigans of camaraderie' – at the heart of all of which, of course, he locates the image of Private Williams (p. 109). What he does not take into account is that Williams himself is a solitary man, more at home among the horses in the stables than among his fellow soldiers, and his 'loafing in the sun' is done in isolation.

We are told that as the obsession develops, Penderton gradually ceases to hate Williams: 'He thought of the soldier in terms neither of love or hate; he was conscious only of the irresistible yearning to break down the barrier between them' (p. 118). In his turn, Williams responds to the captain's obvious but perplexing interest with stoical passivity:

'He accepted the captain as fatalistically as though he were the weather or some natural phenomenon. The captain's behaviour might seem unexpected, but he did not identify it with himself. And it did not occur to him to question it, any more than he would question a thunderstorm or the fading of a flower' (p. 122). He takes no responsibility for a relationship with the older man – he does not even heed the danger of spying on the captain's wife – and he even appears to accept that the captain bears no responsibility for whatever may be his actions towards Williams. Like some natural force, Penderton cannot help what he does, and Williams does not care why he does it. The workings of fate are, supposedly, out of their hands.

When it comes, the ending is no surprise. Williams creeps into the Pendertons' house. The captain finds him in Leonora's bedroom and shoots him in the chest. She wakes up to the incomprehensible scene of the killing: 'As yet she was still only half-awake, and she stared about her as though witnessing some scene in a play, some tragedy that was gruesome but not necessary to believe' (p. 125). Her incomprehension and disbelief may just as well be her husband's, for all the understanding he shows of what he has done. Again, it is as though the shooting was not willed, but inevitable. It is not, strictly, that each man kills the thing he loves, in this case; but that he kills that to which he eventually became so studiously indifferent.

Chapter 19

....

Fantastic Realism

....

Most book reviewers in the Anglo-American gay media, and many gay writers themselves, tend to speak as though all gay fiction should function only according to strictly realist – even Socialist Realist – principles: invariably and unvaryingly plausible, optimistic and heroic. At different periods and in different cultures, such literature should seek to offer a realistic account of the quotidian lives of homosexual men and women and to formulate some kind of critique, however quietly stated, of the sources of the oppression of such people. By holding up a mirror to society, it must not only 'reflect' a social reality, but do so in order to show society the reality of its own reflection as cast back by the mirror of the homosexual consciousness. According to this unimaginative world view, experimentalism would be an elitist irrelevance. (So would poetry.) It would get in the way of the fine ideal of an accessible gay literature which can instantaneously comfort the lonely and the oppressed, and change the minds of homophobes.

This limiting critical dogma is more or less unworkable when applied beyond the limits of the English and North American novel. It also serves to suggest a major limitation at the heart of the Anglo-American gay novel itself, which often seems to have been developed according to a similar set of assumptions. In this chapter, therefore, I am turning my attention to various novelists who, far from being the mavericks they might appear to Anglo-Saxon literalists, actually represent a major, and dominant, cultural strand in other parts of the world and other tongues. But we who have allowed ourselves to be so radically misled about the nature of gay fiction need to teach ourselves how to read such very different texts. At the outset, then, we return to a familiar problem.

It takes more than the identification of a homosexual writer to provide readers with an accessible, recognisably gay literature. Consider, for instance, the limitations of Simon Karlinsky's book *The Social Labyrinth of Nikolai Gogol*, the first study to deal with Gogol's probable homosexuality at length and in serious detail. The crux of Karlinsky's argument (about the strategies which Gogol adopted for conveying something of his sexual world view within the social restrictions of his culture) is stated as follows:

> Both the literary conventions and the social customs of the time would tolerate no sexual expression other than heterosexual, and consequently Gogol has no other choice than to convey his visualisation of sexualised nature in heterosexual terms. But at the same time he invariably selects the kind of imagery and the form of

personification that would effectively preclude the possibility of any sexual consummation.[1]

In other words, his work has no discernible 'gay content'. Although this leaves Karlinsky at something of a loss, he does not compensate by attempting ingenious and fanciful gay readings of Gogol's more fanciful, ingenious stories – though this might be a perfectly laudable thing to do. Instead, he has to concentrate on the strongly negative manner in which Gogol represents heterosexual relations in general, but matrimony in particular. Disregarding the fact that many heterosexual authors, both women and men, offer similarly negative representations, Karlinsky leaves himself with the rather dreary task of demonstrating at length how the homosexual Gogol 'got away with expressing his fear and loathing of heterosexuality in a whole series of remarkable works' (p. 131). By the end of the book, Karlinsky has to fall back on essentially biographical considerations to provide the momentum for his concluding sentence: 'Both the comedy and the tragedy of Gogol's wonderful literary art can be fully appreciated only when we perceive the price in pain and self-repression that had to be paid for bringing this art into existence' (p. 294).

As well as establishing heterophobia and misogyny in Gogol's fiction, Karlinsky also points out his occasional idealisation of male bonding, particularly as it occurs in his saga of Cossack heroism *Taras Bulba* (1835). The theme of comradeship is at its most explicit in the novel's ninth chapter, when Taras addresses his men on the noble tradition of 'our brotherhood', in contrast with which all other relationships look feeble:

> There is no more sacred brotherhood. The father loves his children, the mother loves her children, the children love their father and mother; but this is not like that, brothers. The wild beast also loves its young. . . . There have been brotherhoods in other lands, but never any such brotherhoods as on our Russian soil.

And so on. Taras' passionate advocacy of this peerless brand of nationalistic homosociality brings tears to the eyes of his otherwise obdurately immovable audience. Their conviction that, as Taras says, 'no one else can love in that way' steels their resolve and cements their group consciousness as they prepare for battle.[2] Simon Karlinsky argues that what Gogol saw in the Cossacks 'was an association of beautiful, virile males, united in their love for one another and their distaste and contempt for everyone else' (p. 80). He sees the book's overall theme as being that of an all-male brotherhood which comes to grief when one of its members falls under the spell of a woman (p. 77).

Gogol's stories do, of course, offer plenty of scope for psychoanalytical readings, and Karlinsky repeats some of the more distinguished of these, if without much relish. Indeed, it is true that Freud usually comes off badly – a great laureate of unsubtlety – when applied in all seriousness to the frisky fictions of writers like Laurence Sterne, E.T.A. Hoffmann or Gogol himself: noses invariably become penises, and the rest follows as if automatically. This is a line of investigation which may or may not be fruitful, according to the requirements of the investigator; but whether the intention is to illuminate the texts or merely to use them as evidence in the case history of the author is not always clear. At this stage it may be useful to turn to a better-known but even more interesting example.

It seems to me that Franz Kafka's fiction raises one of the most intriguing sexual conundrums in Modernism. Even as early as the story 'Description of a Struggle' ('*Beschreibung eines Kampfes*', written in 1902–3) his fiction contains sudden, unpremeditated outbursts of intimacy and/or aggression between men. For instance, at the start of this story the narrator kisses a housemaid on his way out of a party. A second man, a complete stranger, follows him and questions him about the girl and the kiss. The narrator imagines the second man being kissed by other girls:

> Let's pray the girls won't spoil him! By all means let them kiss and hug him, that's their duty and his right, but they mustn't carry him off. After all, when they kiss him they also kiss me a little – with the corners of their mouths, so to speak. But if they carry him off, then they steal him from me. And he must remain with me, always. Who is to protect him, if not I?[3]

This possessive protectiveness, imagined as shared moments of hetero-erotic dalliance, is left unexplained. Like so much in Kafka, it is spoken and assumed. The reader may always choose the easy way out and dismiss the narrator, and even the author, as a madman; but this is not an adequate response to the complex strangeness of the unassailable internal logic of Kafka's fiction. The two characters continue their conversation, and the second man smiles at the narrator, who comments:

> So I had already got as far as that. He could tell me things like that and at the same time smile and look at me with big eyes. And I – I had to restrain myself from putting my arm round his shoulders and kissing him on the eyes as a reward for having absolutely no use for me. (pp. 15–16)

One begins to suspect – not unreasonably, I think – that the two characters are involved in an elaborately perverse game of flirtation and denial: they have been cruising each other but now cannot quite bring themselves to be open with each other about what they want to do next. One begins to suspect this, perhaps; but in the end it is a banal suspicion, far too flatly obvious (unless one believes that gay flirtation is inevitably weird) to carry the weight of the whole narrative with all the paraphernalia of its psychological and metaphysical suggestiveness.

Towards the end of the story, the second man says to the narrator, 'You're incapable of loving, only fear excites you. Just take a look at my chest'; and with this curious *non sequitur* he throws open first his overcoat, then his waistcoat, and finally his shirt. The narrator comments: 'His chest was indeed broad and beautiful' (p. 50). Apparently, the bare torso is presented as incontrovertible proof of the man's claims about love and fear. Perhaps it is meant to generate both. It certainly sparks off a revelation. The narrator whispers into the other man's ear, 'I'm engaged, I confess it', thereby clinching the discussion and seemingly closing off whatever erotic possibilities may have been raised by the baring of the chest. But, in the moments that follow, the stranger deliberately stabs himself in the arm. This dramatic gesture seems to do the trick that he requires of it: for the narrator sucks the wound and tenderly binds it ('My dear, dear friend . . . you've wounded yourself for my sake') before leading the man away to whatever destination, whatever fate, one chooses to imagine (pp. 51–2).

I do not want to close off 'Description of a Struggle' by offering my own attempt at a definitive 'gay reading' of it, as if thereby dismissing all other readings. One of the main pleasures of reading Kafka's stories is generated by their refusal of such cocksure closures. Instead, I shall briefly turn to the more famous narrative, *The Castle* (*Das Schloss*, posthumously published in 1926), before then considering one critic's response to all of Kafka's works in relation to the question of homosexuality. Speaking of closure, it is worth remembering that none of Kafka's three novels was finished; so the likelihood of our being able to reach convincingly conclusive conclusions about them is even more severely restricted than by the Modernistic open-endedness they would doubtless have had to share with all the shorter narratives if Kafka had finished them.

K., the central character of *The Castle*, exists in an ambiguous relation to several of the other men he encounters during the course of the novel. In the second chapter, he clearly finds Barnabas attractive – more so than his own assistants, more so even than Barnabas' sister Olga, who merely reminds K. of Barnabas himself. The two assistants, Arthur and Jeremiah, obviously love each other. Their exasperating puerility binds them together – often very closely, hand in hand or cheek to cheek – even while it infuriates K.'s sense of the adult proprieties (a sense which he has brought with him from the outside world and which never really allows him to come to terms with the culture of the castle and its subjects). These two boys are maddeningly intrusive, forever violating what little privacy K. manages to construct for himself and for his relationship with Frieda. The key instance of this is the occasion when K. wakes up in the night and finds in bed next to him not Frieda but one of the assistants. [4] It is only much later in the novel, when he has got rid of them both, that K. is able to be a little more generous about the two boys. He calls them 'good, childish, merry, irresponsible youths, fallen from the sky, from the Castle, a dash of childhood's memories with them too' (p. 236). Little fallen angels, boys prematurely ejected from childhood into the adult world – as such, the two assistants represent, to K., something of the carefree individual he remembers having once been; and at this point, now that he is not trying to get them to work properly for him, he feels a certain affection for them, or for their identical boyishness.

The fact is that, as well as being actively heterosexual, K. experiences moments of intense attraction to other men. When Frieda hears him responding to a knock at the door by calling out Barnabas' name, she says to K.: 'I only wish you had once called out my name as lovingly as for some incomprehensible reason you called that hateful name' (p. 152). This unconscious self-betrayal – or is it just an instance of paranoia on Frieda's part? – is underlined by an episode at the beginning of the additional material (after chapter 18) which Max Brod appended to the definitive German edition of the novel. Listening to Bürgel's long, late-night monologue, the exhausted K. wants nothing more than to creep into bed beside him. When his tiredness gets the better of him he dozes off and has a revealing dream:

> A secretary, naked, very like the statue of a Greek god, was hard pressed by K. in the fight. It was very funny and K. in his sleep smiled gently about how the secretary was time and again startled out of his proud attitude by K.'s assaults and would hastily have to use his raised arm and clenched fist to cover unguarded parts of his body and yet was always too slow in doing so. The fight did not last long; step for step, and they were very big steps, K. advanced. Was it a fight at all? There was no serious obstacle, only now and then a squeak from the secretary. This Greek god squeaked like a girl being tickled.

K. wakes up to find Bürgel still droning on. There is a moment of recognition, identifying the principal source of the dream figure: 'at the sight of Bürgel's bare chest a thought that was part of his dream brushed his awareness: there you have your Greek god! Go on, haul him out of bed!' (pp. 248–9). This dream of a struggle with male beauty, combined with the dangerous moment of waking when K.'s unconscious mind threatens to force its own intervention into Bürgel's monologue, constitutes a much-repeated theme in Kafka, not unlike the central relationship in 'Description of a Struggle'. Are these antagonisms fights at all? Are these barings of male chests, literal and metaphorical, incitements to and acknowledgements of sexual desire? It is not impertinent to build up a list of such questions; but the last question is, should they, or how should they, be answered?

The critic who makes the most sustained attempt to connect and make sense of the many homo-erotic moments in Kafka's fiction – although she concentrates on some of the short stories – is Ruth Tiefenbrun.[5] The gist of her book's argument is stated as follows: 'It is only when one reads the totality of Kafka's writings that it becomes apparent that the predicament of all his heroes is based on the fact that they are all homosexuals' (p. 21). The reason for this can be found in the psychology of the author himself: 'an internal examination of all of Kafka's works . . . reveals that Kafka considered himself to be a homosexual' (p. 22). Indeed, 'he considered his homosexual orientation the best part of himself' (p. 23).

However, because he was unable to write about his homosexuality openly, Kafka developed an elaborate system of codes and symbols – wounds and diseases being prominent among them – to express the unspeakable. As Tiefenbrun puts it, 'Since Kafka spent his entire lifetime deliberately concealing his homosexual orientation, it is not at all surprising that there are relatively few overt references to homosexuality in his personal letters, diaries, notebooks, or in his creative works' (p. 136). There are, however, many coded references: for 'Kafka shares with his fellow-deviants their most distinctive trait: their simultaneous need to conceal themselves and to exhibit themselves' (p. 59). It is these heavily coded references that Tiefenbrun seeks to decode.

She does so by applying the logic of psychoanalysis to certain key texts. For instance, she reads 'Description of a Struggle' as 'a case study in homosexual imagery and paranoid thinking' (p. 53). Similarly, she says that in 'Metamorphosis', the incomparable story in which Gregor Samsa unaccountably wakes up one morning having been transformed into an insect, 'Gregor/Kafka had literally been transformed from a man who had appeared to be heterosexual into a homosexual; therefore metaphorically he had become a vermin in the eyes of his fellowmen' (p. 111). Her elision of Gregor and Kafka, which she does not go far out of her way to justify, is characteristic – but it is also typical of most Kafka criticism: more often than not the author is said to be in some respect represented by those famous, lonely young bachelors who are his central characters: Gregor Samsa, K., Joseph K., Karl Rossmann, the Hunger Artist and so forth. By thus identifying the author more or less indistinguishably with his characters, Tiefenbrun is able to present Kafka as the archetypal homosexual author of the post-psychoanalysis, pre-liberation period.

As well as outlining the case study of a homosexual writer, Tiefenbrun's book itself constitutes a case study in how not to perform gay readings. Alternately irritating and unintentionally hilarious, it states its case – or rather, overstates it – to the self-defeating extent of making Kafka seem interested in only one thing. We are apparently left with a two-dimensional homosexual novelist, when the revelation of his supposed homosexuality not only should have left his third dimension – as Modernism's greatest political and metaphysical novelist – untouched, but also should have had the effect of adding a fourth. This is a shame, because Tiefenbrun's thesis, stripped of its crass psychoanalytic generalisations about 'the homosexual' as a type, is actually very convincing. Regardless of Kafka's own sexuality, which interests me as little as Shakespeare's, the stories and novels are indeed much amplified by reference to both homo-eroticism and the unlawful situation of the male homosexual in early twentieth-century central Europe. 'Metamorphosis' is particularly amenable to such a reading. Interpreted in this spirit, it comes across as one of the most harrowing examples of gay literature you are ever likely to read. Similarly, *The Trial* (*Der Prozess*, posthumously published in 1925) enacts the nightmare of blameless involvement in an unstoppable process of law that might so easily occur to any gay man in a culture where merely to be who he is leaves him open to malicious prosecution.

The question we have to ask ourselves is whether, in order to appreciate the texts in question as gay literature, we have to accept a largely speculative narrative about the author's life. If so, one then has to decide how far it is worthwhile to turn our attention to the pretty forlorn task of biographical detection – in order to end the speculation by proving the homosexual hypothesis – and away from the enjoyment of the literature. In short, why should a text not be its own proof of the readings one performs upon it? This is not an issue I have any intention of concluding in this book: it is still open to queer theoretical discussion. I raise it here because I have to. One cannot read the likes of Kafka as a gay novelist without facing up to such difficult questions. Needless to say, however, not all readers are literary critics or theorists, and it may be that to them the reading of queer Kafka is both productive and serene.

Other cases are less complicated, either because (like, say, the Surrealist writer Raymond Roussel) their homosexuality is provable even if their fantastic texts do not contain obviously homosexual characters or occasions, or else because (like René Crevel) they are both known to have been homosexual and, because their books helpfully contain what you might call homosexual materials, are easily readable as such. In other words, once the biographical enigma has been solved, and the author is to all intents and purposes lost to the anti-homosexual critic, one is allowed to go ahead and read the text as being gay. This seems a ludicrous situation when one is dealing – as we are here – with writers who are not literalists. As in the gossip of queens, speculation can be a formidably creative weapon; but it is wasted on the dead. It works better on the living text.

Although Surrealism was predominantly a movement of bourgeois men attempting and claiming to break the bounds of bourgeois morality, certain rules relating to the sanctity of masculinity were rigorously policed. André Breton, the movement's paternalist disciplinarian, would never relax on this point. In 1928 he wrote in his magazine *Surrealist Revolution*, 'I accuse the homosexuals of affronting human tolerance with a mental and moral defect that tends to advocate itself as a way of life and to paralyze every enterprise I respect'. As an afterthought, Breton felt he had to add: 'I make exceptions, one of which I grant to the incomparable Marquis de Sade'.[6]

This high-handedness did not prevent René Crevel, who admired and respected Breton, from writing fiction which dealt in some detail and depth with the matter of his own homosexuality. Oddly enough, Crevel was not tempted to obscure this theme in fantastic representations of the associative idiosyncrasies of the unconscious mind. For instance, his third novel *Difficult Death* (1926) is, technically speaking, a straightforward narrative, even if moments within it are almost pictorially surrealistic. On her wedding night, a bride 'found herself confronted by a strapping body dressed only in its hair. Her gaze focused on certain details in red which rapidly increased in size to where a naked devil, of which the tender newlywed was horror-struck, inspired in her a sudden vision of a giant coffee-pot in human form' (p. 23).

The distorted echo in this novel's punning title, *La Mort difficile*, announces both the end to which the novel and its protagonist will succumb – suicide – and the immediate cause of that end – *l'amour difficile*, the male protagonist's love for a young American man, his mother's hostility to it, and the American's infidelities with other men. When asked point-blank whether her son is 'abnormal', Mme Dumont-Dufour replies with a good-natured equanimity which conceals her strong resentment that he should have laid her open to this kind of embarrassing scene, 'No, he's simply a bit degenerate' (p. 32). Pierre, the son in question, overhears this exchange and subsequently addresses to himself the all-important question of definitions: 'Abnormal, degenerate, or insane?' (p. 37) His main fear is that the last of these should prove to be the case: for his father is languishing in an asylum. Mere abnormality, or even good old-fashioned degeneracy, would more reassuringly resolve the conundrum.

Crevel's apparently autobiographical representation of Pierre's homosexuality is revealingly expressed at one point in terms which could have been used by many of the anti-bourgeois, heterosexual men who belonged to the Modernist avant-garde:

> He would never be able to stand living like so many others he has seen, looking through their windows from outside, with their ceiling lamps whose light holds happy families at table in a green embrace. He laughs contemptuously. Dining room, ceiling lamps, happy families, green embrace. All it lacks is the soup tureen and what a lovely bouquet, dear. (pp. 54–5)

He has a girlfriend, Diane, but this scene is what she means to him: the threatened anguish of re-imprisonment in a family just like the one from which he has been trying for so long to escape. The menace of the soup tureen, it seems, has clinched the issue; and it is not long before Pierre decides between Diane on the one hand and on the other his American lover, Arthur Bruggle: 'He will have the courage of his own tastes. Resolved: the courage of one's tastes. Exactly' (p. 64).

Pierre's taste for men was confirmed when he met a boxer in a bar – 'this Hercules with a pug nose and pink cheeks' – who offered him lessons in 'physical culture' and taught him a lot more than mere callisthenics. On seeing Pierre naked, the boxer paid him the memorable compliment of saying, 'You're a strange little bird, but that's no reason to say you don't make the grade', and added 'more detailed comments' which, even in memory, still cause the boy to blush (p. 58). The love-making that followed was both the first and the conclusive confirmation that he was not heterosexual: 'the joys of which this athlete was giving him a first inkling seemed to his body more natural than the others which, despite the disillusionment of certain nights spent in bed with women, he had persisted in believing to be the highest, nay, the only joys of love' (p. 60). It is this liberation into new joys which allows Pierre, later, to conceive of a relationship with Arthur Bruggle, and then to turn the concept into reality.

Arthur Bruggle is 'a youth with long hands, the gait of a dancer, a panther's tread, and animal eyes. Quite a phenomenon' (p. 25). But, unfortunately for Pierre, he is not a monogamist, and he resents any sign of possessiveness or jealousy in his lover. The novel reaches its climax at a small party in Bruggle's studio apartment, in which the American has managed to create a purposive impression of erotic Modernism: 'Monsieur Arthur has created an atmosphere, the same as the one found in the dives where small-time boxers, pimps, and prostitutes of both sexes gather round the astonished American, in whose eyes they enjoy the freshness of novelty, curiosities to be used more intimately but otherwise of the same sort as African sculpture, psychoanalysis, and the Ile Saint-Louis' (pp. 113–14). What Pierre fails to see is that, by creating this atmosphere, Bruggle is signalling the Modernism not merely of his sexuality – as 'a homosexual', newly defined – but also of his intended lifestyle. He is offering Pierre not high romance but something more fleshy, more immediate and therefore, perhaps, less enduring. The incompatibility of their requirements leads to the destruction of the weaker of the two. When Pierre starts an argument about Bruggle's demonstrative sexual interest in a beautiful hustler, Bruggles ejects Pierre from the apartment; whereupon, Pierre goes and poisons himself.

Crevel appears to be in two minds – or he puts Pierre into a position of inconclusive suspension – about the desirable status of homosexuality in relation to the dominant culture of the heterosexual bourgeoisie. I have quoted Pierre's fear of the middle-class dining room. Yet in another passage he distances himself from the conspicuous styles associated with men whose homosexuality is regarded, or who regard their own homosexuality, as a 'vice':

> As long as people think it's a vice, as long as they are looking for an amusing spectacle or at the very least an assortment of strange quirks which it is their pleasure to judge reprehensible but rare, like Oscar Wilde's orchids, then the reaction is one of respectful interest. But let someone come along whose sufferings in love are not betrayed by comical eccentricities or increased either by social persecution or the threat of prison or the dictates of fashion, but a man whose sufferings are wordless and quietly eat him up inside, people who were hoping for outlandish scenes, spicy anecdotes, scandalous gossip, will never forgive the commonplace simplicity of such a passion. (p. 98)

What we are offered here is a bifurcation of oppression, whereby the homosexual man is damned whichever way he develops and behaves. He is either forced to become an exotic, in which case he is tolerated – if kept at arm's length – until such time as he ceases to fascinate; or else he gets on with his life in the closet, indistinguishable from his neighbours – at least until they distinguish him, but thenceforth a race apart. To live unacknowledged in the closet is a kind of freedom and a kind of safety; but its freedom is circumscribed, its safety perilous. In the second of the two quoted sentences, Pierre appears to have noticed that the dominant culture likes to be able to see those whom it is dominating. An object of resentment, the invisible queer is all the more vulnerable to scandal, has more to lose, than his flamboyant counterpart – who is so much easier to label and avoid. The closet may seem superficially secure, but the anxieties it fosters in the man it conceals 'eat him up inside': for the fact is, has always been, that a closet door is just as likely to reveal as it is to conceal.

Crevel's subsequent novel *Babylon* (*Babylone*, 1927), although without homosexual characters, is no less interesting as a gay text, particularly once Crevel starts to rhapsodise on the sensual attractions of Marseilles in summer.[7] This is an exquisite book, seamlessly combining orthodox Surrealism with an eroticism and sense of humour which come close to the tone of Ronald Firbank. While its bourgeois men are ineffectual husbands and lovers (one of them, not insignificantly, a psychiatrist; another a magistrate; another a missionary) their wives are forever trying to break out of the bondage of their roles by way of an exploration of sexual fantasy and, they hope, reality. As a young girl hits puberty, her grandmother, too, has a sexual awakening, elopes with her daughter's fiancé, and is eventually institutionalised after allowing sexual frenzy to overcome discretion during Mass and assaulting an attractive priest. It is through his camp representations of such women that Crevel effects a humorous but no less intense tribute to the beauty and vigour of working-class men.

The moment of puberty is signalled when the young girl suddenly finds she can see through men's clothes: 'The child becoming a woman blushed, for she thought that under his canvas jacket, which did not permit a stitch of underwear to be seen, the man who dared to stare at her was perhaps nude. But we are always naked under something, she suddenly realised' (p. 104). Welcome to the world of sexual awareness. By this point the narrative has moved from Paris to the southern port ('The City of Flesh', as a chapter heading describes it) and the women are immediately aware of a difference: for this is a city 'where stevedores with skin the color of their hair, after the bath that cleanses them of the sweat of the docks at the close of day, bulge with far prouder chests than those of the whistling laborers of the capital' (p. 112). The sexy atmosphere of the place also makes itself known to Crevel's rather bewildered bourgeois man. While the missionary is wandering the streets in search of a lost African girl, he is approached by a whore who, when he shows no interest in women, offers him alternative delights:

> If it's titillation you need, gorgeous one, we can oblige. I've got some male colleagues, if that's what you prefer. Want one called Lucien? He's been baptised 'The Warbler' here in the quarter because he sings like a tenor. But the cutie's voice isn't the only good thing about him. One night he made thirteen Japs happy. And those little yellow behinds aren't satisfied with promises. If you don't want The Warbler, he has a brother not so young, but even huskier' (p. 131).

The missionary hurries on, harassed wherever he goes by 'prostitutes and their friends (the muscular ones and the others, the pretty boys with too rosy cheeks)' (p. 132).

Amie, the grandmother, meanwhile continues to cruise the streets of the city of flesh: 'Famished, insatiable, Amie cast about. A butcher boy looked at her and she wanted to suck the blood of animals from his big paws. A young poultry salesman, with his sleeves rolled up, and you too who sold fish and had scales on your fingertips, your thick wrists made promises. Your carnivorous jaws would close on any meat, biting any epidermis with pleasure' (p. 140). The intensity of her cannibalistic sexual hunger is made all the more direct by that switch from the third to the second person in reference to the desirable young men, a strategy which not only seems to put her in direct communication with them, regardless of whether she actually speaks or merely expresses herself with an unambiguous gaze, but also shifts the positions of both author and readers in relation to beautiful male flesh. Furthermore, as in later gay pornography, these men are seen not as significant individuals but as flesh enhanced by particular physical occupations and social status. What they have is muscles; what they lack is manners – they are both able and willing, and have their ways of saying so: 'The hoodlums of the city of flesh did not make eyes, but mouths. In three twists of their thick lips they ran the gamut of all labial, and other, possibilities, and then whistled.' There is a degree of envy of the wolf-whistled woman in this account: for all she need do in this glut of demonstrative, virile desire, is pick out the individual to whom she wishes to respond. The miracle of the city of flesh is sheer quantity – the very same miracle that Marcel Proust witnessed in First World War Paris, Quentin Crisp in Second World War London, and John Rechy in peacetime Los Angeles. Even an elderly woman (or queen) will find a satisfactory response at reasonable cost:

> One lost, ten found, one needed only to choose among these sailors who produced from their seafaring pants splendid handkerchiefs freshly stained with love and perfumed with tobacco and cognac. Each one of these loafers of the old port, with an oblique glance, and for fifty francs, would promise a skilled and robust virility, a ruddy chest, a hard belly, and thighs that, having dispensed with the hypocrisy of underpants, had the good smell of coarse-grained cloth. (p. 141)

I referred to Firbank, but the obvious name to mention in relation to passages like this is Jean Genet. Some of Genet's most explosive moments of homo-eroticism are those which apply the extravagantly metamorphic possibilities of Surrealism to the most mundane incidents of sexual exchange. This is certainly something that the French understand more readily than the prosaic English: that the imagination is by far the most active of the sexual organs, and that sexual pleasure is as much associative as literalist.

Most of the Latin American writers know it, too. While visiting Algiers in 1964, Che Guevara came across a volume of plays in the library of the Cuban embassy. Furious, he flung the book at a wall and shouted at the ambassador, 'How dare you have in our embassy a book by this foul faggot!' (Che's outburst was witnessed by Juan Goytisolo.) The 'foul faggot' in question was Virgilio Piñera (1912–79), who had been a supporter of the Cuban revolution until October 1961, when he was arrested and imprisoned for the 'political and moral crimes' associated with being homosexual.[8]

However, it is from well before the revolution that so many of Piñera's 'cold tales' (*Cuentos fríos*) speak with the oblique voice of an active but circumspect homosexuality. Piñera is especially percipient on the contingencies of appearance, and on the related issue of the distances between appearances and the realities which they obscure but do not leave unaffected. In a story called 'The Face' he restates the fact which Christopher Marlowe had expressed so daringly in the closing scenes of *Edward II*: 'Both the enchanting youth and the fiendish assassin can have a seductive and dreadful face'.[9] They may, of course, have the very same face. For this reason, the prospect of a beautiful face may be enough to petrify the most rational individual. In this particular story, Piñera creates a man whose face has 'a power of seduction so strong that people would shun him' (p. 119). The indiscriminate and oppressive force of his beauty has turned him into an outcast, even from his own family: 'Mankind has shunned me; even my own parents abandoned me some time ago' (pp. 119–20). In an extremity of isolation, he establishes telephone contact with a writer, who increasingly yearns to see the face which has had such an extraordinary effect. When they agree to meet, but in pitch darkness in the beautiful man's house, the writer is immediately overwhelmed with a disruptive desire – 'I was burning with the desire to "see"' him (p. 123) – yet even in darkness blissfully infected by beauty's mere presence: 'Who would dare offend heaven by asking for any greater happiness than this?' (p. 124).

Totally engrossed in the very concept of the other man's beauty, the writer decides to remain permanently at his side – but not, as it were, in the closet; not in the darkness with which he has so far protected himself from dementia. If he is to live in the presence of the other's beauty, the beautiful face must be allowed to flourish in the full light of day. The writer therefore pokes out his own eyes, so that, as he argues, 'his face wouldn't separate our souls' (p. 126). In this grotesque outcome, Piñera invests some of the tragedy inherent in a situation where love is forced to develop unseen; and yet he also acknowledges the great courage – in the face of both adversity and absurdity – of the sacrifices a lover might make, and survive, in order to make sure of a place at the side of the man he loves.

This moment of absurdist self-mutilation is characteristic of Piñera's vision. Sometimes violence is inherent in political institutions and only perversity can break into its automatic routines – as when, in 'The Conflict', the commanding officer of a firing squad raises his sabre to make the fatal command, and freezes 'with his right arm petrified like an inhabitant of Sodom' (p. 152). Many of his stories explode with unmotivated violence. There is one, 'The Actaeon Case', in which two men tear each other to pieces with irresistible energy until they form one undivided mass (pp. 13–15). In another story, 'The Fall' (1944), two mountaineers, roped together, slip and fall off the rock face. As they plummet earthwards and are scythed to pieces by sharp outcrops of rock, each humanely reaches out to protect the other's best asset: the beard in one case, the eyes in the other. At the last moment, however, the hands of one are torn from the eyes of the other; he, in a self-protective spasm, abandons the other's beard and raises his hands to cover his own eyes; but his hands, too, are torn away. Although it seems that all is lost, and the two companions are separated for the first time in their precipitant descent, it happens that the eyes of the one and the beard of the other land safely, a short distance apart on the grassy plain. It is with pleasure that the eyes take in the sight of the companion's beautiful beard (pp. 5–7). I read this as a story of fidelity *in extremis*, absolutely solid until that last moment of reflexive betrayal, which, however, the relationship survives – albeit in somewhat reduced circumstances.

Perhaps the most positive of Virgilio Piñera's stories is 'Swimming' (1957), whose narrator proudly declares that he has learned how to swim on dry land. For all that this is seen as an unacceptable practice ('At first, my friends criticised this decision. They fled from my glances and sobbed in the corners'), the narrator disregards intolerant over-reactions and goes on behaving in a manner that he feels suits him best. In due course, his friends calm down ('Now they know that I am comfortable swimming on dry land') and accept his perversity (p. 165). Not only is it a part of his personality, but one might even say that it is the most interesting part – the most deserving of friendship. Moreover, from the opposite point of view, it is quite clear that a flexible and accepting friend is worth more than a shockable dimwit. The narrator's friends are better friends for the ordeal he and they have put each other through.

Although I have concentrated on a few names in this chapter, many other major writers could have had a place in this section of my account. Leaving aside Jean Genet, to whom I shall return, the most obvious absentees have been, I guess, Juan Goytisolo and Reinaldo Arenas.[10] These two bloody-minded exiles – Arenas from Cuban communism and Goytisolo from Spanish Fascism – vent the splenetic fury of their enforced displacement upon the enforcers, Arenas writing from the United States, Goytisolo from north Africa, Arenas at his most efficiently angry in the dystopian nightmare *The Assault* (*El Asalto*, 1990), Goytisolo perhaps in *Count Julian* (*Reivindicación del conde don Julián*, 1970). Arenas is more consistent than Goytisolo in taking his own homosexuality as the viewpoint from which to make more general observations of political oppression. Indeed, Goytisolo has never written what you could unhesitatingly call a 'gay novel', even if all his writing is so clearly informed by his gayness, whereas by any standard Arenas' two novels *Farewell to the Sea* (*Otra vez el mar*, 1982) and *The Assault* are stunning evocations of the dysfunctional relationship between homosexual desire and the heterosexist state. They bear witness to one of Fidel Castro's biggest mistakes.

With the exception of Gogol – who preceded it and, in some respects, pre-empted it – the writers we have been considering here are all fully involved in continuing the Modernist experiment. That is what gives them the freedom to transform gay experience in various ways that allow them to express it even when to do so might be dangerous. In this sense, contrary to some recent writers and critics, Modernism was not just an elitist, conservative movement, concerned only with internal, psychological processes. Because it developed literatures which were truly transformative, it was unreadable to the mundane.

Chapter 20

Towards the Popular

All canons are naturally élitist, more exclusive than they are inclusive. Paradoxically, they thrive on what they leave out. While attempting to take an overview of gay literature, therefore, it is vital that we do not lose sight of the fact that choices are being made. Thus far, the present study has concentrated mainly on writers and texts which were 'canonical' already – that is, on subjects which had already received various academic imprimaturs which officially proclaimed them worth studying. However, in relation to the twentieth century in particular, it is not sufficient merely to deal with gay 'high' cultural texts and to leave the rest to find their own gay readers. It is embarrassing enough to be dealing only with printed texts, rather than with movies and television programmes as well. Like the movies, modern popular fiction has often made use of (usually minor) homosexual characters, either to convey anti-homosexual jokes or to carry a burden of negative symbolism: the homosexual as sinner, deceiver, criminal, victim, and so forth. That is why, in this chapter, I intend to offer some examples of how homosexual men have been represented in the past by authors who were addressing large, popular audiences; and then to introduce some of those authors' major gay successors.

The fact is that popular novelists have been exploiting homosexual men – to put it in a negative manner – by stereotyping them, or rather by reinforcing popular stereotypes of them, for most of the twentieth century. A good example of such an exploited character is Joel Cairo in Dashiell Hammett's *The Maltese Falcon* (1930).[1] While it is difficult now to read the character without all the oily embellishments brought to him by Peter Lorre's performance in the 1941 film of the novel, the original text offers a fascinatingly concise representation, for popular consumption, of a certain kind of homosexual man. From the moment when he first appears at Sam Spade's office, Cairo involuntarily semaphores his sexual life to all who see him. The book's first comment on him comes from Effie Perine, Spade's secretary, as she hands Spade Cairo's card: 'This guy is queer' (p. 40).

This initial impression of queerness – that is, of both strangeness and homosexuality – is confirmed again and again throughout the narrative by revealing details of appearance and behaviour. The first description of him mentions his 'slightly plump hips' (too womanish for a real man), his 'soft and well cared for' hands and his 'high-pitched thin voice' (pp. 40–41). When he smiles his smile is 'demure' (p. 46) or it betrays 'prim satisfaction' (p. 89). When he walks he takes 'little mincing bobbing steps' (p. 49). For conversational emphasis he holds up 'a wriggling hand' (p. 62). He has a 'round effeminate chest' (p. 163), whatever that may be. And, as on his first appearance, he always has that tell-tale mode of speech, saying things 'primly in his high-pitched thin voice' or his 'brittle excited voice' (pp. 160–1). Also, of course, he is a Levantine, definitively unAmerican.

These personal impressions are further emphasised when either Cairo himself or his hotel room is searched. The contents of his jacket include 'a nail-file in a leatherette case' and 'a half-filled package of violet pastilles' (p. 45). His bathroom cabinet at the hotel is 'stocked with cosmetics – boxes, cans, jars, and bottles of powders, creams, unguents, perfumes, lotions and tonics' (p. 124).

Thus far, one might simply be dealing with some kind of foreign eccentricity, a foppishness too bafflingly effeminate to be trusted by the likes of Sam Spade. Even Effie's use of the word 'queer' (as is so often the case, also, with pre-Stonewall uses of 'gay') is rather too ambiguous to be definitive. So far, the signs have been suspicious but not conclusive. However, Hammett does take things further, confirming both that Joel Cairo is indeed what he appears to be, and that that is what the other characters take him for. It seems that he and Brigid O'Shaughnessy were in competition with each other over the favours of a boy in Constantinople, a competition which Cairo appears to have won (p. 64). But this brief conversational reference is, again, somewhat too glancing to be unambiguously clear. This boy turns out to be a young thing called Wilmer, 'certainly less than twenty years old', with 'very fair' skin and with cheeks 'as little blurred by any considerable growth of beard as by the glow of blood'. When Sam Spade encounters him in the lobby of Joel Cairo's hotel, Spade asks 'Where is he?' To the boy's question 'Who?' Spade replies 'The fairy', meaning Cairo. Having got the hotel detective to eject the boy from the premises, Spade asks the detective about Cairo. 'Oh, that one!' the man replies, leering; but he has no compromising information about Cairo: 'I got nothing against him but his looks' (pp. 85–8).

It later transpires that Wilmer is working for 'the plump man', Gutman. Or rather, he is the fat man's protégé: 'I feel towards Wilmer just exactly as if he were my own son' (p. 164), 'I couldn't feel any different towards Wilmer if he was my own flesh and blood' (p. 165). Be that as it may, as soon as Gutman's own security is under threat he is perfectly willing to abandon the boy: 'You can have him,' he says to Sam Spade, albeit in a sad tone of voice (p. 172). Continuing to press Gutman, Spade threatens: 'we'll give you to the police with your boy-friend', whereupon Gutman protests: 'Oh, come, Mr. Spade . . . that is not – ' (p. 173). He means both 'that is not' the kind of relationship he has with Wilmer and 'that is not' the kind of deal he intends to do with Spade. In both senses, he is betraying the boy: in the first instance by denying their relationship, and in the second by abandoning him to the authorities.

Throughout this scene it is Joel Cairo who is the more demonstratively concerned for Wilmer's welfare. When Sam Spade knocks the boy out with first a left and then a right to the chin, Cairo attacks Spade in a manner as unmanly as the reader must have come to expect, 'clawing at his face' with tears in his eyes (p. 171). All the way through the subsequent negotiations between Spade and Gutman, Cairo sits by the boy, tenderly solicitous: 'Joel Cairo sat beside the boy, bending over him, rubbing his cheeks and wrists, smoothing his hair back from his forehead, whispering to him, and peering anxiously down at his white still face' (p. 172). When Wilmer eventually comes round, Cairo goes and sits next to him again and starts whispering to him, but he only succeeds in antagonising the boy: 'He put his arm on the boy's shoulders and started to say something. The boy rose quickly to his feet, shaking Cairo's arm off.' 'Cairo moved over and whispered in the boy's ear.' 'Cairo had an arm around the boy's shoulders again and was whispering to him', causing Sam Spade to grin (p. 179). 'Cairo edged closer to the boy on the sofa and began whispering in his ear again. The boy shrugged irritably' (p. 182). Wilmer finally loses patience with this persistent courtship: 'Cairo, still muttering in the boy's ear, had put his arm around the boy's shoulders again. Suddenly the boy pushed his arm away and turned on the sofa to face the Levantine. The boy's face held disgust and anger. He made a fist of one small hand and struck Cairo's mouth with it. Cairo cried out as a woman might have cried and drew back to the very end of the sofa.' Grinning again, Sam Spade says sardonically to Brigid O'Shaughnessy: 'The course of true love. How's the food coming along?' (p. 184). When Wilmer sulkily refuses to eat, Cairo takes him a cup of coffee.

Not unexpectedly, when the precious Maltese falcon they have all been trying to get their hands on proves to be a fake, Joel Cairo is effusive in his reactions: 'Tears ran down the Levantine's cheeks and he danced up and down. . . . He put his hands to his face and blubbered' (p. 187). By the time he and Gutman have agreed to resume in Constantinople their search for the real falcon, they and Spade look round and discover that Wilmer has crept out of the hotel room and made good his escape.

It was James M. Cain, of all people, who demonstrated that there was no necessary link between the so-called 'hardboiled' school of men's writing and anti-homosexual hysteria. In his 1937 novel *Serenade* he even risked using a first-person male narrator of somewhat indeterminate sexuality.[2] Since this important book is no longer widely known, a brisk summary of its plot may be useful at this point. The narrator, a one-time classical musician called John Howard Sharp, is leading an aimless existence in Mexico when the young prostitute Juana Montes wins a car with a lottery ticket he once bought her. She invites him to join her in running a classy brothel for Americans in Acapulco. Having nothing to lose, he throws his lot in with hers. They make love in a church in a storm.

Although by the time they get to Acapulco he has decided to ditch Juana and head northward by sea, when he finds that she is about to spend the night with an important local military officer, John Sharp knocks the man down and makes his escape with Juana in tow. Having smuggled her into the United States, he manages to build a successful new career as a popular singer-actor in Hollywood. However, his past now threatens to catch up with him in the person of Winston Hawes, a homosexual conductor with whom he used to have a close professional relationship. It turns out that Winston's family owns a bank with a controlling interest in the movie company John Sharp works for.

As the two men's working relationship becomes closer again, John Sharp tries to keep Winston and Juana apart; but she becomes justifiably suspicious and accuses him of being a 'fairy', in love with the conductor. She admits that she first considered asking him to help her run the projected brothel because she imagined he was homosexual. Her evidence for this suspicion was a flaw she had detected in his singing voice – and she claims that she can now hear it again. He eventually responds with an admission: 'Every man has got five per cent of that in him, if he meets the one person that'll bring it out, and I did, that's all' (p. 213). He adds that whatever once happened between him and Winston is now over – he loves only her. The 'five per cent' in 100 per cent statistic is an interesting one to come from a sympathetic character in a 1937 novel. It is an early variation on the later statistic of 100 per cent homosexuality in 5 per cent of men, a more useful calibration to those homosexual people who took an essentialist line on their definitive difference from a heterosexual majority. The inverted statistic, as stated by John Sharp, is a far more disturbing one to the self-defining heterosexual reader of such a book as this. It posits a universal bisexuality, tilted nineteen to one in favour of heterosexuality but nevertheless offering any individual the fearful possibility of swinging the other way.

John spends two whole days in bed with Juana, confessing to her. Clearly, he needs to affirm his heterosexual credentials even in the very moments when he is admitting homosexuality. However, this act of talkative togetherness fails to settle the issue, because Winston Hawes has not gone away; on the contrary, he moves into an apartment in the same building. At his housewarming party – full of fags and dykes, many of them cross-dressed – it transpires that he has denounced Juana to the immigration service. She responds to this betrayal by publicly stabbing him during a display of her bullfighting skills. She and John escape the country together, eventually ending up in Guatemala, having changed their identities.

The problem they now have to face up to is that if John Sharp should ever sing he will give away his identity. This is doubly problematical, of course: for not only will he be recognised as John Sharp rather than the Italian he is pretending to be, but for those who can hear it the flaw in his voice may also reveal that repressed 5 per cent of himself that is queer. Juana is convinced that the two of them should go their separate ways, so that he can safely return to his old identity and, therefore, his singing career. She takes to sleeping in a separate bed. But to him that old identity has perilous associations of queerness: especially on a particular occasion when he is looking at a baseball pitcher, John is worried that if he loses his woman he will inevitably become queer again. In a misguided attempt to enforce his heterosexuality he visits a brothel, but his response to the women he picks is worryingly ambiguous: 'I didn't want her, and yet I was excited, in some kind of queer, unnatural way' (p. 271). His lack of desire for her is what makes him desire her all the more urgently: he needs to prove himself, not to her but to himself. In effect, he actually desires her homosexually, not for herself but merely to establish desire as a counter to anxiety.

Juana goes back to Mexico City. John Sharp follows her there. He tracks her down in a bar, where he finds her with Triesca, a bullfighter with whom he competed for her favours way back in the novel's opening chapter. When Triesca starts making fun of him – singing to him 'in a high, simpering falsetto, with gestures' suggestive of his secret flaw (p. 282) – and Juana, too, appears to be laughing at him, John gets up and sings. A crowd of people who recognise his voice begins to accumulate. But in the confusion the military man whom John knocked down before he and Juana first fled to the States shoots Juana dead. Her funeral is held in the church they once made love in. John Sharp is asked to sing, but he refuses: never again.

I have summarised this novel in some detail – and incidentally made its structure seem more forced than is actually the case – in order to give a clear sense of the extent to which the theme of homosexuality pervades, and to a certain degree actually drives, its travel-based plot. It is not a particularly positive representation of homosexual men, though many in its day were worse; but it does take the matter seriously, at least to the extent of endangering altogether the manly integrity of its otherwise rather conventional narrator. At the risk of making a facile distinction, I would like to argue that *Serenade* is anxious rather than hysterical. If nothing else, it raises the topic of homosexuality as being worthy of the consideration of the type of reader James M. Cain was generally capable of attracting. Of course, John Sharp's heterosexual 95 per cent is insistently reiterated throughout – not least because he is the book's narrator, trying to justify himself – but the 5 per cent is given space; and, importantly, the space it is given is within a straight man who, by virtue of his straightness (albeit incomplete to the extent of that flawed twentieth part), cannot be simply dismissed as a freak inhabiting some queer region beyond the reach of the straight reader's interest. Above all, this is a serious book, at least as deeply concerned with the intricacies of character as with the pace of its action. It brings the reader considerably closer to empathy with bisexuality than does any of Hemingway's fiction, which, even so, is far more yearningly homo-erotic than Cain's.

One gets the impression, at times, that men's fiction requires the presence of the queer character in order to endorse the heterosexual credentials, not only of the superior (if not necessarily hostile) central character or narrator, but also of the reader himself. Jake Barnes, the narrator of Hemingway's *The Sun Also Rises* (1926), feels distinctly superior to a crowd of gay men he sees in a Paris bar – he wants to plough into them with fists flying – but they also remind him of his own predicament as a war-wounded castrate who will never make love with a woman again. They provide the scale against which he must assess what remains of his masculinity, whether it be expressed by (not) fag-bashing or (not) screwing women. But in the post-war period, under the conditions of McCarthyism in the United States and its American-influenced local variations elsewhere in the West, the homosexual character is often additionally required to symbolise other kinds of unreliability than that of a substandard virility. Espionage fiction offers a case in point.

Alan Sinfield has written that 'Until the Cold War, homosexuality was a submerged discourse, only implicitly subversive of certain institutions. Once it could be linked, in a paranoid way, with communism, it could be invoked to reinforce the Cold War and stigmatised as treachery against the Western Alliance.'[3] In Britain, the defection of the diplomats Guy Burgess and Donald Maclean to the Soviet Union in 1951 served to legitimise public and institutional suspicions of sexual dissidents. The new wave of popular literature about the Cold War shows evidence of this intensified distrust. For instance, Ian Fleming's *From Russia, With Love* (1957) contains two references to Burgess and Maclean.[4] In the second case, at an internal inquiry into the defections, James Bond argues that the Security Service needs to recruit a new breed of agents, rather than just retired army officers, to deal with the new breed of intellectual traitor. Captain Troop, himself a retired naval officer, icily dismisses Bond's argument, saying, 'So you suggest we should staff the organisation with long-haired perverts. That's quite an original notion. I thought we were all agreed that homosexuals were about the worst security risk there is. I can't see the Americans handing over many atom secrets to a lot of pansies soaked in scent.' Of course, his invocation of homosexual men who conform to stereotype both visibly and smellably rather misses the point, which is that Burgess and Maclean went undetected precisely because both espionage and homosexuality may be, as it were, invisible to the naked eye. However, Fleming himself somewhat undermines this point in his crass portrayal of Colonel Rosa Klebb, the obviously lesbian head of operations in the Soviet secret services.

In 1962 Cyril Connolly wrote a mildly interesting send-up of Fleming's James Bond books, a short story called 'Bond Strikes Camp'.[5] Here, M. sends Bond on a mission to a London gay club: dragged-up as 'Gerda', his instructions are to entrap a Soviet agent who is masquerading as a Yugoslav businessman. All goes as planned, and the spy takes 'Gerda' home to his apartment. The due processes of seduction ensue, but just before he might have to surrender his virtue, Bond goes on the attack – and discovers that the supposed spy is, in fact, M. himself, who has always fancied him. Looking forward to taking over M.'s department (and, incidentally, to going back to the gay club), Bond suggests M. commit suicide or face the publicity. Here the story ends. Connolly's squib demonstrates, if little else, that even as soon as they were published, Fleming's novels and Bond's attitudes were equally vulnerable to satirisation on the basis of sexual anxiety.

Without mentioning Burgess and Maclean by name, John Le Carré's *The Spy Who Came in from the Cold* (1963) shows some evidence of the same concerns as Bond's in its representation of Ashe – 'a little bit petulant, a little bit of a pansy', as Leamas characterises him.[6] When the two men first meet, Leamas self-consciously imagines they look like 'a couple of cissies looking at a dirty postcard' (p. 47). Later, reporting back to Control, Leamas says he has made contact with 'A man called Ashe' and adds, as if it sums him up, 'A pansy' (p. 50). We receive another impression of Ashe later, from a different point of view but much the same angle. Liz Gold recalls him as 'that fair, rather effeminate man who was so ingratiating' and who asked her a lot of questions about her boyfriends; 'He hadn't been amorous or anything – she'd thought he was a bit queer to be honest' (p. 137). When seeking some explanation of why Ashe may have recommended her to the attention of the Communists, she considers altering not her first impressions but their meaning: 'Perhaps he had a crush on her, perhaps he wasn't queer but just looked it' (p. 141). That is all Le Carré has to say about the sexuality of this marginal character; but it is interesting that these few references appear to have been both necessary and sufficient: they suggest so much more than they actually say about the psychopathology of espionage. After all, one of the author's most insistent points in this novel is that the secret services on the two sides of the Cold War share the same characteristics, one of which is that agents generally drift into their role for personal rather than ideological reasons. Leamas himself sums up his version of this argument in the penultimate chapter: 'What do you think spies are: priests, saints and martyrs? They're a squalid procession of vain fools, traitors too, yes; pansies, sadists and drunkards, people who play cowboys and Indians to brighten their rotten lives' (p. 210). This is Le Carré's corrective to the James Bond books.

Women's romance novels have generally been no less hostile than men's fiction to the spectre of the unmanly man. The homosexual man is liable to be depicted, if at all, as a failed heterosexual man – a mere waste of the constituent parts of maleness. Moreover, in her overriding need to provide wholesale endorsements of the various institutions of heterosexuality, the romance novelist can no more afford to compromise her vision by including gay men in her narratives than she could afford to introduce her heroine to an attractive and unattached lesbian.

Romance fiction can be seen at its most aggressively formulaic, its least willing to compromise with changing social values and gender roles, in the works of the right-wing, monarchistic pseudo-aristocrat Barbara Cartland, the most prolific novelist in the history of the universe. Cartland has often claimed that the steady growth in her popularity since the 1970s can be explained, in the first place, by the increasing availability of pornography (by which, I think, she simply means the kinds of representations of sex one has found on prime-time television and in mainstream films since the 1960s) and, more recently, by the AIDS epidemic. According to her own mythology, other romantic novelists sold out to the demand for sex. She alone held out against this trend, continuing to write 'a pure type of [heterosexless] romance, with a chaste heroine and a happy ending which is never complete without the couple being married during the last chapter'. All this would be bad enough if she confined her fatuity to writing about an idealised heterosexuality in the eighteenth and nineteenth centuries; but she also chooses to comment publicly on the social consequences of the so-called sexual revolution of the 1960s.

Cartland's right-wing conservative views are entirely consistent with the repressive ethos of her fiction, which is explicitly hostile to all signs of egalitarianism, and rabid about the slightest glimmer of feminism. In 1994 she gave herself the credit for having been the intellectual origin of the British Conservative government's moralistic 'Back to Basics' campaign, which soon fell apart in laughable disarray as the press got to work on the sexual lives of Conservative members of Parliament. Her views on the AIDS epidemic are, characteristically, as uncompromising as they are ignorant:

I won't mention AIDS. I don't have anything to do with AIDS at all. I won't give money towards AIDS because I think the whole thing's disgusting. It only came on because of the queers as you know perfectly well.[7]

So much for love.

Cartland's own representations of homosexual people are revealing. They are stereotypes, of course; but then so are all her characters. They appear to represent a kind of social sophistication, a decadence, which her straight male characters are aware of but which her purest females, even when they witness it, do not recognise for what it is. In Cartland's novel *A Virgin in Mayfair* (published in 1976, nine years after the Sexual Offences Act partially decriminalised male homosexual acts in England and Wales; six years after the first meeting of the London branch of the Gay Liberation Front; four years after *Gay News* was founded) we witness a party in Chelsea at which men in drag are dancing together. Maxine, the eponymous virgin and the novel's narrator, thinks they are women at first; and when she realises they are men she thinks they are in 'fancy dress' rather than drag. She and Mary, the woman with whom she has been taken there, are both discomfited by the fact that they are never asked to dance: for the men keep imploring each other, in 'high, soprano voices', 'Darling, darling, do dance with me!' A bout of face-slapping erupts when 'one awfully good-looking man dressed as a sailor' breaks his promises to dance with two men in drag, choosing instead to partner 'a strange-looking woman who apparently had not bothered to come in fancy dress'. Maxine is disturbed and confused by the whole event, but does not know why. As she reflects afterwards, 'It was a frightfully strange party, and somehow I felt we ought not to have been there; perhaps the people were not frightfully good class.'[8] On a later occasion, demurely passive as ever, Maxine finds her friends have led her into 'the most extraordinary place', an apparently gay nightspot called the Blue Lamp Club. Here, the women are 'all in tweedish clothes, mostly with berets on very straight hair, and hardly made up at all'. They seem to take no interest in the men, whom Maxine considers 'quite amusing' because they are wearing 'absolutely fantastic clothes – red or black shirts, and yellow spotted ties'. Amusing or not, however, these people cannot conceal the failure of their own amusements: for even the obtuse Maxine can see that they all seem 'a little sad, and rather languid – not half as gay as some of the other places I had been to in London'. The word 'gay' is meant in the hetero sense, by Maxine if not necessarily by Cartland. Maxine is, after all, completely unaware of the kind of place the Blue Lamp Club really is (p. 52).

A Virgin in Mayfair opens with the following 'Author's Note':

> I wrote this novel because it is what I discovered Mayfair to be like when I came out in the early twenties.
>
> The Night-Clubs and most of the characters in the story were real people [*sic*] and the atmosphere is correct, only I had fair hair and no money!!

'Came out', of course, is the language of the heterosexual debutante rather than of an emergent lesbian. Whether Cartland uses it with irony in 1976 is unclear; probably not, I guess. More to the point, though, is Cartland's claim to authenticity. She is evoking a 'real' Mayfair of the 1920s, gay clubs and all. If Cartland herself was as naïve at that time as Maxine is, by 1976 she has become better informed. She knows now that what she saw then were inverts; but nothing she knows now persuades her to see them as being any less strange than she then thought them. She is not interested in them as individuals.

However, the book does contain one major homosexual character, even if the naïve narrator is never able to say that that is what he is. Maxine is befriended by an apparently eligible young man called Alec Beattoc – befriended but not, as she would like to imagine, courted. Even though they become close friends, Maxine is vaguely aware that he has placed limits on their intimacy. She wants him to fall in love with her, but 'Somehow he does not seem to want to do that'. He does not try to kiss her and, although he calls her 'darling', '"darling" said by Alec does not mean really anything' (p. 127). On a particular night in his company she gives him ample opportunity to kiss her, but he does nothing and she goes to bed feeling snubbed: 'I cannot think why he did not kiss me, because he must have known that I wanted him to' (p. 128). Maxine's friends notice that she is beginning to make a fool of herself. Her mentor and eventual husband Harry says, 'before you get too involved with that young man I think you ought to know something about him'; but he cannot bring himself to tell her. When he says he does not think Alec is 'a good companion' for her, Maxine understandably demands an explanation. Harry replies, 'it is frightfully difficult to explain to you, but he is no good, you know – take it from me'. He adds: 'Alec Beattoc is no use to you as a young man'. The most Harry is willing to say, when Maxine is angered by his evasiveness, is that Alec is 'a little rotter' (pp. 130–31).

Maxine intransigently insists on continuing to see Alec. So Harry calls in her Uncle Lionel to help:

Uncle Lionel seemed rather embarrassed, and he took up a paper-knife and played about with it.

'You are not a child, Maxine,' he said, 'but there are one or two things in the world which there is no point in your knowing about.

'Certain things which – how shall I put it? – offend against decency, but which are often ignored because people don't wish to make a scandal.' (p. 134)

As a consequence of this policy of reticence, Maxine finds her uncle no more persuasive than Harry. So Uncle Lionel approaches Alec in person and bans him from seing Maxine again. On finding out about this, Maxine infers – rather smartly, considering how obtuse she usually is – that her uncle is blackmailing Alec about something. He responds to her accusation as follows:

There is some blackmail which I consider entirely legitimate. I am sorry to tell you, Maxine, this young man who is outwardly very charming, is utterly worthless to you.

If I had not known his father all my life I should feel obliged to take severer measures than those I have already taken and intend to take. As it is, I can only commiserate with my old friend for having produced such a son.

He adds that Alec is 'a decadent product of a decadent age'. Again, Maxine is left none the wiser, asking herself, 'What is the most awful thing that anyone can do?' (p. 137). Cartland shows every sign of believing that the answer to this question – if we substitute 'be' for 'do' as the last word – is *be* homosexual.

Later, Maxine tells the whole story of the unfortunate liaison with Alec to her friend Tommy, who has been living in Paris. He responds by laughing and telling her that 'that would teach you to keep away from "nice boys"!' This last phrase is said 'with such an affected accent' – presumably to make fun of the queers whose existence Maxine is still unaware of. Thinking back on the whole episode, she believes Harry should have been more frank with her: 'if he had been sensible, and tried to explain to me that Alec belonged to a kind of sect – it sounds like a religion, or something of that sort – of course I should have understood'. What irritates her about the whole business is that the members of Alec's 'sect' are invisible. As a woman, she feels excluded from those in the know: for 'it makes life very difficult if people are peculiar like that [even while she remains in ignorance of what 'that' is 'like'] and you don't know it, while people like Harry and Tommy know it'. What makes Alec so dangerous within Cartland's system of values is that his invisibility as a queer allows him to compromise the institution of matrimony – for he does, after all, turn out to be a fortune-hunter in search of a wife – undetected. He would be a much safer creature, indeed, if he conformed to the effeminate stereotype and signalled his presence by dressing in drag. As Maxine says at this point – and it is hard to imagine that Cartland disagrees – 'It would be so much better if they wore a badge, or something, so that one could know at once, and then no mistakes could be made' (pp. 160–61). I like to pretend this is Cartland's approving response to the post-Stonewall, badge-wearing gay liberationist.

· · ·

There are now many alternatives to the heterosexist norms of mainstream popular fiction. Indeed, some of the most famous of popular novelists are gay or lesbian; it does not get said often enough. The distinguished names of Ursula Le Guin, Samuel Delany and Clive Barker are the first which come to mind. Delany's *Dhalgren* (1975) and his four *Neveryon* novels (1979, 1983, 1985, 1987) contain not only major bisexual or gay characters but also the complex outcomes of the author's meditations on the potential future shape of gender roles and sexual orientations. His own experiences as an African-American gay man clearly influence the depth and extent of his attention to sexually and racially marginalised cultures and individuals. Science fiction's easy accommodation of grand themes is exploited by Delany in a broadly conceived sequence of analyses of heterosexuality's failings and homosexuality's potential strengths.

The fantasy novelist Clive Barker is one of the bestselling gay writers in the world. Although he does not write or publish specifically *as* a gay writer, he makes no secret of his sexuality and has given a number of interviews to gay magazines in the United States and Great Britain. He also gives readings in gay bookshops. Like Stephen King's, Clive Barker's fiction is created in close proximity to the movie industry, and Barker has had to put up with producers' stubborn reluctance to disturb the still surface of their audiences' complacency – even in scenes of extreme horror – by lobbing in questions about sexual values. Like Tennessee Williams long before him, Barker has seen his work emasculated when transferred to the screen. For instance, the short novel *Cabal*, which Barker readily acknowledges as being a gay allegory, was filmed in 1989 as *Nightbreed*. The story's monsters, the Breed, were regarded by the film's eventual producer as 'too sympathetic'. As a consequence, the moral ambiguities of the original story had to be whittled down to the film's clear-cut conflict between good and evil.[9]

Clive Barker makes a strongly argued distinction between his own fiction and that of the two authors with whom he is most often compared:

My books are completely opposed to those of James Herbert and Stephen King. Their books are death-driven, mine are life-driven. I write about the strangeness you see from the corner of your eye – actual adventures waiting to happen. James Herbert and Stephen King want your blood. Their books have a bourgeois mentality manifested by the view that if it's strange, *shoot it*. They're terrified of diversity and think that if it's different, it belongs on the dark side; if anything's different, it's after them. Their books are all about reinforcing the status quo. Deeply conservative.

This advocacy of difference characterises and enlivens Barker's fictions in ways which he relates to his own homosexuality. As he adds, in the same interview, 'I think we as gay people have more space to dream' – clearly, a useful gift for a fantasy novelist. Barker's massive novel *Imajica* (1991) can be read as an allegory about AIDS. But the author is careful not to succumb to the apocalyptic pessimism which so easily afflicts other writers of fantasy and horror. He says: 'I love writing about sex – straight, gay – it's great fun to write about the beauty of it and great fun to have. We mustn't give in to the pessimism. We must make sure we continue to celebrate sex. The flight from sensuality has to be powerfully resisted.'[10]

Each of the popular genres has undergone the major changes which gay liberation exerted on 'mainstream' literature. Many lesbian and gay novelists are now providing the science fiction, the detective novels, the horror stories, the romances and so forth, which gay readers want to read. Gay literature as a whole has been greatly enriched by such work as the detective fiction of Joseph Hansen and, more recently, Michael Nava, or the gay male romances of women novelists like Patricia Nell Warren and Chris Hunt. Indeed, this deliberate post-gay-liberationist appropriation of the various popular genres may one day prove to have been among the happiest outcomes, even among the most useful outcomes, of gay liberation itself.

Chapter 21

The Pink Triangle

The major event in the history of 'the homosexual' is what has come to be known as the Holocaust. At least until the AIDS epidemic, no other event has so clearly – because so extremely – exposed and defined the vulnerable position of homosexual lives under the constraints imposed on them by the dominant culture of institutional heterosexuality. No greater reverse in social conditions has been experienced than by homosexual women and men under Nazism after the spectacular, if limited, advances of the Weimar period. While the idea of a 'homosexual holocaust' has, at times, been rather casually overstated by gay liberationists – since homosexuals were never, as such, included in the 'final solution' (*Endlösung*) – the fact remains that they were transported in large numbers to be 'reformed' or 'cured' in labour camps, and many of them died or were killed there. This may be a very much smaller matter than what was done to the Jews, but it is hardly more trivial.[1]

After the 'liberation' of the camps by the Allies, those survivors who wore the pink triangle – denoting that they had been imprisoned *as* homosexuals – were treated as common criminals who had deserved their incarceration. Many were transferred to prisons proper to serve out their terms. Like the gypsies, and unlike the rest, the pink triangle survivors had to wait until the 1980s before they received either formal recognition of or compensation for their suffering. The pink triangle was left off Holocaust memorials. The Nazis had introduced a stricter version of the anti-homosexual law in Paragraph 175 of the German penal code in 1935. Unlike other Nazi laws, this was not repealed at the end of the war. Indeed, on 10 May 1957, a federal constitutional court (*Bundesverfassungsgericht*) not only upheld the constitutionality of this stricter version, but even doubled its maximum penalty from five to ten years. (It is worth remembering, too, that Paragraph 175 had long pre-dated Nazism: it was introduced in 1871. As Günter Grau has written, 'The anti-homosexual policy of the National Socialists did not therefore start from scratch. Hitler, Himmler and their "national comrades" did not have to invent any new laws, nor establish any new apparatus' in order to carry out their programme aimed at eradicating homosexuality from the body politic.[2]) No less than the Holocaust itself, this narrative of collaborative shame should never be forgotten. It teaches us a useful lesson on the limitation of democratic freedoms.

Given this extension of official persecution of the pink triangle survivors beyond the dismantling of the Third Reich, it is little wonder that there have been few published autobiographical accounts of living in the camps under the stigma of the pink triangle.[3] It seems all the more important, therefore, to take note when other accounts of the concentration camps do – as they very rarely do – refer to pink triangle prisoners and their fate. The literature of the gay holocaust has to be assembled piecemeal, not from accounts by the gay survivors themselves, but from accounts by prisoners from the other categories, and even from the words of the Nazis and their supporters in heterosexism, whatever their nationality.

Many accounts of the genocidal events under Nazi rule simply do not mention the issue of homosexuality.[4] Others mention it only as a circumstantial aspect of sexually segregated mass imprisonment, rather than as one of the reasons for imprisonment in the first place. A typical example is Wieslaw Kielar's memoir of five years spent in Auschwitz, *Anus Mundi*.[5] On one occasion, Kielar reports being sent by Peter, a block supervisor (*Kapo*), to deliver some food to his boyfriend (*Pipel* or *Piepel*) whom Kielar finds recovering from a minor surgical operation 'in connection with his extraordinary relationship with Peter', dressed in 'silk panties' and a colourful dressing-gown (p. 75). Later, Kielar himself is appraised in the showers by 'a short Kapo, who was notorious throughout the camp for his cruelty as well as for his predilection for young men'; he is on the lookout for a new boyfriend (p. 79). These *Kapo/Piepel* relationships are often mentioned in concentration camp memoirs. They do not seem to have involved pink triangle prisoners. *Kapos* tended to be chosen from among the political prisoners or the ordinary criminals, rather than from statusless categories like the Jews or homosexuals; and their boyfriends were chosen for their looks, not for any predisposition to homosexuality. The *Kapos* knew that their patronage was likely to persuade the most heterosexual of boys to agree to sexual relationships, since what was really on offer, along with protection and extra food, was the possibility of survival. These relationships were open and, as it were, institutionalised; it is not surprising that they subsequently attract comment in survivors' memoirs.[6]

When a rumour spreads around the camp that a consignment of women prisoners is about to arrive, Kielar reports that conversation immediately turns to the topic of the *Kapos* and their boyfriends: 'People began to make jokes, particularly concerning the subject of catamites, or *Pipels*, as they were called in the camp, who would presumably fall into disfavor. It may seem strange but it was the German criminals of all people, those who, up until then, had been known as "camp queers", who now displayed the greatest interest in the topic of women' (p. 81). These 'camp queers' are not to be confused with the pink triangle prisoners, whom Kielar never mentions.[7] Whatever the other effects the arrival of women may have had, it did not alter the basic pattern of *Kapo/Piepel* relationships, with protection being offered in exchange for sex. Later in the book, Kielar mentions a man called Bock, the senior prisoner in the camp's hospital, who was reproached by other staff 'for favoring a group of young men who were useless as hospital staff and whom he had been instrumental in turning into homosexuals' (p. 119). When Bock was finally relieved of his post, 'Some of his protégés who thus no longer had anyone to support them, went to seek their fortune elsewhere', presumably by offering themselves to other *Kapos* (p. 160).[8]

Filip Müller's memoir *Auschwitz Inferno* is not untypical in containing only one passing reference to this topic: 'In the centre of our block . . . slept *Kapo* Lajzer, his bum-boy, and his 40-year old cousin whose hand was crippled'. An asterisk leads the reader from the phrase 'bum-boy' to a glossary which offers the following explanation: 'Bum-boy (*Piepel*) A lad corrupted by camp life who served the pleasures of the *Kapos* and block seniors. Sometimes he was sexually abused'.[9] Fleeting glimpses of these boys are also offered in Primo Levi's *If This Is A Man*.[10] For instance: 'Sigi is seventeen years old and is hungrier than everybody, although he is given a little soup every evening by his probably not disinterested protector' (p. 80). Furthermore the numbers of such boys were large enough to merit their appearance in a much more general remark. According to Levi, one of the first 150,000 Jews who arrived in Auschwitz, only a few hundred survived. These survivors were not ordinary prisoners on ordinary rations, but privileged 'doctors, tailors, shoe-makers, musicians, cooks, young attractive homosexuals' and so on (p. 95). Remember, again, that this is not a reference to pink triangle prisoners. In *The Truce*, Levi mentions a boy who survived until the liberation by virtue of his position as the *Lager-Kapo*'s lover, but who even after liberation was crazy with redundant dreams of becoming a *Kapo* himself (p. 201). In his classic memoir *Night*, Elie Wiesel makes a brief, parenthetical mention of homosexuals trading in children, which is presumably another reference to the *Kapo/Piepel* situation rather than to the men with the pink triangles.[11]

One could be forgiven for inferring from the reading of these autobiographical accounts by survivors, that the issue of homosexuality only significantly arose in this context of the granting of favours to pretty boys by privileged men, in situations where neither boy nor man had been imprisoned for sexual reasons. Not one of the books I have referred to so far tells us anything about the imprisoning and killing of homosexual men because they were homosexual. Texts which do acknowledge this fact may do so perfunctorily when describing the system of distinguishing triangular patches by which concentration camp prisoners were visibly categorised.[12] Evelyn le Chêne's *Mauthausen: The History of a Death Camp* takes the same approach, but more slowly and in greater detail. For example: 'PINK. Pink was the colour chosen to distinguish homosexuals, although it varied from a washed-out brown to a washed-out red. There were many more of this category in Mauthausen than the other prisoners would have wished. The "red" or political prisoners were particularly annoyed because rain often washed away their colour and confused them with the "pinks".'[13]

But what are we to make of lists of categories, or lists of patches, which omit the pink triangle prisoners? An HMSO publication of 1939 contains accounts of the jacket-patch system by prisoners released from Buchenwald. They do not mention the pink triangle.[14] Nor, surprisingly, does Primo Levi when listing categories at the beginning of *If This Is A Man* (p. 39). The only categories and patch-colours he includes are: criminals (green), politicals (red) and Jews (red and yellow star). And Martin Gilbert's book *The Holocaust*, published by the Board of Deputies of British Jews, contains a map display entitled 'NON-JEWISH VICTIMS OF NAZI RULE' which does not mention the pink triangle prisoners.[15]

However, a case that I find even more interesting and revealing is that of Walter Poller's memoir *Medical Block, Buchenwald*.[16] Poller had been a journalist on a workers' newspaper in Westphalia before he was imprisoned on a charge of attempted high treason. Among the earliest of his observations of life in the camps is the moment of categorisation: 'We were now classified, the politicals being handed the red triangle, the work-dodgers and anti-socials the black triangle, the Jehovah's Witnesses the violet, the criminals the green, the homosexuals the pink. In addition to their ordinary triangle, the Jews received a yellow one, to be crossed with the other colour and thus form the Star of David' (p. 35). Poller himself wore the red triangle and, therefore, immediately found himself in a privileged position. His comment to this effect is, to say the least, unfortunate: 'I did, for the present, wonder why the politicals received preferential treatment at all. Were these Violets, Blacks, Greens, not also human beings, the same poor wretches we Reds were?' (p. 36). The fact is, of course, that a mere page after his careful listing of all the categories and their badges, he has either completely forgotten two of them – the homosexuals and the Jews – or consciously excluded them from his reckoning of the fully human.

This kind of sleight-of-hand erasure of the Nazi persecution of homosexuals occurs surprisingly frequently. I would like to offer just one more example, this time from Sidra DeKoven Ezrahi's book on the literature of the Holocaust, *By Words Alone*:

> The Jews were not, of course, the only victims of Nazism, and a number of works written by non-Jews reflect the different logic of death and survival that distinguished the fate of the political from the Jewish *Häftling* [prisoner] in the concentrationary universe. The former were, in general, treated with less brutality and could find strength in the fact that they had in large measure chosen their own destiny; the Jews and the Gypsies were the only peoples singled out by *racial* criteria for extermination, and arrested, deported, interned, and gassed simply because of the biological fact of their ancestry. Yet the concentrationary idiom informs the literature written by all the prisoners and binds them in a common linguistic universe.[17]

This line of argument acknowledges the existence of only two categories of prisoner, political and 'racial', and only one category to which the individuals in question, born gypsies and Jews, could not help belonging. Like Poller, Ezrahi has either forgotten or deliberately excluded people imprisoned on the grounds of their sexuality (or, indeed, their religion, like the Jehovah's Witnesses) from her reckoning. Even taking a generous interpretation, one must assume that she has not overlooked thousands of victims altogether, but has opted to include these groups in a portmanteau use of the term 'political' – rejecting essentialist notions of sexuality – and is arguing that, like the communists, homosexuals and Jehovah's Witnesses 'had in large measure chosen their own destiny'. This idea is so obscene in the context of the Holocaust that one wonders how it got through the editing process intact. And yet, one recognises it as being little different from the arguments of those who like to distinguish between the 'innocent' and 'guilty' victims of AIDS.

At the time of the war, and as a consequence since, the association of Fascism with homosexuality was not uncommon – that is, among anti-homosexual anti-Fascists. It is true, of course, that there was a powerful homosexual presence in the Nazis, chiefly among Roehm's Brownshirts; but it is also a matter of fact that these men were violently extirpated from the body politic on the so-called Night of the Long Knives, 29–30 June 1934. It suited Allied propagandists, however, to overlook such events, as well as Himmler's constant anti-homosexual diatribes and the presence of pink triangle prisoners in the concentration camps. Homosexuality was a weapon that could be used against Nazism.

Among certain documents relating to life in Germany just before the war, there is a letter from a Consul-General R.T. Smallbones, dated 14 December 1938. In an attempt to explain Nazism, Smallbones claims to have found a significant flaw in the German character:

> The explanation of this outbreak of sadistic cruelty may be that sexual perversion, and in particular homo-sexuality, are very prevalent in Germany. It seems to me that mass sexual perversity may offer an explanation for this otherwise inexplicable outbreak. I am persuaded that, if the government of Germany depended on the suffrage of the people, those in power and responsible for these

outrages would be swept away by a storm of indignation if not put up against a wall and shot.[18]

This is the authentic voice of the English democrat, right down to that last pugnacious cliché, and it appears to be what Whitehall wanted to hear. Notice that 'the people' of Germany are not afflicted with 'homo-sexuality', even though it is supposedly so 'prevalent' in their society. The 'mass sexual perversity' observed by the good consul-general is somehow confined to 'those in power' and would be swept aside at once by the power of the popular, heterosexual vote.

Smallbones' theory is quoted with approval by Samuel Igra, whose book *Germany's National Vice* (1945) is a sustained and obsessive pursuit of the myth of Fascistic homosexuality. Although eccentric, it is worth considering in some detail, since it makes so clearly the connection which has reappeared at regular intervals ever since the war. Having quoted Smallbones, Igra comments decisively:

> I am convinced that this explanation is the correct one. For, as a matter of fact, the widespread existence of sexual perversion in Germany ... is notorious. And authorities on criminal sociology are agreed that there is a causal connection between mass sexual perversion and the kind of mass atrocities committed by the Germans in the two world wars. Furthermore, there is no doubt that this also explains why the Jews were made the chief victims of German sadistic torture, rapine and murder. That is the main thesis of my book, and I think I have proved it irrefutably.[19]

We know, of course, that the one thing Igra will not be able to mention in his book is the systematic persecution of lesbians and homosexual men by the Nazis. Quite why the presence of homosexuality should result in anti-Semitism is never explained; nor are the 'authorities on criminal sociology' quoted to justify Igra's confident assertions of 'a matter of fact', 'no doubt' and an 'irrefutably' proven thesis. Still establishing the parameters of what pass for an argument, Igra uses the familiar metaphor of infection, 'perversion' being 'that evil which has infected the whole body politic of the German people, breaking out like rabies among them and forcing them in a compulsive urge to spread destruction all round' (p. 8). As in the Smallbones document, Igra suggests, incompatibly, both culpable perversion within a powerful minority and a majority with absolutely no resistance to infection. He subsequently confirms that he is working with an extremely pliable definition of his key word 'homosexualism':

> I have used it throughout the book as a general term, applying not only to the unnatural practices generally associated with the name of Sodom, but also including all forms of anti-natural immorality in sexual conduct, such as rape with violence and other sadistic treatment of women. But there is the further and still more important connotation in the psychological field. This includes the attitude towards human life which expresses itself in that seemingly ineluctable life-destroying urge manifested by the Germans towards helpless persons who have come under their wrath, and also their disrespect for womanhood as the source and guardian of life's beginnings. (p. 10)

So 'homosexualism' here includes not only misogyny – a fairly routine myth even now – but also misanthropy. It is, Igra says later, 'a practical denial of life at its very source, a perversion of nature', whose 'addicts look with cynicism on the whole human race and the normal instincts of mankind' (p. 17).

Igra speaks from a particular subject position with a particular view on sexual issues: 'As a member of the Jewish faith, I have for many years been interested in this question from the standpoint of Biblical teaching' (p. 8). That he is Jewish more convincingly justifies his hatred of Nazism than that of homosexuality, though scriptural fundamentalism does, of course, help to explain the latter. Genesis and Leviticus are quoted in evidence against German cultural history (for, unlike Germany, since Philip the Fair abolished the Knights Templar, 'France has been free from these vices and since then also she has been an object of hatred to the Germans' – pp. 21–2). But, as if the Sodom myth had never been successfully incorporated into Christian thought, Igra argues, in support of his own authoritative credentials, that

> Only a Jew can understand and grasp, with the instinct as well as the intellect, how the vice of homosexualism undermines the very foundations of human existence; and only a Jew, answering the call of his racial blood and traditions, finds himself spontaneously taking up arms against it. In this matter there is no place for compromise. Those who practise homosexualism and defend it are aware of what is at stake. For this reason they strive not only to destroy the persons who oppose them but also discredit the ideas which their opponents stand for. And they know that throughout her long history Israel has been the unrelenting champion of those ideas. (p. 60)

The rest of Igra's argument is concerned to assert – which, he seems to believe, is the same as to prove – that Adolf Hitler was a male prostitute in Vienna from 1907 to 1912, and then in Munich from 1912 to 1914; that his 'sex instincts' were 'abnormal'; but that 'We need not discuss the question whether he was homosexual, impotent or a sadistic pervert, or all three together' (p. 58). This casual sentence may sound peculiar, but its complacency is typical of a tendency among exponents of the Nazism-as-perversion argument to conflate deviancies, treating them as interchangeable. Thus, importantly, Nazi sadism and homo-eroticism are seen as being the same thing: Hitler devised the Final Solution because he was not securely and healthily heterosexual.

The nadir of pseudo-scientific theorisation about homosexuality is reached in the memoirs of the Nazi mass murderer Rudolf Hoess, *Commandant of Auschwitz* (Poland 1951; German translation 1958; English translation 1959). Hoess was no mere academic: his theories had an immediate practical application. The solution to the 'problem' of homosexuality was extreme; and it was capable of expression in the very languages of sexology which the Nazis had been at such pains to suppress when, for instance, they attacked and closed down the Institute for Sexual Science which contained so many of Magnus Hirschfeld's irreplaceable files.

When he addresses the topic of homosexuality in his memoirs, Hoess adopts the tone of the detached expert. Having been imprisoned for murder in 1924, he feels able to make the following observations:

> In my opinion, based on years of experience and observation, the widespread homosexuality [*Homosexualität*] found in these prisons is rarely congenital, or in the nature of a disease, but is rather the result of strong sexual desires which cannot be satisfied in any other way. It arises primarily from a search for a stimulating or exciting activity that promises to give the men something out of life, in surroundings where absolutely no form of moral restraint applies.[20]

Quite what Hoess means by 'experience' [*Erfahrung*] as distinct from 'observation' [*Beobachtung*] is not clear, but he is certainly never associating himself with the men whose imprisonment subjects them to 'strong sexual desires' for each other. (Indeed, since he regards himself as having been a political prisoner, he does not even recognise common ground between himself and the 'mass of criminals' with whom he was confined.) The distinction he makes between, on the one hand, 'congenital' or diseased homosexuality and, on the other, circumstantial homosexual acts returns to govern the ways in which he speaks of his victims at Dachau, Sachsenhausen and, finally, Auschwitz.

As I have suggested, the language of Hoess's book is chillingly deployed. Again and again, George Orwell's coinage 'doublespeak' comes to mind – as when, for instance, Hoess says that some Jehovah's Witnesses who swore not to proselytise were 'eventually – later in the war – immediately set free' (p. 97). However, the interesting thing about this is that his discussions of homosexuality are not conducted in uniquely appalled or disgusted terms. Indeed, Hoess is at ease with the commonplaces of early twentieth-century sexological discourse. Illness is his main metaphor, for instance, and it is a metaphor which helps to determine policy. During the Berlin Olympic Games a particular effort was made to round up visibly homosexual communities and individuals: 'They were to be trained to do more useful work in the camps.' Against Hoess's advice, these prisoners were dispersed around the 'protective custody camp' at Dachau, as a result of which 'It was not long before a constant stream of reports of homosexual activities began to flow in from every block' and 'The epidemic spread' (p. 100). When at last the higher authorities deferred to Hoess' expertise in this field, he had the pink triangle prisoners segregated from the rest – along with some prisoners from other categories who were 'also afflicted with this vice' (itself an interesting phrase, doublespeaking of both culpability and affliction in the same breath) – with the happy consequence that 'the epidemic was at once stopped from spreading. Thereafter only isolated cases of this unnatural intercourse occurred, since a strict watch was kept on these men' (p. 101).

There follows a passage, censored from the 1958 German edition of the book but retained in the following year's English edition, in which Hoess offers the case study of a Romanian prince whose life in Munich 'had become a public scandal owing to his unnatural behaviour. Despite all political and social considerations, the publicity which he had brought on himself had become intolerable and he was brought to Dachau'. In an age of sexological theorisation and speculation, it seems, everyone assumed the right to offer an opinion on such a case. 'The police thought that his excessive debaucheries had wearied him of women, and that he had taken to homosexuality as a pastime in order to get a new thrill. The Reichsführer SS believed that hard work and the strict life of a concentration camp would soon effect a cure.' But neither of these authorities is as authoritative as Hoess himself: 'The moment he arrived, it was obvious to me what was wrong with him. His roaming eyes, the way he started at the slightest noise, his weak and dancer-like movements, all made me suspect the true homosexual at once.' It is as if it had not occurred to this amateur shrink and professional killer that a man might have good cause to show signs of nervousness on being led into Dachau.

As it turns out, the Romanian prince was not simply 'the true homosexual' at all. What made him noteworthy – since he was only one of many pink triangle prisoners – apart from the fact that his body was covered in erotic tattoos (which were routinely and systematically photographed 'for the purposes of the State Criminal Police Office'), was his sexual hyperactivity. He could not be prevented from constantly masturbating. A doctor at the camp judged him beyond hope of reform: 'Any attempt to cure him by hard work was doomed to failure from the start.' In the end, weakened by his experience of the camp, the prince was put to bed and restrained with sedatives. This did not prevent his continuing to masturbate until the time of his death. There is little purpose to be served in speculating on this man's life and mind; my case study is of Rudolf Hoess. I raise the case of the Romanian prince only to comment on the manner of its telling. Hoess' last words on him are striking. Writing after the war, this man who had sent so many prisoners to their deaths and overseen the torture of so many others, commented: 'It makes me shiver even now when I remember this case' (pp. 101–3).

Writing about Sachsenhausen, Hoess considers again the question of the usefulness of hard labour as both a punishment and a cure for men accused of committing homosexual acts or being homosexual. At Sachsenhausen the segregated pink triangle prisoners were put to work in the notorious clay pit of the brickworks. Hoess reports that 'The effect of hard work, which was supposed to make them "normal" again, varied greatly according to the different types of homosexuals.' Notice how the inverted commas around the concept of normality assert Hoess' knowledgeable credentials. Even though he has already muddled his discourses by speaking of homosexuality as 'unnatural', a curable ailment and a 'vice', he here distances himself from the most simplistic arguments of Nazism – that those who show signs of racial, political, mental, religious or sexual abnormality should be removed altogether from the normality of life in the Third Reich – and he continues to lay claim to superior insight into homosexuality in all its categories. He reports that hard labour had 'its most salutary effect' on male prostitutes, who 'could not be classified as true homosexuals: prostitution was just their trade'. They 'were soon brought to their senses' by discipline and work, and did not associate with two of Hoess' other categories, 'the genuine' or 'the viciously depraved type of homosexual'. They might even be reformed and released. Similarly, some of 'those who had become homosexual out of inclination' – which is to say, 'men who through over-indulgence had grown weary of women and sought fresh excitements to enliven their parasitical existence' – might also, mixing metaphors, 'be cured of their vice' (pp. 103–4).

However, men 'who had begun by dabbling in homosexuality for such reasons but had later become deeply addicted to their vice' could be cured by neither work nor close 'supervision'. In this respect they were comparable to 'the genuine homosexuals, of whom there were only a few examples'. Members of the latter type were incorrigible: in spite of the curative properties that make Hoess speak of death camps as if they were merely some kind of rigorous health spa, these men continued to 'fall into one another's arms' at the slightest opportunity. Again laying claim to particular acuteness in this field, Hoess continues:

> They were easy enough to pick out. Their soft and girlish affectations and fastidiousness, their sickly-sweet manner of speech and their altogether too affectionate deportment towards their fellows distinguished them from those who had put their vice behind them and wished to be free of it, and whose steps on the road to recovery were visible to any acute observer. (p. 104)

Since the ideal of 'selection' in the camps meant selection for death, there is a disturbing overlap, in the first sentence quoted here, between Hoess's roles as the ostensibly dispassionate, clinical observer of deviant types and as the Commandant of Auschwitz. In the context of mass extermination, to see an individual in the crowd is to anticipate that person's death. This is how we must reimagine Rudolf Hoess's selective and analytical gaze if we are to understand the horrific implications of these passages on homosexuality. The eye of the sexologist becomes that of the exterminator, and the 'understanding' of homosexuality is deployed to eradicate it.

Perhaps the cruellest and most cynical part of this document, certainly one of its saddest parts, follows on from the above. Still speaking of these intransigent, 'genuine' homosexuals, Hoess goes on:

> Because they could not or would not give up their vice, they knew that they would never be set free. The effect of this psychological burden, on men whose natures were for the most past delicate and sensitive, was to accelerate their physical collapse.
>
> Should one of these lose his 'friend' through sickness, or perhaps death, then the end could be at once foreseen. Many would commit suicide. To such natures, in such circumstances, the 'friend' meant everything. There were many instances of 'friends' committing suicide together. (pp. 104–5)

This passage is awesome in its display of a consciousness of consciousness. Hoess knows that he is dealing with human beings, and he knows the extent of their despair. They in their turn know what it would take to earn a reprieve, but they know that mercy is not on offer to their 'type'. The repulsive equanimity with which Hoess reports the imposition of 'this psychological burden' on 'delicate and sensitive' men, while evincing at last a certain insight into its consequences, shows no sign of an awareness of his own crime.

I do not wish to suggest that homosexual men were uniquely victimised either by Hoess as an individual or by the death camp system as a whole. This is clearly not the case. I have concentrated on a short section of this book in the rest of which there is more and worse. However, this part of the Hoess memoir is uniquely revealing in its appropriation of sexological discourses which had first been developed for essentially liberatory purposes. The discourse of sickness allowed for a concept of temporary, circumstantial homosexuals, and they could eventually be released; but essentialist discourses had provided the concept of 'the homosexual', unchangeable in essence, who was by definition both incurable and irredeemable, and could therefore never be released. Hoess' closing remarks on the topic of homosexuality concern a 'renunciation' test which the SS developed at Ravensbrück in 1944, to ensure that only satisfactorily 'cured' deviants were ever released from the camps. The test involved setting apparently reformed pink triangle prisoners to work alongside female prostitutes and to observe their behaviour when given opportunities for heterosexual contact. Those who passed this stage of the test would then be covertly given opportunities for homosexual contact, which they must reject. It is with some bewilderment that Hoess reports that some men took both opportunities. For once he is only tentatively categorical: 'Whether these men could be described as bisexual [*bisexuell*], I do not know'. Hoess concludes this account of the homosexual Holocaust with a short paragraph containing only the following sentence: 'I can only add that I found the habits and mentality of the various kinds of homosexuals, and the study of their psyches under prison conditions, extremely instructive [*aufschlußreich*]' (p. 105).

It was not until gay liberationists outside Germany in the nineteen-seventies began to publicise the persecution of homosexuals by the Nazis – nor until the pink triangle began to be worn again, willingly and affirmatively this time, throughout the Western world – that a major work was written about the lives and deaths of the pink triangle prisoners. Martin Sherman's play *Bent* (1979) was not the first to deal with the topic – Noel Greig and Drew Griffiths' ambitious historical drama for Gay Sweatshop, *As Time Goes By* (1977), had preceded it – but *Bent*, also written for Gay Sweatshop, was more closely focused on the narrative of what had happened in Germany.[21] The eventual success of Sherman's play, which has since been produced – and has often provoked great controversy, in Israel even rioting – all round the world, has played a major role in alerting gay and straight audiences to the fact of the pink triangle persecutions. It is often criticised as being sensationalist, but, given its topic, it is difficult to imagine how it could not have been. In the end, though, *Bent* has to be seen more as a product of the era of gay liberation than of the Holocaust itself. In a sense – although I do not mean to belittle it by saying this – it hardly qualifies as Holocaust literature proper. As John Clum has said, 'The Holocaust provides a background of brutal oppression, but the real issue of the play is self-oppression' (very much a hot topic in the late 1970s).[22]

I began this chapter with a remark to the effect that gay liberationists have occasionally overstated their speculative statistics in an attempt to persuade people to take seriously the fact that the Nazis were not a bunch of goose-stepping, hyper-masculine queers (though some of them were, of course) but were, on the contrary, stridently anti-homosexual and more than willing to convert that stridency into effective punitive action. Les Wright has pointed out that the phrase 'homosexual genocide' was used in English for the first time in James Steakley's book *The Homosexual Emancipation Movement in Germany* (1975).[23] Wright argues convincingly that this sudden attention to events in Nazi Germany – attention which, even in West Germany itself, was not paid at all widely until the gay movement developed alongside the student movements in the 1970s – coincided with the attempt to establish gay people as constituting a distinct, virtually 'ethnic' minority, with rights in need of defending. In a sense, therefore, the existence of what 'gay holocaust' literature there is can be attributed to the archaeological impulses of the gay liberation movement. The fact that the AIDS epidemic followed so soon after the rediscovery of the extent of Nazi oppression partly accounts for the swiftness with which the gay community resorted to genocidal tropes when reacting, later, to the Reagan regime's spectacular inaction in the face of the multiple deaths of gay men.

Chapter 22

....

The Post-War Starting-Point

....

As homosexuality, particularly male homosexuality, becomes more and more a matter for
open, public debate – as it does in the aftermath of the Second World War – its presences
in and absences from literary texts become increasingly haphazard and unpredictable.
Authors who are not homosexual themselves, and who have no interest in putting forward
arguments either for or against the liberalisation of anti-homosexual laws and conventions,
start using homosexual characters for a broad range of ulterior motives. For instance, such
characters start to appear in American crime fiction as significant contributions to a
generalised depiction of urban moral decay, alongside drug addicts, prostitutes and other
criminal types; or in British spy fiction as the potential enemy within, reds not under the
bed but in it together; or in many different fictional genres as symbols of decadence or
outright evil. Something similar happens in post-war cinema.

These idiosyncratic representations are dependent on the prevailing winds. So many
theories of homosexuality were in circulation by the middle of the twentieth century that
individual novelists could freely choose from a range of common options (call it a cliché-
bank or a stereotype warehouse) which homo was the right one for them: pervert or invert,
struttingly hyper-masculine or mincingly effeminate, sinner or saint, opportunistic
bisexual or compulsive monomaniac, completely unnatural or completely animal-like,
flamboyant or secretive, manipulative or victimised, frivolous or tragic, isolated or hunting
in packs, child molester or harasser of straight men, deviously criminal or mentally ill,
fastidious aesthete or wallower in filth, child in an adult body, woman in a man's, she-wolf
in ram's clothing, or whatever. This masquerade of queer types appears to have no limit.

In the present chapter, however, I shall concentrate on three novels, one from 1945,
barely a post-war book at all, and two from 1949, two containing characters involved in
homosexual activities and/or relationships and one not. None was written by a homosexual
novelist, although the author of the first had certainly – shall we say? – *dabbled* during his
youth. The first is a nostalgic look backwards, mainly to the 1920s, when social categories
were still relatively stable; the second is a retrospective account of the war itself, told entirely
without nostalgia from a German point of view; and the third, at least superficially, is an
extended prophecy of future ills, the first of the great Cold War novels. These are three very
different books. (That is part of the point: they have virtually nothing in common.) But
taken together, they offer us an idea of the place and condition from which the post-war
'heterosexual' novel's representations of homosexuality were setting out.

So, to start with, we look back to upper-class life in the 1920s. It was not unusual at this time – as we are so often told – for a narrow class of English men to be homo-erotically romantic at public school, homosexually active at university (Oxford or Cambridge) and heterosexual thereafter. One thinks of figures like John Betjeman and Evelyn Waugh. Indeed, the latter's novel *Brideshead Revisited* (1945) provides one of the best fictional accounts of the ethos, not only of post-adolescent upper class homo-eroticism between the wars, but also of post-(second)-war nostalgia for its apparent passing.[1] Although Waugh tries to present his central character and narrator's conversion to Catholicism as a spiritual triumph, it is clear that in emotional terms the loss of the male–male romanticism acceptable during the educational years accepts no compensation. The novel is a pastoral romance. As such, it has a far weaker sense of hope for Christianity's afterlife than of regret that even in Arcadia mortality holds sway: *Et in Arcadia ego*, the subtitle of Book 1.

The main body of the book opens in a vulnerable Oxford that no longer exists at the time of narration:

> Oxford, in those days, was still a city of aquatint. In her spacious and quiet streets men walked and spoke as they had done in [John Henry, Cardinal] Newman's day; her autumnal mists, her grey springtime, and the rare glory of her summer days . . . when the chestnut was in flower and the bells rang out high and clear over her gables and cupolas, exhaled the soft airs of centuries of youth. (p. 23)

This is the tonal point, pre-Modernist and pre-heterosexual, away from which the whole narrative will move with a consistent and irreversible force. Even as early as this, the rot is apt to set in at one time of year: 'Here, discordantly, in Eights Week, came a rabble of womankind, some hundreds strong, twittering and fluttering over the cobbles'. In this context, of course, 'Oxford' means an all-male university, cloistered off from the unmentioned Oxford, a city as much of women as of men, and a city of workers more than students. It is in the former that Waugh's narrator, Charles Ryder, meets the embodiment of his Arcadia, Sebastian Flyte. It is Sebastian who, during woman-flooded Eights Week, leads Charles 'out of danger' by driving him into the country for a peacefully womanless picnic (p. 25). Their idyll reaches its defining moment on a knoll beneath some elms: having eaten strawberries with a suitable wine, 'we lit fat, Turkish cigarettes and lay on our backs, Sebastian's eyes on the leaves above him, mine on his profile' (p. 26).

The main point about Sebastian is his beauty: 'he was the most conspicuous man of his year by reason of his beauty' (p. 30); 'He was entrancing, with that epicene beauty which in extreme youth sings aloud for love and withers at the first cold wind' (p. 33). Charles, too, is looking for love, and finds it – but only by postponing adolescence, let alone adulthood: for Sebastian, although he knows how to do such an adult and modern thing as to drive a motor-car, is figured as a child, even by himself. The most visible sign of his retarded spirit is Aloysius, the toy bear from which he is inseparable. Charles looks back on their idyll as if on the happy childhood he never had, but Sebastian did have:

> Now, that summer term with Sebastian, it seemed as though I was being given a brief spell of what I had never known, a happy childhood, and though its toys were silk shirts and liqueurs and cigars and its naughtiness high in the catalogue of grave sins, there was something of nursery freshness about us that fell little short of the joy of innocence. (pp. 45–6)

In a later decade, shrinks might have called this a 'passing phase' – but it does not appear to be, strictly, their kind of phase. It is childish rather than adolescent. Although Charles speaks of a catalogue of sins, the vices he refers to are not sexual. Sex would be too much like growing up, which is what Sebastian most wants to avoid. As he later says to Charles, seemingly in earnest: 'If it could only be like this always – always summer, always alone [together], the fruit always ripe, and Aloysius in a good temper' (p. 77). So sufficient does their relationship eventually become – 'each so much bound up in the other that we did not look elsewhere for friends' (p. 103) – that they do not really have to acknowledge the modern world.

Needless to say, however, theirs is a doomed peacefulness – and not only because the story of it is being told at the time of the Second World War – subject to all the most ordinary ravages of time. As Charles expresses it, Sebastian's disillusionment must come, as inevitably as imperialists to a South Sea island:

> I had no mind then for anything except Sebastian, and I saw him already as being threatened, though I did not yet know how black was the threat. . . . By the blue waters and rustling palms of his own mind he was happy and harmless as a Polynesian; only when the big ship dropped anchor beyond the coral reef, and the cutter beached in the lagoon, and, up the slope that had never known the print of a boot, there trod the grim invasion of trader, administrator, missionary, and tourist – only then was it time to disinter the archaic weapons of the tribe and sound the drums in the hills [.]

I quote this metaphor at length because not only does it represent what Charles takes to be Sebastian's state of mind – prelapsarian, unsullied, contented – but it also marks the moment at which Charles seems fully to realise that Sebastian's state of innocence is by definition insular. Adult human contact of any kind must spoil it. Hence the remark that Charles adds, not unexpectedly, to the above: 'his days in Arcadia were numbered'. The relationship between the two young men ends for Sebastian in the first place, and only then for Charles when he realises that 'I was no longer part of his solitude' (p. 123). Among the demands of adulthood is entry into the social world. Ultimately, for Charles as for the majority of his peers, this will involve heterosexual courtship and matrimony. But, much as Sebastian remains single and only ever forms a close relationship with another man, a German called Kurt, Charles eventually escapes back into bachelorhood from a dry and loveless marriage and forms the second really intimate relationship of his life with the woman who most reminds him of Sebastian – Julia Flyte, Sebastian's sister: 'On my side the interest was keener, for there was always the physical likeness between brother and sister' (p. 172); 'I had not forgotten Sebastian. He was with me daily in Julia; or rather it was Julia I had known in him, in those distant Arcadian days' (p. 288). This dismissive afterthought probably deserves, itself, to be dismissed. It reads like a retrospective rationalisation by Charles, narrating as a Catholic convert, to justify the days when he found Sebastian so enchanting.

There is an occasion when Charles and Sebastian are taken to a brothel by a friend and are assumed by the working women to be homosexual ('Come on . . . we're wasting our time. They're only fairies' – p. 111). The women's mistake is understandable, but Waugh does mean it to be a mistake. Even Sebastian, who never has a heterosexual relationship and ends up in thrall to the abysmal Kurt, is never clearly defined as homosexual: Waugh's intention appears to be to leave him in a limbo of puerile sexlessness, neither one thing nor the other. However, the novel does contain one character, Anthony Blanche, who constitutes Waugh's most important representation of a homosexual man. If the Charles–Sebastian relationship sometimes seems intended as a way of consigning male–male relationships to a region of perpetual immaturity, Waugh's portrayal of Blanche allows for a very different version of homosexuality to flourish.

Of all the characters in *Brideshead Revisited*, Anthony Blanche comes the closest to being Modernism personified. Already, as a student, he has impeccable cultural credentials as that quintessential creation of modernity, 'the homosexual':

> At the age of fifteen, for a wager, he was disguised as a girl and taken to play at the big table in the Jockey Club at Buenos Aires; he dined with Proust and Gide and was on closer terms with Cocteau and Diaghilev; Firbank sent him his novels with fervent inscriptions; he had aroused three irreconcilable feuds in Capri; by his own account he had practised black art in Cefalù and had been cured of drug-taking in California and of an Oedipus complex in Vienna. (p. 47)

He is cultured, sophisticated and, above all, unafraid. He may have been 'cured' of a drug habit and a complex, but one thing he is never in any mood to treat as a complaint is his sexuality itself. When we first encounter him, Charles Ryder refers to him as 'the "aesthete" *par excellence*, a byword of iniquity from Cherwell Edge to Somerville' (not a particularly wide arena in which to be notorious, it is true). Ever up to date with the Modernist avant-garde, he uses a megaphone for reciting *The Waste Land* to hearties on their way to the river for rowing practice. He stutters to the lovely Sebastian, reminding him of the iconic status of his namesake, 'My dear, I should like to stick you full of barbed arrows like a p-p-pin-cushion' (pp. 34–5). This is a man who does not know, or need to know, the meaning of discretion. He has his own sources and resources of defensive strength.

When Blanche is attacked by hearties – in an incident based on many suffered by the likes of Harold Acton and Brian Howard, the two great Oxford 'aesthetes' of Evelyn Waugh's day – he uses his open homosexuality to abash and outwit them. (At least, he *says* he did: he narrates the whole of this sequence himself.) Insults are countered with mock seductiveness: 'Then one of them, a rather juicy little piece, accused me of unnatural vices. "My dear," I said, "I may be inverted but I am not insatiable. Come back when you are *alone*."' And when they threaten to throw him into the fountain in the quadrangle, he takes pre-emptive action:

> Now as you know I have two sculptures by Brancusi and several pretty things and I did not want them to start getting rough, so I said, pacifically, "Dear sweet clodhoppers, if you know anything of sexual psychology you would know that nothing could give me keener pleasure than to be manhandled by you meaty boys. It would be an ecstacy [*sic*] of the very naughtiest kind. So if any of you wishes to be my partner in joy come and seize me. If, on the other hand, you simply wish to satisfy some obscure and less easily classified libido and see me bathe, come with me quietly, dear louts, to the fountain."

So they follow him sulkily to the fountain, where he takes an ostentatious and triumphant bath (pp. 50–51). At a later point in the book, Charles Ryder makes a distinction between 'the intimate feminine, modern world' and 'the august, masculine atmosphere of a better age' (p. 133). Within this scheme, if we are to take it seriously, the presence of Anthony Blanche at Oxford, like the invasion of women in Eights Week, represents the incompatible disturbances of modernity. What they are incompatible with is untroubled masculinity. The problem is, though, that conventional males require their conventional triumphs to be *seen*: that, after all, is why their sisters and girlfriends are invited to Oxford – to watch them rowing – and it is why they do not, simply, leave Blanche alone to get on with his own life. As ever, masculinity cannot just exist: it has to be demonstratively proven.

Unlike Sebastian, or indeed Charles, Anthony Blanche shows no sign of having any difficulty in adjusting to adulthood. We see little of him after Oxford, but there are a few significant reports of his progress. He forms a relationship with a policeman in Munich (p. 102) and then with 'a Jew boy' (Sebastian's phrase) in Constantinople. He has grown a beard and moved into 'a very nice, tumble-down house near the bazaars' with the Jew. Sebastian visits them there (p. 153). Much later, when he is briefly back in London after a long absence from England, Blanche takes Charles into a gay bar ('Blue Grotto Club. Members only') and makes a point of contrasting his own ease with Charles' discomfort in such a place: 'Not quite your milieu, my dear, but mine, I assure you. After all, you have been in your milieu all day' (p. 257); 'You must remember, my dear, that *here* you are just as conspicuous and, may I say, abnormal, my dear, as I should be in B-b-bratt's' (p. 258). He clearly embodies the possibility of living happily as a homosexual man. If he is portrayed as being abnormal – but no less abnormal than modernity itself – he is, nevertheless, shown to be perfectly well adjusted to his abnormality.

In terms of quantity of print, Anthony Blanche is a relatively minor character in the novel. Qualitatively, though, he is of major importance to it. According to Martin Green, the 'major interest' of *Brideshead Revisited* is 'the statement it makes, in mythic form, about Waugh's failure as an artist'. Green elucidates as follows:

Charles Ryder, who represents Waugh, fails as an artist because he turns away from Anthony Blanche (the figure derived from [Harold] Acton and [Brian] Howard, an international dandy-aesthete) to make a friend of Sebastian Flyte (who stands for the pre-war, purely English dandyism of the beautiful Etonian and Oxonian aristocrat). If Ryder had affiliated himself to Blanche (if Waugh had affiliated himself to Acton), he might have become a great artist. Instead he chose charm, playfulness, quaintness, and whimsy – and became the writer of *Brideshead Revisited*.

Nor was this failure of nerve Evelyn Waugh's alone. Green continues:

Another Charles Ryder (John Betjeman) wrote *Summoned by Bells*; another, Cyril Connolly, wrote *The Unquiet Grave*; and so on. For Charles Ryder's wrong choice was the wrong choice of a whole generation of English writers, who preferred the purely playful dandyism of English aristocrats to the dangerously experimental dandyism of international aestheticism.[2]

For all that this is a rather over-schematic rendering of the issue, Green's point is well put. It accurately captures certain envious tones which one can occasionally detect in the novel. Despite being, in all but one scene, out of his milieu as a homosexual, Anthony Blanche is fully in his element as a fearless Modernist. His avant-gardism and his sexuality are of a piece. Hence the references to Proust, Gide, Cocteau, Diaghilev and Firbank – as set against Charles Ryder's one wistful reference to John Henry Newman. Blanche's daring to take on both the 'masculine' world – as antagonist – and 'feminine' or effeminate Modernism – as whole-hearted enthusiast – leaves the impression of his being the most dynamic character in the book.

For the time being the main point I want to emphasise is that, although he is a recognisable stereotype of a kind which gay critics tended to deplore in the first decade after Stonewall, Anthony Blanche constitutes a more vibrant and positive representation of an 'invert' than a canonical English homosexual novelist like E.M. Forster ever dared publish during his lifetime. He is not quite the kind of invisible, pipe-smoking homosexual man envisaged by the Wolfenden Report of 1957 – he is far too indiscreet and in-your-face for that – but he is human. (Coming from Waugh, that is an achievement in itself.) His humanity is never normal, always exotic, but that is not necessarily a bad thing. After all, if the steady spread of suburbanism and bourgeois narrowness are to be the novel's main concluding nightmares, Blanche stands out as the character who has contributed the least to that spread, and who is the least likely to be taken over by it. His individualism has been a greater success than that of Sebastian, which is by contrast whimsical and childish. He may be less normal than Charles Ryder, but in the end he seems to be happier.[3]

•••

Heinrich Böll's novel *The Train Was on Time* (*Der Zug war punktlich*, 1949) consists of a far more dour and depressive narrative. A group of young German soldiers are being transported by rail to the Russian front.[4] It transpires that one of them, never named but always referred to as 'the blonde soldier' [*sic*], is harbouring a terrible secret. The man who has been jammed next to him for forty-eight hours, Andreas, suddenly perceives that behind the blond's eyes, which seem to be 'coated with a kind of greyish-white, slimy film', there lies 'a festering wound'. As soon as he sees that Andreas has understood this, the blond begins to tell the story of his downfall: 'A sergeant corrupted me. Now I'm completely ruined and rotten'. He and six others spent six weeks under the sergeant's control in a remote and dreary spot. 'He corrupted us. What more is there to say? We all did it . . . all but one man. He would not. He was older than the rest of us and was married and had children.' The sergeant went out one night and shot this recalcitrant individual. The other men had to help him dispose of the body in a swamp. Soon afterwards the blond managed to return to headquarters, where he gave false evidence about the death of the older man. 'Since then,' the blond concludes, 'I can find no pleasure in anything. I am afraid to look at a woman.'

Andreas' reaction to this narrative is, arguably, rather extreme, given the context of the war he is involved in: 'Andreas was horrified and disgusted. He thought it was the worst thing he had ever heard. . . . A terrible disgust took possession of him like a poison in his blood.' In a gesture of consolation he tries to take hold of the blond's hand, but the blond recoils 'in horror' and breaks down in tears. 'There's no cure but death,' he sobs. 'I want to die, and that will be the end' (pp. 50–52).

No cure for what? The 'festering wound' of the blond soldier's corruption, presumably. Clearly, the sergeant's sexual offence is figured as being diseased: it leaves his men 'completely ruined and rotten' and morally blind. It festers within them long after the individual sexual event has come to an end. Only a man securely married is morally immune to it – and yet he is the first to die of it. The blond makes no distinction – nor does Andreas – between sexual corruption and the murder of the married man and the concealment of both corpse and murderer. They are all part of the one continuum of immorality. So homosexuality is figured here as both disease and atrocity, to be both cured and punished by the death of the corrupt. There is even a suggestion that this disease can be carried by mere word of mouth. If Andreas has indeed been possessed by 'a poison in his blood' after listening to the blond soldier's confession, it may be that we are expected to believe that his malady, his disgust, will remain with him until he dies.

The blond soldier lies silent for a long time. It is not clear to the others whether he is asleep. However, eventually he gives the game away:

> The blond soldier began to move. One could see that he had only been feigning sleep and that he was now pretending to wake up. He stretched himself slowly, turned over and opened his eyes, but he did not realise that the tear marks on his dirty cheeks were still visible and had left regular furrows in the grime, like those on the face of a little girl from whom a schoolfellow has snatched her buttered sandwich in the playground. Perhaps he had forgotten altogether that he had been weeping. His eyes were red-rimmed and looked ugly, and one could imagine that he really had a venereal disease. (p. 57)

It is not that his confession has much altered his appearance, other than by leaving the traces of tears. But it has changed how his appearance is to be read. In this passage he is presented as being, in turn, a deceiving actor, a whingeing schoolgirl and a syphilitic. Yet one could just as well imagine *the same appearances* being described as follows: he *genuinely* emerges from sleep, the traces of tears on his unwashed cheeks make him look like a grubby school*boy*, and his red-rimmed eyes look as if he has caught *flu*. Obviously, the more sinister version is the one this part of Böll's narrative relies on. It is necessary for the blond soldier not only to feel ruined but also to look it. His appearance must be shown to bear the outward signs of his inward disgrace.

Later on, while the blond soldier is improvising on his mouth-organ 'no recognisable tunes but strange, soft, exciting, formless snatches which made Andreas think of the outpost in the marshes' where the sergeant corrupted his men, Andreas says to himself: 'Tonight I shall pray for the fellows in the outpost at Sivash and also for the man who died for Germany because he wouldn't . . . because he wouldn't do what the others did. All the same, that was a hero's death' (pp. 60–61). The blond, it seems, is beyond being prayed for. Or perhaps Andreas is beginning to feel that, now he has stopped confessing and crying and feigning sleep, he is in some way redeemable after all, and not in need of prayer. When, later, the soldiers find themselves in a house in Lvov which turns out to be a brothel, Andreas does see one path to at least partial redemption for him: 'The blonde soldier blushed and sweated with fear. It must be awful for him, thought Andreas; perhaps it would be better for him to take a girl' (p. 81). To sleep with a woman might be the perfect cure to the homosexuality he contracted from the sergeant. This would not wipe out past shame, but it could at least begin to suggest a viable sexual and social future.

One of the women approaches the blond. 'The blond soldier gave a sob when she touched him, and quivered like a reed in the wind. She caught hold of him and held him up whispering, "Don't be afraid, darling, don't be afraid."' (p. 82). He weeps against her breast. Like the other men he does go upstairs with one of the women, but it later transpires that he has spent his time in her bed asleep (p. 120). But a rest cure, one feels, is never going to be enough for the depth of injury this man has suffered or inflicted on himself. Only the horrors of the Russian front await him. He and his comrades will die. For him – both in his own eyes and according to the moral symbolism of the whole novel – his death will be an appropriate consequence of, and punishment for, the manner of his corruption.

The Train Was on Time is not a novel about homosexuality. Even the section of it I have outlined is not centrally *about* homosexuality. Masculinity would be nearer the mark. As in many later novels, the integrity of an essentially heterosexual young man is demolished by a homosexual assault. As far as one can tell from the tone of the narrative, homosexual activity is conceived of (by the characters if not, perhaps, by their novelist) as contributing to a fate potentially worse than death, and from which death will provide a necessary release. Moreover, this symbolic version of sexual degradation is expected to carry an even heavier moral burden. Homosexual assault is the repulsive emblem of a psychic imbalance induced by the perverse conditions of warfare. But it only seems to affect weak men. True heroes would have buttoned up their lips and resisted. To have given in at all is a sign of moral cowardice which even the cleansing, redefining role of the brothel cannot eradicate.

Ominously, the novel shows no sign that the peacetime legacy of war will be any less extreme in its capacity to destroy the purities of manhood: for in Germany more clearly than anywhere else, in Europe at least, the war would be conspicuous in its failure to end cleanly. German fiction does not envisage a clean peace. The divisions of the Cold War ensure that ideological difference continues to define the status of the individual at least as strongly as it had during the hot war. In this sense, the blond soldier represents a lost characteristic of Germany itself. The only point I wish to make here is an obvious one. In the post-war moment, it seemed appropriate to Heinrich Böll to offer homosexual assault as a more shocking emblem of moral decay than Nazism itself. As the Cold War developed through its various manifestations – the most famously homophobic of which, in the West, would be McCarthyism in the United States – this would prove not to be an isolated case, nor could it seem, among so many other examples of the same tendency, eccentric or extreme.

. . .

We know that much of George Orwell's *Nineteen Eighty-Four* (1949), especially its evocations of urban seediness and squalor, is not dystopian science fiction at all, but a methodically realist representation of London as it emerged from the Second World War, and from the Blitz in particular, into the 'peace' which came to be known as the Cold War.[5] Orwell's novel relied for its emotional effects on the very familiarity of the setting, both physical and social, on to which he imposed the idea of the regime of Big Brother. The contemporary reader was expected to 'identify' with Winston Smith and Julia as people with 1949 values, frighteningly marooned in the nightmare of 1984. Moreover, the fullest effect of this displacement was (and is) conveyed, not in terms of political abstractions, but in relation to the question of love. Although *Nineteen Eighty-Four* has always been most famous for its discussions about the politics of language and the language of politics, its emotional nexus is located where, for the contemporary homosexual reader, the book must have been at its least convincing – that is, in its account of the forbidden love between Winston and Julia. What read as a futuristic nightmare to the heterosexual reader must have seemed to the homosexual reader somewhat paranoid and ignorant, because so close to the reality of homosexual life in England at the time – but showing no sign that Orwell was aware of this fact. (Much the same can be said of the 'Hots', the illicit hetero-romantic minority in Aldous Huxley's 1949 novel *Ape and Essence*, and of Huxley's attitude to them.)

It is worth pausing to remind ourselves of some of the characteristics of the nightmarish 'future' society Orwell describes. Under this regime, what the 1949 reader would have thought of as private life is, in all its aspects, public property. The act of keeping a diary, while not exactly illegal – there being no longer any laws – is punishable either by death or by twenty-five years in a labour camp. (Winston Smith's starting a diary on 4 April 1984 is the first decisive act of his deviancy.) Mere actions, of course, are within the repressive scope of any regime worth its salt. What Orwell identifies as the most frightening refinement achieved by twentieth-century totalitarianism, with the aid of such technological advances as are most visibly represented in the novel by two-way 'telescreens', is thought control. Big Brother's regime can see not only into the individual home, but even into the individual. Moreover, by seeking to control not only people's external behaviour, but even their inner existence – using the 'Thought Police' to patrol for the slightest sign of 'Thoughtcrime' – the regime has opted for an essentialist version of criminality that corresponds with so many modern societies' altered view of the sexual orientations. We note that law and order are the responsibility of the Ministry of Love.

One of the main instruments of social control in the novel, based on Orwell's experiences of BBC propaganda during the Second World War, is language. The regime's development of revolutionary 'Newspeak' to replace reactionary 'Oldspeak' is intended, ultimately, to limit the potential range of people's thoughts. Once an idea becomes unsayable – or so the argument goes – it will be literally unthinkable. Thoughtcrime will have been eradicated along with the words which might have given it voice. As Winston's friend Syme summarises the situation, 'The whole climate of thought will be different. In fact there will *be* no thought, as we understand it now. Orthodoxy means not thinking – not needing to think. Orthodoxy is unconsciousness' (p. 46). In such a society, scientific research has only two aims: to develop more and more efficient ways of killing more and more people (Orwell was thinking of the scientists whose work had already led to Auschwitz and Hiroshima) and to tighten the Party's control over the individual's thoughts. Goldstein's illicit book, which Winston reads, speaks of scientists who are 'a mixture of psychologist and inquisitor, studying with real ordinary minuteness the meaning of facial expressions, gestures, and tones of voice, and testing the truth-producing effects of drugs, shock-therapy, hypnosis, and physical torture' (p. 156). Orwell knew he was writing about a kind of scientist who already existed. No doubt his insight could have been confirmed by the first-hand experience of many of his homosexual readers in the post-war era's golden age of electro-convulsive 'therapy'.

Central to the control of the individual is the need not only to do away with notions of sexuality as a private matter, but even to eradicate sexuality itself. Newspeak contains only two words to denote any kind of sexual behaviour: 'goodsex', meaning only chastity or procreational heterosexual intercourse without pleasure, and 'sexcrime' – which, as the narrative says, denotes 'fornication, adultery, homosexuality, and other perversions, and, in addition, normal intercourse practised for its own sake' (p. 246). Being 'normal', Winston and Julia's relationship comes into the latter category. The explicit aim of the Party is 'to remove all pleasure from the sexual act', or rather from the only sexual act permitted (p. 56). In the end, as O'Brien says, 'We shall abolish the orgasm' (p. 215). (It is in the same passage that O'Brien conjures up the future in the image of 'a boot stamping on a human face – for ever'.)

Given this rigorously policed anti-sexual situation, in which even young children belong to the fanatical Junior Anti-Sex League, anyone who falls in love is at extreme risk of discovery and punishment. This is the source of whatever tension arises – in the reader, if not as greatly as in the characters themselves – when Winston is handed a note by a woman who has been following him and who he suspects is a member of the Thought Police. The note is simple, but complicates their lives: 'I love you.' In order to meet beyond the range of telescreens and microphones, they have to journey separately and secretly out into the countryside. Their subsequent love-making is all the more dramatic, therefore. It is so much more than a release of erotic tension: 'Their embrace had been a battle, the climax a victory. It was a blow struck against the Party. It was a political act' (p. 104).

Both of them feel this, but only Winston is interested in extending the range of his rebelliousness. Julia's dissidence is relatively asocial: 'She hated the Party, and said so in the crudest words, but she made no general criticism of it. Except where it touched upon her own life she had no interest in Party doctrine' (p. 108). She is that figure so common to more recent sexual politics, the 'apolitical' dissident. When Winston tries to speak to her about the Party's falsification of history, she is not interested; nor does she believe that organised opposition is possible. In any case, it was not to have conversations of this kind that she has come to the seedy room which Winston has rented above an antique shop in a restricted, proletarian area of London. When she says she is interested, not in future generations, but in 'us', he accuses her of being merely 'a rebel from the waist downwards' (p. 127). (This would later become a routine leftist response to feminists and gay liberationists.) Winston, on the other hand, is like so many homosexual people who feel their social life has been artificially sexualised by the narrow focus of oppressive circumstances. Although he is Julia's lover, and has no regrets on this score, he is yearning for a less pressurised mode of relating to her:

> He wished that he were walking through the streets with her just as they were doing now but openly and without fear, talking of trivialities and buying odds and ends for the household. He wished above all that they had some place where they could be alone together without feeling the obligation to make love every time they met. (p. 114)

Gay readers may recognise this as a murmur from the closet. Which brings us to the point.

Whenever I read *Nineteen Eighty-Four* I cannot help imagining, between its lines, the spectral presence of another novel, a gay novel called *Nineteen Forty-Eight*, in which two young Londoners called Winston and Julian fall in love with each other and struggle to sustain their relationship under the continuous threat of blackmail, exposure and arrest. This would be an unexceptional homosexual novel of the post-war period, drably realistic and similar to so many which were published in that long period between the end of the war and the first tremors of gay liberation. Like Orwell's depressive heterosexual fantasy, it would end sadly – although probably more so, with the death of at least one of the lovers. It would not be recognised as a reality by heterosexual readers, of whom there would be few. In the two decades after the war, the dystopian realities of homosexual lives under 'the heterosexual dictatorship' (Tom Driberg's phrase) would be described with depressive accuracy by a growing vanguard of courageous homosexual novelists.[6]

Chapter 23

European Poetry on the Left

The polarising effects of the Cold War included the consolidation of an internationalist literature of communism. While the United States was becoming embroiled in the shameful, parochial episode of McCarthyism, resistance to Fascism remained a priority among those in Latin America and Europe who feared that the expansion of American influence during the immediate post-war period threatened an expansionist Fascism under a new flag. The most mature voices of international communism did not emanate from temporary dabblers like W.H. Auden and Stephen Spender, but from committed activists whose politics pre-dated the Cold War yet long outlasted the hot. These are writers whose faith, for better or worse, survived all revelations of Stalinist purges and many other systemic excesses. I am thinking of major figures like the Chilean poet Pablo Neruda (1904–73). Since it is conceivable, if debatable, that Federico Garcia Lorca (1899–1936) might have lived to become such a figure had he not been assassinated so young, a few remarks on him may be relevant at this point.

At a superficial level, Lorca's erotic imagination could appear commonplace. He is, at first, voyeuristic rather than involved. He distinguishes the objects of his desire before he starts to write *to* them. As has so often been the case with gay writers and painters, his mind keeps returning to the sight of boys bathing – not boys bathed *with*, but boys watched from dry land, appreciated secretly. Their enjoyment of their own boyhood's aptness to nature is no less spectacular a manifestation of virility than the artistry of the bullfighter, the point of difference being that the swimmers' beauty involves no artistry at all: nakedness is not a performance, even if it may come to be performed; it may be beautiful but, until described or commented on, it is not art. It has no skill. That said, the nakedness of young men demands not only to be compared with art but also to be made art of. In this respect, Lorca obeys the same impulses as Cavafy before him and Yannis Ritsos after.

But it would not be accurate to speak of Lorca as if he were merely some kind of up-market Spanish Uranian, a wistful sentimentalist with an eye for a boyish curve and a taste for poetic clichés prettified by rhyming, closed verse forms. This brings us nowhere near to a reliable appraisal of Lorca's stature. He is far more interesting than a glib summary of themes could convey. In the first place, he is not really a classicist. (This is relatively rare in homosexual poets of the first half of the twentieth century.) His pretty boys, his dying boys, are much less likely to be Greek Hyacinths or Adonises than named matadors or anonymous civil guards. He once said in an interview, 'I believe that being from Granada

gives me a fellow feeling for those being persecuted. For the Gypsy, the Negro, the Jew . . .
the morisco, whom all granadinos carry inside them'.[1] His poetry is centrally concerned to
protect Spain's racial minorities by invoking their cultures as being essential to Spanish
culture itself. That is to say, for all its apparent otherworldliness, Lorca's poetry is firmly
situated in the cultural and political circumstances leading up to the Spanish Civil War of
1936–39. He was an experimental Modernist and a republican, a Surrealist and a
distinctly modern kind of queer (although in many circumstances closeted). It was as a
republican queer that he was assassinated by Falangists, with an additional bullet up the
arse to emphasise the outrage of the queerness.

When he died in his late thirties he left three major gay texts: the *Oda a Walt Whitman*,
inspired by his 1927 trip to New York and published in a limited edition in Mexico in
1934, but not published in Spain while he was alive; the play *El Publico*, finished in 1930
but not published until 1978; and the eleven *Sonetos de amor oscuro*, written towards the
end of 1935 and suppressed by the poet's family for many decades, until an unofficial
release in 1983 forced them to publish the sonnets properly in 1984. Clearly, Lorca was
making an effort, against great odds, to write openly about his sexuality; clearly, too, the
effort would have had to continue, even if he had lived to a great age.

In spite of its apparent endorsement of a rich store of homophobic insults, the ode to
Whitman is an enthusiastic celebration of queer presence. Lorca was ambivalent about the
queerness he found in Manhattan. It was more open than anything he had seen before,
and the city seemed as a consequence intensely sexy (also because it contained so many
black men); but the development of a distinct subculture worried him, partly because he
was personally attracted to the ambiguity of the ostensibly straight man who has sex with
other men. He was both frightened and fascinated by queens.

Like Jean Cocteau, Lorca tended to think of homosexuality in terms of mirrors and
masks. *El Publico* (usually translated as *The Public* but also meaning 'the audience') is a
play about queer performativity from a moment in history long before that concept came
to be coined and theorised. Among its other events, an audience reacts angrily on realising
that in the performance they are watching Shakespeare's Juliet is being played by a fifteen-
year-old boy opposite an adult male Romeo. The row that ensues comments reflexively on
the drama itself, but also on the relationship between homosexual lovers and a
predominantly heterosexual public catching glimpses of what is going on behind their
masks. Were the two actors really making love on stage, as one member of the audience
alleges, and thereby violating not only propriety but also the conventions of their art; or
was their performance of love-making, because they have both turned out to be male, a
mere travesty of what it was meant to represent? Was their love too real to be a convincing
performance, or was their performance defeated by an inconveniently unmasked reality?
As it happens, the hostile voices in the audience are themselves defeated by the accepting
liberalism of a student in their midst, who says of Juliet: 'She seemed so very beautiful and
even if she was a disguised youth, it doesn't matter at all to me.' He adds: 'I don't have
time to think about whether Juliet's a man or a woman or a child, but only to observe that
I like her with such a joyous desire'. Desire depends on the equanimity of such a willing
suspension of disbelief.[2]

I do not mean to appear to have dismissed homo-erotic classicism as the plaything of
quietists. In Greek culture, for one, it cannot but be freighted with political implications,
many of which are rendered explicit in the poetry of Yannis Ritsos (1909–90). One route
of entry to Ritsos' political poems is, indeed, by way of their enigmatic moments of homo-
eroticism. These incidents are narrated tersely, without description or explanation, and
seem designed to raise questions rather than to provide answers. Less focused and

obsessive than, say, Constantine Cavafy's or Sandro Penna's, the intermittent homo-eroticism of Ritsos' work features as part of a wider vista of thematic concerns, including its antithesis, hetero-eroticism. Consider the following poems.[3] In 'Moment of Devout Concentration' several labourers undress and ride their horses into the sea; one youth cries out and clasps his genitals; the others lay him out on the beach, move his hands aside, and cross themselves at what they see (*SP*, p. 48). In 'Recollection' three young men wash statues, eat figs, and then crouch to shit together in the undergrowth (SP, p96). In 'Indisposition', while a man lies ill, stuffed full of words, the house across the street is being painted white; one of the decorators embraces the chimney 'as if fucking it' and splashes gobs of whitewash on the earth (*SP*, p. 143). In 'Among the Blind' a man wanders among blind men, sometimes naked, sometimes in uniform, sometimes in drag; but he knows, despite his ease in their midst, that they are not really blind at all; his costumes are, as it were, apparent and transparent (*ER*, p. 143). In 'The Lead Actors and the Spectators' two wrestlers move gradually 'from rivalry to consent', and end up making love, with the audience joining in (*ER*, p. 158). In 'Lack of Weight' a corpse's fly-buttons, through overuse, cannot be done up (*CS*, p. 40). In 'Shelters' some men or boys hide behind invisible nude statues; later, each gets inside a statue, wearing it as his disguise, but anxious lest an untimely cough or erection betray his presence to the passers-by (*CS*, p. 41).

Ritsos led what tends to be glibly called 'a tragic life', his family racked by illness, physical and mental, and early death; his nation often lapsing into a political madness with all-too-physical consequences. The tragic nature of his poetic vision is no fiction, no pose. As a communist activist, he was arrested in 1948 and sent to, among other places, the 'Institute for National Re-education' (even more sinister than its name) on Makronisos; he was released for reasons of ill health but rearrested in 1951 and confined for another year. On the first night of the 1967 coup, which ushered in the seven-year dictatorship of the Colonels, he was arrested again. After a year and a half's imprisonment he was then exiled to house arrest on Samos until 1970. Thereafter, in Athens, he effectively shut himself away in his own home, in what his translator Edmund Keeley referred to as 'his version of self-exile'. (I am reminded of Auden's lines, 'In the prison of his days / Teach the free man how to praise.')

Presumably as a consequence of the personal and political tragedies he experienced at first hand, Ritsos wrote poetry in which even the most peaceful scenes evoke a profound sense of unease. As in Auden's early work, everyday life is depicted in terms of heroics and risk. Even the briefest excursion beyond one's front door involves subterfuge; the most mundane of one's deeds is under surveillance, inspected for suspicious signs of sin or crime. National life becomes a struggle between the individual's urge to conceal and the state's imperative that all be laid bare. Even language itself is fundamentally tainted by the terrorism of ordinary life: 'The word is signified by what it would conceal' ('Unfinished', *SP*, p. 119). Meaning is contained in the spaces between and behind bursts of speech. Even poetry 'always begins before the words or after the words' ('The Meaning of Art', *SB*, p. 93). To conduct a survivable social life under such conditions, one must turn oneself into a cross between an actor and a spy. In 'Precautions', the speaker offers a listener practical advice on how to camouflage his real self. The two main instructions are 'control your voice' and 'make sure you lower your cap over your eyes / low, very low,/ so that they will not see where your eyes look' (*SP*, p. 167). The context seems to be political, but its connotations are inevitably personal. To hide the illicit, secret self, the body must be forced into unnatural postures.

Any social dealing contains the seeds of betrayal. Even when someone has 'sworn not to tell' – as in the poem 'Secret Guilt' – 'you can never be sure if and how long he'll keep silent' (*SP*, p. 179). There is always the danger that, in some crowded public place like a restaurant, you will find yourself transfixed as he 'stretches his huge, muscular arm and points at you'. A promise of discretion is thus seen to be, in itself, cause for suspicion and accusation. There is no protection from such dangers, not even in staying at home: absolute privacy can never be guaranteed. You either shut yourself away so securely that your house becomes the very prison from which you are trying to remain free, or you live in constant fear of the rifle butt on the door and the jackboot on the stair. House arrest, although often meant literally, is also metaphorically representative of the imprisoned psyche, the exile within. One can be, as it were, under house arrest within one's own skull, harbouring a secret – political or sexual or whatever – while presenting one's face as a deceptive mask to the outside world. One poem's title presents the outside world's dilemma: 'Face or Façade?' (*SP*, p. 113).

The poem 'Prisoner' is about a man confined to his own home. When he looks out of the window he sees straight into a neighbour's house, where a large mirror throws his gaze back on itself: he sees himself in his neighbour's house, 'clandestine,/ as if he's entered it to steal something'. When he turns back into his own room, he looks in the mirror and finds (of course) the neighbour's reflection. Each is thus imprisoned in his own home, yet present in the other's as a kind of involuntary, watchful jailer. Each can escape his own home only by intruding on the other's, and only by a visual trick (*SP*, p. 114).

Many poems from the late 1960s and early 1970s deal with searches of private property by the public authorities. Most end in arrest. A landlady's indiscretion about her tenants leads to the ominous creaking of a door in the night ('Inactivity', *SP*, p. 105). A man receives a summons and tries to hide it; but when he tears it up and is about to flush it down the lavatory, he is grabbed by three uniformed men ('Summons', *ER*, p. 88). In 'Search', a man shows the police around his home, apparently confident that he has nothing to hide. But they soon start finding incriminating evidence: a forged identity card, some jewellery, a dirty towel, a bloodstained shirt, a photo of himself in drag (inscribed to a stranger in his own handwriting). The poem ends with pathetic repetitions: 'who planted these in here? who planted these in here? who planted these in here?' (*SP*, p. 134).

Although or because Ritsos was also a painter, his poetic effects are primarily visual, his fragmentary narratives cinematic. And, although *to see* is a verb of contemplation – as in the *Twelve Poems for Cavafy* (1963), where there is much attention to Constantine Cavafy's glasses and his lamp, as aids to the seeing of boys and the writing of the poems they inspire – Ritsos also uses it as a verb of action. There are many ways of seeing and, correspondingly, of being seen. This puts the private individual at constant risk of publicity. As in Proust, the window and the mirror are optical instruments of phenomenal power. The window is an outlook on, and even the way to, freedom from house arrest; but it is also a means by which the public world can spy on the private. Similarly, the domestic mirror is an instrument with which both to reveal to oneself and to betray to others one's own most secret self.

Of course, mirrors make us conscious of ourselves. Poets often use them as metaphors for internal self-contemplation. But Ritsos finds that the mirror itself intervenes between object and image. Although, logically, they must reflect what they are given, in strict accordance with the laws of light, Ritsos' mirrors seem to have a life of their own. Like Lorca's and Jean Cocteau's mirrors before them, they often give access to a world of troubled eroticism. They appropriate the images they find, at times distorting them to their own arcane purposes. One will entrap, another betray; none is innocent. The men who look at their reflections find themselves revealed as unnatural, artificial, deviant, shifty. The sheer danger of their beauty undermines whatever satisfaction their vanity might have hoped to derive from the sight of themselves.

Object and image lead separate existences. In 'Normal Occurrence', a man who is meticulously trying to preserve his 'naturalness' is able to present an acceptable front to the world. But 'he knows with a terrible certainty' that, while he is out, 'the same handsome, dark prisoner' in the mirror will remain at home. When the man returns home, he will find his slippers moved and his towels wet. His double, the protagonist of his interior life does not simply disappear when his back is turned (CS, p. 46). 'The Decline of Narcissus' shows a man concentrating on his naked image in the mirror, 'trying / to recapture or to mimic his naturalness'. When he finds that his body alone is not sufficiently natural-looking to give the desired impression, he goes to the absurd length of chewing a lettuce leaf, in the hope that that will do the trick. The implication is that it will not (SP, p. 106). A comparable situation arises in a later poem, 'Known Consequences', where for years a man obsessively undresses whenever he finds himself in front of a mirror, or even a window pane. He does so to 'try out this or that stance in order to choose, to invent / the one most his, the one most natural, so that / his finished statue could be made'. All his carefully studied, 'natural' poses create the effect of a poseur. He has rendered his nudity artificial (ER, p. 105). Even in one's most private and reflexive moments of auto-eroticism, one is perforce an exhibitionist. Moreover, the exhibition of sexual beauty is automatically culpable.

The most explicit portrayals of beauty in Ritsos' poems involve men, usually of the working class. In 'Summer' a youth walks along the beach, followed by a girl who 'devoutly' carries his clothes and by the admiring whispers of both women and men. His skin is, incidentally, 'gold, the colour of clay', as though he were a living sculpture (SP, p. 49). In 'Working-Class Beauty', girls watch as a young man 'with broad, tanned feet, sculptured muscles / on his bare arms' and a powerful back, evident through his shirt, climbs up on to his truck and self-consciously combs his hair (SP, p. 76). In 'Of the Sea', women watch as a 'Dexterous, proud, handsome' fisherman chops up a fish (SP, p. 111). In 'Beauty', a sower stands naked, his underwear and sandals on the table beside him (CS, p. 27). Yet beauty is a mixed blessing, liable to victimise those in whom it is conspicuous, or at least to arouse suspicion about them. The poem 'Red-Handed' (RP, p. 133) begins with the lines:

> Throw the spotlight right on his face;
> hidden like this in the night, let's see him, make him glow;
> he has beautiful teeth – and he knows it[.]

It is as though this beautiful man has been caught red-handed, simply being beautiful and aware of his beauty. Those who trap him in their spotlight do so, as if by erotic impulse, to expose the beauty; and in doing so, both compliment and condemn it.

One of the most characteristic actions of the men in these poems is undressing: to sunbathe, to wash, to swim, to fight, to make love, to face their torturers. And wherever they go they are haunted and reflected by the immortal dead: the naked statues with which the ancient Greece populates the modern. Happy the man who achieves the security of true 'Nakedness' (in a poem of that name): 'Having nothing to hide, he has nothing to expose' (ER, p. 56). But nakedness is a relative condition. Clothing often leaves its traces on Ritsos' most unashamed nudes. As well as reminding us that the human body never exists in a 'wild' or 'natural' condition, void of the social meanings of gender, race and class, but is always fetishised by culture, such marks both emphasise and undermine undress. One teenager looks all the more naked for the pink belt-mark around his waist ('Emergence', SP, p. 72). The sunset traces a ribbon or sash across another man's chest and ties it round his waist, marking him either as the trivially pretty winner of a beauty contest or as the sinisterly masculine wearer, even naked, of military honour and prowess ('Posture', *SP*, p. 74). A young man passes like a ghost through railings which leave their palpable traces – 'broad, gold embroiderings' – like the decorations of a ceremonial uniform on his chest and thighs ('Another Time', *SP*, p. 69).

To be naked is the sign of both freedom and subjugation. Thus, on the one hand, nakedness is the uniform of the escapee – as in 'Horizon', where 'the beautiful deserters are swimming naked' (*ER*, p. 36); in 'Habitual Surprises', where a group of conscripts discard ill-fitting uniforms and climb out of the window, using their belts as a rope (*ER*, p. 96); and in 'The Get-Away', which features 'that handsome, stark-naked fugitive from the insane asylum' (*SB*, p. 153). On the other hand, nakedness is the condition of the humiliated prisoner, vulnerable to the eyes and malice of the uniformed guards around him – as in 'Awaiting His Execution', where a beautiful young man stands naked before the firing squad (*SP*, p. 150); 'Nor This', where a naked deserter, too, goes before the firing squad (*ER*, p. 150); 'Concentration Camp', where prisoners are strip-searched (*SP*, p. 181); and 'How demonstrate . . .', a poem in the Third Series of *Paper Poems*, where a naked man is whipped in front of mocking guards, his genitals shrunken in fear (*ER*, p. 180).

Given the human body's importance to Ritsos, and given his culture's inherited legacy of great sculpture, his most common representation of the artist is as a sculptor, shaping naked human forms in clay and marble. His sculptors almost invariably become the lovers of the bodies they shape, and they shape them with their own bodies as mould (convex to shape a concave opposite sex) or model (to shape a twin or double, the same sex). It follows that making art is an erotic process, and making love an aesthetic. It is not enough simply to make a work of art; one must bring it to life. It is not enough to make a human shape out of stone; one must embrace it, as in 'Experiences', where the speaker makes a statue and then reports: 'I leave my tongue / voluptuously in its marble mouth' (*CS*, p. 61). In 'The Craftsman', a man makes a beautiful statue in clay, perhaps modelled on someone he has seen 'in the café, or in the temple, or among the demonstrators', or it is the figure of 'that swarthy rower'. In any case, he kisses it to breathe life into it, and when he leaves the workshop he is wearing an all too expressive 'guilty smile of secret happiness' (*ER*, p. 101). This is a facial expression we can readily recognise as occurring in the poems of Constantine Cavafy.

In 'Face or Façade?' one man carves another 'with my bare fingers, with my bare eyes,/ with my bare body, with my lips'. Indeed, he identifies so closely with the beloved statue – although he is ugly, it beautiful – that he is no longer certain which of them is which. He walks beside the statue in public, holding it up, trying to persuade observers that it is alive. 'But who believes him?' As this last line implies, the only person taken in by his fiction is the enchanted artist himself (*SP*, p. 113). In 'Cast', a man remembers nothing of a particular summer,

> except for a golden mist and the sensation of warmth from his ring
> and also the bare, broad, sunburnt back of a young farmer
> of whom he had a quick glimpse behind the osiers[.]

And yet that ill-defined atmosphere and the sight of the shirtless farmer stay with him – doubtless, also, coloured by the warmth of the love he feels in the ring on his finger – until long after, when they turn into a productive impulse, a source of artistic inspiration. As the poem's last line says, 'Statues, of course, are made much later' (*SP*, p. 47). It is this lapse of time, perhaps, that makes the artist in Ritsos' poetry so much a figure of valediction and regret. Art is a record of loss, an attempt to stop time when time has already gone by. This may be futile, but it is something that must be done, like breathing itself.

'How can humans live without poetry?' This question, which arises in the poem 'Of the Afternoon', is apparently unironic (*SH*, p. 11). Like sculpture, poetry may be concerned with the past, and it may have a lot of emotion invested in past events which can no longer be undone; but it is all that keeps the past alive. With its help, the past invades the present, conscience to an age that badly needs such haunting. Living statues from ancient Greece and their modern counterparts, young men who could have modelled for them, go hand in hand. Ritsos' project was to reappropriate Greek culture, ancient and modern, from the hands of Fascists and militarists. To him, the heroic spirit of the statuary whose visual language the Fascists found so much to their own taste belonged not to the generals but to the working men and women on whose bodies their splendour, in his view, might have been directly modelled.

By way of a useful contrast at this point, it seems to me that Pier Paolo Pasolini (1922–75) was far less successful than Ritsos at reconciling his communist sympathies and his homosexuality – even if neither faltered until the day of his murder – and at integrating the two to productive effect within his poetry. Pasolini's political commitment was steadfast: it survived not only the murder of his much-loved brother by communist partisans during the war, but also his own eventual expulsion from the Party for being openly and actively homosexual. After his arrest in October 1949 for the corruption of minors and committing obscene acts in a public place, the PCI official Ferdinando Mautino wrote in *L'Unità*, the communist daily paper:

> We take as our cue the events which have brought about a grave disciplinary measure involving the poet Pasolini to denounce once more the deleterious influences of certain ideological and philosophical currents represented by various Gides, Sartres and similarly decadent poets and literary figures, who wish to pose as progressive but in reality are a sum of the most harmful aspects of bourgeois degeneration.[4]

Gide, of course, was all the more decadent for having published not only the pro-homosexual *Corydon* in 1920 but also, worse still, the anti-Stalinist *Retour de l'U.R.S.S.* in 1936.

It is important to keep in mind the fact that Article 154 (later 121) of the Soviet penal code, introduced in 1934, specified a penalty of up to five years' imprisonment with hard labour for sexual acts between consenting adult males, and eight years when force or minors were involved. Soviet writers did not ever perform well on this topic. Maxim Gorky published a virulently anti-homosexual article in both *Pravda* and *Izvestiya* on 23 May 1934, just after Article 154's introduction, in which he associated homosexuality with Nazism and the Western bourgeoisie. He concluded with the fatuous clarion call, 'Destroy homosexuality and fascism will disappear.' Alexander Solzhenitsyn offers no word of support for the homosexual prisoners in his massive, three-volume account of the prison camps, *The Gulag Archipelago* (1973–5). Between Gorky's clamour and Solzhenitsyn's silence lie four decades of unrecorded homosexual history. Gay writers who were victimised by this system include Gennady Trifonov, who was given hard labour from 1976 to 1980 for circulating his gay poems in samizdat form. After his release he was allowed to continue writing only on the condition that he never mention homosexuality. Given the situation in both the Soviet Union and all its subordinate party machines worldwide, it is little wonder that a writer like Pasolini was as deeply despised by the

Kremlin as he was by the equally paranoid Vatican. His expulsion from the PCI was effectively an excommunication.[5]

Like his friend Sandro Penna, with whom he competed in the race to have sex with as many of them as one lifetime could accommodate, Pasolini loved working-class boys. It was they who made the sprawling urban wastes of Rome as attractive to him as tourists find its centre. Their humour, their dialects, their petty criminality and their stringy, overworked and underfed bodies enchanted him. They scented the city's overgrown bombsites with their fragrant piss. And in the same locations they willingly bartered their embraces for a square meal or a pack of cigarettes. In 'Realtà', one of the poems in *Poesia in forma di rosa* (1964), Pasolini's very sense of reality is attributed to contact with gangs of such boys.[6]

In the same poem, he celebrates the abundance of boys and the consequent necessity of promiscuity: 'Thousands of them. It's impossible to love only one of them' ('Sono migliaia. Non posso amarne uno'). Bourgeois boys were altogether lesser creatures, only superficially attractive: it was impossible to love *any* of them. As Enzo Siciliano puts it, 'Pasolini liked to repeat *ad nauseam* that in his eyes the bodies of bourgeois youths evoked nothing but a historical misfortune, a sad destiny: their freshness was illusory. They were all, to his mind, too repressed to admit to themselves the impulses of desire, the raw dreams of eros.'[7] Barth David Schwartz has shown how Pasolini's attitude to proletarian youngsters came to change as a consequence of the swift bourgeoisification of a rebuilt Italy:

> His poetry throughout the fifties and his films up to 1968 were grounded in love of the *borgata*, the slum world no one else wanted to know about. The erotic link he had to the slums was also a utopian vision of the *popolo* and an ideological commitment to the Left. But after 1968 he began to see the young as 'victims' of a consumer culture that turned the willing boys into monstrous hustlers.[8]

(One of them killed him on 1 November 1975.) I suppose he should be accused of hypocrisy, though I am not so sure I want to be the one to do so. He speaks of how capitalism turns the boys he used to consume into mere consumers. What he appears to mean, if one is to be cynical about it, is that as economic conditions in Italy improved during the 1950s and 1960s, his sexual partners demanded more of him – and I do not mean more sex. The sheer foison of male adolescence became commercialised. Mere boys became rent boys.

Chapter 24

Post-War Tragic Fiction

A man's homosexuality amounts to a tragic flaw. What he loves to distraction leads him to destruction. From the moment of his rise, he is fated to fall. The one sexual act which defines him, anal intercourse, inevitably unmans him. Even at its gentlest, it is an act of merciless violence. Ultimately, it will be responsible for his death. Boiled down to its essentials like this, the tragic motif seems ridiculous: it would be laughable if it were not so clearly dangerous. On the other hand, one of the miracles of homosexual representations in the twentieth century has been the production of great (and positive) gay fiction out of such unpromising (and negative) materials.

We have seen that the mythology which represents the invert as an inherently tragic figure materialised in Western culture towards the end of the nineteenth century, and took hold of the imaginations of individual writers like D.H. Lawrence in the early decades of the twentieth. The same mythology is at work in countless novels of the period between the end of the Second World War and gay liberation. By mid-century, the idea of the tragic queer was firmly established in literature, both straight and gay. It can probably be seen at its most forthright, its least compromising, in Jean Genet's *Querelle of Brest* (*Querelle de Brest*, written in 1945–46 but not published until 1953).[1] Genet is not interested in an unassailable, unequivocal masculinity. Indeed, he seems never to have believed that such an aberration could possibly occur. For all his adoration of executioners and murderers, he is mainly concerned with virility, not in a state of complacent repose, but fully engaged in the struggle with its own tendency to undermine itself. In the murderously violent male world he portrays, any victor is a potential victim. In a world where machismo is the ultimate value, even the most aggressively heterosexual hero is liable to be beguiled by the charms of the masculine; the less achieved may seek to prove themselves by default, turning even lesser men into victims by injuring them, or better still into feminised victims by raping them. Anal rape is a conclusive exertion of power, physical and mental; but it must also be symbolic of the fragility of masculinity: for every man has an anus. It is the seat of his manly anxieties. And in some sense these anxieties are never resolved until a man has been fucked.

Genet's siting of a defining streak of femininity at the heart of machismo has become quite a common conceit in gay fiction, although usually to less complex effect. I am reminded of the opening paragraph of Pier Vittorio Tondelli's autobiographical novel about his military service, *Pao Pao* (1982). Tondelli compares the stiffer marching cadets with students of the Bolshoi ('quegli anfibi cosí rigidi e appunto cosí militareschi che dovevano calzare come scarpettine da danzatrici e batterci sopra i ritmi e la grancassa come proprio allievi del Bolscioj'), thereby both mockingly reducing their conceited strutting to the level of the effeminacy they fear and despise and admiringly raising their synchronised movements to the aesthetic heights of classical ballet. That he calls them amphibians (*anfibi*) brings into relief the sexual suggestiveness of the whole comparison: these are men who, for all their posing, are quite capable of moving into a new element.[2]

In *Querelle of Brest*, Querelle's twin roles as murderer and passive queer – the first enacted in partnership with his victim Vic (fated, presumably, even by his very name) and the second with his victimiser Nono – not only overlap, but are actually functions of each other. He kills and is killed in turn. When he first perceives within the integrity of his own physique 'the presence of death throughout his whole body, the presence of a murderer', the feeling dawns on him slowly, 'rather like the mounting of amorous emotion' (p. 73). That this emotion has a basis in anality is suggested when, having just murdered Vic, Querelle slithers down a muddy slope on his backside, thinking up slang expressions for anal intercourse (p. 79). He escapes the scene in the full knowledge that his crime involves his own death as well as Vic's – and yet he willingly chooses this path away from life: the reader is told that 'Querelle must be regarded as a joyous moral suicide' (p. 78).

When he submits to being fucked by Nono, Querelle thinks in terms of performing his own execution: 'This would be capital punishment' (p. 86). They roll dice to decide, according to the dictates of chance, who should fuck whom; but Querelle has every intention of cheating if he does not come out the loser. In the event, he throws a mere two to Nono's five. The imminent loss of his anal virginity scares him, but he treats it virtually as a test of strength. He knows the experience will transform him, perhaps into a monster, perhaps merely into one who gets fucked (*un enculé*). Either way, it seems, his masculine integrity is at stake. And yet, far from feeling unambiguously that he is about to be effeminised, or straightforwardly that, in Leo Bersani's characterisation of the myth, 'To be penetrated is to abdicate power', Querelle feels that he is commanded to bend over to accommodate Nono's invasive prick by 'some imperative authority deep within himself'.[3] Indeed, it is 'his very own strength and vitality commanding him to bend over' (p. 90). Abdication is itself a sign of real power. During a later account of an encounter between Nono and Querelle, the narrator observes: 'It is an intense situation to be held fast by a penis, to retain within one's body, and by the penis, a stalwart who cannot free himself except by discharging inside one's fundament' (p. 267). This paradox of the master being mastered is typical of how Genet tends to represent anal passivity. In effect, he is saying, only real men can do it.

Genet is always questioning received notions of activity and passivity, in relation to execution and murder no less than to sexual intercourse. He is adamant that, in the case of physical violence, the one attacked is complicit in his victimisation, passively enabling the attack or even actively aiding the attacker. Recording a nightmare in his journal, Seblon writes: 'The victim . . . however atrociously he might be suffering, always helped the murderer. He contrived to show him where to strike the next blow. He took an active part in the drama, despite the reproachful look of agonised misery in his eyes' (p. 175). When Querelle murders a homosexual Armenian who picks him up in Beirut, it occurs to him that the face of the strangled man looks like his own face when he is ejaculating. He arranges the dead man's hands so that it looks as though he has died masturbating. While he is doing so the narrator reflects that 'Queers offer a delicate neck to the headsman. One can almost say . . . that the victim becomes his own executioner' (p. 305).

The resulting confusion between anal pleasure and murderous pain lies at the heart of all of Jean Genet's fiction. He cannot conceive of any homosexual act that does not involve

27. The embodiment of heroic
penetrability. (Illustrations attributed to
Jean Cocteau for Jean Genet's
Querelle de Brest)

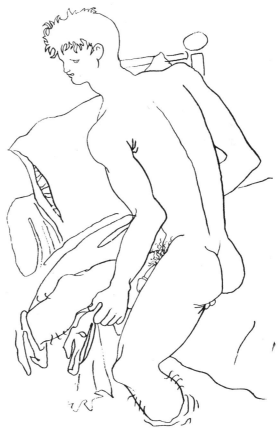

a fundamental struggle between opposed masculinities, or the willing surrender of one to the other. The ultimate end of any such act is always death, whether literal or only symbolic. Seduction is a form of betrayal, and consummation involves no mere *petit mort*, but rather a bloodbath of overblown (if nonetheless repressed) emotionalism, which might have graced the closing moments of some cheap, tragic melodrama. The one thing Genet is not is emotionally subtle.

Towards the end of the *Querelle of Brest*, Lieutenant Seblon picks up a docker and takes him to a dark corner near the city ramparts in order to be fucked by him. However, he makes the mistake of lying down on one of the many turds which litter the place, covering his belly with excrement. Instantly alerted by the stench, the docker makes off into the darkness, leaving Seblon somehow to make his abject way back to his ship without encountering anyone else (pp. 336–7). In connection with this event he subsequently makes the following entry in his journal: 'It is thanks to Jesus that we can extol humility, since He made it a hall-mark of divinity. . . . And humility is born only of humiliation. Otherwise it must be regarded as false vanity' (p. 335). Passages like this achieve a deliberately bogus sublimity which is all the more striking for their author's sang froid. The somewhat arch association of Jesus with the attitude of a disappointed queer with his arse in the air and his belly smeared with shit is a typical manifestation of Genet's insistence on inverting and disrupting moral norms. Whether it does much else with them is open to question.

Moreover, of course, this passage is absolutely reliant on its capacity to shock. In other words, it capitalises on a situation in which the moral norm is left intact. Blasphemy depends on God, after all. Similarly, all of his writing about homosexual activity depends on a situation in which such activity is subject to a powerful taboo. There is no room in Genet for the sanity and balance of liberation. This does not mean, at all, that he is of no use to us as a gay writer. On the contrary, he is one of the most eloquent laureates of the condition of male homosexuality, and men's fears of it, *prior to liberation*. It is precisely the *absence* of liberation that makes the homosexual tragedy plausible.

I think it follows that it would be wrong to suggest that any straight-authored novel which represents the homosexual 'condition' as being, in the proper sense, tragic is automatically an oppressive representation. To take one admittedly exceptional example (and I acknowledge the oxymoron), the tragic model is used to massively impressive effect in William Golding's *Rites of Passage* (1980), a novel which continually and knowingly calls to mind its great predecessor, Melville's *Billy Budd*, while telling the story of the Reverend Robert James Colley, who slowly dies of shame after getting drunk and giving a young sailor (a foretopman, indeed, and likewise called Billy) a blow-job. The narrative of Colley's determined inertia, whereby he condemns himself to the proactive passivity of wasting away without taking sustenance of any kind, is far more plausibly a story of internalised homophobia, or of generalised sexophobia, than one of homosexuality itself as an inherently negative condition.

However, at this point I have chosen to focus on an earlier, but hardly less impressive novel by a straight author, David Storey's exercise in Welfare State Gothic, *Radcliffe* (1963).[4] Storey locates the current of his book's relentless drift towards tragedy in the contrast, and then in the relationship, between two boys, Leonard Radcliffe and Vic Tolson. The former is an intelligent boy whose face has the 'imitative irony of a mask' (p. 7). At school he is treated as a 'natural victim' – indeed, 'the particular victim' of one group of boys (p. 10). He is seen as inviting ill-treatment: his seriousness is supposedly the expression of a 'perverse willingness' to be outraged (p. 11). Storey does not treat this aspect of Leonard's character as simply being visible to nasty little schoolboys. On the contrary, it continues to operate throughout the narrative, determining adults' responses to him and, whether as cause or consequence, his responses to them. Once the boy ceases to suffer from the fits which afflicted him early in life, he develops 'a calm and rather passive nature', somewhat detached from mundane events 'as if he had accepted the intrusion of life and given it reluctant accommodation' (p. 29). Although 'physically docile and acquiescent' for the most part, 'mentally he was quick and alert' (p. 32). This combination of passivity and activity has a crucial bearing on the way his relationship with Vic takes shape.

The novel opens with Leonard's arrival at school, in a scene reminiscent of the openings of both Gustave Flaubert's *Madame Bovary* and Alain-Fournier's *Le Grand Meaulnes*. Although at an opposite extreme from Leonard, Vic is no less of an outsider. This is what brings them together. Vic is first described as 'a large, muscular boy' who, when asked a question in class which he is unable to answer, stands 'facing the teacher as if the question demanded some physical retaliation' with his imposing physique 'set in an instinctively aggressive pose'. The teacher presses him to answer, 'as though disregarding his male pride, or out of some innate desire to take advantage of such an exposed muscular confusion'. Vic looks humiliated, helpless and guilty in turn (p. 9). Needless to say, it is Leonard who is called on to answer the question; and he does so without difficulty. When the two boys' glances meet, Vic's expression is 'one of such incoherent humiliation, half-blinded with reproach' that Leonard blushes, feeling 'peculiarly tortured' (p. 10). This swift exchange of humiliations sets the pattern for what follows.

Vic is far more than just some kind of stupid thug, a lump of brainless brawn. (Indeed, David Storey is renowned for having done without the readiest stereotypes of unintelligent, physical masculinity.) As will become increasingly clear, he has as much mental as physical power. Even as a child he displays 'a kind of cool ferocity which, in its degree of control and direction', is 'as intimidating as his violence itself' (p. 11). He does not have the monopoly on initiatives, however. It is Leonard, not he, who activates a friendship: he asks Vic to come home with him. Vic is troubled by the invitation – 'It was like some loyalty he was being pressed into acknowledging; or a weakness' – but accepts, a little as if he had no alternative (pp. 12–13). As the friendship develops, though, it is the bigger boy, Vic, who reverts to the decisively dominant role. Leonard is a scrupulous and dutiful friend; taking part in the friendship is, to him, 'like a service he willingly and even passionately performed' (p. 36). Vic's attention makes him feel 'unworthily privileged' (p. 37). Although inchoate, their relationship is already physical and vaguely sadomasochistic:

> During that time Leonard was frequently reminded not only of Tolson's remarkable physical strength – often he lay helpless beneath that giant body in some apparently friendly yet vaguely purposeful game – but also of a kind of frustration, a scarcely suppressed antagonism which resulted in sudden and irrational bursts of violence. (p. 36)

It is in negotiations of physical violence that their friendship is both sited and proved. Moreover, despite the fact that it is Vic's which is the violent temperament and the stronger physique, the psychological complications of their tender enmity render it by no means certain that Vic will always emerge the clear victor from a given combative event. One such encounter is narrated in full. On a visit to the Radcliffes' home, a massive and only partly occupied house, Vic knocks Leonard to the floor, kneels astride his chest and forces his mouth open. (To what end? What is he thinking of doing? Although he goes no further, his point is to have shown how far he might have gone. 'I could kill you now if I wanted,' he says; but also apparent is an unvoiced threat of oral rape.) As they are subsequently walking towards Vic's home, Vic suddenly falls to the ground, abasing himself 'Almost as a reconciliatory gesture', and accuses Leonard of tripping him. When Leonard denies this, Vic starts to cry, now sporting a self-inflicted bruise on his forehead. Aggressively and insistently, Vic presses the point until, at last, Leonard agrees that he did, indeed, trip Vic. So, in a sense, the aggressor forces the victim to play the aggressor. Vic bullies Leonard into claiming that bruise as his own doing (pp. 39–41). We are approaching a realm of performative violence, both affectionate and antagonistic, which compares with sadomasochistic role play in which all roles are potentially reversible.

At this point in the narrative Leonard gains a scholarship to grammar school and the two boys are separated. At his new school, again, Leonard is singled out for bullying:

> Now he became the victim of a persecution more subtle and intense than that of mere physical assault, and since he never tried to appease his new tormentors it seemed to them that he secretly invited it. It was as if he recognised within himself the working of a virtually implacable pessimism, for he neither opposed these assaults nor felt the least inclination to deplore his situation. His despair, however acute, never drove him to action, and he began to suspect – and with the slowest yet profoundest shock of his life – that what in fact so hugely dominated his existence, to the extent that he could scarcely recognise it, was an inscrutable sense of guilt. (p. 43)

As at junior school, he is regarded as being different (with regard to his intelligence and his artistic abilities, 'There was an abnormality about his gifts') and also as 'an ideal target for persecution' (p. 44). His very passivity attracts activity: 'No one could tolerate such abject humility' (p. 45). Humility invites humiliation, and there are always plenty of boys and men willing to dole it out to Leonard, throughout his life. His fatalism is itself a goad, encouraging the aggressive instincts of all who encounter him; or all males, at least. We are told of his 'reluctance for action' (p. 46) which, in his community, effectively disqualifies him from manhood, almost even from humanity. Perplexed by his virtually pathological self-effacement, his father says of him 'He seems determined not to exist' (p. 47). This is not true; and nor does the boy live vicariously through other people. But he does appear to require affective and extreme encounters with others to rouse him from what might otherwise become a life of solipsistic inertia. As it turns out, the person best able to offer such encounters in adult life, as once during childhood, is Vic Tolson.

After leaving school, Leonard gets a job with a firm of tent contractors and finds himself unexpectedly working alongside Vic: 'The moment of recognition was like a heat pressing over his nervous body, a fur-like warmth that spread over his back and across his neck. It absorbed his shoulders and his head. His body fell into the warmth and disappeared' (p. 55). By thus imagining the renewal of the two men's friendship as a moment of lycanthropic metamorphosis, Storey both reminds us of Vic's hulking, animal-like virility which exerts such an animating influence over Leonard, and prefigures the descent into instinctive aggression that must follow. Moreover, once he is with Vic, Leonard seems no longer to exist as an individual: he is 'absorbed' and has 'disappeared'. This process gains impetus when, on a particular assignment, the two men share a small tent, with no company but Vic's fetid, equine motorbike. The bike adds to the sense of the bigger man's virile power, 'like an intense part of him, waiting for him, watching for him, another segment of his huge body' (p. 62). As such, it looms over Leonard even more threateningly than Vic himself.

Building up his atmosphere of both menace and pastoral ease, Storey demonstrates that in Leonard's brooding fear and desire there is as much suppressed violence as there appears to be in Vic's physique. At one point, Leonard vents his frustration by attacking a boulder with a sledge-hammer, while gazing at the tent in which Vic is relaxing:

> He lifted the hammer and swung it down on a boulder. He glanced up once more at the tent. He brought the hammer down again, more fiercely. The grey skin split to a yellow-brown core. (p. 63)

This is how he will eventually kill Vic; but at this moment in the narrative it is the prelude to their first love-making. After a frantic bike ride around the field, Leonard clutching on to both Vic and the bike as if they were parts of the same life-enhancing and life-threatening monster, they go back into the tent and undress. Leonard says nothing, for it is the dominant Vic who gives the order – 'Hold me. Hold me!' – which is as much an entreaty as a command (p. 67). Leonard does as he is told – and grants the favour begged for.

There is a lot in what follows that is neither new nor surprising. Much of it, I suppose, is derived from David Storey's readings of D.H. Lawrence. The symbolism is not particularly subtle, but nor is Lawrence's; and one might argue that subtlety would be inappropriate to the book's themes. Certainly, Storey is a much better writer than many who, at roughly the same time, had been drawing a direct line between homosexuality and death; and when he starts to make use of associations of sodomy with excrement one recognises a logic befitting the book's integrity. When the two men's co-worker Shaw accuses Leonard of fucking Vic (an interestingly perceptive comment on how the submissive partner often dominates), he uses a routinely offensive, if oblique, reference to shit: 'What have you been doing the last four days, then? Stuffing it into old Tolson's chocolate box? Rooting it about amongst the raspberry creams?' The topic arises in the first place because Shaw and Leonard, clearing up the site on which they have been working, have arrived at the cesspit. Leonard's response to Shaw's taunts is to drop Shaw's sandwiches one by one into the pit of excrement and to ask 'Are you going to eat them now . . . or later?' A simple retort of 'Eat shit' would have had the same meaning if not quite so elaborate an effect (pp. 101–2). It is not long before Shaw apparently gets his revenge by giving Leonard a shit sandwich (pp. 138–9). Vic later claims, with a 'half-enraptured' expression, that it was not Shaw's shit in the bread, but his own (p. 178). It is on this occasion, too, that he hits Leonard in the face with a sledge-hammer. Humiliation and violence are his most eloquent means of communication.

Leonard's inclination, as the more intellectual of the two, is haltingly to analyse their relationship. Vic is not interested. When Leonard asks, again reversing superficial impressions, 'Are you frightened of me?' Vic replies 'I don't give a sod about you' (p. 125). On a later occasion when Leonard forces one of these analytical conversations on Vic ('Why are you afraid of your feelings? . . . Why must you always destroy them? Why are you always trying to destroy *me*?') Vic gags him with an aggressive kiss (pp. 207–9). In conversation with his father, Leonard points out the fact that Vic is always trying to belittle him, but he adds: 'the worst thing is, half of me wants it' while, on the other hand, 'there's a part of me that won't be reduced'. What Storey seems to be developing here, and throughout the novel, is the idea of the impossibility of balance in a sexual relationship between two men. The meeting of two virilities must become a contest. Harmony requires sexual difference; and, while Leonard and Vic are certainly poles apart, the fact remains that they are men. The whole novel relies on the presence of this 'problem', which can only be resolved in death. Until then, the two men can only express their love in bewildered outbursts of violence. In the same conversation with his father, Leonard says: 'With Vic, it's not something I can let go. Not until it's finished and at an *absolute* end.' He speaks of having a clear choice: 'Either to be loved or to be destroyed' – to which his father adds a third factor: 'Or to be loved *and* destroyed' (pp. 132–3). Whether as a destructive or a defensive impulse, it is just after biting into the sandwich that Leonard steals – and Vic realises he has stolen – a claw hammer.

Neither of the central characters identifies, or considers identifying, as homosexual. The fact remains that any relationship which either of them establishes with a woman must be compromised by the presence, or threatened presence, of the other. While Vic is talking to a young woman on one occasion, he looks not at her but at Leonard, who is looking at him from behind her (p. 144). (This is when Leonard takes the opportunity to steal the hammer, which Vic has been using.) Later, Kathleen manipulates Leonard into making love with her, she being the more active partner. Leonard looks up and sees Vic grinning at him through the window. (One is reminded of Peter Quint at the window, haunting Miles and the governess in *The Turn of the Screw*.) In some sense, each seeks to witness the affirmation of the other's heterosexuality – and his own, therefore – but also to prevent or at least intervene in its consummation. However, the extent to which they are free agents in making such apparent choices is repeatedly brought into doubt by the question of fate.

As in so much classic realist fiction – and *Radcliffe* is firmly in that tradition – each event can be read as foreshadowing some later event, the later one, invariably, being the more crucial or extreme. So often, the carefully plotted nature of such novels gives the impression of characters whose lives are preordained; in *Radcliffe* likewise. Moreover, there are many occasions on which Storey explicitly questions the extent to which his characters are in control of their own destinies. For instance, when the boy Leonard is parted from Vic by his grammar school scholarship, his passivity – or, indeed his fatalism – is explained as follows: 'It was as if he acceded to events in this way because they came from some vague source of authority he knew had to be obeyed' (p. 43). Much later, Kathleen says to him 'There's no accidents in your life' (p. 184). And when Vic appears at the window, he hovers there 'like some imaginary embodiment' before moving away suddenly 'without apparent effort, so that he seemed to be propelled by some impersonal force' (p. 202). Although it looks from early on as if he has plans to kill Vic in the way he does, Leonard claims not to have the capacity for forward planning: he never sees the 'unexpected contingencies' one is meant to be able to anticipate (p. 277). He is unaware of his own meticulous preparations for a specific future event. At the end of the book, when asked why he committed the murder, Leonard replies simply 'Because I had to!' (p. 346). And he protests in court that he should have been tried before God, not men (pp. 347–8).

Uniquely relevant to this whole question of fatedness, as we have seen in other texts, is the story of the Passion of Christ. In *Radcliffe*, too, the conundrum of human divinity is raised, along with that of predetermined free will. Leonard Radcliffe has an intense discussion with the provost about Christ's manhood (which is to say, both his humanity and his virility). Regarding himself as one who has endured his own share of suffering, Leonard questions the extent to which Christ ever felt the true despair of mortality – of being all body: 'Surely He never suffered as a man. As a man *condemned* to this body.' It is clear that sexuality is the issue here, for Leonard continues:

If He could bleed and sweat and be exhausted why couldn't He feel equally the natural desire for a woman or for another man? What is it that a man wants from such love that Christ Himself had no need of? How on earth can we accept Him as an example when He was only half a man Himself? . . . What can He tell us about our lives when He didn't even bother to acquaint Himself with the half of [manhood] that oppresses and confuses us the most? What a wretched and irrelevant thing He must have thought our physical love. He had no need of it. (p. 266)

Oppressed and confused by his own sexuality, Leonard both attacks and empathises with a Christ who, in his view, thought of the human body as a paltry thing. To Leonard, this accounts for the Crucifixion: 'He destroyed his body, showed this contempt for it, hung it up like a bit of canvas. He cast it in the face of men who have to live *within* their bodies, taunting them with salvation' (p. 267). As much confused as pleasured by his physical encounters with Vic and Kathleen, Leonard is nagged by the idea that life might be easier if it were possible to take the option he ascribes to Christ, that of celibacy. At the same time, one can see him approaching a point of self-hatred at which it may seem necessary to destroy his lover (though that is not how Vic is ever described) and, as a consequence, himself. When the provost argues that God has blessed humanity by liberating the soul from the body, Leonard passionately responds by characterising this separation as a curse. Indeed, as he later implies, he sees the body–soul opposition as functioning at the explosive core of his relationship with Vic. In a conversation with Blakeley, he says: 'But just think what if this *separate thing* were in one man, and the body, the acting part in another? What if these two qualities were typified ideally in two separate men? Then, just imagine . . . just imagine the unholy encounter of two such people!' (p. 298). And the unholy encounter he has begun to imagine duly takes place.

The crisis in the relationship between the two men – or rather, the crisis of the relationship, since it has never been in a stable condition – is both verbal and physical; and not surprisingly it takes physical shape as both sex and extreme violence, with sadomasochistic manoeuvres of subjection and dominance connecting the two. Leonard demands explicit notice of the humiliations to which he will be subjected: 'Do you see me lying on the floor, or kneeling down praying to you? . . . I suppose in your imagination you've seen yourself beating me a score of times . . . Is there an even worse, a grotesquer humiliation that you've thought up for me?' (p. 302). But his words are not themselves submissive, of course: they are accusing, taunting, demanding, even imperative. Moreover, given that Leonard is the verbal partner, his forcing of the crisis into verbal expression is itself intended to humiliate his master. Its purpose is to invite or provoke a retributive physical attack. Vic calls his bluff, grabbing his own crotch to identify and prime the weapon he intends to use on Leonard. He forces Leonard to the floor and sits astride his chest. When Leonard refuses to fight – hardly an available choice in his present position – Vic forces his mouth open and thrusts his own erection into it. It is in the following chapter that Vic's victim – his 'frantic sacrifice' – murders him.

When Leonard subsequently suffers another of his epileptic fits, Vic's penis survives in the shape of a scream: 'Leonard lay stiffly in a chair, his head flung back in a curious, distorted foreshortening, his mouth held open as though to accommodate some huge and preposterous shape. From it emerged a hoarse and strangulated wail' (p. 323). But by the time of the trial, Leonard's articulacy is no longer distorted in this way, even if it is still the memory of Vic Tolson's prick that drives him. In a moment of somewhat futile eloquence, he makes a speech of the kind that did nothing to save Oscar Wilde, an irrelevant defence of male love:

You've got to *accept* that there is a love that exists between men which is neither obscene nor degrading, but is as powerful and profound, and as fruitful, as that love which bears children. The love that men have for other men, as *men*, may be beyond some people's powers of comprehension. But it has a subtlety and a flexibility, a power that creates order. Politics, art, religion: these things are the products of men's loving. And by that I mean their hatred, their antagonism, their affection, as *men*, and their curiosity in one another as men. It isn't that women have been deprived of these things, but simply that they can't love *in this way*. They have been given something less abstract, more physical, something more easily understood. Love, art, politics, religion: these are the creation of men as *men*. (p. 346)

This peculiar passage needs to be seen in context for the full extent of its peculiarity to become apparent. In isolation it merely reiterates (in the first sentence) a routine plea for acceptance and (then) an unexceptional argument, based on discrimination between the physical female and the abstract male, which has recently become the stock-in-trade of Camille Paglia but has been a commonplace of male supremacy for centuries. However, in the context of the denouement of David Storey's narrative, the speech is startling. At no point prior to this has Leonard Radcliffe ever been identified as homosexual; nor have his sexual desires ever seemed to be more generally oriented towards other men than just towards a single male individual, Vic Tolson. This speech marks his transformation into a homosexual man in a state of suspension between the Wolfenden Report and the 1967 Sexual Offences Act which partially decriminalised sexual acts between consenting adult males. Although imprisoned for murder, he is nonetheless in prison because of his relationship with another man. While in prison he becomes sexually active and predatory:

> Some while later he was transferred to a mental institution for criminal defectives. His behaviour had become so eccentric that it amounted to the continual and open soliciting of other prisoners and to fits of incoherent moralising whenever he was confined for his behaviour. (p. 348)

As well as being stuck between two dates, he is also in a limbo between definitions, legal and medical. But what makes him most 'eccentric' is that he is neither acceptably heterosexual nor – in the limited way that such a thing was possible at the time – acceptably (which is to say, tolerably) homosexual. For a start, he murders his partner; then, in jail, he openly and promiscuously cruises and solicits other prisoners. (Notice that he apparently does not assault them.) But even at his trial, even in his plea for acceptance, he uses an argument which would have seemed perverse and embarrassing to the kind of discreet and pliable queers whose behaviour the Wolfenden Report had commended. His recommendation of the hatred and antagonism which, he claims, men recognise in each other and put to such profoundly creative uses is a long way from the chintzy aestheticism to be expected of an English pansy. He has a lust for power, if only for the power of a stronger man's physique, which makes him all too visible. Even disregarding the murder, we can see that this is a criminal madness which cannot even be tolerated, let alone accepted.

· · ·

Writing as recently as 1991, on the subject of gay writers' treatment of the family, David Bergman has said:

> If the conclusions of so many gay novels seem inadequate, the reason may be that gay writers have not yet created a myth which is not tragic, which does not follow the received heterosexual conception of gay man's fate. Without some integrating myths that will help bring together the sexual world and the familial world, the gay novel would be forever fractured, divided against itself, without a satisfactory resolution.[5]

As I have already indicated, I am not at all convinced that the gay tragic fate is a 'received heterosexual conception'. On the contrary, it is a major aspect of the way in which homosexual men chose to represent themselves in the late nineteenth and early twentieth centuries, and it continues to be a powerful way of coping with, and representing, oppression. One can think of oneself as being tragic – a tragic hero, indeed – without necessarily ending up as a self-pitying wretch. One can write a novel about such a man without reducing his experience to an account of purposeless sadness and shame (which is how those who begrudge us even the word 'gay' would wish to think of us). On the contrary, it is possible to conceive of a strongly committed literature which makes use of tragedy to argue for, not some bland New Age Arcadia of argument- and dysfunction-free love, but for the maturely rigorous freedom to fuck up one's own life without the interference of envious homophobes. Moreover, no gay literature is ever going to be of the slightest interest to anyone but adolescents in need of an education if it merely portrays sex as a smooth, one-way fast track to ecstasy. No good writer on sex has ever ignored its depths to concentrate solely on its dizzy heights.

One of the most eloquent laureates of homo-erotic control, after Genet, is James Purdy. Ever since the horrendous ending of *Eustace Chisholm and the Works* (1967), in which Captain Stadger disembowels Daniel Haws and then shoots himself, Purdy has continued to explore, at its most extreme, the inbuilt violence within masculinity and its intractable relationship to the ways in which certain kinds of men are capable of loving each other. The other outstanding example of this theme in his work is the narrative which builds up to and beyond the extravagant crucifixion scene in *Narrow Rooms* (1978). It takes a truly banal critic to reduce Purdy's curiously subtle Grand Guignol to an equation of homosexuality with unhappiness. One Henry Chupack claims that Purdy's work is about the 'hellish and frustrating life that homosexuality involves'.[6] This is so crassly reductive as to be barely worth acknowledging. The problem is that it is not an uncommon reaction to complex tragedies concerning homo- or bisexual characters. And some feeble novelists have, indeed, written depressive books about homosexuality on the understanding that it is a depressive condition – any amount of such pulp was published in the 1950s and 1960s – but these writers need to be clearly distinguished and securely quarantined from their betters. This is, perforce, a matter of politicised aesthetics.

Patrick White was another conspicuous 'better'. In White's magnificent novel *Riders in the Chariot* (1961), tragic events derive their impetus from a context of post-Holocaust anti-Semitism, the anti-intellectual and homophobic masculinism of Australian society, and post-colonial racism.[7] It is mainly in the confluence of three men's lives that White's climactic events develop. Mordecai Himmelfarb is a German Jewish intellectual who escaped from a Polish death camp and came to Australia by way of Israel; he now has an unskilled job in a bicycle-lamp factory. An unintelligent but beautifully built youth called Blue, who works in the same factory, is persuaded by his malicious and anti-Semitic 'aunt' (in fact his mother), Mrs Flack, to spy on Himmelfarb at work. The only fellow-worker with whom the Jew forms anything like a friendship is the watchful aborigine Alf Dubbo, secretly a highly talented painter.

Alf is the one whose life story most often and most significantly touches on the subject and the practices of homosexuality. He is brought up by a white clergyman and his sister, Timothy Calderon and Emily Pask. (It is the latter who first teaches him to paint.) When Alf is twelve and Calderon unexpectedly embraces him, the boy immediately visualises 'an old, soft, white worm slowly raising its head, swaying, and lolling, before falling back'. He is neither repelled nor amused by this image of sluggish arousal, but 'fascinated'. However, Calderon breaks the mood by declaring, 'It is wrong to allow our affections to persuade us we are tragic figures', and he pushes the boy away (p. 324). In other words, the thought has occurred to him but he is resisting it. It is important to recall that, prior to this scene, Calderon has discreetly offered Alf a model of virtuous male affection by telling him about John, 'the Beloved Disciple' (p. 320); although this is not made explicit by either the characters or the narrative, the model is, of course, a tragic one, ending in the humiliation, torture and crucifixion of the dominant partner.

When Calderon and Alf do go to bed together, the boy's physical passivity stems from a moment in which the narrative lays bare his *meta*physical passivity: 'At no time in his life was Alf Dubbo able to resist what must happen' (p. 330). He must, as it were, follow his narrative – and the very next preordained step is that he and the clergyman will undress. If Calderon is in control at this moment of daring, he has no influence over what – I am tempted to say, inevitably – happens later: his sister Emily walks into the room. After the first shock of the moment, in which all three protagonists are frozen in silence, she turns not on her brother, whom she instinctively protects, but on the powerless twelve-year-old black boy. She calls him a devil and asks, 'What have you done to my brother?'

Alf has to move on. His new landlady, Hannah, is a prostitute. Her boyfriend Norman, a male nurse, is said to be a 'pufter' (p. 348). And indeed there are nights when Norm holds drag parties in the house, parties which Hannah watches with the 'intelligent interest' which she takes in 'the private life of any perv' (p. 355). It is at one such party that Alf, reluctantly, first shows his paintings to a would-be patron, but refuses to sell them to him. Not long after this occasion, a stranger comes up to Alf in the street and delivers a monologue warning that the Lord will tread under foot those who betray him – including 'the concubines, and sodomites, the black marketeers, and reckless taxi-drivers' (p. 364).

While Patrick White is thus setting Alf Dubbo up in some kind of ambiguous, symbolic relation to a world of 'pufters', 'pervs' and 'queans', he also establishes around Mordecai Himmelfarb both an elaborate pattern of scapegoat images, clearly related to his role as the wandering Jew, and a concomitant association with the novel's themes of tormented homosexuality (by which I mean homosexuality both as a condition of inherent torment and as being likely to become subject to victimisation). There is a scene in Himmelfarb's youth when he laughingly colludes with anti-Semitic mythology in answer to a Christian friend's question about the Passover sacrifice ('we kill the Christian child . . . and cut him up, and drink the blood, and put the slices in a *Brötchen* to send the parents') and the narrator comments, 'Mordecai had learnt how to play'. The two boys then wrestle – but lovingly, as if the antagonism of Christianity and Judaism had been absorbed into a distinctly modern psychosexual complex of yearning and denial, yet a complex informed by the scriptural precedent of Jacob and the Angel:

> They were hitting each other and grunting. Their skins were melting together. They could not wrestle enough on the beds of leaves. Afterwards they lay panting and looked up through the exhausted green to discuss a future still incalculable, except for the sustaining thread of friendship. In the silences they would sigh beneath the weight of their affection for each other. (pp. 104–5)

Not that he is destined to become homosexual; but in a sense, because he is a Jew living in Germany at the worst possible moment in history, he will have his heterosexuality wrested from him. One night, when he is out, the Nazis will come for him but take his wife instead.

As a solitary wanderer, having made his way to Australia and a supposedly new life, he tries to make friends, even to the extent of making 'overtures to many men' and walking the distinctly unfriendly streets at night. Inevitably, he is suspected of being 'some kind of nark or perv' and is cursed and rejected. His problem is, of course, that he is solitary because he has no friends and he has no friends because he is solitary. His foreman at work advises him that 'a man stands a better chance of a fair go if he's got a mate', but by this time Himmelfarb has given up any hope he ever had of integration into white Australian society, and he answers laughingly, 'Anybody is my mate', and then, worse still, 'I shall take Providence as my mate'. His forced equanimity horrifies the foreman, who finds this attitude bafflingly 'educated' and clearly alien (pp. 307–8). The only fellow worker with whom he is able to form anything like a friendship is, of course, Alf Dubbo.

The novel's crisis occurs at the approach of Passover and Easter, when Blue and some of his mates celebrate a lottery win by crucifying Himmelfarb on a tree in the factory yard. As trouble brews, Himmelfarb makes no attempt to escape or defuse it. He says to his boss, 'I have never escaped the consequences by avoiding them' (p. 403), and refuses to leave the premises. '"Nobody but myself," Himmelfarb could have been saying, "will be held to blame for anything that may happen."' Thus shouldering the burden of responsibility for his own fate, he pre-emptively forgives his attackers. When Blue does arrive, he is so drunk he has beer 'running out of his navel' (p. 405), and he is wearing nothing but stained shorts and gumboots. He is described as being 'primarily a torso, an Antinous of the suburbs' (p. 406). Thoughtless, he is not motivated by an idea, but by some kind of inarticulate instinct: 'Reasons which originate in the blood, the belly, or the loins, solicit most persistently. And looking at the Jew, Blue experienced the authentic spasm' (p. 408). What follows as Blue and his mates commence their attack cannot be called a struggle:

> For the Jew did not resist. There was, on one side, the milling of the righteous, even to their own detriment. On the other, the few, who did not flinch, except that he was jostled. His expression remained one almost of contentment. (p. 409)

The juxtaposition of these two personalities, or rather of two personal histories within antagonistic cultural histories, makes the scene predictable, of course; but inevitable. As Blue and his mates haul the Jew up into the tree (Alf Dubbo is watching and visualises it as 'the divine tree'), Blue's body becomes all the more beautiful for its exertions, 'glittering with sweat'. They would use nails if nails were available, but have to make do with a rope.

'Blue was very active.' That is the point. He, his mates and the crowd are goaded by Himmelfarb's passivity, and he is admired by the crowd for translating their collective exasperation into action. In the crowd there is a feeling that could, committed to action, rise to 'heights of tragedy'; but these are low people, content to let Blue's seductive physique act out their petty cruelty. This is a crucifixion scene, but one that Patrick White insists on our seeing as a squalid, small-minded incidence of suburban racism. A woman calls out from the sidelines, 'It is the foreigners that take the homes. It is the Jews. Good old Bluey! Let 'im 'ave it! I'll buy yer one when the job's finished' (p. 410). Hers is the voice of an Australia that Patrick White – who had experienced its racism at second hand, through the experiences of his Greek lover – despised and fought against throughout his career.

Blue is drooling and convulsive in his moment of triumph, his torso 'contorted' too. On the other hand, Himmelfarb appears detached and distant, as if 'removed from them'. So a momentary reversal appears to have taken place: for it is Blue who, insofar as he is capable of moral feeling, is in discomfort: 'the archtormentor himself might have been asking for respite from torments which he had always suffered' (p. 412). After the Jew has been 'raised from the dead' (p. 416), which is to say deposed from the tree, by his crucifiers (who in their own eyes have 'never ceased to be his mates'), Blue goes off into a corner to vomit, his emotional condition suspended somewhere in an ambivalent space 'between longing and revulsion' (p. 417).

Alf Dubbo plays, to some extent, the part of the beloved disciple, John the Evangelist, throughout this sequence of events, visualising them aesthetically as if for some future, painted record. What he sees arouses specifically erotic memories. As Blue crucifies Himmelfarb, Alf Dubbo remembers Calderon ('the old man, the clergyman, searching the boy's body for the lost image of youth') and Hannah and Norm ('Hannah the prostitute curled together with her white capon, Norman Fussell, in their sterile, yet not imperfect, fleshly egg'). This paragraph begins with the sentence, 'And love in its many kinds began to trouble him as he looked' (p. 413). In part, this refers to the compositional relation between the bodies of Himmelfarb and Blue; but it also signals an impulse of guilt at his own painterly (or evangelistic) detachment, both now, as he does not even consider the possibility of intervention, and before, when he held back from association with the other pariah. (He is Peter as well as John.) When the critically injured Jew lies dying in Mrs Godbold's house, having refused the attentions of a doctor, Alf Dubbo peers through the window at the deathbed and feels inspired to paint the Deposition. Early on Good Friday, Mordecai Himmelfarb dies.

Chapter 25

....

The Homosexual in Society

....

The standard version of the 1950s, whether in the United States or Great Britain, gives us a pinched, humourless decade in which the heterosexist institutions of state, all the more powerful for the need to satisfy the requirements of the Cold War, successfully silenced any deviant voices and halted all progress towards sexual liberation, reversing the advances of the war years. To an extent this is a valid representation. But the real story of the 1950s, as well as being about censors, involves many triumphs over, and circumventions of, censorship. Gay writers, among others, ensured that there was an increasing amount of work for the censors to do. Indeed, you might say that, for all their reputation as a time of rigorously enforced conformity ('the tranquillised Fifties', as Robert Lowell called them), the 1950s amounted to a virtual festival of queer self-assertion. The celebrations may have been muted at first, and they were certainly anguished; but who is to say that a frightened whisper cannot be as expressive as a triumphant cheer?

It was in the 1950s rather than the late 1960s that homosexual men truly began to come out – in the sense of emerging into the dominant culture – in sufficient numbers to begin to transform the 'mainstream' itself. The medical model had pathologised the homosexual as an isolated, sick individual with no meaningful social position but only a dysfunctional family history. It was all too easy for literature to follow suit, especially given the fact that it is easier to write novels about individuals than about complex social relations. However, a significant number of writers in the post-war period chose to resist the trend which favoured isolationist representations and, instead, began to explore ways of reintegrating the homosexual character into social fictions.

In the present chapter I am attempting to convey an impression of the variety and strength of homosexual literature in this notorious period. My policy is unsystematic and, perhaps, eccentric. The chapter is centred on two momentous years in Britain and the United States, 1952 and 1953, and on what came out of them. They were productive years, but not uniquely so. We start with a quasi-coincidence of texts, all emerging from much the same subcultural context in the USA. Three remarkable novels by black American writers, two published in 1952, one in 1953, demand that their representations of homosexuality be contrasted. They are Ralph Ellison's *Invisible Man*, Chester Himes' *Cast the First Stone* and, a year later, James Baldwin's *Go Tell It on the Mountain*.[1] Books like these appeared as the first cultural legacy of Alfred Kinsey's monumental study *Sexual Behavior in the Human Male*, first published in 1948; Donald Webster Cory's influential study of *The Homosexual in America* had followed in 1951. Of the three novelists, only Baldwin was gay, and he, of course, would turn out to be one of the most important of post-war gay novelists. Although Himes' novel offers the most detailed account of male–male relationships, its compromised ending offers little scope for further development. Baldwin, on the other hand, is clearly struggling towards a more complete notion of what gay fiction might consist of, beyond (self-) censorship.

In chapter 9 of Ellison's novel, when the narrator, the eponymous but anonymous 'Invisible Man', arrives in New York armed with what he fondly imagines are letters of recommendation from the principal of his college, he calls on one of the addressees of the letters, a Mr Emerson, but is received by Mr Emerson's son, an elegant blond, in a large room richly decorated with works of art. Emerson's son looks at the narrator with 'a strange interest'. He walks with 'a long hip-swinging stride that caused me to frown'. He has been reading Freud's *Totem and Taboo*, which the narrator has never heard of. He appraises the narrator's build while interviewing him. At one point, having momentarily lost his temper, he makes 'an elegant gesture of self-disgust' and explains: 'I had a difficult session with my analyst last evening and the slightest thing is apt to set me off'.

A few moments later, apropos of nothing, he asks the narrator: 'By the way, have you ever been to the Club Calamus?' He explains that this is a Harlem nightclub with 'a truly continental flavour'. (Gay readers, though, will recognise the calamus plant as a distinctly American symbol of homo-erotic desire, straight out of Walt Whitman.) If the narrator is confused by this apparently irrelevant line of talk, he is even more so when Emerson's son tries to establish an inappropriate degree of frankness between them, asking: 'do you believe it possible for us, the two of us, to throw off the mask of custom and manners that insulate man from man, and converse in naked honesty and frankness?' The narrator does not know what he means, and says so. When the young man tries to touch his knee he moves away, and the hand is swiftly withdrawn.

It becomes increasingly clear that Emerson's son, though rich and white, believes he is as heavily endowed with problems as the impoverished, black narrator; or even more so. Completely self-absorbed, he is apparently willing to help, but only on his own terms. He is clearly in conflict with his father – 'I'm afraid my father considers *me* one of the unspeakables' – and seems to come close to tears when he whines, 'You have been freed, don't you understand? I've still my battles'. These last remarks are richly ambiguous, insofar as they can be taken to refer to wider issues than the cases of the two individual young men. On the individual level, Emerson's son – who has read the narrator's dismissive reference letter and shown it to him – is referring to the fact that the narrator has been released from his responsibilities to his college and its principal, and is now free to make his own life, as he chooses, in New York; whereas he, poor little rich boy, is imprisoned in the house and circle of influence of his father. More broadly, however, he appears to be contrasting the emancipation of the slaves – to which the whole narrative keeps strategically referring back – with the continuing oppression of men of his own sort, homosexuals. The comparison is inappropriate to social reality, of course: it wipes out the existence of post-Emancipation racism in the institutions of the Union. But it is entirely appropriate to the speaker's own self-pity.

In a final, desperate flurry of offers, Emerson's son invites the narrator to a party at the Calamus Club. When the narrator interrupts him to turn down the invitation, he instantly changes tack and offers the narrator a job as his valet. The narrator repeats his firm refusal – which is meant, of course, to turn down the sexual proposition implicit in the two offers – and takes his leave. This is all we see, and the last we hear, of the son of Mr Emerson.[2]

Chester Himes (b. 1909) had done time in the Ohio State Penitentiary (1929–36) for armed robbery. The biographical facts lend his prison novel *Cast the First Stone* an authority which is, in effect, pretty much superfluous to the already evident authenticity of its substance. One reference book calls it 'a naturalistic novel about blacks and whites in prison'.[3] This is accurate, but hardly definitive. In fact, the novel is far more centrally concerned with sexuality than with race – and must have seemed all the more so when it was first published. The New Testament reference (John 8: 7) in the title is a commonplace plea for tolerance, and it can be taken as referring not only to the circumstantial homosexuality of its narrator Jim Monroe, but also to the homosexuality proper of Dido, his prison boyfriend.[4]

When Jim is jailed for twenty years for robbery, he is puzzled and disturbed, though not particularly antagonised, by the evidence of circumstantial homosexuality he encounters in all areas of prison life. Being young and pretty himself, he is immediately apprised of the fact that he will have to face up to being desired by men. Later, he will have to acknowledge his own desires for other men. Even very early in this process, he has shown he is susceptible to men's attractions as a substitute for women's. Soon after his arrival in the prison, he and his new friend Mal have a long conversation about their sexual experiences with women:

> We kept talking about it until every time we'd accidentally touch each other we'd feel a shock. I was startled at the femininity a man's face could assume when you're looking at it warmly and passionately, and off to yourselves in prison where there are all men and there is no comparison. (p. 41)

After a long spell in a punishment cell he meets up with Mal again. Mal comments on the fact that Jim has developed a close relationship with a man called Chump. Jim acknowledges this, but denies that their relationship is sexual. However, he has not ruled sex out. He says:

> He's been after me to, but I haven't got to the place where I can do that yet. But give me time. It's so common around this joint it sounds almost natural. It doesn't even shock me any more to find out someone I like is like that. (p. 97)

The phrase 'give me time' apparently constitutes complete acceptance of the likelihood that he is eventually going to have sex with another man: for the one thing they all have, in abundance, is time. Within days, he and a new young convict, Bobby Guy, are on the verge of making love when they are interrupted. Jim is relieved when Bobby is transferred to the hospital block, out of reach.

Some months later, a new man, Duke Dido, arrives. At first he is aggressively stand-offish; but it is not long before he and Jim become passionately interested in each other. The rest of the book tells their love story. They spend a sweet Christmas together, absorbed in each other and ignoring the other cons. They have a break-up, full of suppressed violence, but are soon back together again. Dido has an uncomplicated attitude to queerness: 'It's the feeling that it's wrong that makes it queer.' He has made love with women, but they never satisfied him: 'I needed to swoon. I couldn't surrender; I needed to be conquered' (p. 255). It disturbs Jim to hear that he has worked as a female impersonator: 'But he was in my blood by then. I wanted to erase his past and have him start from scratch with me. I didn't want to admit that he had ever existed before he met me' (p. 259). As his love for Dido develops, Jim rationalises it in ways that his heterosexuality will be able to sustain:

Poor little kid, I thought, too bad he wasn't a woman. He had a woman's fascinating temperament, with a man's anatomy. . . . He was so unstable and theatrical that everything he did seemed posed. But in that place of abnormality of body and mind there was something about his love for me that seemed to transcend degeneracy and even attained, perhaps, a touch of sacredness. Because whatever else he might have felt, he never felt that his love for me was wrong. (p. 262)

But by now it has become clear that, despite being so receptive, in the earlier stages of the novel, to the likelihood that he will end up having sex with men, and despite the fact that he loves Dido more than he has loved any of his earlier prison friends, Jim actually appears to use his sense of superiority to Dido as an instrument for reinforcing his heterosexuality.

What started as an extremely positive novel, in its representations of a range of sexual possibilities in an all-male environment, now closes in; and *Cast the First Stone* ends as so many other homosexual novels of the 1950s had to, with the death of the queer. Jim refuses to make love with Dido. Dido threatens suicide. The other cons complain about them and they are both charged with 'sexual perversion' and sent, separately, to the punishment cells. Jim's case is eventually reinvestigated, but Dido's is not. When Jim is transferred to the prison farm, a half-way house on the road to freedom, Dido kills himself. Jim's reaction is self-centred and complacent:

I knew, beyond all doubt, that he had done it for me. He had done it to give me a perfect ending. It was so much like him to do this one irrevocable thing to let me know for always that I was the only one. Along with the terrible hurt I could not help but feel a great gladness and exaltation. I knew that he would have wanted me to. (p. 302)

As a sop to the self-regard of the heterosexual reader, this may indeed be the 'perfect ending'. But its perfection is manifestly imperfect. Artistically, it is lazy and disappointing. It is far too offhand for such an impressive book. Outside the novels of Jean Genet – whose *Miracle de la rose* was first published in 1951 – it gives the most serious fictional account of prison homosexuality since Balzac.

James Baldwin's *Go Tell It on the Mountain*, like so many gay novels before and since, is an account of a profoundly troubled adolescence.[5] When he is fourteen, John Grimes comes under the influence of a new Sunday School teacher, seventeen-year-old Elisha, the nephew of the pastor. Elisha is saved, and already a preacher. John's reaction is more or less instantaneous: 'John stared at Elisha all during the lesson, admiring the timbre of Elisha's voice, much deeper and manlier than his own, admiring the leanness, and grace, and strength, and darkness of Elisha in his Sunday suit, wondering if he would ever be as holy as Elisha was holy' (pp. 13–14). At roughly the same time, John begins to masturbate – or rather, to 'sin' – to an accompaniment of homo-erotic fantasies: 'In the school lavatory, alone, thinking of the boys, older, bigger, braver, who made bets with each other as to whose urine could arch higher, he had watched in himself a transformation of which he would never dare to speak' (p. 20). This transformation is not only the development of his sexual self at puberty, but also the growing realisation (unexpressed but implicit) that a significant aspect of his burgeoning sexuality is that which is centred on the bodies of older boys, with Elisha's pre-eminent among them. Already guilty about the sexual transgressions forced on him by his body, he is then all the more guilt-ridden when he interprets the fantasies that accompany these moments of transgression. Not only is he becoming an adult sinner, but his sin is that of the sodomite.

In the closing paragraphs of Part One of the novel, John speculates on what Elisha thinks about and does in bed: 'What were the thoughts of Elisha when night came, and he was alone where no eye could see, and no tongue bear witness, save only the trumpet-like tongue of God? Were his thoughts, his bed, his body foul? What were his dreams?' (p. 69). There is a certain degree of hope involved here, that the preacher's bed and body are indeed foul – maybe even foul enough, in an ideal world, to warrant sharing. We have no choice but to infer, here, that when he goes to bed John's own thoughts and body are 'foul' with his fantasies about Elisha.

It is not until close to the end of the novel that John's relationship with Elisha re-emerges as a significant theme, although it is clear that Elisha has remained a significant presence in John's thoughts throughout the narrative. When John is 'saved' he is still trying to negotiate a space in which to live as a (possibly homosexual) man, somewhere between his resentment of his father and his desire for Elisha. It is the latter's voice that guides him part of the way through his confusion; it is his promise of prayers for his 'little brother' that helps to quieten John's anguish, perhaps only temporarily; and it is his kiss that resolves and closes the novel. However, we cannot suppose that Elisha's kiss resolves anything in John but the yearning of the moment. In the sight not only of Elisha's own father but also, of course, of the Lord, Elisha kisses John 'on the forehead, a holy kiss'. The sun has risen over the streets, and as the older boy walks away its light 'fell over Elisha like a golden robe, and struck John's forehead, where Elisha had kissed him, like a seal ineffaceable forever' (p. 254). This is ambiguous. John is either – or both – sealed into his vocation or confirmed in his homosexuality by the kiss. In terms of the former purpose, Elisha's kiss is indeed a permanent, virtually sacramental sign; but in terms of the latter, the kiss is merely an irreversible first step towards complete sexual union with another man or other men, and is no less 'holy' for that. Whether the two types of kiss are compatible is left open.

Baldwin started writing this novel long before it was ever published. In a very real sense, what makes it a suitably representative novel of the early 1950s – instead of the mid-1940s, when it was conceived – is that it bears the scars of a rigorous 'self'-censorship imposed by publishers' rejections. According to the poet Harold Norse, who read the early manuscripts, it was once far more explicitly and centrally concerned with a homosexual relationship. Baldwin had said to Norse, in a moment of despondency, 'Who wants a novel about a black boy anyway, much less a queer one?' And so it proved: 'No publisher would touch it. They flatly rejected it or suggested massive cuts, primarily of the homosexual content.'[6] In the end, they got the cuts they asked for, and the cold, well-ordered book they deserved. In *Giovanni's Room* (1956) he would deal with homosexuality head-on; but not until *Another Country* (1962) would he feel able to combine his central concerns of sexuality and 'race'. The result was a magnificent social novel which has been underrated ever since.[7]

Giovanni's Room is a sophisticated study of what would later come to be known as 'internalised homophobia'. Gay readers who think it is negative about homosexuality itself are wrong – they are making the elementary mistake of confusing author and narrator. Correspondingly, anti-gay readers who see it as an accurate representation of the inevitably destructive nature of homosexuality are also wrong – they are too close to the narrator to notice James Baldwin's distance from him. David, the narrator, is a narrow and complacent hypocrite. His narrative makes for uncomfortable reading. Giovanni, his lover, is not in denial – or not so far in – and therefore seems, at times, more sympathetic. But he is not much better than David: he is, after all, a murderer. Although both have made love with women, both are misogynistic; and both are likewise effeminophobic. This latter characteristic must have its effect on their sexual acts. It must affect how they think of passivity. But *Giovanni's Room* is one of many gay novels of the pre-Stonewall period which are marred by their imposed discretion about sexual acts. Too much of David and Giovanni's relationship is left to the reader's imagination. The extent to which David deflects his self-hatred on to Giovanni is revealed in various moments of frankness – such as: 'His touch could never fail to make me feel desire; yet his hot, sweet breath also made me want to vomit'[8] – but it is never clear quite how they touch each other. Certainly, it is difficult to imagine David putting up with being fucked.

In crude terms, this novel has both an unhappy ending (the execution of Giovanni) and a happy one (the fact that Hella refuses to marry David). David is left on his own, but at least neither he nor Hella is trapped in what would have been a wholly inappropriate marriage. There is a certain optimism apparent in this inconclusiveness. Insofar as David could conceivably come round to accepting himself as being homosexual – as actually belonging to a space which is known here as 'Giovanni's room' – Baldwin offers him some hope of redemption. If, on the other hand, he goes on denying himself, he is likely to destroy his own life, if not also that of any woman he attempts to marry. It is in this manner that *Giovanni's Room* takes an early place in a long sequence of wonderful novels about homosexual self-hatred, often generated by religious guilt, from Julien Green's *Moira* (1950) to Randall Kenan's *A Visitation of Spirits* (1989).

· · ·

In both Britain and the United States, the press, when they mentioned it at all, had a particular angle on deviance: they were increasingly willing to speak of homosexuality as being of news value, but only in the most negative, virtually apocalyptic terms. It was a scandalous perversion endowed with the degenerative capacity to destroy imperial cultures. The British *Sunday Pictorial* carried a major article by Douglas Warth on 25 May 1952. Entitled 'Evil Men', it began:

> The natural British tendency to pass over anything unpleasant in scornful silence is providing cover for an unnatural sex vice which is getting a dangerous grip on this country.
> I have watched it growing – as it grew in Germany before the war, producing the horrors of Hitlerite corruption, and as it grew in classical Greece to the point where civilisation was destroyed.[9]

In the course of the next few years male homosexuality would become solidly established among the moralising mythologies of the print media on both sides of the Atlantic. The Greek and Roman empires had fallen as a consequence of their indulgence in homosexual perversion; so had the Third Reich; and the same could happen to the imperial powers of the NATO alliance if its constituent nations allowed homosexuality to prosper.

One of the jobs of the serious writer – beyond mere aesthetics – appeared to be to give the more complex, less crudely emotive, picture of how the world works. Although the reputation of the British novelist Angus Wilson was built on his perceived willingness and ability to contribute to the Leavisite 'Great Tradition' of the English novel, as evidenced in his clear debt to and development of the nineteenth-century realist tradition, certain sociological aspects of his novels suggest that he also had, in relation to the theme of homosexuality, loosely didactic, even political, aims. It is certainly true that his first novel, *Hemlock and After* (1952), teaches the reader something new about the nature of England, in particular as regards the relation between homosexual men and the society they have to live in. Alan Sinfield goes so far as to say that this book 'launches us into the postwar world, struggling to be born'.[10] In 1953 W.H. Auden remarked on the fact that American reviewers of the novel 'were horrified, not at the subject, but at his portrayal of queers as no more unhappy than anyone else'.[11] For all Wilson's liberal humanist subscription to the idea of the novel as a testing ground for broadly defined moral issues, in *Hemlock and After* he is nonetheless concerned to make a series of didactic points, not only about the social conditions homosexual men endure, but also about how these might be changed for the better. To that extent, at least, this book and some of his others contribute to a long-running debate on sexual politics.

Wilson was also keenly aware of a tradition of representations of homosexuality – a tradition no less 'Great' than Leavis's – to which his own books were contributing. In later years he would lecture on homosexual literature. For instance, on 17 December 1974 he spoke to the law-reform group the Albany Trust on 'Literature and Sexual Freedom'. In Margaret Drabble's account of the event, his coverage of the literature of homosexuality included

> gay frolics in the *Satyricon*, Christian rejection, Chaucerian contempt, Smollett's view of it as a dirty joke, Balzac's macho criminal-hero Vautrin, the mawkish schoolboy dreams of Hugh Walpole and Forrest Reid, the Proustian and Wildean obsession with the working classes, Carpenter's manly clasp of the hand, Gide's sad blind alley in Algiers, John Rechy's City-of-Night obsession with he-men and leathers and his 'disgusting adaptation of shameful anti-woman hatred.[12]

Somewhere between Gide and Rechy we should place Wilson himself.

Hemlock and After illustrates one of Alfred Kinsey's major observations, that human sexual orientations are not straightforwardly classifiable on either side of a binary divide, unambiguously homo- or heterosexual, but that they feature as points on a 'spectrum' or 'continuum' of multiple possibilities *between* exclusive homosexuality at one end and exclusive heterosexuality at the other.[13] So Wilson's 'gay characters' tend not to be exclusively homosexual, or not continuously so. Bernard Sands comes to homosexuality relatively late in life, and Terence Lambert describes himself as being 'not completely one-tracked' (p. 237).

Secondly, like most other homosexual novelists of the post-war period, Wilson is at pains to demonstrate that not all homosexual men conform to the camp, effeminate stereotype – although, unlike some writers, he is sophisticated enough to affirm that *many do*, and that they are no less deserving of rights than their less visible peers. Stephen Adams once made the useful point about Angus Wilson that, 'In common with writers such as Gore Vidal and James Purdy, he contradicts the notion that camp involves a purely aesthetic view of the world, one which is incompatible with moral analysis.'[14] Wilson shows that homosexual men constitute a range of types, and come from all social classes. As such, indeed, they are a perfect subject group for the attention of traditionalist English fiction, with its heavy concentration on character and class. In *Hemlock and After*, the clearest expression of this interest in homosexual variety occurs in a scene (pp. 102–3) when two incompatible groups of queens attend the same social event and gravitate to opposite ends of the room – 'respectability' at one end and '*loucherie*' (note the impression of un-Englishness) at the other. Bernard Sands' unwaveringly liberal sympathies make him attempt to intervene in the awkward 'borderland' between the two groups and reconcile them. Needless to say, in the situation that existed before law reform – as, to some extent, ever since – it was never going to be easy to get invisible homosexuals to identify readily with the more visible, and therefore more vulnerable and dangerous, type.

Thirdly, although Wilson consistently shows that individuals are fearful of being singled out for blackmail or arrest, he demonstrates that there is, in fact, such a thing as a homosexual *community* from which the individual may derive strength and support. (Contrast this with the apparently total isolation of a young man like Geof in Shelagh Delaney's 1958 play *A Taste of Honey*.) What I find especially moving about the ways in which Wilson makes this point is his insistence that this community's main strength comes from the solidarity of camp men. Indeed, in this novel unlike so many others from the same period, campness is a sign of strength, mutuality, exclusivity, self-identification as homosexual, and co-identification with other homosexuals. It should be of some interest that this community is referred to, simply, as 'the gay scene' (p. 56).

If a narrative can be said to hold an opinion – and I see no reason why not – this book takes it for granted that law reform is long overdue. In all its representations, positive and negative, of homosexual men, it shows that even if there are negative aspects to homosexual men as they exist and behave in England at the time of the book's writing, most of these are caused by outlaw status, which serves no useful social purpose at all. Even rural conservative, heterosexual characters are enlisted to state that 'the courts are choc-a-bloc with these cases [of homosexual offences] every day, wasting the time of the police. If it wasn't for this damned Nonconformist government [Clement Attlee's Labour administration of 1945 to 1951] the law would have been changed long ago' (p. 18). Bernard Sands' daughter says, 'I quite like queers if it comes to that, so long as they're not on the make', and adds, 'I'd abolish all those ridiculous laws any day' (p. 57). Distaste and discomfort on the part of heterosexual people are shown to be insufficient reasons for the continuation of the unlawful status of consenting relationships between adult men.

Although I have presented this novel as having, to a limited extent, a political programme, I would not wish to exaggerate either its radicalism or its effectiveness. Certainly Wilson's decision to include among its characters Hubert, a child molester who is unequivocally heterosexual, is quite combative. Moreover, one should acknowledge the bravery of publishing such a first novel at all – even dedicating it to his lover Tony Garrett, albeit somewhat stiltedly: 'TO ANTHONY / *most gratefully*' – when contrasted with E.M. Forster's continued inability to bring himself to do anything public with *Maurice*. The fact remains, though, that Wilson's artistic interests take precedence over any political point he wishes to make. Essentially, *Hemlock and After* is an aesthetic performance. Who can tell if it was at all effective in changing people's minds about the 'problem', as it tended to be called, of homosexuality? All we can say for certain is that, although Wilson clearly sees law reform as a matter of some urgency, the law remained unreformed for a further fifteen years after the book's publication. Of course, we can hardly blame Angus Wilson for that.

Wilson's third novel, *The Middle Age of Mrs Eliot* (1958), contains one of the period's most affirmative representations of the stable possibilities of homosexual coupledom.[15] Its portrayal of Meg Eliot's brother David and his lover Gordon is perfectly suited to the requirements of the post-Wolfenden assessment of whether homosexual lifestyles could ever be compatible with heterosexist versions of respectability. Margaret Drabble comments on the novel's relation to Wilson's involvement in the campaign for law reform: 'Angus's fiction made its own contribution: David and Gordon could be seen as excellent prototypes of Good Caring Homosexuals – music-loving, garden-loving, law-abiding decent citizens, unlike the gilded riff-raff of *Hemlock* and the dangerous underworld of *Anglo-Saxon Attitudes*.'[16] But what Drabble does not mention – and it is a detail that makes this couple all the more palatable to those who are only tolerant with effort – is that David and Gordon's relationship is platonic. Wolfenden would have been proud of them, perhaps, but David eventually knows better. After Gordon's death he reflects that Gordon 'had deprived himself, deprived them both, of what could have been a transforming friendship and had twisted it by his obsessive guilt into a copy-book lesson of moral maxims' (p. 285). The author distances himself from this moralised but immoral travesty of a loving relationship.

As ever, Wilson shows his fascination with heterosexual characters' responses to their homosexual counterparts. Some are scrupulously liberal, if awkwardly so. For instance, Meg herself, when David phones her, is a little disconcerted when he mentions Gordon before she manages to do so (p. 60). Others, like Meg's old friend Jill, have become conscious of increasing public discussion of homosexuality and, even if they are uncomfortable about it, feel under some pressure to demonstrate their tolerance. But they do so under slight protest. When Meg tells her that David has 'never had any feelings for women', Jill replies, 'Oh! I see. Well, I suppose that's something we have to accept too. The papers are always telling us so nowadays. I can't see it matters very much anyway now that the whole world's gone to pot' (p. 245).

Wilson's later homosexual characters like Ray Calvert in *Late Call* (1964) and Marcus Matthews in the family saga *No Laughing Matter* (1967) are examined within the context of their own families, which are in turn examined in the wider social context. The distance thus created between the homosexual individual and the social circumstance has the effect of leaving him without significant peers – or rather, since neither Ray nor Marcus is a solitary creature, without homosexual friends or lovers who are examined in anything like the detail which Wilson reserves for family members. However, at the end of *Late Call*, Wilson is insistent that, whereas even the most liberal of families in the newest of the post-war New Towns (like the Calverts in Carshall) may unwittingly stifle and isolate their gay sons (like Ray), such a son may decide to move to a city (London, in this case) and become, instead of a homosexual oddity adrift in a sea of heterosexual normality, an active participant in *homosexual society*. Ray's overbearingly liberal father, Harold, only finds out about his son's gayness after the boy has left home. Harold misses the point of his own paternal failure when he says, 'If a community like Carshall can't help a decent chap like Ray to make a more normal life for himself, then we've failed. We want him back and we want him with the family. I'll have no narrow-minded censoriousness in this house.'[17] Harold's reaction to Ray's gayness becomes increasingly hostile over the next few pages; and Wilson allows the fact that Ray sends his family a postcard from Milan (where he is attending a textile exhibition, for he has gone into the fashion trade) to represent the scale of his liberation from Carshall.[18] He has moved, if not quite to Italy, into a new subculture.

· · ·

1952 was the year of Terence Rattigan's play *The Deep Blue Sea*, which started out as the story of a gay relationship (Rattigan's own affair with Kenneth Morgan) but ended up dealing with a Battle of Britain hero's affair with a judge's wife.[19] 'Self'-censorship again. Similarly, Major Pollock in Rattigan's 1954 play *Separate Tables* was originally conceived of as being accused of a homosexual crime. This was the playwright's response to his friend John Gielgud's conviction for cruising in a public toilet in 1952; instead, in the final version of the play, Pollock has a record of molesting women in the darkness of cinemas.

1953 was the year of Robert Anderson's *Tea and Sympathy*, successful on Broadway but banned by the British Lord Chamberlain. Censorship again. The history of gay drama in the twentieth century is, far more obviously than the equivalent histories of fiction and poetry, a story of negotiations with censors. And not only explicitly homosexual plays were cut or banned. *Tea and Sympathy* is about a student who cannot live up to the standards of machismo required of him by his college. He has all the hallmarks of the sissy – except, as we eventually discover when the housemaster's wife offers him considerably more than the tea and sympathy she has already provided, homosexuality itself. This is a play about homosexuality from which homosexuality is absent. But its implicit presence as a mere topic – unvoiced yet demanding to be discussed, perhaps after the curtain has fallen – is enough to have made the play potentially scandalous.[20]

Between Mordaunt Shairp's *The Green Bay Tree* (1933) and Mart Crowley's *The Boys in the Band* (1968), drama in English more or less consistently portrays homosexuality as illness, or at least as the prime cause of acute mental frailty. In the best of the plays in question, however, the depressive certainty of illness is somewhat mitigated by passion. I am referring to the neurasthenic tragedies of Tennessee Williams, in which the appreciation of male beauty manifests itself, in both women and men, as a worrying symptom. John Clum reminds us that of the four major post-war American playwrights – Arthur Miller, Tennessee Williams, William Inge and Edward Albee – only the first was heterosexual; and that the plays of Williams and Inge are full of iconic youths to whose bodies other characters cannot resist being attracted.[21] (In a good production, nor can the audience.)

In his 1953 play *Camino Real* (block 3) Tennessee Williams resurrects Proust's Baron de Charlus as 'an elderly foppish sybarite' cruising 'a wild-looking young man of startling beauty called Lobo'. Charlus forewarns the proprietor of a seedy flophouse that he may be needing a room for two:

> You know the requirements. An iron bed with no mattress and a considerable length of stout knotted rope. No! Chains this evening, metal chains. I've been very bad. I have a lot to atone for.

This crude reprise of the flagellation scene in Jupien's brothel, in *Le Temps retrouvé*, is virtually all Williams allows Charlus by way of self-definition. Whether a 1953 audience was meant to find this passage horrifying, thrilling, or just plain funny is not clear; perhaps all three. (Such indeterminacy is, in any case, characteristic of the whole play.) Charlus gives a more literal account of himself a short while later. Responding to Kilroy's mistaken identification of him as 'A normal American. In a clean white suit', he replies: 'My suit is pale yellow. My nationality is French, and my normality has been often subject to question'. Presumably, this line *should* be played for laughs. Charlus complains about the standard gay bar in town: 'They stand three-deep at the bar and look at themselves in the mirror and what they see is depressing. One sailor comes in – they faint!' He himself prefers an establishment with the evocative name 'the Bucket of Blood'. Clearly turned on by the Grand Guignol of sadomasochism, Charlus is led with a sense of theatrical inevitability towards the climax of his brief appearance in the play: he disappears down a dark alley, where he is apparently beaten to death. Not that Williams presents this as a deplorable queer-bashing. On the contrary, it is treated lightly, with a sense of the inevitability I have already mentioned, as if it were something that semi-comical figures like Charlus called down, half willingly, on themselves.

When Williams comes to treat the topic of homosexuality in more considered detail, the comedy evaporates and we are left with the (literal) bare bones of a tragic victim. The preposterous play *Suddenly Last Summer* (1958) is an appropriate monument to its times, when, in some mental dictionaries, secrecy and shame were virtually definitive concomitants of the very concept of homosexuality. Another play about homosexuality with no homosexual character on stage, like *Tea and Sympathy*, it is an exercise in voyeuristic cod-Freudianism and overblown emotion. It teeters thrillingly on the line between aesthetic disaster and camp. The spectre at this unwholesomely rich feast is the late Sebastian Venable, a rich mother's boy who reached middle age, his early forties, without having achieved anything more than writing one poem a year since he was in his teens. (We have only his mother's word for the suggestion that these poems are any good.) Or rather, his achievements were secret, personal ones, managed within the mercenary embraces of poverty-stricken rent boys. The play builds up to an account, in front of his bereft mother, of how a group of boys killed him and then 'devoured' various unspecified parts of his anatomy. (The speaker is Catherine, the cousin whom Sebastian made use of to attract the boys he wanted to have sex with.) The boys' literal consumption of his meat operates, paradoxically, as the symbolic response to his metaphorical consumption of theirs.

Mrs Venable, the mother, wants to have Catherine, the bearer of these unthinkable tidings, lobotomised in order to censor her memory of any trace of Sebastian's very public, sexual death. John Clum has observed that 'the conflicting stories of his mother and cousin present the public and private selves', and goes on to ask 'whether his mother's fierce protection of Sebastian's closet, or Catherine's truthful narrative, does more violence to Sebastian's memory'.[22] So two women fight over the sexuality of the man who had no sexual interest in women – other than through the Oedipal yearnings which kept him so close to his mother for so long – even as the boys he had been excessively interested in picked over his corpse. Other than in the two women's memories – for the boys are not important enough to be represented as individuals with minds – hardly anything remains of him but his poetry. It is not gay literature, but the kind of work a closeted homosexual is able to present to his self-deluding mother: an elaborately crafted suppression of desire.

Williams never shows any sign of believing that a homosexual man could be happy, other than in fits of momentary pleasure for which the inevitable come-uppance would be swift and brutal. Sebastian Venable does have a sex life – at the time of his death he had had a surfeit of dark, Latin boys and he was dreaming of a trip to the north in search of pallid blonds – but he was unable to reconcile his puerile subjection to his mother with his adult thirst for other boys. For Williams, sexuality is destiny; and the destiny of the homosexual is tragic. There are no happy endings for these kinds of men. Their fate is inscribed with either violent death or the madhouse.

Playwrights like Williams and Joe Orton were operating within a universe created by Freud. While I agree that he takes many steps beyond Williams' guilt-ridden and self-hating position, towards the sexual carnivalesque one retrospectively associates with gay liberation, I do not believe that Joe Orton is the radical subversive that some gay critics like to imagine him.[23] This must surely be clear to anyone who has seen a provincial, straight, bourgeois audience splitting their sides at one of his plays as though it were a farce, blithely unaware or unconcerned that it is supposed to be a *parody* of a farce. Gay spectators may well find that their own laughter is out of sync with that of the rest of the auditorium – but perhaps, therefore, out of sync with the play itself. Orton was, after all, a commercial playwright. He wrote for the West End, not for a gay audience or for the fringe. What Alan Sinfield has said of Noël Coward seems true, also, of Orton: 'the breadth of Coward's audiences, of itself problematizes any claim that the plays fundamentally disconcerted. People generally are titillated, up to a point, by ideas and attitudes that they find improper; beyond that point, they repudiate them. So it is very difficult actually to catch and influence actual readers and audiences.'[24]

Moreover, it is difficult to imagine Orton's being, had he lived, at ease with the gay liberation movement; and he would almost certainly have reacted against the seriousness of the new wave of feminism – particularly in its disapproval of jokes about mothers-in-law, illegitimacy, rape and so forth – in the 1970s. A new kind of theatre was needed to meet the requirements of a new kind of gay man; and it was always clear that this new drama would not be producible in the established spaces. There would be no dress circle, no velvet plush, hardly ever any curtain, in the Manhattan cafés where Robert Patrick and Lanford Wilson's plays were first staged in the mid-1960s,[25] or in the British municipal halls and students' unions where Gay Sweatshop would tour work by men like Noël Greig and Martin Sherman (Robert Patrick, too) in the mid-1970s. More importantly, there would be no more deference to the Freudian fathers.

. . .

There must have been many times in the 1950s when, to the homosexual writer, merely to write at all was to break an embargo on speaking the unspeakable. The press were particularly likely to remain silent when the usually reliable scandalousness of perversion appeared to have been undermined. In Los Angeles in 1952 the two-year-old gay organisation the Mattachine Society mounted the defence of the writer Dale Jennings, a homosexual man entrapped in his own apartment by a police officer. However, the ground-breaking case, in which the defence lawyer successfully demolished the notion that homosexuality and lewdness were one and the same thing, went completely unreported in the media.[26]

And yet it was not only the mainstream media that adopted a censorious line. The literary/academic establishment in the United States was no more liberal when the question of homosexuality arose. The San Franciscan poet Robert Duncan was certainly indiscreet in ways that alienated him from America's literary and academic mandarins. The New Critical establishment, already during the 1940's conspicuously antique in its attitudes, never forgave him his sexual openness. John Crowe Ransom, the editor of the *Kenyon Review*, refused one of his poems on the grounds that 'I read the poem as an advertisement or a notice of overt homosexuality, and we are not in the market for literature of this type'.[27] Similar attitudes prevailed at the *Hudson, Partisan, Sewanee* and *Southern* reviews. Allen Ginsberg experienced them in 1952 when he sent the manuscript of his collection *Empty Mirror* to *Hudson Review, Partisan Review, Commentary* and *Poetry Chicago*, as well as to publishers Random House and New Directions; but no one would publish any of it.[28]

It was not only heterosexual feathers that Robert Duncan ruffled. In his famous essay 'The Homosexual in Society' (1944), the appearance of which prompted Ransom's rejection slip, he had attacked other gay intellectuals for prostituting themselves to false values. They had been all too willing, he wrote, 'to convert their deepest feelings into marketable oddities and sentimentalities'. He deplored what he saw as the self-defeating separatism of the 'homosexual cult'. He therefore hated gay men's fascination with the language of camp ('a tone and a vocabulary that is loaded with contempt for the human').[29] While he believed homosexual writers should come out, and should never compromise their integrity *as* homosexuals, he nevertheless thought they should strive to make a place for their sexual identity within the broader culture rather than in some coterie on its edge. Those writers who, not openly gay, were making a literature of 'marketable oddity' did little more than confirm the common view of homosexuality as a personality disorder.

However, across the continent in New York in the early 1950s, Frank O'Hara was starting to transfer gay slang from his everyday speech into his poems. For instance, in his 1952 poem 'Easter' he uses the adjectival phrase 'all cruisy and nelly' and the adverbial phrase 'without swish/without camp'. The poem 'Day and Night in 1952' includes a variety of similar argot, including the phrase 'just camp it up a bit'.[30] As we have seen, Angus Wilson was just beginning his long-term defence of the camp personality.[31] Frank O'Hara was interested in integrating the quotidian tones of camp – which he shared with friends like fellow poets James Schuyler and John Ashbery – into his experiments with 'high' cultural languages such as those of Surrealism. Camp is a social (and sociable) mode of behaviour and speech: to use it, you have to know it; to know it, you have to have learned it from someone else; to practise it satisfactorily, you have to feel in need of some kind of audience. Camp signals the existence of a gay subculture. That is, presumably, why so many heterosexual people find it so threatening and offensive. Much of Frank O'Hara's poetry assumes the presence of incompatible audiences. 'Easter' is his answer to Lorca's 'Oda a Walt Whitman', all the more convincing for being expressed in the authentic tones of a New York queen. By contrast, Robert Duncan's disapproval seems inhibited and inhibiting.

Duncan's poetry is solidly rooted in what people whimsically call the 'real' world; his subjects are as often definably political as aesthetic or religious. Indeed, if one were to seek out a single literary work that most convincingly and confidently distilled into words the dynamic terror of the Vietnam period, it would make as much sense to choose *Bending the Bow* (1968) as Allen Ginsberg's *Planet News*, which came out in the same year. In Duncan's book – as in Ginsberg's – the very concept of Americanness is spoiled by the war. Even the nation's poetry is implicated in, and defiled by, its militant involvement in Asia. In 'Passages 26: The Soldiers', he speaks of 'the bloody verse America writes over Asia'. And he then quotes Whitman's proud remark from the 1855 Preface to *Leaves of Grass*, 'The United States themselves are essentially the greatest poem'. Of course, what made perfect sense in 1855, by 1968 sounds thrombosed with patriotic vanity. Duncan's finely tuned ear for the apt quotation thus, at a stroke, shows how far his nation's culture has erred since Whitman's day; the dead poet's words are enough. Duncan need add little but the scorch-mark of his irony.[32] Duncan may have been a pioneer in his 1944 essay, but it was Ginsberg who, by adding not irony but activism, would become the most prominent, socially concerned gay poet of the 1960s and 1970s. And it was Frank O'Hara who, by allowing his verse to consist of *nothing but* irony, resisted the heterosexist imperative to muffle or tone down the voices of effeminacy and camp.

Chapter 26

Black African Poetry

Theorists of African culture are quick to point out, as a first principle which ought not to need stating, that Africa is not the West; and its culture is one in which Western standards do not necessarily apply. To apply a concept as recent and Western as 'homosexuality', or even as apparently broad but actually restrictive as 'sexuality' itself, to African patterns of behaviour and discourse cannot pass with impunity. These are problematic issues within our own culture, let alone when transplanted wholesale to Africa. Quite apart from any other consideration, we are always being told that homosexuality barely exists at all in sub-Saharan Africa, except among the white population and those blacks they have corrupted and westernised; or else, circumstantially, in situations of enforced segregation of the sexes, as in prisons or the South African mining camps.[1] We must distinguish, however, between homosexual identities as they have come to be experienced in the West and patterns of homosexual behaviour that may occur in Africa's developing nations. As Neil McKenna has written, 'if you look for a Western homosexual identity in a developing country, you are unlikely to get anything like a true picture of male-to-male sex, because all too often male-to-male sexual behaviour bears little or no relationship to a "homosexual" sexual identity'.[2]

While the post-imperial cultures have been coming to terms with both their own colonial disempowerment and the acceptance of once subject black peoples as supposedly equal citizens on European soil, the 'new' African nations have had to endure more than three post-war decades of painful adjustment to their ambivalent condition as 'independent' states at once self-governed – albeit by institutions shaped to the prior needs of Europe and administered in European languages – and yet, as debtors to the West, still economically subject.

To impose on this troubled zone of adjustments a new burden of Western values and assumptions – such as, say, the expectation that each African nation might show its own signs of an incipient 'gay culture' – could be seen as both arrogant and foolish. But it does not seem beyond the acceptable remit of gay studies to watch for signs of black African proximity to, and distance from, ideas which we in the West take for granted as pertaining to the sexual life, if only to conclude that the notion of a distinct 'gay culture' in certain African nations would be alien and absurd. The truth is, though, that post-colonial African literature does indeed show anxieties clustering around familiar sexual topics, often expressed in rhetoric which echoes that of what were until so recently the imperial cultures, at times even amplifying those original sources.[3] After all, it is Christianity that has provided many of the attitudes in question and much of the rhetoric with which they are habitually expressed.

The poetry of black African men provides a case in point.[4] Africa is, conventionally, written of as a woman, mother of humanity. Only rarely, as in J.N. Kanyua Mugambi's 'Letter to My Child', does the continent appear as a man: 'Africa, you are now a man of age,/ For you have borne your initiation rites / Like a hero sanely bred from your mother's breast'.[5] Far more common is Syl Cheney-Coker's habit, in *The Graveyard Also Has Teeth*, of speaking of Africa in terms of fertilisation and husbandry. He berates the continent 'for permitting a perpetual butchery of her womb'. He mentions a farmer who sows his sperm in both his wife and Africa. He calls Africa 'mother womb of the earth'; her 'fertile womb wastes down the nile' [*sic*]. He addresses his own Sierra Leone as 'my woman!'[6]

Similarly, in *Sacred Hope*, Agostinho Neto speaks to 'oh Africa mother' and refers to 'our beautiful Angolan homeland' as 'our land, our mother'.[7] It is as part of much the same train of thought that Jean-Joseph Rabéarivelo, in his poem 'Cactus', mentions 'The blood of the earth, the sweat of the stone,/ and the sperm of the wind'.[8] This Mother Earth is hardly different from the European version, although more highly revered. Where, perhaps, Mother Africa differs is in the way she is seen as having political meaning, however fanciful. In *Cascades*, Jared Angira uses the image of a barren bride surrounded by exploitative suitors to describe, not Africa itself, but the Organisation of African Unity.[9]

Overt heterosexuality is common in its most unsubtle manifestations. Single and childless men and women are often described in terms of lack or loss. These sentiments from Okot p'Bitek's *Song of Lawino* are not untypical:

> You may be a giant
> Of a man
> You may begin
> To grow grey hair
> You may be bold
> And toothless with age,
> But if you are unmarried
> You are nothing.[10]

Correspondingly, in the case of the other sex, according to a traditional Swahili poem included in Wole Soyinka's *Poems of Black Africa*, 'Woman cannot exist except by man, what is there in that to vex some of them so?' Of course, it cannot be over-emphasised that if this sentiment is 'traditional', so too is the incipient feminism it dismisses. Neither sexism nor anti-sexism is exclusive to the West. A Yoruba poem in the same collection goes further: 'A woman cannot look at the penis – without being glad'. An entirely negative version of both female and male childlessness is presented in Kittobe's poem 'To the Childless', also in the Soyinka anthology.[11]

The thought of lesbianism, not unexpectedly, calls forth some of the most strident mating-calls of straight male poets. Consider, for instance, Taban lo Liyong's 'The Marriage of Black and White', which includes these unequivocal lines:

> I go for
> The woman who does not answer
> When Sappho calls the tune;
> The woman who hasn't spilled an egg,

> The woman who knows that equality
> Places her below her husband.
> Automatically.[12]

Liyong would doubtless approve of p'Bitek's Lawino, who, tiring of her husband's unmanliness, cries out: 'I am sick / Of sharing a bed with a woman!'[13] Lesbianism is, then, an affront to men: for the call of Sappho is an attempt to undermine the natural authority of husbands. If a woman should answer the call, her defection may be seen as proof of her husband's failing to maintain his virility.[14]

Heterosexual woman proves man's manhood. Out of her he shapes sons in his own image. She is the pliant material out of which he devises issue: 'I longed to carve my child upon that woman's womb'.[15] In her care he leaves his sons to grow into men: 'the milk of woman / Brings up men / Who are supermen'.[16] It is her voice that coaxes him to achieve his most virile feats: 'our minds / Drone with the voices of women / Harassing our loins / To force courage into the heart'.[17]

The potential for virility is established at birth. Virility itself is established by circumcision and initiation. Prior to that defining moment, boyhood is a period which allows for a certain amount of intimacy between boys. Indeed, having grown out of the capacity for such closeness may be perceived as a loss, as when, in A.W. Kayper-Mensah's poem 'The Happy and the Free', an adult voice comments on puerile affections with wistful bewilderment:

> We did not understand
> quite why
> the young boy wept
> deprived of his friends.
> But now we know.
> The seeds of the happy
> flower as the free!
> And that which links
> the boy's [sic] is stronger
> far than our grown-up power
> to understand'.[18]

Lack of understanding is a two-way street: for there are plenty of men whose needs boys cannot fathom. In a brief rhapsody of remembered adolescence – hetero wet dreams and skinny-dipping in the river – Kofi Anyidoho recalls how certain kinds of adults drifted into the boys' consciousness and conversations:

> Sometimes we talked of funny old men with
> the waist of the wasp. They kept asking
> useless questions sending boring greetings
> to your parents casting sly glances
> at things too fresh for their souring tastes.[19]

These wasp-waisted queens are represented here as being strange, funny and boring, but not as a threat. The fresh fruits their glances light on are the uncircumcised penises of males who are not yet masculine in any official sense; who, despite their nocturnal emissions, are still regarded, functionally, as children.

When it is due, according to J.N. Kanyua Mugambi's poem 'Circumcision', the ceremony of circumcision is preceded by boyish displays of near-manhood: 'Glistening bodies / Of huge dancing boys / Boil their courage / With manly songs'.[20] Although, according to one of Christopher Okigbo's poems, 'The bleeding phallus,/ Dripping fresh from the carnage cries out for the medicinal leaf', it is soon healed into awesome potency.[21] So, while L.S. Senghor can write an 'Elegy of the Circumcised', nostalgic for boyhood, his elegiac tone gives way, of necessity, to one of celebration.[22]

From this bloody moment of ancient ritual, the adult rules apply. Manhood needs defending, often by attack. The genitals, fully grown, hang heavy with warlike significance. In Wole Soyinka's 'Idanre', therefore, the god Ogun goes to war with gourds containing gunpowder, charms, palm wine, and his own sperm, as though semen were a kind of sexual ammunition.[23] (In the anthology *Poems of Black Africa*, Soyinka includes a Yoruba poem in which the belligerent Ogun molests first a girl, then a boy, until their genitals bleed.[24]) Virility is now a matter of public reputation and may not be compromised. As p'Bitek's *Song of Lawino* has it:

> A man's manliness is seen in the arena,
> No one touches another's testicles.

To Lawino, this is public proof – in the arena, where the traditional dances of Uganda take place – of natural sexual relations, untainted by the West.[25]

Of course, manhood is, of its nature, an erotic condition, no less worthy of celebration by the heterosexual man than by the homosexual. Arthur Nortje's 'Joy Cry', a poem expressing desire for someone of unstated sex, presumably female, consists of three stanzas on the 'joy cry of virility', the first of which reads as follows:

> Apollo's man-breasts smooth and gold-blond
> hold between in the fine-boned cleft
> the kernel of radiant light. Like wind
> youth's madness streams through orifices. The swift
> vivacious morning shoots along the ripples:
> in my loins the swelling pearl moves.[26]

Such a text celebrates the sheer heroism of male beauty (in this instance, white), static, simply existing, *seen* and admired. The 'joy cry' of virility comes from both seer and seen. Even in the most earnest and violent struggle, such as the fight for Angola as recorded in *Sacred Hope* by Agostinho Neto, real tension gives rise to symbolic beauty; speaking of the Angolan heroes, Neto writes: 'I arrived to see the resurrection of the seed / dynamic symphony of the growth of joy in men'.[27]

It is clear, then, that African poetry is littered with symbolic homo-erotic moments, when virility is beautified in an atmosphere implicitly exclusive of homosexuality as such. As in European poetry, we find 'gay poetry' written by straight men. Taban lo Liyong, no champion of homosexuality, has a poem in *Frantz Fanon's Uneven Ribs* called 'Normalcy, Normalcy, I Detest Thee!' Its paradoxical assertion is that virility is dependent on abnormality. He offers his 'complications' (abnormalities) as proof that he is *not* like a harem eunuch.[28]

The conventional friendship elegy, with no suggestion of erotic interest, is not uncommon. I would include in this tradition Kojo Gyinaye Kyei's 'Dammirifa Due Due!' ('Shadows have lengthened / And Kofi Ankonam, my friend,/ Has taken the long long road'), Roderic B. Roberts's 'On Friendship and War', and Mazisi Kunene's 'For a Friend who was Killed in the War'.[29] But there are equivalent moments even in poems which start in the relatively detached realm of friendship. One such occurs in Syl Cheney-Coker's 'Night of Absinthe', a drunken vision of his brother as a suicide. Drink breaks down the barriers thus: 'thus do I declaim him, love him, knead him / and fall vertical with him in his slime' – but there is, clearly, as much humiliation here as humility.[30]

If the elegy on a lost friend is arguably derived from an English tradition, other non-African sources provide points of reference which we may recognise as constituting part of a gay cultural store. The myth of Sodom, of course, enters Africa on missionary tongues; it then reappears in such texts as L.S. Senghor's marvellous poem 'To the American Negro Soldiers':

> Brothers, I do not know if it was you who bombed the cathedrals, the
>   pride of Europe
> If you are the lightning that in God's hand burnt Sodom and Gomorrah.

But notice that Senghor characterises blacks as the instruments of God's vengeful power; implicitly, the Sodomites are white.[31] In 'Fragments out of the Deluge', Christopher Okigbo compares his poem's hero with Gilgamesh, and makes passing reference to Gilgamesh's 'Companion and second self' Enkidu.[32] The eighteenth of Jean-Joseph Rabéarivelo's 'Translations from the Night' is a pastoral poem in which Corydon is still waiting for his beloved Alexis; it is explicitly modelled on Virgil's second Eclogue.[33]

In cultures where virility is as highly valued as we have seen, it may not be surprising to find among male writers a nagging castration anxiety. A broad range of situations and experiences is described in terms of unmanning. In *Katchikali*, Lenrie Peters, a surgeon by profession, seems disturbed by the circumcision he has to carry out on a boy, mainly because 'mother would have it deprived'.[34] A similar sense of losing one's manhood to woman arises in Joe de Graft's poem 'Platinum Lou', where marriage comes to one of the poet's friends 'like a castrating angel', because his wife insists he wear a condom when they make love.[35]

In p'Bitek's *Song of Lawino*, educated men are seen as eunuchs: 'Their manhood was finished / In the class-rooms,/ Their testicles / Were smashed / With large books!'[36] In a more obvious way, men confined to prison are pitied as castrates, even in poems which make no mention of jailhouse homosexuality (a subject to which I shall return). Speaking of men in South African jails, in 'At Rest from the Grim Place', Arthur Nortje combines images of soldiers disarmed and genitals disabled:

> Those bayonets are silent,
> the spear of the nation gone to the ground.
> Warriors prowl in the stars of their dungeons.
> I've seen the nebulae of a man's eyes
> squirm with pain, he sang his life
> through cosmic volleys. They call it
> genital therapy, the blond bosses.[37]

This sense of white men as the emasculators of black men is also to be found in Taban lo Liyong's poem 'Laurels for [Stokely] Carmichael in Prison': 'You walk like a eunuch / In a harem / Unable to bark – or bite./ Your manhood is taken / Leaving you a race of women'.[38] Even when black men are admired for their potency – in the invasive, voyeurist myth of the big, black penis – the white gaze is judged to be demeaning and, precisely by virtue of its admiration, defeating. (After all, historically, the envy that white men show in this myth has sought resolution in lynch-mob castrations, particularly in the southern United States.) Thus, when in the *Song of Ocol*, Okot p'Bitek writes: 'White women came to discover,/ To see with their naked eyes / What manhood could be', an insult is intended to white men; yet true potency, real power, is seen to be theirs *despite* the roving eyes of their women. The tourist-as-colonist uses desire and the camera to turn African manhood into a quaint fetish, of little value save as a white woman's souvenir.[39]

Fear of castration is one aspect of the anxiety built into masculinity; another, more specifically if not exclusively to be associated with heterosexual masculinity, is anal rape. The threat may be relatively urgent in prison life (as we shall see), but is much less so elsewhere. Even so, the image of male rape is used in a wide variety of circumstances. In 'Viaticum', for instance, Tchicaya U Tam'si speaks of silences which 'ravage us / with lecherous resolves / for my beardless conscience / ravage us alone'.[40] Presumably, the beardlessness denotes the ravaging of a pre-pubescent boy. In Jared Angira's poem 'Braying On and On', the rape fantasy arises as part of a more generalised narrative of being

> Imprisoned
> in this dark cocoon
> in sarcasm
>   deranged
> in dishonour
>   defiled
> in agony
>   tortured
> in male degradation
>   raped
> hands in sisal ropes behind my back'.[41]

And anal rape comes to Wole Soyinka's mind when he gives an account of riding the New York subway: he refers to the train's 'rape / Of motion through Manhattan's bowels'.[42] In all such instances, homosexual intercourse is seen as a dangerous threat, to which no man is immune so long as he remains weaker than any other who might turn rapist. Once put to political uses, this can become a compellingly persuasive metaphor.

Neil McKenna has written that 'the Western construction of "homosexuality", "bisexuality" and "gay" has allowed many countries, many populations and, most importantly, many governments to label sex between men (as, indeed, they have labelled Aids) as a cultural and behavioural import from the West, a contamination, a contagion, which has little or nothing to do with the sexual behaviour of the indigenous culture'.[43] It is with a confident sense of African virility, and with homophobic pride, that certain male poets of the black diaspora refer to imperialists and colonists as homosexuals. In *Return to My Native Land*, Aimé Césaire lists 'the exacerbated odour of corruption, the monstrous sodomies of the host and the slaughterer, the unscalable ship's prow of prejudice and stupidity, the prostitutions, hypocrisies, lusts, betrayals, lies, swindles, concussions – ' as symptoms of both the colonial misrule of his native Martinique and the inertia of the misruled.[44] In a similar manner, David Mandessi Diop, speaking of the colonial period and addressing the colonists, writes in 'The Vultures':

> Strange men who were not men
> You knew all the books you did not know love
> Or the hands that fertilise the womb of the earth[.]

These lines associate the physical work of black Africans with reproductive heterosexual love, while the book-learning of the 'Strange' colonists is seen to be sterile and unmanly, implicitly homosexual in a most negative sense.[45] In 'Come down Sunjiata', Lenrie Peters speaks of the need for 'a mass uprising', not just in the Gambia but

> from the Atlas to the Cape
> to ravage the puppets,
> perverts, Iconoclasts.

As though Africa had been weakened by the political equivalent of sexual 'perverts', Peters calls for a kind of moral clean-up; 'We need heroes worthy of the name'.[46] Whether these 'perverts' and so on are white outsiders or white-influenced blacks is not clear: for the imperial age has had lastingly debilitating effects on the Africans themselves. Thus, the Ugandan poet Okot p'Bitek has the female singer of his *Song of Lawino* complain about her westernised husband as follows:

> He borrows the clothes he wears
> And the ideas in his head
> And his actions and behaviour
> Are to please somebody else.
> Like a woman trying to please her husband!
> My husband has become a woman![47]

Unmanned not by empire itself but by the commercial and cultural waves that have followed, this African man is no longer able to perform conjugally for a wife who is implicitly as proud not to be lesbian as he should be to be heterosexual. So the appeal to be manly operates in a broad political context and is more than a mere call to deepen the voice and broaden the shoulders. Frantz Fanon recognised this when he wrote about virile fitness as the embodiment of resistance to colonialism:

> The native is a being hemmed in; apartheid is simply one form of the division into compartments of the colonial world. The first thing which the native learns is to stay in his place, and not to go beyond certain limits. This is why the dreams of the [male] native are always of muscular prowess; his [sic] dreams are of action and of aggression. I dream I am jumping, swimming, running, climbing; I dream that I burst out laughing, that I span a river in one stride, or that I am followed by a flood of motorcars which never catch up with me. During the period of colonisation, the native never stops achieving his freedom from nine in the evening until six in the morning.[48]

As post-colonial literature shows, this psychological effect of colonisation can hardly be wiped out overnight by the moment of independence. Indeed, the dream of macho achievements may be even more urgent during the period of national renewal after colonial withdrawal. In a poem called 'Non-commitment', Chinua Achebe goes further: denouncing the uncommitted as diaphragms over the womb of 'seminal rage', he directly associates political engagement with (male) reproductive fertility.[49]

A number of poets use imagery of pre-industrial warfare to denote many different aspects of manly activity in modern society, including a specifically sexual type of approved virility. Typically, the active phallus is associated with the traditional spear. Okot p'Bitek's

Song of Lawino has several of these references. For instance, when Lawino deplores the Protestant habit of segregating boys and girls, she says of the boys' genitals: 'The trusted right-hand spears / Of young bulls / Rust in the dewy cold / Of the night'. Later, her mother shows her some medicines 'For men whose spears / Refuse to stand up,/ Lazy spears / That sleep on their bellies / Like earthworms!' And Lawino recommends to her husband Ocol, castrated by Western culture, that he pray to his ancestors:

> Ask for a spear that you will trust
> One that does not bend easily
> Like the earth-worm.
> Ask them to restore your manhood!
> For I am sick
> Of sharing a bed with a woman![50]

In one of his poems, Christopher Okigbo mentions a 'nude spear'.[51] And in 'Post Mortem', echoing Lawino's image of the soft penis as an earthworm when it should be a spear, Wole Soyinka speaks of a dead man's 'man-pike / shrunk to a sub-soil grub'.[52] Given this frequent emphasis on the desirability of a weapon-like penis, it comes as no surprise to find sexual intercourse treated as a form of combat. Here, again, African tradition is no different from the European. Thus, to take a random example, Mbella Sonne Dipoko shows a whole city trying to see into a single window, 'As if in order to referee the impending love-making / To see who wins and who loses'.[53]

Explicit poetic references to sexual activity between African men tend to occur mainly in the context of life in all-male environments like prisons and, to a lesser extent, camps for migrant workers. It follows from the social structures that enforce the populating of such places that, in the literatures of colonial oppression and of apartheid, such poems are far more likely to be political than erotic (although, needless to say, these two modes are not mutually exclusive). The sexual activities themselves tend to be seen, then, as the violent and coercive fruits of colonial racism. Hence Kenneth Kaunda's attention to the detail of prison life in his book *Zambia Shall Be Free* (1962):

> When these poor boys come in for the first time (aged 15 to 20) they are so scared, they respond very quickly to anyone offering them protection and in many cases they will need it. . . . If a boy tries to resist, his so-called protector arranges with others to thrash him so that by coming to the boy's protection at the right moment, he will submit to his unnatural desires. The organisation of these incorrigibles is so effective, that warders will either explicitly or implicitly approve of the action. From this time, the boy is treated like a 'housewife'. Food as well as many other requirements in ordinary life which find their way into prison, in spite of the strict rules, the boy now receives.[54]

Kaunda was, of course, himself imprisoned by the British before Zambian independence. One assumes he speaks from observed experience. Although Kaunda clearly deplores the behaviour of the 'incorrigibles' who thus make housewives of Zambian youths, his account is not an attack on homosexuality as such, but on the system that creates the circumstances in which such 'incorrigibles' can impose themselves on the captive boys. The point I infer is crucial, and cannot be over-emphasised: it is quite likely that prison was the context in which various post-independence national heads of state like Robert Mugabe learned their hostile attitudes to male homosexuality (see below). Another putrescent legacy of empire.

In Oswald Mbuyiseni Mtshali's poem 'Amagoduka at Glencoe Station', some migrant workers heading for the South African gold mines say: 'We'll live in compounds / where young men are pampered / into partners for older men'.[55] This inevitability is taken for granted, as is the lack of privacy in work camp or jail; which is not to say that they are accepted. One of Wole Soyinka's prison poems, 'Live Burial', complains about a voyeur who keeps watch in the latrines.[56] In 'The Vultures', Musaemura Bonas Zimunya shows how, in certain cases, mere lack of privacy extends to humiliating and violent intrusion, by the prison guards themselves, into prisoners' (and their families') sexual identities. In this poem the guards continually go on

> about Fernando's behind,
> about his father's stub
> about his sister's hot fork
> about his saliva-washed penis –
> how they all knew this!
> They laughed
> said his face was like a pregnant woman's
> organs'.

They complete the humiliation by beating him up.[57]

The poet one cannot ignore in this context, and in whose work this context cannot be ignored, is Dennis Brutus. In his *Letters to Martha, and Other Poems from a South African Prison*, Brutus offers graphic images of a debased homosexuality which seems to have left a scar of fear and abhorrence across the worst of his prison memories.[58] Sex is always yoked to violence. Sharpened fragments of metal, to be used as weapons, can at any moment be unsheathed 'from some disciplined anus' – an image which, while evoking an anality empowered by its hidden phallicism, is more likely to bring to mind the sheer vulnerability of flesh (letter 2). A fight is caused ('strange, most strange!') by 'love, strange love' between prisoners (letter 3). In this matter of erotic threat, Brutus begins to become obsessive about 'Coprophilism; necrophilism; fellatio;/ penis-amputation' – a list which leaves us in no doubt about about the extremes of sexual violence and violation with which he is associating oral sex (letter 5).

One prisoner goes mad – 'so great the pressures to enforce sodomy' (letter 6). Another too, or perhaps the same, flees into madness 'from the battering importunities / of fists and genitals of sodomites' (postscript 6). Brutus constructs in this enclosed world a moral hierarchy, at the foot of which lie those who sink so low as to volunteer for assault: 'Perhaps most terrible are those who beg for it,/ who beg for sexual assault' (letter 7). Some men are routinely used as 'girls'; of these, the most popular sleeps with several men a night. But when he grows older, too old to be a 'girl', he becomes 'that most perverse among / the perverted:/ a "man" in the homosexual embrace / who had once been the "woman"' (letter 8).[59]

For gay readers in search of positive images, much of this may seem inexcusably negative. It is as well to dismiss such sentimental idealism at once, with a quotation from one of Brutus' prose accounts of life on Robben Island:

The criminal prisoners were placed in charge of the political prisoners, with responsibility for feeding them, taking them to work, overseeing the work . . . and disciplining them. At the instigation of the warders (all of them white), they used sexual assault to break an individual's morale and self-esteem, and were themselves rewarded with marijuana. Prisoners were starved into submission, beaten if necessary, then when on the point of consent to homosexuality left alone without food or water, though with an occasional beating. Most then found themselves begging for sexual assault in order to get food and water.[60]

It is in the light of this kind of account that one has to read Brutus' later poem 'I Would Not Be Thought Less Than A Man', in *Stubborn Hope*. Here, he is starting to come to terms with the idea that, among the horrific bursts of manipulation and violence, there might be genuinely positive sparks of love. Hesitant and reluctant, Brutus nevertheless makes an effort to accept 'the hints of tenderness and passion / not blazoned forth as the false and insincere / the genuine concern and anxiousness / between two men whom sexual bonds had linked'. On the grounds that he 'would not be thought less than a man / in feeling and understanding', he decides he must admit that

> not all of it was evil it must seem
> (we except of course, seduction, outrage, rape)
> or some of it had graces that I know not of[.]

The overall impression this poem gives is of moral confusion tempered by the uncomfortable honesty of a man who is trying hard to stifle abhorrence with tolerance. For all its limitations, this is a vital step in his psychic recovery from the prison ordeal.[61]

Another admission of incomprehension, though springing from less extreme circumstances than those of enforced incarceration, occurs in Lenrie Peters's *Katchikali*. While observing the English sunning themselves on Primrose Hill, he interrupts the following scene:

> Hairy-limbed Sodomite
> fixes Narcissus by the tree;
> frowns with cold winter passion
> because I intercept his glance.
>
> I confess embarrassment and pay attention to the leaves.
> Forgive me: I did not mean to intrude.

Peters seems unsure of where, between the spontaneous hostility of his first reaction ('Hairy-limbed Sodomite') and the rather abject embarrassment in which he retreats from the scene, he should place himself; and this unsureness seems to occur at the time both of the encounter and of the subsequent writing. It is not clear what mood asserted itself after the first wave of embarrassment had broken; but surely not one of enthusiastic approval.[62]

What I have been outlining in this chapter is a debate around standards of virility and femininity which are, as far as one can tell, beginning to be strongly questioned and destabilised, if only in certain cosmopolitan, urban centres. Potentially, the debate offers a context in which African gay literatures might develop, if writers who chose to define themselves as lesbian or gay were to make the further choice of focusing their writing on that definition, thereby sharing with each other what they felt set them apart from the broader culture. Whether such literatures would follow the gay models we have been developing in Western Europe and North America, thus establishing points of identity between gay people across continental boundaries – cultural and 'racial' as well as merely geographical – is not yet clear.

It is clear, though, that the gay movement as we know it has, indeed, arrived (from the United States) on the African continent and elsewhere in the developing world. As Neil McKenna has observed, 'Today, all over the developing world, gay and lesbian organisations are forming and emerging, often with fear and trepidation. In Africa alone, gay and lesbian groups have recently been formed in South Africa, Zimbabwe, Ghana and Nigeria, and are in the process of emerging in Botswana.'[63] There is no good reason to suppose that lesbian and gay writers of the black African nations will not follow where African-Americans and other groups within the diaspora have already made their mark. One of the most encouraging developments in post-war gay literature has been the development of the non-white literatures, which have increasingly forced white gay men into the position of having to question their own habits of sex-based colonialism and orientalism.

However, in some African nations the struggle to establish an indigenous gay and lesbian culture is going to be protracted and hard-fought. Consider the example of Zimbabwe. In July 1995, Robert Mugabe, the Zimbabwean President, opened a book fair on the theme of 'Human Rights and Justice' with an outspoken attack on Gays and Lesbians of Zimbabwe, a group who had originally been invited to have a stall at the fair but who were subsequently disinvited. In his opening speech, Mugabe said:

> I find it extremely outrageous and repugnant to my human conscience that such immoral and repulsive organisations, like those of homosexuals who offend both against the law of nature and the morals and religious beliefs espoused by our society, should have any advocates in our midst and even elsewhere in the world. . . . If we accept homosexuality as a right, as is being argued by the Association of Sodomites and Sexual Perverts what moral fibre shall our society ever have to deny organised drug addicts, or even those given to bestiality, the rights they might claim and allege they possess under the rubrics of 'individual freedom' and 'human rights' including freedom of the press to write, publish and publicise their literature on them? . . . We don't believe they have any rights at all.

The following month, at a conference in remembrance of the heroes of Zimbabwe, Mugabe warmed to his new theme, urging people to arrest lesbians and gay men, whom he described as being 'worse than dogs and pigs'. There is evidence that a campaign of active oppression followed on from these speeches.[64] Mugabe's attitudes deserve to be contrasted with the fact that equal rights for lesbians and gay men were explicitly inscribed in the new, post-apartheid South African Bill of Rights.[65]

Unlike Mugabe, the great Angolan poet Agostinho Neto allowed his celebrations of revolutionary heroism and comradeship a carnal edge. He was unafraid to affirm, for example, that he wanted to write a poem 'sculpted in love / exhaling the hope of that friend of mine / at this hour with loincloth soaked / in the sweet [sic] of his back'. He wrote of how 'the deadly lightning of revolution / pulverises the submission of men / and in the force of friendship hands meet / [and] faces are kissed'. And he celebrated the revolution's capacity to satisfy certain fundamental needs in men: 'the uncontained desire to realise oneself / to be a man / to find the supreme heat of the carnal surface of another'.[66] Here, being a man – in the senses both of being human and of achieving one's virility – is actually predicated upon the heat of another man's touch. These and other sentiments expressed in Neto's poetry remain a vibrant alternative to Mugabe's thrombotic revolutionary fervour.

Chapter 27

....

From Solitary Vice to Circle Jerk

....

In André Gide's great Modernist novel *The Counterfeiters* (*Les Faux-monnayeurs*, 1926), the schoolboy Boris, at the age of nine, comes under the influence of a boy called Baptistin, a year or two older, with whom he enjoys certain 'clandestine practices' – mutual masturbation – which they both, understandably, consider to be magical. Although Boris cures himself of this 'vice' for a while, he later takes it up again, masturbating alone, essentially as a consequence of being bullied. His sexual pleasure (*volupté*) is all the more intense for the recidivism it involves ('mais il prenait plaisir à se perdre et faisait, de cette perdition même, sa volupté').[1] Gide himself had been removed from school at the tender age of eight because of certain 'bad habits' which he made no attempt to cover up, being naïvely unaware that there was any need to do so. Prior to this, he and the son of the concierge had been in the habit of masturbating – not each other but themselves in each other's close company – underneath his parents' dining table.[2]

No book so intensely redolent of the frenzy of male puberty could well avoid mention – or implication, at least – of masturbation. But there is more to the raising of this topic than the dully mirroring requirements of realist plausibility. The whole of *The Counterfeiters* is vibrant with onanistic promise. Its complex of intrigues and affairs between adolescent boys thrives upon the purposive conjunction of hands and penises. The motivation for this is not just Gide's indulgence of a personal interest – although that is likely to be a part of the matter. Given that the novel is so profoundly and extensively concerned with education and socialisation, masturbation takes its place in a thematic whole as the definitive exercise in sexual self- or co-education. It constitutes the boys' best way of establishing a firm (and pleasurable) mode of relation to the physical world. This is no incidental detail in Gide's broader, intellectual explorations of criminality and liminality: for the perception of physical matter is, as it always has been, sited near the base of all metaphysics.

In the earlier novel *The Immoralist* (*L'Immoraliste*, 1902), between boy-loving trips to north Africa, Gide's *alter ego* Michel drains a lake on his country estate with the seventeen-year-old (but fifteen-looking) Charles, the son of his gamekeeper. Although many other people are present, the scene which follows is narrated as if Michel and Charles are alone together:

> I called him after a moment to help me catch a big eel; we joined hands in trying to
> hold it. . . . Then came another and another; our faces were splashed with mud;

sometimes the ooze suddenly gave way beneath us and we sank into it up to our waists; we were soon drenched. In the ardour of the sport, we barely exchanged a shout or two, a word or two; but at the end of the day, I became aware I was saying 'thou' to Charles, without having any clear idea when I had begun.[3] [Ellipsis in the original.]

The supposed intimacy that develops here between the two men bridges the gaps between their ages and classes. The formal relation of employer to employee breaks down – yet remains intact – at an imperceptible point among the inarticulate utterances which accompany a sequence of ardent physical actions. Their bucolic interlude of mud-wrestling with eels is the closest they come to the sexual consummation it represents. Its filthiness and wetness are haphazardly polymorphous and teeter on the verges of perversity. When they join hands around the slippery girth of an ungraspable eel, it is not so much the eel itself they are trying to capture as the eeliness of phallic pleasure.

Michel's inadvertent shift from *vous* to *tu* expresses nothing so straightforward as physical pleasure, however. It momentarily appears to dissolve social distinctions. (We have to note, though, that such literary moments of cross-class fellowship tend to be related from the bourgeois point of view only: we are not told what Charles thinks of his master's impertinent intimacy.) It raises the possibility of a corresponding linguistic shift in the opposite direction, from singular to plural, in the introspective first person: from solitary *je* to mutual *nous*. This is a question of the very possibility of love between men, or between men and boys.

While the 'tragic' motif in gay fiction relies so heavily and so often on a perception of anal intercourse as a fundamental defeat of the receptive partner's masculinity – a very positive defeat if you regard traditional standards of masculinity as an unnecessary evil, a negative one otherwise – positive representations of boys who grow up gay and turn into gay men, through a gradual and self-aware metamorphosis of both body and mind, tend to give a central role, instead, to masturbation. (Fellatio, surprisingly, does not have a very prominent role in the symbolic arsenal of gay literature.)

Now, it is all very well to dismiss masturbation, whether solitary or mutual, as mere puerility – mere foreplay to both adulthood and penetrative intercourse proper – but such dismissiveness will inevitably overlook those aspects of masturbation, both physical and mental, which are distinctly adult. Moreover, in a subculture where being like a boy is not always regarded as a bad thing for an adult male to aspire to, to retain supposedly boyish sexual modes during adulthood may come to be seen as a viable way of resisting the bourgeois imperative that adulthood should deteriorate into stability and respectability. Certainly, gay culture often lays claim to a dynamism that the straight paterfamilias, that master of mortgages, is said to have lost.

The adolescence of boys is important to gay literature not merely because adolescent boys are desirable – though they are, and that is no trivial thing – but also because it is so intensely in the passing stage of adolescence that not all but so many young men learn that they are going to be gay. Masturbation, whether solitary or mutual, is the outward sign of this moment of grace. The typical act of solitary masturbation is, in one sense, completely self-absorbed: a dialogue of pleasure between one body and its mind, self-regarding (often literally: in the mirror or glassy pool) and definitively self-satisfying. In another respect, however, when one takes into account the question of fantasy, masturbation directs the genitals beyond the self, not merely towards the actual physique of one actual person, but idealistically into the dream of perfect multitudes. For all its participation in a kind of libidinous celibacy, masturbation abhors monogamy. It is kleptomaniac in its appropriation of bodies, whether seen or imagined, complete or rendered down to their fetishised parts. The masturbator's vicious solitude conjures up a dream of encounters with willing crowds, serial or simultaneous.

This intellectual Don Juanism is not a particularly accurate way for a youth to come to terms with the adult world. The contriving of masturbatory fantasy is not a realistic art, even if it has to appear to be so for the duration of the telling. It is, however, structurally precise: there is an art to the co-ordination of the respective climaxes of fantasy and act. If the two fail to coincide, the mistiming of the mental image may diminish the pleasure of the physical climax. Puberty constitutes a crash course in such autodidactic lessons in technique.

The success of a fantasy, then, being measured in seismic terms relating to the pleasure of the orgasm it facilitates, is not predicated upon mere plausibility. Pornography in general – except when filmed, and then screened unedited, as it were raw – does not follow the conventions of likelihood. Thinking only of the male genitals, one sees that size, endurance and copiousness of sperm are all invariably exaggerated in good porn. Likewise, the masturbatory fantasy is a tall tale for one's own – and only one's own – consumption, with the self as origin, protagonist and sole destination. Above all, it is likely to be generous about one's own powers of attraction.

Literary representations of masturbation by homosexual authors have tended to be less censorious than those by heterosexual authors. There would seem to be little point, after all, in men who have already been labelled as deviant attempting to shift the same label on to mere masturbators. Moreover, since it involves a male hand on a penis, male masturbation is, in a particular sense, already a homosexual act, even if the masturbator is fantasising about women at the time. The male hand is joined to the penis, as it were, by way of a male brain which recognises the feelings experienced by both parts. This entirely male familiarity is what makes the whole act progress so smoothly. The gay author who invites gay readers to witness such an event is invoking a commonality of erotic feeling with which to intensify the emotion conveyed by his text. The gay reader of the scene mixes memory and desire: remembering his own masturbatory experience, and desirous of the masturbating protagonist. You wish you could render your solo masturbation mutual; and you wish your own masturbatory sessions, too, could so easily slide over from solitude into solidarity.

In the present chapter I have limited myself to French fiction, not because the French are much more likely to write about masturbation than, say, the British or the Germans, but because they tend to do so in a more intensive spirit of intellectual enquiry. I chose the French for the revealing rigour of even their most celebratory representations of onanism. The narrator of Marcel Proust's *A la recherche du temps perdu*, like Proust himself before him, habitually masturbates in the lavatory at the top of his parents' home.[4] He goes there, since it is the only room he can lock, to indulge in all of his solitary pleasures: 'reading or dreaming, secret tears or paroxysms of desire' ('la lecture, la rêverie, les larmes et la volupté', Proust's incipient experience of Baudelaire's 'luxe, calme et volupté'). But what might, in other houses, be experienced as a confined, cellular activity, in this case has prospects, not only temporal – insofar as masturbation will develop into his adult heterosexual experiences, which sometimes consist of mere frottage against a sleeping woman's body – but also spatial: this lofty water closet is a room with a view. From here Marcel can see the distant prospect of a romantic past, in the shape of the castle keep at Roussainville and the thick woods out of which he expects, in his definitively phallocentric vanity, a village girl to walk into his arms.[5]

What does, however, burst into arms' reach, in one of the natural world's routinely flamboyant gestures, is the intrusive branch of a flowering currant-bush (*cassis*) which fills the little room with its scent. In a manner prefiguring Jean Genet, petals are associated with the scattered drops of Marcel's semen; indeed, he seems to ejaculate on to the plant.[6] The novel thus begins as it means to go on, making close comparisons between botany and human physiology with a view to questioning the designation of marginalised sexualities – female and male inversion in particular – as 'unnatural'.

The other myth Proust discards here is that masturbation so weakens the moral fibre that the physical fibre, too, is put at risk, even to the extent of a slow descent into imbecility and death. As the cheerfully flourishing currant, spattered with cum, might suggest, and as the novel goes on to confirm at great length, Marcel will not die of his furtive dissipation. The boy manipulates himself 'with the heroic scruples of a traveller setting forth for unknown climes, or of a desperate wretch hesitating on the verge of self-destruction, faint with emotion', convinced that what he is doing 'might lead me to my death'. But, of course, no harm is done.

Dominique Fernandez recognises this scene in his gay liberationist novel *L'Etoile rose* (1978) during a passage about his narrator's schooldays and early adolescence. The discursive narrative passes, with clear associative logic, from Latin lessons, through the Proust episode, to masturbation; or rather, since this is a novel which so insistently asserts its characters' place in a continuous cultural tradition,[7] the passage moves bibliographically from Petronius' *Satyricon*, through Proust, to Voltaire's essay on onanism in the *Dictionnaire philosophique*. Petronius arises here as a significant absence from the narrator's Latin lessons, themselves a token of middle-class respectability ('Le latin occupait une place centrale dans nos horaires: signe distinctif de notre instruction bourgeoise'). Instead, the schoolboys are made to read Cicero, in whose work there is no danger that they will be aroused by playfulness or homo-eroticism. A mention of the latter element leads straight into the narrator's own haunted and unpoetic experiences of masturbation. The suggestion is that he would have had a far less anguished fantasy life if he had been allowed to read Petronius.

It is at this juncture that the narrator contrasts the early masturbatory life of Proust's Marcel with his own. From his own subject position there was no panorama, no blossom reaching through his window, and no poetic comparisons came to mind at the sight of semen stains on his linen. ('Ni donjon de Roussainville ni porche de Saint-André-des-Champs pour moi; les branches du cassis sauvage ne se penchaient pas vers ma fenêtre.') Fear and shame, we are told, accompanied the solitary sexual pleasures of this generation: for they laboured in the shadow of the formidable authority of Voltaire, that name so closely, and in this context so unjustifiably, associated with 'enlightenment' and 'reason'. The narrator refers to Voltaire's article on onanism as the most stupid text ever written on the topic – the most reactionary, ignorant and harmful – because of its (subsequently commonplace) insistence that masturbation weakens not only the moral fibre but even one's very physique. Fernandez establishes a clear link between the reading habits of the bourgeois boy and his masturbatory life, and appears to suggest that this link is all the more effective, more potentially harmful or helpful, in the case of a boy who, like the narrator, is destined to turn out homosexual as an adult.[8]

There is a further echo of the Proust scene in Hervé Guibert's autobiographical novel *My Parents* (*Mes Parents*, 1986):

In six months I have grown up, I let my hair grow a bit and it's getting curly, I have pubic hair and by persevering I managed to make myself come, between noon and two o'clock, sitting on the toilet amid the smell of lavender paper, astounded by the simplicity of the action and the growing tickle in this slightly smelly tumescence which friction causes to fill the skin with blood then finally spit as it gives me an orgasm.[9]

As if setting the experience up as a suitable candidate for a hypothetical future moment in which the protagonist's Proustian memories of his adolescence are, involuntarily and by chance, triggered by a fleeting sensory stimulus, Guibert represents the memorable pleasures of the first ejaculation as occurring just as intensely in the nose as in the genitals. The combined odours of the lavender paper and Hervé's erection ('cette turgescence un peu odorante') intoxicate the boy to a far greater degree than the simple, albeit effortful, mechanics of the act might appear to merit. The mundane progression from 'tickle' to 'friction' to 'spit' is given a complex, emotional third dimension by the totality of the sensory experience of sitting locked away in the privacy of the lavatory with only the residual fragrance of lavender to romanticise the act and only his parents' lavender paper to wipe up the consequence.

A further dimension is added to the masturbation scenes in Proust's *Recherche* by the fact that the adult Marcel has indiscreetly granted an audience access to the adolescent Marcel's erotic sanctum. His cell has a glass wall of which he is unaware, and which he is unaware that he himself, as an adult, will have installed in his apparently secure privacy. Such is the self-betraying nature of retrospective confession: the boy is unaware that the man will make an exhibition of him.

This narrative moment is, as it were, rendered literal or actual in a later text, published anonymously at first, but in fact by Jean Cocteau, *Le Livre blanc* (1928). At one stage in his autobiographical account, the narrator frequents a bathhouse/brothel full of working-class youths.[10] The place is similar in some respects to Jupien's establishment in the *Recherche*; and, indeed, Cocteau makes a joke at Proust's expense by having him visit this brothel in the person of a man '(a moralist)' who 'could only find enjoyment in the spectacle of a Hercules killing a rat with a red-hot needle'. One of the bathrooms in this place is equipped with a two-way mirror, behind which the narrator watches as boys come there to bathe and jerk off. A particular occasion stands out in his mind:

> Once, a Narcissus who was pleasuring himself brought his mouth up to the mirror, glued it to the glass and completed the adventure with himself. Invisible as a Greek god, I pressed my lips against his and imitated his gestures. He never knew that the mirror, instead of reflecting, was participating, that it was alive and loved him.

And yet, the narrator too, complacently satisfied that he has taken his pleasure from the unknowing boy, seems ignorant of the fact that, instead of participating, he is merely reflecting. Masturbation is a meditative act.

The boy imagines making love with himself – while making love with himself. The narrator imagines making love with the boy – while making love with himself. The text's masturbating consumer – its assumed gay male reader – imagines himself in the place of the narrator (for it is not strictly possible to identify with the boy), imagining himself making love with the boy while making love with himself – while making love with himself. Desire is thus depicted as a *mise-en-abîme* of willing self-deception, wherein the hand of the self represents all parts of the body of the other. Self-love conquers all.

This boy is being watched but does not know it. A completely new dynamic is introduced when a masturbatory scene centres on someone who knows he is being watched and acts accordingly. In such a case, the crucial focus is, depending on the psychology of the watched individual, exhibitionistic pride or abject humiliation. On these alternatives depends the nature of the watcher's pleasure, whether co-operatively appreciative or mockingly sadistic.

There is a scene of great symbolic and erotic force in Jean Genet's *Miracle of the Rose* when Bulkaen is ritually humiliated by eight other convicts.[11] He is forced to stand with his mouth open while the others, each in turn, attempt to spit into him from a distance of fifteen metres. Bulkaen responds to the first shot, which hits its mark with impressive accuracy, by submissively, almost unconsciously, swallowing the other man's spit. After this first conspicuous success, the other aggressors join in, and Bulkaen's face is soon streaming with their spit as if with their semen: he describes himself as having become 'slimier than a prickhead under the discharge'.

The condition of his head corresponds to that of his penis, which, as the aggressors now notice, is erect and leaking in his pants. The spitters have not only wet him, and caused him to wet himself with desire; they have effectively *turned him into* his desire, which, as a cascading phallus, is the focus of what, ideally, he would seek from each of them. He comments, 'I was no longer the adulterous woman being stoned. I was the object of an amorous rite.' As such, he has become not only his own penis, but that of each of his amorous tormentors, and his own ejaculation is symbolically harmonised with theirs: he imagines himself caught in a shower of sperm.[12]

What started, therefore, as a rite of humiliation soon turns into one of sexual homage. Contempt has been transformed into venery and veneration. It is as if the spitters were jerking off in a circle around a pornographic icon: the close-up of a cumming cock. Bulkaen has mesmerised them to the extent that all their emissions (literally saliva, symbolically semen) have taken him as their aim. He is no longer humiliated; indeed, his gaping throat is yearning for them 'to spit more and thicker slime'. He is beyond mockery. The worst they can do to him now is stop. They do so, therefore.

This scene reaches the reader by an indirect route. It is narrated in the first person, as if by Bulkaen himself in a final act of brazen self-exposure. In 'fact', it is Genet himself who, for the duration of the scene, has adopted the viewpoint and voice of Bulkaen, taking on himself the other man's suffering and bliss. Genet learned about the scene not from Bulkaen but from Divers, one of the spitters. It is as though Divers had emitted the story into Genet, from whose mouth and in whose first person it must then overflow in a gesture of sympathetic identification with Bulkaen, whom Genet loves. In the original, every line of the account begins with the opening punctuation of direct speech, reminding us again and again that what we are reading has already been passed from mouth to mouth. Such gossip is tasty but nasty: pleasurable, of course, but ultimately unhygienic.

In Tony Duvert's novel *Strange Landscape* (*Paysage de fantaisie*, 1973) a somewhat similar scene takes place, in which a number of boys masturbate into a glass and then force an isolated victim to drink the outcome.[13] Of the perverse pleasures enjoyed by these boys, the greater is that afforded by the cruelty involved. Participation in this ritual seeks to prove, not only the maleness of the ejaculating individual and the virile solidarity of the gang, but also the domination of the weakest individual by all the rest. Each boy's laughter includes a note of relief that he was not picked to be victimised; mockery is a release from the possibility of being mocked. This is definitively but not properly a homosexual event. The concerns of the participants are less to do with sexual attraction to each other's bodies than with mutual homosocial affirmation, at the expense of the victim; their semen, brimming over the edges of the glass, is not so much an outcome of orgasmic pleasure as an instrument and sign of sadistic abuse. Yann is attacked as a faggot in a manner considered appropriate to his desires ('don't complain faggot [*monsieur d'la pédale*] here's something you're sure to like'), on the assumption that his effeminisation will be confirmed thereby. So if this circle jerk must be considered a homosexual orgy, it is, nevertheless, one from which all homo-eroticism has been expunged; the thrills it offers its participants (rather than its readers, for whom it is, of course, intended to convey an erotic *frisson*) are those of straight male self-affirmation over women and queers: that is to say, the pleasures of heterosexual homophobia. Likewise, for Yann himself, who is indeed gay, this semen has lost all erotic force – unless, perhaps, in future memory. Instead of eagerly gulping it down, he retches and throws it up.

The narrative's rapturous lingering on the semen in the glass ('the glass circulating from hand to hand little by little filling with globules dancing melting candle wax boils that burst like far-off flights of doves caught in sticky nets stretched stringy between the spout-holes of young cocks and the rim of the glass') bypasses the characters' viewpoints on a direct line from the enraptured narrator to the reader, who seems to be offered one of two responses: an equivalent rapture or total disgust. Perhaps, however, Duvert's ideal reader is one who experiences both extremes – a homosexual man who, uncomfortable with his own sexuality, masturbates while reading the scene and passes, in the long moment of ejaculation, from the extremes of pleasure to those of shame; from a short-lived appreciation of himself into the depths of self-disgust.

It may be that to speak of an ideal reader implies an unnecessarily restrictive intentionality on the part of the author. Rather, one should speak in terms of the ideal reading strategy: namely, with the book in one hand and the cock in the other. This is not a facetious point. It is clear that, unlike Proust, the other three authors are seeking to excite a readership consisting of homosexual men. These masturbation scenes are intended to encourage the reader in his own solitary enjoyment. In a tenuous sense, they temper his solitude: for, alone though he may be, he is nonetheless being manipulated, as surely as by his own hand, by the author of the piece he is reading.

Furthermore, the higher degree of excitement is liable to be stimulated, in the case of the Genet and Duvert passages, not by sympathy with the aggressors, the abusive self-abusers, but by an abject process of identification with the humiliated victim. The *frisson* comes less from imagining oneself as the triumphant spitter/ejaculator than in the thought of the taste, warmth and texture of his spit/cum. The reader is asked to explore the theory of his own masochism. Acting upon his own body, he imagines having no choice but to endure having his body acted upon by other men. He thus activates his own passivity.

It does not take a circle jerk to provide such an impressive munificence of cum as Duvert's episode celebrates. A scene from the schooldays of Alexandre, the most striking character in Michel Tournier's *Gemini* (*Les Météores*, 1975), reminds us that the sexual acts most likely to occur in school dormitories are collective acts of solitary pleasure. Notwithstanding the privacy of what happens in each individual bed, collectively these orgasms add to an already stimulating atmosphere of burgeoning sexuality shared. By morning the whole place stinks:

> The rule was that we had to give our sheets a shake before making up the beds. This simple action, performed simultaneously by forty boys, shook out the crust of dried sperm from the sheets and filled the air with a seminal dust. This vernal aerosol got into our eyes, noses, and lungs, so that we were impregnating one another as if by a pollen-bearing breeze.[14]

This daily rite, like the ostentation of stained linen the morning after a wedding night, marks the public acknowledgement of a significant passage of time: not only from night into morning, but from winter into spring, from childhood into adolescence, and from private growth into public adulthood. However, the process is by no means complete. These boys are not yet fully functioning patriarchs. The theme of cross-fertilisation (*une brise pollinique*) makes that clear: for boyhood still has a passive, receptive capacity which, lest any individual should turn into a queer like Alexandre, must atrophy before the youth can turn into a father. For all the separateness of their beds, the boys in this dormitory have not outgrown the capacity for mutual masturbation. Invulnerable to hay fever, they remain bewitched by the pollen of their own and each other's emissions.

The scenes I have cited from Cocteau, Genet and Duvert all involve displaced or interrupted oscular pleasures. In the Cocteau, the pane of the mirror comes between two pairs of kissing lips; in the Genet, a distance of fifteen metres comes between two mouths engaged in the salivary negotiations of a kiss by remote control; in the Duvert, glass again mediates, or intercedes, this time between penis and lips. This cannot help but remind us that solo masturbation is, after all, a kind of psychic *coitus interruptus,* with its break not exactly between desire and execution – since the act is an expression of desire culminating in a related orgasm – but perhaps between desire and any but a superficial kind of satisfaction. One is left, as it were, with the memory of a dream rather than the aftertaste of another man's body.

It may be, then, that we must include the Proust case in our catalogue of kisses denied. His is, of course, the massive book which so notoriously arises out of the tears he sheds when his mother omits to kiss him good night. This omen of the end of childhood should, I suppose, be paired with the masturbation scenes (though the former is dwelt on at far greater length) as constituting instances of loss and gain, respectively, in the transitions of puberty. A masturbating boy, distancing himself from his parents (perhaps literally, by locking the toilet door), gives shape to the future of his sexuality. (Engaged in the same act, a man may be looking to the past, with wistful regret.)

It is at this adolescent moment, perhaps long before he ever 'loses his virginity' with another man or boy, that a homosexual youth becomes actively homosexual – by a process, just starting, of self-definition.[15] It is in this sense that a gay man's masturbatory act may differ radically in depth of significance from that of a straight man. For one thing, it is an act of 'deviant' self-recognition, a physical confirmation and focusing of desires involving other males. To ejaculate while fantasising about men confirms that one wishes to ejaculate while not fantasising about them, but actually touching them. The masturbator may not yet admit to being gay, but he knows what he likes.

Secondly, in his identification with the bodies in his fantasies, he is forging a network of solidarity in gay pleasures. From his solitary confinement he enacts a future, if only a dream future, of promiscuous sexual relations with other men. This is a deed, albeit unconscious, of momentous sexual-political significance, which censorious approaches to pornography – from whichever direction – threaten to disrupt. The isolated gay man who identifies with pornographic representations of the pleasure of other gay men has taken a major step towards his sexual 'community'. He knows what he wants.

Chapter 28

....

Boys and Boyhood

Twentieth-century homosexual writers have been foremost among those who have analysed and described boyhood, either in memories of their own early years or in observations of the boys they admire and desire. The classic opening section of Marcel Proust's *Du Côté de chez Swann* (1913) sets a standard of complexity and depth to which few others have aspired. (By contrast, the Uranian poets in England were, for the most part, writing sentimental doggerel about the kissable but generally unkissed faces of schoolboys.) Some gay writers – like, for instance, the Australian novelist David Malouf in such books as *Johnno* (1975) and *An Imaginary Life* (1978) – have taken boyhood as their primary imaginative arena. This is not a parochial interest; or it need not be, especially when taken up by a writer as good as Malouf. It may be a temporary or intermittent interest, or it may constitute the spine of a whole career.

In this context I think of several major Italian writers. Sandro Penna's poetry has virtually no other subject than boys: he watches them, he listens to them, he talks to them, and whenever possible he makes love with them. Indeed, he explicitly asserts that every other topic is boring to him ('le altre cose son tutte noiose').[1] Similarly, most of Pier Paolo Pasolini's fiction – unlike his more complex and wide-ranging poetry – is about boys, either as remembered from the early stages of his own sex life in Friuli, or boys as later observed in and pursued through the urban waste lands around Rome. Umberto Saba is the third great Italian connoisseur of boys. His account of sexual awakening, *Ernesto* (written in 1953), merely renders in more or less explicit prose some of the erotic themes which he had already dealt with more subtly in his poetry.

A significant amount of homosexual writers' fiction deals with isolated boys who, in the absence of friends of their own age, turn their attention with some bewilderment to the adult world. Some, like Hurtle Duffield in the childhood section of Patrick White's *The Vivisector* (1970), watch with the early detachment of the artist-to-be. But what such a boy may see of adult sexuality is likely both to confuse and excite him. In Truman Capote's *Other Voices, Other Rooms* (1948), while peeking through windows in New Orleans, Joel sees, 'most puzzling of all, two grown men standing in an ugly little room kissing each other.'[2] Another good example of the boy as compulsive but bewildered voyeur would be Leo Colston, the twelve-year-old inadvertent Cupid in L.P. Hartley's *The Go-Between* (1953). When he realises that his two adult friends are enjoying a sexual liaison behind his back, and that his own goings-between were the instrument of their coming together, it is not clear by which of them, the man or the woman, he feels the more betrayed, and which he envies more. That is Hartley's point: the adolescent boy hovers in a limbo of undifferentiated sexual orientations from which he eventually has to emerge into the emotional and sexual rigidities of adulthood.

It is not always the boy who is the isolated observer. Often he is watched, from a greater or lesser distance, by a man who would like nothing more than to become his lover, carnal or spiritual – or even just his admiring friend: for men can just as often hero-worship boys as vice versa. Thomas Mann's *Death in Venice* (*Der Tod in Venedig*, 1913) is the obvious model here.[3] In the sickly child of this book – as distinct from the robust youth in Luchino Visconti's 1971 film – Aschenbach sees both his own past and his future, his childhood and his death. Tadzio's fragile translucency is, in a precise sense, angelic: his beauty is barely of this world. And yet, worldly it is. As both flesh coming into being and flesh under threat of fatal infection, as evanescent as it is solid, it is carnality incarnate. Like Phaedrus and Charmides and their pals in the *palestra* – what could be less spiritual than a growing boy?

Tadzio and Aschenbach are respectively pre- and post-sexual. (At least, they are pre- and post-sexually active.) But, far from leaving sexuality out of the reckoning, the story actually *frames* it: Tadzio is all anticipation, Aschenbach all remembrance, even if the former is inchoate and the latter somewhat desiccated. Aschenbach sees nothing but art in the artlessness of Tadzio's carnal beauty. This is a matter of choice – a turning away from the dangerous alternative. He dare not go so close as to feel the heat of life in limbs he considers orderly and cool. He dare not smell – still less taste – the sheer boyishness of the boy he is miscasting as a platonic ephebe. Tadzio, meanwhile, is simply growing up. Neither miracle nor masterpiece, he is just a kid.

Aschenbach's adventitious encounter, as he is first arriving in Venice on the ferry, with an old man who initially appears to be young but who from the instant of revelation seems all the more grotesquely old, is more than just disturbing. It is momentous and fateful. Of course, there is something banal about Mann's representation of this 'young-old man': at the most simplistic level of meaning, his presence is required merely to show the reader that Aschenbach, by contrast, is not a libidinous old queen. It has to be recalled that negative portrayals of homosexual men often occur in books which seek to explore male–male relationships which are not themselves supposed to be labelled homosexual. (An example which springs to mind is the sodomite monk in Nikos Kazantzakis' 1946 novel *Zorba the Greek*, otherwise one of the great modern celebrations of intimate male friendships.) But the young-old man is more than just a point of comparison – or more than that single point. More than merely what Aschenbach is not, he is also what he might well have become.

Even more disturbingly, he appears to be Mann's nightmare of what *Tadzio* might become. The boy desired will eventually desire boys, long after his own physical beauty has deserted him. The young-old man's coquettishness, which so appals Aschenbach, inevitably foreshadows the moment when Tadzio himself breaks into a confidential smile:

> and just at this moment it happened that Tadzio smiled. Smiled at Aschenbach, unabashed and friendly, a speaking, winning, captivating smile, with slowly parting lips. With such a smile it might be that Narcissus bent over the mirroring pool, a smile profound, infatuated, lingering, as he put out his arms to the reflection of his own beauty; the lips just slightly pursed, perhaps half-realising his own folly in trying to kiss the cold lips of his shadow – with a mingling of coquetry and curiosity and a faint unease, enthralling and enthralled.[4]

This is not unambiguously an innocent smile. There is a long distance – a moral distance, it might be – between 'unabashed and friendly' on the one hand and 'profound, infatuated, lingering' on the other. There is a distance between friendliness and coquetry. Moreover, the comparison with Narcissus, especially in its closing phrase, 'enthralling and enthralled', implies an exactly mirrored mutuality which can only exist in Aschenbach's feverish imagination. It is the paedophile reading of a boy's smile.

Death in Venice is one of the most extraordinary of all autobiographical texts by respectably married scions of the bourgeoisie.[5] It reveals so much. But it cannot be said to be particularly daring if we conclude that its revelations are inadvertent. (It may be that Aschenbach is deceiving himself about the purity of his feeling for Tadzio – but did Mann know he was?) Certainly, Mann did not hesitate to publish the story and did not fear that it would compromise his reputation. This tells us a lot about how he expected the story to be read. The fact remains that there is little but sensual promise in the description of Tadzio's smile. Those 'slowly parting lips' are 'slightly pursed', as if for a kiss; and that slight opening of the mouth is in both senses 'profound': physically deep and psychologically meaningful. One thinks back to the repulsively flirtatious mouth of the young-old man – that grotesque embodiment of inter-generational union – with its cheap false teeth and unceasingly suggestive tongue. The contrast between the two mouths is not between purity and lust – the Narcissus comparison is enough to have located Tadzio in the ranks of those who experience physical desire – but, rather, between beauty and ugliness. Where the young-old man repels, Tadzio attracts. It is by contrast with the repulsive mouth that Tadzio's lips seem all the more kissable.

The author's own past is so often the key to gay men's texts about boys. English gay writers like Paul Bailey, James Kirkup and Tom Wakefield have written autobiographies of childhood; and many homosexual novelists have produced important autobiographical novels on the process of growing up gay. Yukio Mishima's *Confessions of a Mask* (1949) is one of the first such books that spring to mind. It is particularly good on the relationship between hero-worship and the development of a boy's masturbatory iconography. Hubert Fichte's *The Orphanage* (*Das Waisenhaus*, 1965) and *Detlev's Imitations* (*Detlevs Imitationen*, 1971) go into even greater depth in their attempts to recapture how boyhood felt and how the growing awareness of the boy's own gayness both threatened and then affirmed the integrity of his growth. Similar projects include Reinaldo Arenas' lyrically surrealistic novel *Singing from the Well* (*Cantando en el pozzo*, 1982) and Hervé Guibert's clinical dissection of bourgeois family life, *My Parents* (*Mes parents*, 1986). Regardless of whether such novelists are interested in the aetiology of homosexuality – and most, I think, are not – their works are ruthlessly efficient at laying bare the earliest memories they have which can be even remotely linked to the subsequent development of their sexual personalities. These books reward the reader far more lavishly than the equivalent 'scientific' texts.

Clearly, if boyhood itself is going to be of interest to a gay novelist, it follows that many gay novels are going to concern themselves with the various kinds of loving relationship which may develop between boys. Some of the key examples of texts of this kind come from France. Roger Peyrefitte's *Special Friendships* (*Amitiés particulières*, 1945) is an account of a sentimental friendship – a platonic love affair – which develops between a fourteen-year-old and a twelve-year-old in a Catholic boarding-school run by priests. As a result of adult disapproval and interference (based on the assumption that no such relationship could possibly be anything but impure) the affair ends tragically with the suicide of the younger boy. The important thing about this sequence of events is that the boys' love for each other is portrayed as being both incomparably intense and totally pure.

28. Boyhood active in its element, watched by the adult artist. (Henry Scott Tuke, *Ruby, Gold, Malachite*, 1902)

This fact is contrasted with the general shallowness and impurity of adult relationships. Between children, friendship and love may be the same thing, and both have a spiritual dimension which is capable of raising two handsome, aristocratic boys far above the envy of mere priests and parents (or novelists, indeed). Although one of the priests gives a sermon in which he plays on the connection between the Latin word *puer* (boy) and 'pure', it is quite clear that he remembers nothing about boys, and still less about the true nature of their purity.

Henry de Montherlant's play *La Ville dont le prince est un enfant* (the first version of which dates from 1951 and which also exists as the novel *Les Garçons*) has a similar theme – a sentimental friendship which develops between a sixteen-year-old and a fourteen-year-old and is subsequently disrupted by envious priests. As in *Special Friendships*, the boys' affair is seen as a triumph of youthful spirituality over adult moral hypocrisy. Friendship is presented as a sacramental marriage of souls, in which sentiment and chivalry raise the mind above the body, whose beauty serves only as a pale imitation of the soul.

The boarding-school genre flourishes, of course, in English fiction too. Alec Waugh's *The Loom of Youth* (1917), written when the author was himself only a teenager, set both the parameters and the standard. The English 'public' (that is, private) school has proved fertile ground for the development of narratives of upper-middle-class adolescent homosexuality.[6] Implicit in most such narratives, and explicit in some, is the idea that whatever homosexual behaviour occurs in boarding-schools is not likely to extend into the later lives of their old boys. The institution serves a dual purpose of containment: having segregated hundreds of boys from female company – and even to a large extent from adult company – thereby encouraging the very kinds of intimacy which are officially most

29. Boarding school is the citadel of the passing phase.(Late eighteenth-century schoolboy illustrations)

frowned upon, these schools isolate adolescent homosexuality, keeping it hidden from the outside world – especially from the attention of fee-paying parents – but also, even more importantly, confine homosexual behaviour, within the progress of individual boys' lives, to its own artificial micro-culture and to the short duration of the individual boy's school career. A boy may love boys in such a place without, once he leaves it, ever being tarnished by actually having to *be* homosexual. Boarding-school is the citadel of the passing phase.

Of course, a boy need not be sent away from his family before striking up an intimate relationship with another boy. Indeed, he may well find his emotional counterpart within the very bosom of the family itself. Several major novels have given detailed attention to the ways in which brothers might relate to each other. I am thinking of the childhood passages in Patrick White's *The Solid Mandala* (1966) and Michel Tournier's *Gemini* (*Les Météores*, 1975), and the whole of Agustin Gomez-Arcos' *The Carnivorous Lamb* (*L'agneau carnivore*, 1975), which deals with two brothers who are also each other's passionate lovers. Although such relationships can only exist in violation of the conventional codes of familial behaviour, nevertheless the family home may be the safest place for a boy to test out his capacity for intimacy.[7] (After all, schools have a strong reputation for the bullying of sensitive boys. Think of the sadistic sexual episodes in Robert Musil's *Young Törless* [*Die Verwirrungen des Zöglings Törleß*, 1906].) Once the parental gaze has been ducked, the family home may become a more effective type of refuge than a school from the expectations of the outside world. And for lack of a sibling, a family servant might do. Michael Schmidt's *The Colonist* (1980) deals with a loving relationship between one boy and the son of his parents' gardener. Their two worlds, house and garden, while corresponding with the differences in their class status, are for a while united and enfolding. While the parents are absent, the parental home is an even more protective space for sexual and emotional development.

I make no apology for having had to list titles here. The proliferation of all major fiction on boyhood needs to be noted. Sheer quantity is a significant issue. If I have sounded a little like a bibliographer during the above passage it is because even the more important of the writers on boyhood constitute something of a crowd. In what follows, however, I shall look at one classic short novel in some considerable detail. My aim is now to address the issue of the child's supposed innocence, and the adult child-lover's supposed guilt. Does the lover of boys molest victims or does he liberate his protégés into their dormant but already present sexualities? Are boys inherently nice or – to use the simplistic opposite that sometimes appears to be on offer in William Golding's *Lord of the Flies* (1954) – are they just nasty? It may be that we shall have to settle on the muddled but plausible compromise, that they are not either but both.

· · ·

The text which first set out some of these key issues is Henry James' *The Turn of the Screw* (1898).[8] James received the idea for the tale in a conversation with the Archbishop of Canterbury in 1895, the year of the Wilde trials, but the written narrative did not really begin to take shape until the idea of the corruption of children by ghosts had troubled James for two years. The first thing to be said about the two children, Miles and Flora, is that they look beautiful: the narrator, their governess, describes Flora as 'the most beautiful child I had ever seen' (p. 14) – though this is before she has seen Miles. When the two appear together she says, 'I was dazzled by their loveliness' (p. 37).

Miles and Flora attract the eye, the lips and the enfolding arms. But from the moment when the governess admits to being 'lifted aloft on a great wave of infatuation and pity' (p. 27) – or, perhaps, from the very earliest moment, when one sees that the tale is by

Henry James – the reader is forced to consider adopting a sceptical attitude to virtually anything she says. Dazzled and infatuated as she admits to being, it often appears that she is an unreliable witness to the children's lives. The reader only ever receives images of the children as seen by the governess and the housekeeper, Mrs Grose. They are always seen from without. In that respect this is a book not about children but about adult responses to them.

It soon becomes clear that the governess is taking the children's physical perfection to be representative of their moral condition. Flora's 'radiant image' is 'beatific', her beauty 'angelic' (p. 15). Both children radiate a 'positive fragrance of purity'. Miles first strikes her as being 'incredibly beautiful' to an extent that immediately – despite his having been sent home from school for some unspecified but apparently extreme transgression – demands the homage of moral hyperbole:

> What I then and there took him to my heart for was something divine that I have never found to the same degree in any child – his indescribable little air of knowing nothing in the world but love. It would have been impossible to carry a bad name with a greater sweetness of innocence [.] (p. 25)

The governess is so perplexed by his dismissal from school that she uses it in his favour as proof that a boy's school is not the right place for 'something divine'. Since he simply cannot have been behaving too badly to be allowed to stay there, he must have been too good: 'he was only too fine and fair for the little horrid, unclean school-world, and he had paid a price for it'. Not only are both children 'quite unpunishable' but Miles – again, judging merely by his appearance – has 'never for a second suffered'. Combined with the earlier impression that he has never known anything but love, this inference of the boy's painless history leads the governess to a conclusion which is extreme, even perverse:

> He had never for a second suffered. I took this as a direct disproof of his having really been chastised. If he had been wicked he would have 'caught' it, and I should have caught it by the rebound – I should have found the trace, should have felt the wound and the dishonour. I could reconstitute nothing at all, and he was therefore an angel. (p. 36)

The problem is, of course, that the governess is not as clear-sighted as she imagines or claims. If one is to take seriously the epithet 'angel' in reference to a child one must also start to entertain the possibility, not only that children can be corrupted, but that they can in turn corrupt other people. The point is that once there are angels, there can be *fallen* angels. As popularly mythologised, childhood is a prelapsarian condition, subsequently lapsing through puberty into adulthood. Children are thought to be innocent, fresh and uncorrupted but not, being mortal, incorruptible. They are *at risk*. Childhood is not a state of unruffled peacefulness, but a moral battleground on which the future of the child as an adult is mapped out.

As she gets to know them better the governess is increasingly inclined to judge Miles and Flora in terms as extremely negative as her earliest impressions of them were positive. Once she begins to conceive of the possibility that the children are fully aware that their home is being haunted, and by whom, her descriptive epithets veer to the opposite reach of the moral scale. Suddenly the children are 'monstrous' (p. 56). Miles might well have been 'a fiend at school' after all (p. 67). Where once there were only the pure effects of unremitting love, she speaks of Miles' 'dreadful little mind' (p. 84). Soon both children have become 'little wretches' (p. 96). And yet, in a wonderfully Jamesian moment, the governess concedes that having adopted this new perspective on their behaviour, having accepted that they are morally imperfect, she now finds them 'so immensely more interesting' (p. 69). In effect, she is now able, at last, to see Miles and Flora as complex, ambiguous characters rather than icons of idealised childishness. From this point onwards she begins to be appalled by the very qualities which first attracted her to the children: for she starts to believe that these are deliberate. As she says to Mrs Grose, 'Their more than earthly beauty, their absolutely unnatural goodness. It's a game . . . it's a policy and a fraud!' (p. 89).

For the most part of the story, then, we have to think of Miles and Flora as classic cases of ambiguity. They are not good or bad, but both or either. This is the real seat of the book's horror: it is located in the governess' and Mrs Grose's *indecision* about the children. Every charming thing about them may be an act. Every smile or kiss may be cynically calculated to deceive. Where once their games seemed charmingly 'contrived' and inventive (pp. 52–3) they start to show disturbing 'signs of subtlety' (p. 63) – surely a more appropriate quality to Satan than to little children. Their charm becomes 'beguilement' – another Satanic term, suggesting both seduction and trickery – in as far as it has raised 'the possibility that it was studied'. Like the 'method' of Hamlet's 'madness', it may have 'a purpose in it' (p. 70). Even their sweetest kisses may be possessed of 'a wild irrelevance' stemming from their calculated nature (p. 98). This moral ambiguity attains a climactic pitch at the moment when, according to the governess, Miles plays the piano with a deliberately seductive charm so as to distract the governess from noticing that Flora has wandered down to the lakeside to meet the ghost of Miss Jessel. As the governess says to Mrs Grose, 'He found the most divine little way to keep me quiet while she went off' – but she immediately amends 'divine' to read 'Infernal' (pp. 120–22). By this stage in the tale, the children are represented as being more than just passively attractive: they are knowingly and actively seductive.

The most solid evidence of the children's corruption, particularly Miles', is in their use of 'bad' language. These usages go further than the telling of lies. They seem to involve profanities or obscenities which can only have been learned by inappropriately close contact with members of a lower class – specifically, in this instance, by contact with Peter Quint and Miss Jessel, both now dead. Some, if not all, of these utterances may be conjured up only in the imagination of the governess: at one point she conveys to Mrs Grose the strange accusation, 'They say things that, if we heard them, would simply appall us' (p. 125). When Flora is accused of having conversed with the dead woman, she replies 'exactly as if she had got from some outside source each of her stabbing little words' (p. 133). In her subsequent delirium this apparently supernatural ventriloquism loses all restraint: Mrs Grose reports having heard 'horrors' coming from Flora's lips, horrors about the governess. When Mrs Grose says, rather predictably, 'I can't think wherever she must have picked up – ' the governess intervenes with: 'The appalling language she applies to me? I can, then!' (pp. 140–41). It is not clear whether she means Flora has learned these new habits of speech from Miss Jessel herself – and thereby from Quint – or merely from her foul-mouthed brother Miles; but whichever is the case, Quint is the ultimate point of origin. It is his corruption that the tale's lesser corrupters pass on.

Bad language turns out to have been the cause of Miles' expulsion from school. In the last chapter he confesses as much: 'Well – I said things' (p. 157). But that is not all; nor is it all that appears to have developed between Miles and Quint. Miles has 'said things' not to all and sundry but to certain select individuals: 'only a few. Those I liked.' And he confidently adds: 'they must have repeated them. To those *they* liked.' These brief remarks establish the momentary suspicion of a murmur of corruption spreading across the school by word of mouth from each boy to those he likes. Was it in much the same way that Quint first whispered his affection into Miles' ear? And was what each boy whispered not only *to* boys he liked but *about* the very topic of liking boys? These can only be suspicions. Indeed, Henry James leaves them as weak ones – if nonetheless insistently present within the climax of the tale. It is while Miles is making his confession of guilt that the governess gets the strongest inkling of his perhaps having been innocent all along. Even as the spectre of homosexuality at school comes so close to explicitness, she is stricken by 'the appalling alarm of his being innocent' – and in all conscience she has to ask herself, 'if he *were* innocent what then on earth was *I*?' (p. 158). She would, of course, be the repressed spinster first identified by Edmund Wilson – a woman so twisted by her own inadequacies that she has apportioned guilt to those least able to oppose her: children and the dead.

Although Miles gets the majority of the attention, it is Quint who is cast as the tale's source of corruption. When he was alive, according to Mrs Grose, he zeroed in on Miles with a certain single-mindedness: 'It was Quint's own fancy. To play with him, I mean – to spoil him . . . Quint was much too free' (p. 48). When he died the tenor of local gossip was that 'there have been matters in his life – strange passages and perils, secret disorders, vices more than suspected, that would have accounted for a good deal more' than a drunken, accidental death on an icy slope (p. 51). Strangeness and secrecy, perils, disorder and vice – this is a strongly suggestive catalogue of defects in a character who is a corrupter of boys. (Miss Jessel exerts influence on Flora.) It is no wonder that Mrs Grose 'ventured to criticise the propriety, to hint at the incongruity, of so close an alliance' as developed between Quint and Miles when, 'for a period of several months', they were 'perpetually together' (p. 65). Even after death, according to the governess, Quint waits 'hungrily' for Miles (p. 84). When, at last, the governess considers openly confronting Miles with her suspicions of his willingly being haunted by Quint, she states her fear of the potential consequences in what may appear to be sexual terms:

> To do it in *any* way was an act of violence, for what did it consist of but the obtrusion of the idea of grossness and guilt on a small, helpless creature who had been for me a revelation of the possibilities of beautiful intercourse? (p. 152)

A little earlier in her narrative, the governess came up with an even more plain-speaking phrase to convey the kind of 'grossness and guilt' that she is afraid has developed between the man and the boy. Revealingly she says: 'what I had to deal with was, revoltingly, against nature' (p. 146). Few mature readers in 1898 could have missed the particular meaning of those last two words.

· · ·

Henry James never develops Peter Quint as a character, so the reader gets no clear idea, other than by unreliable hearsay, of what he was like when he was alive. We do not hear him speak, and we certainly never enter his mind. In twentieth-century fiction we begin to see, if only in small cameos, a little more of the so-called 'child molester' as a social being. It is not really until Vladimir Nabokov's *Lolita* (1959) that the heterosexual Humbert Humbert comes to represent in such detail – and often sympathetic detail, at that – the consciousness of the lover of 'nymphets'. Outside paedophile fiction itself, representations of boy-lovers tend to be brief and negative. In some cases the reasons for these fleeting appearances – that is, why these men are mentioned at all – remain obscure. The spectre of the child molester crops up in James Joyce's story 'An Encounter', collected in *Dubliners* (1914). Rather than have priests fill them with Latin, two boys who are more interested in Red Indians play truant for the day. After a series of modest explorations and adventures they are approached by a man who asks them about their sweethearts, goes a little way away and either masturbates or merely exposes himself, and then returns and talks to them about corporal punishment:

> He said that if ever he found a boy talking to a girl or having a girl for a sweetheart he would whip him and whip him; and that would teach him not to be talking to girls. And if a boy had a girl for a sweetheart and told lies about it then he would give him such a whipping as no boy ever got in this world. He said that there was nothing in this world he would like so well as that. He described to me how he would whip such a boy as if he were unfolding some elaborate mystery. He would love that, he said, better than anything in this world; and his voice, as he led me monotonously through the mystery, grew almost affectionate and seemed to plead with me that I should understand him.[9]

At this point the boys make their excuses and leave. The stranger's prohibitions on the early forming of heterosexual relationships serve two purposes: in the first place, to raise the topic of sex in the company of boys who excite him; and secondly, of course, to capitalise upon young boys' tendency to consider themselves superior to girls and all things girlish. He is trying to get the boys to think about sex in a context which excludes the female. His interest in corporal punishment at once expresses the only kind of physical contact a man might respectably have with the body of a boy – as so many schoolmasters have known and put into practice – and asserts his power, as an adult, over such bodies and their behaviour. He wants the boys to begin to associate heterosexual relations with pain – thereby attempting to dissuade them from ever entering into such relations – but in the same breath he wants to evoke, in their minds as well as his own, the image of boys' bottoms, sensitised by a good whipping.

This episode is tonally uncertain. Joyce appears to be trying to make it both shocking and funny at once. His interest in the man does not extend as far as his interest in the boys' reactions to him. To that extent, it is entirely to be expected that he does not make much of the man as a character. His presence in the story is necessarily sketchy. Remember that he is being portrayed from the boys' point of view, and can therefore in any case be only partially understood, if at all. A simplistic objection to stereotyping does not seem to me to achieve anything useful here. In a much fuller exploration of a paedophile character, such as the one we turn to now, such objections may appear to be even less convincing.

Christopher Robinson accuses 'the heterosexual Sartre' of trivialising male homosexual desire 'in an obtuse and patronising fashion' in *Nausea* (*La Nausée*, 1938).[10] Specifically, Robinson is referring to 'the caricature of Gidean pederasty in the person of "l'Autodidacte"'.[11] These few dismissive phrases do not seem to be an adequate response to one of the few prominent characters in such an important novel. Indeed, Robinson's approach is itself trivial. It is true that, if we must take the Autodidact as being representative of 'male homosexual desire', he will emerge as a familiar stereotype: he is a timid, loveless and sad figure with 'beautiful curved lashes – a woman's eyelashes' (p. 49) and a habit of staring at schoolboys in the public library. As well as being self-taught to the extent that he has spent several years working his way through half the library's significant books in alphabetical order of their authors' names, he is also implicitly a sexual autodidact: he is a fantasist and masturbator, but not, apparently, a rapist of children. There is no reason to believe he has ever had a sexual relationship – or, indeed, sex – with anyone, adult or child. He probably has masturbated in the presence of boys – assuming that what happens in the library at the end of the book is not happening for the first time – but Roquentin, the disinterested narrator, seems to think him pretty harmless.

The first hint of the Autodidact's sexual tastes materialises in the following passage:

> He was sitting right at the end of the table at the back; he had put a book in front of him, but he wasn't reading. He was looking with a smile at his neighbour on the right, a filthy-looking schoolboy who often comes to the library. The schoolboy allowed himself to be looked at for a while, then suddenly put his tongue out at him and pulled a horrible face. The Autodidact blushed, hurriedly plunging his nose back into his book, and became engrossed by his reading. (p. 60)

Boys are the one topic that distracts him from his systematic pursuit of knowledge. Where Roquentin sees only a distasteful filthiness, the Autodidact is mesmerised by the beauty of boyishness. On this occasion, it is the schoolboy who is in control, using a childish method to evoke embarrassment, if not fear, in the adult. He knows he has the upper hand. And the Autodidact knows that no amount of book-learning will ever make the wooing of schoolboys any easier, except insofar as an open book is as good a place as any in which to conceal the embarrassment of defeat.

Roquentin is quite sympathetic to the Autodidact's paedophilia. He is neither surprised nor shocked when the Autodidact finally, inevitably, gets into trouble:

> To tell the truth, I was scarcely surprised when the thing happened: for a long time I had felt that his gentle, timid face was positively asking scandal to strike it. He was guilty in so small a degree: his humble, contemplative love for little boys is scarcely sensuality – rather a form of humanism. (p. 228)

The latter is not a trivial word in the hands of a philosophical novelist; indeed, it grants the Autodidact's 'humble, contemplative' sexuality a certain weight of dignity. What occurs in the subsequent section of the book is another attempt to woo a boy in the library, another manoeuvre of tentative humanism doomed to falter in its nondescript space between real sensuality and real intellectual endeavour. Intermittently looking up from his work, Roquentin sees the incident developing: two schoolboys come into the library; they sit on either side of the Autodidact; he starts speaking to the younger of them and seems infected with the boy's youthfulness ('I had never seen him look so young before'); the boys appear to be in conspiracy together; another reader, a woman, starts watching; after a quarter of an hour, the Autodidact starts whispering again. Roquentin observes the boy's hand: 'Now it was lying on its back, relaxed, soft, and sensual, it had the indolent nudity of a woman sunning herself on the beach. A brown hairy object approached it hesitantly. It was a thick finger yellowed by tobacco; beside that hand, it had all the grossness of a male organ. It stopped for a moment, rigid, pointing at the fragile palm, then, all of a sudden, it timidly started stroking it.' By now, Roquentin is furious with the man – not for what he is doing, publicly stroking a boy's hand, but for not stopping doing so before it is too late. Roquentin tries to save him – he coughs and tries to catch his eye – 'But he had closed his eyes, he was smiling. His other hand had disappeared under the table.'

It is at this point that the character of the incident changes; or, at least, it is from this point that Roquentin narrates with a change of tone. A kind of courtship has turned into an assault – the Autodidact is masturbating under the table while continuing to stroke the boy's hand, which the boy is too frightened to withdraw. Some angry adult readers intervene. Like Roquentin, the Autodidact is unsurprised at their reaction: 'He must have been expecting this to happen for years. . . . And yet he came back every evening, he feverishly went on with his reading, and then, from time to time, like a thief, he stroked the white hand or perhaps the leg of a little boy.' Both narrator and author appear to give him credit for single-mindedness, if for nothing else. When the Corsican starts hitting the Autodidact in the face, Roquentin angrily intervenes and is accused of being another 'fairy' (*pédé*) (pp. 232–9). Later in the day, Roquentin wonders if the humiliated Autodidact, now expelled from the library which provides his two purposes in life, books and boys, will kill himself; but he reckons not. 'No: that gentle, hunted soul cannot think of death.' No mere academic theorist, he is far too embroiled in life, albeit humiliated, to be in need of an escape.

Sartre's portrayal of the Autodidact looks all the less careless when contrasted with such fragmentary appearances as that of Joyce's disciplinarian. There is an even more fearfully intrusive moment towards the end of Saul Bellow's *Herzog* (1964)[12] when we are informed for the first time that Moses Herzog was raped when he was a child:

> The man clapped his hand over his mouth from the back. He hissed something to him as he drew down his pants. His teeth were rotten and his face stubbled. And between the boy's thighs this red skinless horrible thing passed back and forth, back and forth, until it burst out foaming.

It hardly needs saying that this passage uses extremely familiar strategies in its deployment of images of physical and moral corruption. Both the rapist's hiss and his serpent-like penis, foaming as if with venom or as if rabid, evoke the narrative of the Fall. The rotten teeth, stubbled face and skinless penis add to the man's ugliness implications of dirt and disease. The account of the attack goes on:

> The dogs in the back yards jumped against the fences, they barked and snarled, choking on their saliva – the shrieking dogs, while Moses was held at the throat by the crook of the man's arms. He knew he might be killed. The man might strangle him. How did he know! He guessed. So he simply stood there.

These dogs give the impression of a natural world outraged by the sexual crime it is witnessing. They have also, symbolically, been infected by the perpetrator: in their howling and drooling they seem as rabid as the offending penis. The violated boy's stillness at the heart of this moral chaos is all the more touching for his instinctive wisdom. Self-protectively, he endures the assault without response. As he buttons himself up again, the rapist says 'I'm going to give you a nickel. But I have to change this dollar' and makes his escape, 'walking swiftly, with bad feet; bad feet, evil feet'. Like the boyhood assault on Snaith in *South Riding* (see p. 207–8), this is an underdeveloped incident which, in terms of its function in the narrative, is apparently expected to bear a huge burden of moral and psychological import on the strength of nothing more than the implications within a single paragraph. It is not fully integrated into the narrative; its consequences are left unstated, only to be imagined. The violator is never developed as a character: we know nothing of him at all. For all Saul Bellow's reputation as a moralist – a reputation richly deserved, perhaps especially by *Herzog* itself – there is something glib about the way in which this scene flashes before us as a moment of pure evil but is never otherwise developed as having a functioning relation to the novel's other moral themes (of which child-molesting is not one).

Yet another example of a paedophile character only fleetingly developed is Soaphead Church, in Toni Morrison's *The Bluest Eye* (1970).[13] Here we find an eccentric depiction of the heterosexual paedophile as a homosexual man *manqué*: 'He could have been an active homosexual but lacked the courage. Bestiality did not occur to him, and sodomy was quite out of the question, for he did not experience sustained erections and could not endure the thought of somebody else's. And besides, the one thing that disgusted him more than entering and caressing a woman was caressing and being caressed by a man'. In any case, he is disgusted by the filth of physicality. 'His attentions therefore gradually settled on those humans whose bodies were least offensive – children. And since he was too diffident to confront homosexuality, and since little boys were insulting, scary, and stubborn, he further limited his interests to little girls'.[14]

Finally, at an early point in Salman Rushdie's *The Satanic Verses* (1988), twelve-year-old Salahuddin Chamchawala is assaulted on the rocks at the aptly-named Scandal Point:

In a hollow of black stone Salahuddin saw a man in a dhoti bending over a pool. Their eyes met, and the man beckoned him with a single finger which he then laid across his lips. *Shh*, and the mystery of rock-pools drew the boy towards the stranger. He was a creature of bone. Spectacles framed in what might have been ivory. His finger curling, curling, like a baited hook, come. When Salahuddin came down the other grasped him, put a hand around his mouth and forced his young hand between old and fleshless legs, to feel the fleshbone there. The dhoti open to the winds. Salahuddin had never known how to fight; he did what he was forced to do, and then the other simply turned away from him and let him go.[15]

It is this traumatic and mysterious event that persuades the boy Salahuddin that he must leave Bombay or die. It is impossible for a child to take such an event as being anything but momentous: even if the abuser himself turns away abruptly, as if nothing much had happened between them, to the violated boy their collision has to have been of significance. The apparent indifference of the adult, once his inexplicable act of intrusiveness has come to its end, is itself an education of sorts.

· · ·

Against these characters we must set self-representations by writers who are boy-lovers themselves. Virtually all paedophile artists, homosexual or not, share a collective (rather than selective) approach to children, whereby it is childhood itself that attracts, rather than the individual child. Given that this is so, we can see that their work will have a number of common themes. For a start, if boyhood is so important, age will be a crucial theme. And wherever age is important, the theme of time is inescapable. Paedophile relationships are by definition short-lived, and their art is forever poised on the brink of nostalgia. So all boy-loving literature, like that of the *Greek Anthology* or of the medieval Islamic civilisations, contains a recurrent anxiety about the growth of body hair and facial hair, the ominously virile development of muscles and genitals, the breaking of the voice, and the possibility of a complete change of sexual orientation – or loss of docile pliability – at puberty.

Along with the physical characteristics of boyhood come all the allurements of puerility, the attractions of the *puerile personality*: the innocence, the enthusiasm, the flexibility, the spontaneity, the experimentation, the misbehaviour, the silliness and so forth. All or any of these may vanish at any moment, and the boy's personality fade into the uniform greyness of mere adulthood. So the literature of paedophilia is even more obsessed with the *carpe diem* theme than is love poetry in general. The paedophile *carpe diem* usually means: eat, drink and be merry – for tomorrow I die and you reach puberty.

André Gide's novel *The Immoralist* (*L'Immoraliste*, 1902) is a very succinct autobiographical portrayal of the intellectual boy-lover and his quest, which leads him not only southward – through the length of Italy and Sicily to Tunisia and the healthy colouring of dark skin – but also into the past: a social past, in which the loving of boys is highly valued; a literary past (because he spends much of his time, especially in Sicily, reading Theocritus) in which the loving of boys is celebrated; and a personal past, the past of his own infancy and puberty, still operative in the psychological present. In this way, loving involves reliving. But it is to a more recent French writer that I now want to turn, for a more explicit and detailed polemic about living as a lover of boys.

Where Peyrefitte and Montherlant found, or claimed to find, the heights of purity and piety, Tony Duvert finds an explosion of polymorphous sexuality (which, one suspects, is what Peyrefitte and Montherlant would have preferred to find). Duvert's boys are still conspicuously innocent, but not in the sense that means sexless: these boys are innocent of guilt and guile. In that sense, their indefatigable sexuality is the epitome of *pure pleasure*. In Duvert's paedophile universe, boys are two-sexed, insofar as they are both concave and convex, both fucked and fucking. But they are also *multi*-sexed: firstly, because of their mental and physical pliancy – their flexibility – and their lack of shame. They can perform many more sexual feats than adults can, because they have not yet learned not to. Secondly, they are still individuals, and have not yet got stuck in single sexual roles. So, Duvert asserts, there is only one way of finding out in detail what any particular boy's sexuality consists of: that is, by making love with him. You cannot judge one child by another. Add to this certain physical advantages such as the relative durability of boys' erections and (after puberty) the copiousness of their ejaculations, and you will see that the lover of boys is necessarily involved in a process of constant comparison between himself and the boys he makes love with – a comparison in which he is always notably the loser.

Like Casanova and Don Giovanni – and like the narrator, also, of Michel Tournier's *The Erl-King* (*Le Roi des aulnes*, 1970), who bathes in luxuriant heaps of boy-hair – the Duvert narrator tends to be a collector of erotic encounters rather than the lover of a single boy.[15] But Duvert makes what seems to me an important point about this obsessive habit. This kind of collecting is not a materialist obsession – no house is emptier, he says, than that of a man who goes cruising. It does not lead to an accumulation of boys, because, as we have seen, time passes and each boy becomes a man. Boy-collection leads only to an accumulation of memories of boys.

Although Tony Duvert often argues that the ideal location for a collector of boys is a large city – mainly for the obvious reason that, the higher the population, the more the boys – much of his fiction is set in isolated, non-urban landscapes. Three typical settings for his novels are the following: the conventional pastoral landscape of fields and streams and a temperate climate; the seemingly endless forest, interrupted occasionally by straight firebreaks doubling as roads, or by clearings around foresters' cottages; and the desert island. What these three types of landscape have in common is not a topographical reality, but a psychological one. They are all erotic landscapes – that is to say, not just places where erotic things happen, and not just places inhabited or frequented by lovers; but they are *erotic in themselves*. Part of their function is to represent and evoke certain characteristics of the human body itself, and thereby to contribute to human sexual pleasure. To make love with someone in a landscape whose caves and springs and woods and rolling pastures and crags echo the forms of the lover's physique is, in some way, to enter the world of the lover, to live within him as a part of him. And there is a very real sense in which a boy who wanders into (say) one of Tony Duvert's dark and shaggy forests – so reminiscent of the forests of fairytale, the bear- and witch-ridden spaces in which children like Goldilocks, Red Riding Hood and Hansel and Gretel wandered about – is *entering manhood* – and not necessarily only his own. What this frankly sexual version of the world of boyhood has in common with the more patrician and sentimental traditions adhered to by the likes of Roger Peyrefitte are two related beliefs: that the individual boy encapsulates boyhood and its beauty; and that adult authority, as typified by parents and teachers, is a form of colonialism from which children should be granted their independence.

The paedophile world-view depends heavily upon a view of the child as the embodiment of certain ideals which transcend the sordid and cynical realities of adult life. Boys represent the height from which human life then descends into confusion, self-repression and decay. Without their reserves of all the qualities which go together to make up puerility, they may seem like lifeless husks – or capable of being very easily reduced to such a condition. Once innocence and idealism have been drained off, one is left with something like the boys in Dennis Cooper's novels: dulled by drugs and void of interests, they fall prey to any man with the money for the next fix and a bed for the night. In narratives from 'A Herd' (in *The Tenderness of the Wolves*, 1982) to *Frisk* (1991) Cooper represents with chilling detachment the way in which the desire for an observable, physical beauty might become so analytically obsessive as to require the literal reduction of a boy to his constituent parts. As in Bret Easton Ellis' emetically brilliant novel *American Psycho* (1991), once the logic of desire is taken to its most insane limit, the desired body no longer has any connection to personality (a mere complication which can be erased by the simple expedient of drugging or otherwise incapacitating the victim), the skin becomes an obstacle to entry, mucous membranes demand to be extended – and making love becomes a process which passes through anal rape to the inexorable business of separating out bones from meat, liquids from solids, and scientifically exposing the mystery-less banality of life-as-meat. These are only intermittently novels about fear. For all their screaming when pain finally penetrates the haze of their self-absorption, Cooper's boys barely register what is happening to them. Given this fact – given the defining passivity of a boy who is half-way to becoming mere offal – they can be seen as representing, at its extreme, a certain kind of perverse ideal.

It hardly needs saying: literary representations of boyhood have come a long way since J.M. Barrie met a small boy in Clifton Grove near Nottingham and was inspired to write *Peter Pan, Or the Boy Who Wouldn't Grow Up*, the play for children which was first performed in 1904 and published as a story in 1911. It has to be said, even if it is not strictly accurate, that the boy who never grows up represents the paedophile's only real chance of a lasting relationship. He is also, however, a simulacrum of the psychology of the man who desires him: the man who chooses not to relate to adults, but seeks to return, whether literally or not, to the playgrounds of boyhood and their pleasurable games. If the body must age, it may be that the puerile mind, at least, can be preserved. By playing with boys, the man remains boyish. Whether you regard this as a way of retreating from life or, on the contrary, as a way of engaging with it at its most honest and least corrupted level, depends on which writer you consult at any given time.

Chapter 29

....

The Age of Antibiotics

....

In his 1976 memoir *Christopher and His Kind*, Christopher Isherwood raises what turns out to have been – and perhaps still is – one of the major difficulties faced by both gay and lesbian novelists in the twentieth century. It leaves a massive fault line all the way through the fiction of Marcel Proust, for instance. Writing about the composition of his novel *Mr Norris Changes Trains* (1935), and referring to himself in the third person, Isherwood says: '*Was* Christopher claiming that the Narrator of this novel was, in every respect, himself? No. Most importantly, he wasn't prepared to admit that the Narrator was homosexual. Because he was afraid to? Yes, that was one reason.' His aim was to protect his family, particularly his mother, from social embarrassment.

But that was, as he says, only one reason. The second is a literary one, which Isherwood was able to articulate in the 1970s, but which he thought 'must have influenced his decisions' if only 'subconsciously' when he was writing *Mr Norris*: 'Christopher wanted to keep the reader's attention concentrated on Norris; therefore the Narrator had to be as unobtrusive as possible'. Homosexuality would have been obtrusive, distracting. Elaborating his point with reference to any narrator who does not share the 'ordinariness' of the 'ordinary reader', Isherwood adds: 'The ordinary reader may be repelled by, or sympathetic to such a Narrator's reactions, but he [*sic*] will never identify with him. He will always remain aware that the Narrator is an individual who is very different from himself.'

One might ask, so what? Is 'identification' between two or more ordinarinesses the only way of relating to a novel's narrator? Be that as it may, however, Isherwood's point gives us a useful insight into the artistically inhibiting effects of social homophobia. If the narrator of *Mr Norris* had shared the author's sexuality, he 'would have become so odd, perhaps so interesting, that his presence would have thrown the novel out of perspective. It could no longer have been exclusively a portrait of Mr Norris. The Narrator would have kept upstaging Norris's performance as the star.' Again, one could raise objections here, relating to the degree of attention an author would have to pay to the narrator's sexuality. Could it not simply be taken for granted, without necessarily entailing the distraction of superfluous homosexual subplots, characters, conversations or whatever? Isherwood's presumable reply to such an easy question would be that, no, the 'ordinary' heterosexual reader of the mid-1930s could not so easily have allowed the presence of homosexuality to pass without generating an acute anxiety. The mere presence would itself seem virtually pornographic.

On one point, though, Isherwood was not willing to compromise: 'Christopher dared not make the Narrator homosexual. But he scorned to make him heterosexual. That, to Christopher, would have been as shameful as pretending to be heterosexual, himself. Therefore the Narrator could have no explicit sex-experiences in the story.' This must have seemed the ideal solution. It avoided the destructive trap into which Marcel Proust had wandered long before he could see what its consequences would be – the apportioning of his own experiences of love to heterosexual characters, leaving little for the homosexual characters other than relationships (or sexual encounters) paid for in money or influence. However, the main problem with Isherwood's policy is that it left a somewhat airbrushed, sexless impression of his narrator. Some perceptive reviewers noticed this straight away. One referred to the narrator as a 'sexless nitwit'.[1]

Although they have different names (William Bradshaw and Christopher Isherwood) the narrators of *Mr Norris Changes Trains* and *Goodbye to Berlin* are essentially the same man, the same emasculated simulacrum of their author. The latter book contains this narrative voice's defining statement of nature and intent: 'I am a camera with its shutter open, quite passive, recording, not thinking'.[2] This classic remark could be taken as merely stating, in a forthright manner, the voyeuristic function of a great many fictional narrators. But it can also be read as referring to the lack of engagement which was, as it were, forced on the author by what he felt to be the incompatibility between his own homosexuality and public expectation of 'ordinariness' in an acceptably transparent narrator. Detachment may simply be the sign of an unexceptionally efficient, self-effacing narrator; or it may, on the other hand, be detected as the scar remaining after an autobiographical novelist has had to excise all reference to his or her sexuality. That said, we need to ask if it is indeed true that the narrator of *Goodbye to Berlin*, nitwit or not, is as entirely sexless as the reviewer called his predecessor in *Mr Norris*.

Although both *Goodbye to Berlin* and *Christopher and His Kind* refer to the same physical space, the city of Berlin, there is a great distance between the opening page of the earlier book (1939) and the second page of the later (1976). This brings me to the exciting changes which gay readers have been able to observe across the careers of certain twentieth-century authors, changes brought about, to a large degree, by gradual liberalisations in state control of both sexuality itself and expressions of it. Certain authors have come out as gay, and their publications have marked the various stages in that process. This is true of Isherwood, but not W.H. Auden; of Thom Gunn, but not John Cheever. I mention the excitement of gay readers as distinct from many straight-identified critics because the latter have often proved petulantly 'disappointed' by the later books of gay authors who were at first so unthreateningly closeted. They will never admit that the later books of (say) Isherwood or Gunn could be better than the earlier ones.

Isherwood famously opens *Goodbye to Berlin*, not only with his claim to the passive objectivity of a camera, but also with an account of sitting alone in his rented room, listening to boys outside, whistling up to the windows of their girlfriends:

> Because of the whistling, I do not care to stay here in the evenings. It reminds me that I am in a foreign city, alone, far from home. Sometimes I determine not to listen to it, pick up a book, try to read. But soon a call is sure to sound, so piercing, so insistent, so despairingly human, that at last I have to get up and peep through the slats of the venetian blind to make quite sure that it is not – as I know very well it could not possibly be – for me. (p. 7)

This is the first of several moments in the book when he comes close to making an open statement of his need for a boyfriend – close, but not quite. He wants a whistled serenade to be directed at himself, but knows that 'it could not possibly be' for him, firstly because these are German boys and he is a solitary foreigner, but secondly because these are heterosexual boys summoning their girlfriends. Both national and sexual difference have isolated him. More than thirty-five years later, in *Christopher and His Kind*, Isherwood dismisses this passage as a cheap appeal for the reader's sympathy. He adds: 'In real life, the whistling would only have worried Christopher on some occasion when a boy *was* whistling for him and he was afraid that [his boyfriend] Otto, who had a key, might show up unexpectedly and find them together and make a scene' (p. 50).

In *Goodbye to Berlin*, Isherwood describes Otto's physique as follows: 'Otto certainly has a superb pair of shoulders and chest for a boy of his age – but his body is nevertheless somehow slightly ridiculous. The beautiful ripe lines of the torso taper away too suddenly to his rather absurd little buttocks and spindly, immature legs' (p. 81). In *Christopher and His Kind*, Isherwood comments that he 'nearly gives himself away' in the positive phrase about the torso, and he admits that he *therefore* included the remark about the legs, 'lest the reader should suspect him of finding Otto physically attractive'. In fact, he adds, his German boyfriend had 'an entirely adequate, sturdy pair of legs' (p. 38). There is something rather pathetic about this minor betrayal of truth; and yet, not only must it be one among many, but it should surely be allowed, here, to represent infinitely more, similar adjustments made by other homosexual writers before and since. That change from the phrase 'spindly, immature' to 'adequate, sturdy' looks unimpressive out of context. But it shows a gay writer doing what the homosexual writer he used to be could not.

One partial solution to the problem of unwanted self-revelation may be to publish anonymously or – so as not to *seem* closeted – pseudonymously. Of course, historically, the closer a text has come to being pornographic, the more likely it was to have to remain anonymous. I am thinking of *Le Livre blanc*, a beautiful little book now known to be by Jean Cocteau and generally reissued under his name; and 'The Platonic Blow' (or 'A Day for a Lay'), the pornographic narrative poem of great technical virtuosity (parodying the dreary Catholic poet Charles Williams) by W.H. Auden. One can understand why Auden was furious when the poem was published under his name in 1965; it is less obvious why Faber & Faber refused to give permission for a reprint in 1995 and the notoriously prickly Auden Estate threatened to sue the anthologist who had wanted to use the poem.[3] The most famous post-Stonewall example of pseudonymity is 'Andrew Holleran', author of the novels *Dancer from the Dance* (1978) and *Nights in Aruba* (1983). Gregory Bredbeck begins an essay on him as follows: 'Andrew Holleran may or may not have been born around 1943; he more than likely is white, American, and middle class; he probably lives in New York'.[4] These deductions are based on the known fact that Holleran's fiction is largely autobiographical. By the late 1970s this paradox, the gay liberationist message voiced through a pseudonym, really is more than, politically, Holleran's novels are able to sustain. By this point in our history, being *out* becomes one of the first requirements of the gay writer, as opposed to the writer who just happens to be homosexual. We might call this the main legacy of the confessional tradition of the pre-Stonewall period.

· · ·

Once the effectiveness of penicillin in fighting infectious diseases had been clinically demonstrated in 1941, the age of antibiotics began. Soon thereafter, for the first time in human history, sex became safe. I recognise that this sweeping statement is far truer for men than for women. I exclude all the other risks, physical and emotional, that sex and love so often involve – risks related to violence and poverty in particular. With this reservation in mind, sex nevertheless remained safe for forty years, until the AIDS epidemic began. For heterosexuals the Pill was definitive; for homosexuals – notwithstanding McCarthyism and its equivalents – the sexual revolution had started two decades previously. What others regarded, often showing classic signs of envy, as rampant promiscuity became, in certain urban centres in the United States and Western Europe, a way of living, a way of *being gay*. Quantity of sexual contacts came to seem more important than quality, regardless of how the latter might be measured.

In the meantime, homosexuality was becoming increasingly visible from beyond the enclaves of what paperback book-jackets often referred to as the 'twilight world' of its Mafia-run and police-harassed urban bars. And among those who began to comment on homosexual men, their behaviour and its implications were women to whom either gay sexual habits represented what straight men would be like if only they could – gay men could be taken as the symbolic representation of phallicism run rampant – or, in terms of their capacity for relating to women, gay men's intense interest in virility represented straight men's lack of empathic interest in femininity and female sexuality.

Feminist fiction of the 1960s and 1970s was uneasily ambivalent about homosexual men. They may be homosexual, and consequently less likely to cause direct harm to women in personal relationships; but they are still men, and therefore no less deeply implicated in patriarchy. The figure of the homosexual misogynist – or the apparently heterosexual man whose suppressed or latent homosexuality expresses itself in a streak of misogyny – looms large in women's fiction of the period. In Doris Lessing's monumental novel *The Golden Notebook* (1962) certain passages wax Lawrentian both in their contempt for the unmanliness of Englishmen and in the labelling of that shortfall as being related to homosexuality. For instance, at one point England is described as 'a country full of men who are little boys and homosexuals and the half-homosexuals'.[5] American men, also, are accused of being too interested in each other to be able to sustain mature relationships with women. When Anna looks at her naked body reflected in a mirror and reacts with disgust, at first she is reminded of a straight man who once told her that 'sometimes he looked at his wife's body and hated it for its femaleness'; but as this paragraph continues her revulsion is more strongly associated with male homosexuality, which is treated as being definitively misogynist: 'I was experiencing, imaginatively, for the first time, the emotions of a [male] homosexual. For the first time the homosexual literature of disgust [for women] made sense to me' (p. 590). Lessing gives no further details, so it is not really clear which homosexual writers she is referring to.

Not much has changed by the time we come to Erica Jong's *Fear of Flying* (1973), in which Isadora Wing wanders the earth in quest of the perfect 'Zipless Fuck'. Despite a certain interest in the idea that two straight men in a woman's bed might be able to explore that aspect of themselves which is homosexual, the prevailing view in the novel is that men should be good at fucking women, and that anything less – any other sexual interest or ability – is just funny. Jong's book explicitly refers back to Lessing's book's central concept of 'free women' and Isadora Wing shares Lessing's tendency to dismiss straight men who do not come up to scratch as crypto-homosexuals: 'I'd have thought he'd be impotent, or else homosexual. At any rate, it's clear he hates women'.[6]

In 1970 Kate Millett had published *Sexual Politics*, her withering and cogent attack on patriarchy. A large part of the book was taken up by a critical analysis of four major masculinist novelists of the twentieth century: D.H. Lawrence, Henry Miller, Norman Mailer and Jean Genet. Millett's inclusion of the homosexual Genet among the other laureates of what she called 'the pathology of virility' did not go unnoticed by those gay male writers who were bothering to pay attention to the new wave of feminist debate.[7] The political context of the liberation movements, of which gay liberation was only one, demanded a certain sensitivity to the needs of other groups and solidarity with them in their respective struggles for fair cultural representation. 'Political correctness' came to be used in the 1980s as a pejorative phrase by right-wing journalists. The same concept, when it developed in the 1970s, was a matter of meaningful courtesy. There is no question that its influence on the literatures of oppressed groups, minority or otherwise, has been both dynamically positive and yet, ultimately, restrictively negative. I shall return to this point in a short while.

One thing is undeniable. The age of antibiotics produced some intensely boring fiction. To my mind, the most obvious examples are John Rechy's *Numbers* (1967) and Renaud Camus' *Tricks* (1981).[8] The former, at least, had the virtue of novelty. The two novels' titles say it all: no potential character other than the author's own *alter ego* – Johnny Rio or 'Renaud Camus' – will ever be more than a 'number' or 'trick', and the narrative structure will consist of little more than a linear ramble from sex act to sex act. For the reader this is a frustrating experience: one is left in the situation of the cruiser deprived of the sex. The experience would be more satisfying if the books were simply pornographic – gay liberationist versions of the Marquis de Sade's *The 120 Days of Sodom* – and the drudgery of cruising at second hand could be alleviated with the occasional first-hand ejaculation. The odd thing about both books – contrary to the arguments of those who attacked them as pornography appropriate to the lifestyle of the 'promiscuous' faggot – is that they offer the reader a rather joylessly mechanistic experience of what could, in actuality, be a thrilling way of life.

It is true that Renaud Camus presents his book as having certain ambitions which need to be taken into account. In his foreword he writes: 'Sex has its joys, certainly, which are among the finest: but none which deserves to make it the secret *par excellence*. If this book helps to make its subject banal *as subject*, it will not have been written in vain.'[9] Aiming to make one's subject banal is, of course, a risky business; succeeding in doing so may be disastrous. Much as the 'we are just the same as you' lobby of respectable homosexuals makes for duller television viewing than do the more raucous transgressions of 'in your face' queers, so too does the belief that sex is banal make for more boring reading than the idea that nothing could be more extraordinary than the ways in which human beings routinely go about generating bodily pleasure – nothing except, perhaps, the subsequent ways in which they try to convey that pleasure to an audience of others.

On the other hand, it may be that the structural characteristics of novels like these are perfectly suited to the conditions, and indeed the aspirations, of the 'sexual revolution' and the first post-Stonewall decade. The sheer plotlessness of lives committed to a continuous round of hectic pleasures and the recovery therefrom – lives deliberately set up in opposition to the heterosexual plot of courtship and stable domesticity – might best be represented by some kind of urban picaresque. Remorselessly postmodern in its shallowness, such a structure could symbolically liberate its characters into new ways of living. A few light-hearted picaresque novels emerged from within the gay liberationist ethos, among them Daniel Curzon's *The Misadventures of Tim McPick* (written 1970–71, published 1975). However, this plotless aspect of individual gay lifestyles has most consistently been dealt with by literature which closely approaches the characteristics of travelogue. I do not literally mean travel books like Edmund White's *States of Desire: Travels in Gay America* (1980) – though that is a classic of its kind, now very revealingly dated – or Duncan Fallowell's staggeringly innovative *One Hot Summer in St Petersburg* (1994); but, rather, novels in which travel is presented with largely symbolic intent. Geographical movement, often apparently haphazard, comes to represent the roving of the liberated mind and the multi-directional cruising of the randy physique. It is also opposed to the stasis of domesticity. I have in mind books like the deliberately rambling (and long) novels which Aldo Busi wrote in the 1980s, and Desmond Hogan's beautiful novel *A Farewell to Prague* (1995).

The literature gay men produced in the 1970s was often ill-received by heterosexual-identified critics for reasons other than, or additional to, any obvious lack of quality. For one thing, most gay literature had more or less ceased to offer apologetic, 'respectable' representations of homosexual men for heterosexual readers; instead, it was written for gay readers, often offering them role models for use in the pursuit of the kinds of happiness that post-liberation gay life was meant to consist of. This was not unrelated to the second major point of heterosexist objection: happiness itself. It can seem that the sex in homosexuality is felt to be less threateningly transgressive than the happiness it may generate. Michel Foucault was probably right in 1988 when he said that 'People can tolerate two homosexuals they see leaving together, but if the next day they're smiling, holding hands and tenderly embracing one another, then they can't be forgiven. It is not the departure for pleasure that is intolerable, it is waking up happy.'[10] It is worth remembering the strength of anger that our reappropriation of the word 'gay' provoked in the 1970s: they wanted us to be sad.

However, there is a serious sense in which one can suggest that our happiness came to plague us, too. From the late 1960s to the early 1980s, nothing so severely limited the range of out gay novelists as the imperative to provide relentlessly positive images and unambiguously happy endings. Anything less would have been dismissed by gay reviewers as negative at best, at worst self-hating. All signs of unhappiness had to be given causes which were clearly distinguished from homosexuality itself. To the more dim-witted of writers, this meant avoiding representations of unhappy same-sex relationships. Above all, gay critics made gay writers self-conscious about their sense of appropriate endings. No central gay character could be murdered or commit suicide, even if for reasons clearly represented as being other than homosexuality itself, for fear of reinforcing the myth of the tragic queer.

Perhaps the most acceptable deaths in gay fiction at the time were those which occurred in Joseph Hansen's crime novels starring the insurance claims investigator Dave Brandstetter. The series started in 1970 with *Fadeout*. By centring each novel on the unwaveringly well-adjusted investigator, Hansen was at liberty not only to have gay characters killed by homophobic psychopaths – which was unlikely to cause offence to rigorously gay liberationist readers – but even to create murderers who were themselves gay, as in *Death Claims* (1973) and *Troublemaker* (1975). In cases like these, though, Hansen took care to demonstrate the perverting tendencies of heterosexism, which might drive self-hating homosexual men to commit murder. The problem was not homosexuality so much as excessive pride in heterosexuality. Always positive about homosexuality itself, and never apologetic, it was novels like these that met with most equanimity the conditions imposed on gay literature by the social demands of the gay movement.

On the other hand, Larry Kramer's much-reviled novel *Faggots* (1978) was, among other things, an implicit attack on the expectation that gay literature should offer the gay reader nothing but unambiguously positive role models. Kramer said in an interview: 'I purposely made the chief characters in my book intelligent, educated, and affluent men who should be role-models for the rest of us. Instead, they're cowardly and self-pitying persons who retreat into their own ghetto because they feel the world doesn't want them. . . . It just seems that we should be angry at our own cowardice instead of the world's cruelty.'[11] As so often, Kramer overstates his case by insisting on a clear choice between two alternatives, rather than allowing that it would be possible to produce a literature of resistance to 'the world's cruelty' at the same time as taking a critical view of gay complacency and cowardice. But it occurs to me that he would have been better equipped to do this through characters who were *not* necessarily 'intelligent, educated, and affluent' and who, therefore, *had* to struggle rather than rest on their laurels.

More recent novelists have continued the debate on the policing of lesbian and gay literature by its closest (lesbian and gay) critics. In her hard-hitting 1986 essay 'Is Lesbian Culture Only for Beginners?', Sarah Schulman writes: 'In what appears to me to be an attempt to manufacture, rather than reflect lesbian culture, like the Stalinists we have developed a sort of lesbian Socialist Realism which has come to dominate lesbian fiction.'[12] The implication is that there is a 'party line', if only a metaphorical one, dictating what a lesbian is and how she must be represented in fiction. Moreover, in representing her, all lesbian writing is expected to be transparently realist and, therefore, accessible to the greatest number of readers. This *reductio*, whereby all literature ends up being both shallow and relentlessly simplistic about lesbian lives, leads Schulman to complain that 'There is virtually no experimentation in language and form in contemporary lesbian novels' (p. 167). This is overstated, of course; but it usefully points up a potential problem in the literature of the pressure group. Aesthetics must never be allowed to obfuscate the clarity of the propagandist point.

Schulman is especially vehement on the limitations of so-called 'positive images':

> In terms of content, it appears that the main purpose of our fiction is not . . . to depict lesbian lives, but rather to argue for a specific point of view. . . . Succinctly stated, content is required to show morally superior, oppressed people confronting forms of social oppression. In order to show morally conflicted protagonists or characters with cruel or negative aspects, the author must qualify these descriptions by implying that their ambiguities are the result of social oppression. In other words, lesbian characters are not allowed to be real (p. 167).

The coming-out novel, in particular, whether lesbian or gay, soon came to rely on stock characters whose individuality was secondary to their social role. A prominent example in gay men's fiction is the unsympathetic, macho elder brother who eventually marries and has kids. Fathers were often similarly simplistic caricatures: they beat their wives, they drank, they talked about ball games and they despised their pansy sons. The son himself, the central character, was almost invariably good looking.

One began to think that gay fiction's only purpose was to serve adolescent readers, gently guiding them towards uncomplicated bliss in the arms of their first boyfriends. Far more novels were substantively set in schools and colleges than in the adult workplace. Some writers like David Rees in Britain wrote as much 'teenage' as 'adult' fiction, and it was generally difficult to tell the difference between the two.[13] Indeed, I am inclined to suggest that the coming-out novel was *always* teenage fiction, in terms of its ideal readership as well as its central topic. Little gay liberationist fiction dealt with (say) the kinds of adult relationships which men who live in suburbs or small towns have to lead, lacking access to the backrooms and bathhouses of the Golden Age. Even books with elderly narrators were likely to be nostalgically concerned with a remembered adolescence. Despite the fact that the 'clone' look of the 1970s (denim jeans, plaid shirt, facial hair) was, as fashions go, uncommonly kind to older men, even to the extent that pornographic magazines and films from the period feature a high proportion of middle-aged models (or 'stars', as they like to call themselves), fiction was still largely preoccupied with the problems and joys of youth. Even the relatively complex fictions of the Violet Quill group (Edmund White, Robert Ferro, Felice Picano, Michael Grumley, George Whitmore, Andrew Holleran and Christopher Cox) sometimes seemed like Bloomsbury for Boys.[14] It was always surprising to find that Malone, the alluring but elusive central character of Andrew Holleran's *Dancer from the Dance* (1978), is thirty-eight years old. This makes him virtually double the age of most central characters of gay novels from this period.[15] This was the other somewhat innovative aspect of Joseph Hansen's Dave Brandstetter novels: Brandstetter is not a beautiful young man. Beautiful perhaps, but certainly no longer young.

The gay *Bildungsroman* leading from adolescent masturbation – solitary and then mutual, guilt-ridden and then celebratory – to adult sexual liberation threatened, for a while in the 1970s, to limit gay liberationist writing to the repetition of a few well-rehearsed scenes. Some very prominent gay novelists began to seem narrow. It was not until the 1980s that they disproved this, both by demonstrating a manifest ability to deal with the subject of AIDS and by turning their attention to history: Robert Ferro to nineteenth-century Manhattan in the sub-plot of *The Blue Star* (1985); Christopher Bram to wartime Manhattan in *Hold Tight* (1988), to McCarthyite Washington and to thirty years of recent history of the Philippines in *Almost History* (1992), and to 1930s Hollywood in *Father of Frankenstein* (1995); David Leavitt to pre-war England in *While England Sleeps* (1993);[16] Neil Bartlett to 1920s London in *Mr Clive and Mr Page* (1996); Felice Picano to several decades of gay history from the Cold War to AIDS in *Like People in History* (1995), a novel far more wide-ranging in its time-scale than in the social spread of its characters. As Dale Peck has put it, gay novelists are 'trying to script themselves into history'.[17] One of the finest examples of this new ambitiousness is Patrick Gale's novel *The Facts of Life* (1995), which spans the period between the Holocaust and AIDS, and suddenly shifts Gale's career, impressive as it had already become, into a higher gear. With such changes, gay novelists have effectively broken out of the inertia which the age of antibiotics temporarily required of them.

As I have pointed out elsewhere, straight-identified critics, if they speak about gay literature at all, tend to deplore its increasing explicitness. This is one of the threads of George Steiner's 1975 essay 'Eros and Idiom'. In his 1977 book on *Homosexuality and Literature*, Jeffrey Meyers says that 'The emancipation of the homosexual has led, paradoxically, to the decline of his art.' In a 1989 book review, Meyers returns to the same theme: 'Explicit homosexual poetry . . . which rarely mentions love and emphasises the sexual organs and the satisfaction of lust, lacks both a transcendent beauty and a universal appeal' – as if lust itself were not 'universal' enough.[18] This insistence that books which are outspoken about sex are automatically lesser achievements than the rest, leaves Meyers in the absurd position, in the 1977 book, of having to imply – for he never does fully argue the case – that T.E. Lawrence ('of Arabia') is a more interesting writer than Jean Genet; or even, indeed, than Marcel Proust, who is far more explicit than, in his main argument, Meyers ever allows. If these implied attacks on the very idea of a gay literature had not been so ill thought out, they might have hit the very easy target their authors seemed to have known was somewhere available. The explicitness of the literature of 'emancipation' is not the point. After all, it is not unknown for great literature to be about sex. If there was a flaw which could be generalised across gay literature, it did not lie in explicitness as such. It was a problem of range and tone – and it was soon resolved.

Chapter 30

The Family and Its Alternatives

Once homosexuality comes to be seen and spoken of as incompatible with family life, and particularly once homosexual people are expected not to marry into the system or to take part in its perpetuation by producing children – as they used to – the family itself inevitably becomes a battleground on which are fought out various issues central to the struggle for gay liberation and gay subcultural autonomy.

As perceived threats to children, even sometimes to those of their own siblings, gay men and lesbians have often been made to feel unwelcome in those areas of modern Western life which are believed to be the exclusive province of families. Furthermore, having been made unwelcome in the first place, we ourselves are often militantly resistant to the seductive wiles of family life: we no longer wish to be inveigled into a system which so profoundly mistrusts us and all our motives.

And yet, no matter how often and how rudely we, as gay men and lesbians, have been denied our place within the family as defined by certain political and religious interests, we continue to have a vested interest in the future of the family, whether that future involves its ossification as an artificial instrument of social control, its development in productive new directions of supportive interrelation, or its complete collapse.

The cultural answer to the family lobby – that is, to those who claim the heterosexual, nuclear family to be the only moral (indeed, holy) way of conducting one's life, and who seek by control of laws and taxes to enforce that narrowly conceived morality – is to make representations of the family in all its possible forms. Gay and lesbian fiction represents the family variously: as a place of neglect, violence and sexual abuse; as a potential place of alternative ways of caring and loving; even, at times, and even in its most traditional manifestations, as a place in which genuine happiness can be achieved in spite of external pressures to discriminate against its homosexual members. Some of the greatest novelists of family life have been homosexual men. I am thinking of Marcel Proust and Henry James, Patrick White and Angus Wilson, and of particular books: Yves Navarre's *Cronus' Children* (*Le Jardin d'acclimatation*, 1980), David Plante's trilogy *The Francoeur Family* (*The Family*, 1978; *The Country*, 1981; *The Woods*, 1982) and Paul Bailey's entrancing account of a father-son relationship in *Gabriel's Lament* (1986). I am also thinking of literal brotherhood as represented in two extraordinary fictional accounts of the lives of male twins: Jean and Paul in Michel Tournier's *Gemini* (*Les Météores*, 1975), Lewis and Benjamin in Bruce Chatwin's *On the Black Hill* (1982).[1]

The fact is that gay literature has had a great deal to say about families. Indeed, the family is one of our principal themes. In the first place, it has constantly to be reiterated that homosexual women and men actually come from within families. Families create us, for the most part (though I am not saying that they *cause* us). In the second, we either come to an accommodation with those families, or we distance ourselves from them, or they reject and eject us. In the third, many of us create families of our own, or we find ourselves inventing new configurations of relationship which might be called alternative families or alternatives to the family.

When lawmakers under the Thatcher regime in the United Kingdom conjured up an anti-gay sub-clause (variously remembered, from different moments in its history, as Clause or Section 28 or 29) of the Local Government Act 1988, with a view to banning the use of public money to 'promote homosexuality', they explicitly denounced our living arrangements, whenever those arrangements involved our trying to be anything other than isolated individuals, as 'pretended families'. Not much imagination or information seems to have gone into this phrase: it appears to refer to nothing more adventurous than the homosexual couple, which was to be denied the rights assumed by even its unmarried, heterosexual counterpart. This is despite the fact that the very people who originated the clause were also those who, so often, so insistently, deplored the supposed fact that gay men are incapable of forming lasting, monogamous relationships.

The family is a weapon used by politicians to bash the supposed 'minority' of adults who live by other arrangements: single parents, same-sex couples, and even the broad array of people who, for whatever reason, choose to lead their lives unmarried, as single individuals. So, to repeat the point: in the face of official denials of our right to exist except as isolated spinsters and bachelors who secretly, occasionally end up in each other's (sometimes) legally tolerated beds, lesbian and gay novelists have kept returning to the subject of the family.

Take the example of Christopher Isherwood's novel *A Single Man* (1964), or rather of its homosexual protagonist George, who is consistently hostile to the conventional family of the American bourgeois suburb. George's hatred of his neighbours' ill-behaved children combines with his misogyny in silent rants against heterosexual breeding habits – 'litter after litter after litter' – and the liberal indulgence of modern motherhood. The presence of the neighbouring families combines with the absence of his late lover Jim, who was killed in a motoring accident, to enforce his sense of isolation within American life. The nuclear family next door is the outward sign of the excluded homosexual's disgrace. The very title of *A Single Man* signals George's irredeemable difference – far more foreign, even, than his British origins. The book's problem, to my mind, is that its central character is as single-dimensional as he is single. More sophisticated in the conception than in the execution, this most explicitly gay-affirmative of its author's novels is undermined by the fact that George's jaundiced anti-heterosexualism is unrelieved by any sense of the homosexual as a social being: George has no gay friends.

Looking back at gay fiction from the period since the onset of gay liberation, and thinking of the topic of the family, one immediately calls to mind the novels of David Leavitt, whose principal subject has been the effect of homosexuality on the affluent, white, bourgeois, American family. Most of the stories in *Family Dancing* (1984) concern relationships between parents and their children, and several of them with the ways in which the coming-out process intervenes in family life as a test of allegiances and an agent of change. *The Lost Language of Cranes* (1986) deals with a son who comes out to his mother and father, and with the latter's having to face up to the fact, hitherto concealed even from himself, that he too is gay. In *Equal Affections* (1989) a family has to come to terms with the fact that both son and daughter have turned out to be gay. To say the least, the presence of homosexuality is shown to complicate family life, or rather to complicate the most widely accepted, hetero-mythical version of it.

The coming-out novel, the gay equivalent of the *Bildungsroman*, is, almost inevitably, almost invariably, an account of the move away from the family – a move which, if not literal and physical, is at least psychological and in that respect irreversible. Take the example of Edmund White's two connected novels, initially planned as the first half of a tetralogy, *A Boy's Own Story* (1982) and *The Beautiful Room is Empty* (1988). Taken together, these two narratives lead their gay narrator from a family summer holiday when he is fifteen, through his college years, to his move to New York and his participation in the Stonewall riot. This is clearly a narrative of gradual and eventual self-empowerment, the first step of which involves negotiating a way to grow up in spite of, or by somehow sidestepping, parental power and its related instruments of discipline. To an extent, as in so much gay fiction, this involves keeping secrets. Call this the first sign of disloyalty to the family; it is also the first sign of an incipient, adult independence.

Of course, the gay adolescent himself is acutely sensitised to the new presence within himself which homosexuality represents: as in the title of Timothy Ireland's first novel (1984), such a boy may suddenly feel that his boyhood has been invaded by a gay stranger *Who Lies Inside*. The defining moment of estrangement is usually that of the first homosexual encounter, which in some cases coincides with the moment of self-definition as gay. In James Baldwin's *Giovanni's Room* (1956), when the teenaged David wakes up the morning after having made love with his friend Joey, his feelings of shame are closely connected to family: 'I wondered what Joey's mother would say when she saw the sheets. Then I thought of my father, who had no one in the world but me, my mother having died when I was little.'[2] In Rudi van Dantzig's *For a Lost Soldier* (*Voor een Verloren Soldaat*, 1986), when eleven-year-old Jeroen has a meal with the family he has been billeted with, just after having made love with the American serviceman Walt, incompatible thoughts – 'The finger moves from his prick to my mouth and rubs along my lips' – keep springing to mind.[3] A graphic account of how a sense of such unbridgeable incompatibilities can overwhelm the young gay character occurs in Jonathan Ames' novel *I Pass Like Night* (1989), when the narrator, at the age of nineteen, comes home after his first sexual experience with another man:

> I walked home, the sun had come up, and my mother was making eggs. It seemed incredible to me that I could return home from being fucked and my mother would still be making breakfast. My ass was burning, I had shit out the man's white sperm and I wanted to hold my mother to cry into her neck, to tell her that I had been fucked and didn't know why I let it happen. But instead I sat down and ate my breakfast, how can you tell your mother that her son feels like a daughter[?][4]

The supposed distance between motherhood and anal intercourse has been securely internalised by a youth who is still deeply ashamed of his own pleasures – though he will not be for long. He contrasts his mother (feeding and comfort) with sodomy (shitting and pain). If it were as simple as that, there would be no problem: for he could abandon the prospect of further sexual encounters in favour of loyalty to his family. But he is perfectly well aware – and the awareness is spelt out in his unwillingness to say anything about his dilemma to his mother – not only that his life consists of both aspects, but that his future life will commit itself more to the sexual than to the familial. His anus may be burning now, but there will come a time when it will burn for *lack* of being fucked.

At one point in White's *The Beautiful Room is Empty* the narrator's mother tries to persuade him to undergo hormonal treatment for his homosexuality. Gay fiction tends to portray such betrayals as being the common currency of gay youths' relations with their parents. But of the two parents it is generally the father who is seen as representing the greater problem.[5] Consider the following typical scenes, in which the sins of the fathers attain varying degrees of seriousness. In Frank Mosca's *All-American Boys* (1983), when Paul comes out, his father strikes him and threatens never again to acknowledge him as his son. In Robert Ferro's *The Family of Max Desir* (1983), Max is forced to give up dance classes when his father says they will turn him into a fairy. In George Whitmore's *Nebraska* (1987), Craig is abducted from his life with his grandparents by his own father, who confiscates his artificial leg so that he cannot escape. When Craig does manage to get away, his father catches up with him and breaks his arm. In Will Aitken's *Terre Haute* (1989), fourteen-year-old Jared McCaverty's father catches him masturbating over a copy of *Physique*. Seven months later Jared's father catches him again, this time making love with a friend, the suitably named Randy Sparks, and gives him a punitive belting. Likewise, in Larry Duplechan's *Blackbird* (1986), Ephrem is hospitalised when his father finds him in bed with a man and assaults him. In Jim Grimsley's *Dream Boy* (1995), Nathan's first affair with another boy is haunted by memories of systematic sexual abuse at the hands of his own father, an alcoholic and a Christian fundamentalist. In some books this vengeful, almost terroristic role is taken by an elder brother. In others it is the mother. In Stephen Benatar's *The Man on the Bridge* (1981), thirty-nine-year-old Oliver Cambourne's mother vainly attempts to bribe his nineteen-year-old boyfriend John to leave him. In Patricia Powell's *A Small Gathering of Bones* (1994), Ian Kaysen is disowned by his mother because he is gay. Later, when he is dying of a mysterious disease afflicting gay men – it is 1978 – he rejects his own gayness and has himself baptised; then he goes home to his mother. Intransigent, she rejects him still, causing him to fall backwards down her stairs to his death.

On the other hand, when parents get to be too much to handle, some extended families are represented as including one or two more sympathetic members – perhaps located in the family's distant outer reaches – such as Billy's aunt, in John Fox's *The Boys on the Rock* (1984), who allows Billy to stay in her house with his boyfriend Al, and only complains to them when their nocturnal fucking disturbs her sleep. In Tom Wakefield's short story 'A Bit of Shrapnel', when Malcolm is thrown out by his parents who have discovered he is gay, he is looked after by his sympathetic aunt Bertha, who knew about him all along. In Wakefield's story 'Gypsies', it is even a father who willingly gives up his bed to accommodate his homeless son John and his lover Alan.[6] Sometimes these guardians of the intimacy which is purported to flourish in families are themselves lesbian or gay, or are suspected of being so by the youngsters who come under their benign influence. (In Steven Corbin's 1993 novel *Fragments that Remain* it is Skylar Whyte's gay uncle Aubrey who takes him to his first gay bar.) When this is the case, they exist either as role models of how a homosexual adult might productively relate to the family they came from and contribute to the futures of its new generations; or they stand as lonely warnings of how a family will exile its unattached gay members to outposts beyond harm's reach.

Rejection by the family, or the gay character's rejection *of* it, returns as an insistent motif throughout recent gay fiction. Typically, a central character's biological family may even be dismissed from the narrative – if they are mentioned at all – on its very first page. In that sense, a lot of contemporary gay men's fiction is about what happens *after* the family, once parents and siblings have been escaped and, if not yet forgotten, at least left behind. Geoffrey Rees' novel *Sex with Strangers* (1993) opens with the following sentence: 'I had a thousand foolish, romantic reasons for taking the train to Chicago, but most of all I wanted to savor every inch of every mile of the distance that would separate me from my hometown'. This narrator, Thomas Hobart, is heading westward to college. He explicitly associates this move with the mythology of the West in the closing sentences of this first paragraph:

> I pictured myself in a black-and-white film, waiting in the dead of night at the depot in a desolate prairie town for the one train a day headed to the big city, and I was that innocent, bright-eyed farm boy who had saved up my pennies and was leaving the family homestead to seek fame and fortune in the great metropolis. The train would give me the time I needed to reinvent myself.[7]

Although he is moving from prairie to city, his journey is equivalent to Huck Finn's lighting out for the territories: Thomas Hobart is on a journey from confinement to freedom, a journey which constitutes the end of puberty. It is also equivalent to the moment at which one James Gatz transforms himself into 'the great' Jay Gatsby. Hobart starts to 'reinvent' himself – that is, to shape himself as a single gay man, unencumbered by family – on the journey itself. He strikes up a friendship with the gay sleeping-car attendant.

The first paragraph's point about leaving 'hometown' and 'family homestead' is made with even more efficient brevity at the start of Christopher Coe's novel *Such Times* (1993). In this book's second paragraph the narrator, Timothy Springer, states without any trace of regret: 'I had a mother, of course, a father, grew up in a house, was educated, but all that is behind me now'.[8] The rest of the novel concerns Timothy's relationships with a small number of friends and a lover. The family is no longer of any significance whatsoever, not even being mentioned when Timothy is very ill with AIDS. As a gay man, he has broken free not only of the Springer family itself, but of what *The* appropriated *Family* has come to mean in the right-wing rhetoric of the United States.

Even more summarily, Pai Hsien-yung's *Crystal Boys* (*Nieh-Tzu*, revised edition, 1984) opens with the sentence, 'Three months and ten days ago, on a spectacularly sunny afternoon, Father kicked me out of the house.' This first chapter, a mere short paragraph in length, only reports the moment at which A-qing's father, brandishing a pistol and yelling abuse, expels him from family life for ever. The second, equally short chapter reports the boy's expulsion from school after being caught *in flagrante* with the lab supervisor in the chemistry laboratory. Thus, the boy goes from being a son and schoolboy to his new status as queer outlaw within the space of a single page. No lengthy explanation or analysis is required. The consequence of queerness, in the context of home and school, is taken as read. Subsequently, when A-qing has developed a network of friendships with other rejected homosexual youths, most of them working as hustlers from a city park, one clause of their shared etiquette is to banish the family from all conversation: 'The one thing we denizens of the park never talk about is our own family backgrounds. And even if we do, we don't say much, since every one of us has his own private anguish that can never be told to anyone.'[9]

Abandonment can work both ways, however. One parent (generally the father) may do the rejecting, thereby leaving the other (generally the mother) bereft. Or a pair of parents may both be left suddenly and sadly childless by the single son's gay-related quitting of their home for the big city. In Desmond Hogan's first novel *The Ikon Maker* (1976), Susan O'Hallrahan spends most of her time searching for her much-loved son Diarmaid, often arriving at some address of his a day after he has left. By the end of the book she has to reconcile herself to the fact that he has gone to Yugoslavia with another man and set up home there. In Adam Mars-Jones' short story 'The Brake' (1987), a boy called Gregory begins his long trek away from his own family by using an assumed name, Roger, when he first starts meeting gay men: '"Gregory" actually contained "Roger", albeit back to front. All he had done was set it free from its confines, reading his name against the grain of his parents' intentions.'[10]

A homosexual offshoot will often signal the ending of a family tree. Something of the sort is implicit in this elegiac passage from the opening of Desmond Hogan's novel *A New Shirt* (1986):

> This bungalow where I live, the last remnant of my mother's and my father's combined wealth, enjoyed by an aged, well-nigh celibate man, who parades his genitals among those of other men on the slab which constitutes the men's bathing place on the Vico Road. Naked old men saunter among the nudes ready for autopsy. Occasionally a young man starts out of the white sheets of my bed in the morning. I have attracted him with liquor, with Swiss chocolates, with perhaps the relics of my youthful handsomeness.[11]

The bungalow, such a demonstratively suburban type of home, perfectly tailored to the requirements of the bourgeois family, is really no place to lure young men back to; and yet, as the home of a gay man, it is just that. The parental bedroom has become a boudoir, the site of the ageing queen's wheedlingly coercive seductions. I suppose one is reminded of the sacrilege of Marcel Proust deliberately donating his mother's furniture to a friend of his, the proprietor of a male brothel. The loss of Hogan's narrator's youth signals, also, the end of any chance that he might, after all, change his mind (or even his sexuality) and father a new bud on the family tree. He is more than just negligently what used to be called a confirmed bachelor: he is irreversibly committed to being childless.

In Robert Ferro's *The Family of Max Desir* (1983), much fuss is caused when a niece makes a tapestry of the family tree and includes not only Max himself, but also his lover Nick, with whom he has lived for fifteen years. A feud ensues, in which Max threatens to leave the family altogether unless the tapestry is restored to its place on the wall. Eventually, he gets his way. Ferro's novel usefully reminds us that not all families are nuclear. Not all are shaped in uniform accordance with the post-war Anglo-American model. In certain ethnic and cultural groups, such as the Italo-Americans in Ferro's background, it is the extended family which still holds sway. Although the extended family is less easy to escape than the nuclear family, it appears to give its gay members less reason to wish to escape. Indeed, as often represented in the fiction of various non-white cultures, the family is an entity which one could not possibly conceive of wanting to leave. It is, after all, the surest anchor to one's cultural background.

One sees this in any number of African-American novels; one sees it in Caribbean fiction. As an example, H. Nigel Thomas' *Spirits in the Dark* (1993) is not untypical. At the age of forty-five, having at last come to an accommodation with his homosexuality, Thomas' central character Jerome contemplates emigrating from his native Isabella Island in order to escape local homophobia. However, he hallucinates a trip 'back' to Africa with his grandmother, whose intention is to teach him to respect, and remain attached to, his roots. She persuades him not only to stay put, but to fight for his right to do so as a gay man. By implication, there is more to be lost to the white racism he would experience as an isolated black man elsewhere than to the black homophobia he will continue to experience, but which he will increasingly become able to resist, as a gay man within his own relatively protective culture.

Although a gay youth's alienation from the extended family is likely to seem no less acute than that of some other youth in a more exposed position in the smaller, nuclear family in the first moments of gay self-awareness, the external pressure of racism ensures that the family is still the safest place to be. The Tamil Canadian writer Shyam Selvadurai examines this situation in his first novel, *Funny Boy* (1994). While still at school, Arjie becomes the lover of another boy, Shehan, and instantly realises that this will affect his relationship with his family:

> My eyes came to rest on my parents. As I gazed at Amma [his mother], I felt a sudden sadness. What had happened between Shehan and me over the last few days had changed my relationship with her forever. I was no longer a part of my family in the same way. I now inhabited a world they didn't understand and into which they couldn't follow me.[12]

In part, of course, this sense of change can be found in the literature of male adolescence in general: the move away from the mother, the affectation of a detached, 'manly' attitude to those one loves, and so on. But Selvadurai emphasises that the above reaction occurs immediately after Arjie embraces Shehan, and that it is the nature of the embrace, rather than puberty itself, that effects the change. Despite the acknowledged sadness, there is no sign that Arjie thinks he will actually have to leave the family. The key word is 'changed', not ended. Indeed, it would probably be fair to say that he cannot conceive of life without them. He remains a part of his family, and will accompany them when they enter Canada as refugees; but he can no longer relate to them 'in the same way'. From now on, he will be a gay man – and a Canadian one at that, increasingly acculturated in a North American fashion. But the implication seems to be that, like his counterparts in other novels from the various non-white diasporas, he will not abandon his roots: for these tend to be cultures in which 'family' is not yet a dirty word – or a right-wing word, which amounts to the same thing.

However, once the family *has* been left behind – typically, once the gay son has left home and moved to a big city, perhaps even a foreign city – his new life as a gay man takes shape, firstly, of course, around the meeting of and having sex with other gay men; but secondly, often, with the meeting of and confiding in that stock character who provides gay men with a non-familial substitute for, or alternative to, sisterhood: the woman friend. She is usually heterosexual (though some novels deal with the loving relationship which develops between a gay man and a lesbian, as happens between David and Beth in Gary Glickman's 1987 novel *Years from Now*). She is often either a workmate or a fellow tenant in cheap accommodation. She often begins by being romantically or sexually interested in him, at least until she realises he is gay. She is often the first person he has dared to talk to about his sexuality. The most famous early example of this type of relationship – even if the man is not openly presented as being gay – is between Christopher Isherwood's Christopher Isherwood and Sally Bowles.

There is a moment in *Goodbye to Berlin* when Christopher has the following exchange with Sally:

> 'Then you do like me, Christopher darling?'
> 'Yes, of course I like you, Sally. What did you think?'
> 'But you're not in love with me, are you?'
> 'No. I'm not in love with you.'
> 'I'm awfully glad. I've wanted you to like me ever since we first met. But I'm glad

you're not in love with me, because, somehow, I couldn't possibly be in love with you – so, if you had been, everything would have been spoilt.'
'Well then, that's very lucky, isn't it?'[13]

These brisk negotiations institute the platonic intimacy of their friendship. In *Christopher and His Kind*, Isherwood misquotes himself when providing a gloss on this dialogue: 'The "somehow or other" may be taken to suggest that Sally knows instinctively that Christopher is homosexual – or it may not.'[14] The rather complacent playfulness of this remark airily conflates *Goodbye to Berlin* and real life in an unhelpful way; but unlike the fictional version of the conversation, it does at least acknowledge that homosexuality is the unspoken gist of what is being said. What I mean is that the famous relationship between Christopher Isherwood and Sally Bowles depends on its being between a gay man and a straight woman. It may not actually be the model of so many similar relationships in later gay fiction, but it is certainly their major precursor. The unspoken dynamic in the relationship as represented in *Goodbye to Berlin* lies in their shared appreciation of the sexiness of young men. What sets them apart is that Sally can become pregnant as a consequence of her affairs, whereas Christopher cannot.

Also worth recording in this context is Shelagh Delaney's play *A Taste of Honey* (1958). The effeminate, homosexual Geof is the only friend available to Jo, as she is to him. She gives him shelter in her flat and he returns the favour by treating her with the gentle respect she has never received from others who were supposedly close to her. This is not to say that she is always kind to him – on two occasions, for instance, she demands that he tell her exactly what he does in bed, or she will throw him out of her flat – but her teasing of him is certainly affectionate, for the most part, unlike that of her mother, Helen, and Helen's lover, Peter. Jo says that Geof is like a sister to her, and that he would make somebody a wonderful wife. She describes him and Helen as a couple of old women. As in the case of Sally Bowles, the threat of becoming a single mother temporarily brings the heterosexual woman even closer to the homosexual man. Jo is pregnant; Geof is palpably not the father; and for a while they happily fantasise about the possibility of bringing up the child together. Complete freedom from sexual relations, it is often implied in such texts, could be the making of a properly respectful relationship between the sexes. But this is no less of a whimsical fantasy in authors than it is in Jo and Geof: the sanctity of heterosexual relations is never allowed to fall. This new family unit is never more than proposed before more practical closures are devised.

Among the more famous recent examples of this type of relationship are Michael 'Mouse' Tolliver's friendship with Mona Ramsay and then Mary Ann Singleton in Armistead Maupin's *Tales of the City* sequence; and the intermittently sexual – and almost marital – relationship between the narrator and Maria in Edmund White's *The Beautiful Room is Empty*. A less well known but no less interesting example occurs in Stephen McCauley's *The Object of My Affection* (1987), which opens with Nina Borowski announcing to her gay flatmate George Mullen that she is pregnant. Indeed, she tells George before she tells her boyfriend Howard. After an initial period of depression, Nina decides to have the baby but not to marry Howard; instead, she says she would like to bring the child up with George. This does not happen. George sees Nina through her pregnancy but then, as prearranged, leaves her (but not before they have made love once, when she is heavily pregnant). After a good deal of gentle re-education, Howard turns out to be the kind of caring babysitter that no single mother could afford to discard lightly. By the end of the book, Nina is sharing a flat with Molly, who is the mother of Paul, with whom George is starting a relationship, and Howard is minding his own baby.

A surprisingly large number of gay novels include temporary interludes with babies, as in chapter 9 of Christopher Bram's wonderful novel *Surprising Myself* (1987), when gay lovers Joel and Corey look after the baby of Joel's sister Liza, who has just walked out on her husband. Other novels have taken the juxtaposition of baby and gay man as their comical but still basically serious starting point. At the beginning of Patrick Gale's *Kansas in August* (1987) a gay man called Hilary Metcalf finds an abandoned baby and takes him home. Much of the rest of the novel concerns his efforts, firstly, to look after the child and, secondly, to persuade the authorities to allow him to do so, officially and for good. Eric Shaw Quinn's novel *Say Uncle* (1994) is entirely built upon the premise of a gay man assuming responsibilities *in loco parentis* when his sister and brother-in-law are killed in a car crash but their baby son survives. As the rear cover of the Plume paperback edition puts it, 'the author celebrates the many forms a family can take and the triumph of individualism over straightlaced conformity'.

In Michael Cunningham's *A Home at the End of the World* (1990), the contingencies of postmodern love produce a triangle of two men and a woman: gay Jonathan, straight Bobby, and Clare. Often they parody a more conventional arrangement, thinking of themselves as a family called 'the Hendersons', with Clare playing 'Mom', Bobby 'Junior', and Jonathan 'uncle Jonny'. But reality overtakes them in the shape of a child. Clare is her mother and Bobby the biological father, but little Rebecca is born into a family with two fathers. Later, the four of them are joined by Erich, a lover of Jonathan's, whom they all nurse towards his AIDS-related death. Although this is a relentlessly positive representation of alternative familial configurations, Cunningham does not allow it to last. Erich, of course, has to die; and Clare decides to exchange her life as maternal wife to two adult men for the rigours of single motherhood.

In Greg Johnson's *Pagan Babies* (1993), gay Clifford Bannon and straight Janice Rungren remain friends long after they have attended Catholic school together. At the end of the first half of the novel, Janice is pregnant by Clifford and they are about to get married, in spite of all of his misgivings: 'And, he thought, he did love Janice, however guardedly, however fearfully at times, and surely this baby would bring them closer, maybe they would be a blithe carefree "counterculture" family – Clifford working at his art, Janice happy at home in her long hair and sandals, the baby plump, naked, babbling'.[15] However, on their way to Atlanta to get married, they have a car crash and she has a miscarriage.

Throughout the novel, Janice is eager to forge familial bonds with close groups of her friends and lovers. Even when having dinner with her lover Jack Lassiter and her friends Belinda and Graham, a dinner rendered particularly awkward by Graham's alcoholism, Janice thinks of the four of them as having become 'a family of sorts, a group she thought would remain close to one another all their lives' (p. 213). In this second half of the book, Clifford has come out to Janice as gay – but not, later, as being in the habit of sleeping with her lover. At one point, Clifford receives a phone call in which Janice 'talked in her usual way of their being a "family" of sorts, of how much she wanted them to grow closer as time passed'. Meanwhile, Clifford is lying in bed with Jack, both naked, still sweaty from love-making, and exchanging panic-stricken glances (pp. 246–7). Later, when she walks in on them one day and realises they are lovers, she miscarries her and Jack's baby.

The novel ends with a rather disturbing display of what we might want to call 'family-envy'. (There is a need for some such term, given how often this syndrome crops up in recent fiction, both gay and lesbian.) Janice and Clifford, the latter against his better judgement, attend Mass together. They hold hands. Both of them are mesmerised by the members of an apparently perfect family, who are sitting directly in front of them:

Between the woman and her husband are their small children, a boy and two girls, all under age eight. The children are exquisite replicas of the parents, their hair dark and shining, pink faces glowing with health. Every few seconds the mother bends down, smiling, her own face pink and glowing, to answer one of their questions, or to straighten a hair bow or collar. (p. 307)

Before the service has come to a close, Janice has deposited her IUD in the collection plate and decided to ask Clifford to father her child. Some readers might take this ending, far from being happy, as a rather sinister capitulation to 'family values', and as such a jarringly unsuitable ending to a gay novel. Although one has a certain amount of sympathy with it, this would be an unfortunate response, especially since it appears to suggest that gay writers must toe a particular ideological line when closing their narratives; and we have already seen what an impoverishing effect the demand for happy endings had on gay fiction during the age of antibiotics. The point is, not that Janice and Clifford must now go forth and multiply in accordance with a narrow version of God's will, but that they can have a child – along with all the new joys and problems that it would bring into their lives – in *their own* manner, according to their own will. Read as such, then, this ending would constitute a symbolic reappropriation of the family to alternative uses.

The other common reaction to the closed unit of the heterosexual family is sceptical and negative. It is well represented in chapter 9 of David Plante's novel *The Catholic* (1985), when the depressed narrator, seeking distraction, calls on a straight couple, Roberta and Charlie, and their small baby. He cannot believe that they find the necessary restrictions of their present life sufficient. He writes: 'I began to imagine it was more dangerous for me to be among them than to be alone, because they were a family, and as a family all their relationships were fixed and everything they said and did was predictable. I sensed that among them nothing could be different.' This contrasting of the fluidity of gay lives with the constraints of the nuclear family depends on a consciousness and acceptance of the gay man's own difference. It is not conducive to assimilationist conclusions.

The fact is, also, that the narrator cannot believe that Charlie, whom he desires, finds heterosexuality sufficient to his emotional and sexual needs. He thinks in Charlie's direction, demonstratively, as if attempting an experiment in sexually predatory ESP: 'I could show you a time you've never even dreamed of'. As if to convey a little of the same thought in words, he asks them both, 'Don't you two ever get bored being a family?' Charlie seems bewildered by the question – he simply repeats the key word as if it had never heard it spoken out loud, 'Bored?' – but Roberta, who is feeding the baby, dismissively replies, 'Of course we get bored.' Her pragmatism may be taken as a sign of maturity in such a moment of practical maternalism – fit to be contrasted with the puerile restlessness of the gay man, or perhaps even of manhood in general – or it may be a signal that Roberta and Charlie have, indeed, made the wrong choices by circumscribing their youthfulness with conventional, predetermined roles. There is also the baby itself to be taken into account. What are the futures which families offer their children? What are their choices? The unsuitability of the conventional family as a space for the nurturing of young gay children has already been expressed in the regretful opening sentence of chapter 2: 'Walt Whitman's poetry never appeared in the house I grew up in.'[16]

This is not merely a point about Whitman in particular or even poetry in general. It relates to heterosexual parents' unreadiness (in the sense of their lacking both the preparation and the will) to bring up homosexual children. Indeed, it is thought to be the first duty of the good parent to ensure that the first and faintest signs of deviancy be instantly suppressed. Given this fact of how we are brought up in an atmosphere of enforced sexual conformity, it is entirely conceivable that a man who is trying to suppress his gayness, or who has not recognised it yet, may get married and raise children. David Leavitt's *The Lost Language of Cranes*, as we have seen, deals centrally with this situation, when the father realises that his son is gay. In *Out of the Winter Gardens* (1984), David Rees' novel for teenagers, partly based on the author's own experiences of parenthood, a gay father comes out to his straight sixteen-year-old son and develops their relationship from there.

. . .

There comes a point at which it seems impossible for some gay writers to take these things – matrimony, the family, parenthood and whatnot – with the sanctimonious seriousness that is generally expected. It is in such a mood that one might turn to Joe Orton's farcical demolition of the supposed proprieties of family life in *Entertaining Mr Sloane* (1964), which ends with such a gloriously cynical family arrangement, whereby brother and sister Ed and Kath blackmail Mr Sloane into remaining with them, not only as part of their family but as a sexual partner to each of them in turn; and in *What the Butler Saw* (1969), where it appears that the only family members who do not end up having sex with each other are the father and mother, husband and wife.

Orton is by no means an isolated case. But most outright gay opposition to the family is stated in far more serious, often angry tones. The names of other major gay writers come to mind in this context of hostility to the family: William Burroughs, Jean Genet, Pierre Guyotat, Gerard Reve – all the most self-conscious and self-confident transgressives. Consciousness of outlaw status has often generated great hostility to the very idea of family, partly because the family is itself likely to have been one of the first excluding instruments which framed the (literal or metaphorical) law in the first place. (Outlaws and inlaws are, simply, not compatible.) Such hostility may be particularly acute in paedophile writing. One thinks of the case of the militantly paedophile Tony Duvert, according to whom the motto of conventional parenthood is always 'No!' He remembers his father saying, 'If I had a homosexual son I would kill him!' and his mother more conciliatorily interposing that it might be better to kill the homosexuality and keep the son. His counter-argument has since been that children need protection not so much from paedophiles as from the heterosexual dictatorship. The homosexual boy, too, is in need of protection – from his own family.[17]

Most AIDS-related drama has its crucial family scenes. For instance, in William M. Hoffman's *As Is* (1985) the brother of Rich, the gay man with AIDS, slowly comes to be able to speak to him about his illness, and to touch him, even though he never quite manages to memorise the name of Rich's long-term lover Saul.[18] In Howard Schuman's television play *Nervous Energy* (1995) Tom, who has AIDS, returns to his native Glasgow in a vain attempt to come to some kind of reconciliation with his family before he dies. They turn out to be still homophobic and, even worse, unsympathetic to the vagaries of his illness. His lover has to rescue him and take him back to the care of their friends in London. These are merely two random, though prominent, examples, written a decade apart. I could have chosen others. David Bergman has strongly argued a case that Larry Kramer's work has the family (indeed, the author's own family) as the locus of all its central arguments and emotional conflicts:

In [the play] *The Normal Heart* and [the collection of essays and speeches] *Reports from the Holocaust*, Kramer weaves in his conflicts with his brother as if the AIDS epidemic were an episode in a continuing family squabble. Indeed, both of these books end, not with Kramer addressing the gay community, but with him embracing his brother and sister-in-law. Kramer's tendency to place the gay community within the bosom of the heterosexual family is, I think, the reason his work speaks so powerfully and uneasily to gay readers, for it suggests a vision of reconciliation both keenly desired and frustratingly delayed.[19]

More of the same could be said of Kramer's later play *The Destiny of Me* (1992).

In the end, few gay writers seem to believe that the family can survive gay liberation unchanged – that is, if gay liberation itself is to survive unharmed. The experience of the AIDS epidemic has often underscored the family's inability – or rather, in many cases, its unwillingness – to deal with its own responsibilities where gay men have been concerned. Two of the great nightmares of the epidemic have been the related possibilities, either that a dying man might be uprooted by his parents from his urban environment and transported 'home' to his middle-American origins, to die alone in the midst of a hostile family and at a great distance from any gay friends; or that a dead gay man might be given an entirely inappropriate funeral by his family, hijacked back to godliness by a hostile religion in the strict absence not only of gay friends and lovers but even of references to the very topic of his gayness. Both of these narratives have occurred, with depressing regularity, wherever gay men have succumbed to the syndrome.

On the other hand, in the context of the services which the gay communities developed during the 1980s to support people with HIV or AIDS, one starts to see all kinds of other ways of conceiving of protective, familial relationships. (One of the key members of the new alternative to the hostile family and disloyal friends, for instance, is the entirely artificial – but no less impressively effective – figure of the volunteer 'buddy'.) The urban American experience of the epidemic has started to produce a literature which explores the emotional resonances of such alternatives. A good example would be Thom Gunn's *The Man with Night Sweats* (1992) which, contrary to the majority of its reviewers, is as centrally concerned with gay families (including the author's own household of lovers) as with AIDS itself. Similarly, Sarah Schulman's novel *People in Trouble* (1990) is about new communities and altered definitions of family. At the funeral of Jeffrey, a gay man who had AIDS, his biological family is left on the margins of the obsequies celebrated by his lovers and friends. Only when a more conventional element is introduced at the end of the service do they become involved: 'Then the family moved to the front and brought in a rabbi who got to stand up at the end and say, "Yiskadol veh yiskadosh shemay rabah," which seemed to be the only part of the whole event that they could understand. That was when they cried.' A short while later, Kate observes the mourners emerging from the service: 'The family stuck out. They looked miserable, crunched together shrinking from the community of mourning friends, not understanding any of it. They were denying themselves the comfort within arms' reach.'[20]

Once the gay family comes to be seen as consisting of more than just a male or female couple – or, increasingly, a female couple, less often a male one, with a child or children – the possibilities of communal intimacy become endless. The gay family may be small or large, nuclear or extended. In *Widows and Children First* (1979), the third part of Harvey Fierstein's *Torch Song Trilogy*, we are offered one possible version of the gay nuclear family when Arnold adopts a gay teenager, fifteen-year-old David, and Ed moves back in with Arnold. Although this looks dangerously close to a parody of the norm – with Arnold as Mom, Ed as Pop and David as Junior – Fierstein makes some effort to demonstrate that this little family is being created, as far as is possible, on Arnold's own terms. The fact that he is dramatically breaking with his own dominant mother at the same time helps to underline this.

The most popular of the fictional communes – if that has not become too pejorative a word – is Mrs Madrigal's household in Armistead Maupin's San Franciscan soap opera, the *Tales of the City* sequence of novels (1978, 1980, 1982, 1984, 1987, 1989). From the moment that Mrs Madrigal says to her new tenant Mary Ann Singleton, 'I have no objection to anything', her household becomes *the* fantasy home for gay readers to retreat to (or advance to), even if only in their reading lives. Her motley collection of waifs and strays – notably not just gay ones – becomes Maupin's model of a kind of evolving permanence, a way of maintaining long-term relationships without chaining anybody to the floor. The landlady's maternal advice and regular gifts of rolled joints on special occasions leave her tenants, whom she invariably refers to as her children, with a sense of privileged belonging, and they reciprocate with various displays of affectionate gratitude. Although they live in their own separate apartments, the inhabitants of 28 Barbary Lane, with one or two exceptions, behave as though in some way they belong to each other. At the same time as taking a close personal interest in each other's affairs, they allow each other the space in which to develop separate relationships. When their concern for each other threatens to teeter over into nosiness, it is considered reasonable etiquette to say so.

In fact, though, it becomes clear that few of her tenants feel comfortable at Barbary Lane except when they are more or less single. This is a household for young people, twenty-somethings, who have to leave it when they mature and form lasting one-to-one relationships, whether hetero or homo. To that extent if no further, Mrs Madrigal's family home is no different from those they all left in the first place, the homes of their parents. However, once they have left, they do tend to keep in touch more with her than with their parents.

In the last volume of the sequence, *Sure of You* (1989), thinking of his mother, Michael Tolliver remembers the time 'years before when she'd lobbied annually for him to spend Christmas "with the family" in Orlando. It had never even occurred to her that his family might be elsewhere'. When she now starts dropping hints that there is a place for Michael, who is HIV-positive, in the family plot in Orlando, where his father is buried, he writes to her with a firm refusal. He intends to be cremated in San Francisco. He adds: 'This wouldn't be so important to me if I didn't believe in families just as much as you do. I have one of my own, and it means the world to me. If there are goodbyes to be said, I want them to be here, and I want Thack [his lover] to be in charge.'[21] So it is not so much the physical reality of 28 Barbary Lane, the house itself, as the network of relationships it represents that is presented by Maupin as having provided so effective an alternative to the nuclear family. Even heterosexual characters like Mary Ann and Brian benefit by it, though Mary Ann sacrifices all her relationships to her career in the end. Nobody in the book entertains any nostalgia about childhood and their relationships with their parents. All the nostalgia is reserved for memories of Anna Madrigal's more than maternal hospitality. And that nostalgia continues to warm the relationships between her ex-lodgers when they meet up later in their lives.

In plotting the course of how an isolated gay teenager might become socialised into the urban gay subculture, Neil Bartlett's novel *Ready to Catch Him Should He Fall* (1990) examines various notions of family, some of which Bartlett had already explored in his extraordinary book on Oscar Wilde, *Who Was That Man?* (1988). The titles of the novel's three sections map out the progress of the two central characters, Boy and O (for Older man): 'Single', 'Couple' and 'Family'.[22] As the narrative begins, nineteen-year-old Boy lives alone, renting a room in a highrise apartment – the main point being that he no longer lives in his parents' home. So the novel figures the long and complicated process of coming out as a journey from one type of family to another: from the structurally heterosexist nuclear unit to the more flexible arrangements of the gay subculture.

The main location for these changes in Boy's life is the Bar – in homophobic mythology that shamed inferno of cross-dressing and promiscuous sodomy, but in actuality the potential centre of the subculture's social networks. (As Audre Lorde says of a New York lesbian bar in the mid-1950s, 'It had a feeling of family'.[23]) The Bar is managed by a formidable woman called Madame or Mother – that is, she is both procurer and nurturer; her establishment is both a house of 'ill repute' and a home from home. It is Madame/Mother who matchmakes Boy into his relationship with O. It is she who helps finance the home they set up together. And it is she who, finally, performs the secular ceremony by which they are 'married'. When there are confidences to be shared, if not with each other, it is in Mother that both Boy and O confide.

As the novel's title suggests, love – and not just the love of the lover, but also that of the community of friends – acts as a safety net against the risks run by openly gay men in contemporary urban life. (Throughout the book, people are falling victim to racist and homophobic attacks.) The narrator, an unnamed regular at the Bar, seems to regard all gay men as having been set adrift by their own families, and therefore as being in particular need of mutual support: 'Sometimes I think we're all parentless, and that The Bar is just one big orphans' home anyway, and that's why we use all those words all the time to each other, Mother, Daddy, Baby, Sister' (p. 235). The existence of these kinds of 'pretend families' is seen as being a defence against the isolation imposed by a heterosexist society.

Writing in *Who Was That Man?* about his own move to London as a young gay man, Neil Bartlett says that 'for the longest time imaginable I experienced my gayness in complete isolation, just like any other gay child in a small town. And now, gradually, I've come to understand that I am connected with other men's lives, men living in London with me. Or,' he adds, 'with other, dead Londoners.'[24] Coming out as gay involves networking – sexually, socially, politically – with the living and identifying with the dead. Gay men have gay fathers, even if their natural fathers are generally straight. (To Bartlett, Oscar Wilde is the biggest daddy of them all.) But in *Ready to Catch Him Should He Fall*, Bartlett offers the ambiguous figure of the Father who may be the natural father but is also gay; or it may be that he is an ex-lover who has elected to take the place and the role of the father. Either way, the Father figure, who writes letter after letter to Boy without expecting any reply, and who is then brought to live with Boy and O in their apartment, represents not only Boy's past but its reconciliation with his present.

Boy nurses Father through increasing dementia and physical decline. This section of the narrative could as well be a representation of a man nursing his lover through a sequence of advanced AIDS-related illnesses; only O's continued presence as lover, helper and observer reinforces the distinction between lover and father. But role definitions continue to blur and invert until, at the moment of Father's death, Bartlett sets up a theatrical – and vividly unsubtle – tableau of his central characters as the Holy Family of Christian mythology. Instead of a *pietà*, this is a nativity, with the dead Father as the newborn Jesus, O as the somewhat usurped patriarch Saint Joseph, Boy as the Virgin Mother, and, to one side, gazing out at the viewer (represented by some startled ambulancemen), Mother as the picture's donor/patron.

The problem with this scene is, in a sense, as much the reader's problem as the author's. The book offers no secure guidance as to how seriously one should take the introduction of Christian iconography at this point in the narrative. In one of Bartlett's distinguished theatrical performances it would have been climactic and spectacular, all the more thrilling for the operatic ease with which Bartlett is able to reconcile emotional seriousness with elements of unapologetic kitsch. Here, though, the Christian symbolism is intrusive. If it is to be taken seriously, at face value, it jars with the absent history of Christianity's often murderous oppression of sodomites. If, on the other hand, the nativity scene is merely played out here to evoke some kind of anti-religious camp recognition – a beautiful queen in drag as the Virgin Mary, an emaciated old man as the baby Jesus – it is just facile. The Christian archetype of the Holy (nuclear) Family obviously bears on the whole issue of the Christian Right's appropriation of what it calls 'family values', but its appearance in this novel is not successfully integrated into the system of signs of which Neil Bartlett is otherwise so impressively in control.

Chapter 31

The AIDS Epidemic

It may be timely to remind ourselves of a sequence, in random order, of quotations and brief narratives relating to queers and death. Socrates kills himself by taking hemlock when charged with the corruption of minors. The Maenads dismember Orpheus for the evangelical fervour of his sexual interest in boys. The Theban Band, lovers of men to a man, fight to the death lest they be discredited in one another's eyes. The cultures of the cities of the plain attract the divine Final Solution, genocide. 'Each man kills the thing he loves' (Oscar Wilde). Dennis Nilson dismembers, and boils the meat off the bones of, the boys he has strangled. A gentleman convicted of 'indecency' takes his pistol into a private room to 'do the decent thing'. 'Kill a queer for Christ' (Florida bumper sticker). 'If a man also lie with mankind, as he lieth with a woman, both of them have committed an abomination: they shall surely be put to death' (Leviticus 20: 13). 'AIDS is a pain in the ass' (toilet wall graffito). 'When I was in the military they gave me a medal for killing two men and a discharge for loving one' (epitaph of Leonard P. Matlovich, 1943–88).

Gay culture has been acquainted with death for a long time. More than any of the other so-called 'high-risk groups', gay men were well prepared, albeit unwittingly, to cope with the AIDS epidemic. It was not the first time we had died for no good reason. Even our poets, whom we might have expected to be a relatively privileged and protected species, had not escaped danger: Paul Verlaine shot Arthur Rimbaud in the wrist; Oscar Wilde was given hard labour, from the effects of which he eventually died; Wilfred Owen was shot dead, aged twenty-five, in November 1918; Hart Crane threw himself off the stern of a liner; Fascists assassinated Federico García Lorca, giving him a homophobic *coup de grâce* up the arse; Pier Paolo Pasolini was beaten to death by a hustler, and then repeatedly run over with his own car.

As we have seen, throughout this century – or, to be a little more accurate, since the Wilde débâcle of 1895 – homosexual men have been thought of as inherently tragic figures. Think of homophobic reactions to the reappropriation of the word 'gay' in the late 1960s: there's nothing *gay* about a queer. Look at how we were marketed on the bleak, black covers of paperback novels in the 1950s and 1960s. Think of how those novels, and the films based on them, almost invariably ended in murder or suicide. Many homosexual men and women internalised this opinion of themselves, and set about living out a tragic destiny of loneliness and shame.

But in the literature of post-Stonewall gayness, the tragic motif came to be seen as redundant and reactionary. Novelists made a conscious effort *not* to end their plots with death. Only when politically justifiable, in terms of the aims and complaints of the gay movement, did death enter the most right-on of our narratives. The suicides of scared teenagers or exposed adults, for instance, often resonated in gay verse lamenting homophobic malice. Certain events, caused by accident or chance, could not go unrecorded: the death of Frank O'Hara, run over by a beach buggy on Fire Island in 1966; the disastrous fire at the Everard Baths in New York on 25 May 1977.

It is easy to forget that a lot of writing from the Golden Age between Stonewall and AIDS was filled with foreboding. Larry Kramer's novel *Faggots* (1978) is an obvious example. So is Andrew Holleran's *Dancer from the Dance* (also 1978), which even begins with the sentence, 'It's finally spring down here on the Chattahoochee – the azaleas are in bloom, and everyone is dying of cancer'; another character responds by mail, 'I'm sorry everyone is dying of cancer; I'm beginning to think cancer is contagious.'[1] The implicit point is made explicit in Lluís Fernàndez's *The Naked Anarchist* (*L'Anarquista Nu*, 1979): 'The price of indulgence will always be cancer in one form or another.'[2] In Armistead Maupin's *Tales of the City* (1978), gay men swap urban legends about men who pick you up and kill you. Later, straight Brian Hawkins tells gay Michael Tolliver he reckons the pendulum of public morality is about to swing back to where it was before the 1960s.[3] It is clear that gay writers had a nagging suspicion that the sexual festival of gay liberation was too good (to those to whom it was good) to be true: it could not continue indefinitely.

A less famous example of a gay liberationist book written in this ominous mood is Michael Rumaker's *A Day and a Night at the Baths* (1979), which starts with a clear suggestion that the bad old days are not yet over. Heading for his first visit to the Everard Baths, Rumaker's narrator passes the scene where a suicide has landed after jumping off the Empire State Building. He comments: 'As I turned away, heading down Fifth, my first impulse was to suppose, intimate with suicide among us, that the victim had perhaps been gay.' His subsequent sojourn in the baths is heavy with as much dread as desire, with constant negative references to the stale reek of bodies, poppers, chlorine and marijuana. Even the healthiest-looking bodies remind him of the likelihood of disease. One passage is representative:

> The shapely posteriors parading by in the hall I imagined rampant with hepatitis, the penises that flamed with passion flaming with spirochetes as well; and scabies, and yaws, and all the other parasites carried here, along with desire, by the sailors of love from every port of the globe, the lonely and flesh-hungry from every corner of the nation and from every borough in the city; carrying here centuries-old infections of the fathers, their gay sons infected hosts, carriers in blind desire of invisible flesh-eating stowaways on bodies innocent of contaminating, and, in imperative yearning riding out the fears of infection, driven to this contagious harbor again and again, myself among them now, there are so few unrestricted havens, no ports free of the contaminating fathers.

In spite of this reaction, the narrator enjoys what he came here for – sexual intercourse – and stores it up against an indistinct but unpromising future: 'I could hold all the unexpected visitations throughout my day here, like gifts, always, in any dark times to come'. This is ambiguous: he seems to mean memories of sexy moments; but he could just as well be speaking, again, of viruses or germs. The novel ends with a note by the author, referring to actual events:

Dedicated to the nine who died,
and to those injured,
and to those present,
in the fire that destroyed the Everard Baths
on West 28th Street in Manhattan on the morning
of May 25, 1977.
And, out of the ashes and ruin of all despair,
and in spite of it,
to the spirit of the rainbow gay and lesbian phoenix, rising.[4]

This novel, then, shows a clear awareness, even when dreaming of its future 'phoenix', of dangers past and to come. Bathhouses catch fire; bodies catch diseases. Rumaker offers no secure emergence, for gay men, from the 'tragic' nightmare of their past. It may be that we are facing, in such texts, evidence of undercurrents of guilt: a lingering suspicion that, just as our straight critics were never missing an opportunity to state, we were having too good a time of it. The sweatshirt slogan 'So many men, so little time' was our contemporary version of *carpe diem*: seize the day; eat, drink and be merry, for tomorrow you die. It was a covert acknowledgement that, even at the heights of physical pleasure, we were nonetheless conscious of mortality.

If this is true of the sexually celebratory lifestyle and literature of the late period in the age of antibiotics after Stonewall, it should come as no surprise to find, in the subsequent era of the AIDS crisis, that gay men have started referring back to those homophobic myths of their own tragic status. As Bill Becker says, punning on his own first name at the start of one of his poems about living with AIDS,

> For years
> I've been billing myself
> as a tragic figure
> Now it seems
> I fit the bill[.][5]

It is Becker's task, in the rest of his book, to deny this suggestion. His main concern is, not an acceptance of inevitable death, but, as his acronymic title puts it, *An Immediate Desire to Survive*. There is a poem by Rob Hamberger, 'The Moments', in which the desire for survival is all the more touching for the simplicity of both the ideal and its expression: 'Wanting to be two / old queens: surviving this, having the time of your life'.[6]

In an appalling way, just as AIDS has returned us to the position in which hostile straights are most happy to confine us, it has returned many of us – particularly those of older generations – to a place where we once felt, if not happiest, most at home. It is where so many of us were brought up, a place we call the 'closet', a lonely space where nothing is (in the 'old' sense) gay. It is not a new place; we recognise it. Some never ceased to be nostalgic about it. One of the central purposes of a seriously reflective gay literature is to reach such readers and win them back to the outside world. Writing poetry is not a waste of time. The notorious volatility and inaccuracy of written responses to AIDS – notably in the press and on toilet walls – have underscored, in the eyes of those whose communities have been affected, the need for a considered and considerate literature of the crisis.

It is not easy – perhaps it is not even possible – to convey in measured tones the sense of betrayal gay men feel as a result of the way AIDS has been used against us. It is not just the open glee of bigots, wreaking their revenge for the years of gay liberation, that has hurt.

Equally painful is the way even humane and liberal eyes have discreetly turned away from the crisis as though it did not really exist. (This was always easy with regard to drought or earthquake victims in the so-called Third World; but what theatrical gestures of indifference are needed when the problem exists right under one's nose.) People have ostentatiously been waiting for AIDS to spill over into the 'general population' before engaging their care.

In reaction to these reactions, gay men have made a gay cultural festival out of our acts of remembrance. The emergency role of gay culture is clear. While giving his account of the illness and death of his own lover, Paul Monette has made the appropriate point very cogently:

> Loss teaches you very fast what cannot go without saying. The course of our lives had paralleled the course of the movement itself since Stonewall, and now our bitterness about the indifference of the system made us feel keenly how tenuous our history was. Everything we had been together – brothers and friends beyond anything the suffocating years in the closet could dream of – might yet be wiped away. If we all died and all our books were burned, then a hundred years from now no one would ever know. So we figured we had to know and name it ourselves, tell each other what we had become in coming out.[7]

Simon Watney has written of how 'gay men have learned to celebrate the achievements of the living, and mourn our dead, *on the terms of our own culture*. Anyone who has heard the frequent juxtaposition of disco-music by Grace Jones or Donna Summer played at AIDS funerals alongside arias from the Verdi *Requiem* or *Der Rosenkavalier* will appreciate this point very well.'[8] It is in this context that we should site all elegiac cultural productions to have emerged from the epidemic. It may be that such poems – for it is with poetry that I am, at present, primarily concerned – turn out to be sentimental, nostalgic, backward-looking and, in a narrow sense, conservative. That is, perhaps, their first function. But the most thoughtful of them will, while refusing to forget, turn to the requirements of the present and forge, out of the disappointments of the past, hopes for the future.

A predominantly secular age such as – in the industrialised West – our own, clearly, does not offer easy opportunities for statements of faith in an eternal afterlife. It may be that we must piece together our eternities out of temporal fragments far more mundane. Curiously, in his poem 'Kip', which elegises the well-known American porn star Kip Noll, Marc Almond does not take up this opportunity.[9] One could argue, after all, not only that Kip lives on in glory, naked and at his best, on our video screens, but also that he may thereby be helping to preserve the lives of those of us who 'love' him, by inspiring us to the safest form of sex – in a salutary solitude gladdened by his company – solo masturbation. The poem is conspicuously failing to give Kip the 'immortality' that his own videos do. Andrew Holleran once ironically lamented the fact that 'The Mayans left temples in the Yucatán; we seem to have left pornography.'[10] However, in my opinion, this may not be such a poor legacy as he imagines.

There is also, of course, a second type of elegy, less common but no less important than the first. This is the elegy, not on an individual who has died, but on a way of life. A good example of this sort is Oliver Goldsmith's 'The Deserted Village' (1770) which argues passionately against the enclosure of common land by landowners; deserted villages are the consequence of such action. A controversial recent example of the general elegy is Tony Harrison's *v.* (pronounced *versus*), in which the poet complains about the daubing of his parents' gravestone with obscene graffiti. Modelled on Gray's elegy, the poem widens out from family concerns to a critique of the social and economic reasons for such vandalism.[11]

In its accumulation of types, and taken as a whole, Robert Boucheron's *Epitaphs for the Plague Dead* (1985) becomes an elegy of this second sort, commemorating an era. Its contents page lists such poems as 'Epitaph for a Bodybuilder,', 'Epitaph for an Atheist', 'Epitaph for a Disco Bunny', 'Epitaph for a Bureaucrat', 'Epitaph for a Stammerer', and so on. All are modelled on the measure of Alfred Tennyson's *In Memoriam*, and each works as a discrete unit, a record of one life: unique in its idiosyncrasies, yet representative of others. Like fictional characters, each person is an individual and a type. But, taken together as a series, the poems acquire broader significance as records of an era. This strikes me as a somewhat embittered collection, with a strong undertow of retrospective moralising. Suspicions on this score are confirmed when one encounters a poem about a baby which was infected before birth, by a mother who was infected, in turn, by her haemophiliac husband. The poem is called 'Epitaph for an Innocent' – an apparently unironic reflection on the other lives the book outlines.[12]

No matter which type of elegy a poet chooses to write, the nature of AIDS prevents an entirely conventional lament. Death by water, the most common origin of the traditional elegy, does not place the poet himself at risk; it is not transmitted sexually (unless you count, say, the death of Ophelia as an instance of venereal drowning). In poems about AIDS, on the other hand, the mourner may know that he is, or must suspect that he may be, infected with the HIV which, apparently, led to or hastened his lover's death. His elegy may, therefore, become, to some extent, reflexive: grieving for his own death to come – yet, perhaps, all the more willing to accept his fate, since his lover has gone ahead of him.

Roy Gonsalves, in a poem called 'The Photograph', consults a photo of himself and two friends at Christmas, and concludes:

> Benny died last year.
> Les died last month.
> Tomorrow I go for the results of the blood test.[13]

At its most negative, the implication of this characteristically stark sequence of facts is: by this time next year all three of us will be dead. (And, indeed, some of the poets with whom I am here concerned have already died.) Much of Paul Monette's book of elegies *Love Alone* consists of the poet's realisation of the need to prepare for his own death. The poem 'Readiness' speaks of his arrangements for his own funeral and for his interment in his lover's grave; the poem includes the epitaph he has written for himself.[14]

The very nature of desire has become embroiled in the crisis. Thom Gunn's 'In Time of Plague' starts with another expression of this awareness of personal vulnerability:

> My thoughts are crowded with death
> and it draws so oddly on the sexual
> that I am confused
> confused to be attracted
> by, in effect, my own annihilation.[15]

To an extent, then, desire itself, fixed on the future, becomes prematurely elegiac, morbidly anticipating a time when the encounter desired will be in the past and the desirer will have died of its effects. One overcomes this dread, not by turning away from the object of desire and sublimating one's physical and emotional needs in good works, but by negotiating a safe sexual encounter with him. This is how we release our desires into viable futurity.

Nor is it only from AIDS itself that the living are under threat. They who mourn require our attention, to be protected from despair. Therefore, in 'Elijah and Isaac', John McRae expressly turns from the dead to the living – though with no intention of forgetting the dead. The poem ends as follows:

> This June Elijah died of AIDS.
> This is not a poem about Elijah dying of AIDS.
> I love the memory of him.
>
> But God I weep for Isaac.[16]

One weeps for the weeping. Lamentation concerns the living as well as the dead – or even the living *rather than* the dead: to lament is to negotiate a mode of survival. It is itself an acknowledgement that the one who sheds tears *has a future*.

In other respects, too, the nature of the death, the dying, has its effect on the continuing life of the mourner. In his poem 'Anon', Pat O'Brien remembers a man with whom he had a three-week affair. To him, the poet says:

> You died gay
> you died with dignity
> that makes me proud.[17]

The ideas of dignity and pride are linked: the dignity of the dying contributes to the pride of the mourner. But the important phrase implicit in these lines is *gay pride*. What does it mean to say a man 'died gay'? Well, as the bigots would rush to remind us, he died because he was gay. He chanced to be performing the wrong kinds of sexual act at the wrong moment in history. But there is far more than mere bad luck to having 'died gay'. It is the fact that the subject of the poem 'died gay' that is the first cause of his mourner's pride – which is itself (since the mourner is an ex-lover of the dead man) not just pride but *gay* pride.

Most of these writers know of AIDS as an inscribed cluster of social texts, with no immunity to issues like sexism, homophobia and racism. Their work is often concerned to emphasise the continuity and contiguity of such issues. Craig G. Harris' poem 'Our Dead Are Not Buried Beneath Us' (*'for Marc-Steven Dear, 1953–1986'*) implicitly demonstrates how the dying enter history, in the following observation:

> I noticed the tribal markings
> of his face
> multiplied
> grown larger than when I'd last seen
> constant reminders of
> dimly lit liaisons[.][18]

One can take these markings as literal scars, on an African face – tribal markings accentuated by the lesions of disease – or as a metaphor for lesions on a face previously unmarked. Either way, the point is that the illness brings the ill man ever closer to his African roots, perhaps stigmatising him even more than his black skin, in American society, already does. The man's origins and his AIDS are associated here, but not in the bigot's manner ('he is African, therefore he has AIDS'). What connects these two aspects of his being is, on the contrary, racism itself. Having AIDS makes him, in the eyes of a racist society, *more African* (where the name of the continent is meant as a term of abuse). So, as a matter of defence, let his lesions proclaim him to be, in racist eyes, defiantly more African indeed (where the name of the continent connects with a long and proud history of civilisations pre-dating those even of Europe, let alone of white America). Let him wear his identity, though it kill him, with pride.

As on Washington's memorial to the dead of the Vietnam war; as on so many patches of the Names Project's quilt: a naming of names may be sufficient commemoration. The quilt itself – that massive artefact whose symbolism reminds us, both that it was beneath our bed covers that we loved those who have died, and that gay men symbolically *know how to embroider* – is fast becoming a mobile yet immovable monument, inscribed not merely with the names of those we have lost, but also with certain chosen aspects of their personalities. Even if words fail us, we can ensure that our dead do not, like those of the Black Death or the Holocaust or the Killing Fields, go anonymously to mass graves. Andrew Holleran has said:

> Someday writing about this plague may be read with pleasure, by people for whom it is a distant catastrophe, but I suspect the best writing will be nothing more, nor less, than a lament. . . . The only other possible enduring thing would be a simple list of names – of those who behaved well, and those who behaved badly, during a trying time.[19]

This highlights one of the weaknesses of Robert Boucheron's book of epitaphs. None of his characters have names. They are all identified by occupation, or habit, or quirk; which may not be enough. In contrast, Section III of Sam Ambler's 'After the Howl' (following in the wake of Allen Ginsberg's 'Howl') is all the more powerful for the straightforwardness of its strategy. Each three-line unit consists of the clause 'I will not let you die', followed by the name of an individual; a second line bearing only the birth and death dates of this person; and a third, more expansive, briefly outlining some unforgettable aspect of his/her life. For example:

> I will not let you die Michael Calvert
>   born 1958 died January 1987
>   crafting floral epithets into bouquets of people poems for AIDS
>   commiseration[.][20]

The accumulation of names and lives takes on the character of a formal act of remembrance, a litany of ordinary saints.

One does not have to make a roll-call of the dead, though, to open out from the particular to the general. So many of the elegies about named individuals seem, as if by unavoidable accident, to become the more general sort of lament. For instance, Michael Lassell's 'How to Watch Your Brother Die' includes an account of the brother's funeral, attended by 'several hundred men / who file past in tears, some of them / holding hands'. And one says to another, 'I wonder who'll be next'. The funeral, like the poem itself, is centred on the loss of the individual, but acutely aware of the wider crisis. Not just one man is dying, not just one generation, but whole ways of life.[21] Honor Moore's 'Memoir' ('*For J.J. Mitchell, dead of AIDS 4/26/86*') ends with a revealing, retrospective scene of dementia:

> Jimmy said
> your last days the virus at your brain had you

in summer at the door on Fire Island
offering refreshment as guests arrived –
beautiful men, one after another.[22]

Here, even before his own imminent funeral, the demented subject revisits lost friends – or rather, he allows them to visit him – for a valedictory house party on Fire Island, the *locus* of the Golden Age, gay urban America's Arcadia, a place which can now only support nostalgia. Dementia takes the dying man back to the past. The suggestion is, perhaps, that any similar regression on *our* part (we being the living) would signify a comparable descent into dementia. To remain sane, while not forgetting the past, we must look to the present and its future.

In the middle of his poem 'Readiness', which I have already mentioned, Paul Monette's consideration of his own gravestone and epitaph leads to a brief vision of such a future. He imagines a chance visit to his and his lover's grave, at some indeterminable point in the distant future:

> if we're lucky some far-off
> men of our sort generations hence a pair
> of dreamy types strolling among the hill graves
> for curiosity's sake this well may be
> in a time when dying is not all day and every
> house riven and they'll laugh *Here's 2 like us*
> won't that be lovely Rog[?]

That anything could still prove 'lovely' *in the future tense* is indicative of a sort of triumph, here. The epidemic will end. Love will, after its own dreamy fashion, prevail. It is an act of real courage for a man with HIV to reach this conclusion. The best of the volumes of AIDS poetry should work in similar ways. To the extent that they serve any commemorative functions, they are firmly rooted in the past; but one has to imagine them being read in the future by new generations of gay men. (This is a sentimental notion, but there is plenty of room in an epidemic for the productive indulgence of sentimentality.) Some, like Tim Dlugos' *Strong Place* (1992) or Adam Johnson's *The Playground Bell* (1994), will be memorials to their own authors; others, like Mark Doty's *My Alexandria* (1995) and *Atlantis* (1996), will commemorate their authors' lovers.[23] Yet we build memorials not for the past, but *of* the past *for* the future.

Without that sense of a future, it might have been that only silence would beckon. It might have seemed that the best reaction to despair would be an elegy for rational speech – something keened to the melody of John Cage's '4'33"'. Yet, although a Francis Bacon scream or the self-denying mouth of Beckett's *Not I* (1973) were felt to be appropriate modes for the late Modernists, the very fact that we have not been reduced to minimalist silence is itself a triumph of eloquence. Silence = Death.[24] The future tense is a mode of resistance in itself – as is the act of commemorating the past for the sake of an implicit future generation. What is now emerging, in a confident, gay literature of the crisis, is that if future generations of gay men can go dancing, freely and healthily, that is enough. That *is* our future. This is not a trivial matter; not some frivolous question of making the future safe for disco-bunnies. It is a question of the survival of – to use a dated phrase – gay liberation.

· · ·

HIV will be seen to have shaped, not only the subjects of gay art, but also its forms. Activist artists have had to develop new methods, new combinations of materials – I am thinking of the propagandists of ACT-UP, in particular. But even those who are working in traditional forms and genres – the novel, the elegy – have had strategies dictated to them by the state of their health. The simplest and yet the most extreme of these effects has been the need to trim one's artistic ambition to the possibility that one has not long to live. Many gay writers are writing short books. A writer like Proust, although bedridden for long periods, nevertheless clearly had confidence in his own ability to survive: this is asserted every time he writes, as he often does, a sentence a page long or a paragraph of ten pages or more. It is asserted in his notorious reluctance to release proofs to his publishers without massive and complex – not to mention barely legible – revisions. Proust did not, as it happened, live to see his novel published in full; but he does not seem to have been in any great hurry to do so. He felt he had time to indulge his expansive artistic integrity. AIDS literature, on the other hand, is generally still characterised by a sense of urgency.

If the term 'gay literature' is to have any practical significance during the present epidemic, it must be defined in such a manner as to include documents relating to the health of gay men. AIDS has had the effect of bringing the language of pornography out of the sex shops and into the wider marketplace; but this same language has been transformed by usage, from a Mafia-controlled discourse of seduction into a major instrument of care and responsibility within the gay subcultures. If we are to take this proposition seriously in a literary-critical discussion, then we must alter our sense of the types of text it is appropriate to include within our canons. At any rate, there can be no doubt that certain texts from the epidemic deserve recognition as having played crucial roles in developing our understanding of the nature of the epidemic and how we might strive to survive it. Two examples which spring readily to mind are Larry Kramer's article '1,112 and Counting' (*New York Native*, 7 March 1983) and Richard Berkowitz and Michael Callen's booklet *How to Have Sex in an Epidemic* (1983).[25]

Correspondingly, many of the most effective narratives of the individual's struggle within the AIDS universe have been factual: essay collections like Emmanuel Dreuilhe's *Mortal Embrace* (*Corps à corps*, 1987), autobiographies like Paul Monette's *Borrowed Time* (1988) and Mark Doty's *Heaven's Coast* (1996), journals like Derek Jarman's *Modern Nature* (1991) and more or less fictionalised autobiography like so many of the later books of Hervé Guibert. Guibert's accounts of undergoing such medical processes as an incompetently carried-out fibroscopy or an alveolar lavage, both described in *The Compassion Protocol* (*Le Protocole compassionel*, 1991), give an extraordinarily direct impression of the intolerable crises a person with AIDS has to tolerate virtually as a matter of routine.[26] Collections of AIDS-related journalism have made some of the most persuasive contributions to the lasting literature of the epidemic without necessarily proving any more ephemeral than 'creative' writing on the same themes. Here, I would include Larry Kramer's *Reports from the Holocaust* (1989) and David Feinberg's *Queer and Loathing* (1994).

Unlike the poetry, which was mainly commemorative, the first spate of AIDS narratives in drama or fiction had what might loosely be called didactic aims. Most sought to persuade either a straight audience to begin to take the epidemic seriously and humanely, or a gay audience not to succumb to despair but to agitate positively for more effective political instigation of medical research and health care. Larry Kramer's play *The Normal Heart* (1985) is both an account of such agitation and an effective agitation in itself. To an extent the same goes for Randy Shilts' pugnacious history of the early stages of the epidemic, *And the Band Played On* (1987). Other texts make didactic historical analogies:

for instance, by its use of the figure of Roy Cohn, Tony Kushner's sequence of plays *Angels in America* (1990, 1991) instructively places AIDS in the context of American homophobia both during the McCarthyite period of the 1950s and since; Michael Arditti's novel *The Celibate* (1993) draws comparisons between AIDS and both the Black Death and the serial murders of Jack the Ripper.

Of more immediately practical use, some of the early fiction inspired – if that is the word – by AIDS attempted to reassure gay men that sex could still be safe, and safety could still be sexy. John Preston, the well-known writer of stories on gay sadomasochistic themes, edited a collection called *Hot Living: Erotic Stories about Safer Sex* in 1985. The point of the book is stated in Preston's introduction: 'Sex has always been a special means of communication and self-affirmation for gay men. The idea that it was going to be denied us by AIDS was one of the greatest concerns we had.' He goes on to speak of 'sensible sex' and 'responsible sex'. In the end, he addresses the reader directly: 'It is up to you to decide to act responsibly. We can only suggest the various ways that that is possible.'[27]

The obvious AIDS-related structure gives us a novel in two parts: the first, in which the central character grows up, comes out and enjoys the sexual carnival of gay liberation in the 1970s; and the second, in which the epidemic is heard of in the early 1980s, affects distant acquaintances, and then kills a lover or close friend or even the central character himself. This is before-and-after fiction. It is a structure which is possibly to be seen at its most clear-cut in David Feinberg's novel *Eighty-Sixed* (1989): the book is in two halves, the first, set in 1980, called 'Ancient History'; the second, set in 1986, fully immersed in the epidemic – whence the ironic title of the first. The shift from the age of antibiotics to the AIDS era is generally represented as involving significant alterations in attitude and behaviour, plus, of course, a major change in mood. On a small scale, there is a nice moment at the end of Adam Mars-Jones' short story 'The Brake' (1987) when Roger understands that he is going to have to give up unhealthy foods and unhealthy sexual habits at the same time. The story is concluded with the sentence: 'In the end, he found it easier to give up men than to give up the taste, even the smell, of fried bacon.'[28]

According to Suzanne Poirier, 'all writing today is AIDS writing in that it must consciously choose how to respond to the epidemic, whether by direct involvement or evasion'.[29] I think it should be possible to soften some of the edges of this remark. Many straight writers do not seem to me to be evading the topic so much as to have forgotten that it exists at all. And there may well be ways of responding to AIDS which cannot strictly be characterised as 'direct involvement'. There is, I think, a literature of indirection which is not evasive. For instance, while Adam Mars-Jones' novel *The Waters of Thirst* (1993) is directly 'about' kidney dialysis, no one could deny that its concerns are very similar to those of more explicitly AIDS-related fiction. And who is to say that a book like Christopher Bram's novel *Father of Frankenstein* (1995), in its depiction of one man's preparation for his own death – albeit in 1957 and of 'unnatural causes' – is not in any way informed by the epidemic? Are books which do not actually name AIDS – books like Frans Kellendonk's *The Mystical Body* (*Mystiek lichaam*, 1986) and Robert Ferro's *Second Son* (1988) – direct or evasive?[30] Surely there must be some alternative, or alternatives plural, to these two possible extremes.

The British novelist Alan Hollinghurst has adopted two different strategies of 'evasion'; or rather, to phrase it more positively, he has twice refused to submit to the considerable pressure, from gay readers and straight critics, on all gay male writers, to write about AIDS. His first novel, *The Swimming-Pool Library* (1988), is a lusty celebration of pre-AIDS freedoms, already a 'historical novel' at the time of its publication by virtue of being set in London in the 1970s, a decade so radically different from the 1980s in the common experience of urban gay men. Other major gay novels of the 1980s and 1990s were, similarly, 'historical': for example, Christopher Bram's *Hold Tight* and Edmund White's *The Beautiful Room Is Empty* (both 1988), Robert Patrick's *Temple Slave* (1994) and Neil Bartlett's *Mr Clive and Mr Page* (1996). It does not seem adequate to dismiss such a variety of fictional works, as some journalistic reviewers have, as wallowing in nostalgia. None of the books listed here does that.

Alan Hollinghurst's somewhat over-written second novel, *The Folding Star* (1994), appears to be set in the 'present' of the time of its writing, and certainly refers to AIDS, but only glancingly. The book's narrator and central character Edward Manners is visited in Belgium, where he is teaching English, by his friend Edie. Passing on news of a mutual friend, a gay man called Dawn, Edie says, 'he's put on a bit of weight. The AZT seems to have made him rather hilarious', to which Edward replies, 'I so want him to be all right'.[31] Presumably this means nothing to any reader who has been living in an AIDS-free haze for the duration of the epidemic; to anyone else, little more need be said: the presence of the syndrome is firmly established by the use of the acronym denoting its most well-known interventive drug. A few pages later the narrative implies that Dawn's illness has not been an isolated case in this social group: Edward says of Edie that she has 'looked after friends of ours who were dying. Dawn was one of them' (p. 155).

AIDS is explicitly mentioned for the first and last time when Dawn actually does die. Edward reports Dawn's father's having said, 'Well, no one can say he died of AIDS, Edward' – for the fact is that, true to the perverse contingency that often shifts the plots of Hollinghurst's novels in unexpected directions, Dawn dies not 'of AIDS' but in a car crash (p. 194). Apart from these few references, the novel's only other concession to the universe of HIV occurs during its lavishly celebrated climactic sexual event, when Edward's detailed description mentions 'the slicked and rubbered pumping of my cock in his arse' (p. 337). Not that Hollinghurst pauses in his elaboration of sexual gymnastics for the rubber to have been unpackaged, 'slicked' and put on; or, later, to be taken off and thrown away. It is characteristic of his strategically oblique approach to the epidemic throughout this book, that the reader is expected to be awake to such glancing references, and to register that Edward knows the requirements of safer sex. He is not putting his beloved Luc (with the inverted *cul*) at risk.

The question of directness and evasion obviously also arises in relation to homosexuality itself. The fact is that it has not generally been possible to make useful cultural interventions from the closet. No amount of discreet metaphor can convey the messages of safer sex so efficiently and memorably as an explicit – some would say pornographic – statement of physical mechanics. AIDS has not only outed figures whose illness became known to the press or to family and friends/enemies, and who would not otherwise have come out (Rock Hudson and Roy Cohn spring to mind); it has also forced writers, finally, to choose whether to become usefully committed to the struggle for health, by openly bearing witness, or to continue a lifetime's habit of cloaking themselves in metaphor. (The most extreme of these is the self-representation of the gay writer as being heterosexual or as having another name than that of his family.) This strategy of deception is most warmly appreciated by straight-identified critics. To the rest of us, it may seem to be a betrayal of integrity, and it represents a profound misunderstanding of what the purpose of metaphor should be: to *reveal*.

But if one comes and stays out, one has to take the consequences. The AIDS epidemic has not radically altered the ways in which homosexual men are perceived by the rest of society, but it has shifted perceptions of us further in the directions of two tendencies which were already apparent before the epidemic began. It simultaneously confirmed two models of the homosexual man which had been current for half a century at least: the self-destructive pervert whose sexual acts are so extremely and obviously 'against Nature' as to call down the righteous wrath of God more or less exactly in the manner of the eradication of Sodom; and, on the other hand, the diseased victim whose condition demands not blame but compassion, not punishment but prayers. It would not be quite accurate to distinguish between the two as if one were the 'moral' model and the other the 'medical' model, the former with a history at least as old as Leviticus and the latter dating only from the late nineteenth century's mental health movement and the coining of so many psychoanalytically based defining terms, including 'homosexuality' itself. In fact, both models contain suggestions of sickness – indeed, even of plague – but both are far more clearly based in religious history and correspond with distinct ideologies within the Christian Churches (not to mention, for instance, Judaism and Islam) today. Very loosely, one is fundamentalist, the other liberal, while both are moralistic. It should go without saying that – depending on your preferred terminology – both are heterosexist, homophobic, anti-gay. Hardly any non-gay commentators responded neutrally to the so-called 'gay plague'.

We know perfectly well that straight critics like gay writers to write about AIDS. They tend not to be interested in other aspects of our lives. We only move them when we talk about death. Alan Sinfield has scathingly reported the reception of Thom Gunn's collection *The Man with Night Sweats* (1992), which received far better reviews than the two openly gay – and equally good – collections which preceded it, *Jack Straw's Castle* (1976) and *The Passages of Joy* (1982). The reviewer for the *Economist* frankly acknowledged having been unimpressed by the 1982 collection because it 'deals with homosexuality happily', whereas by the time of the 1992 collection, AIDS 'has given his poetry more life and more raw human vigour than it has ever had before'.[32]

· · ·

One does not have to subscribe to the myth of the tragic queer to recognise that the theme of mortal danger – along with *carpe diem*, its corollary – has recurred throughout the history of the literature I have been calling 'gay'. In the literature of AIDS we return, as it were, to our roots. Inevitably, while so doing, we find our way back to the most complex and memorable of our writers. Canons are centripetal. They lead us back to the centre – to Virgil, to Dante, to Goethe, to Shakespeare – even when we can see that the centre is itself shifting and only intermittently stable. There is no escaping the big names. Since my argument throughout this book has depended on literary hit parades – even if I have sought to question certain criteria by which books have been judged and consequently to adjust their respective positions in the qualitative listings – it seems only apt that I should feel obliged to go back to the top of the conventional rankings at this late stage. In British culture, whether or not critics like the idea of a gay Shakespeare, it is nevertheless against Shakespeare's stature that modern gay literature tends to be measured and found wanting. As Jeffrey Meyers once wrote when denouncing gay poets of the twentieth century,

> What I consider to be the greatest love poetry, by Shakespeare and Donne, is not graphic but idealistic. ... Explicit homosexual poetry, however, which rarely mentions love and emphasises the sexual organs and the satisfaction of lust, lacks both a transcendent beauty and a universal appeal.[33]

By this exacting standard, of course, most heterosexual literature of the twentieth century would also seem to be rubbish. So, for that matter, would most literary criticism. Be that as it may, it is to the iconic Shakespeare that, briefly but obediently, we now return.

Shakespeare is continually referring to poxes and plagues. He does so not obsessively but as a matter of routine. He retrieves them not from morbid fantasy but from the conditions of everyday life in his time. These references are not mere bawdy jokes, as they are so often treated by the critics. On the contrary, they are deeply fearful. Many, perhaps most, of the characters in his plays are at risk, some more so than others. Not only are their lives, as *life*, distinctly fragile; but it is clear that certain turns in the narratives of their lives expose that fragility to even greater, perhaps fatal, risk. One such turn is love.

It may be that we have grown so accustomed to certain poetic tropes that we now take them for granted and they pass us by. For example, the love-as-sickness metaphor has long seemed naturalised within the English language. It was already something of a cliché by Shakespeare's time: love had been referred to as a malfunction of the heart since long before Ovid twice complained that it could not be cured by herbal remedy.[34] Shakespeare could draw on a broad range of phrases to conjure up this emotional angina. The *OED*'s first quoted instance of 'lovesick' dates from 1530. Other expressions such as 'heartsick', 'heartache' and 'heartbreak' derive from the same conceit. Shakespeare's contemporary Samuel Daniel declared, in *Hymen's Triumph* (1614), that

> Love is a sickness full of woes
> All remedies refusing[.]

I quote this sentiment as being wholly unexceptional. It would not seem conspicuously out of place in any of the Shakespearean comedies.[35] The very existence of love, in Shakespeare, is predicated on risk. Courtship involves negotiations of safety. Marital infidelity invokes the spectre of the pox. More than just a conventional conceit or naturalised cliché, the love-as-sickness metaphor serves as an indicator of genuine anxieties at the very heart of Elizabethan sexual life. Shakespeare's attitudes to love developed within a context of medical uncertainties. English culture was as extensively affected by the arrival of syphilis in the late fifteenth century as continental cultures were. The disease encouraged epidemiological speculation and medical experimentation whilst exerting even broader influences on sexual attitudes and behaviour. The combination of clinical observation, intelligent hypothesis, and myth-making which constituted the version of the disease shared by medical practitioners, once mediated by the equally authoritative yet more erratic pronouncements of a range of moral arbiters, descended to common understanding in distinctly frightening forms. In particular, speculation on means of transmission led to a more widespread sense of risk in daily life than had actually been proved or was even plausible.

Johannes Fabricius has pointed out that 'many Elizabethans reacted to the growing venereal plague in the same way that modern Americans react to the epidemic of AIDS'.[36] At the Diet of Worms in 1495, the Emperor Maximilian had offered the view that syphilis was God's punishment for humanity's blasphemies – as commonplace an account of the aetiology of AIDS as of that of the earlier epidemic. Having deduced that syphilis could be transmitted in human sweat, Phillipp Hermann's *Excellent Treatise Teaching How to Cure the French Pockes* (1590) concluded: 'Therefore let euery man take heede, that he doo not lye with them whom he knoweth not, for that it is very dangerous.'[37] No one who has observed the AIDS crisis can have missed similar warnings against sleeping with strangers. One could go on making comparisons indefinitely. In his book on Renaissance representations of sodomy, Jonathan Goldberg writes:

> The lethal energies directed against those who have AIDS or are HIV-positive are the latest episode in the persecution of sodomites; people with AIDS are our culture's

version of the Elizabethan monster with his heretical beliefs, or the colonialist's promiscuous natives and degenerate underclasses. In our culture, at this moment, in many quarters, AIDS and homosexuality are considered to be synonymous, and AIDS serves as the present site for the lethal confusions that, in the Renaissance, were called *sodometries*.[38]

This is why it has become important not to end the present book straightforwardly in the present day, as if the AIDS epidemic had no precedent in our cultural history. There is nothing straightforward about the present day. Nor is its 'presence' ever entirely clean of the accretions of the past – far from it. AIDS is continually reminding us of this. It returns us, as I have said, to our roots.

One theory about the transmission of syphilis – that it could be carried on the air – has not been particularly prevalent during the AIDS era, yet exercised so strong an influence on Shakespeare's imagination that its pervasion of his work has what I believe to be a striking relevance to our own age. Hans Widmann, who in 1497 gave the first account of the sexual transmission of syphilis, nevertheless argued that it could also be contracted from corrupted air or 'miasma'. Ulrich von Hutten saw 'unholsom blastes of the ayre' as the disease's origin. Girolamo Fracastoro, too, categorised syphilis among the airborne diseases. Cardinal Wolsey was accused of 'blowing upon' Henry VIII with 'his perilous and infective breath', thereby putting the king at risk of catching 'the foul and contagious disease of the great pox'.[39] Given such fearful possibilities, Shakespeare treats the air not merely as a space between individuals, a distance defining their apartness, but as a dense medium of high conductivity across which all interpersonal communications are effected. The glance, the voice and the breath may combine to transmit impressions which are powerfully seductive.

Think of how love operates in *Twelfth Night*. From its famous opening line onwards, the play is, like Prospero's island, full of noises. As any production's musical director must be aware, its music is always associated with two compelling emotional themes – love and death – which, as often as not, unite in the plaintive singing of *carpe diem* songs:

> Then come kiss me, sweet and twenty,
> Youth's a stuff will not endure.
> (II. iii, 49–50)

In Shakespeare, music often reduces the listener to a mood of silent pensiveness, as when Orsino calls for music and speaks to 'Cesario' of love, but then stops to listen to Feste's rendition of 'Come away, death'. Music is a leisure activity, which may appear to involve the wasting of time – the plot of a play cannot proceed during a song – and yet it always has its effect. For instance, after Feste's song on love (II. iii) Sir Andrew refers to 'A mellifluous voice' and Sir Toby to 'A contagious breath', the latter being the kind of phrase which might more usually be applied to a perceived risk of pestilence or plague. The two men have caught a disease, or unease at least, from the song. But Sir Andrew continues: 'Very sweet and contagious, i' faith'. The very sweetness of the plague is the instrument of its virulence: people actively want to catch it.

Pestilence is in the mind throughout the play, from the opening moments when Orsino says:

> O, when mine eyes did see Olivia first
> Methought she purged the air of pestilence.
> (I. i, 20–21)

Here, beauty is imagined as a disinfectant air-freshener. To love such a creature must be to engage in a uniquely safe manner of intercourse. However, this is a delusion: for from the moment when she is first seen, deeply in mourning for the loss of her brother, one knows that even Olivia cannot fend off death. Indeed, part of her beauty consists of her weeds. It is a kind of beauty that contains both death and grief: you can see them in the look of her. And it is the presence of death, the fact of her mourning, that makes her beauty all the more rare, all the more precious, by rendering it unattainable. When 'Cesario' (Viola in drag) is wooing her (on Orsino's behalf), 'he' says:

> Lady, you are the cruell'st she alive,
> If you will lead these graces to the grave
> And leave the world no copy.
> (I. v, 230–32)

Her beauty's destiny and destination will be the grave, death, unless she marries and has children. (This is, of course, the insistent theme of Shakespeare's first seventeen sonnets.)

In answer to 'Cesario'/Viola's argument, Olivia bitterly – or, at least, ironically – inventories her own beauty: two lips, 'indifferent red', two grey eyes and their lids, one neck, one chin, 'and so forth'. This dismembering or mutilation of her own face is intended to show, by separating its parts, that her beauty is unremarkable: she possesses no part that is more than virtually anyone else possesses. Then, when 'Cesario' leaves the stage, Olivia proceeds to inventory the features of '*his*' beauty:

> Thy tongue, thy face, thy limbs, actions, and spirit
> Do give thee fivefold blazon.
> (I. v, 281–2)

That is to say, 'his' parts prove 'him' a gentleman, worthy of a coat of arms: she is attracted to 'his' class, which she reads as being inscribed in his physique, even though (as we know) she sees nothing there about 'his' actual gender. In the next breath, having thus articulated 'Cesario''s charms, Olivia suddenly and unexpectedly finds them working on her: she is beginning to fall in love. And she refers to love *as a plague*:

> How now?
> Even so quickly may one catch the plague?
> Methinks I feel this youth's perfections
> With an invisible and subtle stealth
> To creep in at mine eyes.
> (I. v, 283–7)

She catches the disease of love through her eyes – yet she catches it when the 'boy' is no longer visible to her. So love is being imagined, here, as an airborne pestilence that lingers in the atmosphere even after the carrier has left the room. In effect, love works its charm much as music does. It is like the lingering breath of Feste's song, 'Very sweet and contagious, i' faith'.

The bodies of lovers are the most feigning: that is how they seduce you. Shakespeare appears to have thought of beauty, routinely, as potentially hiding death. Any number of images can be quoted as evidence of this conviction. Since any beautiful body may have a corrupt interior, beauty itself begins to seem a risky condition, both to the beautiful themselves and to their admirers. One of the loveliest lines in the sonnets, in Sonnet 106, is one of the least conventionally poetic, even though it satirises the conventional love poetry of the time:

Of hand, of foot, of lip, of eye, of brow[.]

Although he is disowning the catalogue effect of the love poems of lesser poets – and remember that there is a lot of writerly vanity on show in the sonnets – Shakespeare is, nevertheless, also allowing his mind to wander over the body of his boyfriend. There is nothing to say so in the line in question, but to take it out of its context and display it on its own, as above, is yet to bring with it all the laudatory hyperbole, not only of the rest of the poems about the boy, but also of the heritage of lesser poetry which Shakespeare is seeking to transcend. The body parts he lists here are the parts of a beautiful youth, and one has to imagine them as such. The line represents the lover-poet at both his most and least expressive: all he can say is the physique, yet this admission conveys far more than a mere list of parts.

However, contrast this vision of desirable masculinity with another: in *Troilus and Cressida*, having accused Patroclus of being the 'male varlet' and 'masculine whore' of Achilles, Thersites drives his point home with the following invective: 'Now, the rotten diseases of the south, the guts-griping, ruptures, catarrhs, loads o' gravel i'th'back, lethargies, cold palsies, raw eyes, dirt-rotten livers, wheezing lungs, bladders full of impostume, sciaticas, limekilns i'th'palm, incurable bone-ache, and the rivelled fee-simple of the tetter, take and take again such preposterous discoveries!' (V. i, 15–23). The grammar of the sentence is ambiguous: either there is an implicit 'may' between the first and second words, in which case Thersites is calling down a curse on the practitioners of sodomy; or else he is making a simple statement, that these are the illnesses sodomites catch. Either way, he constructs a prejudicial representation of the body of the 'male varlet' in a definitively degenerate condition. To the peak of Achilles' and Patroclus' youthful virility he applies the jaundiced eye of envy and reveals a sodomite's body assailed in all its organs by the punishments it deserves. Actually, of course, his own body is closer than theirs to this state.

Shakespeare's view of sexual risk allows us to suppose that Patroclus and the addressee of the sonnets might be physically identical. In one case this physique inspires a sonnet sequence; in the other a stream of insults. To one viewer the body is desired above all other aspects of life; to the other it is a foul bag of corruption. This contingency of desire and disgust is what makes Shakespeare's sexual comedies seem so ripe for explicit restaging within the context of AIDS. Let the comedies represent a central truth of the 'gay tradition' I have been outlining. Desire and laughter belong in the same place as revulsion and grief. Any drag queen knows this. It is worth remembering.

Chapter 32

Poetry and Paradox

In Canto XXVI of the *Purgatorio*, Dante watches in amazement as a band of (literally) flaming faggots passes by. He recognises the sexual transgressives, not by any particular mannerism or stigma, but by their two distinct ways of communication. Among themselves their language is physical: they are constantly kissing one another, in brief signs of greeting as chaste as the embraces of angels, yet as suggestive as any sinful gesture can be. This sensual language of solidarity reminds Dante of how, by promiscuous contact of antennae, a community of ants will disseminate vital information in a manner private to itself:

> così per entro loro schiera bruna
> s'ammusa l'una con l'altra formica,
> forse ad espiar lor via e lor fortuna.
> (34–6)

(Thus within their brown ranks / one ant toys with another,/ perhaps to determine their way and their fortune.) For all its joyousness, this eloquent dalliance is a very serious pastime. The French might call it *jouissance*, a kind of sexually aware fore-and-aft-play of the intellect. That Dante seems to trivialise this exchange as mutual amusement need not trouble us here, since it usefully underlines the fact that their priorities are not his, and that he is not included in their discourse. As a heterosexual observer, he is an outsider to outsiders.

The passing sinners are not silent, however. They seem to be in competition to see which of them can most loudly proclaim where they come from: '*Soddoma e Gomorra*'. This ostentation of identity, a collective coming-out, is both a confession of the nature of their sin – presumably, a requirement of their sojourn in Purgatory – and an expression of 'citizenship' at least as proud as it is ashamed. Like the confessional gay literature of the pre-Stonewall period in the twentieth century, the most substantial message of these voices lies in the fact that they are heard at all: to speak is to act. What they are shouting is, in effect, a political slogan.

I mention Canto XXVI partly because it was T.S. Eliot's favourite bit of the *Divina Commedia* and, as such, became a central text in the genesis of Anglo-American Modernism. But what concerns me more about it is its attribution of these two modes of speech to Sodomites: the sensual mode in their private relationships, and the public shout in their confrontations with the outside world. We should be able to find similar stratagems being used in modern gay literature; and, as in the Dante, we may find both being used at once, either alternately or, as in a palimpsest, as text and subtext, one on top of the other.

In the course of this chapter, I shall try to establish that poetry (which so many people dismiss as incredible, unreadable and unreal, suited only to eggheads and sissies) is the ideal medium for a creativity that liberates. Within the miracle of its release from the restrictions of prose, verse allows for a world in which not all rules apply – not even the so-called 'laws' of nature. I hope to show how modern gay poets have reflected the peculiarity of their social status by adopting correspondingly peculiar linguistic strategies. My main topic is their use of paradox, as weapon and shield, against a world in which heterosexuality is taken for granted as being exclusively natural and healthy. Given that our lives as gay men are thought to be anomalous, contradictory, obsessive and obscene, we have taken up paradoxical ways of speaking, both to reflect the way we are seen and to stamp our own more accurate logic on the world. We strive to make sense of the conflict between the negative versions of our lives and our own more positive versions: to forge some kind of unity out of our contrary needs to be different and to fit in.

I do not like to be categorical about the nature of gay poetry. That would be to conform to the requirements of those who see homosexuality as being definitively – and negatively – *other*. Much of what gay authors do is – like what they do in bed – hesitant, improvised, polymorphous, messy, impassioned and (as such) indistinguishable from the efforts of their heterosexual counterparts.

I have shown elsewhere that there is an enormous common space of themes shared by the literatures of gay and straight men, a space in which men of whatever sexual orientation experience their masculinity in variations on three favourite roles: the male as Warrior, Lover and Father (inseminator, not parent).[1] However, if the concept of gay literature is to have any useful meaning whatsoever, it must also imply a needed space beyond (or, perhaps, fenced off within) the place in which most of us are forced to lead our daily lives: the waste land of heterosexual self-esteem. So, for the duration of this chapter, I am more concerned with the expression of difference, which is where paradox comes into play.

How convenient it would be for critics and readers, sympathetic and hostile alike, if gay and straight authors really wrote in different languages: if their tongues were different shapes. The world of speech could be cleanly divided up and labelled – the danger being (as is usually true of such instances) that the two categories thereby formed would be arranged by rank, like concentration camp inmates, with the homosexual populace underneath. Speaking in another context altogether, Jonathan Culler has pithily described the relevant process: 'When reducing the continuous to the discrete, one calls upon binary oppositions as the elementary devices for establishing distinctive classes.'[2]

Culler's use of the word 'classes' is particularly suggestive: for, as many commentators have pointed out, binary oppositions almost invariably end up ranked: white above black, good above bad, man above woman, heterosexual above homosexual. (This 'organising' tendency of the patriarchal mind has been severely and cogently attacked on gender grounds by a number of women; Hélène Cixous argues that it should be replaced by a system of multiple differences.) In exactly this manner, religious moralists and civil legislators and medical theorists – each group in its own way, yet all in much the same – have turned the world's spectrum of sexual variety into a confrontation between homosexuals and heterosexuals. Where language itself is forced into a divided state under contrary banners (natural–unnatural, logical–illogical, proper–improper, orthodox–unorthodox), such is the battleground of paradox.

In the opening chapter of *The Well Wrought Urn* (1949), Cleanth Brooks suggests that paradox is 'the language appropriate and inevitable to poetry'. The assumption is that scientific and poetic logic are mutually exclusive. 'The tendency of science is necessarily to stabilise terms, to freeze them into strict denotations; the poet's tendency is by contrast disruptive. The terms are continually modifying each other, and thus violating their dictionary meanings.' If we apply Brooks' argument to our own purposes, we can deduce correspondences between heterosexuality and science, homosexuality and poetry. Of course, this is to take Brooks closer to the carnal world outside a given text than he intends; but there are tantalising moments when his train of thought does threaten to address the question of the languages of sexuality. Paradox, he says, 'is an extension of the normal language of poetry, not a perversion of it'. For good measure, he adds that 'most of the language of lovers' is paradoxical.[3]

Our word 'paradox' is derived from the Greek *pará* and *dóxa*, meaning contrary to, or opposed to, public opinion. It is, by definition, the speech pattern of a minority; and it is, by definition, out of step with the complacent *dogma* (same etymological root) of the *Doxa*. It is deviant speech. With paradox as its natural tongue, therefore, poetry is not only miraculous and incredible – or, to the *Doxa*, incomprehensible – but also open to sexual irregularity. Only when the eloquence of poetry is thought to fail does scientific tautology regain authority. This happens in Shakespeare's sonnets, for instance, when the poet gives up trying to replicate the beauty of the boy he loves in words. He pretends he is reduced to such insignificant, phatic utterances as 'you alone are you' (84) and 'best is best' (101).

It may have been a consequence of a decision to fight the dubious (anti-homosexual prejudice) with the dubious, that homosexual men became masters of the paradox. Paradox would be the invincible weapon of their tongues: a doubtable hypothesis which always turned out to be true. Once you have accepted as perfectly reasonable and desirable the sexual union of two penised creatures, your world is released from the chains of heterosexual tautology (whereby penis and vagina are defined by one another's shape, and 'love' and 'sex' and 'reproduction' are synonyms). Then, where the body has gone, language must follow. Paradox affirms the possibility of a world in which humanity – like a living language – invents itself continuously, according to usage, rather than rotting – like Latin – within a cage of proscriptive rules. Paradox is syntactical logic working 'against nature'. It offers us the lovely world in which Quentin Crisp can write a book called *How to Become a Virgin*.

There can be no doubt that Oscar Wilde's love of paradoxical utterances about the state of the world is connected to a sense of social absurdity aggravated, or enriched, by his sexuality. Most of his paradoxes are generalisations, stated with all the confidence of a scientist establishing natural law: 'There is only one thing in the world worse than being talked about, and that is not being talked about', 'It is a terrible thing for a man to find out suddenly that all his life he has been speaking nothing but the truth', 'It is only shallow people who do not judge by appearances', 'Each man kills the thing he loves'. Behind them all is a strong sense that the speaker has an uncommon view of the world; and if we accept the paradox itself, we also have to accept that, compared with the common view, the uncommon is based on superior intelligence. 'Each man *loves* the thing he loves' would, after all, be a stupid thing to say, even if it is perfectly logical.

It is not difficult to see why paradox would be thought a superior creative mode to tautology. Insofar as each leads to either a repetition or an apparent negation of its starting point, both are circular; but, whereas tautology invariably returns to an unchanged point of departure, paradox moves on, spiral-wise, to a modified (often inverted) version of its origin. Whilst tautology involves itself in an endless reiteration of dictionary definitions, paradox redefines. It seeks to modify the world – especially that part represented by the timid status quo of definitions.

In much gay literature, the subversion of logical discourse by the use of paradox is compounded by an unrelenting irony, often dangerously close to being overlooked. I am thinking, particularly, of the way in which writers like Wilde and Ronald Firbank distinguish between the naïve and the knowing, not only among their characters, but among their readers as well: those who get the joke (or, indeed, the serious point) and those who are assumed not to. This is the kind of irony which radicalises half of its readers/listeners at the other half's expense. It sets those who recognise it against those who do not, by attacking the prejudices of the latter, while often seeming (to them) to confirm them. (Of course, when it tires, it tends merely to confirm the complacent 'radicalism' of the first half, and to patronise the second.) At its best, it sets the ignorant against the knowing, and then undercuts both. Above all, it deflates emotion, thereby amusing itself at the expense of solemn objections to homosexuality, which, at their most irrational, are fired by nothing but blunt emotionalism. At the same time, its aesthetic antidote to emotion is as artificial as it sets out to be, but remains emotionally (often passionately) committed to its fight for the 'decadent', which in so many cases is a cover for something as mundane as love. The ironic style is often unaware that its own artifice is artificial, its emotionlessness is emotional, and its lack of commitment is committed.[4]

Like this kind of irony, every paradox assumes a divided audience. Indeed, it takes on itself the relatively straightforward task of dividing them. It will not make any sense at all to the literal-minded, whose best reaction to it may be grudging and embarrassed laughter, as though at an *odd* sense of humour: for, to them, paradox is *nonsense*.[5] When a character in Joe Orton's play *What the Butler Saw* says 'You can't be a rationalist in an irrational world. It isn't rational', Orton is addressing a hypothetical audience, half of which are expected to think 'How ridiculous!' and the other half 'How true!' Thus, one side of any audience will dismiss a given statement as logically preposterous; the other will either accept it at once, or at least accept that, with a little further thought, it *might* be acceptable. Never egalitarian, paradox ranks its audience accordingly, setting its own sympathisers above simpler minds. It relies on a divided world.

In order to understand the role of gay poetry on the battlefield of hetero–homo confrontation, we need to discard the typically English association of poetry with the gentility, serenity and sensitivity of tea-time in a vicarage garden. On the contrary, poetry is the most violent of the written arts: consistently cruel to language, vicious with logic, swift to the jugular of politics. The word 'verse' itself, in common with 'versus', has a Latin root, relating to the turning of a plough at the end of its furrow. To embark on verse constitutes *going against* a direction previously established, in opposition to ordinary syntax. Thus, most poetry assumes into its very structure an understanding that the two major subdivisions of written discourse are in conflict: prose *versus* verse.[6] The one contra-dicts the other. In *Don Juan* (1819–24), Byron had said, 'if a writer should be quite consistent, / How could he possibly show things existent?'[7] And Walt Whitman may have been a world away from the epigrammatic Oscar ('Who wants to be consistent?') Wilde, but even he saw, and celebrated, the innate deviancy of verse. As he says in 'Song of Myself' (Section 51):

> Do I contradict myself?
> Very well then . . . I contradict myself[.]

He is talking not only about the direction of his argument, but also, as we shall see, about fundamental questions of personality and physique.

Pier Paolo Pasolini also knew that this matter of contradicting oneself is not to be taken lightly. In 'Le ceneri di Gramsci' (1957), he writes of

30. The scandal of the
contradictory physique.
(Drawing by Czanara of the
*Hermaphrodite Angel of
Peladan*)

Lo scandolo del contraddirmi, dell'essere
con te e contro te; con te nel cuore,
in luce, contro te nelle buie viscere[.][8]

(The scandal of contradicting myself, of being / with you and against you; with you in the
heart,/ in light, against you in my dark bowels.) The 'you' is generally Gramsci himself;
but there are times when, as here, 'you' is also Italy, *patria* and patriarchy, to which the
double agent Pasolini is a traitor, by virtue of his interdependent communism and
homosexuality. (No matter that these are the very virtues which affirm his *love* of country.)
He is, simply, not to be trusted. Note that he sites his contrariety as much in his body as
in his speech: for sexuality is the crux of the issue, and a particular type of sexuality at that.
The 'problem' is not in the misdirection of his phallus so much as in the darkness of his
bowels.

It is at moments like this that texts act out the equivocation of the homosexual body as
one which – to put it in terms both archaic and inaccurate – is either simultaneously or
alternately 'female' and 'male', while remaining ('scientifically'/'objectively') the sex it
would unequivocally have been, were it heterosexual: in a man's case, male. Straight men
are definitively male: their heterosexuality and their maleness are mutually proven, since a
man *is* the penised creature whose defining organ becomes erect when he sees (desires) a
person without such an organ, a woman. Gay men, on the other hand, confuse the issue.

Our desire responds to the wrong object and, notoriously, we turn ourselves into women by allowing ourselves to be penetrated by other men. Like whores, we become *all cunt* (where this noun is wielded as the most extreme obscenity imaginable), the vagina being, by etymological definition, a sheath for penises.

This tedious reasoning, dependent on the 'logical' wit of lexicographers, seems to me one of the more creative sources of the gay literature that departs from it. Good gay literature *denies* the fallacies with which we are ourselves denied; yet it often then uses that same fallacious material in building our alternative view of reality. Out of an intercourse between our own bodies and other people's versions of them, we express our disadvantaged relation to the societies that fear us.

The archetype of homosexual paradox is the notion of two sexes existing simultaneously in one body. For a while around the turn of the century this theme appeared as a *psychological* metaphor for male homosexuality: a woman's soul trapped in a man's body. (This is the metaphor Proust takes to literal conclusions in *La Prisonnière*, where his own love for his chauffeur is represented in terms of a possibly lesbian Albertine imprisoned in the apartment of a shakily heterosexual Marcel.) The two sexes appear, also, as a *sexual* metaphor for the things we do 'in bed', and whom we do them with. We are the men-not-men who can fuck and be fucked. (We contradict ourselves; very well then, we contradict ourselves.) It is as if our anatomy differs completely from that of the two-dimensional straight: for bisexual and homosexual men consist of *both front and back*. What this physical monstrosity invokes is a complicated choice followed by a simple action: a turning-over or bending-over. This is what is happening when Shakespeare's Achilles and Patroclus go to their tent 'to make paradoxes'. It is also why Balzac's Vautrin is said to be 'an expert in paradox'.[9] It is what Oscar Wilde meant when he said, 'What the paradox was to me in the sphere of thought, perversity became to me in the sphere of passion'.[10] Think of all the anti-gay jokes with which straight men use this elementary transformation scene to effeminise gay men. Stephen Coote prints some in *The Penguin Book of Homosexual Verse*. A twelfth-century fragment of doggerel by Godfrey the Satirist is a perfect expression of the unorthodoxy of the bisexual body (which is *of* and *desires* both sexes):

> Who sees you, G, surprises two in one:
> A boy behind, your front as man must rate.
> You play the lad for your illicit fun,
> But on the turn, you're virile true and straight!

A more modern version, a limerick, goes as follows:

> A hermaphrodite fairy of Kew
> Offered boys something new in a screw,
> For they both looked so sweet
> On the front and back seat
> Of a *bisexual built for two*.[11]

To the unconfident straight, this is a metamorphosis more awesome than anything in Ovid.[12] It has the terrible power to compromise his definition of himself: he may be, and be convinced that he is, a Real Man; but there is always, in the seat of his pants, the worry that he possesses one part which could – if he were to *turn* at the wrong/right time – *turn* him into a woman, a mere sheath for men more Real than himself. (Here lies his true contempt for the women he 'desires'.) He is fooling himself, of course, about the extent of his virile virtue: for no one who has ever defecated is an anal virgin.

Nothing could be more disturbing to the sexual status quo – which keeps male divided from female, and hetero- from homosexual, in watertight compartments – than the homosexual body. Men-who-love-men-instead-of-women can do two monstrous things in the social arena of sexual choice: (a) they turn men-who-love-women into objects of male desire, and (b) they may themselves become womanly enough to deflect from women proper the desires of men-who-love-women. In other words, homosexuality is itself a threat to the binary system that invented it: for its equivocal relation to the proprieties of discrete gender constantly cause it to break the bounds of its own definition. Once 'homosexuality' exists, thereby creating 'heterosexuality', the latter is already under threat. In a society which sees all women as seductresses, the most dangerous woman of all will be the least visible and most sly: the female soul within a male body. It is she who will persuade him to *turn*.

The metamorphic capacities of the homosexual body extend to perversities of behaviour and thought. There is a fine poetic example of this when Wilfred Owen admits that an impulse of homo-erotic humaneness has overcome his formal duty to religious symbolism. As he reports in 'Maundy Thursday', a cold metal crucifix is held out to him in church, so that he may kiss the feet of the dead Christ. The sonnet ends as follows:

> And yet I bowed, yea, kissed – my lips did cling
> (I kissed the warm live hand that held the thing.)[13]

Perhaps 'unorthodox' is the best word for this moment of irreligious eroticism. (The *orthos* in *orthos-dóxa* means 'straight', in the sense of 'correct'. To turn against, or be contrary to, this straightness, is to be bent.) With this simple action, Owen puts himself beyond the pale. Others have kissed the cross before him, and different groups' kisses have had different meanings: men have paid homage to 'the emblem of a creed'; women have embraced Christ's body; children have kissed 'a silver doll'. But Owen's kiss sets him apart from them all: society, the nuclear family, institutional religion, heterosexuality, reproduction, artifice, even art. This does not leave him isolated or lonely: the very act of separation forges a new union – with life, warmth, beauty, youth, flesh, humanity, the present tense . . . all united in the figure of the altar boy. Owen is kissing goodbye to the Church, identifying himself as a member of the Sodomite diaspora, and greeting the possibility of love, homosexual love. His planting of the paradoxical kiss is a coming-out scene. The lips say 'I am gay' to whom it concerns – the original paradox: 'I-a-man desire you-a-boy'.

The second major paradox of our lives is the one forced on us by social decree. Paul Goodman expresses it clearly in the opening words of one of his untitled poems:

> Almost everything lovely in my eyes
> is banned to me by law or circumstance
> or impractical people.[14]

We learn this, most of us, during adolescence; and it shapes our relationships with heterosexuals for the rest of our lives. What we love they loathe. It distances us at once from even our closest kin, unless they too are gay. As we fumble our way through tentative first relationships, sighing and starry-eyed at the ordinary thrill of love, the occasional sneer or giggle or threat intrudes on our mood, reminding us that what we call beauty is 'really' only filth. Our love is just lust, like our lust. At the very luckiest, those of us who were nurtured in the 'liberal' bourgeoisie are policed with embarrassment – merely a diluted form of what we are still under pressure to feel: shame.

Given the extent of heterosexual people's ineradicable (often clinically phobic) terror of homo-eroticism, the gay space will be *defined* as one in which all is per-verse (or a-verse, ad-verse, con-verse, di-verse, in-verse, ob-verse, re-verse, sub-versive, trans-verse): a natural territory, in fact, for *verse* itself. And it will be defined as such from both sides of the fence. As with women, blacks, Jews, the working class, so too with gay men: not only are the disadvantaged defined as the Other, but they are forced into the defensive cultural position of having to define *themselves* as such. If my love is an abomination, so be it: I shall be abominate with defiant pride.[15] 'Very well then . . . I contradict myself.'

Once one finds oneself to be *para-dóxa*, freed from the 'logic' of linguistic 'common sense' and the 'natural' urges of the syntax we have been taught, all kinds of poetic dialects struggle to unfurl the tongue. We become immature again, the adulthood of our homosexuality leading us back through an inverted puberty into the creative, drooling babble of infancy. Language becomes assertively puerile. It is entirely appropriate that the greatest exemplar of this passing phase is the eternal adolescent Arthur Rimbaud, a gorgeous poet by the age of fifteen, but dead to both poetry and male love by twenty.[16]

How far this perverse teenager, with a body as beautiful and filthy as his verse, can be judged relevant to the lives and literature of post–1970 mature gay men depends on how we view the crucial area of the way we seem to the straight hegemony. A remark of Herbert Blau's looks as if it should help:

> To the extent that gays still pretend to be a challenge to the superstructure of bourgeois capitalism, they can't afford the accentuation of the difference, and with it a more than theoretical deference to the old illicit energies of the homosexual underworld, and its canonical rhetoric of abominations.[17]

While I accept that the challenge is largely pretentious, I would have thought that it was precisely those 'old illicit energies' and the 'rhetoric of abominations' that make for some of the most vibrant – and politically effective – gay culture: for the fact is that the hegemony is not liberal; it is not possible to live as an innocent homosexual: they will not allow us to do so. If any of us holds subversive power, it is the sodomite, not the kind of submissive, virile, quiet man's-man (and one-man man at that) the law would like us to be: the kinds of invisible homosexuals Britain's Sexual Offences Act of 1967 envisaged, while still expecting us to be stigmatised as filth. Thus, in considering Blau's point, we must be drawn back to those two words 'difference' and 'deference'. They recapitulate the one choice open to the gay personality emergent in the emergency of adolescence. We must defer to the requirements of the majority, or make a conscious decision to confirm and affirm our difference and our right to it.

Later in the same essay, Blau says that 'the really determining factor in what . . . you choose for yourself sexually, is *disgust*' (p. 249). This is a resonant thought, but not half as simple as it looks. Whose disgust is he talking about, ours or theirs? For the moment, I am mainly interested in things that disgust *them* (they being heterosexuals). Lautréamont – that other wild, young, French poet of Rimbaud's day – says in *Les Chants de Maldoror* (1868), 'Pigs vomit when they look at us' ('Les pourceaux, quand ils nous regardent, vomissent'). This strikes me as a nicely defiant attitude to heterosexual disgust: we make them sick because they are so porcine.

One could not stray further from deference than this. It obviously brings us to the question of propriety. Rudeness is not an innocent concept. It depends on all the usual social factors: age, gender, race, class. What it boils down to is a question of relative power.[18] A man is allowed more latitude in his speech than a 'lady' is. The middle class can make far more polite use of impolite terms than the working class – even though, contrariwise, the workers are *expected* to be rude: their accents (not to mention diction and grammar) are themselves obscene or, at the very least, 'vulgar'. Likewise with the sexual orientations: heterosexuals can be ruder than homosexuals, because straight bad language is less bad than gay bad language. Polite gay fiction stands on the 'Adult' shelves, blushing amongst the obscene straight novels.

Even when we are at our most polite, we are adjudged to be being rude. Because we take part in sexual acts which were known in the Middle Ages as the *lingua mala* (or *langue méchante*), we cannot but use bad language. Be it physical or spiritual, our love is seen as *inappropriate* to the proper relation of man and man, and is therefore *improper*.[19] And when we use 'their' phrases, they think we are using the wrong language. (How can such a beautiful heterosexual expression as 'love' be suited to our lewdness?[20])

There are times when we decide to exploit this fact – that everything we say about ourselves will be thought rude – by lacing the fruit-cup of our lyricism with the headier spirits of obscenity: an 'inappropriate' mixture of proper and improper languages that results in the intoxicant effects of Rimbaud and Genet. We even go so far as to pervert grammar in order to express our alienation: 'I is someone else.' (Rimbaud: 'Je est un autre'.)

Once this other-ness becomes ingrained in a particular writer – as a mannerism, or a pathological flaw, or subversive diversity, or whatever you like to call it – we may find that everything written in his name needs placing in 'inverted' commas. (I believe this is true of W.H. Auden, who wrote poetry of the most private sort and then, the more famous and popular it became, distanced himself from it with self-chastising cruelty.) More extreme still is the case of the writer who does not even use his own name: Anon. or the legions of the pseudonymous. But what of a man like Fernando Pessoa, who wrote in both Portuguese and English, and turned himself into *four* major poets – Alberto Caeiro, Ricardo Reis, Àlvaro de Campos and 'Fernando Pessoa' – only one of them (to me) identifiably gay?

But to return to Rimbaud: his poems are pungent with what, in the age of safer sex, have come to be called the bodily fluids: not just semen, but sweat and urine too; and not just fluids: for much of what he writes is presented as excrement. He needs to pass it, he enjoys passing it, and he is glad to get rid of it, preferably on to the heads of his parents' generation. His reaction to it combines a sense of inert waste with a coprophile's thrill to terrible riches. Thus, when, at sixteen, Rimbaud scrawled *Merde à Dieu* on public benches, he not only performed a gauche act of blasphemy, but he also bade farewell (*adieu*) to the words he was writing as though they were turds. An infantile joke, but one which retained its power over him throughout his precocious poetic career.

Later in life, when asked about his poetry, he would reply with something to the effect of 'Absurd! Ridiculous! Disgusting!'[21] This does not mean that he had changed his mind about his poems. They were always intended to arouse such reactions. Any Rimbaud poem – and many gay poems – should be read on the understanding of a silent background chorus of stuffy, bourgeois voices, grunting 'Absurd! Ridiculous! Disgusting!' This is the sound of Lautréamont's pigs throwing up.

It may be that the only language truly suited to our marginality is some kind of filthy slang – that transitory dialect which does not conform to the 'standard' social usage. When Genet says 'the word balls is a roundness in my mouth', he means not just the testicles but a particular way, a rude way, of mouthing them: 'balls' (*couilles*).[22] Paul Verlaine says 'Stop metaphoring; let's fuck' ('Ne métaphorons pas, foutons').[23] W.H. Auden launches into a narrative poem – the usual pornographic narrative passage from first sight to ejaculation – with the immortal words:

> It was a spring day, a day, a day for a lay, when the air
> Smelled like a locker-room, a day to blow or get blown[.][24]

This gay playfulness is easy enough to dismiss. But one dismissed text is the same as all the others. Once there is censoring to be done, who cares whether the offending passage is extremely or only mildly transgressive? Either way, it must be excised. Auden's *The Platonic Blow* was no more unpublishable, for all its explicitness and joy, than E.M. Forster's much more circumspect and anguished *Maurice*. It does not matter to the scissor-wielders whether I am sighing after a boy's soul or lusting after his prick; whether I whisper in his ear or come in his rear makes little difference. My politeness and my rudeness sound the same: for I am speaking the language of Sodom in the presence of xenophobes. It does not matter *how* I am other; I simply am. This is why it is so important to so many critics to deny the homo-eroticism of Shakespeare's poems, or ignore that of Auden's: for once a text is 'homosexual' it is, to all intents and purposes, obscene.

An interesting commentary on this theme of appropriate languages occurs between the lines of James Mitchell's poem 'Gay Epiphany'.[25] The poem is, as it were, a speechless ode to the male genitals, addressed to them in the adoring vocative, but with nothing to say to them beyond naming, from anus to prepuce, their parts. It is a roll-call of the kind of scientific terminology which would never normally appear in either a romantic lyric or a pornographic narrative; yet it is curiously expressive:

> o symphysis pubis! tunica albuginea! vasa efferentia!
> corpus cavernosum et spongiosum! o ampulla of vas!

This certainly does not read as drily as a medical text. Despite the respectable pedigree of its diction, it sounds thoroughly rude. The combined effect of the vocatives and the exclamation points is to return medical language to its Latin origins and to restore the enthusiasm of Catullan eroticism to it. Thus, the danger that all this technical language might give the impression of genitals in need of medical care does not arise; on the contrary, they seem in fine working order and ready for action.

Implicit in the act of addressing the lover's genitals (speaking of them to them) is an approach to fellatio. The speaking mouth's dance of lips and tongue draws ever nearer the object of its concentration until finally, either by word of mouth or by mouth itself, the poet consumes the penis. It takes its place in his throat, shaped to the sound of his voice, in harmony.

There is also a grotesque aspect to the poem: for, by examining the genitals in detail, part by part, it takes them apart. To read it aloud is to dissect it with one's tongue and teeth, to spread out the pieces as though on a laboratory bench. This is fellatio reduced to cannibalism, perhaps, but also raised to the status of sacrament. I mention this aspect because there seems to be a kind of violence in much of the work paradoxical language achieves. It is, certainly, not a pacific mode of speech. It exists *in order to* disturb; at times even to damage; at times even to destroy. It may be a joke, but a joke with a deadly serious edge.

'Gay Epiphany' ends with the line 'Boy, at the lovely tip of your external urethral orifice, all my poetries terminate' – with no terminal punctuation. Depending on the direction from which we imagine the poet approaching the end of the boy's cock, this line can mean either that he is rendered speechless by it (both with wonder at its beauty and, then, by taking it into his mouth, the place of speech, in place of speech), or, on the contrary, that his poetry (like this poem) consists *only* of praise of the lover's cock, and comes to an end when he comes to its end.

So – a frequent motif in the verse of gay fellatio – the sucked cock is *paradoxically* both a gag and a voice. As such, it is the model subject for all gay utterance, the physical emblem of social requirement: the gay poet's opposed needs to be discreet and to be expressive. Like homosexuality itself, it prompts him to speak yet is not, according to public opinion, the kind of thing one speaks about. It embodies the paradox of a love which, while perhaps not daring to speak its name, *must* do so in order that the name, and consequently the love, continue to exist. Fellatio is not the done thing; but it must be done.

I am not trying to make out a case for this poem as a special work of the lyric imagination. Precisely *because* its one-off wit (in both senses 'unrepeatable') does not strike out in any new direction, the poem has a range of backward reference to what other gay poems have already tried to do. Far from being experimental, it relies heavily on the tradition of all phallus-fetishistic literature by gay men: in that sense, it is orthodox, hidebound. Its quality is not at issue; of more interest to me is its representative obsession with linguistic doublespeak that requires a doublehearing by ears receptive to *double entendre*. Not that it ever hides the object of its admiration: this penis is hardly being euphemised or in any way merely suggested, hinted at. But the poem is duplicitous about the way it presents speech as oral intercourse: although it never says so, when I read it aloud I have a cock in my mouth; which is why I take such pleasure in reading it.

Double entendre is the verbal expression of an imposed (double-) lifestyle. A façade of expedient respectability conceals the erotic joke which explodes within. A man who is wrongly assumed to be heterosexual (because he looks ordinary) is a living pun, whose second meaning makes itself known only to the perceptive, and only after office hours. There is a point in Joe Orton's *Loot* (1966) when Dennis says to Mr McLeavy, referring to Mrs McLeavy's death, 'The exit of a loved one is always a painful experience.'[26] This textbook example of innuendo exactly mimics the way in which respectable social behaviour conceals unrespectable sexual truth. The line is one text with two meanings: effectively two texts, therefore. To the innocent McLeavy it is Dennis' compassionate and formal expression of condolence, comforting him on the death of his wife. As such, it is discreet and tasteful. But to Dennis himself, who says it, the subtext has a mischievous sexual meaning, referring to the withdrawal of a penis from an orifice: in Dennis' case, Hal's from his. The line's humour exists in neither of its texts alone. The respectable meaning is a dull cliché, a formulaic way of dealing with death; and the unrespectable meaning, made explicit, is a rather obvious statement of emotional and physical fact. The humour comes from the interplay of the two meanings. It is a social joke, about the need, above all, to hide one's actual feelings behind the requirements of social expediency.

Impoliteness thus festers and flourishes in a closet of politeness. Although I have just offered a joke as my main example, I prefer not to think of the *double entendre*, along the lines of common usage, as being necessarily humorous. All gay literature consisting of text and subtext works in a similar way, and (like the discovery that a man previously assumed to be straight is, in fact, gay) can be devalued to the status of a mere risqué joke by any hostile reader aware of the two levels. If such a reader judges gay seriousness to be 'inappropriate' to his world, it can always be laughed at.

If seriousness is at such risk, a gay writer may adopt a pre-emptive laughter of his own. The assumption behind this stratagem is that straight people will find it more difficult to laugh at gays who are themselves already laughing. So, along with lexical propriety goes the question of the proper *register*. I have already mentioned gay irony; one of its effects, if it is maintained at any length, is to open its author to the charge of frivolity. (Think of Wilde or Firbank or Orton; just how serious are they generally credited with being?) Like that of Lord Byron, the reputation of W.H. Auden has suffered at the hands of readers who think he wrote too much 'light verse'. The most consistently intellectual English poet of this century was too clever by half, yet not quite earnest enough. Take the notorious ending of 'Lakes', the fourth of seven 'Bucolics' which date from 1952 and 1953:

> It is unlikely I shall ever keep a swan
> Or build a tower on any small tombolo,
> But that's not going to stop me wondering what sort
> Of lake I would decide on if I should.
> Moraine, pot, oxbow, glint, sink, crater, piedmont, dimple . . .?
> Just reeling off their names is ever so comfy.[27]

The critics tend to treat this ending as a kind of senile lapse into an inappropriate register. Given the nominative pomp of the penultimate line, what with its thesaurus erudition and its capitulation of poetic syntax to a mere list of technical ('scientific') names, the poem's last four words seem to some readers a virtual abdication of responsibility. The poem is spoilt, they argue, by such frivolous bathos.

It is violated, to be sure – or rather, the expected version of it is. But since when were expected versions those which must prevail? The disturbance Auden inflicts here can, I think, adequately be characterised by the critical term 'camp', which straight critics are reluctant to use in any realm other than that of cross-dressing.[28] The poem suffers a deflation of tone at the hands of its own maker, in such a manner as demands we question the tone of all that has gone before. There is a kind of infection in the ending that spreads back to the rest of the poem. Perhaps we have 'lower' expectations when we get round to rereading it.

Stan Smith has said, of the ending of 'Lakes', that the speaker 'withdraws into a petty privacy'.[29] While I can see what he means, and agree with it to an extent, I think one also needs to take into account a move in the opposite direction: from a specialist to a common language – that is, from esoteric privacy into the *comfort* of public pleasantry, however worn smooth of precise meaning. But which of the two is the more rhetorical: the technical nouns denoting the physical shapes and origins of lakes, or the fake cosiness the last line puts on like carpet slippers? Auden is at home in both, of course, but, having set one against the other, seems genuinely at peace in neither. Both are borrowed languages, in each of which the poet has learned an apparently effortless fluency. But there is at least as much unease here as comfort: the comfiness is posed.

The question I kept coming back to when first reading Auden was: when is he going to use his own voice? (This, despite his being so often so chatty and informal.) The question was naïve: for what poet ever does use his/her 'own' voice? All speech is conveyed in borrowed tones, indistinct against the background noises of race, class, gender, sexuality and so on. Even our most private 'I love you' is a quotation heavy with the messy histories of other people's attempts at intimate communication. Like Eliot, Auden was always aware of this problem with language: you think it, you speak it, you write it, but what you say is never truly 'in your own words'. You put your name to an arrangement of quotations. So, as one of Auden's titles has it, '"The Truest Poetry is the Most Feigning"' (which is itself a quotation from a love scene in *As You Like It*).

Given how our mouths tend to fill up with other people's speech, the struggle not to become a mere ventriloquist's dummy is not only a concern for mediocre writers. To the likes of Auden, if true originality is not available in an old and much-weathered language, the writer's best choice is to try to give an 'original' impression; knowingly to feign or fake it. But as spontaneity recedes and the studied poses of aestheticism take over, there is a danger that the less careful of such writers will retreat into a rarefied haze at ever greater distances from 'everyday life' and 'ordinary people'. The worst of them will look down on 'real life' with a voluble sneer. (It is a mark of Auden's humaneness, and measure of his achievement, that this does not happen in his verse, even after he has firmly decided that 'poetry makes nothing happen'.[30])

It may be that paradox is particularly friendly to poets who, like Auden himself and John Ashbery after him, are quite open about being homosexual but do not wish to be read as gay writers. There is a defining moment in the poem 'Qualm' when the oblique trajectory of Ashbery's view comes clearly into evidence.[31] The poem, which appears in the 1982 collection *Shadow Train*, is ostensibly about Warren G. Harding, the 29th President of the United States (1921–23). The prime point Ashbery makes about this undistinguished politician is that he invented two words: 'bloviate', whose meaning is unclear, and the unnecessary 'normalcy'. Both the vagueness of the former and the fact that the latter is a perversion of 'normality' suggest that Harding was not the man to be granted custody of the American language; and yet, as Ashbery has accepted by the very fact of having included them in his poem, for all their crassness both words are strangely expressive, especially on the manner of their own coining. Ashbery's supposition of what 'bloviate' means – 'to spew aimless verbiage' – instantly sticks to Harding as the perfect word to describe his linguistic activities. And the word's perfection, its aptness to purpose, is clearly self-contradictory, a paradox. The same goes for 'normalcy', which in some sense – indicated by the fact that the word has always been so sniffily received by English-speaking intellectuals – is not a normal word at all.

Ashbery presents Harding as a dull man, at least by presidential standards: he never even wanted to be President; he died undramatically, in a hotel, while his wife was reading to him from a newspaper. From this portrayal one infers that he would have been happier in, and better suited to, a more modest, bourgeois career. Ashbery sums him up – some might say, dismisses him – as follows: 'Poor Warren. He wasn't a bad egg, / Just weak. He loved women and Ohio.'

This put-down is worth examining in detail, since it tells us a great deal about the direction from which Ashbery's irony is launched. The phrase 'Poor Warren', which is repeated later as the poem's last words, would be unexceptional on the lips of the bereaved wife; otherwise, it sounds patronising, even impertinent. Similarly, 'bad egg' is not strictly the poet's own phrase but the kind of vague judgement one might have heard from a man like Harding himself, or from one of his provincial cronies. Everything in the poem so far has contributed to the impression of Harding as being what Ashbery calls him next, 'Just weak'. Readers who want to know the exact nature of that weakness are offered the succinctly definitive sentence: 'He loved women and Ohio'.

To love Ohio when you have so many other states to choose from, not to mention other nations, is either wilfully perverse or just unimaginatively narrow-minded. It is provincial – an east coast word, as judgmental coming from a New York poet as from a Washington-based civil servant. But what is most interesting, here, is the way in which Ashbery has yoked the love of Ohio to the love of women. By association, heterosexuality itself is branded as a weakness, as dull a taste as an affection for Ohio. Why love women when you might love . . . Manhattan?

In effect, Harding's 'normalcy' is presented as being predictable and banal – a view which would itself be banal if it were not clear, too, that Ashbery paradoxically characterises Harding as being so extremely normal (if we accept that norms can be superlative) as to have become, on the page, virtually exotic, the object of fascination and even, perhaps, a touch of revulsion. The subsequent association of confetti with golf stars, in the manner in which the appearance of both tends to grace the summer months, gives further emphasis to the poem's fascination with suburban, heterosexual values.

Ashbery's written view of the world is no less paradoxical than Oscar Wilde's. In the same collection as 'Qualm' he even has a love poem called 'Paradoxes and Oxymorons', which expresses something of the tenderness which can be borne on lovers' tongues. Although the poem begins with the claim 'This poem is concerned with language on a very plain level', which it immediately seeks to demonstrate in a sentence which could have appeared in a children's reading primer – 'Look at it talking to you' – it plots a distinctly sinuous course towards the linguistically simple, but conceptually less straightforward, conclusion, 'The poem is you'.[32] The process by which words addressed to the lover – words in verse, masquerading as speech – actually become the lover may not be new (it is a trick Shakespeare managed in the sonnets), but it may be that it works to a somewhat new effect here, where paradox is seen as normative. 'The poem is you' does not mean anything so syntactically banal as 'you are the poem'. It comes much closer to Rimbaud's 'je est un autre'.

A much earlier poem, 'Soonest Mended', in the 1969 collection *The Double Dream of Spring*, opens by speaking of the experience of being 'Barely tolerated, living on the margin / In our technological society'.[33] The speaker appears not to identify with that 'our' which is so closely yoked to technological logic. Moreover, the same speaker's later avowal of the practice of 'sowing the seeds crooked in the furrow' indicates both an awareness of being watched and judged wanting, and a determination to continue sowing seeds in the same perversely individualistic manner. It is from such margins, and with such awareness and determination, that what I have been referring to as a paradoxical point of view is developed.

Some people might regard such a statement as 'he loved women' as a tautology, given that loving women is what human males are meant to do. It is what defines the male, just as loving Ohio should define the mind-set of the orthodox Ohioan. By setting his own discourses so emphatically against the grain of such tautological orthodoxies, Ashbery puts himself into a position, ideal for any writer, from which the ordinary looks extraordinary and the mundane sublime.

Given the political complacency of many gay writers – who assume that anything they write will automatically express dissent, simply because they are gay – a word of warning is needed with respect to the politics of the texts I have been referring to. Paradox may be subversive, but it makes for unsound political discourse if ever required to move the very public it defies. Beware of orators bearing paradox: they are unlikely to be democrats.

According to Roland Barthes, whose own career was proof, 'Lavish use of paradox risks implying . . . an individualist position, and one might say: a kind of dandyism.'[34] If so, it can suffer from all the available defects of the dandy: his self-absorption, his shallowness (masquerading as depth), the *feux d'artifice* of his arrogance, and, most dangerous of all, his contempt for the ordinary.

It is all very well to fashion an ornate superiority to people or things or ideas that the *Doxa* considers 'normal' (a word which tends to be used, by both sides of the divide, with cavalier disregard for statistical likelihood); but to allow one's mental languor to obscure any distinction between the normal and the ordinary is a very serious lapse of care. At some point, if the public are wrong, they must be put right. Simply to despise them may be temporarily satisfying; but, sooner or later, our literature needs to evangelise. And paradox may not be quite the right language for that. Thus, we are wedged in a situation where, our lives being seen from outside as paradoxical, paradox is the proper language with which to affirm our identity, but inappropriate to making ourselves understood by those who hold a so-called 'public' opinion.[35]

It follows from all I have been saying that paradox is in the eye of the beholder. Its meanings depend on whether the reader has a tautological or a paradoxical relation to the world; which roughly, in the present context, means whether the reader is straight or gay. Take, for example, the climax of Robert Duncan's love poem 'The Torso'.[36] The penultimate line carries an explicit message to readers who have not yet caught on to what is implicit in the previous two pages:

> For my Other is not a woman but a man[.]

In a world undivided, this would sound banal. Here, though, as one in a career-long series of comings-out, it is dignified and meaningful. But what *does* it mean? To the 'innocent' heterosexual reader whom it takes by surprise, this line – like homosexuality itself – may seem to be an exotic paradox. To me, knowing that Duncan was gay, and assuming his gayness was as natural to him as mine to me, the line is profoundly tautological: it goes without saying. Knowing Duncan as a gay poet, I infer 'my Other is not a woman but a man' from his every use of the first person singular; and as a gay reader, I do not think his homosexuality odd.

Insofar as paradox is thus a response to circumstances in which homosexuality is seen as being strange, it has to be read as the argot of an oppressed group. Its very existence acknowledges the oddness imposed on us from outside, and is a response to outsiders. It is, as I hope I have shown, structured along the lines of erroneous heterosexual versions of homosexuality. From the myth that we are double-sexed, we have derived a duality of speech, a habit of self-contradiction: to the extent that we are physically bi-sexed, we are also bi-lingual, double-tongued. While sticking out one tongue contemptuously at the homophobe, we apply the other, in depth and at length, to the bodies of our lovers. Even our silences may be contra-dictory, compliant and sulky at once.

Which brings us back to Dante's 'ants'. They have been labelled as deviants and transported to the camps of Purgatory in order to purge their deviancy. Adopting this label of sin, they adapt it to their own purposes, passing the duration of their internment in a curious competition to see who can confess the loudest. Although they are thus, presumably, acting within the terms of their sentence, it is difficult not to hear a note of conspiratorial irony in their cries. After all, at the same time as they are proclaiming their sinfulness, they seem to be undermining penitence with more kisses.

Thus, each of their two languages (cries and kisses) is conveying two incompatible messages, one to themselves and the other to others; the former defiantly positive, the latter submissively negative. Their harmonious incompatibility is, as I see it, the consistent distinguishing mark of the culture of Sodom, throughout the history of its oppression. Much of the poetry of gay men is energised by this paradoxical simultaneity of deferential and differential speech. Even when gagged, we have had voices. Muffled and distorted, perhaps, but eloquent with the very effort of speech.

Notes

Chapter 1

1 Hubert Kennedy, *Ulrichs: The Life and Works of Karl Heinrich Ulrichs, Pioneer of the Modern Gay Movement* (Boston: Alyson, 1988), pp. 87–8, 62.

2 *New Songs from a Jade Terrace* (Harmondsworth and New York: Penguin, 1986), p. 165.

3 Byrne R.S. Fone (ed.), *Hidden Heritage: History and the Gay Imagination* (New York: Irvington, 1981), p. 163.

4 The poem is reprinted in Fone, pp. 169–79. This reference is on p. 175.

5 Edward Carpenter, *Selected Writings, Volume 1: Sex* (London: GMP, 1984), p. 200.

6 See Fone, p. 287. Sometimes an author will pass on a gay reading list via a fictional character. For instance, in Klaus Mann's *The Pious Dance (Der Fromme Tanz, 1925)* the homosexual Andreas reads his way through Knut Hamsun, Walt Whitman, Stefan George, Hermann Bang, Paul Verlaine and Oscar Wilde.

7 Michael Elliman and Frederick Roll (eds), *The Pink Plaque Guide to London* (London: GMP, 1986).

8 John Rechy, *The Sexual Outlaw: A Documentary: A Non-fiction Account, with Commentaries, of Three Days and Nights in the Sexual Underground* (London: Futura, 1979), p. 31.

9 Holly Johnson, *Legendary Children (All of Them Queer)* (Club Tools CLU 6045–9), 1994. Johnson's list includes Alexander the Great, Michelangelo, Leonardo, Shakespeare, Oscar Wilde, Nijinsky, Gustav Mahler, Leonard Bernstein, Jean Cocteau, Truman Capote, W.H. Auden, Christopher Isherwood, Jean Genet, William Burroughs and Joe Orton, among others.

10 Eric Hobsbawm, 'Introduction: Inventing Traditions', in Eric Hobsbawm and Terence Ranger, *The Invention of Tradition* (Cambridge: Cambridge University Press, 1983), pp. 1–14; pp. 1, 4, 6.

11 Linda Dowling, *Hellenism and Homosexuality in Victorian Oxford* (Ithaca, NY and London: Cornell University Press, 1994), p. xiii.

12 This remark is retained in the third edition: B. Jowett, *The Dialogues of Plato Translated into English with Analyses and Introductions, Vol. I* (Oxford: Clarendon Press, 1892), p. 406. Jowett adds, rather presumptuously, 'Had [Plato] lived in our times he would have made the transition himself.' As Frank Turner comments, on this and other passages in Jowett, 'Ancient pederasty posed to the appreciation of some Greek literature and philosophy [by Victorian readers] a moral difficulty analogous to that presented by slavery to the defenders of the Athenian constitution' – *The Greek Heritage in Victorian Britain* (New Haven and London: Yale University Press, 1981), p. 424.

13 Dowling, p. 86.

14 Richard Jenkyns, *The Victorians and Ancient Greece* (Oxford: Blackwell, 1980), p. 282.

15 David Halperin, *One Hundred Years of Homosexuality, and Other Essays on Greek Love* (New York and London: Routledge, 1990). Alan Sinfield, *The Wilde Century: Effeminacy, Oscar Wilde and the Queer Moment* (London: Cassell, 1994).

16 Humphrey Carpenter, *The Brideshead Generation: Evelyn Waugh and His Generation*

(London: Faber, 1989), p. 81.

17 Edward Carpenter, *Anthology of Friendship: Ioläus* (London: George Allen and Unwin, 1906).

18 The first of these chapters gathers together extracts of anthropological prose about the customs of 'primitive peoples' (extracts from Herman Melville's *Omoo* and *Typee*, for instance); followed by historical accounts of 'comradeship', mainly from ancient Greek culture (the Theban band, Harmodius and Aristogeiton, Orestes and Pylades, Damon and Pythias). The second chapter contains extracts from Plato (*Symposium* and the *Phaedrus*) and Plutarch. The third turns to 'literary' texts in Greek and Latin, offering selections from Homer (Achilles and Patroclus), Theognis, Anacreon, Meleager, Theocritus, Bion, Ovid, Virgil, Catullus and Martial. In the fourth chapter, alongside selections from Saint Augustine's *Confessions*, one finds brief examples of 'Eastern' love poetry by the likes of Hafiz of Shiraz, together with fragments of J.S. Buckingham's travel writing. Chapter 5 has an enormous span, moving from Montaigne's essays to Michelangelo's sonnets; from Richard Barnfield, through Sir Francis Bacon, to Shakespeare (sonnets 18, 20, 104, and 108 plus brief extracts from *The Merchant of Venice* and *Henry V*). The rest of this chapter is a haphazard mixture of items, ranging from Winckelmann's letters to the poetry of August von Platen; from Wagner's letters to poems by K.H. Ulrichs; and from Byron and Shelley, through Alfred Tennyson's *In Memoriam*, to Walt Whitman. The enlarged edition of *Ioläus* which Carpenter published in 1926 contained an appendix covering the same breadth as that of the body of the book, from Aristotle to Edward Fitzgerald, via Prussia and Ceylon. In the preface to the first edition, Carpenter had acknowledged that the collection was 'only incomplete, and a small contribution, at best, towards a large subject'. Knowing as well as anyone how very large the subject was indeed, Carpenter left the apology to stand even in the enlarged edition.

19 Patrick Anderson and Alistair Sutherland, *Eros: An Anthology of Male Friendship* (London: Anthony Blond, 1961).

20 Cécile Beurdelay's lavishly illustrated anthology *L'Amour bleu* (first published in 1977) is avowedly 'a survey of the different attitudes towards male homosexuality' from 'Antiquity' to the present (Köln: Evergreen, 1994, p. 7). Its seven chapters are, by now, fairly predictable: 'Budding Youths, or Love – Chaste and Unchaste – in Ancient Greece';

'When the Gods Played', a sequence of summaries of the most pertinent of the Greek myths; 'Love, the Roman Way'; 'The Return of Plato', a brief selection of Renaissance Neoplatonism, rounding up the usual suspects; 'The Philosophers' Sin', a selection from the Enlightenment, including Rochester, Voltaire, Rousseau and the Marquis de Sade; 'Aesthetes and Poets Accursed', including the strange mixture of Balzac, Verlaine and Rimbaud, Oscar Wilde, Walt Whitman, Henry James and Paul Gauguin; and, finally, 'To a Happier Year', for the most part a selection of the great Modernists, plus a handful of post-war American figures such as Tennessee Williams, Gore Vidal, William Burroughs and James Baldwin. Byrne R.S. Fone's anthology *Hidden Heritage* is divided into five more or less self-explanatory sections: 'Arcadia: The Greek Experience'; 'The Great God Pan is Dead', on biblical texts and Bible-based traditions; 'The Middle Ages and the Renaissance', from Peter Abelard through Michelangelo, Shakespeare, Marlowe and Richard Barnfield to John Addington Symonds' essay on Dante; 'The Eighteenth and Nineteenth Centuries', from Walter Pater's essay on Winckelmann to Xavier Mayne's sexological treatise *The Intersexes* (1910); and 'The Twentieth Century', which only contains prose on homosexuality by Gide and Eric Bentley.

21 Stephen Coote (ed.), *The Penguin Book of Homosexual Verse* (Harmondsworth: Penguin, 1983), p. 29.

22 Of the main English-language poets who, by now, simply could not be left out of such a collection, Coote made the following selections: Shakespeare (sonnets 20, 29, 35, 36, 53, 55, 57, 60, 67, 87, 94, 104, 110, 116 and 144), Tennyson (*In Memoriam*, sections 7, 9, 13, 27 and 80), Whitman ('We Two Boys Together Clinging', 'A Glimpse', 'Vigil Strange I Kept on the Field One Night', 'O Tan-Faced Prairie-Boy' and 'The Beautiful Swimmer'). On the other hand, there are problematic major omissions from the collection. Of these, the most glaring is Hart Crane. Also compromising is the fact that of W.H. Auden's poems, Coote includes only the relatively trivial 'Uncle Henry'.

23 Winston Leyland (ed.), *Orgasms of Light: The Gay Sunshine Anthology* (San Francisco: Gay Sunshine, 1977), p9.

24 See James W. Jones, *'We of the Third Sex': Literary Representations of Homosexuality in Wilhelmine Germany* (New York: Peter Lang, 1990).

25 See Timothy d'Arch Smith, *R.A. Caton and*

the Fortune Press: A Memoir and a Hand-List (London: Bertram Rota, 1983). I am very grateful to Simon Wright for letting me read his unpublished research on the Fortune Press.

26 For the most part, these ventures involved white gay men. It was not until 1986 that the African-American Blackheart Collective started the *Other Countries* magazine. In the same year, Joseph Beam's anthology *In the Life* was published. Essex Hemphill's sequel to the latter, *Brother to Brother*, appeared in 1991, the same year as Assoto Saint's *The Road Before Us*, a collection of work by no fewer than one hundred gay black poets; ten of the same poets were represented in Saint's later collection, *Here to Dare* (1992). In 1988, Will Roscoe's *Living the Spirit* became the first major anthology of gay American Indian texts.

27 Robert K. Martin, *The Homosexual Tradition in American Poetry* (Austin: University of Texas Press, 1979). Martin begins his account by establishing in great detail the textual evidence of Walt Whitman's homo-erotic concerns. Thus, as ever in gay re-evaluations of American literature, Whitman stands as the presiding and defining 'father' of the tradition. A second chapter discusses the 'Academic Tradition' of Fitz-Greene Halleck, Bayard Taylor, and George Santayana. Chapter 3 is entirely devoted to Hart Crane, the 'bridge' between Whitman and Modernism. Chapter 4 offers brief analyses of the work of Allen Ginsberg, Robert Duncan, Thom Gunn, Edward Field, Richard Howard, James Merrill and Alfred Corn. Finally, an end-note discusses 'The Future', in relation to which Martin speaks of 'a tradition that seems certain to grow, confident in its readers and lovers' (p. 220).

28 Alan Sinfield, *Cultural Politics – Queer Reading* (London: Routledge, 1994), p. 64. The following books of textual criticism deal with the following canonical writers: Jeffrey Meyers, *Homosexuality and Literature 1890–1930* (London: Athlone, 1977): Oscar Wilde, André Gide, Thomas Mann and Robert Musil, Marcel Proust, Joseph Conrad, E.M. Forster, T.E. Lawrence and D.H. Lawrence. Stephen Adams, *The Homosexual as Hero in Contemporary Fiction* (London: Vision, 1980): Gore Vidal, James Baldwin, Truman Capote and Carson McCullers, James Purdy, John Rechy, William Burroughs, E.M. Forster, J.R. Ackerley, Christopher Isherwood, Angus Wilson, Iris Murdoch and Jean Genet. Gregory Woods, *Articulate Flesh: Male Homo-eroticism and Modern Poetry* (New Haven and London: Yale University Press, 1987): D.H. Lawrence, Hart

Crane, W.H. Auden, Allen Ginsberg and Thom Gunn. Claude J. Summers, *Gay Fictions: Wilde to Stonewall, Studies in a Male Homosexual Literary Tradition* (New York: Continuum, 1990): Oscar Wilde, Willa Cather, E.M. Forster, Gore Vidal, Truman Capote, Tennessee Williams, Mary Renault, James Baldwin and Christopher Isherwood. Mark Lilly, *Gay Men's Literature in the Twentieth Century* (London: Macmillan, 1993): Byron and Wilde, Constantine Cavafy, E.M. Forster, the poets of the First World War, Jean Genet, Tennessee Williams, Yukio Mishima, James Baldwin, Joe Orton, Christopher Isherwood, Andrew Holleran and David Leavitt. In *Love's Litany: The Writing of Modern Homoerotics* (Stanford: Stanford University Press, 1994), Kevin Kopelson deals with Oscar Wilde, André Gide, Ronald Firbank, Virginia Woolf, Gertrude Stein, Marguerite Yourcenar, Mary Renault and Roland Barthes. Texts with a greater degree of theoretical focus tend to be no less interested in a given canon. So, for example, Eve Kosofsky Sedgwick's *Epistemology of the Closet* (New York and London: Harvester Wheatsheaf, 1991) gives its most detailed and respectful attention to Herman Melville, Oscar Wilde, Henry James and Marcel Proust. Jonathan Dollimore's *Sexual Dissidence* (Oxford: Clarendon Press, 1991) concentrates, though not exclusively, on William Shakespeare, Oscar Wilde and André Gide. In *Homos* (Cambridge, Mass.: Harvard University Press, 1995), Leo Bersani homes in on Marcel Proust, André Gide and Jean Genet. Bersani is, of course, a French specialist; but the Anglocentric canon which is generally promoted by gay studies specialists in Britain and the United States is starting to look distinctly threadbare. It has been left to continental Europeans to widen the field. Wolfgang Popp's *Männerliebe: Homosexualität und Literatur* (Stuttgart: Metzler, 1992) is far more generous to European writers with its space. Thus, alongside the expected Walt Whitman and Oscar Wilde, we find August von Platen, Pier Paolo Pasolini, Paul Verlaine and Arthur Rimbaud; next to William Burroughs and James Purdy, we find Hubert Fichte, Josef Winkler, Gerard Reve, Yves Navarre, Guido Bachmann and many others. One impressively ambitious chapter deals with Hans Christian Andersen, Stefan George and Franz Kafka.

29 David Bergman, *Gaiety Transfigured: Gay Self-Representation in American Literature* (Madison: University of Wisconsin Press, 1991), p. 11.

30 Harold Bloom, *The Western Canon: The Books and School of the Ages* (New York, San Diego and London: Harcourt Brace, 1994), pp. 531–67.

31 Thomas Hardy, *The Return of the Native* (Oxford: Oxford University Press, 1990), pp. 22–4; p. 417, n. 24; p. 446, n. 23

32 Ibid., pp. 222–3.

33 Wayne Koestenbaum points to various interesting uses of 'queer' by Joseph Conrad and Ford Madox Ford, in *Double Talk: The Erotics of Male Literary Collaboration* (New York and London: Routledge, 1989), pp. 167–73. I wonder whether the word 'queer' is beginning to take on its sexual connotation in the penultimate paragraph of Virginia Woolf's strange short story about deviant aestheticism, 'Solid Objects' – *A Haunted House* (Harmondsworth: Penguin, 1973), pp. 85–92.

34 Joseph Conrad, *Three Short Novels: Heart of Darkness, Youth, Typhoon* (New York: Bantam, 1960), pp. 159, 162–5, 134.

35 Edith Wharton, *The Age of Innocence* (London: Everyman, 1993), p. 139.

36 Meanwhile, the English 'homosexual novel' – in which homosexuality itself is treated, by a homosexual writer, as the central social issue or 'problem' – was taking shape. E.M. Forster completed *Maurice* in July 1914; Radclyffe Hall's *The Well of Loneliness* was published in 1928. Both novels adopt the deliberately ambiguous use of 'queer' which became a distinguishing mark of the genre.

37 John Sutherland, *Is Heathcliff a Murderer? Puzzles in 19th-Century Fiction* (Oxford and New York: Oxford University Press, 1996), p. 198.

Chapter 2

1 Byrne R.S. Fone (ed.), *Hidden Heritage: History and the Gay Imagination* (New York: Irvington, 1981) p. 148. The essay was first collected in Symonds' book *In the Key of Blue* (1893).

2 Quoted in Eva Cantarella, *Bisexuality in the Ancient World* (New Haven and London: Yale University Press, 1992), p. 77.

3 Hans Licht, *Sexual Life in Ancient Greece* (London: Routledge and Kegan Paul, 1932), p. 451.

4 Theognis, *Hesiod and Theognis,* trans. Dorothea Wender (Harmondsworth: Penguin, 1973), p. 145.

5 Robert Graves, *The Greek Myths* I (Harmondsworth: Penguin, 1960), p. 117. As

Graves adds, Plato himself used the Zeus–Ganymede justification in *Phaedrus* 79.

6 I am using Benjamin Jowett's influential translations in their five-volume third edition: *The Dialogues of Plato* (Oxford: Clarendon Press, 1892). The dialogues I quote here are all in the first volume.

7 Cantarella, p. 51.

8 K.J. Dover, *Greek Homosexuality* (London: Duckworth, 1978), p. 97.

9 If we allow ourselves to assume an equal distribution of the original sexes, we can conclude that Aristophanes thinks of homosexual halves as outnumbering heterosexual halves by two to one.

10 On Diotima, see David M. Halperin, 'Why is Diotima a Woman?', in *One Hundred Years of Homosexuality* (New York and London: Routledge, 1990),pp. 113–51.

11 Dover, p. 148.

12 Anthony Holden (ed. and trans.), *Greek Pastoral Poetry: Theocritus, Bion, Moschus, The Pattern Poems* (Harmondsworth: Penguin, 1974).

13 Longus, *Daphnis and Chloe* (New York: Prestel, 1994).

14 Quoted in Licht, pp. 492–3.

15 Michel Foucault, *The Use of Pleasure: The History of Sexuality, Volume Two* (New York: Random House, 1985), p. 221.

16 Ibid., p. 245.

Chapter 3

1 In what is meant to be an 'explanatory note' to this poem, the editor and translator Guy Lee glosses the accusation that both Caesar and Mamurra are likewise diseased ('morbosi pariter') as follows: '"diseased" because pathic'. No further explanation is considered necessary, here or anywhere else in Lee's edition – which was published not in the late nineteenth century but in 1990. This appears to be a clear case of a modern scholar imposing his own prejudices on the reader, or at least assuming that his post-AIDS readers share a given prejudice, which was actually not a strong characteristic of Roman society. Lee's footnotes on the subject of homosexuality are all unreliable; see *The Poems of Catullus* (New York and Oxford: Oxford University Press, 1990). Compare Lee's remark with the following, equally eccentric quotation from Peter Whigham's introduction to his 1966 Penguin edition of Catullus: 'homosexuality was not then considered either as a vice, an aberration, or a disease, as it is now' (p. 42).

2 Guy Lee becomes so uncomfortable when translating this poem that he feels the need to append the 'explanatory' footnote: 'Such demonstrations of affection were common between friends in the ancient world' (p. 151).

3 *The Poems of Tibullus*, trans. Constance Carrier (Bloomington and London: Indiana University Press, 1968).

4 *The Greek Anthology* (London: Heinemann, 1956), IV, p. 281.

5 Christopher Gill cites 'several' uses of the words *inguina*, *scortum*, *clunes* and *coitus*; and also individual appearances by *anus*, *cinaedus*, *spatalocinaedus*, *spintria* and *pigiciaca* – 'The Sexual Episodes in the "Satyricon"', *Classical Philology* 68 (1973), p. 177.

6 Cecil Wooten, 'Petronius and "Camp"', *Helios* 11, 2 (1984), p. 136.

7 Peter Green's notes to Ovid, *The Erotic Poems* (Harmondsworth: Penguin, 1982), p. 380. One should also take into account that, as in Greece, the well-bred boy exercised restraint in his relations with an adult lover: while the lover's pleasure was paramount, the boy was required only to be dutifully passive; he should not compromise his purity with overt enthusiasm. Needless to say, then as now, not all boys are well-bred.

8 Ovid, *The Metamorphoses* (New York: Viking, 1958), Horace Gregory's translation.

Chapter 4

1 John Boswell, *Christianity, Social Tolerance, and Homosexuality: Gay People in Western Europe from the Beginning of the Christian Era to the Fourteenth Century* (Chicago and London: University of Chicago Press, 1980), p. 218. Writing in the late 1970s, Boswell was more at ease than later cultural historians when applying the terminology of gay liberation to the Middle Ages. He is, however, scrupulous in explaining his policy (pp. 41–6) and pointing out that 'gay' has an extremely old pedigree, especially in its Provençal manifestation as 'gai' (p. 43, n. 6).

2 Ibid., pp. 333–4. I am quoting from the summary digest of his findings, expressed as the book's conclusion.

3 Ibid., pp. 92–9.

4 Thomas Stehling (ed.), *Medieval Latin Poems of Male Love and Friendship* (New York and London: Garland, 1984), pp. xx, xxii).

5 Boswell, p. 188.

6 Ibid., p. 210.

7 Ibid., p. 253.

8 Joseph Pequigney, 'Dante Alighieri', in Claude J. Summers (ed.), *The Gay and Lesbian Literary Heritage: A Reader's Companion to the Writers and Their Works, from Antiquity to the Present* (New York: Holt, 1995), pp. 186–7; p. 187.

9 Joseph Pequigney, 'Sodomy in Dante's *Inferno* and *Purgatorio*', *Representations* 36 (1991), pp. 22–42; p. 39.

10 Ibid., p. 26.

11 *The Mabinogion* (Harmondsworth: Penguin, 1976), pp. 104–6.

12 Boswell, p. 55.

13 *The Decameron of Giovanni Boccaccio* (New York: Modern Library, n.d.), p. 459.

14 Monica E. McAlpine, 'The Pardoner's Homosexuality and How it Matters', *PMLA* 95 (1980), pp. 8–22; pp. 10, 13.

15 Glenn Burger, 'Kissing the Pardoner', *PMLA* 107 (1992), pp. 1143–56; p. 1145.

Chapter 5

1 Edward Carpenter, *Anthology of Friendship: Ioläus* (London: Allen and Unwin, 1906), p. 109.

2 Edward W. Said, *Orientalism* (London: Penguin, 1991), p. 103. The *Description* Said refers to is the encyclopaedic outcome of the Napoleonic occupation of Egypt, published in 23 volumes (1809–28).

3 'An Adventure of the Poet Abu Nuwas', *The Book of the Thousand Nights and One Night*, Vol. 2 (London: Routledge and Kegan Paul, 1986), pp. 170–75.

4 'Girls or Boys?', ibid, Vol. 2, pp. 409–15.

5 'Tale of Kamar al-Zaman and the Princess Budur, Moon of Moons', ibid., pp. 1–68.

6 Ibn Hazm, *The Ring of the Dove* (London: Luzac and Co., 1953).

7 These are the five chapters so usefully translated and introduced by the poet Edward A. Lacey in Ahmad al-Tifashi, *The Delight of Hearts, Or What You Will Not Find in Any Book* (San Francisco: Gay Sunshine, 1988).

8 Ibid., p. 60.

9 As the work of A.R. Nykl has conclusively shown, the literature which emerged in the period of the Muslim conquest of the Iberian peninsula included countless pederastic love poems. Nykl's introductory remarks hardly prepare the reader for this wealth of gay literature. He merely says: 'The Muslims, and especially the Syrian Arabs, brought into Al-Andalus their tender, passionate love for women and children, which was enriched later with all the nuances of Hindu, Persian and Greek love feelings and exaltations, – the

unique poetic *sensibilité'* of the Abbasid period in Baghdad – A.R. Nykl, *Hispano-Arabic Poetry and Its Relations with the Old Provençal Troubadours* (Baltimore: [no publisher named], 1946), p. 16. But the body of this book includes some extremely intense homoerotic poetry, albeit rather flatly translated. Some examples of typical pederastic themes are worth quoting. At-Taliq (*c.* 961–*c.* 1009), who wrote most of his poetry about female blondes, could turn his hand nevertheless to a conventional comparison of a boy and a beautiful garden: 'The dew of the garden was mixed in the morning / With the sweet fragrance of remembrances of him,/ The flowers are his mouth, the breeze his breath,/ The rose has been moistened by the dew of his cheeks:/ Therefore I love gardens so madly, for at all times / They make me remember the one whom I adore!' (p. 63). Remembering a night spent with a similarly enchanting boy, Ibn Ammar (1031–83/4) combines the garden comparison with the even commoner simile comparing boyfriend and full moon: 'His glamor surpassed the beams of the full moon,/ His face put the moon's firmament to shame! / During the night of union there was wafted / To me, in his caresses, the perfume of its dawns,/ My tears streamed over the beautiful garden / Of his cheeks to moisten its myrtles and lilies,/ Until Fate gave me to drink the cup of sad parting,/ Which intoxicated me with fumes that clear not away' (p. 157). The pleasures boys afford the men who court them are frequently likened to the less complicated pleasure of drinking wine – wine often served by the very boy whose intoxicating beauty is being celebrated. The typical shape of the simile is manifest in this fragment by Abu 's-Salt Omayya (b. 1067–8): 'Oh slender youth, whose handsome face does share / The beauty of wine he pours into the cup:/ Its effects are those of his eyes, its color is / That of his cheeks, its taste is that of his lips' (pp. 238–9). A slightly more complex version occurs in a poem by Al-Waqqasi (1017–96): 'Wonderful, how wine has borrowed from / The character and qualities of him who tortures me / The odor of his breath, the sweetness of his kiss,/ The inebriating sugar of his looks,/ The brightness of his face, the redness of his cheeks,/ The pleasant charm of his colorful robe!' (p. 309). Wine, of course, has always been a useful instrument to aid the strategies of seduction. It lowers the object's inhibitions – or it sends him to sleep, in which condition he can be either raped or, by the more gentlemanly suitor, simply gazed upon. Alternatively, as in the following lines by Ibn

Suhaid (992–1035), the matter may be left ambiguous: 'When he was fully intoxicated,/ And fell asleep and the watchers too,/ I drew near him, though he was far away,/ Like a companion who knows what he wants:/ Creeping toward him as sleep does creep,/ Going up to him as breath does rise:/ Thus I spent my night with him in joy,/ Until the mouth of dawn began to smile:/ Kissing the whiteness of his charming neck,/ Sipping the redness of his scented lip!' (p. 104). Certainly, the speaker has done more than merely watch the sleeping boy; who, indeed, may have been woken up. The precise nature and extent of the joy are left unstated; as is the question of whether joy was one-sided or mutual.

10 Annemarie Schimmel, *The Triumphal Sun: A Study of the Works of Jalaloddin Rumi* (London and The Hague: East-West Publications, rev. ed 1980), p. 23.
11 See also Andrew Harvey's impressive versions of Rumi's love poems in *Love's Fire: Recreations of Rumi* (London: Cape, 1988).
12 Minoo S. Southgate, 'Men, Women, and Boys: Love and Sex in the Works of SA'DI', *Iranian Studies* 17 (Autumn 1984), pp. 413–52. For Sa'di's works, see *The Gulistan or Rose Garden of Sa'di*, trans. Edward Rehatsek, (London: Allen and Unwin, 1964). Southgate refers the reader to W.G. Archer's preface to Rehatsek's translation for an account of bowdlerised versions of the *Gulistan*.
13 Schimmel, p. 434.
14 Schimmel, 'Hafiz and his Critics', *Studies in Islam* (January 1979), pp. 1–33; this quotation, p. 15. A noted gay imitator of Hafiz was August von Platen (1796–1835). His *Ghaselen* were published in 1821.
15 Cited in Annemarie Schimmel, *Mystical Dimensions of Islam* (Chapel Hill: University of North Carolina Press, 1975), p. 300.
16 Nermin Menemencioglu (ed.), *The Penguin Book of Turkish Verse* (Harmondsworth: Penguin, 1978), pp. 40–41.
17 Although this tradition has been allowed to die out in the People's Republic, it is being kept alive by some members of the Chinese diaspora. For instance, there is an Anglo-Asian gay group in London called the Long Yang Club.
18 Bret Hinsch, *Passions of the Cut Sleeve: A History of the Male Homosexual Tradition in China* (Berkeley: University of California Press, 1990), p. 72.
19 A slightly different version of this poem is available in *New Songs from a Jade Terrace* (Harmondsworth and New York: Penguin, 1986), p. 213.
20 Hinsch, pp. 80–85.
21 Ibid., p. 87.

22 Ibid., pp. 88–9.
23 Bret Hinsch in Wayne R. Dynes, *Encyclopaedia of Homosexuality*, Vol. 1 (Chicago and London: St James Press, 1990), p. 218.
24 Hinsch, *Passions*, p. 125.
25 Ibid., pp. 121–36. See also Vivien W. Ng, 'Homosexuality and the State in Late Imperial China', in Martin Bauml Duberman, Martha Vicinus and George Chauncey, Jr. (eds), *Hidden from History: Reclaiming the Gay and Lesbian Past* (Harmondsworth: Penguin, 1991), pp. 79–85.
26 Much of the information that follows is derived from Tsuneo Watanabe and Jun'ichi Iwata, *The Love of the Samurai: A Thousand Years of Japanese Homosexuality* (London: GMP, 1989).
27 I have dealt with this story elsewhere, as one of three archetypal narratives of homo-eroticism in warfare. See Gregory Woods, *Articulate Flesh: Male Homo-eroticism and Modern Poetry* (New Haven and London: Yale University Press, 1987), pp. 59–61, 65–9.
28 Ihara Saikaku, *The Great Mirror of Male Love* (Stanford, Calif.: Stanford University Press, 1990).
29 Watanabe and Iwata, p. 79.
30 The majority of these and the book's many other Western references are conveyed by way of the viewpoint of Shunsuké Hinoki, a highly educated novelist. It is he who has, as it were, imported them into Japan and who conveys them to the Japanese, as Mishima himself did, in both his conversations and his writing. This is not simply a question of Mishima attributing a heavily Westernised erudition to Shunsuké and contrasting this wealth of knowledge with a hermetically Japanese culture around him. In fact, the third person narrative voice itself, which cannot be attributed to any character in the book, is continually dropping references to the kinds of mythic tradition and literary source I have already mentioned in relation to Shunsuké. The adolescent Yuichi, we are told, kept his body pure by involving himself in mathematics and sport; it is obviously not from his viewpoint that the narrator, speaking from a position of greater erudition, adds: 'He did not realise particularly that this option of his was a Greek option' – Yukio Mishima, *Forbidden Colours* (Harmondsworth: Penguin, 1971), p. 32. Yuichi is constantly being associated with the mythical figure of Narcissus (pp. 168, 218, 264, 297, 312, 313). But on only one such occasion does Yuichi himself raise the comparison, and he immediately dismisses its validity: 'I am not

Narcissus, he rationalised proudly' (p. 246).
31 Mutsuo Takahashi, *Poems of a Penisist* (Chicago: Chicago Review Press, 1975), pp. 47–108; and revised in *A Bunch of Keys* (Trumansburg, New York: Crossing Press, 1984), pp. 27–73.

Chapter 6

1 On Michelangelo, see James M. Saslow's introduction to his annotated edition of *The Poetry of Michelangelo* (New Haven and London: Yale University Press, 1991). For a more general overview of male homosexuality in the Italian Renaissance, see James M. Saslow, *Ganymede in the Renaissance: Homosexuality in Art and Society* (New Haven and London: Yale University Press, 1986).
2 Giovanni Dall'Orto, '"Socratic Love" as a Disguise for Same-Sex Love in the Italian Renaissance', in Kent Gerard and Gert Hekma (eds), *The Pursuit of Sodomy: Male Homosexuality in Renaissance and Enlightenment Europe* (New York: Haworth Press, 1988), pp. 33–65; p. 39.
3 Ibid., p. 58.
4 Bruce R. Smith, *Homosexual Desire in Shakespeare's England: A Cultural Poetics* (Chicago and London: University of Chicago Press, 1991), p. 14. The key introductory text on male homosexuality in the period of the English Renaissance, even if some of its details have since been contested, remains Alan Bray, *Homosexuality in Renaissance England* (London: Gay Men's Press, 1982).
5 Smith, p. 112.
6 Ibid., p. 138.
7 H. Montgomery Hyde, *The Other Love: An Historical and Contemporary Survey of Homosexuality in Britain* (London: Mayflower, 1972), p. 56.
8 Wayne R. Dynes (ed.), *Encyclopedia of Homosexuality* (Chicago and London: St James Press, 1990), p. 103.
9 Joseph Cady, '"Masculine Love", Renaissance Writing, and the "New Invention" of Homosexuality', in Claude J. Summers (ed.), *Homosexuality in Renaissance and Enlightenment England: Literary Representations in Historical Context* (New York: Harrington Park Press, 1992), pp. 9–40; p. 15. Cady also tries to make something, if only a hint, of the fact that Bacon, although married, did not marry until he was forty-five, and had no children.
10 On friendship, see Alan Bray, 'Homosexuality and the Signs of Male Friendship in

Elizabethan England', in Jonathan Goldberg (ed.), *Queering the Renaissance* (Durham, NC and London: Duke University Press, 1994), pp. 40–61. Michel de Montaigne's essay 'De l'amitié', celebrating his intimate relationship with Etienne de la Boëtie, distinguishes adult male friendship from both heterosexual matrimony and the age imbalance of Graeco-Roman pederasty. This does not inhibit him from lavishly quoting Horace and Catullus, among other writers from the ancient world.

11 Phillip Stubbes, *The Anatomie of Abuses* (New York: Garland, 1973), N8r–v. Jonathan Goldberg quotes this passage tellingly on p. 118 of his essay 'The Transvestite Stage: More on the Case of Christopher Marlowe', in *Sodometries: Renaissance Texts, Modern Sexualities* (Stanford, Calif.: Stanford University Press, 1992), pp. 105–43.

12 Juliet Dusinberre, *Shakespeare and the Nature of Women* (London: Macmillan, 1975), p. 233.

13 John Day, *The Ile of Gvls* (London: Shakespeare Association, 1936).

14 L.A. Beaurline, 'Introduction' to Ben Jonson, *Epicoene, or The Silent Woman* (London: Edward Arnold, 1966), p. xiii.

15 Ben Jonson, *Sejanus His Fall* (London: Ernest Benn, 1966), p. 83. The editor, W.F. Bolton, goes on to footnote 'catamite' (line 404) as meaning 'sodomite'.

16 In his introduction to the play, Bernard Harris writes that 'Coupler, though a homosexual, is a professional marriage-arranger' – John Vanbrugh, *The Relapse or, Virtue in Danger* (London: Ernest Benn, 1971), p. xxii.

17 Paul Hammond lists the play's uses of the word 'love' in reference to male–male relationships, but then adds: 'Nowhere does this vocabulary suggest sexual relationships between the men' – *Love Between Men in English Literature* (London: Macmillan, 1996), p. 61.

18 Roland Barthes, *On Racine* (New York: Hill and Wang, 1964), p. 13. Raymond Picard complained that Barthes' book forces one 'to reread Racine to persuade oneself that his characters are different from D.H. Lawrence' – which is a roundabout way of deploring Barthes' speculations on the sexuality of Racine's characters; quoted in Jonathan Culler, *Barthes* (London: Fontana, 1983), p. 65.

Chapter 7

1 Richard Barnfield's 'affectionate Shepheard' Daphnis adopts the same approach in his wooing of Ganimede. Having listed all the lavish gifts at his disposal, he repeats that the boy can have them 'If thou wilt come and dwell with me at home'; and 'All these, and more, Ile giue thee for thy loue'. By the time of 'The Second Dayes Lamentation', he has thought of further gifts, including a nightingale in a cage. Not mincing his words, he says: 'Her shalt thou haue, and all I haue beside; / If thou wilt be my Boy, or else my Bride'.

2 For another echo of these words, see *The Jew of Malta* IV. ii, 106–16.

3 This usage of 'ring' reverberates throughout the last scene of Shakespeare's *The Merchant of Venice*: Bassanio and Gratiano have given away Portia and Nerissa's respective rings to the doctor and the clerk – who were Portia and Nerissa themselves, cross-dressed as men. All of the play's themes relating to the price of flesh culminate, here, in a cascade of bawdy jokes which depend on the double meaning in 'ring', a word which Shakespeare places at the ends of lines 193–7 and 199–202 by way of comic, ringing emphasis. The main joke is about men who turn from the sacred, conjugal bed to homosexual intercourse. Heterosexual order is restored, however, in the play's closing line, when Gratiano pledges himself once more to the pleasurable duty of 'keeping safe Nerissa's ring'.

4 Once the body is scripted – whether with public declamation or the introspection of soliloquy – love, too, grows loud with significance. Marlowe's versions of love invariably involve (as whose do not?) a measure of discourse. Like heart and genitals, the tongue is an organ convulsed by desire. As he writes in *Hero and Leander*, 'Love always makes those eloquent that have it' (II. 72). This does not necessarily contradict what he has already said – 'True love is mute, and oft amazèd stands' – since even the silences of lovers are gushingly expressive. Lovers can speak with 'dumb signs', a kind of unspoken speech, just as Hero and Leander 'parlèd by the touch of hands' (I. 185–7).

5 Other major works on the Edward-Gaveston relationship include Michael Drayton's poem *Piers Gaveston* (*c.* 1593) and Elizabeth Cary's play *The History of the Life, Reign and Death of Edward II* (1627). On Marlowe's and Drayton's versions, see Paul Hammond, *Love Between Men in English Literature* (London: Macmillan, 1996), pp. 47–57.

6 John E. Cunningham, *Elizabethan and Early Stuart Drama* (London: Evans Brothers, 1965), p. 44.

7 Judith Cook, *At the Sign of the Swan: An*

Introduction to Shakespeare's Contemporaries (London: Harrap, 1986), p. 107.

8 Harry Levin, *Christopher Marlowe: The Overreacher* (London: Faber, 1961), p. 116. But this shift, by sleight-of-hand, from Edward to Marlowe, needs to be regarded with a degree of scepticism.

9 A.L. Rowse, *Christopher Marlowe: A Biography* (London: Macmillan, 1964), p. 134.

10 Terence Michael Stephenson, 'Sweet Lies', *Gay Times* August 1990, p. 36. Beale's last remark is not strictly true of this production, since Act II scene i began with Baldock and young Spenser getting out of bed, apparently having just made love while spectacularly, if anachronistically, dressed in Calvin Klein knickers.

11 Cunningham, p. 48. This seems to be a modern and heterosexual reading of the 'problem'. Shakespeare, after all, seems to have had no significant difficulty in presenting on stage a Cleopatra who, although likewise played by a boy, was allowed both movement and speech, and still seemed devastatingly beautiful. However, for a modern audience of unreconstructed heterosexual men, Cunningham's point may, indeed, be apt.

12 William Tydeman, *Doctor Faustus: Text and Performance* (London: Macmillan, 1984), p. 76.

13 Michael Scott, *Renaissance Drama and a Modern Audience* (London: Macmillan, 1982), p. 30. The worry here is Scott's claim to read a whole audience's – or, rather, a whole *series* of audiences' – reactions, and the hint of moralising in his use of the word 'rightly'. But might the unease (if that is what it was) not simply have been the reaction of an audience unused to a convention taken for granted in Marlowe's theatre, rather than unconvinced that a boy could be sufficiently beautiful to impersonate Helen of Troy? In any case, if the audience were to be left *at ease* by this scene, could the production really be said to have succeeded at all?

14 This instance of Marlowe's quoting himself is of changeable significance, according to whether we believe *Dido* precedes *Faustus* – as I am assuming here – or vice versa.

15 Edward, too, has a fantasy of re-enacting the Trojan wars, when he is forced to send Gaveston into exile. In a soliloquy he threatens Rome: 'I'll fire thy crazed buildings, and enforce / The papal towers to kiss the lowly ground' (I. iv, 101–2).

16 Joseph A. Porter, 'Marlowe, Shakespeare, and the Canonization of Heterosexuality', in Ronald R. Butters, John M. Clum and Michael Moon (eds), *Displacing Homophobia:*

Gay Male Perspectives in Literature and Culture (Durham, NC and London: Duke University Press, 1989), pp. 127–147; p. 128. This is, of course, a much simplified version of the spread of Italian Renaissance images and ideas; but Porter's point about Marlowe's post-medieval carnality is, nonetheless, worth considering.

17 Claude J. Summers, 'Sex, Politics, and Self-realization in *Edward II*', in Kenneth Friedenreich, Roma Gill and Constance B. Kuriyama (eds), *'A Poet and a filthy Play-maker': New Essays on Christopher Marlowe* (New York: AMS Press, 1988), pp. 221–40; p. 231.

18 Levin, p. 124. Levin refers here to a book review in which William Empson wrote: 'The last act of "Edward II" is a crescendo of horror, seen as a punishment deserved by Edward because of his exorbitant love of his favorites. The obscene torture by which he is at last killed is an appalling parody of the homosexual act [*sic*]' – 'Two Proper Crimes', *Nation* 163 (1946), pp. 444–5.

19 Alan Bray, 'Lovers or Just Good Friends?', *The Guardian* 6 July 1990, p. 37.

20 Simon Shepherd, *Marlowe and the Politics of Elizabethan Theatre* (Brighton: Harvester, 1986), pp. 179, 198.

21 Purvis E. Boyette has said, in relation to the play's closing scenes, 'From the King's bowels, a new king is born' – 'Wanton Humour and Wanton Poets: Homosexuality in Marlowe's *Edward II*', *Tulane Studies in English* 21 (1977), pp. 33–50; pp. 47–8. The boy was, of course, born of woman (albeit a woman played by an older boy), and the young warrior and statesman has been shaped by the constraints of courtly machismo; but the new king emerges in the moment of Edward's horrendous scream, as it reverberates through the bowels of the castle and beyond. The new king is the offspring of his father's tragedy, which itself stemmed from Edward's love of Gaveston.

Chapter 8

1 Paul Hammond, *Love between Men in English Literature* (London: Macmillan, 1996), p. 59. See also Joseph A. Porter, 'Marlowe, Shakespeare, and the Canonization of Heterosexuality', in Ronald R. Butters, John M. Clum and Michael Moon (eds), *Displacing Homophobia: Gay Male Perspectives in Literature and Culture* (Durham, NC and London: Duke University Press, 1989), pp. 127–47.

2 Jonathan Goldberg, *Sodometries: Renaissance Texts, Modern Sexualities* (Stanford, Calif.: Stanford University Press, 1992), pp. 161, 163.

3 For an account of Bill Alexander's 1987 production of the *Merchant* for the Royal Shakespeare Company, see John M. Clum, *Acting Gay: Male Homosexuality in Modern Drama,* revised edn. (New York: Columbia University Press, 1994), pp. 5–7.

4 Alan Sinfield, *Cultural Politics – Queer Reading* (London: Routledge, 1994), p. 4. Needless to say, the Nazi persecution of homosexuals will never come to mind if the history of that persecution has been suppressed.

5 Seymour Kleinberg, '*The Merchant of Venice*: The Homosexual as Anti-Semite in Nascent Capitalism', in Stuart Kellogg (ed.), *Essays on Gay Literature* (New York: Harrington Park Press, 1983), pp. 113–26; p. 113.

6 Kleinberg, p. 120.

7 Ibid., p. 124.

8 Clum, pp. 114–15.

9 Gregory W. Bredbeck, *Sodomy and Interpretation: Marlowe to Milton* (Ithaca, New York and London: Cornell University Press, 1991), pp. 33–4. The notes in question are on pp. 156 and 263 of the Arden edition.

10 I have seen *Troilus and Cressida* only twice, both times performed by the Royal Shakespeare Company at Stratford-upon-Avon, but at a distance of twenty years from each other. In 1970 Achilles was famously played by Alan Howard as a somewhat hysterical queen with his hair swept back in a bun. In 1990 he was played by Ciaran Hinds in full leather, all man but also every inch the queen.

11 Leslie A. Fiedler, *The Stranger in Shakespeare* (St Albans: Paladin, 1974), pp. 128–9.

12 Jonathan Dollimore, *Sexual Dissidence: Augustine to Wilde, Freud to Foucault* (Oxford: Clarendon Press, 1991), p. 157.

13 Jonathan Dollimore, 'Shakespeare Understudies: The Sodomite, the Prostitute, the Transvestite and Their Critics', in Jonathan Dollimore and Alan Sinfield (eds), *Political Shakespeare: Essays in Cultural Materialism* (Manchester: Manchester University Press, 2nd ed., 1994), pp. 129–52; p. 134. At this point, Dollimore is paraphrasing a longer passage from Bruce R. Smith's *Homosexual Desire in Shakespeare's England: A Cultural Poetics* (Chicago and London: University of Chicago Press, 1991), pp. 61–3.

14 Jody Greene, '"You Must Eat Men": The Sodomitic Economy of Renaissance Patronage', *GLQ* 1, 2 (1994), pp. 163–97; p. 165.

15 Ibid., pp. 178, 186.

16 Simon Shepherd, 'Shakespeare's Private Drawer: Shakespeare and Homosexuality', in Graham Holderness (ed.), *The Shakespeare Myth* (Manchester: Manchester University Press, 1988), pp. 96–109; p. 97.

17 Eric Partridge, *Shakespeare's Bawdy: A Literary and Psychological Essay and a Comprehensive Glossary* (London: Routledge and Kegan Paul, revised and enlarged edn 1968), pp. 11–12.

18 But there were major homosexual exceptions: W.H. Auden, for instance. See his introduction to the Signet Classics edition of the Sonnets (New York, 1965).

19 Alfred Harbage, *Shakespeare Without Words, and Other Essays* (Cambridge, Mass.: Harvard University Press, 1972), p. 75.

20 Katharine M. Wilson, *Shakespeare's Sugared Sonnets* (London: George Allen and Unwin, 1974), p. 355.

21 Alan Sinfield, *Cultural Politics – Queer Reading*, p. 19.

22 Fiedler, p. 32.

23 Joseph Pequigney, *Such Is My Love: A Study of Shakespeare's Sonnets* (Chicago: University of Chicago Press, 1985), p. 186.

24 Eve Kosofsky Sedgwick, *Between Men: English Literature and Male Homosocial Desire* (New York: Columbia University Press, 1985), p. 35.

25 Paul Ramsey, *The Fickle Glass: A Study of Shakespeare's Sonnets* (New York: AMS Press, 1979), p. 32.

26 Valerie Traub, *Desire and Anxiety: Circulations of Sexuality in Shakespearean Drama* (New York and London: Routledge, 1992), p. 143.

27 Stephen Booth claims that Sonnet 87 also uses feminine rhymes throughout. This is not the case. In Sonnet 87, Booth misreads the '-ate' syllables of 'estimate' and 'determinate' (lines 2 and 4) as being unstressed – *Shakespeare's Sonnets* (New Haven: Yale University Press, 1977), p. 163.

28 Quoted in E.A.M. Colman, *The Dramatic Use of Bawdy in Shakespeare* (London: Longman, 1974), p. 163. Colman himself rather sensibly hedges his bets by saying that the addressee of the bulk of the sequence is 'a male friend who is, in one sense or another, the poet's lover' (p. 161).

29 *The Collected Works of Samuel Taylor Coleridge, vol. 12: Marginalia* (Princeton, NJ: Princeton University Press; London: Routledge, 1980), pp. 42–3. The marginal note appears in Coleridge's copy of Robert Anderson's *The Works of British Poets* (1792–5). It was written at 3.30 a.m. on 2

November 1803 at Greta Hall, Keswick. I am grateful to Tim Fulford for this reference.

30 H. M. Young, *The Sonnets of Shakespeare: A Psycho-Sexual Analysis* (1963), p. 11. Quoted in Colman, pp. 163–4.

31 Hallet Smith's introduction to the *Sonnets* in G. Blakemore Evans' edition of *The Riverside Shakespeare* (Boston: Houghton Mifflin, 1974), Vol. II, pp. 232–9. Quoted in Purvis E. Boyette, 'Shakespeare's *Sonnets*: Homosexuality and the Critics', *Tulane Studies in English* 21 (1974), pp. 35–46; pp. 36–7.

32 Ramsey, p. 29.

33 Peter Levi, *The Art of Poetry, The Oxford Lectures 1984–1989* (New Haven and London: Yale University Press, 1991), pp. 137 and 320, n. 4.

34 Robert Giroux, *The Book Known as Q: A Consideration of Shakespeare's Sonnets* (London: Weidenfeld and Nicolson, 1982), p. 20.

35 'Introduzione', William Shakespeare, *Sonetti* (Torino: Einaudi, 1974), p. c).

36 Martin Seymour-Smith, 'Shakespeare's Sonnets 1–42: A Psychological Reading', in Hilton Landry (ed.), *New Essays on Shakespeare's Sonnets* (New York: AMS Press, 1976), p. 25.

37 Martin Seymour-Smith (ed.), *Shakespeare's Sonnets* (London: Heinemann, 1963), p. 34.

38 Gregory Woods, *Articulate Flesh: Male Homo-eroticism and Modern Poetry* (New Haven and London: Yale University Press, 1987), p. 9.

39 Sedgwick, pp. 34–5. Martin Green made this point a few years before Sedgwick, but then elaborated on it in an idiosyncratic manner: 'Shakespeare is saying . . . that Nature added to his friend one thing which was, for his purpose, a vulva. Obviously, a penis is not like a vulva to the extent that a vulva can receive a penis, but it could for a homosexual be like a vulva to the extent that it acts as a focal point for sexual desire. Thus this *nothing* added to the friend is in reality for Shakespeare a *something*' – *The Labyrinth of Shakespeare's Sonnets: An Examination of Sexual Elements in Shakespeare's Language* (London: Skilton, 1974), pp. 77–8.

40 Smith, p. 248.

41 Claude J. Summers, 'Homosexuality and Renaissance Literature, or the Anxieties of Anachronism', *South Central Review* 9 (Spring 1992), pp. 2–23; p. 15.

42 Rictor Norton, *The Homosexual Literary Tradition: An Interpretation* (New York: Revisionist Press, 1974), p. 250.

43 Seymour-Smith (ed.), *Shakespeare's Sonnets*, p. 130.

44 Pequigney, p. 49.

Chapter 9

1 Gray ends his 'Sonnet on the Death of Richard West' (not published until after Gray's own death) with the lines: 'I fruitless mourn to him that cannot hear,/ And weep the more because I weep in vain.' This self-perpetuating effect characterises elegy's representation of the earlier stages of grief. But the point is that the mourner eventually discovers that he has not mourned in vain after all. No tears are wasted. They lead towards an emotional equilibrium that comes with the eventual understanding that *nothing dies*. So tears are then associated with the effects of rain on plant life. The fact that Gray writes his 'Elegy Written in a Country Church-Yard' about himself – imagining his own rustic funeral rites – does not detract from the fact that the poem's essential mood is determined by the loss of his closest friend.

2 The first record of my acquaintance with this material is a group edition of *Lycidas* in J.B. Broadbent's edition of John Milton, *Odes, Pastorals, Masques* (Cambridge: Cambridge University Press, 1975), pp. 183–238.

3 *The Epic of Gilgamesh* (Harmondsworth: Penguin, 1960), p. 91.

4 C.S. Lewis, *A Preface to "Paradise Lost"* (Oxford: Oxford University Press, 1961), p. 112.

5 Gregory W. Bredbeck, *Sodomy and Interpretation: Marlowe to Milton* (Ithaca, New York and London: Cornell University Press, 1991), p. 227.

6 Ibid., p. 191.

7 I quote from the prose translation provided in John Carey's edition of John Milton, *Complete Shorter Poems* (London: Longman, 1971), pp. 279–83.

8 This question is debated in Barbara Breasted, '*Comus* and the Castlehaven Scandal', *Milton Studies* 3 (1971), pp. 201–24, and John Creaser, 'Milton's *Comus*: The Irrelevance of the Castlehaven Scandal', *Milton Quarterly* 4 (1988), pp. 24–34.

9 Reprinted in James A. Notopoulos, *The Platonism of Shelley: A Study of Platonism and the Poetic Mind* (Durham, NC: Duke University Press, 1949), pp. 404–13.

10 Alan Sinfield, *Alfred Tennyson* (Oxford: Blackwell, 1986), p. 132.

11 Richard Dellamora, *Masculine Desire: The Sexual Politics of Victorian Aestheticism* (Chapel Hill, NC and London: University of North Carolina Press, 1990), p. 34.

12 Most readers are familiar only with the work of the canonised poets. But it is in the work of lesser names that reliance on the English

elegiac tradition is seen at its most slavish. Martin Taylor's wonderful collection *Lads: An Anthology of Comradeship* (London: Constable, 1989) reprints a lot of such material. Taylor's introduction is extremely useful. On homo-eroticism and war poetry in general, see Gregory Woods, *Articulate Flesh: Male Homo-eroticism and Modern Poetry* (New Haven and London: Yale University Press, 1987), pp. 51–80. On the poets of the First World War in particular, see Mark Lilly, 'The Love Poetry of the First World War', in *Gay Men's Literature in the Twentieth Century* (London: Macmillan, 1993), pp. 64–82. All three of these items were much influenced by Paul Fussell's classic essay 'Soldier Boys', on homo-eroticism and Wilfred Owen, in *The Great War and Modern Memory* (New York and London: Oxford University Press, 1975), pp. 270–309. The best fictional account of the lives of Sassoon and Owen is in Pat Barker's *Regeneration Trilogy: Regeneration* (1991), *The Eye in the Door* (1993) and *The Ghost Road* (1995).

13 John Peter, 'A New Interpretation of *The Waste Land* (1952)', *Essays in Criticism* 19, 2 (April 1969), pp. 140–75. Mark Lilly provides us with a relevant fragment of autobiography: 'As a young undergraduate, my first lecture on T.S. Eliot was given by a lecturer (now a poet), who commented on "the filthy lie" that Eliot "loved" Jean Verdenal' – Lilly, *Gay Men's Literature* , p. 3.

14 Peter, p. 143.

15 Eliot's favourite cantos from Dante's *Divina Commedia* were *Purgatorio* XXVI and *Inferno* XV, which happen to include the two main encounters with sexual sinners. *Purgatorio* XXVI provided the title of Eliot's 1920 volume *Ara Vos Prec*, the dedication of *The Waste Land* to Ezra Pound, *il miglior fabbro*, and important fragments of *The Waste Land*, 'Ash Wednesday' and 'Little Gidding'. *Inferno* XV is another important source for 'Little Gidding'.

16 Quoted in Peter, p. 167, from the *Criterion* 13, p. 452.

17 Saint Augustine, *Confessions* (Harmondsworth: Penguin, 1961), pp. 55, 75.

18 In his suggestive exploration of Eliot and Ezra Pound's collaborative work on this poem, Wayne Koestenbaum writes: 'It was once fashionable to say that *The Waste Land* portrays a crisis in Western civilization. That interpretation still holds: through Tiresias, Eliot describes (from the inside) an epoch we might call The Age of Inversion, when heterosexuality was in the process of being undermined and traduced by its eerie opposite.' So the elegiac theme takes its place, alongside those which have been more widely disseminated by the critics and teachers, as having urgent relevance to the condition of modern culture – Wayne Koestenbaum, *Double Talk: The Erotics of Male Literary Collaboration* (New York and London: Routledge, 1989), p. 128. Koestenbaum, incidentally, does not seem to have read John Peter's essay.

19 John Unterecker, *Voyager: A Life of Hart Crane* (New York: Blond, 1970), p. 240.

20 It is important to remember that not all gay writers are obliged to deal with the same themes, or to make the same job of similar themes. In the matter of elegies, W.H. Auden's career is instructive. Auden's great elegies on named individuals are 'In Memory of W.B. Yeats' (1939), 'In Memory of Ernst Toller' (1939), 'In Memory of Sigmund Freud' (1939) and 'At the Grave of Henry James' (1941). These are not, and do not claim to be, love elegies, however. They are acts of homage to intellectual masters, expressed in a coolly intellectual register; and Auden was no pastoralist – he was far too interested in the industrial revolution for that. The opening of the poem on Yeats is a deliberate violation of the expected imagery – 'He disappeared in the dead of winter: / The brooks were frozen, the airports almost deserted' – and this refusal to be caught gushing about (say) lovely Irish landscapes is entirely consonant with the poem's emotional tone as a whole: it is a refusal to mourn as a lover a man whom he did not love – W.H. Auden, *Collected Poems* (London: Faber, 1976), pp. 197–8.

But other gay writers have tried to follow the tradition of the love elegy. Allen Ginsberg wrote important elegies on Frank O'Hara ('City Midnight Junk Strains', 1966), Che Guevara ('Elegy Ché Guévara', 1967) and Neal Cassady ('Elegy for Neal Cassady', 1968). The one on Che is no less intimate than those on O'Hara, whom he knew, and Cassady, whom he had loved. For Ginsberg the body was the main sign of life, and he was constantly reminding us that public figures such as politicians are bodily the same as we are: they shit like us, their love lives are as sexy but as messy as ours. Ginsberg had learned from 'When lilacs last' that the best policy for the public elegist was to affect a personal involvement. So the fact that he found Che Guevara sexually attractive is presented as reason enough to mourn his passing. In the O'Hara poem, written on 29 July 1966, four days after O'Hara's accidental death, Ginsberg complains that he 'hear[s] of one funeral a year nowadays'. Needless to say, there would come a time when one funeral a year would seem luxuriously rare. By far the best of the pre-AIDS, gay liberationist love elegies, Thom Gunn's 'Talbot Road', is actually about a heterosexual friend, Tony White – see Thom Gunn, *The Passages of Joy* (London: Faber, 1982), pp. 80–89.

University Press, 1985), p. 91.

13 Matthew Lewis, *The Monk* (London: Oxford University Press, 1973), p. 17.

14 Eve Kosofsky Sedgwick, *The Coherence of Gothic Conventions* (New York and London: Methuen, 1986). This is a reissue of the 1980 edition, with a useful preface added. The book was itself a revised version of a 1975 dissertation.

15 Sedgwick, *Between Men*, pp. 91, 92.

Chapter 10

1 Claire Lynn Gaudiani, *The Cabaret Poetry of Théophile de Viau: Texts and Traditions* (Tübingen: Gunter Narr; Paris: Jean-Michel Place, 1981), pp. 103–4.

2 *The Complete Poems of John Wilmot, Earl of Rochester* (New Haven: Yale University Press, 1968), p. 39.

3 John Wilmot, Earl of Rochester, *Sodom, or The Quintessence of Debauchery* (N. Hollywood, Calif.: Brandon House, 1966).

4 The Marquis de Sade, *The 120 Days of Sodom, and Other Writings*, trans. Austryn Wainhouse and Richard Seaver(New York: Grove, 1966).

5 The whole of this essay, first published in *Les Temps modernes*, is printed in translation in Sade, *The 120 Days of Sodom*, pp. 3–64; this quotation, p. 36.

6 *The Complete Marquis de Sade* I (Los Angeles, Calif.: Holloway House, 1966), pp. 211–12.

7 Philip Core, *Camp: The Lie that Tells the Truth* (London: Plexus, 1984), pp. 32–3.

8 Mark Booth, *Camp* (London: Quartet, 1983), p. 125.

9 William Beckford, *Vathek,* in Philip Henderson (ed.), *Shorter Novels: Eighteenth Century* (London and New York: Everyman, 1930), p. 213.

10 George E. Haggerty, 'Literature and Homosexuality in the Late Eighteenth Century: Walpole, Beckford, and Lewis', *Studies in the Novel* 18 (1986), pp. 341–52: pp. 343, 350.

11 Charles Maturin, *Melmoth the Wanderer* (London: Oxford University Press, 1968), p. 108. We learn in the following paragraph that this naked novice becomes 'delirious with shame and agony', refuses food and dies eight nights after the scene described.

12 Leslie A. Fiedler, *Love and Death in the American Novel* (New York: Criterion, 1960), p. 466. Of closely related significance is a point made by Eve Kosofsy Sedgwick, that 'traces of the Gothic are ubiquitous in Freud's writing' – *Between Men: English Literature and Male Homosocial Desire* (New York: Columbia

Chapter 11

1 Cited in Rictor Norton, *Mother Clap's Molly House: The Gay Subculture in England 1700–1830* (London: GMP, 1992), pp. 119–20, 139–40.

2 Pamela Bacarisse, 'Chivalry and "Camp" Sensibility in *Don Quijote,* with Some Thoughts on the Novels of Manuel Puig', *Forum for Modern Language Studies* 26, 2 (1990), pp. 127–43.

3 Jane Austen, *Northanger Abbey* (London: Penguin, 1985).

4 Jane Austen, *Mansfield Park* (London: Oxford University Press, 1934), p. 60.

5 This point was made by Jonathan Bate in a review essay, 'Nothing but Officers', *Times Literary Supplement* 4818 (4 August 1995), p. 7.

6 Anne Brontë, *The Tenant of Wildfell Hall* (Harmondsworth: Penguin, 1979), pp. 51–8.

7 Alexandre Dumas, *The Count of Monte Cristo* (London and Glasgow: Collins, 1955), pp. 354–81.

8 Théophile Gautier, *Mademoiselle de Maupin,* trans. Joanna Richardson (Harmondsworth: Penguin, 1981).

9 Honoré de Balzac, *Lost Illusions,* trans. Herbert J. Hunt (Harmondsworth: Penguin, 1971) and *A Harlot High and Low,* trans. Rayner Happenstall (Harmondsworth: Penguin, 1970).

10 Charles Dickens, *Oliver Twist* (London: Wordsworth, 1992), p. 174.

11 For further work on Dickens, see Eve Kosofsky Sedgwick, *Between Men: English Literature and Male Homosocial Desire* (New York: Columbia University Press, 1985): chapter 9 on *Our Mutual Friend* (pp. 161–79) and chapter 10 on *Edwin Drood* (pp. 180–200). See also Geoffrey Thurley, *The Dickens Myth: Its Genesis and Structure* (London: Routledge and Kegan Paul, 1976), pp. 126–31, on *Dombey and Son*.

12 Leo Tolstoy, *Resurrection,* trans. Louise Maude (London: Oxford University Press,

1916), pp. 283–4, 291–3; Book II, chapters 21 and 24. In *Anna Karenin* (1873–7), Tolstoy endorses the manliness of the friendship between Vronsky and Captain Yashvin by briefly contrasting them with another pair of officers in the mess: 'Two officers appeared in the doorway: one, a young fellow with a weak, thin face, who had recently joined the regiment from the Corps of Pages; the other, a plump, elderly officer with a bracelet on his wrist and sunken little eyes.' Vronsky will not speak civilly to either of them. As they leave the room, Yashvin sneers, 'There go the inseparables' – *Anna Karenin* (Harmondsworth: Penguin, 1954), pp. 193–4. According to Simon Karlinsky, 'The theme of homosexuality in the life of Leo Tolstoy . . . deserves a special study which will undoubtedly be written one day. In his childhood, Tolstoy kept falling in love with boys and girls' – in Wayne R. Dynes, *Encyclopedia of Homosexuality* II (Chicago and London: St James Press, 1990), p. 1136.

Chapter 12

1 Greenhorn [George Thompson], *City Crimes* (Boston: William Berry, 1849), pp. 64–5.
2 Ibid., pp. 138–9.
3 David S. Reynolds, *Beneath the American Renaissance: The Subversive Imagination in the Age of Emerson and Melville* (Cambridge, Mass., and London: Harvard University Press, 1989), p. 328.
4 Michael Moon, *Disseminating Whitman: Revision and Corporeality in 'Leaves of Grass'* (Cambridge, Mass., and London: Harvard University Press, 1991), p. 21.
5 Camille Paglia, *Sexual Personae: Art and Decadence from Nefertiti to Emily Dickinson* (New Haven and London: Yale University Press, 1990), p. 607.
6 Joel L. Swerdlow, 'America's Poet: Walt Whitman', *National Geographic* 186, 6 (December 1994), pp. 106–41. Photographs by Maria Stenzel. I am grateful to Susie Daniel for drawing this item to my attention.
7 F.O. Matthiessen, *The American Renaissance: Art and Expression in the Age of Emerson and Whitman* (London: Oxford University Press, 1941).
8 See, for instance, David Bergman, 'F.O. Matthiessen: The Critic as Homosexual', in *Gaiety Transfigured: Gay Self-representation in American Literature* (Madison: University of Wisconsin Press, 1991), pp. 85–102; and Michael Cadden, 'Engendering F.O.M.: The

Private Life of *American Renaissance*', in Joseph A. Boone and Michael Cadden (eds), *Engendering Men: The Question of Male Feminist Criticism* (New York: Routledge, 1990), pp. 26–35.
9 Leslie A. Fiedler, *Love and Death in the American Novel* (New York: Criterion, 1960), p. 209.
10 Leslie A Fiedler, *The Return of the Vanishing American* (London: Paladin, 1972), p. 117.
11 Walter L. Williams, *The Spirit and the Flesh: Sexual Diversity in American Indian Culture* (Boston: Beacon, 1988). Will Roscoe (ed.), *Living the Spirit: A Gay American Indian Anthology, Compiled by Gay American Indians* (New York: St Martin's Press, 1988).
12 Robert K. Martin, *Hero, Captain, and Stranger: Male Friendship, Social Critique, and Literary Form in the Sea Novels of Herman Melville* (Chapel Hill and London: University of North Carolina Press, 1986), p. 49.
13 Herman Melville, *Moby-Dick* (Harmondsworth: Penguin, 1972), p. 527. The editor of this edition, Harold Beaver, comments that the longing to 'squeeze ourselves into each other' is 'repulsive to one part of the normal personality' – whatever that may be – but concedes that it is 'seductive to another' (p. 876).
14 Herman Melville, *Billy Budd, Sailor, and Other Stories* (New York and London: Penguin, 1970).
15 Robert K. Martin, 'Melville, Herman', in Claude J. Summers (ed.), *The Gay and Lesbian Literary Heritage: A Reader's Companion to the Writers and their Works, from Antiquity to the Present* (New York: Henry Holt, 1995), pp. 471–5; p. 475.

Chapter 13

1 Brian Reade (ed.), *Sexual Heretics: Male Homosexuality in English Literature from 1850 to 1900* (London: Routledge & Kegan Paul, 1970), pp. 388–91.
2 Ibid., p. 83.
3 See Richard Dellamora, 'An Essay in Sexual Liberation, Victorian Style: Walter Pater's "Two Early French Stories"', in Stuart Kellogg (ed.), *Essays on Gay Culture* (New York: Harrington Park Press, 1983), pp. 139–50.
4 Walter Pater, *Plato and Platonism: A Series of Lectures* (London: Macmillan, 1893), pp. 280–81.
5 H. Montgomery Hyde (ed.), *Trials of Oscar Wilde* (London: William Hodge, 1948), p. 236.

6 David Hilliard, 'UnEnglish and Unmanly: Anglo-Catholicism and Homosexuality', *Victorian Studies* 25, 2 (Winter 1982), pp. 181–210; p. 185.

7 Ibid., pp. 198–200. For further details on the Uranians, see Timothy d'Arch Smith, *Love in Earnest: Some Notes on the Lives and Writings of the English 'Uranian' Poets from 1880 to 1910* (London: Routledge and Kegan Paul, 1970).

8 Ronald Chapman, *Father Faber* (London: Burns and Oates, 1961), p. 16.

9 See Renée V. Overholser, '"Looking with Terrible Temptation": Gerard Manley Hopkins and Beautiful Bodies', *Victorian Literature and Culture* 19 (1991), pp. 25–53.

10 Quoted ibid., p. 42.

11 Joseph Bristow, '"Churlsgrace": Gerard Manley Hopkins and the Working-Class Male Body', *ELH* 59 (1992), pp. 693–711; p. 708.

12 Oscar Wilde, *Complete Works of Oscar Wilde* (Glasgow: Harper Collins, 1994), p. 790.

13 Brigid Brophy, *Prancing Novelist: A Defence of Fiction in the Form of a Critical Biography in Praise of Ronald Firbank* (London: Macmillan, 1973).

14 Neil Bartlett, *Who Was that Man? A Present for Mr Oscar Wilde* (Harmondsworth: Penguin, 1993), p. 93.

15 Alan Sinfield, *The Wilde Century: Oscar Wilde, Effeminacy and the Queer Moment* (London: Cassell, 1994), p. 72.

16 Bartlett, pp. 201–2.

17 Ibid., p. 112.

18 Hyde, p. 344.

19 Sinfield, p. 103.

20 Quoted in Ed Cohen, *Talk on the Wilde Side: Toward a Genealogy of a Discourse on Male Sexualities* (New York and Routledge, 1993), p. 200.

21 See Eve Kosofsky Sedgwick, *Between Men: English Literature and Male Homosocial Desire* (New York: Columbia University Press, 1985), pp. 201–217.

22 Richard Ellmann, *Oscar Wilde* (London and New York: Penguin, 1988), pp. 160–64. An imagined account of the meeting is given in Richard Howard's wonderful poem 'Wildflowers' in his *Selected Poems* (London and New York: Penguin, 1991), pp. 81–98.

23 Quoted in Reade, *Sexual Heretics*, p. 6.

24 Reade, pp. 275–82.

25 For further details, see Richard Dellamora, *Masculine Desire: The Sexual Politics of Victorian Aestheticism* (Chapel Hill, NC and London: University of North Carolina Press, 1990), pp. 44–45, 49, 87–9; and Robert Bernard Martin, *Gerard Manley Hopkins: A Very Private Life* (London: Flamingo, 1992), pp. 350–52.

26 Reade, pp. 344–5.

Chapter 14

1 James W. Jones, *'We of the Third Sex': Literary Representations of Homosexuality in Wilhelmine Germany* (New York: Peter Lang, 1990), p. 115. On Ulrichs, see Hubert Kennedy, *Ulrichs: The Life and Works of Karl Heinrich Ulrichs, Pioneer of the Modern Gay Movement* (Boston: Alyson, 1988).

2 Edward Carpenter, *Selected Writings, Volume 1: Sex* (London: GMP, 1984), p. 244.

3 Quoted by Ernst Morwitz in his introduction to Stefan George, *Poems* (New York: Schocken, 1967), p. 27.

4 Rex Warner's introduction to John Mavrogordato's translation of *Poems by C.P. Cavafy* (London: Chatto and Windus, 1951), p. 8. In what follows page references to this edition will be marked by the abbreviation *P*. I also use Edmund Keeley and George Savidis' edition of C.P. Cavafy, *Passions and Ancient Days: Twenty One New Poems* (London: Hogarth, 1972), page references to which will be marked *PAD*.

5 Mark Lilly, *Gay Men's Literature in the Twentieth Century* (London: Macmillan, 1993), p. 49.

6 See Gregory Woods, *Articulate Flesh: Male Homo-eroticism and Modern Poetry* (New Haven and London: Yale University Press, 1987), p. 233, n. 25.

Chapter 15

1 See Gregory Woods, 'The Injured Sex: Hemingway's Voice of Masculine Anxiety', in Judith Still and Michael Worton (eds), *Textuality and Sexuality: Reading Theories and Practices* (Manchester: Manchester University Press, 1993), pp. 160–72.

2 See Don Merrick Liles, 'William Faulkner's *Absalom, Absalom!*: An Exegesis of the Homoerotic Configurations in the Novel', in Stuart Kellogg (ed.), *Essays on Gay Literature* (New York: Harrington Park Press, 1983), pp. 99–111.

3 On *Victory*, see Jeffrey Meyers, *Homosexuality and Literature, 1890–1930* (London: Athlone, 1977), chapter 6. James Lansbury's novel *Korzeniowski* (1992) is, in effect, an extended

gay reading of Conrad's short story 'The Secret Sharer'. On the other hand, one cannot fail to be interested in the fact that, despite being largely set in a seedy pornographic bookstore, Conrad's *The Secret Agent* shows no hint that its English sexual underworld contains any inverts.

4 Volume numbers and page numbers refer to the twelve-volume Chatto and Windus edition of the translation of *Remembrance of Things Past* by C.K. Scott Moncrieff and Andreas Mayor. The elegance and eccentricities, even the errors, of the Scott Moncrieff translation contribute to its status as a camp classic in its own right.

5 André Gide, *Corydon* (New York: Farrar, Straus, 1950), pp. 193–4. Note Gide's recognition, from which Proust did not demur, that the *Recherche* had a propagandist purpose.

6 On Gide's attitudes to Proust, see Patrick Pollard, *André Gide: Homosexual Moralist* (New Haven and London: Yale University Press, 1991), pp. 253–8.

7 Roland Barthes, *A Lover's Discourse* (London: Cape, 1979), pp. 26–7.

8 Ibid., p. 138.

Chapter 16

1 Naomi Mitchison, 'Krypteia' and 'O Lucky Thessaly!' in *Black Sparta: Greek Stories* (London: Cape, 1928), pp. 16–25, 27–56; and 'A Matter of No Importance' in *Barbarian Stories* (London: Cape, 1929), pp. 81–95.

2 Another, later, short story worth reading is Karen Blixen's 'The Sailor-Boy's Tale', in which male love is represented as being at least as dangerous as it may be enigmatic and even magical – Isak Dinesen, *Winter's Tales* (New York: Random House, 1942), pp. 89–103).

3 On desert island narratives, see Gregory Woods, 'Fantasy Islands: Popular Topographies of Marooned Masculinity', in David Bell and Gill Valentine (eds), *Mapping Desire: Geographies of Sexualities* (London and New York: Routledge, 1995), pp. 126–48.

4 Quoted in C. Harman, *Sylvia Townsend Warner: A Biography* (London: Chatto and Windus, 1989), pp. 69–70.

5 Sylvia Townsend Warner, *Mr Fortune's Maggot* (London: Virago, 1978), pp. 192–3, 247.

6 Virginia Woolf, *The Waves* (London: Hogarth, 1963).

7 Ernest Hemingway, *A Moveable Feast*

(London: Cape, 1964), pp. 25–6. In fairness to Stein, one ought to acknowledge the possibility that, in making these ludicrous remarks, she may have been deceiving Hemingway. The stated view about homosexual men is so close to what he would have wanted to hear, that he may have overlooked any trace of irony in its tone.

8 Gertrude Stein, *Two: Gertrude Stein and Her Brother and Other Early Portraits (1908–1912)* (New Haven: Yale University Press, 1951), pp. 310–15.

9 By the shorthand term 'non-Modernist' I mean, in brief, writers who were content to write realist fiction on predominantly social themes, without much concerning themselves with the kinds of innovation which one associates with the fiction of the inner individual as practised by Virginia Woolf, or the reflexive stylistic experimentation of writers like Gertrude Stein.

10 Blair Niles, *Strange Brother* (London: GMP, 1991), p. 193.

11 Radclyffe Hall, *The Well of Loneliness* (London: Virago, 1982). It is true that Stephen Gordon is sufficiently maladjusted to her lesbianism to be constantly pleading the cause of normality, but the fact remains that she has to admire the garden of the norm from the other side of the fence.

12 Djuna Barnes, *Nightwood* (London: Faber, 1979).

13 Shari Benstock, *Women of the Left Bank: Paris, 1900–1940* (London: Virago, 1987), p. 266.

14 Winifred Holtby, *South Riding* (London: Collins, 1936), pp. 134–5.

15 Katharine Burdekin, *Swastika Night* (London: Lawrence and Wishart, 1985).

Chapter 17

1 Eric Garber, 'A Spectacle in Color: The Lesbian and Gay Subculture of Jazz Age Harlem', in Martin Bauml Duberman, Martha Vicinus and George Chauncey, Jr. (eds), *Hidden From History: Reclaiming the Gay and Lesbian Past* (Harmondsworth: Penguin, 1991), pp. 318–333; p. 318. See also George Chauncey, *Gay New York: Gender, Urban Culture, and the Making of the Gay Male World 1890–1940* (New York: Basic Books, 1994), pp. 244–67.

2 Emmanuel Nelson, 'Critical Deviance: Homophobia and the Reception of James Baldwin's Fiction', *Journal of American Culture* 14, 3 (Fall 1991), pp. 91–6; p. 92. This should not distract us from the fact that

the main impetus behind the current recovery of the Harlem Renaissance as a gay cultural phenomenon is coming from gay African-American critics. The record of white gay critics has not always been impressive. To give myself as an example, my book *Articulate Flesh* names only one black poet, Langston Hughes, in a primary bibliography of over a hundred poets. The text itself does not refer to Hughes once. For a trenchant report on many issues raised by white critical responses to black cultural products, see Michael Awkward's essay 'Negotiations of Power: White Critics, Black Texts, and the Self-Referential Impulse', *American Literary History* 2, 4 (Winter 1990), pp. 581–606.

3 Daniel Garrett, 'Other Countries: The Importance of Difference', *Other Countries: Black Gay Voices* 1 (Spring 1988), pp. 17–28; p. 17.

4 See Essex Hemphill's interview with Isaac Julien and Hemphill's own short essay 'Undressing Icons', in Essex Hemphill (ed.), *Brother to Brother: New Writings by Black Gay Men* (Boston: Alyson, 1991), pp. 174–180, 181–3. In the latter, Hemphill refers to the Langston Hughes estate as Hughes's 'sacred closet' (p. 181) and reaches the following angry conclusion about the Estate's involvement in the affair: 'Perhaps black assimilation into Western culture is more complete than we realise. It was common at one time to openly silence and intimidate outspoken black people. Now black people practice these tactics against each other – just like white men' (p. 183). See also Bad Object-Choices (eds), *How Do I Look? Queer Film and Video* (Seattle: Bay Press, 1991), pp. 17–19.

5 Langston Hughes, *Selected Poems* (London: Pluto, 1986).

6 Langston Hughes shows no sign of linking this trade, ironically or otherwise, with the commodification of flesh which first brought African slaves on ships to the Americas.

7 Claude McKay, *Selected Poems of Claude McKay* (New York: Harcourt, Brace and World, 1953), p. 76.

8 Countee Cullen, *On These I Stand: An Anthology of the Best Poems* (New York: Harper and Row, 1947), pp. 104–37.

9 Blair Niles, *Strange Brother* (London: T. Werner Laurie, 1932), p. 234.

10 When McKay introduced his own reading of the poem on Arna Bontemps' disc *Anthology of Negro Poets* (Folkways Record, FP91) he spoke of it as a universal poem, intended for all people who are 'abused, outraged and murdered, whether they are minorities or nations, black or brown or yellow or white,

Catholic or Protestant or Pagan, fighting against terror' – Nathan Irvin Huggins, *Harlem Renaissance* (New York: Oxford University Press, 1971), p. 72.

11 Cullen uses the seed image again in 'Ultimatum' (p. 69), where he states his determination to plant his chosen seed – an activity which inevitably has a sexual resonance – regardless of whether it will subsequently grow upwards ('to heaven') or downwards ('to hell'). I am inclined to read this as a moment in which the poet decisively washes his hands of the 'moral' issues which other people have imposed on his life. In any case, as one sees in the perversely paradoxical 'More Than a Fool's Song' (p. 67), Cullen was happy to hypothesise that the people who are commonly thought virtuous may actually be vicious, and vice versa.

12 Huggins, p. 212. This argument can also be applied to non-specific love lyrics. Wayne Cooper mentions poems by McKay which 'celebrated brief affairs with partners whose sex is never explicitly stated. They could well have been either men or women' – Wayne F. Cooper, *Claude McKay: Rebel Sojourner in the Harlem Renaissance, A Biography* (Baton Rouge and London: Louisiana State University Press, 1987), p. 75. Cooper lists the following poems, all in *Home to Harlem*, as examples: 'Romance', 'The Snow Fairy', 'Tormented' and 'One Year After' (p. 388, n. 39).

13 Eric Garber's assertion that 'Even Langston Hughes touched upon the topic' of black lesbian and gay experience in the poem 'Café: 3 A.M.' takes an unnecessarily narrow view of what constitutes a reference to the topic – Garber, p. 330. While it may be true that, as Allen D. Prowle has said, 'Hughes rarely allowed himself to indulge in personal poetry', I would argue that the sensuality and enthusiasm which Hughes conveys in his work are easily read as representations of the atmosphere of subcultural life in Harlem as he experienced it – Allen D. Prowle, 'Langston Hughes', in Chris Bigsby (ed.), *The Black American Writer, Volume II: Poetry and Drama* (DeLand, Fla: Everett/Edwards, 1969), pp. 77–87; p. 84.

14 David Levering Lewis, *When Harlem Was in Vogue* (New York and Oxford: Oxford University Press, 1989), p. 77. There are even more negative ways of putting this. For instance: 'Nor can there be any doubt that his feeling of inferiority is also derived . . . from his partial or total inability to lead a normal sex life' – Jean Wagner, *Black Poets of the United States from Paul Laurence Dunbar to*

Langston Hughes (Urbana: University of Illinois Press, 1973), p. 295.

15 I do not mean to endorse what Amitai Avi-Ram has rightly referred to as 'the relatively simplistic association of "conventional" poetic forms (such as the sonnet) with political conservatism and of "free verse" with liberation' – Amitai F. Avi-Ram, 'The Unreadable Black Body: "Conventional" Poetic Form in the Harlem Renaissance', *Genders* 7 (Spring 1990), pp. 32–46; p. 33. But there is, arguably, a real problem of inappropriate archaisms in Cullen and McKay's formal verse, especially when they force themselves into awkward inversions, which makes Hughes, by contrast, seem far more in touch with the *Zeitgeist* of Modernist Harlem.

16 Alain Locke (ed.), *The New Negro* (New York: Boni, 1925), pp. 113–14.

17 Langston Hughes, *The Big Sea* (London: Pluto, 1986), p. 237.

18 Nugent himself said, of the *Fire!!* story, 'I didn't know *it was gay* when I wrote it' – Charles Michael Smith, 'Bruce Nugent: Bohemian of the Harlem Renaissance', in Joseph Beam (ed.), *In the Life: A Black Gay Anthology* (Boston: Alyson, 1986), pp. 209–20; p. 214. But his readers could then, and can now, immediately perceive a clearly gay voice which, in its unguarded flamboyance and flair, even in its breathily queeny ellipses, briefly defied the dominant culture's threats in order to voice the desires of the emergent gay sub-subculture.

Chapter 18

1 Quoted in James M. Saslow (ed. and trans.), *The Poetry of Michelangelo: An Annotated Translation* (New Haven and London: Yale University Press, 1991), p. 18.

2 Joseph Bristow, *Effeminate England: Homoerotic Writing after 1885* (Buckingham: Open University Press, 1995) p. 22.

3 E.M. Forster, *Maurice* (Harmondsworth: Penguin, 1972), pp. 32–3.

4 Very valuable recent discussions of Forster and Maurice have included the following: Joseph Bristow, 'Against "Effeminacy"' [*sic*]: the Sexual Predicament in E.M. Forster's Fiction', in Bristow, *Effeminate England*, pp. 55–99; John Fletcher, 'Forster's Self-Erasure: *Maurice* and the Scene of Masculine Love', in Joseph Bristow (ed.), *Sexual Sameness: Textual Differences in Lesbian and Gay Writing* (New York and London: Routledge, 1992), pp.

64–90; Paul Hammond, 'E.M. Forster and *Maurice*', in his *Love between Men in English Literature* (London: Macmillan, 1996), pp. 195–203; and Claude J. Summers' entry on Forster in his *The Gay and Lesbian Literary Heritage* (New York: Holt, 1995), pp. 280–85.

5 D.H. Lawrence, *The Prussian Officer* (Harmondsworth: Penguin, 1945), p. 8.

6 Carson McCullers, *Reflections in a Golden Eye* (Harmondsworth: Penguin, 1967), p. 7.

Chapter 19

1 Simon Karlinsky, *The Sexual Labyrinth of Nikolai Gogol* (Cambridge, Mass: Harvard University Press, 1976), pp. 41–2.

2 Nikolai Gogol, *Taras Bulba* (London: Everyman, 1918), pp. 95–6.

3 Franz Kafka, *Description of a Struggle and Other Stories* (Harmondsworth: Penguin, 1979), pp. 13–14.

4 Franz Kafka, *The Castle* (Harmondsworth: Penguin, 1957), p. 124.

5 Ruth Tiefenbrun, *Moment of Torment: An Interpretation of Franz Kafka's Short Stories* (Carbondale and Edwardsville: Southern Illinois University Press, 1973).

6 See David Rattray, introduction to René Crevel, *Difficult Death* (San Francisco: North Point, 1986) p. xviii.

7 René Crevel, *Babylon* (London: Quartet, 1988).

8 See G. Cabrera Infante, 'The Death of Virgilio', in Virgilio Piñera, *Cold Tales,* trans. Mark Schafer (Hygiene, Colo.: Eridanos, 1988), pp. xi–xiv. See also G. Cabrera Infante, *Mea Cuba* (London: Faber, 1994), p. 355.

9 Piñera, p. 121.

10 Nor should we overlook Virgilio Piñera's Cuban contemporary José Lezama Lima, in the middle chapters of whose novel *Paradiso* (1966) gay Latin American fiction attains its first peak.

Chapter 20

1 Dashiell Hammett, *The Maltese Falcon* (Harmondsworth: Penguin, 1963).

2 James M. Cain, *Serenade* (London: Cape, 1938).

3 Alan Sinfield, *Literature, Politics and Culture in Postwar Britain* (Oxford: Blackwell, 1989), p. 76.

4 Ian Fleming, *From Russia, With Love*

(London: Pan, 1959), pp. 36, 82–3.

5 Cyril Connolly, 'Bond Strikes Camp', in *Previous Convictions* (London: Hamish Hamilton, 1963), pp. 354–71.

6 John le Carré, *The Spy Who Came in from the Cold* (London: Coronet, 1990), p. 46.

7 Tim Heald, *A Life of Love: The Life of Barbara Cartland* (London: Sinclair-Stevenson, 1994), pp. 171, 60.

8 Barbara Cartland, *A Virgin in Mayfair* (London: Arrow, 1976), pp. 26–7.

9 Paul Burston, 'Dream Demon', *Attitude* (November 1995), p. 61.

10 Peter Burton, 'The Candyman Cometh (Out)', *Gay Times* 202 (July 1995), pp. 48–51.

Chapter 21

1 On the Nazi treatment of homosexual men, see Jean Boisson, *Le Triangle rose: La déportation des homosexuels 1933–1945* (Paris: Robert Laffont, 1988); Günter Grau (ed.), *Hidden Holocaust? Gay and Lesbian Persecution in Germany 1933–45* (London: Cassell, 1995); Richard Plant, *The Pink Triangle: The Nazi War against Homosexuals* (New York: Holt, 1986); Frank Rector, *The Nazi Extermination of Homosexuals* (New York: Stein and Day, 1981). The latter, by far the weakest of these accounts, was only temporarily useful at the time of its publication.

2 Grau, p. 1.

3 One relevant – but curiously pornographic – example is Heinz Heger, *The Men with the Pink Triangle* (London: GMP, 1980). Far more impressive is Pierre Seel's *I, Pierre Seel, Deported Homosexual: A Memoir of Nazi Terror* (New York: Basic Books, 1995).

4 See, for instance, Walter Laqueur, *The Terrible Secret: Suppression of the Truth about Hitler's 'Final Solution'* (London: Weidenfeld and Nicolson, 1980); Dr Miklos Nyiszli, *Auschwitz: A Doctor's Eye-Witness Account* (London: Panther, 1962); Jona Oberski, *A Childhood* (London: Hodder and Stoughton, 1983); Richard Rashke, *Escape from Sobibor* (London: Michael Joseph, 1983). It is important to acknowledge that these silences are entirely justifiable in certain cases. For instance, Oberski's book is a fictionalised autobiography from a child's point of view, and we may have no reason to expect a child to understand or even be aware of homosexuality. Rashke's book deals with Sobibor, which was an extermination camp

for Jews only, so pink triangle prisoners are not relevant to his account. On the other hand, given its title and subtitle, Laqueur's book might be expected not, by intention or default, to have secrets of its own.

5 Wieslaw Kielar, *Anus Mundi: Five Years in Auschwitz* (Harmondsworth: Penguin, 1982).

6 Female survivors have testified to similar arrangements in the women's sections of the camps. See, for example, Fania Fénelon, *The Musicians of Auschwitz* (London: Sphere, 1979), p. 206; and Kitty Hart, *Return to Auschwitz* (London: Granada, 1983), p. 95. Hart also reports having heard of the *Kapo/Piepel* relationships in the men's compounds (p. 163).

7 In a short story by Tadeusz Borowski, criminal prisoners who are due to be transferred from Auschwitz to the trenches ask in dismay, 'out there, who will polish our boots, and how are we going to get pretty young boys?' – *This Way for the Gas, Ladies and Gentlemen* (Harmondsworth: Penguin, 1976), p. 123.

8 Bock is also mentioned in Jóseph Jarlínski's memoir *Fighting Auschwitz*: 'The SS-men discovered that on Block No. 21 Hans Bock, the Senior Prisoner of the Hospital, had a small camouflaged room in which he met young boys, mostly Polish male nurses' – (Greenwich, Conn.: Fawcett Crest, 1975), p. 243. Like Kielar, Jarlínski only mentions circumstantial homosexuality, and only briefly: 'Amongst the men homosexuality was spreading, practised mainly by German criminal prisoners, who had been there for many years. They would entice or force young boys to spend time with them. These were nevertheless isolated incidents' (p. 151).

9 Filip Müller, *Auschwitz Inferno* (London: Routledge and Kegan Paul, 1979), pp. 56, 178.

10 Primo Levi, *If This Is A Man/The Truce* (Harmondsworth: Penguin, 1979).

11 Elie Wiesel, *Night* (Harmondsworth: Penguin, 1981), p. 59.

12 Other accounts sometimes list the categories without mentioning the patches. See Primo Levi, *Moments of Reprieve* (London: Abacus, 1987), p. 92. Levi mentions homosexuals here, but some of the other categories vanish into an uncharacteristically careless 'etc'.

13 Evelyn le Chêne, *Mauthausen: The History of a Death Camp* (London: Methuen, 1971), p. 40. This authoritative account gives useful statistics on the numbers of prisoners in each category on specific dates at Mauthausen. 1 December 1939: 688 politicals, 143 Jehovah's Witnesses, 51 homosexuals (that is, imprisoned *as such*), 13 emigrants, 1 Jew, 946

criminals, 930 asocials – 2,772 in total. 1 January 1940: 648 politicals, 143 Jehovah's Witnesses, 48 homosexuals, 12 emigrants, 827 asocials, 925 criminals and 3 miscellaneous – 2,606 in total. 1 May 1940: 749 politicals, 66 Jehovah's Witnesses, 63 homosexuals, 870 criminals, 1,043 asocials, 12 emigrants – 2,803 in total. 31 December 1943: 6,574 politicals, 23 Jehovah's Witnesses, 30 homosexuals, 3,702 Poles, 2 Jews, 754 prisoners of war, 1,944 young Russian civilians, 710 long-term criminals, 1,942 short-term criminals, 287 asocials, 1,738 miscellaneous – 17,706 in total. 31 December 1944: 34,955 politicals, 85 Jehovah's Witnesses, 66 homosexuals, 9,075 Jews, 153 Gypsies, 5,214 prisoners of war, 15,924 young Russians, 1,320 long-term criminals, 2,811 short-term criminals, 468 asocials, 2,355 miscellaneous – 72,426 in total. 4 May 1945: 28,256 politicals, 96 Jehovah's Witnesses, 67 homosexuals, 9,822 Jews, 165 Gypsies, 4,502 prisoners of war, 15,020 young Russians, 1,253 long-term criminals, 2,721 short-term criminals, 441 asocials, 2,457 miscellaneous – 64,800 in total. I offer these figures in order to keep the homosexual situation in context, never forgetting that some of the other categories, notably the Russians, were far greater in number. It is also important to note that members of certain categories (for instance the politicals) were less likely to be killed than others (principally, of course, the Jews). However, the comparing of numbers is not necessarily productive if it leads different groups to compete in the degree of their oppression. I refer readers to a story told by Gore Vidal: 'In the German concentration camps, Jews wore yellow stars while homosexualists wore pink triangles. I was present when Christopher Isherwood tried to make this point to a young Jewish movie producer. "After all," Isherwood said, "Hitler killed six hundred thousand homosexuals." The young man was not impressed. "But Hitler killed six *million* Jews," he said sternly. "What are you?" asked Isherwood. "In real estate?"' – 'Pink Triangle and Yellow Star', in Gore Vidal, *Pink Triangle and Yellow Star, and Other Essays (1976–1982)* (London: Granada, 1983), p. 213.

14 *Papers Concerning the Treatment of German Nationals in Germany 1938–1939* (London: HMSO, 1939), Cmd. 6120 xxvii 429; pp. 10, 12. A later document from a former Buchenwald prisoner does mention this category: 'The fourth category consisted of the homo-sexuals, or at least of those against

whom the Gestapo thought fit to bring charges of homo-sexuality. To charge those it dislikes with this offence is a favourite tactic of the secret police. At the time I was there [for six weeks in 1938] Buchenwald contained no representative of this group' in a total of 8,000 prisoners (p. 35).

15 Martin Gilbert, *The Holocaust* (London: Board of Deputies of British Jews, 1978), p. 20. On the other hand, Martin Gilbert's *Atlas of the Holocaust* (London: Michael Joseph, 1982) mentions homosexuals among those killed in the last months at Mauthausen, the last camp liberated by the Americans. A map entitled 'Homosexuals Murdered, January-May 1945' shows 62 brought to Mauthausen from Germany, 3 from Czechoslovakia and 2 from Poland; 67 in all (map 302, p. 233).

16 Walter Poller, *Medical Block, Buchenwald: The Personal Testimony of Inmate 996, Block 36* (London: Souvenir Press, 1961).

17 Sidra DeKoven Ezrahi, *By Words Alone: The Holocaust in Literature* (Chicago: University of Chicago Press, 1980), pp. 10–11.

18 *Papers Concerning the Treatment. . . .* p. 20

19 Samuel Igra, *Germany's National Vice* (London: Quality Press, 1945), p. 7.

20 Rudolf Hoess, *Commandant of Auschwitz* (London: Pan, 1974), p. 48.

21 For an account of events leading up to, and critical reactions to, the first production of *Bent*, see Nicholas de Jongh, *Not in Front of the Audience: Homosexuality on Stage* (London and New York: Routledge, 1992), pp. 145–56.

22 John M. Clum, *Acting Gay: Male Homosexuality in Modern Drama*, revised edn. (New York: Columbia University Press, 1994), p. 227.

23 Les Wright, 'Gay Genocide as Literary Trope', in Emmanuel S. Nelson (ed.), *AIDS: The Literary Response* (New York: Twayne, 1992), pp. 50–68; p. 52.

Chapter 22

1 Evelyn Waugh, *Brideshead Revisited* (Harmondsworth: Penguin, 1962).

2 Martin Green, *Children of the Sun: A Narrative of 'Decadence' in England after 1918* (London: Pimlico, 1992), pp. 220–21.

3 Evelyn Waugh's other homosexual Modernist – but if no less homosexual somewhat less successfully Modernist than Anthony Blanche – is Ambrose Silk in *Put Out More Flags* (1942). He once knew

Diaghilev, Cocteau and Gertrude Stein. However, at Oxford he recited not *The Waste Land* but Tennyson's *In Memoriam* through a megaphone; and there is a hint of Wilde and Beardsley about his style. Modern though he is, he has been left behind by events. Like his German lover, Hans, who is consigned to a concentration camp by the Nazis, he seems bewildered by the fact that he cannot 'fit the old love into the scheme of the new' – *Put Out More Flags* (Harmondsworth: Penguin, 1943), p. 187.

4 Heinrich Böll, *The Train Was on Time* (London: Sphere, 1967).

5 George Orwell, *Nineteen Eighty-Four* (Harmondsworth: Penguin, 1954).

6 Anthony Burgess partially recognised what Orwell appears not to have – that one could create a dystopian nightmare for heterosexual readers by imposing on heterosexual characters the routine conditions governing the lives of real homosexual people in the time of writing – when he wrote his novel *The Wanting Seed* (1962). In this rather uncomfortably comic, post-Wolfenden narrative, Burgess portrays a society passing through a liberal 'Pelagian' period, in which the values of homosexuality, infertility, infanticide and perpetual peace are raised above those of heterosexuality, fertility, motherhood, God and war.

Chapter 23

1 Quoted in Ian Gibson, *Federico García Lorca: A Life* (London: Faber, 1989), p. 29.

2 On the homosexual Lorca, see Paul Binding, *Lorca: The Gay Imagination* (London: Gay Men's Press, 1985) and Angel Sahuquillo, *Federico García Lorca y la cultura de la homosexualidad masculina* (Alicante: Instituto de Cultura Juan Gil-Albert, 1991).

3 I am using the following Ritsos editions and abbreviations of their titles: *Corridor and Stairs* (The Curragh, Ireland: Goldsmith, 1976), *CS. Exile and Return* (London: Anvil, 1989), *ER. Ritsos in Parentheses* (Princeton, NJ: Princeton University Press, 1979), *RP. Scripture of the Blind* (Columbus: Ohio State University Press, 1979), *SB. Selected Poems* (Harmondsworth: Penguin, 1974), *SP. Subterranean Horses* (Athens, Ohio: Ohio University Press, 1980), *SH*.

4 Quoted in Nico Naldini's introduction to *The Letters of Pier Paolo Pasolini, Volume I: 1940–1954* (London: Quartet, 1992), p. 78.

5 On the PCI's record in relation to homosexuality, see Fabio Giovannini,

Comunisti e diversi: il PCI e la questione omosessuale (Bari: Dedalo, 1980). On Pasolini, see pp. 54–7, 74–8, 93–4. For an excellent overview of homosexual writing in Russia see Kevin Moss (ed.), *Out of the Blue: Russia's Hidden Gay Literature, An Anthology* (San Francisco: Gay Sunshine, 1997). See also Ursula Owen (ed.), *Gay's the Word in Moscow*, a special issue of *Index on Censorship* 24, 1 (January/February 1995), pp. 14–85.

6 Pier Paolo Pasolini, *Selected Poems* (London: Calder, 1984), pp. 110–137.

7 Enzo Siciliano, *Pasolini: A Biography* (London: Bloomsbury, 1987), p. 203.

8 Barth David Schwartz, *Pasolini Requiem* (New York: Pantheon, 1992), p. 35.

Chapter 24

1 Jean Genet, *Querelle of Brest* (London: Panther, 1969).

2 Pier Vittorio Tondelli, *Pao Pao* (Milano: Feltrinelli, 1989), p. 7.

3 Leo Bersani, 'Is the Rectum a Grave?', in Douglas Crimp (ed.), *AIDS: Cultural Analysis/Cultural Activism* (Cambridge, Mass. and London: MIT Press, 1988), pp. 197–222; p. 212.

4 David Storey, *Radcliffe* (Harmondsworth: Penguin, 1965).

5 David Bergman, *Gaiety Transfigured: Gay Self-Representation in American Literature* (Madison: University of Wisconsin Press, 1991), p. 196.

6 Henry Chupack, *James Purdy* (Boston: Twayne, 1975), pp. 102–3.

7 Patrick White, *Riders in the Chariot* (Harmondsworth: Penguin, 1964).

Chapter 25

1 Other gay-related literary publications of these two years include the following. In 1952: Ernest Frost's *The Lighted Cities*, G.F. Green's *In the Making*, John Clellon Holmes's *Go*, Jay Little's *Maybe – Tomorrow*, Helen Mahler's *Empress of Byzantium*, Douglas Sanderson's *Dark Passions Subdue* and George Sylvester Viereck's *Men into Beasts*. In 1953: Jocelyn Brooke's *The Passing of a Hero*, Donald Webster Cory's anthology of homosexual fiction *Twenty-One Variations on a Theme*, John Cromwell's *A Grain of Sand*, Rodney Garland's *The Heart in Exile*, L.P. Hartley's *The Go-Between*, John Clellon Holmes' *The*

Horn, William Lee's *Junkie* (that is, William Burroughs' first book), Mary McLaren's *The Twisted Heart*, Mary Renault's *The Charioteer* and Gore Vidal's *The Judgment of Paris*.

2 Ralph Ellison, *Invisible Man* (Harmondsworth: Penguin, 1965), pp. 147–58.

3 James D. Hart (ed.), *The Oxford Companion to American Literature* (New York and Oxford: Oxford University Press, 1983), p. 334.

4 Chester Himes, *Cast the First Stone* (London: Allison and Busby, 1990).

5 Baldwin had published fiction on the topic of adolescent homosexuality even before *Go Tell It on the Mountain*. His story 'The Outing' first came out in 1951, though it was republished much later in *Going to Meet the Man*. Of three boys torn between their bodies' sinful persuasiveness and their families' pressures to sacrifice their lives to Jesus, one, Johnnie, is going to turn out to be homosexual. Baldwin had published an essay on homosexuality and literature as early as 1949: 'Preservation of Innocence: Studies for a New Morality', *Zero* 1, 2 (1949), pp. 14–22. See Jonathan Ned Katz, *Gay/Lesbian Almanac: A New Documentary* (New York: Harper and Row, 1983), pp. 647–51.

6 Harold Norse, *Memoirs of a Bastard Angel* (London: Bloomsbury, 1990), pp. 114–15. None of this appears in James Campbell's *Talking at the Gates: A Life of James Baldwin* (London: Faber, 1991).

7 The really impressive thing about *Another Country* is Baldwin's speculative eagerness to examine in 'practice' a number of major and complex issues which, at various times, he raised in his essays: the conundrum of bisexuality; the correlation between queer-bashing and repressed homosexuality; the similar correlation between racism and the erotic fetishisation of the black body and Negro culture; the inadequacy of all definitive labels when applied to the routine instabilities of human existence; and so forth. This is a relentlessly serious novel – somewhat too mature for many of its early readers – even if its prose is often overblown to the extent of inadvertent self-imitation.

8 James Baldwin, *Giovanni's Room* (Harmondsworth: Penguin, 1990), p. 101.

9 See Patrick Higgins, *Heterosexual Dictatorship: Male Homosexuality in Post-War Britain* (London: Fourth Estate, 1996), pp. 288–93.

10 Alan Sinfield, *Literature, Politics and Culture in Postwar Britain* (Oxford: Blackwell, 1989), p. 74.

11 Richard Davenport Hines, *Auden* (London: Heinemann, 1995), p. 276.

12 Margaret Drabble, *Angus Wilson: A Biography* (London: Secker and Warburg, 1995), p. 380.

13 Angus Wilson, *Hemlock and After* (Harmondsworth: Penguin, 1956).

14 Stephen Adams, *The Homosexual as Hero in Contemporary Fiction* (London: Vision, 1980), p. 160.

15 Angus Wilson, *The Middle Age of Mrs Eliot* (Harmondsworth: Penguin, 1961).

16 Drabble, p. 243.

17 Angus Wilson, *Late Call* (London: Granada, 1982), p. 288.

18 In *As If By Magic* (1973), which contains the most explicitly sex-related of Angus Wilson's homosexual representations and was consequently ill received by the British critics, the homosexual character, Hamo Langmuir, is sent off, away from his family, on a picaresque sequence of more or less grotesque, boy-hunting adventures in the Far East. This removal from the contexts of both family and English liberal society leaves Wilson at a loss to do much with homosexuality itself as a morally serious topic. There is evidence that he realised this and was saddened by the relative failure of what was, sexually, his most daring book. When he came to write *Setting the World on Fire* (published in 1980), Wilson made a conscious decision to limit the amount of gay material he used, so as not to risk a repetition of *As If By Magic*'s lukewarm reception.

19 Nicholas de Jongh, *Not In Front of the Audience: Homosexuality on Stage* (London and New York: Routledge, 1992), p. 56.

20 Because drama is, of necessity and by definition, such a public art, dramatic texts lagged behind their twentieth-century equivalents in fiction and poetry when it came to the explicit representation of homosexuality. Oscar Wilde's comedies may be read now as knowingly perverse, even queer, but the fact remains that they speak with cunning obliquity. They may relate strongly to homosexuality in certain themes and stylistic effects, but they are not in any clear sense actually *about* it. Strictly speaking, they do not contain any homosexual characters. No drama in English had the daring of the scene in Frank Wedekind's *Spring Awakening* (*Frühlings Erwachen*, 1891) when two adolescent boys, Ernst and Hänschen, declare their love for each other, but recognise that when they are married adults they will look back on this day with some amusement. Wilhelmine Germany offered the productive conditions in which other dramatists were able to stage plays even more centrally and openly concerned with homosexuality. In Ludwig Dilsner's

Jasminblüthe (1898), a boy called Rudolf goes to confession to admit having homosexual feelings but he refuses to accept the idea that such feelings are themselves intrinsically sinful. When he falls in love with a man he is subjected to blackmail and considers killing himself. He decides to get married to cure himself, but then changes his mind. When his fiancée refuses to release him from their engagement, he does commit suicide after all. Based on Magnus Hirschfeld's theories, this play shows the homosexual protagonist to be subject to oppression by the institutions of Church, law, medicine and family. In the face of all these pressures, the play unambiguously argues in favour of homosexual rights. Herbert Hirschberg's play *Fehler* (1906) argues a similar case in a context of medical discourses. See James W. Jones, *'We of the Third Sex': Literary Representations of Homosexuality in Wilhelmine Germany* (New York: Peter Lang, 1990), pp. 174, 183. Nothing comparable happens in drama in the English language until the appearance of Mordaunt Shairp's *The Green Bay Tree* (1933). (This play is reprinted in Michael Wilcox [ed.], *Gay Plays* [London: Methuen, 1984].) But even this is what John Clum has referred to as 'a play about a homosexual character and possible homosexual relationship that never mentions or even directly alludes to homosexuality'. The central premise of the play is the competition between Leonora and Mr Dulcimer, a rich and elegant bachelor, for the love of the latter's ward, twenty-six-year-old David Owen, alias Julian Dulcimer. Although Mr Dulcimer is eventually shot by David's father, the younger man does not end up with Leonora; instead, he turns into a version of his own guardian, effetely arranging flowers and, as John Clum suggests, planning to seek out and corrupt a young ward of his own. For Clum, this ending is ambiguous: 'A gay audience could see the denouement not as a sinister picture of corruption but as the survival of the homosexual. Only a portion of the audience will read flower-arranging as a sign of degeneracy' – John M. Clum, *Acting Gay: Male Homosexuality in Modern Drama*, revised edn. (New York: Columbia University Press, 1994), pp. 92, 97. 1933 was also the year of Noël Coward's *Design for Living*.

21 Ibid., pp. 149, 22–3. Among these young men in Williams' plays are Stanley Kowalski in *A Streetcar Named Desire* (1947), Brick in *Cat on a Hot Tin Roof* (1955), Val Xavier in *Orpheus Descending* (1957) and Chance Wayne in *Sweet Bird of Youth* (1959).

22 Clum, pp. 155–6.

23 The most intelligent of the gay promotions of Orton's case is Simon Shepherd, *Because We're Queers: The Life and Crimes of Kenneth Halliwell and Joe Orton* (London: GMP, 1989). Shepherd is particularly good on the ways in which John Lahr has misappropriated Orton.

24 Alan Sinfield, 'Private Lives/Public Theater: Noel Coward and the Politics of Homosexual Representation', *Representations* 36 (Fall 1991), pp. 43–3; pp. 57–8.

25 This period is dealt with in detail in Robert Patrick's own novel *Temple Slave* (1994).

26 Stuart Timmons, *The Trouble with Harry Hay: Founder of the Modern Gay Movement* (Boston: Alyson, 1990), pp. 163–71.

27 Ekbert Faas, *Young Robert Duncan: Portrait of the Poet as Homosexual in Society* (Santa Barbara, Calif.: Black Sparrow, 1983), pp. 152–3.

28 *Empty Mirror* eventually came out in 1961. See Barry Miles, *Ginsberg: A Biography* (London: Viking, 1990), p. 147.

29 Robert Duncan, 'The Homosexual in Society', *Politics* 1 (August 1944), pp. 209–11. The essay is reprinted in full in Faas, pp. 319–22.

30 Frank O'Hara, *The Selected Poems of Frank O'Hara* (New York: Vintage, 1974), pp. 38–45.

31 In 1954 Christopher Isherwood would follow with the two-page essay on camp in his novel *The World in the Evening*.

32 Robert Duncan, *Bending the Bow* (New York: New Directions, 1968), p. 113.

Chapter 26

1 See, for instance, Philip J. Hilts, 'Dispelling Myths about AIDS in Africa', *Africa Report* 33, 6 (November–December 1988), pp. 27–31: 'there is virtually no anal sex reported among the people of Central Africa. Researchers are firmly convinced that there are few homosexuals in that part of Africa because survey after survey involving thousands of interviews in several nations has turned up few responses indicating homosexual or bisexual activity' (p28). However, for examples to the contrary, see Gerald W. Kleis and Salisu A. Abdullahi, 'Masculine Power and Gender Ambiguity in Urban Hausa Society', *African Urban Studies* 16 (Spring 1983), pp. 39–53; and Gill Shepherd, 'Rank, Gender, and Homosexuality: Mombasa as a Key to Understanding Sexual Options', in Pat Caplan (ed.), *The Cultural Construction of*

Sexuality (London: Routledge, 1989), pp. 240–70. On circumstantial male prostitution necessitated by poverty, see Robert Peake, 'Swahili Stratification and Tourism in Malindi Old Town, Kenya', *Africa* 59, 2 (1989), pp. 209–220. On the mining camps, see T. Dunbar Moodie, 'Migrancy and Male Sexuality on the South African Gold Mines', *Journal of Southern African Studies* 14, 2 (January 1988), pp. 228–56.

2 Neil McKenna, *On the Margins: Men Who Have Sex With Men and HIV in the Developing World* (London: Panos Institute, 1996), p. 12.

3 My use of the phrase 'African literature', and, indeed, my skimming the surfaces of many national cultures in the space of a short chapter, are mere conveniences, which clearly threaten to overlook or eradicate all signs of cultural difference within Africa. However, I hope that my use of the expression 'post-colonial' does suggest a certain cultural commonality which I wish to highlight here. As Frantz Fanon once put it, 'There is no common destiny to be shared between the national cultures of Senegal and Guinea; but there *is* a common destiny between the Senegalese and Guinean nations which are both dominated by the same French colonialism' – *The Wretched of the Earth* (New York: Grove, 1968), p. 234.

4 On African fiction, see Chris Dunton, '"Wheyting Be Dat?": The Treatment of Homosexuality in African Literature', *Research in African Literatures* 20, 3 (Fall 1989), pp. 422–48; Robert B. Marks Ridinger, 'African Literatures', in Claude J. Summers (ed.), *The Gay and Lesbian Literary Heritage: A Reader's Companion to the Writers and their Works, from Antiquity to the Present* (New York: Holt, 1995), pp. 5–8; and Shaun de Waal, 'A Thousand Forms of Love: Representations of Homosexuality in South African Literature', in Mark Gevisser and Edwin Cameron (eds.), *Defiant Desire: Gay and Lesbian Lives in South Africa* (New York and London: Routledge, 1995), pp. 232–45.

5 J.N. Kanyua Mugambi, *Carry It Home* (Kampala/Nairobi/Dar es Salaam: East African Literature Bureau, 1974), p. 86. Even rarer is a moment in 'Mine is the Silent Face', by Lenrie Peters, when the earth is imagined as male and the male poet's union with it as a sexual act: 'my youth burrows into the yearning / entrails of the earth; dessicated' (*sic*) – in Wole Soyinka (ed.), *Poems of Black Africa* (London: Heinemann, 1975), p. 298. This implies buggery, but other acts are possible. In *Return to My Native Land* (1956), Aimé Césaire, having imagined 'earth great sex raised in the sun', a few lines later goes on to say: 'One mouthful of your milk-spurt would let me discover always at the distance of a mirage on earth . . . a fraternal earth where all is freed, my earth' (Harmondsworth: Penguin, 1969), p. 50.

6 Syl Cheney-Coker, *The Graveyard Also Has Teeth* (London: Heinemann, 1980), pp. 11, 14–15, 16, 78, 60.

7 Agostinho Neto, *Sacred Hope* (Dar es Salaam: Tanzania Publishing House, 1974), pp. 45, 77.

8 Gerald Moore and Ulli Beier (eds), *Modern Poetry from Africa* (Harmondsworth: Penguin, 1968), p. 40, and *The Penguin Book of Modern African Poetry* (Harmondsworth: Penguin, 1984), p. 132.

9 Jared Angira, *Cascades* (London: Longman, 1979), p. 91.

10 Okot p'Bitek, *Song of Lawino* (Nairobi: East African Publishing House, 1966), p. 105.

11 Soyinka, *Poems of Black Africa*, pp. 174, 342, 155.

12 Taban lo Liyong, *Frantz Fanon's Uneven Ribs* (London: Heinemann, 1971), p. 102.

13 P'Bitek, p. 213.

14 Only rarely is a reference to a lesbian either neutral (as in Dennis Brutus' 'After the Entertainment') or positive (as in Jared Angira's 'Sonata for Sappho', where Sappho herself personifies love).

15 Cheney-Coker, p. 6.

16 Liyong, p. 103.

17 Mafika Mbuli, 'The Miners', in Robert Royston (ed.), *Black Poets in South Africa* (London: Heinemann, 1973), p. 70.

18 A.W. Kayper-Mensah, *The Drummer in Our Time* (London: Heinemann, 1975), p. 19.

19 Kofi Anyidoho, *A Harvest of Our Dreams* (London: Heinemann, 1984), pp. 16–17.

20 Mugambi, p. 7.

21 Christopher Okigbo, *Labyrinths* (London: Heinemann, 1971), p. 65.

22 Soyinka, *Poems of Black Africa*, pp. 159–61.

23 Wole Soyinka, *Idanre and Other Poems* (London: Methuen, 1967), p. 72.

24 Soyinka, *Poems of Black Africa*, p. 54.

25 P'Bitek, p. 33.

26 Cosmo Pieterse (ed.), *Seven South African Poets: Poems of Exile* (London: Heinemann, 1971), p. 122.

27 Neto, p. 71.

28 Liyong, pp. 34–5.

29 Kyei in Kofi Awoonor and G. Adali-Mortty (eds), *Messages: Poems from Ghana* (London: Heinemann, 1971), p. 126. Roberts and Kunene in Soyinka, *Poems of Black Africa*, pp. 172–4, 278.

30 Cheney-Coker, p. 97.

31 John Reed and Clive Wake (eds), *A Book of African Verse* (London: Heinemann, 1964), p. 76.

32 Okigbo, p. 28.

33 Jean-Joseph Rabéarivelo, *Translations from the Night* (London: Heinemann, 1975), pp. 51–3.

34 Lenrie Peters, *Katchikali* (London: Heinemann, 1971), p. 46.

35 Joe de Graft, *Beneath the Jazz and Brass* (London: Heinemann, 1975), p. 24; reprinted in Awoonor and Adali-Mortty, p. 29.

36 P'Bitek, p. 208.

37 Moore and Beier, p. 275.

38 Liyong, p. 91

39 Okot p'Bitek, *Song of Ocol* (Nairobi: East African Publishing House, 1970), p. 49.

40 Tchicaya U Tam'si, *Selected Poems* (London: Heinemann, 1970), p. 60.

41 Jared Angira, *Soft Corals* (Nairobi: East African Publishing House, 1973), p. 118.

42 Wole Soyinka, 'New York, U.S.A.', in *Mandela's Earth and Other Poems* (London: Methuen, 1989), p. 39.

43 Neil McKenna, 'Men Loving Men: Towards a Taxonomy of Male-to-Male Sexualities in the Developing World', per*versions* 5 (Summer 1995), pp. 54–101; pp. 56–7. See also McKenna, *On the Margins*, pp. 13–14.

44 Césaire, p. 41.

45 David Mandessi Diop, *Hammer Blows* (London: Heinemann, 1975), p. 5.

46 Lenrie Peters, *Selected Poetry* (London: Heinemann, 1981), p. 96.

47 P'Bitek, *Song of Lawino*, p. 207.

48 Fanon, p. 52.

49 Chinua Achebe, *Beware, Soul Brother* (London: Heinemann, 1972), p. 31.

50 P'Bitek, *Song of Lawino*, pp. 124, 161, 213. In Ocol's reply, the spear – the literal spear, this time – is seen as the symbol of African warriors' backwardness: *Song of Ocol*, p. 48.

51 Okigbo, p. 23.

52 Soyinka, *Idanre and Other Poems*, p. 31.

53 Mbella Sonne Dipoko, *Black and White in Love* (London: Heinemann, 1972), p. 70.

54 Quoted in Bahadur Tejani, 'Can the Prisoner Make a Poet? A Critical Discussion of *Letters to Martha* by Dennis Brutus', in *African Literature Today, 6: Poetry in Africa* (London: Heinemann, 1973), pp. 130–44; p. 136.

55 Soyinka, *Poems of Black Africa*, p. 185.

56 Wole Soyinka, *A Shuttle in the Crypt* (London: Collins/Methuen, 1972), p. 61.

57 Musaemura Bonas Zimunya, *Thought Tracks* (London: Longman, 1982), p. 40.

58 Dennis Brutus, *Letters to Martha, and Other Poems from a South African Prison* (London: Heinemann, 1968).

59 Commenting on this sequence, literary critic R.N. Egudu dismisses 'homosexuality in the prison' as 'one of the worst human aberrations' without taking into account the social or political circumstances – *Modern African Poetry and the African Predicament* (London: Macmillan, 1978), p. 60.

60 Quoted in Ken Goodwin, *Understanding African Poetry: A Study of Ten Poets* (London: Heinemann, 1982), p. 13.

61 Dennis Brutus, *Stubborn Hope* (London: Heinemann, 1978), pp. 21–2.

62 Peters, *Katchikali*, p. 18.

63 McKenna, *On the Margins*, p. 104. McKenna adds: 'Paradoxically, the spread of AIDS among men who have sex with men has acted as a catalyst in the formation of a social and political identity in several countries in the developing world.'

64 'Human Rights Yes, Gay Rights No: Mugabe', *Gay Times* 204 (September 1995), p. 38. Vicky Powell, 'Zimbabwean Gay Man's Home Burnt to the Ground', *Gay Times* 205 (October 1995), pp. 35–6.

65 See Gevisser and Cameron, pp. 94–7. The newspaper of South Africa's National Coalition for Gay and Lesbian Equality reported the inclusion of sexual orientation in the final version of the Constitution under the headline 'VICTORY!!! SEXUAL ORIENTATION PROTECTED IN FINAL CONSTITUTION' – beneath which is printed the subclause in question, 9 (3): 'The state may not unfairly discriminate directly or indirectly against anyone on one or more grounds, including race, gender, sex, pregnancy, marital status, ethnic or social origin, colour, SEXUAL ORIENTATION, age, disability, religion, conscience, belief, culture, language, and birth' – *Equality* 3 (May 1996), p. 1.

66 Neto, pp. 50–51, 81, 83.

Chapter 27

1 André Gide, *Les Faux-monnayeurs* (Paris: Gallimard, 1972), pp. 202, 366.

2 André Gide, *Si le grain ne meurt* (Paris: Gallimard, 1954), pp. 7–8.

3 André Gide, *The Immoralist* (Harmondsworth: Penguin, 1960), pp. 74–5.

4 Marcel Proust, *Swann's Way* (London: Chatto and Windus, 1966), pp. 13–14, 216–17.

5 Writing this sentence, I am reminded of the atmosphere of Alain-Fournier's *Le Grand Meaulnes* (1912), a novel so sticky with the romantic eroticism of adolescence that its silent *lack* of masturbation scenes sounds

positively suppressive.

6 Ronald Hayman, *Proust: A Biography* (London: Minerva, 1991), pp. 22–3.

7 This is the tradition which Dominique Fernandez deals with in his idiosyncratic history of gay culture, *Le Rapt de Ganymède* (Paris: Grasset, 1989).

8 Dominique Fernandez, *L'Etoile rose* (Paris: Grasset, 1978), pp. 51–2.

9 Hervé Guibert, *My Parents* (London: Serpent's Tail, 1993), pp. 78–9.

10 Jean Cocteau, *Cocteau's World: An Anthology of Writings* (London: Peter Owen, 1972), pp. 136–7.

11 Jean Genet, *Miracle of the Rose* (Harmondsworth: Penguin, 1971), pp. 255–7. This scene is dramatised in the 'Homo' section of Todd Haynes' film *Poison* (1991).

12 A spitting episode in Hervé Guibert's narrative of sadomasochism, *Les Chiens* (Paris: Minuit, 1982), reaches a similarly amorous climax: '*il m'a craché au visage, il a resserré ses lèvres pour que son crachat soit pulvérisé et au moment un peu pénible de la jouissance cette pluie fine et musquée a été comme la brumisation d'un mot d'amour*' (p. 22).

13 Tony Duvert, *Strange Landscape* (New York: Grove, 1975), pp. 121–3.

14 Michel Tournier, *Gemini* (London: Collins, 1981), p. 36.

15 Denis, the protagonist of Denis Belloc's *Néon* (Paris: Lieu Commun, 1987) has a more direct and literal masturbatory introduction to sexual and homosexual pleasure. His first ejaculation happens when a man jacks him off in a public toilet.

Chapter 28

1 Sandro Penna, *Tutte le Poesie* (Milano: Garzanti, 1984), p. 305.

2 Truman Capote, *Other Voices, Other Rooms* (London: Heinemann, 1968), p. 65.

3 Gilbert Adair's *Love and Death on Long Island* (1990) is a significant follower, tracing its narrator's obsession with a young American actor. More interestingly, however, in the title story of *A Sense of Loss* (1993), Martin Foreman rewrites *Death in Venice* from Tadzio's point of view.

4 Thomas Mann, *Death in Venice* (Harmondsworth: Penguin, 1955), p. 58.

5 On the origins of the story in Mann's 1911 trip to Venice, see Ronald Hayman, *Thomas Mann: A Biography* (London: Bloomsbury, 1996), pp. 248–54.

6 These include Roy Fuller's *The Ruined Boys* (1959), Michael Campbell's *Lord Dismiss Us* (1967), Simon Raven's *Fielding Gray* (1967) and Christopher Dilke's *The Rotten Apple* (1968). Among the best of recent additions to the genre are William Corlett's *Now and Then* (1995) and William Sutcliffe's *New Boy* (1996). An outstanding American equivalent would be John Knowles' *A Separate Peace* (1960), in which a love affair develops between two schoolboys, an intellectual and an athlete. Canaan Parker's *The Color of Trees* (1992) offers an interesting variation on the usual themes in its depiction of an African-American scholarship boy from Harlem at a white private school in Connecticut. On the English public schools, see Simon Raven, *The Old School: A Study in the Oddities of the English Public School System* (London: Hamish Hamilton, 1986) and Alisdare Hickson, *The Poisoned Bowl: Sex and the Public School* (London: Duckworth, 1996).

7 In James Baldwin's *Just Above My Head* (1979), two brothers, Arthur and Hall, one gay and the other straight, manage a consistently supportive and loving relationship for many years. Theirs is the central relationship of the novel, interrupted by absences, but ended only by Arthur's death.

8 Henry James, *The Turn of the Screw and The Aspern Papers* (London: Everyman, 1935) On the theme of homosexuality in James' work see Mildred E. Hastock, 'Henry James and the Cities of the Plain', *Modern Language Quarterly* 29 (1968), pp. 297–311; Viola Hopkins Winner, 'The Artist and the Man in "The Author of Beltraffio"', *PMLA* 83 (1968), pp. 102–8; Robert K. Martin, 'The "High Felicity" of Comradeship: A New Reading of *Roderick Hudson*', *American Literary Realism* 11 (Spring 1978), pp. 100–118; Richard Hall, 'Henry James: Interpreting an Obsessive Memory', *Journal of Homosexuality* 8, 3/4 (1983), pp. 83–97; Michael Moon, 'Sexuality and Visual Terrorism in *The Wings of the Dove*', *Criticism* 28, 4 (1986), pp. 427–43; Melissa Knox, '*Beltraffio*: Henry James's Secrecy', *American Imago* 43, 3 (Fall 1986), pp. 211–27; Eric Savoy, 'Hypocrite Lecteur: Walter Pater, Henry James and Homotextual Politics', *Dalhousie Review* 72, 1 (1992), pp. 12–36; Cheryl B. Tornsey, 'Henry James, Charles Sanders Pierce, and the Fat Capon: Homoerotic Desire in *The American*', *Henry James Review* 14 (Spring 1994), pp. 166–78; Leland S. Person, 'James's Homo-Aesthetics: Deploying Desire in the Tales of Writers and Artists', *Henry James Review* 14 (Spring 1994), pp. 188–203. For a detailed biographical study, see Shelden M. Novick, *Henry James:*

The Young Master (New York; Random House, 1996).

9 James Joyce, *Dubliners* (London: Triad Grafton, 1977), pp. 23–4.

10 Jean-Paul Sartre, *Nausea* (Harmondsworth: Penguin, 1965).

11 Christopher Robinson, *Scandal in the Ink: Male and Female Homosexuality in Twentieth-Century French Literature* (London: Cassell, 1995), p. 222.

12 Saul Bellow, *Herzog* (Harmondsworth: Penguin, 1965), pp. 295–6.

13 Toni Morrison, *The Bluest Eye* (London: Chatto and Windus, 1979), pp. 153–4.

14 Salman Rushdie, *The Satanic Verses* (London: Viking, 1988), p. 38.

15 This is not the case in Duvert's *Quand mourut Jonathan* (1978), the story of one man's love for one small boy. Other notable examples of this genre are Angus Stewart's *Sandel* (1968) and Joseph Geraci's *Loving Sander* (1997).

Chapter 29

1 Christopher Isherwood, *Christopher and His Kind* (London: Eyre Methuen, 1977), pp. 141–2.

2 Christopher Isherwood, *Goodbye to Berlin* (Harmondsworth: Penguin, 1945), p. 7.

3 Humphrey Carpenter, *W.H. Auden: A Biography* (London: Allen and Unwin, 1981), pp. 358–60. David Laurents, introduction to Laurents (ed.), *The Badboy Book of Erotic Poetry* (New York: Badboy, 1995), pp. 12–14.

4 Gregory W. Bredbeck, 'Andrew Holleran', in Emmanuel S. Nelson (ed.), *Contemporary Gay American Novelists: A Bio-bibliographical Critical Sourcebook* (Westport, Conn.: Greenwood, 1993), pp. 197–204; p. 197.

5 Doris Lessing, *The Golden Notebook* (London: Panther, 1973), p. 395.

6 Erica Jong, *Fear of Flying* (London: Minerva, 1994), pp. 109, 307 and 149.

7 In *Le Deuxième Sexe* (1949), Simone de Beauvoir had performed a similar type of critique of Henry de Montherlant, D.H. Lawrence, Paul Claudel, André Breton and Stendhal. The presence of Montherlant on the list constituted a similar shot across the bows of male homosexual writers.

8 Another might be the Mexican novelist José Ceballos Maldonado's *Después de todo* (1969), the middle-aged narrator of which works his way through an album of snapshots of the many boys he has had sex with.

9 Renaud Camus, *Tricks* (New York: Ace Charter, 1982), p. xii.

10 Quoted in Leo Bersani, *Homos* (Cambridge, Mass. and London: Harvard University Press, 1995), p. 77. Translated from an interview with Jean Le Bitoux in *Mec* 5 (June 1988), p. 35.

11 *Chicago Tribune* interview with Richard Christiansen, quoted in Joel Shatzky, 'Larry Kramer', in Nelson, pp. 244–7; p. 245.

12 Sarah Schulman, *My American History: Lesbian and Gay Life during the Reagan/Bush Years* (New York: Routledge, 1994), p. 165.

13 The more sophisticated Philip Ridley writes both about childhood (or rather, boyhood) and for children.

14 For more detail on this group, see David Bergman (ed.), *The Violet Quill Reader* (New York: St Martin's Press, 1994).

15 For a list of ages in gay literature, see Gregory Woods, *Articulate Flesh: Male Homo-eroticism and Modern Poetry* (New Haven and London: Yale University Press, 1987), pp. 233–4.

16 *While England Sleeps* was reviewed in Britain with a certain amount of scorn and not a little laughter. While it may be that some of the latter was deserved, it is clear that some commentators on the controversy about Stephen Spender's objections to Leavitt's book were motivated by their objection to the wrong kind of queer. The anti-Americanism of the British literary establishment, usually quite carefully suppressed, also came bubbling up. An anonymous news item in the *Independent* newspaper contrasted 'the discreet homosexuality of Sir Stephen, 84' with 'the aggressive approach of gay Americans today' – 'Poet set for court fight over novel', 28 October 1993, p. 8. Similarly, Simon Tisdall wrote in the *Guardian* that Leavitt 'is a prominent spokesman for his aggressively glad-to-be-gay generation' – 'Literary love that speaks its name in too strident a voice', 27 October 1993, p. 20. Most of these items were written as if their authors had never heard of Leavitt – which they should have done – and never met a British gay man – which they must have done. Also, I think they misrepresented Spender's position: he hated Leavitt's book, but he did not necessarily hate either 'aggressively glad-to-be-gay' men or their culture. For example, he was very helpfully instrumental in getting my own book *We Have the Melon* published.

17 Dale Peck, 'Tacky Dress', *London Review of Books* 18, 4 (22 February 1996), pp. 27–31; p. 27.

18 Woods, *Articulate Flesh*, pp. 2–3. George Steiner, *On Difficulty, and Other Essays* (Oxford: Oxford University Press, 1978), pp. 95–136. Jeffrey Meyers, *Homosexuality and Literature, 1890–1930* (London: Athlone, 1977), p. 3. Jeffrey Meyers, untitled review of

Gregory Woods, *Articulate Flesh*, in *Journal of English and German Philology* 88, 1 (January 1989), pp. 126–9; p. 127.

Chapter 30

1 Other twins worth considering are Dave and Theo in Philip Ridley's novel *Crocodilia* (1988) and the Kray brothers in Ridley's screenplay for Peter Medak's 1990 film *The Krays*. See, also, the twin brothers, Angel and Sphinx, in Derek Jarman's 1978 film *Jubilee*.

2 James Baldwin, *Giovanni's Room* (London: Penguin, 1990), p. 14.

3 Rudi van Dantzig, *For a Lost Soldier* (London: GMP, 1996), p. 142.

4 Jonathan Ames, *I Pass Like Night* (London: Mandarin, 1989), p. 91.

5 The two teenage lovers in Jonathan Harvey's play *Beautiful Thing* (1993) both come from 'broken homes', one living with a brutal father, the other with an eventually understanding mother, in neighbouring apartments. It is with the functioning family of mother and son that the brutalised boy takes refuge on leaving his father.

6 'A Bit of Shrapnel' and 'Gypsies', in Tom Wakefield, *Drifters* (London: GMP, 1984).

7 Geoffrey Rees, *Sex with Strangers* (Harmondsworth: Penguin, 1994), p. 3.

8 Christopher Coe, *Such Times* (London: Penguin, 1994), p. 3.

9 Pai Hsien-yung, *Crystal Boys* (San Francisco: Gay Sunshine, 1995), pp. 13, 86.

10 Adam Mars-Jones and Edmund White, *The Darker Proof: Stories from a Crisis* (London: Faber, 1987), pp. 128–9.

11 Desmond Hogan, *A New Shirt* (London: Faber, 1987), pp. 1–2.

12 Shyam Selvadurai, *Funny Boy: A Novel in Six Stories* (London: Cape, 1994), pp. 284–5.

13 Christopher Isherwood, *Goodbye to Berlin* (Harmondsworth: Penguin, 1945), p. 38.

14 Christopher Isherwood, *Christopher and His Kind* (London: Eyre Methuen, 1977), p. 53.

15 Greg Johnson, *Pagan Babies* (New York: Plume, 1994), p. 160.

16 David Plante, *The Catholic* (London: Paladin, 1988), pp. 70, 6.

17 These views are most pugnaciously yet coherently expressed in Tony Duvert, *L'Enfant au masculin* (1980). On the other hand, in Duvert's *Quand mourut Jonathan* (1978), Jonathan's love for Serge involves a continuous sequence of negotiations with Barbara, the boy's mother. Similarly, in Joseph Geraci's *Loving Sander* (1997), Will's

relationship with Sander is negotiated via the mother, Marijke, and to a lesser extent with her estranged husband, the boy's father, Niek.

18 *As Is* is included in Don Shewey (ed.), *Out Front: Contemporary Gay and Lesbian Plays* (New York: Grove Weidenfeld, 1988).

19 David Bergman, *Gaiety Transfigured: Gay Self-Representation in American Literature* (Madison: University of Wisconsin Press), 1991), p. 128.

20 Sarah Schulman, *People in Trouble* (London: Sheba, 1990), pp. 94, 99–100. In a similar moment in his novel *The Waters of Thirst* (1993) the context of a British AIDS ward gives Adam Mars-Jones the opportunity to make a distinction between the biological family and its alternatives. As his narrator observes: 'I noticed that biological family, old-fashioned next-of-kin, tended to visit at old-fashioned visiting hours – ten to twelve in the morning, two in the afternoon till eight in the evening – while at other times a small irregular army of lovers and semi-official functionaries seemed to have the run of the place. These unofficial or semi-official people seemed almost to supplement the staff. Sometimes the orthodox families were escorted, even cordoned off, by these intermediate people, as if the families were intruding in a place where they had no rights, and were only allowed in on condition of best behaviour' (London: Faber, 1993), pp. 163–4.

21 Armistead Maupin, *Tales of the City, Volume Two* (London: Chatto and Windus, 1990), pp. 647–8, 703.

22 Neil Bartlett, *Ready to Catch Him Should He Fall* (Harmondsworth: Penguin, 1992).

23 Audre Lorde, *Zami: A New Spelling of My Name* (London: Pandora, 1996), p. 184.

24 Neil Bartlett, *Who Was That Man? A Present for Mr Oscar Wilde* (Harmondsworth: Penguin, 1993), p. xx.

Chapter 31

1 Andrew Holleran, *Dancer from the Dance* (London: Corgi, 1980), pp. 1, 6.

2 Lluís Fernàndez, *The Naked Anarchist* (London: GMP, 1990), p. 87.

3 Armistead Maupin, *Tales of the City, More Tales of the City, Further Tales of the City: An Omnibus* (London: Chatto and Windus, 1989), pp. 85, 218. However, in the next volume, *More Tales of the City* (1980), Chuck Lord hatches a plan for the 'first gay nursing home in the history of the world', reckoning that the 120,000 gays in San Francisco 'are

going to grow old together' (pp. 344–5). At the beginning of the fourth novel in the sequence, *Babycakes* (1984), we find that Michael is working for the local AIDS hotline. By the beginning of the fifth novel, *Significant Others* (1988), Michael has tested positive and his lover, Jon, is dead.

4 Michael Rumaker, *A Day and a Night at the Baths* (Bolinas, Calif.: Grey Fox, 1979) pp. 2, 27–8, 78, 81.

5 Bill Becker, '6 Sep 84', in *An Immediate Desire to Survive* (Bryn Mawr, Penn.: Dorrance, 1985), p. 6.

6 Robert Hamberger, *The Wolf's Tale* (North Leverton, Nottinghamshire: Waldean Press, 1995), p. 13. *New Statesman and Society* 24 November 1995, p. 49.

7 Paul Monette, *Borrowed Time* (London: Collins Harvill, 1988), pp. 227–8.

8 Tessa Boffin and Sunil Gupta (eds), *Ecstatic Antibodies: Resisting the Aids Mythology* (London: Rivers Oram Press, 1990), p. 166.

9 Marc Almond, *The Angel of Death in the Adonis Lounge* (London: GMP, 1988), pp. 21–26. Many of these laments for out gay men will not, of course, be pastoral elegies, since the lost way of life is likely to have been urban. (Pastoral can, though, be written retrospectively by a poet of rural origins, as Theocritus wrote about his native Sicily while living in Alexandria.) However, while on the subject of pornography, it occurs to me that many gay American porn videos, among them some of Kip Noll's, constitute a kind of suburban pastoral: a poolside world of perfect weather, near perfect physiques, and guiltless polymorphous perversity.

10 Andrew Holleran, *Ground Zero* (New York: Plume, 1988), p. 23.

11 Tony Harrison, *v.* (Newcastle: Bloodaxe, 1985).

12 Robert Boucheron, *Epitaphs for the Plague Dead* (New York: Ursus Press, 1985), p. 32.

13 *Other Countries Journal: Black Gay Voices* 1 (Spring 1988), p. 51.

14 Paul Monette, *Love Alone: 18 Elegies for Rog* (New York: St Martin's Press, 1988), pp. 13–15.

15 Thom Gunn, *Undesirables* (Durham: Pig Press, 1988), p. 11; *The Man with Night Sweats* (London: Faber, 1992), p. 59.

16 Martin Humphries (ed.), *Not Love Alone: A Modern Gay Anthology* (London: GMP, 1985), p. 76.

17 Anthony William Mann, Stewart Charles and Pat O'Brien, *Respectively . . .* (London: Oscars Press, 1987), p. 43. Pat O'Brien offers some remarkable further contributions to the literature of living with HIV, in his own chapbook *'I'm Afraid This Time Love, It's*

Positive' (London: Oscars Press, 1989).

18 Dirg Aaab-Richards, Craig G. Harris, Essex Hemphill, Isaac Jackson and Assotto Saint, *Tongues Untied* (London: GMP, 1987), p. 30.

19 Holleran, p. 18.

20 *City Lights Journal* 2 (1988), pp. 36–38.

21 Carl Morse and Joan Larkin (eds), *Gay and Lesbian Poetry in Our Time: An Anthology* (New York: St Martin's Press, 1988), pp. 224–226.

22 Ibid., pp. 260–61.

23 Still others, like my own collection *We Have the Melon* (1992), will simply be dedicated to the memory of friends who have died.

24 Lee Edelman gives a coherent and acute theoretical account of this slogan in his essay 'The Plague of Discourse: Politics, Literary Theory, and AIDS', in Ronald R. Butters, John M. Clum and Michael Moon (eds), *Displacing Homophobia: Gay Male Perspectives in Literature and Culture* (Durham, NC and London: Duke University Press, 1989), pp. 289–305.

25 Richard Berkowitz and Michael Callen, *How to Have Sex in an Epidemic: One Approach* (New York: News from the Front, 1983).

26 On Guibert, see Jean-Pierre Boulé, *Hervé Guibert, À l'ami qui ne m'a pas sauvé la vie, and Other Writings* (Glasgow: University of Glasgow French and German Publications, 1995) and the Hervé Guibert edition of *Nottingham French Studies* 34, 1 (Spring 1995), edited by Boulé.

27 John Preston (ed.), *Hot Living: Erotic Stories about Safer Sex* (Boston: Alyson, 1985), p. 13.

28 Adam Mars-Jones and Edmund White, *The Darker Proof: Stories from a Crisis* (London: Faber, 1987), p. 162.

29 Suzanne Poirier, 'Writing AIDS: Intro-duction', in Timothy F. Murphy and Suzanne Poirier (eds), *Writing AIDS: Gay Literature, Language, and Analysis* (New York: Columbia University Press, 1993), pp. 1–8; p. 7. There are searching questions to be asked of some established gay writers who did not pay significant attention to the epidemic. Would it be invidious to name John Ashbery or Allen Ginsberg or Gore Vidal?

30 On this issue, see James W. Jones, 'Refusing the Name: The Absence of AIDS in Recent American Gay Male Fiction', in Murphy and Poirier, pp. 244–64. On Kellendonk, see Gert Hekma, 'The Mystical Body: Frans Kellendonk and the Dutch Literary Response to AIDS', in Emmanuel S. Nelson (ed.), *AIDS: The Literary Response* (New York: Twayne, 1992), pp. 88–94.

31 Alan Hollinghurst, *The Folding Star* (London: Chatto and Windus, 1994), p. 152.

32 Alan Sinfield, *Cultural Politics – Queer Reading* (London: Routledge, 1994), p. 81. The ref-

erence is to the *Economist*, 22 February 1992.

33 Jeffrey Meyers, untitled review of Gregory Woods, *Articulate Flesh*, in *Journal of English and German Philology* 88, 1 (January 1989), pp. 126–9; p. 127.

34 See *Heroides* V, line 149 ('Me miserum, quod amor non est medicabilis herbis!') and *Metamorphoses* I, line 523 ('Ei mihi! quod nullis amor est sanabilis herbis').

35 The theme continues, of course, in later poetry. Dryden says 'Love's a malady without a cure' (*Palamon and Arcite* II, line 110). Pope says love is 'the sole disease thou canst not cure' (*Pastorals: Summer*, line 12).

36 Johannes Fabricius, *Syphilis in Shakespeare's England* (London: Jessica Kingsley, 1994), p. 264.

37 Quoted ibid., p. 20 n.

38 Jonathan Goldberg, *Sodometries: Renaissance Texts, Modern Sexualities* (Stanford, Calif.: Stanford University Press, 1992), p. 26. My main reservation on reading these remarks is that people with HIV/AIDS may have replaced the heretical monster, but they exist alongside the 'promiscuous natives' and the underclasses who remain with us, all ripe for continued persecution.

39 Widmann: Greg W. Bentley, *Shakespeare and the New Disease: The Dramatic Function of Syphilis in 'Troilus and Cressida', 'Measure for Measure', and 'Timon of Athens'* (New York: Peter Lang, 1989), p. 25. Ulrich von Hutten: ibid., p. 10. Fracastoro: ibid., pp. 10–11; Fabricius, p. 14. Wolsey: Fabricius, p. 14; Richard Davenport-Hines, *Sex, Death and Punishment: Attitudes to Sex and Sexuality in Britain since the Renaissance* (London: Fontana, 1991), pp. 28–9.

Chapter 32

1 Gregory Woods, *Articulate Flesh: Male Homo-eroticism and Modern Poetry* (New Haven and London: Yale University Press, 1987).

2 Jonathan Culler, *Structuralist Poetics* (London: Routledge and Kegan Paul, 1975), p. 14.

3 Cleanth Brooks, *The Well-Wrought Urn* (London: Dobson, 1949), pp. 3, 8, 10, 16. In the arguments that follow I adhere to the *Concise Oxford Dictionary*'s definition of paradox: 'Statement contrary to received opinion; seemingly absurd though perhaps really well-founded statement; self-contradictory, essentially absurd, statement; person, thing, conflicting with preconceived notions of what is reasonable or possible'.

4 Susan Sontag once called 'homosexual estheticism and irony' one of the two 'pioneering forces of modern sensibility' (the other being 'Jewish moral seriousness') – 'Notes on Camp', *Partisan Review* 31, 4 (Fall 1964), p. 529. The presence or absence of such irony may form one of several areas of difference between two otherwise superficially similar poets like the heterosexual Thomas Hardy and the homosexual A.E. Housman.

5 At this point in a more detailed version of my argument, I would need to introduce Edward Lear, one of many gay masters of the inconsequential.

6 The sense of poetry as *turning* is recognised, also, in the concept of the 'strophe', which derives from the Greek *strephein*, meaning 'to twist'. But turning is at its most tenacious and perverse in 'boustrophedon' poetry – with alternate lines running left-to-right and right-to-left – named, again, after the alternating directions of a plough on a field.

7 Lord Byron, *Don Juan* XV, 87. He continues, in 88, 'If people contradict themselves, can I / Help contradicting them and everybody, / Even my veracious self? But that's a lie; / I never did so, never will. How should I?'

8 Pier Paolo Pasolini, *Selected Poems*, trans. Norman MacAfee and Luciano Martinengo (London: Calder, 1984), p. 10. Pasolini's open desire for proletarian youths led to his expulsion from the Italian Communist Party in 1949. In his 'Phrases and Philosophies for the Use of the Young', Oscar Wilde said 'The wise contradict themselves'; and in 'The Truth of Masks' he said 'A truth in art is that whose contradictory is also true'. André Gide was another self-conscious self-contradictor: 'Je suis un être de dialogue; tout en moi combat et se contredit'.

9 Honoré de Balzac, *Lost Illusions* (Harmondsworth: Penguin, 1971), p. 645.

10 Oscar Wilde, *De Profundis*, in *The Works of Oscar Wilde* (London and Glasgow: Collins, 1948), p. 857.

11 Stephen Coote (ed.), *The Penguin Book of Homosexual Verse* (Harmondsworth: Penguin, 1983), pp. 117, 381.

12 But an inopportune act of turning the wrong way may also dismay gay men, as is suggested in this little poem:

> With a tube of grease in his pocket
> he walked the avenue to get fuckèd
> but every queen in town mistook it
> for the hard-on which it lookèd.
> – Paul Goodman, *Hawkweed*
> (New York: Vintage, 1967), p. 101.

13 *The Collected Poems of Wilfred Owen* (London: Chatto and Windus, 1963), p. 136.

14 Goodman, p. 41. Another important paradox in Goodman concerns the object of desire, the

beautiful youth. Watching boys surfing, at the time of the Vietnam War, the poet comments:

how beautiful they are
their youth and human skill
and communion with the nature of things,
how ugly they are
already sleek with narrow eyes.

(p. 24: 'Surfers at Santa Cruz'). The future of youth does not bear thinking about. Appearances, even beautiful ones, are often deceptive.

15 Of course, this decision underlies a lot of homosexual camp. As Mark Booth has said of the camp man, 'He pays dearly for his emancipation from bourgeois dreariness and conformity; he sees himself with his enemies' eyes.' Oppression internalises self-oppression, with the result that 'Camp self-love is securely grounded in self-hatred' – *Camp* (London: Quartet, 1983) pp. 93–4.

16 Rimbaud tends to bring out the worst in the critics. It would be hard to find a sillier sentence than this: 'I do not think that his homosexuality matters nearly as much as what sort of person he was' – Oliver Bernard, 'Introduction' to Arthur Rimbaud, *Collected Poems* (Harmondsworth: Penguin, 1962), p. xxx.

17 'Disseminating Sodom', in Robert Boyers and George Steiner (eds), *Homosexuality: Sacrilege, Vision, Politics*, special issue of *Salmagundi* 58–9 (Fall 1982-Winter 1983), p. 237.

18 Politeness has a lot to do with ownership. Both 'propriety' and 'property' are derived, via Old French, from the Latin root *proprius*, meaning 'one's own'. Hence the fact that our 'propriety' and 'property' share a single word in both Italian (*proprietà*) and French (*propriété*). It seems to follow from this association that the *insolvent* are so widely thought to be *insolent*.

19 Saint Thomas Aquinas, not a noted immoralist, understood perfectly this hypocritical link between personal choice and moral judgement. As he says in the *Summa theologiae*: 'Because of the diverse conditions of humans, it happens that some acts are virtuous to some people, as appropriate and suitable to them, while the same acts are immoral for others, as inappropriate to them.' John Boswell uses this as one of three telling epigraphs to *Christianity, Social Tolerance, and Homosexuality: Gay People in Western Europe from the Beginning of the Christian Era to the Fourteenth Century* (Chicago and London: University of Chicago Press, 1980).

20 Received (heterosexual) opinion tends to overlook the extent to which the modern Western version of 'love' is derived, firstly, from boy-loving theorists and practitioners like Plato, and then from celibate Christians. It has taken the ingenuity of more recent philosophers like Russell and Ortega to squeeze the swollen issue of Reproduction into the little glass slipper of Love. See Bertrand Russell, *The Conquest of Happiness* (London: Unwin, 1930) pp. 186–207, and Jose Ortega y Gasset, *On Love . . . Aspects of a Single Theme* (London: Cape, 1967) pp. 33–4.

21 Bernard, Introduction to Rimbaud: *Collected Poems*, p. xxv.

22 Jean Genet, *Journal du voleur* (Paris: Gallimard, 1949), pp. 261–2.

23 Paul Verlaine, 'O mes amants..', *Men and Women* (London: Comet, 1985), p. 186.

24 W.H. Auden, *The Platonic Blow* (New York: Fuck You Press, 1965), [p. 1].

25 Coote, pp. 330–31.

26 Joe Orton, *The Complete Plays* (London: Eyre Methuen, 1976), p. 212.

27 W.H. Auden, *Collected Poems* (London: Faber, 1976), p. 431.

28 Auden himself is happy to use 'camp' as a critical term: in reference to baroque architecture, for instance, or, pejoratively, to the sentimentality of the *Stabat Mater* – *A Certain World* (London: Faber, 1971) pp. 28, 169. I think it is also useful to recall that the 'Letter to Lord Byron' gives Ronald Firbank and Edward Lear high rank in the pantheon of Auden's personal masters.

29 Stan Smith, *W.H. Auden* (Oxford: Blackwell, 1985), p. 189.

30 Auden, *Collected Poems*, p. 97.

31 John Ashbery, *Selected Poems* (London: Paladin, 1987), p. 296.

32 Ibid., p. 291.

33 Ibid., pp. 91–3.

34 Roland Barthes, *Roland Barthes* (London: Macmillan, 1977), p. 106.

35 There is, of course, a debate on ordinariness among the gay communities. But Quentin Crisp reminds us that to say you are ordinary is itself to lay claim to a kind of distinction: 'Public interest was beginning to be focussed on me just when the new image of gayness . . . was being advertised. Homosexuals had not only modified their appearance, they were forever popping up on television to explain that they were really quite ordinary. In my opinion this ploy will never work. Except in Illinois, ordinary people do not go about claiming – nay, boasting – that they are humdrum. The declaration is chiefly interesting because it is the reverse of a previous posture.' – *How to Become a Virgin* (London: Fontana, 1981) p. 85.

36 Robert Duncan, *Bending the Bow* (New York: New Directions, 1968), pp. 63–5.

Bibliography

Aaab-Richards, Dirg, Craig G. Harris, Essex Hemphill, Isaac Jackson and Assotto Saint, *Tongues Untied* (London: GMP, 1987)

Abelove, Henry, Michèle Aina Barale and David M. Halperin (eds), *The Lesbian and Gay Studies Reader* (New York and London: Routledge, 1993)

Achebe, Chinua, *Beware Soul Brother* (London: Heinemann, 1972)

Ackroyd, Peter, *T.S. Eliot* (London: Hamish Hamilton, 1984)

Adair, Gilbert, *Love and Death on Long Island* (London: Heinemann, 1990)

Adams, Stephen, *The Homosexual as Hero in Contemporary Fiction* (London: Vision, 1980)

Aitken, Will, *Terre Haute* (New York: Dell, 1989)

Alain-Fournier, *Le Grand Meaulnes* (London: Harrap, 1968)

Aldrich, Robert, *The Seduction of the Mediterranean: Writing, Art and Homosexual Fantasy* (London: Routledge, 1993)

Almansi, Guido, *L'estetica dell'osceno* (Torino: Einaudi, 1974)

Almond, Marc, *The Angel of Death in the Adonis Lounge* (London: GMP, 1988)˙

Al-Tifashi, Ahmad, *The Delight of Hearts, or What You Will Not Find in Any Book* (San Francisco: Gay Sunshine, 1988)

Altman, Dennis, *Homosexual Oppression and Liberation* (London: Allen Lane, 1974)

Ambler, Sam, 'After the Howl', *City Lights Journal* 2 (1988), pp. 36–38

Ames, Jonathan, *I Pass Like Night* (London: Mandarin, 1989)

Amory, Richard, *Song of the Loon* (London: Tallis, 1969)

Anderson, Patrick, and Alistair Sutherland (eds), *Eros: An Anthology of Male Friendship* (London: Anthony Blond, 1961)

Anderson, Reed, *Federico García Lorca* (London: Macmillan, 1984)

Anderson, Robert, *Tea and Sympathy* (New York: Random House, 1953)

Andrew, Malcolm, and Ronald Waldron (eds), *The Poems of the Pearl Manuscript: Pearl, Cleanness, Patience, Sir Gawain and the Green Knight* (London: Edward Arnold, 1978)

Angira, Jared, *Cascades* (London: Longman, 1979)

——, *Soft Corals* (Nairobi: East African Publishing House, 1973)

Anon., 'Human Rights Yes, Gay Rights No: Mugabe', *Gay Times* 20 (September 1995), p. 38

——, 'Poet Set for Court Fight over Novel', *The Independent* 28 October 1993, p. 8

Anyidoho, Kofi, *A Harvest of Our Dreams* (London: Heinemann, 1984)

Aprile, Giuseppe, *Dante, inferni dentro e 'Fuori': omosessualità, antifemminismo e sadomasochismo del Poeta* (Palermo: Editrice de 'Il Vespro', 1977)

Apter, Emily S., *André Gide and the Codes of Homosexuality* (Saratoga, Calif: ANMA Libri, 1987)

Aquinas, Saint Thomas, *Basic Writings of Saint Thomas Aquinas* (New York: Random House, 1945)

Arditti, Michael, *The Celibate* (London: Sinclair-Stevenson, 1993)

Arenas, Reinaldo, *The Assault* (New York: Viking, 1994)

——, *Before Night Falls* (New York: Viking Penguin, 1993)

——, *Farewell to the Sea* (New York: Viking Penguin, 1986)

——, *Singing from the Well* (New York: Viking Penguin, 1987)

Aretino, Pietro, *The Ragionamenti* (London: Panther, 1971)

Aristophanes, *The Complete Plays* (London: Bantam, 1962)

Arnold, Matthew, *Selected Poems and Prose* (London: Everyman, 1993)

Ashbee, Henry Spencer, *Index of Forbidden Books* (London: Sphere, 1969)

Ashbery, John, *Selected Poems* (London: Paladin, 1987)

Auden, W.H., *A Certain World* (London: Faber, 1971)

——, *Collected Poems* (London: Faber, 1976)

——, *The English Auden* (London: Faber, 1977)

——, *The Orators: An English Study* (London: Faber, 1966)

——, *The Platonic Blow* (New York: Fuck You Press, 1965)

Augustine, Saint, *Confessions* (Harmondsworth: Penguin, 1961)

Austen, Jane, *Mansfield Park* (London: Oxford University Press, 1934)

——, *Northanger Abbey* (Harmondsworth: Penguin, 1985)

——, *Pride and Prejudice* (Harmondsworth: Penguin, 1972)

Austen, Roger, *Playing the Game: The Homosexual Novel in America* (Indianapolis: Bobbs-Merrill, 1977)

Avi-Ram, Amitai F., 'The Unreadable Black Body: "Conventional" Poetic Form in the Harlem Renaissance', *Genders* 7 (Spring 1990), pp. 32–46

Awkward, Michael, 'Negotiations of Power: White Critics, Black Texts, and the Self-Referential Impulse', *American Literary History* 2, 4 (Winter 1990): 581–606

Awoonor, Kofi, and G. Adali-Mortty (eds), *Messages: Poems from Ghana* (London: Heinemann, 1971)

Bacarisse, Pamela, 'Chivalry and "Camp" Sensibility in *Don Quijote*, with Some Thoughts on the Novels of Manuel Puig', *Forum for Modern Language Studies* 26, 2 (1990), pp. 127–43

Bacon, Francis, *Essays* (London: Dent, 1906)

Bad Object-Choices (eds), *How Do I Look? Queer Film and Video* (Seattle: Bay Press, 1991)

Bailey, Derrick Sherwin, *Homosexuality and the Western Christian Tradition* (London: Longman, 1955)

Bailey, Paul, *Gabriel's Lament* (London: Cape, 1986)

Baldwin, James, *Another Country* (Harmondsworth: Penguin, 1990)

——, *Giovanni's Room* (Harmondsworth: Penguin, 1990)

——, *Going to Meet the Man* (London: Michael Joseph, 1965)

——, *Go Tell It On the Mountain* (London: Corgi, 1963)

——, *Just Above My Head* (London: Michael Joseph, 1979)

——, 'Preservation of Innocence: Studies for a New Morality', *Zero* 1, 2 (1949), pp. 14–22.

——, *The Price of the Ticket: Collected Non-fiction 1948–1985* (London: Michael Joseph, 1985)

Balzac, Honoré de, *A Harlot High and Low,* trans. Rayner Heppenstall (Harmondsworth: Penguin, 1970)

——, *Lost Illusions,* trans. Herbert J. Hunt (Harmondsworth: Penguin, 1971)

——, *Le Père Goriot* (London: University of London Press, 1967)

Barker, Clive, *Cabal: The Nightbreed* (London: Fontana, 1989)

——, *Imajica* (London: HarperCollins, 1991)

Barker, Deborah E., and Ivo Kamps (eds), *Shakespeare and Gender: A History* (New York and London: Verso, 1995)

Barnes, Djuna, *Nightwood* (London: Faber, 1979)

Barnfield, Richard, *Poems 1594–1598* (Westminster: Archibald Constable, 1896)

Barrie, J.M., *Peter Pan, or The Boy Who Wouldn't Grow Up* (London: Hodder and Stoughton, 1951)

Barthes, Roland, *A Lover's Discourse* (London: Cape, 1979)

——, *On Racine* (New York: Hill and Wang, 1964)

——, *Roland Barthes* (London: Macmillan, 1977)

Bartlett, Neil, *Mr Clive and Mr Page* (London: Serpent's Tail, 1996)

——, *Ready to Catch Him Should He Fall* (Harmondsworth: Penguin, 1992)

——, *Who Was That Man? A Present for Mr Oscar Wilde* (Harmondsworth: Penguin, 1993)

Bassani, Giorgio, *Gli occhiali d'oro* (Milano: Einaudi, 1958)

Bataille, Georges, *L'Érotisme* (Paris: Minuit, 1957)

Bate, Jonathan, 'Nothing but Officers', *Times Literary Supplement* 4818 (4 August 1995), p. 7.

Beam, Joseph (ed.), *In the Life: A Black Gay Anthology* (Boston: Alyson, 1986)

Becker, Bill, *An Immediate Desire to Survive* (Bryn Mawr, Pa: Dorrance, 1985)

Bellezza, Dario, *Morte di Pasolini* (Milano: Mondadori, 1995)

Belloc, Denis, *Néon* (Paris: Lieu Commun, 1987)

Bellow, Saul, *Herzog* (Harmondsworth: Penguin, 1965)

Benatar, Stephen, *The Man on the Bridge* (Brighton: Harvester, 1981)

Benstock, Shari, *Women of the Left Bank: Paris, 1900–1940* (London: Virago, 1987)

Bentley, Greg W., *Shakespeare and the New Disease: The Dramatic Function of Syphilis in 'Troilus and Cressida', 'Measure for Measure', and 'Timon of Athens'* (New York: Peter Lang, 1989)

Bergman, David (ed.), *Camp Grounds: Style and Homosexuality* (Amherst: University of Massachusetts Press, 1993)

——, *Gaiety Transfigured: Gay Self-Representation in American Literature* (Madison: University of Wisconsin Press, 1991)

—— (ed.), *The Violet Quill Reader: The Emergence of Gay Writing after Stonewall* (New York: St Martin's Press, 1994)

Berkowitz, Richard, and Michael Callen, *How to Have Sex in an Epidemic: One Approach* (New York: News from the Front, 1983)

Bernardin de Saint-Pierre, Jacques-Henri, *Paul and Virginia* (London: Peter Owen, 1982)

Bersani, Leo, *Homos* (Cambridge, Mass. and London: Harvard University Press, 1995)

——, *The Freudian Body: Psychoanalysis and Art* (New York: Columbia University Press, 1986)

Beurdelay, Cécile, *L'Amour bleu* (Köln: Evergreen, 1994)

Bien, Peter, *Three Generations of Greek Writers: Cavafy, Kazantzakis, Ritsos* (Athens: Efstathiadis, 1983)

Bigsby, Chris (ed.), *The Black American Writer, Volume II: Poetry and Drama* (DeLand, Fla: Everett/Edwards, 1969)

Binding, Paul, *Lorca: The Gay Imagination* (London: Gay Men's Press, 1985)

Bloom, Harold, *The Western Canon: The Books and School of the Ages* (New York, San Diego and London: Harcourt Brace, 1994)

Boccaccio, Giovanni, *The Decameron of Giovanni Boccaccio* (New York: Modern Library, n.d.)

Boffin, Tessa, and Sunil Gupta (eds), *Ecstatic Antibodies: Resisting the Aids Mythology* (London: Rivers Oram Press, 1990)

Boisson, Jean, *Le Triangle rose: La déportation des homosexuels 1933–1945* (Paris: Robert Laffont, 1988)

Böll, Heinrich, *The Train Was on Time* (London: Sphere, 1967)

Bolsterli, Margaret, 'Studies in Context: The Homosexual Ambience of Twentieth Century Literary Culture', *D.H. Lawrence Review* 6 (1973), pp. 71–85

The Book of the Thousand Nights and One Night (London: Routledge and Kegan Paul, 1986)

Boone, Joseph A., and Michael Cadden (eds), *Engendering Men: The Question of Male Feminist Criticism* (New York: Routledge, 1990)

Booth, Mark, *Camp* (London: Quartet, 1983)

Booth, Stephen, *Shakespeare's Sonnets* (New Haven: Yale University Press, 1977)

Borowski, Tadeusz, *This Way for the Gas, Ladies and Gentlemen* (Harmondsworth: Penguin, 1976)

Boswell, John, *Christianity, Social Tolerance, and Homosexuality: Gay People in Western Europe from the Beginning of the Christian Era to the Fourteenth Century* (Chicago and London: University of Chicago Press, 1980)

——, *The Marriage of Likeness: Same-Sex Unions in Pre-modern Europe* (London: Fontana, 1996)

Boucheron, Robert, *Epitaphs for the Plague Dead* (New York: Ursus Press, 1985)

Boulé, Jean-Pierre, *Hervé Guibert, À l'ami qui ne m'a pas sauvé la vie, and Other Writings* (Glasgow: University of Glasgow French and German Publications, 1995)

——, (ed.), *Nottingham French Studies: Hervé Guibert* 34, 1 (Spring 1995)

Boyers, Robert, 'The Ideology of the Steambath', *Times Literary Supplement* (30 May 1980), pp. 603–4

Boyers, Robert, and George Steiner (eds), *Homosexuality: Sacrilege, Vision, Politics*, special issue of *Salmagundi* 58–59 (Fall 1982–Winter 1983)

Boyette, Purvis E., 'Shakespeare's *Sonnets*: Homosexuality and the Critics', *Tulane Studies in English* 21 (1974), pp. 35–46

——, 'Wanton Humour and Wanton Poets: Homosexuality in Marlowe's *Edward II*', *Tulane Studies in English* 22 (1977), pp. 33–50

Bram, Christopher, *Almost History* (New York: Donald I. Fine, 1992)

——, *Father of Frankenstein* (New York: Plume, 1995)

——, *Hold Tight* (London: GMP, 1990)

——, *Surprising Myself* (New York: Donald I. Fine, 1987)

——, *In Memory of Angel Clare* (London: GMP, 1991)

Bray, Alan, *Homosexuality in Renaissance England* (London: Gay Men's Press, 1982)

——, 'Lovers or Just Good Friends?', *The Guardian* (6 July 1990), p. 37

Breasted, Barbara, '*Comus* and the Castlehaven Scandal', *Milton Studies* 3 (1971), pp. 201–224

Bredbeck, Gregory W., *Sodomy and Interpretation: Marlowe to Milton* (Ithaca, New York, and London: Cornell University Press, 1991)

Bristow, Joseph, '"Churlsgrace": Gerard Manley Hopkins and the Working-Class Male Body', *ELH* 59 (1992), pp. 693–711

——, *Effeminate England: Homoerotic Writing after 1885* (Buckingham: Open University Press, 1995)

——, 'Introduction: Texts, Contexts', *Textual Practice. Special Issue, Lesbian and Gay Cultures: Theories and Texts* 4, 2 (Summer 1990), pp. 165–178.

——, *Sexuality* (London and New York: Routledge, 1997)

——, (ed.), *Sexual Sameness: Textual Differences in Lesbian and Gay Writing* (London and New York: Routledge, 1992)

Broadbent, John, *Poetic Love* (London: Chatto and Windus, 1964)

Broch, Hermann, *The Death of Virgil* (New York: Vintage, 1995)

Bronski, Michael, *Culture Clash: The Making of Gay Sensibility* (Boston: South End Press, 1984)

Brontë, Anne, *The Tenant of Wildfell Hall* (Harmondsworth: Penguin, 1979)

Brooke, Rupert, *1914, and Other Poems* (London: Sidgwick and Jackson, 1916)

Brooks, Cleanth, *The Well Wrought Urn* (London: Dobson, 1949)

Brophy, Brigid, *Prancing Novelist: A Defence of Fiction in the Form of a Critical Biography in Praise of Ronald Firbank* (London: Macmillan, 1973)

Brown, Norman O., *Love's Body* (New York: Vintage, 1966)

Brutus, Dennis, *Letters to Martha, and Other Poems from a South African Prison* (London: Heinemann, 1968).

——, *Stubborn Hope* (London: Heinemann, 1978)

Buchen, Irving (ed.), *The Perverse Imagination: Sexuality and Literary Culture* (New York: New York University Press, 1970)

Bullough, Vern L., *Sexual Variance in Society and History* (New York: John Wiley, 1976)

Burdekin, Katharine, *Swastika Night* (London: Lawrence and Wishart, 1985)

Burger, Glenn, 'Kissing the Pardoner', *PMLA* 107 (1992), pp. 1143–56

Burgess, Anthony, *The Wanting Seed* (London: Heinemann, 1962)

Burroughs, William, *The Place of Dead Roads* (New York: Holt Rinehart, 1983)

——, *The Wild Boys: A Book of the Dead* (New York: Grove, 1971)

Burston, Paul, 'Dream Demon', *Attitude* (November 1995), p. 61

Burton, Peter, 'The Candyman Cometh (Out)', *Gay Times* 202 (July 1995), pp. 48–51

Busi, Aldo, *Seminario sulla gioventù* (Milano: Adelphi, 1984)

——, *Sodomie in Corpo 11* (Milano: Mondadori, 1988)

——, *Vita standard di un venditore provvisorio di collant* (Milano: Editore S.p.A., 1985)

Butler, Judith, *Gender Trouble: Feminism and the Subversion of Identity* (New York and London: Routledge, 1990)

Butters, Ronald R., John M. Clum and Michael Moon (eds.), *Displacing Homophobia: Gay Male Perspectives in Literature and Culture* (Durham, NC and London: Duke University Press, 1989)

Byron, Lord, *Don Juan* (Harmondsworth: Penguin, 1982)

Cain, James M., *Serenade* (London: Cape, 1938)

Campbell, James, *Talking at the Gates: A Life of James Baldwin* (London: Faber, 1991)

Campbell, Michael, *Lord Dismiss Us* (London: Heinemann, 1967)

Camus, Renaud, *Tricks* (New York: Ace Charter, 1982)

Cantarella, Eva, *Bisexuality in the Ancient World* (New Haven and London: Yale University Press, 1992)

Capote, Truman, *Other Voices, Other Rooms* (London: Heinemann, 1968)

Carpenter, Edward, *Anthology of Friendship: Ioläus* (London: Allen and Unwin, 1906)

——, *Days with Walt Whitman* (London: George Allen, 1906)

——, *The Intermediate Sex: A Study of Some Transitional Types of Men and Women* (London: Allen and Unwin, 1916)

——, *Intermediate Types among Primitive Folk: A Study in Social Evolution* (London: Allen and Unwin, 1919)

——, *My Days and Dreams* (London: Allen and Unwin, 1916)

——, *Selected Writings, Volume 1: Sex* (London: GMP, 1984)

——, *Towards Democracy* (London: GMP, 1985)

Carpenter, Humphrey, *The Brideshead Generation: Evelyn Waugh and His Generation* (London: Faber, 1989)

——, *W.H. Auden: A Biography* (London: Allen and Unwin, 1981)

Carter, Erica and Simon Watney (eds), *Taking Liberties: AIDS and Cultural Politics* (London: Serpent's Tail, 1989)

Cartland, Barbara, *A Virgin in Mayfair* (London: Arrow, 1976)

Casi, Stefano (ed.), *L'Homosexualité dans l'oeuvre de Pier Paolo Pasolini* (Lille: Cahiers Gay-Kitsch-Camp, 1977)

Catullus, Gaius Valerius, *The Poems of Catullus*, trans. Peter Whigham (Harmondsworth: Penguin, 1966)

——, *The Poems of Catullus*, trans. Guy Lee (New York and Oxford: Oxford University Press, 1990)

Cavafy, C.P., *Poems by C.P. Cavafy*, trans. John Mavrogordato (London: Chatto and Windus, 1951)

——, *Passions and Ancient Days: Twenty One New Poems*, ed. E. Keeley and G. Savidis (London: Hogarth, 1972)

Ceballos Maldonado, José, *Después de todo* (Mexico City: Premiá, Red de Jonás, 1986)

Cervantes, Miguel de, *Don Quixote* (Harmondsworth: Penguin, 1950)

Césaire, Aimé, *Return to My Native Land* (Harmondsworth: Penguin, 1969)

La Chanson de Roland (Oxford: Blackwell, 1946)

Chapman, Ronald, *Father Faber* (London: Burns and Oates, 1961)

Chatwin, Bruce, *On the Black Hill* (London: Cape, 1982)

Chaucer, Geoffrey, *The Works of Geoffrey Chaucer* (London: Oxford University Press, 1966)

Chauncey, George, *Gay New York: Gender, Urban Culture, and the Making of the Gay Male World 1890–1940* (New York: Basic Books, 1994)

Cheever, John, *Oh What a Paradise It Seems* (London: Cape, 1982)

Cheney-Coker, Syl, *The Graveyard Also Has Teeth* (London: Heinemann, 1980)

Chupack, Henry, *James Purdy* (Boston: Twayne, 1975)

Cleto, Fabio, 'Biografia, ideologia, autor-ità interpretativa (con un caso esemplare)', *Textus: English Studies in Italy* 6 (1993), pp. 179–220

——, '"Camp": l'estetismo nella cultura di massa', in Franco Marenco (ed.), *Storia della civiltà letteraria inglese*, Vol. 3 (Torino: Utet, 1996), pp. 529–69

——, 'Theoretical Issues in Camp Aesthetics (with a Working Bibliography of Secondary Material)', in Marialuisa Bignami and Caroline Patey (eds), *Moving the Borders: Papers from the Milan Symposium, Varenna, September 1994* (Milano: Unicopli, 1996), pp. 120–148

——, 'An Updated Bibliography of Firbank Criticism', *Quaderni del Dipartimento di Linguistica e Letterature Comparate, Bergamo* 9 (1993), pp. 37–51

Cleugh, James, *Love Locked Out: A Survey of Love, Licence and Restriction in the Middle Ages* (London: Tandem, 1964)

Clum, John M., *Acting Gay: Male Homosexuality in Modern Drama*, revised edn. (New York: Columbia University Press, 1994)

Cockshut, A.O.J., *Man and Woman: A Study of Love and the Novel, 1740–1940* (London: Collins, 1977)

Cocteau, Jean, *Cocteau's World: An Anthology of Writings* (London: Peter Owen, 1972)

——, *Le Livre blanc* (Paris: Erotika Biblion, 1970)

——, *Poèmes 1916–1955* (Paris: Gallimard, 1956)

Coe, Christopher, *Such Times* (Harmondsworth: Penguin, 1994)

Cohen, Ed, *Talk on the Wilde Side: Toward a Genealogy of a Discourse on Male Sexualities* (New York and London: Routledge, 1993)

Coleridge, Samuel Taylor, *The Collected Works of Samuel Taylor Coleridge, Vol. 12: Marginalia* (Princeton, NJ: Princeton University Press; London: Routledge, 1980)

Colette, *The Pure and the Impure* (Harmondsworth: Penguin, 1971)

Colman, E.A.M., *The Dramatic Use of Bawdy in Shakespeare* (London: Longman, 1974)

Connolly, Cyril, *Previous Convictions* (London: Hamish Hamilton, 1963)

Conrad, Joseph, *The Secret Agent* (Harmondsworth: Penguin, 1963)

——, *Three Short Novels: Heart of Darkness, Youth, Typhoon* (New York: Bantam, 1960)

——, *Victory: An Island Tale* (London: Dent, 1923)

Cook, Judith, *At the Sign of the Swan: An Introduction to Shakespeare's Contemporaries* (London: Harrap, 1986)

Cooper, Dennis, *Closer* (New York: Grove Weidenfeld, 1989)

——, (ed.), *Discontents: New Queer Writers* (New York: Amethyst, 1992)

——, *Frisk* (New York: Grove Weidenfeld, 1991)

——, *Idols* (New York: Sea Horse, 1979)

——, *The Tenderness of the Wolves* (Trumansburg, New York: Crossing Press, 1982)

——, *Try* (New York: Grove, 1994)

——, *Wrong* (New York: Grove Weidenfeld, 1992)

Cooper, James Fenimore, *The Last of the Mohicans* (Oxford: Oxford University Press, 1990)

Cooper, Wayne F., *Claude McKay: Rebel Sojourner in the Harlem Renaissance, A Biography* (Baton Rouge and London: Louisiana State University Press, 1987)

Coote, Stephen (ed.), *The Penguin Book of Homosexual Verse* (Harmondsworth: Penguin, 1983)

Corbin, Steven, *Fragments that Remain* (London: GMP, 1993)

Core, Philip, *Camp: The Lie that Tells the Truth* (London: Plexus, 1984)

Corlett, William, *Now and Then* (London: Abacus, 1995)

Cory, Donald Webster, *The Homosexual in America* (New York: Greenberg, 1951)

Craft, Christopher, *Another Kind of Love: Male Homosexual Desire in English Discourse, 1850–1920* (Berkeley: University of California Press, 1994)

Creaser, John, 'Milton's *Comus*: The Irrelevance of the Castlehaven Scandal', *Milton Quarterly* 4 (1988), pp. 24–34

Crevel, René, *Babylon* (London: Quartet, 1988)

——, *Difficult Death* (San Francisco: North Point, 1986)

Crew, Louie (ed.), *The Gay Academic* (Palm Springs, Calif.: Etc Publications, 1978)

——, and Rictor Norton (eds) 'The Homosexual Imagination – in Literature – in the Classroom – in Criticism: A Special Issue', *College English* 36, 3 (November 1974), pp. 271–404

Crimp, Douglas (ed.), *AIDS: Cultural Analysis/Cultural Activism* (Cambridge, Mass. and London: MIT Press, 1988)

Crisp, Quentin, *How to Become a Virgin* (London: Fontana, 1981)

——, *The Naked Civil Servant* (London: Fontana, 1977)

Croft-Cooke, Rupert, *Feasting with Panthers: A New Consideration of Some Late Victorian Writers* (London: W.H. Allen, 1967)

Crompton, Louis, *Byron and Greek Love: Homophobia in 19th-Century England* (Berkeley: University of California Press, 1985)

Crowley, Mart, *The Boys in the Band* (New York: Farrar, Straus and Giroux, 1968)

Cullen, Countee, *On These I Stand: An Anthology of the Best Poems* (New York: Harper and Row, 1947)

Culler, Jonathan, *Barthes* (London: Fontana, 1983)

——, *Structuralist Poetics* (London: Routledge and Kegan Paul, 1975)

Cunningham, John E., *Elizabethan and Early Stuart Drama* (London: Evans Brothers, 1965)

Cunningham, Michael, *A Home at the End of the World* (New York: Farrar, Straus, Giroux, 1990)

Cunningham, Valentine, *British Writers of the Thirties* (Oxford: Oxford University Press, 1988)

Curtin, Kaier, *We Can Always Call Them Bulgarians: The Emergence of Lesbians and Gay Men on the American Stage* (Boston: Alyson, 1987)

Curzon, Daniel, *The Misadventures of Tim McPick* (Los Angeles: John Parke Custis Press, 1975)

Daniels, Peter (ed.), *Take Any Train: A Book of Gay Men's Poetry* (London: Oscars Press, 1990)

Dante Alighieri, *Inferno* (London: Macmillan, 1933)

——, *Paradiso* (London: Macmillan, 1943)

——, *Purgatorio* (London: Macmillan, 1938)

D'Arcangelo, Angelo, *The Homosexual Handbook* (London: Olympia, 1971)

D'Arch Smith, Timothy, *Love in Earnest: Some Notes on the Lives and Writings of the English 'Uranian' Poets from 1880 to 1910* (London: Routledge and Kegan Paul, 1970)

Davenport-Hines, Richard, *Auden* (London: Heinemann, 1995)

——, *Sex, Death and Punishment: Attitudes to Sex and Sexuality in Britain since the Renaissance* (London: Fontana, 1991)

Davidson, Michael, *The World, the Flesh and Myself* (London: Arthur Barker, 1962)

Day, John, *The Ile of Gvls* (London: Shakespeare Association, 1936)

De Beauvoir, Simone, *The Second Sex* (Harmondsworth, Penguin, 1972)

De Becker, Raymond, *The Other Face of Love* (London: Neville Spearman and Rodney, 1967)

De Graft, Joe, *Beneath the Jazz and Brass* (London: Heinemann, 1975)

De Jongh, Nicholas, *Not in Front of the Audience: Homosexuality on Stage* (London and New York: Routledge, 1992)

Delaney, Shelagh, *A Taste of Honey* (London: Methuen, 1990)

Delany, Samuel R., *The Bridge of Lost Desire* (New York: Arbor House, 1987)

——, *Dhalgren* (New York: Bantam, 1975)

——, *Flight from Neveryon* (New York: Bantam, 1985)

——, *The Motion of Light in Water: East Village Sex and Science Fiction Writing, 1960–1965* (London: Paladin, 1990)

——, *Neveryona, or The Tale of Signs and Cities* (New York: Bantam, 1983)

——, *Tales of Neveryon* (New York: Bantam, 1979)

Delavenay, Emile, *D.H. Lawrence and Edward Carpenter: A Study in Edwardian Transition* (London: Heinemann, 1971)

Dellamora, Richard, *Masculine Desire: The Sexual Politics of Victorian Aestheticism* (Chapel Hill, NC, and London: University of North Carolina Press, 1990)

D'Emilio, John and Estelle B. Freedman, *Intimate Matters: A History of Sexuality in America* (New York: Harper and Row, 1988)

De Mott, Benjamin, '"But He's a Homosexual"', *New American Review* 1 (September 1967), pp. 166–82

Dickens, Charles, *Great Expectations* (Harmondsworth: Penguin, 1996)

——, *The Old Curiosity Shop* (London: Everyman, 1995)

——, *Oliver Twist* (London: Wordsworth, 1992)

Dickinson, G. Lowes, *Plato and His Dialogues* (London: Allen and Unwin, 1931)

Di Fonzo, Giulio, *Sandro Penna: La luce e il silenzio* (Roma: Edizioni dell'Ateneo, 1981)

Dilke, Christopher, *The Rotten Apple* (London: Macdonald, 1968)

Dinesen, Isak, *Winter's Tales* (New York: Random House, 1942)

Diop, David Mandessi, *Hammer Blows* (London, Heinemann, 1975)

Dipoko, Mbella Sonne, *Black and White in Love* (London: Heinemann, 1972)

Dlugos, Tim, *Strong Place* (New York: Amethyst, 1992)

Dolben, Digby Mackworth, *The Poems of Digby Mackworth Dolben* (London: Frowde, 1911)

Dollimore, Jonathan, *Sexual Dissidence: Augustine to Wilde, Freud to Foucault* (Oxford: Clarendon Press, 1991)

—— and Alan Sinfield (eds), *Political Shakespeare: Essays in Cultural Materialism* 2nd edn. (Manchester: Manchester University Press, 1994)

Dos Passos, John, *Manhattan Transfer* (London: Constable, 1927)

Doty, Mark, *Atlantis* (London: Cape, 1996)

——, *Heaven's Coast: A Memoir* (New York: HarperCollins, 1996)

——, *My Alexandria* (London: Cape, 1995)

Dover, K.J., *Greek Homosexuality* (London: Duckworth, 1978)

Dowling, Linda, *Hellenism and Homosexuality in Victorian Oxford* (Ithaca, NY and London: Cornell University Press, 1994)

Drabble, Margaret, *Angus Wilson: A Biography* (London: Secker and Warburg, 1995)

Dreuilhe, Emmanuel, *Corps à corps* (Paris: Gallimard, 1987)

Duberman, Martin Bauml, Martha Vicinus, and George Chauncey, Jr. (eds), *Hidden from History:*

Reclaiming the Gay and Lesbian Past (Harmondsworth: Penguin, 1991)

Dumas, Alexandre, *The Count of Monte Cristo* (London and Glasgow: Collins, 1955)

Duncan, Robert, *Bending the Bow* (New York: New Directions, 1968)

——, *Caesar's Gate* (Berkeley, Calif.: Sand Dollar, 1972)

——, *Derivations: Selected Poems 1950–1956* (London: Fulcrum, 1968)

——, *The First Decade: Selected Poems, 1940–1950* (London: Fulcrum, 1968)

——, *The Opening of the Field* (London: Cape, 1969)

——, *Roots and Branches: Poems* (London: Cape, 1970)

——, *Selected Poems* (Manchester: Carcanet, 1993)

——, *The Years as Catches: First Poems (1939–1946)* (Berkeley, Calif.: Oyez, 1966)

Dunton, Chris, '"Wheyting Be Dat?": The Treatment of Homosexuality in African Literature', *Research in African Literatures* 20, 3 (Fall 1989), pp. 422–48

Duplechan, Larry, *Blackbird* (New York: St Martin's Press, 1986)

Dusinberre, Juliet, *Shakespeare and the Nature of Women* (London: Macmillan, 1975)

Duvert, Tony, *Le Bon sexe illustré* (Paris: Minuit, 1974)

——, *L'Enfant au masculin* (Paris: Minuit, 1980)

——, *Interdit de séjour* (Paris: Minuit, 1971)

——, *Journal d'un innocent* (Paris: Minuit, 1976)

——, *Paysage de fantaisie* (Paris: Minuit, 1973)

——, *Quand mourut Jonathan* (Paris: Minuit, 1978)

——, *Strange Landscape* (New York: Grove, 1975)

Dynes, Wayne R. (ed.), *Encyclopedia of Homosexuality* (Chicago and London: St James Press, 1990)

Edwardes, Allen, *The Jewel in the Lotus: A Historical Survey of the Sexual Culture in the East* (London: Tandem, 1965)

—— and R.E.L. Masters, *The Cradle of Erotica: A Study of Afro-Asian Sexual Expression and an Analysis of Erotic Freedom in Social Relationships* (New York: Julian, 1962)

Eglinton, J.Z., *Greek Love* (London: Spearman, 1971)

Egudu, R.N., *Modern African Poetry and the African Predicament* (London: Macmillan, 1978)

Eliot, T.S., *Collected Poems 1909–1935* (London: Faber, 1936)

——, *The Waste Land: A Facsimile and Transcript of the Original Drafts* (London: Faber, 1971)

Elliman, Michael and Frederick Roll (eds), *The Pink Plaque Guide to London* (London: GMP, 1986)

Ellis, Bret Easton, *American Psycho* (New York: Vintage, 1991)

Ellis, Havelock, *Studies in the Psychology of Sex* (Philadelphia: Davis, 1928)

Ellison, Ralph, *Invisible Man* (Harmondsworth: Penguin, 1965)

Ellmann, Richard, *Oscar Wilde* (London and New York: Penguin, 1988)

Empson, William, *Seven Types of Ambiguity* (London: Chatto and Windus, 1930)

——, 'Two Proper Crimes', *Nation* 163 (1946), pp. 444–5

The Epic of Gilgamesh (Harmondsworth: Penguin, 1960)

Evans, David T., *Sexual Citizenship: The Material Construction of Sexualities* (New York and London: Routledge, 1993)

Ezrahi, Sidra DeKoven, *By Words Alone: The Holocaust in Literature* (Chicago: University of Chicago Press, 1980)

Faas, Ekbert, *Young Robert Duncan: Portrait of the Poet as Homosexual in Society* (Santa Barbara, Calif.: Black Sparrow, 1983)

Faber, Frederick William, *Poems* (London: Thomas Richardson, 1856)

Fabricius, Johannes, *Syphilis in Shakespeare's England* (London: Jessica Kingsley, 1994)

Fallowell, Duncan, *One Hot Summer in St. Petersburg* (London: Cape, 1994)

Fanon, Frantz, *The Wretched of the Earth* (New York: Grove, 1968)

Farrar, F. W., *Eric or Little by Little* (London: Adam and Charles Black, 1905)

Faulkner, William, *Absalom, Absalom!* (Harmondsworth: Penguin, 1971)

Feinberg, David B., *Eighty-Sixed* (New York: Viking Penguin, 1989)

——, *Queer and Loathing: Rants and Raves of a Raging AIDS Clone* (New York and Harmondsworth: Penguin, 1995)

Fénelon, Fania, *The Musicians of Auschwitz* (London: Sphere, 1979)

Fernandez, Dominique, *L'Etoile rose* (Paris: Grasset, 1978)

——, *Le Rapt de Ganymède* (Paris: Grasset, 1989)

Fernàndez, Lluís, *The Naked Anarchist* (London: GMP, 1990)

Ferro, Robert, *The Blue Star* (New York: Dutton, 1985)

——, *The Family of Max Desir* (New York: Dutton, 1984)

——, *Second Son* (New York: Crown, 1988)

Fichte, Hubert, *Detlev's Imitations* (London: Serpent's Tail, 1992)

——, *The Orphanage* (London: Serpent's Tail, 1990)

Fiedler, Leslie A., *An End to Innocence: Essays on Culture and Politics* (New York: Stein and Day, 1972)

——, *Love and Death in the American Novel* (New York: Criterion, 1960)

——, *The Return of the Vanishing American* (London: Paladin, 1972)

——, *The Stranger in Shakespeare* (St Albans: Paladin, 1974)

——, *Waiting for the End: The American Literary Scene from Hemingway to Baldwin* (London: Cape, 1965)

Fierstein, Harvey, *Torchsong Trilogy* (New York: Gay Presses of New York, 1980)

Firbank, Ronald, *The Complete Ronald Firbank* (London: Duckworth, 1961)

Fitzgerald, Edward, *Rubáiyát of Omar Khayyám* (London: Siegle, Hill and Co., n.d.)

Fitzgerald, F. Scott, *Tender is the Night* (New York: Scribner's, 1934)

Fitzroy, A.T., *Despised and Rejected* (London: GMP, 1988)

Flaubert, Gustave, *Madame Bovary: moeurs de province* (Paris and London: Nelson, 1944)

Flecker, James Elroy, *Hassan* (London: Folio Society, 1966)

Fleming, Ian, *From Russia, With Love* (London: Pan, 1959)

Fondazione Sandro Penna, *Orgoglio e pregiudizio: L'eros lesbico e omosessuale nella letteratura del Novecento* (Torino: Fondazione Sandro Penna: 1983)

Fone, Byrne R.S. (ed.), *Hidden Heritage: History and the Gay Imagination* (New York: Irvington, 1981)

Foreman, Martin, *A Sense of Loss* (London: GMP, 1993)

Forster, E.M., *The Life to Come, and Other Stories* (London: Edward Arnold, 1971)

——, *Maurice* (Harmondsworth: Penguin, 1972)

Foster, David William, *Gay and Lesbian Themes in Latin American Writing* (Austin, Texas: University of Texas Press, 1991)

Foucault, Michel, *The History of Sexuality, Volume One: An Introduction* (Harmondsworth: Penguin, 1981)

——, *The Use of Pleasure: The History of Sexuality, Volume Two* (New York: Random House, 1985)

Fowlie, Wallace, *Love in Literature: Studies in Symbolic Expression* (Bloomington: Indiana University Press, 1965)

Fox, John, *The Boys on the Rock* (London: Arena, 1985)

Frankl, George, *The Failure of the Sexual Revolution* (London: New English Library, 1975)

Freeman, Gillian, *The Undergrowth of Literature* (London: Nelson, 1967)

Freud, Sigmund, *An Infantile Neurosis, and Other Works* (London: Hogarth, 1955)

——, *Three Contributions to the Theory of Sex* (New York: Nervous and Mental Disease Publishing Co., 1920)

Friedenreich, Kenneth, Roma Gill and Constance B. Kuriyama (eds), *'A Poet and a filthy Play-maker': New Essays on Christopher Marlowe* (New York: AMS Press, 1988)

Fryer, Jonathan, *Isherwood* (London: New English Library, 1977)

Fuller, Roy, *The Ruined Boys* (London: Deutsch, 1959)

Furbank, P.N., *E.M. Forster: A Life* (Oxford: Oxford University Press, 1979)

Fuss, Diana (ed.), *Inside/Out: Lesbian Theories, Gay Theories* (New York and London: Routledge, 1991)

Fussell, Paul, *The Great War and Modern Memory* (New York and London: Oxford University Press, 1975)

Gadda, Carlo Emilio, *That Awful Mess on Via Merulana* (London: Quartet, 1985)

Gale, Patrick, *The Facts of Life* (London: Flamingo, 1995)

——, *Kansas in August* (London: Century, 1987)

Garboli, Cesare, *Penna Papers* (Milano: Garzanti, 1984)

Garrett, Daniel, 'Other Countries: The Importance of Difference', *Other Countries: Black Gay Voices* 1 (Spring 1988), pp. 17–28

Gaudiani, Claire Lynn, *The Cabaret Poetry of Théophile de Viau: Texts and Traditions* (Tübingen:

Gunter Narr; Paris: Editions Jean-Michel Place, 1981)

Gautier, Théophile, *Mademoiselle de Maupin,* trans. Joanna Richardson (Harmondsworth: Penguin, 1981)

Gay Left Collective (eds), *Homosexuality: Power and Politics* (London: Allison and Busby, 1980)

Genet, Jean, *Journal du voleur* (Paris: Gallimard, 1949)

——, *Miracle of the Rose* (Harmondsworth: Penguin, 1971)

——, *Querelle of Brest* (London: Panther, 1969)

George, Stefan, *Poems* (New York: Schocken, 1967)

Geraci, Joseph, *Loving Sander* (London: GMP, 1997)

Gerard, Kent, and Gert Hekma (eds), *The Pursuit of Sodomy: Male Homosexuality in Renaissance and Enlightenment Europe* (New York: Haworth Press, 1988)

Gevisser, Mark, and Edwin Cameron (eds), *Defiant Desire: Gay and Lesbian Lives in South Africa* (New York and London: Routledge, 1995)

Gibbon, Edward, *The History of the Decline and Fall of the Roman Empire* (London: Folio Society, 1983)

Gibson, Ian, *Federico García Lorca: A Life* (London: Faber, 1989)

Gide, André, *Corydon* (New York: Farrar, Straus and Co., 1950)

——, *Les Faux-monnayeurs* (Paris: Gallimard, 1972)

——, *The Immoralist* (Harmondsworth: Penguin, 1960)

——, *Si le grain ne meurt* (Paris: Gallimard, 1954)

Gilbert, Martin, *Atlas of the Holocaust* (London: Michael Joseph, 1982)

——, *The Holocaust* (London: Board of Deputies of British Jews, 1978)

Gill, Christopher, 'The Sexual Episodes in the "Satyricon"', *Classical Philology* 68 (1973), pp. 172–85

Ginsberg, Allen, *Collected Poems 1947–1980* (London: Viking, 1985)

Giovannini, Fabio, *Comunisti e diversi: il PCI e la questione omosessuale* (Bari: Dedalo, 1980)

Giroux, Robert, *The Book Known as Q: A Consideration of Shakespeare's Sonnets* (London: Weidenfeld and Nicolson, 1982)

Glickman, Gary, *Years from Now* (London: Heinemann, 1988)

Gogol, Nikolai, *Taras Bulba* (London: Everyman, 1918)

Goldberg, Jonathan, *Sodometries: Renaissance Texts, Modern Sexualities* (Stanford, Calif.: Stanford University Press, 1992)

——, 'Sodomy and Society: The Case of Christopher Marlowe', *Southwest Review* 69 (1984), pp. 371–78

—— (ed.), *Queering the Renaissance* (Durham, NC and London: Duke University Press, 1994)

Golding, William, *Lord of the Flies* (London: Faber, 1954)

——, *Rites of Passage* (London: Faber, 1980)

Goldstein, Bill, 'Andrew Holleran: A Trilogy of Divided Lives', *Publishers Weekly*, 17 June 1996, pp. 42–3

Gomez-Arcos, Agustin, *The Carnivorous Lamb* (London: GMP, 1984)

Gonsalves, Roy, 'The Photograph', *Other Countries Journal: Black Gay Voices* 1 (Spring 1988), p. 51

Gooch, Brad, *City Poet: The Life and Times of Frank O'Hara* (New York: Knopf, 1993)

Goodich, Michael, *The Unmentionable Vice: Homosexuality in the Later Medieval Period* (Santa Barbara, Calif. and Oxford: ABC–Clio, 1979)

Goodman, Paul, *Hawkweed* (New York: Vintage, 1967)

Goodwin, Ken, *Understanding African Poetry: A Study of Ten Poets* (London: Heinemann, 1982)

Goytisolo, Juan, *Count Julian* (London: Serpent's Tail, 1989)

Grau, Günter (ed.), *Hidden Holocaust? Gay and Lesbian Persecution in Germany 1933–45* (London: Cassell, 1995)

Graves, Robert, *The Greek Myths* (Harmondsworth: Penguin, 1960)

The Greek Anthology, trans. W. R. Paton (London: Heinemann, 1956)

Green, Julien, *Moira* (London: Quartet, 1988)

Green, Martin, *Children of the Sun: A Narrative of 'Decadence' in England after 1918* (London: Pimlico, 1992)

——, *The Labyrinth of Shakespeare's Sonnets: An Examination of Sexual Elements in Shakespeare's Language* (London: Skilton, 1974)

Greenberg, David R., *The Construction of Homosexuality* (Chicago: University of Chicago Press, 1988)

Greene, Jody, '"You Must Eat Men": The Sodomitic Economy of Renaissance Patronage', *GLQ* 1, 2 (1994), pp. 163–97

Greenhorn [George Thompson], *City Crimes; or, Life in New York and Boston, A Volume for Everybody: Being a Mirror of Fashion; a Picture of Poverty, and a Startling Revelation of the Secret Crimes of Great Cities* (Boston: William Berry, 1849)

Greig, Noël, and Drew Griffiths, *As Time Goes By: Two Gay Sweatshop Plays* (London: Gay Men's Press, 1981)

Grimsley, Joe, *Dream Boy* (London: Black Swan, 1996)

Guibert, Hervé, *A l'Ami qui ne m'a pas sauvé la vie* (Paris: Gallimard, 1990)

——, *Les Chiens* (Paris: Minuit, 1982)

——, *L'Homme au chapeau rouge* (Paris: Gallimard, 1992)

——, *My Parents* (London: Serpent's Tail, 1993)

——, *Le Protocole compassionel* (Paris: Gallimard, 1991)

Gunn, Thom, *Jack Straw's Castle* (London: Faber, 1976)

——, *The Man With Night Sweats* (London: Faber, 1992)

——, *The Occasions of Poetry: Essays in Criticism and Autobiography* (London: Faber, 1982)

——, *The Passages of Joy* (London: Faber, 1982)

——, *Shelf Life: Essays, Memoirs and an Interview* (London: Faber, 1994)

——, *Undesirables* (Durham: Pig Press, 1988)

Guyotat, Pierre, *Eden, Eden, Eden* (London: Creation, 1995)

Hafiz of Shiraz, *Fifty Poems of Hafiz* (Cambridge: Cambridge University Press, 1947)

——, *Thirty Poems* (London: Murray, 1952)

Haggerty, George E., 'Literature and Homosexuality in the Late Eighteenth Century: Walpole, Beckford, and Lewis', *Studies in the Novel* 18 (1986), pp. 341–52

Hall, Radclyffe, *The Well of Loneliness* (London: Virago, 1982)

Hall, Richard, 'Henry James: Interpreting an Obsessive Memory', *Journal of Homosexuality* 8, 3/4 (1983), pp. 83–97

Hallam, Paul, *The Book of Sodom* (London: Verso, 1993)

Halperin, David, *One Hundred Years of Homosexuality, and Other Essays on Greek Love* (New York and London: Routledge, 1990)

Hamberger, Robert, *The Wolf's Tale* (North Leverton, Nottinghamshire: Waldean Press, 1995)

Hammett, Dashiell, *The Maltese Falcon* (Harmondsworth: Penguin, 1963)

Hammond, Paul, *Love between Men in English Literature* (London: Macmillan, 1996)

Hansen, Joseph, *Death Claims* (New York: Harper, 1973)

——, *Fadeout* (New York: Harper and Row, 1970)

——, *Troublemaker* (New York: Harper, 1975)

Harbage, Alfred, *Shakespeare Without Words, and Other Essays* (Cambridge, Mass.: Harvard University Press, 1972)

Hardy, Thomas, *The Return of the Native* (Oxford: Oxford University Press, 1990)

Härle, Gerhard, *Männerweiblichkeit: Zur Homosexualität bei Klaus und Thomas Mann* (Frankfurt am Main: Athenäum, 1988)

Harman, C., *Sylvia Townsend Warner: A Biography* (London: Chatto and Windus, 1989)

Harold, John (ed.), *How Can You Write a Poem When You're Dying of AIDS?* (London: Cassell, 1993)

Harrison, Tony, *v.* (Newcastle: Bloodaxe, 1985)

Harstock, Mildred E., 'Henry James and the Cities of the Plain', *Modern Language Quarterly* 29 (1968), pp. 297–311

Hart, James D., *The Oxford Companion to American Literature* (New York and Oxford: Oxford University Press, 1983)

Hart, Kitty, *Return to Auschwitz* (London: Granada, 1983)

Hartland, Claude, *The Story of a Life, for the Consideration of the Medical Fraternity* (London: Brazen Books, 1989)

Hartley, L.P., *The Go-Between* (London: Hamish Hamilton, 1953)

Harvey, A.D., 'The Outsider: E.M. Forster 91 Years Ago', *London Magazine* (October/November

1996), pp. 63–71

——, 'Prosecutions for Sodomy in England at the Beginning of the Nineteenth Century', *The Historical Journal* 21, 4 (1978), pp. 939–48

Harvey, Andrew, *Love's Fire: Re-creations of Rumi* (London: Cape, 1988)

Harvey, Jonathan, *Beautiful Thing* (London: Methuen, 1996)

Harwood, Lee, *Crossing the Frozen River: Selected Poems* (London: Paladin, 1988)

Hawthorne, Nathaniel, *The Scarlet Letter* (Harmondsworth: Penguin, 1983)

Hayman, Ronald, *Proust: A Biography* (London: Minerva, 1991)

——, *Thomas Mann: A Biography* (London: Bloomsbury, 1996)

Hazm, Ibn, *The Ring of the Dove* (London: Luzac, 1953)

Heald, Tim, *A Life of Love: The Life of Barbara Cartland* (London: Sinclair-Stevenson, 1994)

Heger, Heinz, *The Men with the Pink Triangle* (London: GMP, 1980)

Hemingway, Ernest, *A Moveable Feast* (London: Cape, 1964)

——, *The Sun Also Rises* (London: Cape, 1927)

Hemphill, Essex (ed.), *Brother to Brother: New Writings by Black Gay Men* (Boston: Alyson, 1991)

Henderson, Philip (ed.), *Shorter Novels: Eighteenth Century* (London and New York: Everyman, 1930)

Henderson, William Haywood, *Native* (New York: Plume, 1994)

Hesse, Hermann, *The Glass Bead Game* (London: Cape, 1970)

Hickson, Alisdare, *The Poisoned Bowl: Sex and the Public School* (London: Duckworth, 1996)

Higgins, Patrick, *Heterosexual Dictatorship: Male Homosexuality in Post-War Britain* (London: Fourth Estate, 1996)

—— (ed.), *A Queer Reader* (London: Fourth Estate, 1993)

Hilliard, David, 'UnEnglish and Unmanly: Anglo-Catholicism and Homosexuality', *Victorian Studies* 25, 2 (Winter 1982), pp. 181–210

Hilts, Philip J., 'Dispelling Myths about AIDS in Africa', *Africa Report* 33, 6 (November–December 1988), pp. 27–31

Himes, Chester, *Cast the First Stone* (London: Allison and Busby, 1990)

Hinsch, Bret, *Passions of the Cut Sleeve: A History of the Male Homosexual Tradition in China* (Berkeley: University of California Press, 1990)

Hobsbawm, Eric, and Terence Ranger, *The Invention of Tradition* (Cambridge: Cambridge University Press, 1983)

Hocquenghem, Guy, *Homosexual Desire* (London: Allison and Busby, 1978)

Hoess, Rudolf, *Commandant of Auschwitz* (London: Pan, 1974)

Hogan, Desmond, *A Farewell to Prague* (London: Faber, 1995)

——, *The Ikon Maker* (London: Pulsifer, 1987)

——, *A New Shirt* (London: Faber, 1987)

Holden, Anthony (ed.), *Greek Pastoral Poetry: Theocritus, Bion, Moschus, The Pattern Poems* (Harmondsworth: Penguin, 1974)

Holderness, Graham (ed.), *The Shakespeare Myth* (Manchester: Manchester University Press, 1988)

Holleran, Andrew, *Dancer from the Dance* (London: Corgi, 1980)

——, *Ground Zero* (New York: Plume, 1988)

——, *Nights in Aruba* (New York: William Morrow, 1983)

Hollinghurst, Alan, *The Folding Star* (London: Chatto and Windus, 1994)

——, *The Swimming-Pool Library* (London: Chatto and Windus, 1988)

Holtby, Winifred, *South Riding* (London: Collins, 1936)

Homer, *The Iliad* (Chicago and London: University of Chicago Press, 1961)

——, *The Odyssey* (London: Heinemann, 1962)

Hopkins, Gerard Manley, *The Notebooks and Papers of Gerard Manley Hopkins* (New York and London: Oxford University Press, 1937)

——, *Poems* (London: Oxford University Press, 1948)

Horace, *The Odes of Horace*, trans. James Michie (Harmondsworth: Penguin, 1967)

Horovitz, Michael (ed.), *Children of Albion: Poetry of the 'Underground' in Britain* (Harmondsworth: Penguin, 1969)

Housman, A.E., *The Collected Poems of A.E. Housman* (London: Cape, 1960)

Howard, Richard, *Selected Poems* (London and New York: Penguin, 1991)

Howe, Lawrence, 'Critical Anthologies of the Plague Years: Responding to AIDS Literature', *Contemporary Literature* 35, 2 (1994), pp. 395–416

Hsien-yung, Pai, *Crystal Boys* (San Francisco: Gay Sunshine, 1995)

Huggins, Nathan Irvin, *Harlem Renaissance* (New York: Oxford University Press, 1971)

Hughes, Langston, *The Big Sea* (London: Pluto, 1986)

——, *Selected Poems* (London: Pluto, 1986)

Hughes, Thomas, *Tom Brown's Schooldays* (London: Macmillan, 1898)

Humphreys, Laud, *Out of the Closets: The Sociology of Homosexual Liberation* (Englewood Cliffs, NJ: Prentice-Hall, 1972)

——, *Tearoom Trade: Impersonal Sex in Public Places* (Chicago: Aldine, 1975)

Humphries, Martin (ed.), *Not Love Alone: A Modern Gay Anthology* (London: GMP, 1985)

Huxley, Aldous, *Ape and Essence* (London: Flamingo, 1994)

Huysmans, Joris-Karl, *À Rebours* (Paris: Fasquelle, 1974)

Hyde, H. Montgomery, *A History of Pornography* (London: Heinemann, 1964)

——, *The Other Love: An Historical and Contemporary Survey of Homosexuality in Britain* (London: Mayflower, 1972)

——, (ed.) *Trials of Oscar Wilde* (London: William Hodge, 1948)

Igra, Samuel, *Germany's National Vice* (London: Quality Press, 1945)

Infante, G. Cabrera, *Mea Cuba* (London: Faber, 1994)

Ireland, Timothy, *Who Lies Inside* (London: GMP, 1984)

Irwin, Robert, *The Arabian Nights: A Companion* (London: Allen Lane, 1994)

Isherwood, Christopher, *Christopher and His Kind* (London: Eyre Methuen, 1977)

——, *Goodbye to Berlin* (Harmondsworth: Penguin, 1945)

——, *Mr Norris Changes Trains* (Harmondsworth: Penguin, 1942)

——, *A Single Man* (New York: Simon and Schuster, 1964)

——, *The World in the Evening* (New York: Random House, 1954)

James, Henry, *The Turn of the Screw and The Aspern Papers* (London: Everyman, 1935)

Jarlínski, Jóseph, *Fighting Auschwitz* (Greenwich, Conn.: Fawcett Crest, 1975)

Jarman, Derek, *Modern Nature* (London: Century, 1991)

Jay, Peter (ed.), *The Greek Anthology and Other Ancient Greek Epigrams: A Selection in Modern Verse Translations* (London: Allen Lane, 1973)

Jeffery-Poulter, Stephen, *Peers, Queers and Commons: The Struggle for Gay Law Reform from 1950 to the Present* (London and New York: Routledge, 1991)

Jenkyns, Richard, *The Victorians and Ancient Greece* (Oxford: Blackwell, 1980)

John of the Cross, Saint, *The Mystical Doctrine of St John of the Cross* (London: Sheed and Ward, 1944)

Johnson, Adam, *The Playground Bell* (Manchester: Carcanet, 1994)

Johnson, Greg, *Pagan Babies* (New York: Plume, 1994)

Jones, James W., *'We of the Third Sex': Literary Representations of Homosexuality in Wilhelmine Germany* (New York: Peter Lang, 1990)

Jong, Erica, *Fear of Flying* (London: Minerva, 1994)

Jonson, Ben, *Epicoene, or The Silent Woman* (London: Edward Arnold, 1966)

——, *Sejanus His Fall* (London: Ernest Benn, 1966)

Jowett, Benjamin (ed.), *The Dialogues of Plato Translated into English with Analyses and Introductions* (Oxford: Clarendon Press, 1892)

Joyce, James, *Dubliners* (London: Triad Grafton, 1977)

——, *Ulysses* (London: Bodley Head, 1937)

Jullian, Philippe, *Oscar Wilde* (London: Granada, 1971)

Juvenal, trans. Peter Green, *The Sixteen Satires* (Harmondsworth: Penguin, 1967)

Kafka, Franz, *The Castle* (Harmondsworth: Penguin, 1957)

——, *Description of a Struggle and Other Stories* (Harmondsworth: Penguin, 1979)

——, *The Trial* (Harmondsworth: Penguin, 1953)

Kaplan, Justin, *Walt Whitman: A Life* (New York: Bantam, 1982)

Karlínsky, Simon, *The Sexual Labyrinth of Nikolai Gogol* (Cambridge, Mass.: Harvard University Press, 1976)

Katz, Jonathan Ned, *Gay American History: Lesbians and Gay Men in the USA* (New York: Crowell, 1976)

——, *Gay/Lesbian Almanac: A New Documentary* (New York: Harper and Row, 1983)

Kayper-Mensah, A.W., *The Drummer in Our Time* (London: Heinemann, 1975)

Kazantzakis, Nikos, *Zorba the Greek* (London: Faber, 1961)

Kellendonk, Frans, *Mystiek lichaam* (Amsterdam: Meulenhoff, 1986)

Kellogg, Stuart (ed.), *Essays on Gay Literature* (New York: Harrington Park Press, 1983)

Kelly, Dennis, *Size Queen, and Other Poems* (San Francisco: Gay Sunshine, 1981)

Kenan, Randall, *Let the Dead Bury Their Dead* (San Diego, Calif.: Harcourt, 1992)

——, *A Visitation of Spirits* (New York: Grove, 1989)

Kennedy, Hubert, *Ulrichs: The Life and Works of Karl Heinrich Ulrichs, Pioneer of the Modern Gay Movement* (Boston: Alyson, 1988)

Kielar, Wieslaw, *Anus Mundi: Five Years in Auschwitz* (Harmondsworth: Penguin, 1982)

Kiernan, Robert F., *Frivolity Unbound: Six Masters of the Camp Novel* (New York: Continuum, 1990)

King, Edward, *Safety in Numbers: Safer Sex and Gay Men* (London: Cassell, 1993)

Kinsey, Alfred C., Wardell B. Pomeroy and Clyde E. Martin, *Sexual Behavior in the Human Male* (Philadelphia: Saunders, 1948)

Kipling, Rudyard, *Kim* (London: Macmillan, 1951)

Klein, Michael (ed.), *Poets for Life: Seventy-Six Poets Respond to AIDS* (New York: Crown, 1989)

Kleinberg, Seymour (ed.), *The Other Persuasion* (New York: Random House, 1977)

Kleis, Gerald W. and Salisu A. Abdullahi, 'Masculine Power and Gender Ambiguity in Urban Hausa Society', *African Urban Studies* 16 (Spring 1983), pp. 39–53

Klusacek, Allan and Ken Morrison (eds), *A Leap in the Dark: AIDS, Art and Contemporary Cultures* (Montreal: Véhicule, 1992)

Knowles, John, *A Separate Peace* (New York: Macmillan, 1960)

Knox, Melissa, '*Beltraffio*: Henry James's Secrecy', *American Imago* 43, 3 (Fall 1986), pp. 211–27

Koestenbaum, Wayne, *Double Talk: The Erotics of Male Literary Collaboration* (New York and London: Routledge, 1989)

Kopelson, Kevin, *Love's Litany: The Writing of Modern Homoerotics* (Stanford, Calif.: Stanford Uniforia Press, 1994)

Krafft-Ebing, Richard von, *Psychopathia Sexualis* (New York: Putnam, 1965)

Kramer, Larry, *The Destiny of Me* (New York: NAL Dutton, 1993)

——, *Faggots* (New York: Random House, 1978)

——, *The Normal Heart* (London: Methuen, 1986)

——, *Reports from the Holocaust: The Making of an AIDS Activist* (New York: St Martin's Press, 1989)

Kushner, Tony, *Angels in America, Part One: Millennium Approaches* (London: National Theatre/Nick Hern, 1992)

——, *Angels in America, Part Two: Perestroika* (London: National Theatre/Nick Hern, 1994)

Laclos, Choderlos de, *Les Liaisons Dangereuses* (Harmondsworth: Penguin, 1961)

Lahr, John, *Prick Up Your Ears: The Biography of Joe Orton* (London: Allen Lane, 1978)

Landry, Hilton (ed.), *New Essays on Shakespeare's Sonnets* (New York: AMS Press, 1976)

Langland, William, *Piers Plowman* (London: Edward Arnold, 1967)

Lansbury, James, *Korzeniowski* (London: Serpent's Tail, 1992)

Laqueur, Walter, *The Terrible Secret: Suppression of the Truth about Hitler's 'Final Solution'* (London: Weidenfeld and Nicolson, 1980)

Laurents, David (ed.), *The Badboy Book of Erotic Poetry* (New York: Badboy, 1995)

Lauritsen, John and David Thorstad, *The Early Homosexual Rights Movement (1864–1935)* (New York: Times Change, 1974)

Lautréamont, Comte de, *Oeuvres complètes* (Paris: Garnier-Flammarion, 1969)

Lawrence, D.H., *The Complete Poems of D.H. Lawrence* (London: Heinemann, 1972)

——, *The Prussian Officer* (Harmondsworth: Penguin, 1945)

——, *Women in Love* (London: Secker, 1921)

Leavitt, David, 'Did I Plagiarise His Life?', *New York Times Book Review* 3 April 1994, pp. 36–7

——, *Equal Affections* (New York: Weidenfeld and Nicolson, 1989)

——, *Family Dancing* (New York: Knopf, 1984)

——, *The Lost Language of Cranes* (New York: Knopf, 1986)

——, *While England Sleeps,* revised edn. (New York and Boston: Houghton Mifflin, 1995)

Le Carré, John, *The Spy Who Came in from the Cold* (London: Coronet, 1990)

Le Chêne, Evelyn, *Mauthausen: The History of a Death Camp* (London: Methuen, 1971)

Lessing, Doris, *The Golden Notebook* (London: Panther, 1973)

Leverenz, David, *Manhood and the American Renaissance* (Ithaca, New York and London: Cornell University Press, 1989)

Levi, Peter, *The Art of Poetry: The Oxford Lectures 1984–1989* (New Haven and London: Yale University Press, 1991)

Levi, Primo, *If This Is A Man/The Truce* (Harmondsworth: Penguin, 1979)

——, *Moments of Reprieve* (London: Abacus, 1987)

Levin, Harry, *Christopher Marlowe: The Overreacher* (London: Faber, 1961)

Levin, James, *The Gay Novel: The Male Homosexual Image in America* (New York: Irvington, 1983)

Lewis, C.S., *A Preface to "Paradise Lost"* (Oxford: Oxford University Press, 1961)

Lewis, David Levering, *When Harlem Was in Vogue* (New York and Oxford: Oxford University Press, 1989)

Lewis, Matthew, *The Monk* (London: Oxford University Press, 1973)

Leyland, Winston (ed.), *Angels of the Lyre: A Gay Poetry Anthology* (San Francisco: Panjandrum/Gay Sunshine, 1975)

—— (ed.), *Gay Sunshine Interviews, Volume One* (San Francisco: Gay Sunshine, 1978)

—— (ed.), *Gay Sunshine Interviews, Volume Two* (San Francisco: Gay Sunshine, 1982)

—— (ed.), *Orgasms of Light: The Gay Sunshine Anthology* (San Francisco: Gay Sunshine, 1977)

Licht, Hans, *Sexual Life in Ancient Greece* (London: Routledge and Kegan Paul, 1932)

Liddell, Robert, *Cavafy: A Critical Biography* (London: Duckworth, 1974)

Lilly, Mark, *Gay Men's Literature in the Twentieth Century* (London: Macmillan, 1993)

—— (ed.), *Lesbian and Gay Writing: An Anthology of Critical Essays* (London: Macmillan, 1990)

Liyong, Taban lo, *Frantz Fanon's Uneven Ribs* (London: Heinemann, 1971)

Locke, Alain (ed.), *The New Negro* (New York: Boni, 1925)

Longus, *Daphnis and Chloe* (New York: Prestel, 1994)

Lorca, Federico García, *Poet in New York* (Harmondsworth: Penguin, 1990)

——, *The Public and Play Without a Title* (New York: New Directions, 1983)

——, *Selected Poems* (Newcastle upon Tyne: Bloodaxe, 1992)

——, *Selected Poetry* (Harmondsworth: Penguin, 1960)

Lorde, Audre, *Zami: A New Spelling of My Name* (London: Pandora, 1996)

Lowenfels, Walter (ed.), *Walt Whitman's Civil War* (New York: Knopf, 1960)

Lucas, Ian, *Impertinent Decorum: Gay Theatrical Manoeuvres* (London: Cassell, 1994)

The Mabinogion (Harmondsworth: Penguin, 1976)

McAlpine, Monica, 'The Pardoner's Homosexuality and How it Matters', *PMLA* 95 (1980), pp. 8–22

McCaffrey, Joseph A. (ed.), *The Homosexual Dialectic* (Englewood Cliffs, NJ: Prentice-Hall, 1972)

McCauley, Stephen, *The Object of My Affection* (New York: Simon and Schuster, 1987)

McCullers, Carson, *Reflections in a Golden Eye* (Harmondsworth: Penguin, 1967)

McKay, Claude, *Selected Poems of Claude McKay* (New York: Harcourt, Brace and World, 1953)

McKenna, Neil, 'Men Loving Men: Towards a Taxonomy of Male-to-Male Sexualities in the Developing World', per*versions* 5 (Summer 1995), pp. 54–101

——, *On the Margins: Men Who Have Sex with Men and HIV in the Developing World* (London: Panos Institute, 1996)

McLynn, Frank, *Burton: Snow Upon the Desert* (London: John Murray, 1990)

Magee, Bryan, *One in Twenty: A Study of Homosexuality in Men and Women* (London: Secker, 1966)

Malouf, David, *An Imaginary Life* (London: Chatto and Windus, 1978)

——, *Johnno* (Ringwood, Victoria: Penguin, 1976)

Mann, Anthony William, Stewart Charles, and Pat O'Brien, *Respectively . . .* (London: Oscars Press, 1987)

Mann, Klaus, *The Pious Dance* (London: GMP, 1988)

Mann, Thomas, *Death in Venice, Tristan, Tonio Kröger* (Harmondsworth: Penguin, 1955)

——, *Doctor Faustus* (Harmondsworth: Penguin, 1968)

——, *The Magic Mountain* (Harmondsworth: Penguin, 1960)

Marcus, Steven, *The Other Victorians: A Study of Sexuality and Pornography in Mid-Nineteenth-Century England* (New York: Basic Books, 1974)

Marlowe, Christopher, *The Complete Poems and Translations* (Harmondsworth: Penguin, 1971)

——, *The Complete Plays* (Harmondsworth: Penguin, 1969)

Marr, David, *Patrick White: A Life* (London: Cape, 1991)

Mars-Jones, Adam (ed.), *Mae West is Dead: Recent Lesbian and Gay Fiction* (London: Faber, 1983)

——, *The Waters of Thirst* (London: Faber, 1993)

—— and Edmund White, *The Darker Proof: Stories from a Crisis* (London: Faber, 1987)

Martial, *The Epigrams of Martial* (London: Hart-Davis, MacGibbon, 1973)

Martin, Robert Bernard, *Gerard Manley Hopkins: A Very Private Life* (London: Flamingo, 1992)

Martin, Robert K. (ed.), *The Continuing Presence of Walt Whitman: The Life after the Life* (Iowa City: University of Iowa Press, 1992)

——, 'Criticising the Critics: A Gay Perspective', *Gay Sunshine* 35 (Winter 1978), pp. 24–25

——, *Hero, Captain, and Stranger: Male Friendship, Social Critique, and Literary Form in the Sea Novels of Herman Melville* (Chapel Hill and London: University of North Carolina Press, 1986)

——, 'The "High Felicity" of Comradeship: A New Reading of *Roderick Hudson*', *American Literary Realism* 11 (Spring 1978), pp. 100–118

——, *The Homosexual Tradition in American Poetry* (Austin: University of Texas Press, 1979)

Marvell, Andrew, *The Complete Poems* (Harmondsworth: Penguin, 1972)

Masters, William Howell and Virginia E. Johnson, *Human Sexual Response* (Boston: Little, Brown, 1966)

Matthiessen, F.O., *The American Renaissance: Art and Expression in the Age of Emerson and Whitman* (London: Oxford University Press, 1941)

Maturin, Charles, *Melmoth the Wanderer* (London: Oxford University Press, 1968)

Maupin, Armistead, *Tales of the City, More Tales of the City, Further Tales of the City: An Omnibus* (London: Chatto and Windus, 1989)

——, *Tales of the City, Volume Two* (London: Chatto and Windus, 1990)

Mecke, Günther, *Franz Kafkas offenbares Geheimnis: Eine Psychopathographie* (Munchen: Wilhelm Fink, 1982)

Melville, Herman, *Billy Budd, Sailor, and Other Stories* (New York and London: Penguin, 1970)

——, *Moby-Dick* (Harmondsworth: Penguin, 1972)

Menemencioglu, Nermin (ed.), *The Penguin Book of Turkish Verse* (Harmondsworth: Penguin, 1978)

Meyers, Jeffrey, *Homosexuality and Literature, 1890–1930* (London: Athlone, 1977)

——, [untitled review of Gregory Woods, *Articulate Flesh*], *Journal of English and German Philology* 88, 1 (January 1989), pp. 126–9

Michelangelo, *The Poetry of Michelangelo,* ed. and trans. James Saslow (London and New Haven: Yale University Press, 1991)

Mieli, Mario, *Homosexuality and Liberation: Elements of a Gay Critique* (London: Gay Men's Press, 1980)

Miles, Barry, *Ginsberg: A Biography* (London: Viking, 1990)

Miller, Jr., James E., *T.S. Eliot's Personal Waste Land* (University Park: Pennsylvania State University Press, 1977)

Miller, Neil, *Out of the Past: Gay and Lesbian History from 1869 to the Present* (New York and London: Vintage, 1995)

Millett, Kate, *Sexual Politics* (London: Hart-Davis, 1971)

Milton, John, *Complete Shorter Poems,* ed. J. Carey (London: Longman, 1971)

——, *Odes, Pastorals, Masques,* ed. J. B. Broadbent (Cambridge: Cambridge University Press, 1975)

——, *The Poetical Works of John Milton* (London: William Tegg, 1848)

Mishima, Yukio, *Confessions of a Mask* (New York: New Directions, 1958)

——, *Forbidden Colours* (Harmondsworth: Penguin, 1971)

Mitchison, Naomi, *Barbarian Stories* (London: Cape, 1929)

——, *Black Sparta: Greek Stories* (London: Cape, 1928)

Moi, Toril, *Sexual/Textual Politics: Feminist Literary Theory* (London: Methuen, 1985)

Monette, Paul, *Borrowed Time* (London: Collins Harvill, 1988)

——, *Love Alone: 18 Elegies for Rog* (New York: St. Martin's Press, 1988)

Montaigne, Michel de, *The Essays of Michel de Montaigne* (New York: Heritage, 1946)

Montherlant, Henry de, *La Ville dont le prince est un enfant* (Paris: Gallimard, 1967)

Moodie, T. Dunbar, 'Migrancy and Male Sexuality on the South African Gold Mines', *Journal of Southern African Studies* 14, 2 (January 1988), pp. 228–56

Moon, Michael, *Disseminating Whitman: Revision and Corporeality in 'Leaves of Grass'* (Cambridge, Mass. and London: Harvard University Press, 1991)

——, '"The Gentle Boy from the Dangerous Classes": Pederasty, Domesticity, and Capitalism in Horatio Alger', *Representations* 19 (Summer 1987), pp. 87–110

——, 'Sexuality and Visual Terrorism in *The Wings of the Dove*', *Criticism* 28, 4 (1986), pp. 427–43

Moore, Gerald and Ulli Beier (eds), *Modern Poetry from Africa* (Harmondsworth: Penguin, 1968)

——, *The Penguin Book of Modern African Poetry* (Harmondsworth: Penguin, 1984)

Morgan, Ted, *Literary Outlaw: The Life and Times of William S. Burroughs* (New York: Holt, 1988)

Morrison, Toni, *The Bluest Eye* (London: Chatto and Windus, 1979)

Morse, Carl and Joan Larkin (eds), *Gay and Lesbian Poetry in Our Time: An Anthology* (New York: St Martin's Press, 1988)

Mosca, Frank, *All-American Boys* (Boston: Alyson, 1983)

Moss, Kevin (ed.), *Out of the Blue: Russia's Hidden Gay Literature, An Anthology* (San Francisco: Gay Sunshine, 1997)

Mugambi, J.N. Kanyua, *Carry It Home* (Kampala, Nairobi and Dar es Salaam: East African Literature Bureau, 1974)

Müller, Filip, *Auschwitz Inferno* (London: Routledge and Kegan Paul, 1979)

Murphy, Dennis, *The Sergeant* (London: Frederick Muller, 1958)

Murphy, Timothy F. and Suzanne Poirier (eds), *Writing AIDS: Gay Literature, Language, and Analysis* (New York: Columbia University Press, 1993)

Musil, Robert, *Young Törless* (London: Secker and Warburg, 1955)

Nafzawi, Shaykh, *The Glory of the Perfumed Garden* (London: Panther, 1978)

Nava, Michael, *Finale* (Boston: Alyson, 1988)

——, *Goldenboy* (Boston: Alyson, 1988)

——, *How Town* (New York: Harper and Row, 1990)

——, *The Little Death* (Boston: Alyson, 1986)

Navarre, Yves, *Le Jardin d'acclimatation* (Paris: Flammarion, 1980)

Nelson, Emmanuel S. (ed.), *AIDS: The Literary Response* (New York: Twayne, 1992)

——, *Contemporary Gay American Novelists: A Bio-Bibliographical Critical Sourcebook* (Westport, Conn.: Greenwood, 1993)

——, 'Continents of Desire: James Baldwin and the Pleasures of Homosexual Exile', *James White Review* 50 (Fall 1996), pp. 8, 16

——, 'Critical Deviance: Homophobia and the Reception of James Baldwin's Fiction', *Journal of American Culture* 14, 3 (Fall 1991), pp. 91–6

——, 'Towards a Transgressive Aesthetic: Gay Readings of Black Writing', *James White Review* 11, 3 (Spring 1994), pp. 15–17

Neto, Agostinho, *Sacred Hope* (Dar es Salaam: Tanzania Publishing House, 1974)

Newman, Jenny (ed.), *The Faber Book of Seductions* (London: Faber, 1988)

Newman, John Henry, *The Dream of Gerontius, and Other Poems* (London: Oxford University Press, 1914)

New Songs from a Jade Terrace (Harmondsworth and New York: Penguin, 1986)

Niles, Blair, *Strange Brother* (London: GMP, 1991)

Norse, Harold, *Memoirs of a Bastard Angel* (London: Bloomsbury, 1990)

Norton, Rictor, *The Homosexual Literary Tradition: An Interpretation* (New York: Revisionist Press, 1974)

——, *Mother Clap's Molly House: The Gay Subculture in England 1700–1830* (London: GMP, 1992)

Notopoulos, James A., *The Platonism of Shelley: A Study of Platonism and the Poetic Mind* (Durham, NC: Duke University Press, 1949)

Novick, Shelden M., *Henry James: The Young Master* (New York: Random House, 1996)

Nyiszli, Dr. Miklos, *Auschwitz: A Doctor's Eye-Witness Account* (London: Panther, 1962)

Nykl, A.R., *Hispano-Arabic Poetry and Its Relations with the Old Provençal Troubadours* (Baltimore: [no publisher named], 1946)

Oberski, Jona, *A Childhood* (London: Hodder and Stoughton, 1983)

O'Brien, Pat, *'I'm Afraid This Time Love, It's Positive'* (London: Oscars Press, 1989)

O'Hara, Frank, *The Selected Poems of Frank O'Hara* (New York: Vintage, 1974)

Okigbo, Christopher, *Labyrinths* (London: Heinemann, 1971)

——, *Song of Ocol* (Nairobi: East African Publishing House, 1970)

Ortega y Gasset, Jose, *On Love . . . Aspects of a Single Theme* (London: Cape, 1967)

Orton, Joe, *The Complete Plays* (London: Eyre Methuen, 1976)

Orwell, George, *Nineteen Eighty-Four* (Harmondsworth: Penguin, 1954)

Otway, Thomas, *Venice Preserved, or, A Plot Discovered* (London: Edward Arnold, 1969)

Outland, Orland, '"Lord of Illusions" Clive Barker: Gay Heroism, Tales of Transcendence', *Frontiers* 14, 9 (8 September 1995), pp. 44–5

Overholser, Renée V., '"Looking with Terrible Temptation": Gerard Manley Hopkins and Beautiful Bodies', *Victorian Literature and Culture* 19 (1991), pp. 25–53

Ovid, *The Erotic Poems* (Harmondsworth: Penguin, 1982)

——, *The Metamorphoses* (New York: Viking, 1958)

Owen, Ursula (ed.), 'Gay's the Word in Moscow', *Index on Censorship* 24, 1 (January/February 1995), pp. 14–85

Owen, Wilfred, *The Collected Poems of Wilfred Owen* (London: Chatto and Windus, 1963)

Paglia, Camille, *Sexual Personae: Art and Decadence from Nefertiti to Emily Dickinson* (New Haven and London: Yale University Press, 1990)

Painter, George D., *Marcel Proust: A Biography, Volume One* (London: Chatto and Windus, 1959)

——, *Marcel Proust: A Biography, Volume Two* (London: Chatto and Windus, 1965)

Papers Concerning the Treatment of German Nationals in Germany 1938–1939 (London: HMSO, 1939)

Paris, Renzo and Antonio Veneziani (eds), *L'amicizia amorosa: Antologia della poesia italiana dal XIII Secolo a oggi* (Milano: Gammalibri, 1982)

Parker, Canaan, *The Color of Trees* (Boston: Alyson, 1992)

Partridge, Eric, *Shakespeare's Bawdy: A Literary and Psychological Essay and a Comprehensive Glossary,* revised and enlarged edn. (London: Routledge and Kegan Paul, 1968)

Pasolini, Pier Paolo, *The Letters of Pier Paolo Pasolini, Volume I: 1940–1954* (London: Quartet, 1992)

——, *Selected Poems*, trans. Norman MacAfee and Luciano Martinengo (London: Calder, 1984)

Pater, Walter, *Plato and Platonism: A Series of Lectures* (London: Macmillan, 1893)

——, *The Renaissance: Studies in Art and Poetry* (London: Macmillan, 1922)

Patrick, Robert, *Temple Slave* (New York: Richard Kasak, 1994)

p'Bitek, Okot, *Song of Lawino* (Nairobi: East African Publishing House, 1966)

——, *Song of Ocol* (Nairobi: East African Publishing House, 1970)

Peake, Robert, 'Swahili Stratification and Tourism in Malindi Old Town, Kenya', *Africa* 59, 2 (1989), pp. 209–20

Pearson, Hesketh, *The Life of Oscar Wilde* (London: Methuen, 1946)

Peck, Dale, 'Tacky Dress', *London Review of Books* 18, 4 (22 February 1996), pp. 27–31

Pecora, Elio, *Sandro Penna: Una cheta follia* (Milano: Frassinelli, 1984)

Penna, Sandro, *Confuso sogno* (Milano: Garzanti, 1980)

——, *Remember Me, God of Love* (Manchester: Carcanet, 1993)

——, *Tutte le poesie* (Milano: Garzanti, 1984)

Pequigney, Joseph, 'Sodomy in Dante's *Inferno* and *Purgatorio*', *Representations* 36 (1991), pp. 22–42

——, *Such Is My Love: A Study of Shakespeare's Sonnets* (Chicago: University of Chicago Press, 1985)

Person, Leland S., 'James's Homo-Aesthetics: Deploying Desire in the Tales of Writers and Artists', *Henry James Review* 14 (Spring 1994), pp. 188–203

Pessoa, Fernando, *The Book of Disquiet* (London: Serpent's Tail, 1991)

——, *Selected Poems* (Harmondsworth: Penguin, 1974)

Peter, John, 'A New Interpretation of *The Waste Land* (1952)', *Essays in Criticism* 19, 2 (April 1969) pp 140–75

Peters, Lenrie, *Katchikali* (London: Heinemann, 1971)

——, *Selected Poetry* (London: Heinemann, 1981)

Petronius, *The Satyricon, and the Fragments* (Harmondsworth: Penguin, 1965)

Peyrefitte, Roger, *The Exile of Capri* (London: Secker and Warburg, 1961)

——, *Special Friendships* (London: Secker and Warburg, 1958)

Pezzana, Angelo (ed.), *La politica del corpo: antologia del 'Fuori', movimento di liberazione omosessuale* (Roma: Savelli, 1976)

Picano, Felice, *Like People in History* (New York: Viking, 1995)

Pieterse, Cosmo (ed.), *Seven South African Poets: Poems of Exile* (London: Heinemann, 1971)

Pindar, *The Odes*, trans. C.M. Bowra (Harmondsworth: Penguin, 1969)

Piñera, Virgilio, *Cold Tales*, trans. Mark Schafer (Hygiene, Color.: Eridanos, 1988)

Plant, Richard, *The Pink Triangle: The Nazi War against Homosexuals* (New York: Holt, 1986)

Plante, David, *The Catholic* (London: Paladin, 1988)

——, *The Francoeur Family* (London: Chatto and Windus, 1984)

Plato, *The Dialogues of Plato* (Oxford: Clarendon Press, 1892)

Pollard, Patrick, *André Gide: Homosexual Moralist* (New Haven and London: Yale University Press, 1991)

Poller, Walter, *Medical Block, Buchenwald: The Personal Testimony of Inmate 996, Block 36* (London: Souvenir Press, 1961)

Popp, Wolfgang, *Männerliebe: Homosexualität und Literatur* (Stuttgart: Metzler, 1992)

Porter, Roy and Lesley Hall, *The Facts of Life: The Creation of Sexual Knowledge in Britain, 1650–1950* (New Haven and London: Yale University Press, 1995)

Powell, Neil, 'The Case of Rossiter's Rabbit: Gay Publishing, Poetry, and AIDS', *PN Review* 58 (1987), pp. 40–43

Powell, Patricia, *A Small Gathering of Bones* (London: Heinemann, 1994)

Powell, Vicky, 'Zimbabwean Gay Man's Home Burnt to the Ground', *Gay Times* 205 (October 1995), pp. 35–6

Praz, Mario, *The Romantic Agony* (London and New York: Oxford University Press, 1970)

Preston, John (ed.), *Hot Living: Erotic Stories about Safer Sex* (Boston: Alyson, 1985)

Proust, Marcel, *Remembrance of Things Past* (London: Chatto and Windus, 1966)

——, *Time Regained* (London: Chatto and Windus, 1970)

Purdy, James, *Eustace Chisholm and the Works* (New York: Farrar, Straus and Giroux, 1967)

——, *Narrow Rooms* (New York: Arbor, 1978)

Quinn, Eric Shaw, *Say Uncle* (New York: Dutton, 1994)

Rabéarivelo, Jean-Joseph, *Translations from the Night* (London: Heinemann, 1975)

Racine, Jean Baptiste, *Oeuvres complètes* (Paris: Gallimard, 1950)

Ramsey, Paul, *The Fickle Glass: A Study of Shakespeare's Sonnets* (New York: AMS Press, 1979)

Rashke, Richard, *Escape from Sobibor* (London: Michael Joseph, 1983)

Ratcliffe, Michael, 'From the Closet to the Ghetto', *Prospect* (November 1996), pp. 66–8

Rattigan, Terence, *The Deep Blue Sea; Harlequinade; Adventure Story; The Browning Version* (London, Pan, 1955)

——, *Separate Tables* (London: Samuel French, 1956)

Raven, Simon, *Fielding Gray* (London: Blond, 1967)

——, *The Old School: A Study in the Oddities of the English Public School System* (London: Hamish Hamilton, 1986)

Reade, Brian (ed.), *Sexual Heretics: Male Homosexuality in English Literature from 1850 to 1900* (London: Routledge and Kegan Paul, 1970)

Rechy, John, *City of Night* (New York: Grove, 1963)

——, *Numbers* (New York: Grove, 1968)

——, *The Sexual Outlaw: A Documentary: A Non-fiction Account, with Commentaries, of Three Days and Nights in the Sexual Underground* (London: Futura, 1979)

Rector, Frank, *The Nazi Extermination of Homosexuals* (New York: Stein and Day, 1981)

Reed, John and Clive Wake (eds), *A Book of African Verse* (London: Heinemann, 1964)

Rees, David, *Out of the Winter Gardens* (London: Olive Press, 1984)

Rees, Geoffrey, *Sex With Strangers* (Harmondsworth: Penguin, 1994)

Renault, Mary, *The Charioteer* (London: Longmans Green, 1953)

——, *The Mask of Apollo* (New York: Pantheon, 1966)

——, *The Persian Boy* (New York: Pantheon, 1972)

Reve, Gerard, *Parents Worry* (London: Minerva, 1991)

Reynolds, David S., *Beneath the American Renaissance: The Subversive Imagination in the Age of Emerson and Melville* (Cambridge, Mass. and London: Harvard University Press, 1989)

Rice, Anne, *Interview with the Vampire* (London: Raven, 1976)

Richards, Jeffrey, *Happiest Days: The Public Schools in English Fiction* (Manchester: Manchester University Press, 1988)

Richmond, Len and Gary Noguera (eds), *The Gay Liberation Book* (San Francisco: Ramparts, 1973)

Ridley, Philip, *Crocodilia* (London: Brilliance, 1988)

——, *Flamingoes in Orbit* (London: Hamish Hamilton, 1990)

——, *In the Eyes of Mr Fury* (Harmondsworth: Penguin, 1989)

——, *The Krays* (London: Methuen, 1997)

Rimbaud, Arthur, *Collected Poems* (Harmondsworth: Penguin, 1962)

—— and Paul Verlaine, *A Lover's Cock, and Other Gay Poems* (San Francisco: Gay Sunshine, 1979)

Ritsos, Yannis, *Corridor and Stairs* (The Curragh, Ireland: Goldsmith, 1976)

——, *Erotica* (Old Chatham, New York: Sachem Press, 1982)

——, *Exile and Return* (London: Anvil, 1989)

——, *The Moonlight Sonata* (New Malden, Surrey: Tangent, 1975)

——, *Ritsos in Parenthesis* (Princeton, NJ: Princeton University Press, 1979)

——, *Scripture of the Blind* (Columbus: Ohio State University Press, 1979)

——, *Selected Poems* (Harmondsworth: Penguin, 1974)

——, *Subterranean Horses* (Athens: Ohio University Press, 1980)

Robb, Peter, 'Poise of the Powerless', *Times Literary Supplement* (23–29 March 1990), p. 327

Robinson, Christopher, *Scandal in the Ink: Male and Female Homosexuality in Twentieth-Century French Literature* (London: Cassell, 1995)

Rochester, John Wilmot, Earl of, *The Complete Poems of John Wilmot, Earl of Rochester* (New Haven: Yale University Press, 1968)

——, *Sodom, or The Quintessence of Debauchery* (N. Hollywood, Calif.: Brandon House, 1966)

Rodgers, Bruce, *The Queen's Vernacular: A Gay Lexicon* (London: Blond and Briggs, 1972)

Rolfe, Frederick, *Collected Poems* (London: Woolf, 1974)

Roscoe, Will (ed.), *Living the Spirit: A Gay American Indian Anthology, Compiled by Gay American Indians* (New York: St Martin's Press, 1988)

Rowse, A.L., *Christopher Marlowe: A Biography* (London: Macmillan, 1964)

——, *Homosexuals in History: A Study of Ambivalence in Society, Literature and the Arts* (London: Weidenfeld and Nicolson, 1977)

Royston, Robert (ed.), *Black Poets in South Africa* (London: Heinemann, 1973)

Rumaker, Michael, *A Day and a Night at the Baths* (Bolinas, Calif.: Grey Fox, 1979)

Rushdie, Salman, *The Satanic Verses* (London: Viking, 1988)

Russell, Bertrand, *The Conquest of Happiness* (London: Unwin, 1930)

Russo, Vito, *The Celluloid Closet: Homosexuality in the Movies,* revised edn. (New York: Harper and Row, 1987)

Saba, Umberto, *Ernesto* (Milano: Einaudi, 1979)

——, *Poesie scelte* (Milano: Mondadori, 1976)

Sade, The Marquis de, *The Complete Marquis de Sade* (Los Angeles: Holloway House, 1966)

——, *The 120 Days of Sodom, and Other Writings,* trans. Austryn Wainhouse and Richard Seaver (New York: Grove, 1966)

Sa'di, *The Gulistan or Rose Garden of Sa'di*, trans. Edward Rehatsek (London: Allen and Unwin, 1964)

Sahuquillo, Angel, *Federico García Lorca y la cultura de la homosexualidad masculina* (Alicante: Instituto de Cultura Juan Gil-Albert, 1991)

Said, Edward, *Culture and Imperialism* (London: Chatto and Windus, 1993)

——, *Orientalism* (Harmondsworth: Penguin, 1991)

Saikaku, Ihara, *The Great Mirror of Male Love* (Stanford, Calif.: Stanford University Press, 1990)

Saint, Assotto (ed.), *Here to Dare: 10 Gay Black Poets* (New York: Galiens Press, 1992)

——, *The Road Before Us: 100 Gay Black Poets* (New York: Galiens Press, 1991)

Sarotte, Georges-Michel, *Like a Brother, Like a Lover: Male Homosexuality in the American Novel and Theatre from Herman Melville to James Baldwin* (Garden City, New York: Doubleday, 1978)

Sartre, Jean-Paul, *The Age of Reason* (Harmondsworth: Penguin, 1961)

——, *Iron in the Soul* (Harmondsworth: Penguin, 1963)

——, *Nausea* (Harmondsworth: Penguin, 1965)

——, *The Reprieve* (Harmondsworth: Penguin, 1963)

Saslow, James M., *Ganymede in the Renaissance: Homosexuality in Art and Society* (New Haven and London: Yale University Press, 1986)

Savoy, Eric, 'Hypocrite Lecteur: Walter Pater, Henry James and Homotextual Politics', *Dalhousie Review* 72, 1 (1992), pp. 12–36

Savran, David, *Communists, Cowboys, and Queers: The Politics of Masculinity in the Work of Arthur Miller and Tennessee Williams* (Minneapolis: University of Minnesota Press, 1992)

Saylor, Douglas B., *The Sadomasochistic Homotext: Readings in Sade, Balzac and Proust* (New York: Peter Lang, 1993)

Schimmel, Annemarie, 'Hafiz and His Critics', *Studies in Islam* (January 1979), pp. 1–33

——, *Mystical Dimensions of Islam* (Chapel Hill: University of North Carolina Press, 1975)

——, *The Triumphal Sun: A Study of the Works of Jalaloddin Rumi*, revised edn. (London and The Hague: East-West Publications, 1980)

Schmidt, Michael, *The Colonist* (London: Frederick Muller, 1980)

Schulman, Sarah, *My American History: Lesbian and Gay Life during the Reagan/Bush Years* (New York: Routledge, 1994)

——, *People in Trouble* (London: Sheba, 1990)

Schwartz, Barth David, *Pasolini Requiem* (New York: Pantheon, 1992)

Schwartz, Kessel, 'Homosexuality and the Fiction of Reinaldo Arenas', *Journal of Evolutionary Psychology* 5, 1–2 (March 1984), pp. 12–20

Schwenger, Peter, *Phallic Critiques: Masculinity and Twentieth-Century Literature* (London: Routledge and Kegan Paul, 1984)

Scott, Michael, *Renaissance Drama and a Modern Audience* (London: Macmillan, 1982)

Sedgwick, Eve Kosofsky, *Between Men: English Literature and Male Homosocial Desire* (New York: Columbia University Press, 1985)

——, *The Coherence of Gothic Conventions* (New York and London: Methuen, reissued 1986)

——, *Epistemology of the Closet* (New York and London: Harvester Wheatsheaf, 1991)

——, *Tendencies* (London: Routledge, 1994)

Seel, Pierre, *I, Pierre Seel, Deported Homosexual: A Memoir of Nazi Terror* (New York: Basic Books, 1995)

Seidler, Victor J., *Unreasonable Men: Masculinity and Social Theory* (New York and London: Routledge, 1994)

Seidman, Steven, *Embattled Eros: Sexual Politics and Ethics in Contemporary America* (New York and London: Routledge, 1992)

Selvadurai, Shyam, *Funny Boy: A Novel in Six Stories* (London: Cape, 1994)

Sergent, Bernard, *Homosexuality in Greek Myth* (Boston: Beacon, 1986)

Seymour-Smith, Martin, *Guide to Modern World Literature* (London: Wolfe, 1973)

——, (ed.), *Shakespeare's Sonnets* (London: Heinemann, 1963)

Shakespeare, William, *The Riverside Shakespeare*, ed. G. Blakemore Evans (Boston: Houghton Mifflin, 1974)

——, *Sonetti* (Torino: Einaudi, 1974)

——, *The Sonnets,* ed. William Burto (New York: Signet, 1965)

——, *Troilus and Cressida,* eds. J. Dover Wilson and Alice Walker (Cambridge: Cambridge University Press, 1957)

——, *Troilus and Cressida* (London: Methuen, 1982)

——, *Twelfth Night,* ed. M. M. Mahood (Harmondsworth: Penguin, 1968)

——, *The Works of William Shakespeare,* ed. J. Payne Collier (London: Whittaker, 1844)

Shapiro, Michael, *Gender Play on the Shakespearean Stage: Boy Heroines and Female Pages* (Ann Arbor: University of Michigan Press, 1994)

Shelley, Percy Bysshe, *Poetical Works* (London: Oxford University Press, 1907)

Shepherd, Gill, 'Rank, Gender and Homosexuality: Mombasa as a Key to Understanding Sexual Options', in Pat Caplan (ed.), *The Cultural Construction of Sexuality* (London: Routledge, 1989)

Shepherd, Simon, *Because We're Queers: The Life and Crimes of Kenneth Halliwell and Joe Orton* (London: GMP, 1989)

——, *Marlowe and the Politics of Elizabethan Theatre* (Brighton: Harvester, 1986)

—— and Mick Wallis (eds), *Coming On Strong: Gay Politics and Culture* (London: Unwin Hyman, 1989)

Sherman, Martin, *Bent* (London: Amber Lane Press, 1979)

Shewey, Don (ed.), *Out Front: Contemporary Gay and Lesbian Plays* (New York: Grove, Weidenfeld, 1988)

Shilts, Randy, *And the Band Played On: Politics, People, and the AIDS Epidemic* (New York and London: Penguin, 1988)

Shively, Charley, *Calamus Lovers: Walt Whitman's Working-Class Camerados* (San Francisco: Gay Sunshine, 1987)

——, *Drum Beats: Walt Whitman's Civil War Boy Lovers* (San Francisco: Gay Sunshine, 1989)

Siciliano, Enzo, *Pasolini: A Biography* (London: Bloomsbury, 1987)

Signorile, Michelangelo, *Queer in America: Sex, the Media and the Closets of Power* (New York: Random House, 1993)

Silko, Leslie Marmon, *Almanac of the Dead* (New York: Simon and Schuster, 1991)

Simpson, Mark, *Male Impersonators: Men Performing Masculinity* (London: Cassell, 1994)

Sinfield, Alan, *Alfred Tennyson* (Oxford: Blackwell, 1986)

——, *Cultural Politics – Queer Reading* (London: Routledge, 1994)

——, 'Diaspora and Hybridity: Queer Identities and the Ethnicity Model', *Textual Practice* 10, 2 (1996), pp. 271–93

——, *Faultlines: Cultural Materialism and the Politics of Dissident Reading* (Oxford: Oxford University Press, 1992)

——, *Literature, Politics and Culture in Postwar Britain* (Oxford: Blackwell, 1989)

——, 'Private Lives/Public Theater: Noel Coward and the Politics of Homosexual Representation', *Representations* 36 (Fall 1991), pp. 43–63

——, 'Thom Gunn and the Largest Gathering of the Decade', *London Review of Books* (13 February 1992), pp. 16–17

——, *The Wilde Century: Effeminacy, Oscar Wilde and the Queer Moment* (London: Cassell, 1994)

Smith, Bruce R., *Homosexual Desire in Shakespeare's England: A Cultural Poetics* (Chicago and London: University of Chicago Press, 1991)

Smith, Stan, *W.H. Auden* (Oxford: Blackwell, 1985)

Smollett, Tobias, *Peregrine Pickle* (London: Oxford University Press, 1964)

——, *Roderick Random* (Oxford: Oxford University Press, 1979)

Solzhenitsyn, Alexander, *The Gulag Archipelago* (London: Collins, Harvill and Fontana, 1974, 1976, 1978)

Sontag, Susan, *AIDS and Its Metaphors* (New York and London: Penguin, 1990)

——, 'Notes on Camp', *Partisan Review* 31, 4 (Fall 1964), pp. 515–30

——, 'The Pornographic Imagination', *Partisan Review* 34, 2 (Spring 1967), pp. 181–212

Southgate, Minoo S., 'Men, Women, and Boys: Love and Sex in the Works of SA'DI', *Iranian Studies* 17 (Autumn 1984), pp. 413–452

Soyinka, Wole, *Idanre and Other Poems* (London: Methuen, 1967)

——, *Mandela's Earth and Other Poems* (London: Methuen, 1989)

—— (ed.), *Poems of Black Africa* (London: Heinemann, 1975)

——, *A Shuttle in the Crypt* (London: Collins/Methuen, 1972)

Spalding, P.A. (ed.), *A Reader's Handbook to Proust* (London: George Prior, 1975)

Spanbauer, Tom, *The Man Who Fell in Love with the Moon* (London: Secker and Warburg, 1992)

Spender, Stephen, 'My Life Is Mine; It Is Not David Leavitt's', *New York Times Book Review* (4 September 1994), pp. 10–12

Spenser, Edmund, *The Poetical Works of Edmund Spenser* (London: Oxford University Press, 1912)

Stacpoole, H. de Vere, *The Blue Lagoon* (London: Benn and Fisher Unwin, 1908)

Stambolian, George and Elaine Marks (eds), *Homosexualities and French Literature: Cultural Contexts/Critical Texts* (Ithaca, NY and London: Cornell University Press, 1979)

Steakley, James, *The Homosexual Emancipation Movement in Germany* (New York: Arno, 1975)

Stehling, Thomas (ed.), *Medieval Latin Poems of Male Love and Friendship* (New York and London: Garland, 1984)

Stein, Gertrude, *Two: Gertrude Stein and Her Brother and Other Early Portraits (1908–1912)* (New Haven: Yale University Press, 1951)

Steiner, George, *On Difficulty, and Other Essays* (Oxford: Oxford University Press, 1978)

Stephenson, Terence Michael, 'Sweet Lies', *Gay Times* August 1990, p. 36

Stewart, Angus, *Sandel* (London: Hutchinson, 1968)

Stoker, Bram, *Dracula* (Harmondsworth: Penguin, 1994)

Stone, Brian (ed.), *Medieval English Verse* (Harmondsworth: Penguin, 1964)

Storey, David, *Radcliffe* (Harmondsworth: Penguin, 1965)

Stubbes, Phillip, *The Anatomie of Abuses* (New York: Garland, 1973)

Suetonius, *The Twelve Caesars* (London: Penguin, 1957)

Summers, Claude J., *Christopher Isherwood* (New York: Ungar, 1980)

——, *E.M. Forster* (New York: Ungar, 1983)

—— (ed.), *The Gay and Lesbian Literary Heritage: A Reader's Companion to the Writers and their Works, from Antiquity to the Present* (New York: Holt, 1995)

——, *Gay Fictions: Wilde to Stonewall, Studies in a Male Homosexual Literary Tradition* (New York: Continuum, 1990)

——, 'Homosexuality and Renaissance Literature, or the Anxieties of Anachronism', *South Central Review* 9 (Spring 1992), pp. 2–23

—— (ed.), *Homosexuality in Renaissance and Enlightenment England: Literary Representations in Historical Context* (New York: Harrington Park Press, 1992)

Sutcliffe, William, *New Boy* (Harmondsworth: Penguin, 1996)

Sutherland, John, *Is Heathcliff a Murderer? Puzzles in 19th-Century Fiction* (Oxford and New York: Oxford University Press, 1996)

Swerdlow, Joel, 'America's Poet: Walt Whitman', *National Geographic* 186, 6 (December 1994), pp. 106–41

Tacitus, *The Annals of Imperial Rome* (Harmondsworth: Penguin, 1956)

Takahashi, Mutsuo, *A Bunch of Keys* (Trumansburg, New York: Crossing Press, 1984)

——, *Poems of a Penisist* (Chicago: Chicago Review Press, 1975)

Taylor, G. Rattray, *Sex in History* (London: Panther, 1965)

Taylor, Martin (ed.), *Lads: An Anthology of Comradeship* (London: Constable, 1989)

Tejani, Bahadur, 'Can the Prisoner Make a Poet? A Critical Discussion of *Letters to Martha* by Dennis Brutus', in *African Literature Today, 6: Poetry in Africa* (London: Heinemann, 1973)

Tennyson, Alfred, Lord, '*Enoch Arden*' and '*In Memoriam*' (London: Macmillan, 1888)

Theognis, *Hesiod and Theognis,* trans. Dorothea Wender (Harmondsworth: Penguin, 1973)

Thody, Philip, 'Jean Genet and the Indefensibility of Sexual Deviation', *20th Century Studies* 2 (November 1969), pp. 68–73

Thomas, H. Nigel, *Spirits in the Dark* (London: Heinemann, 1993)

Thurley, Geoffrey, *The Dickens Myth: Its Genesis and Structure* (London: Routledge and Kegan Paul, 1976)

Thurman, Wallace (ed.), *Fire!!* (New York: The Fire!! Press, 1926)

Tibullus, *The Poems of Tibullus,* trans. Constance Carrier (Bloomington and London: Indiana University Press, 1968)

Tiefenbrun, Ruth, *Moment of Torment: An Interpretation of Franz Kafka's Short Stories* (Carbondale and Edwardsville: Southern Illinois University Press, 1973)

Timmons, Stuart, *The Trouble with Harry Hay: Founder of the Modern Gay Movement* (Boston: Alyson, 1990)

Tisdall, Simon, 'Literary Love That Speaks its Name in Too Strident a Voice', *The Guardian* (27 October 1993), p. 20

Tolstoy, Leo, *Anna Karenin* (Harmondsworth: Penguin, 1954)

——, *Resurrection,* trans. Louise Maude (London: Oxford University Press, 1916)

Tondelli, Pier Vittorio, *Pao Pao* (Milano: Feltrinelli, 1989)

Tornsey, Cheryl B., 'Henry James, Charles Sanders Pierce and the Fat Capon: Homoerotic Desire in *The American*', *Henry James Review* 14 (Spring 1994), pp. 166–78

Tourneur, Cyril, *The Atheist's Tragedy* (London: Methuen, 1964)

——, *The Revenger's Tragedy* (Manchester: Manchester University Press, 1996)

Tournier, Michel, *Gemini* (London: Collins, 1981)

——, *Le Roi des aulnes* (Paris: Gallimard, 1970)

——, *Vendredi ou les limbes du Pacifique* (Paris: Gallimard, 1972)

Traub, Valerie, *Desire and Anxiety: Circulations of Sexuality in Shakespearean Drama* (New York and London: Routledge, 1992)

Turner, Frank, *The Greek Heritage in Victorian Britain* (New Haven and London: Yale University Press, 1981)

Twain, Mark, *The Adventures of Huckleberry Finn* (Harmondsworth: Penguin, 1966)

——, *The Adventures of Tom Sawyer* (Harmondsworth: Penguin, 1986)

Tydeman, William, *Doctor Faustus: Text and Performance* (London: Macmillan, 1984)

Unamuno, Miguel de, *The Tragic Sense of Life* (London: Fontana, 1962)

Unterecker, John, *Voyager: A Life of Hart Crane* (New York: Blond, 1970)

U Tam'si, Tchicaya, *Selected Poems* (London: Heinemann, 1970)

Vaglio, Anna, *Invito alla lettura di Penna* (Milano: Mursia, 1993)

Vanbrugh, John, *The Relapse or, Virtue in Danger* (London: Ernest Benn, 1971)

Van Dantzig, Rudi, *For a Lost Soldier* (London: GMP, 1996)

Verlaine, Paul, *Men and Women* (London: Comet, 1985)

——, *Selected Poems* (Harmondsworth: Penguin, 1974)

Veyne, Paul, *Roman Erotic Elegy: Love, Poetry, and the West* (Chicago: University of Chicago Press, 1988)

Vidal, Gore, *The City and the Pillar* (New York: Dutton, 1948)

——, *Pink Triangle and Yellow Star, and Other Essays (1976–1982)* (London: Granada, 1983)

——, *United States: Essays 1952–1992* (New York: Random House, 1993)

Virgil, *The Aeneid* (New York: Bantam, 1972)

——, *The Eclogues,* trans. Guy Lee (Harmondsworth: Penguin, 1984)

Voltaire, *Dictionnaire philosophique* (Paris: Flammarion, 1964)

Waddell, Helen, *Medieval Latin Lyrics* (Harmondsworth: Penguin, 1952)

Wagner, Jean, *Black Poets of the United States from Paul Laurence Dunbar to Langston Hughes* (Urbana: University of Illinois Press, 1973)

Wakefield, Tom, *Drifters* (London: GMP, 1984)

Walter, Aubrey (ed.), *Come Together: The Years of Gay Liberation (1970–73)* (London: Gay Men's Press, 1980)

Warner, Sylvia Townsend, *Mr Fortune's Maggot* (London: Virago, 1978)

Warren, Patricia Nell, *The Beauty Queen* (London: Corgi, 1979)

——, *The Fancy Dancer* (New York: Morrow, 1976)

——, *The Front Runner* (New York: Morrow, 1974)

Watanabe, Tsuneo and Jun'ichi Iwata, *The Love of the Samurai: A Thousand Years of Japanese Homosexuality* (London: GMP, 1989)

Watney, Simon, *Policing Desire: Pornography, AIDS and the Media* (London: Methuen, 1987)

Waugh, Alec, *The Loom of Youth* (London: Grant Richards, 1917)

Waugh, Evelyn, *Brideshead Revisited* (Harmondsworth: Penguin, 1962)

——, *Put Out More Flags* (Harmondsworth: Penguin, 1943)

Weatherby, W.J., *James Baldwin: Artist on Fire* (New York: Laurel, 1990)

Webster, John, *The White Devil,* (London: Methuen, 1966)

Wedekind, Frank, *Spring Awakening* (London: Calder and Boyars, 1969)

Weeks, Jeffrey, *Coming Out: Homosexual Politics in Britain, from the Nineteenth Century to the Present* (London: Quartet, 1977)

——, *Sex, Politics and Society: The Regulation of Sexuality since 1800* (London: Longman, 1981)

——, *Sexuality and Its Discontents* (London: Routledge and Kegan Paul, 1985)

Weinberg, Martin S. and Alan P. Bell, *Homosexuality: An Annotated Bibliography* (New York: Harper and Row, 1972)

Weiss, Andrea and Greta Schiller, *Before Stonewall: The Making of a Gay and Lesbian Community* (Tallahassee, Fla: Naiad, 1988)

West, D.J., *Homosexuality* (London: Duckworth, 1955)

West, Nathanael, *Miss Lonelyhearts* (Harmondsworth: Penguin, 1961)

Wharton, Edith, *The Age of Innocence* (London: Everyman, 1993)

White, Edmund, *The Beautiful Room Is Empty* (London: Picador, 1988)

——, *A Boy's Own Story* (London: Picador, 1983)

—— (ed.), *The Faber Book of Gay Short Fiction* (London: Faber, 1991)

——, *Genet* (London: Chatto and Windus, 1993)

——, *States of Desire: Travels in Gay America* (New York: Dutton, 1980)

White, Patrick, *Riders in the Chariot* (Harmondsworth: Penguin, 1964)

——, *The Solid Mandala* (London: Jonathan Cape, 1976)

——, *The Twyborn Affair* (London: Cape, 1979)

——, *The Vivisector* (London: Cape, 1970)

Whitman, Walt, *Leaves of Grass* (New York and Oxford: Oxford University Press, 1990)

Whitmore, George, *Nebraska* (New York: Washington Square, 1989)

Wiesel, Elie, *Night* (Harmondsworth: Penguin, 1981)

Wilcox, Michael (ed.), *Gay Plays* (London: Methuen, 1984)

Wilde, Oscar, *The Works of Oscar Wilde* (London and Glasgow: Collins, 1948)

——, *Teleny, or the Reverse of the Medal* (London: GMP, 1986)

——, *Complete Works of Oscar Wilde* (Glasgow: HarperCollins, 1994)

Williams, Tennessee, *Five Plays* (London: Secker and Warburg, 1962)

——, *Memoirs* (New York: Doubleday, 1975)

——, *The Rose Tattoo and Other Plays* (Harmondsworth: Penguin, 1976)

Williams, Walter L., *The Spirit and the Flesh: Sexual Diversity in American Indian Culture* (Boston: Beacon, 1988)

Wilson, Angus, *Anglo-Saxon Attitudes* (Harmondsworth: Penguin, 1968)

——, *As If By Magic* (London: Secker and Warburg, 1973)

——, *Hemlock and After* (Harmondsworth: Penguin, 1956)

——, *Late Call* (London: Granada, 1982)

——, *No Laughing Matter* (London: Secker and Warburg, 1967)

——, *The Middle Age of Mrs Eliot* (Harmondsworth: Penguin, 1961)

——, *Setting the World on Fire* (London: Secker and Warburg, 1980)

Wilson, Katharine M., *Shakespeare's Sugared Sonnets* (London: Allen and Unwin, 1974)

Winner, Viola Hopkins, 'The Artist and the Man in "The Author of Beltraffio",' *PMLA* 83 (1968), pp. 102–8

Woods, Gregory, *Articulate Flesh: Male Homo-eroticism and Modern Poetry* (New Haven and London: Yale University Press, 1987)

——, 'Fantasy Islands: Popular Topographies of Marooned Masculinity', in David Bell and Gill Valentine (eds), *Mapping Desire: Geographies of Sexualities* (London and New York: Routledge, 1995), pp. 126–48

——, 'The Injured Sex: Hemingway's Voice of Masculine Anxiety', in Judith Still and Michael Worton (eds), *Textuality and Sexuality: Reading Theories and Practices* (Manchester: Manchester University Press, 1993), pp. 160–72

——, *This Is No Book: A Gay Reader* (Nottingham: Mushroom, 1994)

——, *We Have the Melon* (Manchester: Carcanet, 1992)

Woolf, Virginia, *A Haunted House* (Harmondsworth: Penguin, 1973)

——, *Mrs Dalloway* (London: Hogarth, 1925)

——, *The Waves* (London: Hogarth, 1963)

Wooten, Cecil, 'Petronius and "Camp"', *Helios*, 11, 2 (1984), pp. 133–9

Wright, Stephen (ed.), *Different: An Anthology of Homosexual Short Stories* (New York: Bantam, 1974)

Yingling, Thomas E., *Hart Crane and the Homosexual Text: New Thresholds, New Anatomies* (Chicago: University of Chicago Press, 1990)

Young, Ian (ed.), *The Male Homosexual in Literature: A Bibliography* (Metuchen, NJ: Scarecrow, 1975)

—— (ed.), *The Male Muse: A Gay Anthology* (Trumansburg, New York: Crossing, 1973)

—— (ed.), *The Son of the Male Muse: New Gay Poetry* (Trumansburg, New York: Crossing, 1983)

Young, Wayland, *Eros Denied* (London: Corgi, 1968)

Yourcenar, Marguerite, *Memoirs of Hadrian* (London: Secker and Warburg, 1955)

Zimunya, Musaemura Bonas, *Thought Tracks* (London: Longman, 1982)

Illustration Credits

Index

Maupin, Armistead, 351, 356, 360, 417–18
Maurois, André, 200
Mautino, Ferdinando, 273
Maximilian, Emperor, 371
Mayne, Xavier, 4, 391
Medak, Peter, 417
Melchiori, Giorgio, 105
Meleager, 34, 391
Melville, Herman, 6, 11, 159, 163–6, 391, 392;
    Billy Budd, 97, 164–6, 278; *Moby-Dick*, 160,
    163–4; *Redburn*, 164; *White-Jacket*, 164
Menemencioglu, Nermin, 59
Merrill, George, 218
Merrill, James, 11, 392
Meyers, Jeffrey, 343, 370, 392
Michelangelo Buonarroti, 3, 4, 68–9, 89, 102, 159,
    167, 217, 390, 391
Michelangelo the Younger, 102
Military cultures, 24, 66, 91, 98
Mill, John Stuart, 6
Miller, Arthur, 298
Miller, Henry, 339
Millett, Kate, 339
Milton, John, 108, 110, 113–16, 118, 119, 120,
    131, 212
Mishima, Yukio, 66–7, 323, 392, 396
Misogyny, 19, 23, 45, 65, 68, 103–4, 125, 127, 159,
    160, 168, 208, 227, 232, 252, 293, 339, 345
Mitchell, James, 384–5
Mitchison, Naomi, 201–2
Moldau, Siegfried, 10
Molière, 4
Moll, Albert, 67
Moncrieff, C.K. Scott, 405
Monette, Paul, 362, 363, 366, 367
Montaigne, Michel de, 4, 391, 397
Montesquiou, Robert de, 193
Montherlant, Henry de, 324, 334, 416
Moon, Michael, 155
Moore, Honor, 365–6
Morgan, Kenneth, 297
Morrison, Toni, 11–12, 333
Morse, Carl, 9
Mosca, Frank, 347
Moschus, 24, 27, 112, 120
Mousa Paidiké, 7, 28–30, 121
Mouth of the Dragon, 10
Mozart, Wolfgang Amadeus, 127
Mozzi, Andrea de', 48
Mtshali, Oswald Mbuyiseni, 310
Mugabe, Robert, 309, 312
Mugambi, J.N. Kanyua, 303, 305
Müller, Filip, 248
Murasaki, Lady, 63
Murdoch, Iris, 392
Murphy, Dennis, 166
Murphy, Gerard, 87
Musil, Robert, 326, 392
Muzio, Girolamo, 69

Nabokov, Vladimir, 329
Nafzawi, Shaykh, 54
Names Project, 365
Narcissus, 66, 74, 86, 116, 174, 271, 317, 322–3,
    396

Nava, Michael, 246
Navarre, Yves, 344, 392
Nelson, Emmanuel, 209
Nero, 4, 82–3, 124
Neruda, Pablo, 267
Neto, Agostinho, 303, 305, 312
Newman, John Henry, 169, 170, 171, 258, 261
Newton, Sir Isaac, 4
Nijinsky, Vaslav, 390
Niles, Blair, 204–5, 212–13
Nilson, Dennis, 359
Nisus, 39
Noh theatre, 65
Noll, Kip, 362, 418
Norse, Harold, 293
Nortje, Arthur, 305, 306
Norton, Rictor, 11, 106, 136
Nugent, Richard Bruce, 209, 216, 407
Nykl, A.R., 394–5

Oberski, Jona, 408
O'Brien, Pat, 364, 418
Octavius, 3
Odysseus, 17, 18
Oedipus, 17, 217
O'Hara, Frank, 11, 300–301, 360, 401–2
Okigbo, Christopher, 305, 306, 309
Olivier, Laurence, 97
Orestes, 3, 113, 133, 391
Orpheus, 1, 17, 28, 40, 44, 80, 108–9, 120, 359
Ortega y Gasset, José, 420
Ortleb, Chuck, 8
Orton, Joe, 175, 299–300, 354, 378, 385, 386,
    390, 392
Orwell, George, 253, 264–6
Otway, Thomas, 80–81, 146
Ovid, 39–40, 44, 86, 91, 371, 380, 391
Owen, Wilfred, 121, 204, 359, 381
Oxford Movement, 169–70
Oxford University, 3, 4–5, 5–6, 120, 169–71, 258,
    260–61

Paglia, Camille, 156–7, 284
Pai Hsieng-yung, 348
Palmer, Kenneth, 95
Palmer, Roundell, 171
Paperback Library, 10
Parker, Canaan, 415
Partridge, Eric, 100–102
Pasolini, Pier Paolo, 273–4, 321, 359, 378–9, 392
Pater, Walter, 3, 167–9, 171, 391
Paton, W.R., 34
Patrick, Robert, 300, 369
Patroclus, 3, 8, 17–18, 21, 39, 95–7, 109, 190, 212,
    374, 380, 391
Pausanias, 4, 21–2
P'Bitek, Okot, 303, 304, 305, 306, 307, 308,
    308–9
Pearson, Hesketh, 101
Peck, Dale, 343
Penna, Sandro, 269, 274, 321
Pequigney, Joseph, 47–8, 103, 107
Pessoa, Fernando, 383
Peter, John, 121–2
Peters, Lenrie, 306, 308, 311, 413